Supreme Court Asserts as Conscience Keeper of the Constitution of India

The daring publisher, Universal Law Publishing Company, among the foremost in the law publishing field and progressive in venturing to bring out rare legal literature of avant garde *character has rightly enriched the* corpus juris *of India*

Justice V R Krishna Iyer
Random Reflections, page 14

SUPREME COURT ASSERTS AS CONSCIENCE KEEPER OF THE CONSTITUTION OF INDIA

Justice S.N. Aggarwal
Former Judge, Punjab & Haryana High Court
Former President, Punjab State Consumer Disputes Redressal Commission

Universal
Law Publishing Co.
NEW DELHI - INDIA

2014 Edition

ISBN: 978-93-5035-433-9

Published by

Universal
Law Publishing Co. Pvt. Ltd.
NEW DELHI - INDIA

A-58, G.T. Karnal Road Industrial Area,
(Near Azadpur Metro Station), Delhi-110033
Tel. : 011-47082254, 27458529, 27215334 Fax : 011-27458529
e-mail: unilaw@vsnl.com

- Showroom : C-27, Connaught Place, New Delhi-110001
- Sales : sales@unilawbooks.com
- Editorial : edit@unilawbooks.com
- Website : **www.unilawbooks.com**

Join us on Facebook www.facebook.com/unilawbooks

Recommended citation: Justice S.N. Aggarwal, *Supreme Court Asserts as Conscience Keeper of the Constitution of India* (New Delhi: Universal Law Publishing Co. Pvt. Ltd., 2014).

Computer Typeset at Aesthetic and *Printed* at Glorious Printers, Delhi.

DEDICATION

Dedicated to their Lordships of the Supreme Court who handed down these and similar judgments and strengthened the People's faith in this Institution.

Justice Ashok Bhan
Former Judge,
Supreme Court of India

Kothi No. 302
Sector – 10B
Chandigarh

FOREWORD

The controversy as to who is the final authority as the custodian or interpreter of the Constitution of India, whether the Parliament or the Judiciary, or for that matter, the Supreme Court of India, has been going on right from the day of inception of the Constitution of India on 26th January, 1950. It was finally put on rest by the Seven Judge Bench judgment of the Supreme Court in *A.K. Gopalan's* case[1] in which it was held that the last word on the interpretation of the Constitution vested in the Supreme Court of India.

The Chief Justice and Judges of the Supreme Court of India, by virtue of the oath of their office as prescribed in Form number IV in the THIRD SCHEDULE of the Constitution of India, are to uphold the Constitution without any affection or ill-will, fear or favour.

On the other hand, the Ministers in the Central Cabinet including all the other higher Constitutional functionaries by virtue of the Constitutional oath of their office are supposed to work in accordance with the Constitutional provisions but since the Judiciary is to uphold the Constitution, therefore the Judges of the Supreme Court are given an extra mileage in the Constitution to oversee if the actions of the other organs of the State namely the Executive and the Legislature are in accordance with the Constitutional provisions and to set aside the decisions which are violative of it.

The Supreme Court, therefore, is the guardian of the Constitution of India which is the *Megna Carta* for the good governance of our country and the Supreme Court jealously safeguards it.

Public Interest Litigation has cropped up as another jurisdiction of the Supreme Court which in recent years has got momentum. The awakened citizens resort to this remedy to assail the abuse and misuse of authority by the State. Although not all the PILs are in public interest but many of them are genuine and clearly expose the actions and inactions of the Executive which are in violation of the Constitutional provisions.

The Judgments reproduced in this book, given by the Supreme Court of India in the last ten years, clearly prove that in the litigation initiated by way of Public Interest Litigation, very big scams and scandals have been unearthed and the misuse of power by the Executive has been exposed. If the enlightened citizens had not resorted to the PIL jurisdiction and the Supreme Court had not passed the orders and quashed the decisions of the Executive and the Legislature, the Nation and its people would have been the sufferers and the future generations would not

1. *A.K. Gopalan* v. *State of Madras*, AIR 1950 SC 27: 1950 SCR 88.

have forgiven us for such colossus loss and social evils which grew during our times after independence.

The judgment on black money reveal the inaction and silence of the State at the cost of the nation, the judgment in 2G scam reveals the motivated actions of the top Executive which caused loss to the National exchequer worth lakhs of crores of rupees. The judgments in Rameshwar Prasad and P.J. Thomas clearly prove the misuse of power by the Executive. The judgment in P. Venugopal and the judgment setting aside the provision of sub-section (4) of section 8 of the Representation of the People Act, 1951 reveal the illegal enactments passed by the Parliament. Some other judgments reproduced in this book are on electoral reforms, one judgment on reservation for the benefit of disabled persons shows how the Executive worked contrary to the law passed by the Parliament and the last one is to protect the administrative Executive from political interference in their functioning in the national interest.

All the judgments reproduced in this book show that the Supreme Court had to set aside the decisions of the Executive and quash the Parliamentary enactments which were contrary to the Constitutional provisions.

I really appreciate the efforts made by the enlightened citizens who resorted to the PIL jurisdiction for no personal interest, but in the interest of the society in general and the country at large.

I also appreciate the pains taken and the hard work done by Justice S.N. Aggarwal in bringing out all these judgments in the form of a book for the benefit of its readers. But for his efforts these judgments of the Supreme Court had remained un-noticed in the Law Journals.

I wish this book all success.

20th December, 2013

JUSTICE ASHOK BHAN

Justice N.K. Mehrotra
Lok Ayukta
Uttar Pradesh

P. Box : 172 (G.P.O.)
T.C. 46/V-1, Vibhuti
Khand, Gomti Nagar,
Lucknow-226010
Phone : (0522) 2305760
Fax : (0522) 2306647

MESSAGE

Corruption affects the good governance at all levels of Government decision making. Besides affecting the quality of governance, corruption threatens the very foundation of democracy and Statehood and it is anti-poor. In India, corruption attacks the very fabric of human values, dignity and political equality of people. It deprives the common man from the welfare schemes of the Government; as well as causes great hardship to the individuals. Therefore, there is a demand to formulate human rights to corruption free service.

In India, civil and political rights were incorporated in the Constitution as "Fundamental Rights". Although Directive Principles of State Policy were also included in the Constitution but, these attempts have not been able to bring much fruits, because of corruption in implementing the same.

Fundamental right to live with dignity was not possible without realization of economic and social rights, that is why the Supreme Court of India in a landmark case of *Francis Coralie Mullin* v. *Administrator, Union Territory of Delhi*, AIR 1981 SC 746 has given the interpretation that the right to life includes the right to live with human dignity.

The Indian Judiciary has played a major role in extending right to life concept to include numerous economic and social rights which were earlier only policy guidelines in the form of Directive Principles of the State Policy. But, still a day has to come when Judiciary would interpret the fundamental right to corruption free service also in the right to life.

In our system in India both Judiciary and Legislature can play a vital role in establishing corruption free society. In the matter of corruption, it is always the Judiciary which takes the lead to check corruption through public interest litigations and the Legislature as well as the Executive are forced, by seeking writ from Judiciary, in that direction. In view of these attempts, to check corruption, the Indian Judiciary has given several judgments from time to time in the public interest litigations only with a view to expose corruption and to get the culprit punished.

Justice S.N. Aggarwal has made an attempt to compile all such important judgments of the Supreme Court at one place for the convenience of those, who deal in the matter of corruption by the public servants. The book should be useful to those who have been entrusted the work of investigation in the matter of

Residence: Sai Kripa, 2/381, Vishal Khand-2, Gomti Nagar, Lucknow-226010 Phone: 2396469, 3200399
Mobile: 9839080828, 9415013739 **Website:** www.lokayukta.up.nic.in **Email:** lokayukta@hotmail.com

corruption by the public servants. Therefore, the work of authoring this book by Justice S.N. Aggarwal is worth appreciation.

I wish that in future also Justice S.N. Aggarwal should continue to revise this book by adding further the attempts of Judiciary in eradicating corruption from the Indian society.

(Justice N.K. Mehrotra)

DEDICATION

Dedicated to their Lordships of the Supreme Court who handed down these and similar judgments and strengthened the People's faith in this Institution.

Justice Ashok Bhan
Former Judge,
Supreme Court of India

Kothi No. 302
Sector – 10B
Chandigarh

FOREWORD

The controversy as to who is the final authority as the custodian or interpreter of the Constitution of India, whether the Parliament or the Judiciary, or for that matter, the Supreme Court of India, has been going on right from the day of inception of the Constitution of India on 26th January, 1950. It was finally put on rest by the Seven Judge Bench judgment of the Supreme Court in *A.K. Gopalan's* case[1] in which it was held that the last word on the interpretation of the Constitution vested in the Supreme Court of India.

The Chief Justice and Judges of the Supreme Court of India, by virtue of the oath of their office as prescribed in Form number IV in the THIRD SCHEDULE of the Constitution of India, are to uphold the Constitution without any affection or ill-will, fear or favour.

On the other hand, the Ministers in the Central Cabinet including all the other higher Constitutional functionaries by virtue of the Constitutional oath of their office are supposed to work in accordance with the Constitutional provisions but since the Judiciary is to uphold the Constitution, therefore the Judges of the Supreme Court are given an extra mileage in the Constitution to oversee if the actions of the other organs of the State namely the Executive and the Legislature are in accordance with the Constitutional provisions and to set aside the decisions which are violative of it.

The Supreme Court, therefore, is the guardian of the Constitution of India which is the *Megna Carta* for the good governance of our country and the Supreme Court jealously safeguards it.

Public Interest Litigation has cropped up as another jurisdiction of the Supreme Court which in recent years has got momentum. The awakened citizens resort to this remedy to assail the abuse and misuse of authority by the State. Although not all the PILs are in public interest but many of them are genuine and clearly expose the actions and inactions of the Executive which are in violation of the Constitutional provisions.

The Judgments reproduced in this book, given by the Supreme Court of India in the last ten years, clearly prove that in the litigation initiated by way of Public Interest Litigation, very big scams and scandals have been unearthed and the misuse of power by the Executive has been exposed. If the enlightened citizens had not resorted to the PIL jurisdiction and the Supreme Court had not passed the orders and quashed the decisions of the Executive and the Legislature, the Nation and its people would have been the sufferers and the future generations would not

---

1. *A.K. Gopalan* v. *State of Madras*, AIR 1950 SC 27: 1950 SCR 88.

have forgiven us for such colossus loss and social evils which grew during our times after independence.

The judgment on black money reveal the inaction and silence of the State at the cost of the nation, the judgment in 2G scam reveals the motivated actions of the top Executive which caused loss to the National exchequer worth lakhs of crores of rupees. The judgments in Rameshwar Prasad and P.J. Thomas clearly prove the misuse of power by the Executive. The judgment in P. Venugopal and the judgment setting aside the provision of sub-section (4) of section 8 of the Representation of the People Act, 1951 reveal the illegal enactments passed by the Parliament. Some other judgments reproduced in this book are on electoral reforms, one judgment on reservation for the benefit of disabled persons shows how the Executive worked contrary to the law passed by the Parliament and the last one is to protect the administrative Executive from political interference in their functioning in the national interest.

All the judgments reproduced in this book show that the Supreme Court had to set aside the decisions of the Executive and quash the Parliamentary enactments which were contrary to the Constitutional provisions.

I really appreciate the efforts made by the enlightened citizens who resorted to the PIL jurisdiction for no personal interest, but in the interest of the society in general and the country at large.

I also appreciate the pains taken and the hard work done by Justice S.N. Aggarwal in bringing out all these judgments in the form of a book for the benefit of its readers. But for his efforts these judgments of the Supreme Court had remained un-noticed in the Law Journals.

I wish this book all success.

20th December, 2013

JUSTICE ASHOK BHAN

Justice G.C. Mital
Former Chief Justice
Delhi & Rajasthan High Courts

Kothi No. 7
Sector – 9A
Chandigarh

APPRECIATION

I feel proud in writing APPRECIATION as the author of this book, Justice Som Nath Aggarwal has worked in my office as an advocate in the High Court, Punjab and Haryana, Chandigarh from 1970 to 1972 before his entry into P.C.S. (Judicial). I could see in him even at that time, the desire to work hard, with sincerity of purpose and with total dedication. The author has already written three books on Law (Law on Religious and Charitable Endowments, Law on Maintenance and the Supreme Court on Consumer Protection Act). He has also written two books on the Revolutionary Patriots who remained incarcerated in the Cellular Jail (The Heroes of Cellular Jail) originally published by the Punjabi University, Patiala and the revised edition published by M/s Rupa Publications. The book on this subject in concise form was later on published by the National Council for Educational Research and Training, New Delhi under the title 'The Cellular Jail in our Freedom Struggle' as supplementary reading for the students. This book is the sixth, or we may say, seventh book in line. I have gone through this book. It contains the Judgments of the Supreme Court with separate headings carved out by the author.

These judgments clearly reveal the misuse of power, especially by the top executive who have sworn by the Constitution but have taken decision contrary, not only to the oath of their office but also in violation of the Constitutional provisions.

Some of these judgments reveal the inaction of the State in a matter which even causes threat to the national economy and national security while one of it reveals the misuse of power by the top executive which has caused loss to the nation in lakhs of crores of rupees. Other judgments also reveal that the State has taken decisions which were found to be contrary to the Constitutional provisions.

I really appreciate the Supreme Court for performing its duty in the national interest to protect the Constitution and the awakened citizens who by way of PILs attracted the attention of the Supreme Court to the misuse of power by the Executive.

Above all I appreciate the efforts made by Justice S.N. Aggarwal in bringing out this book to draw the attention of the readers on these judgments. I also appreciate the publishers of this book.

I also wish this book to be all success.

JUSTICE G.C. MITAL

PREFACE

It was the far-sightedness and wisdom of the Founding Fathers of the Constitution of India, that they prescribed a binding oath in its *Third Schedule* for the high Constitutional appointees who govern the destiny of the Nation. The oath calls upon them to "d*o right to all manner of people in accordance with the Constitution and the law, without fear or favour, affection or ill will.*"

The Founding Fathers further vested the judiciary with powers of judicial scrutiny of all acts of other organs of the State in order to determine their legality and constitutionality. The Supreme Court by making a large number of interventions and by quashing the Executive decisions and Legislative enactments, which were violative of the Constitutional provisions, has indeed proved itself to be supreme. It has risen up to the expectation of the Founding Fathers by guarding the Constitution and protecting the rights of our countrymen.

In the last one decade, the Hon'ble Supreme Court of India, delivered the judgments, reproduced in this book, in which it was held that the decisions taken by the Union Government or by a particular Ministry of the Central Government or the parliamentary enactments were illegal and unconstitutional and were thus set aside. These judgments deal with very significant areas in the history of our country and lives of our countrymen.

For example, the judgment in 2G Scam case sets aside the arbitrary decision of the Executive in the allocation of spectrum, a natural resource, which caused loss to the nation worth lakhs of crores of rupees. The judgment in black money's case adversely commented on the inaction of the Central Government and black money was held as a threat to the country's economy and national security. The judgments in *Dr. P. Venugopal's* case and Lily Thomas's case struck down the offending provisions of the Acts of Parliament relating to those cases. The judgment in P.J. Thomas's case sets aside his appointment as CVC, holding wrong application of mind by the top Executive in his selection. Some judgments are on the electoral reforms. In one judgment, the Office Memorandum issued by the Executive was held contrary to the Legislative enactment and was set aside. The last judgment was to ensure transparency and accountability in Executive functioning and to save the Administrative Executive from political interference.

I hope this book will serve as an eye-opener for our countrymen and push them to fight for a Government which would, in the words of Mahatma Gandhi, 'wipe every tear from every eye'.

JUSTICE S.N. AGGARWAL

Chandigarh
23rd January, 2014

ACKNOWLEDGEMENTS

I have always had the blessings of Param Pujya Sudhanshu Ji Maharaj. When I went to Param Pujya Guru Ji to present my last book, 'The Supreme Court on the Consumer Protection Act', I was advised to write something on the subject of corruption prevailing in the Country. When I expressed my limitations, I was blessed and told, 'No, You can'. This book is, thus, an attempt to fulfil Guru Ji's wish.

I was also prompted to some extent to write this book when my son-in-law, Pankaj Goyal and daughter Ruchika Goyal told me in 2011 that they were shifting back to America on finding the all pervasive corruption, uncleanliness, terrorist occurrences, indiscipline, lack of work culture, little opportunity for the youth to grow and blossom in order to give their best to their motherland and above all the lack of political will to tackle all these and many other unbearable conditions. They had returned to India in 2006 after spending nearly 10 years in USA. My daughter-in-law Poonam also endorsed their view. I am thankful to them for igniting fire in me for writing this book.

My great friend Shri T. C. Gupta, immediately after the release of the book, 'The Supreme Court on Consumer Protection Act' on 15th March, 2013 in Delhi, where he was also present, enquired from me what next? When I told him that it was difficult to undertake any onerous work, he agreed, but after a pause, he also told me that sitting idle was still more difficult. He suggested that I could do something on legal matters without much labour. I am also grateful to him for lending his assistance in the production of this book.

My friend Shri Iqbal Singh Sidhu always exhorted me to write something unique and memorable. I am grateful to him for his moral support.

I am grateful to Hon'ble Mr. Justice G. C. Mital, Former Chief Justice, High Courts of Delhi and Rajasthan for adding 'Appreciation' to the book. Justice Mital had been kind to me since the days I started professional life in his office in 1970 when he was the practicing Advocate in the High Court at Chandigarh.

I am also grateful to Hon'ble Mr. Justice Ashok Bhan, Former Judge, Supreme Court of India for adding grace to the book by very kindly contributing the 'Foreword'. He always treated me very kindly, since the day I came into his contact for more than four decades ago. He was helpful in very many ways in my build-up

Hon'ble Mr. Justice G. S. Singhvi, former judge, Supreme Court of India is an icon for me ever since I got an opportunity to work under his supervision when he was Judge in the Punjab and Haryana High Court, a few years before his elevation to the Supreme Court of India. His valuable advice helped me to bring about improvement in the Book. I am extremely grateful to Hon'ble Mr. Justice G.S.Singhvi former Judge Supreme Court of India.

Last of all but not the least, I am also grateful to Dr. Manish Arora, Director, Universal Law Publishing Co. Pvt. Ltd., New Delhi for very kindly undertaking the publication of this book. I am also grateful to Shri Hasan Imam of M/s Universal Law Publishing for his pains-taking efforts in editing the book.

Justice S. N. Aggarwal

Chandigarh
23rd January,2014

CONTENTS

Ram Jethmalani v. Union of India 153

TABLE OF CASES

C

D

E

F

G

H

I

J

M

N

P

R

S

T

U

V

Z

INTRODUCTION

Our country won freedom on 15th August, 1947. It is indeed sad that even after 66 years, our leadership has failed to fulfill the dreams of the father of the nation Mahatma Gandhi *i.e.*, wiping out tears from every eye. Millions of our countrymen have no access to clean drinking water or a roof over their heads. They have no proper clothes to cover their bodies. Health and educational facilities are woefully beyond their reach. Lacs of our children start their life journey by picking up rags from the heaps of waste. Slums and Jhuggies are growing by the day. The rising prices are breaking the backs of even middle income families. Lacs of people become homeless during rains. Millions of our youth are unemployed. They are driven by such circumstances towards social evils like drugs or crime or they pick up the gun. The incidents of rape followed by murders or suicides are going up every day.

Environment is getting polluted. Dirty industrial waste flows into the sacred rivers like *the Ganges and the Yamuna*. Cows are slaughtered in thousands every day, little caring for the Directive Principles of the State Policy. In the independent India, red-tapism is the order of the day. Adulteration even in items of food prevails unhindered. Illegal mining is being done even in broad day light. The exploitation of other natural resources is galore. Corruption is not a part of the system but it is the system in every walk of life.

Commonwealth Games scam, Adarsh Housing scam, 2G scam, Coalgate scam, VVIP Chopper scam, IPL betting scam are only few of the scandals which shook the nation in recent times. The Coalgate scam is being monitored directly by the Hon'ble Supreme Court. The reader would be able to easily imagine the reasons for all these maladies by going through the judgments reproduced in this book.

We take pride in the fact that our civilization is one of the oldest in the world. Our motherland was known as *Sone ki Chirhya*. It is the land of *Rishis and Munis*, Prophets and Saints who gave us the *Vedas, Upnishads, the Bhagvad Gita and Ramayana.*

Hundreds of Revolutionary patriots, who were fighting the imperialist rulers to get our country released from the colonial shackles were deported to *Kala Pani* and incarcerated in the dungeons of the Cellular Jail to undergo tortuous life. Veer Savarkar, a leading revolutionary patriot was confined in a solitary cell of this prison house for more than 10 years. The Revolutionary patriots sacrificed their lives for the independence of our country so that the countrymen and future generations may live the life of happiness, but alas! India is not the same after independence, as was thought of by the revolutionaries. Our country got freedom, but it forgot its martyrs, not to speak of honouring their memory or educating our children about the sacrifices made by them.

In the beginning after independence, there are very fine examples where the Ministers in the Government have acted with a mission and with moral conviction for the welfare of the country and its people. The name of Sardar Vallabhbhai Patel is written in words of gold in the history of our country who worked honestly with iron hand to unite the hundreds of small kingdoms, into one India. Lal Bahadar

Shastry was also a Gem in the crown of mother India as he had resigned as Railway Minister when a train accident had taken place owning moral responsibility. He died as a Prime Minister in January, 1966 without leaving any bank balance. Patriotism, Simplicity and integrity were his way of life. Such was also the life story of Gulzari Lal Nanda who officiated twice as Prime Minister.

There was still a fine example of Shri Gopinath Bardoloi, Chief Minister of Assam, who died in harness on 6.8.1950 without leaving any 'savings'. It is recorded in SARDAR PATEL'S CORRESPONDENCE 1945-50. In its 9th Volume is the letter dated 13.8.1950 received by Sardar Patel from Jairamdas Doulatram, Governor of Assam, which was forwarded by Sardar Patel to Pandit Jawaharlal Nehru, Prime Minister of India, New Delhi *vide* his letter dated 24.8.1950. These letters are reproduced in original for the benefit of the reader as under:—

218

New Delhi
24 August, 1950

My dear Jawaharlal,

The other day I spoke to you about Bardoloi's family. I am sending herewith an extract of a letter which I have received from Jairamdas. I should be glad if you would kindly let me know your views in the matter.

Yours sincerely,
Vallabhbhai Patel

The Hon'ble Pandit Jawaharlal Nehru
Prime Minister of India
New Delhi"

"Enclosure
EXTRACT

Government House
Shillong
13 August, 1950

My dear Sardar,

Shri Bardoloi's family is in a very difficult situation. He had made absolutely no provision for them as he had made no savings. He has 4 sons and 5 daughters. Two eldest daughters are married; 3 sons are at school and college. One, the youngest, will, go next year. The three unmarried daughters are at school. He has left the building incomplete. Even the performance of the Shraddh ceremony is beyond the means of the family. All friends are putting their heads together to deal with the situation. Government will probably sanction scholarships for the children at school and college. Some amount may be contributed for the Shraddh ceremony as it is going to have a public character. But the maintenance of the family is going to be a very awkward problem. People had great affection for him because of his temperament. Regard for him has grown more after his death. I wish it were possible for the Government to sanction a pension for his wife. In military life this is done. In the case of civil servants, their pensions and provident funds come to the rescue of the family. But in the case of men who have given their lives for political work, as Bardoloi did, his family is now to face very hard times. The lack of money itself would mean a big drop in the social status of the family with its effect on the mind of the growing children. He had two brothers, but both of them are men of very low income, one with a family also of 8 children. On the first day, one of the brothers broke out as he explained to me the situation which they had all to face. The brothers used to live together, in all a family of four, with one widowed sister of Bardoloi also with them. Could you suggest a way out?

Yours sincerely,

Jairamdas Doulatram

The Hon'ble Sardar Vallabhbhai Patel
New Delhi"

Nehru sent the following reply to Sardar Patel:-

219

New Delhi
24 August, 1950

My dear Vallabhbhai,

Thank you for your letter of 24 August about Bardoloi's family. Jairamdas has written to me also. He informed me that the Assam Government had agreed to give scholarships to Bardoloi's children. That I think is good. Personally I think that a pension to Bardoloi's widow is justifiable. How it can be arranged, I do not know.

I suggested to Jairamdas that if he thought it fit I would arrange to send some money to him for Bardoloi's family. He replied yes, but did not indicate any sum. In any event, I cannot send much but I could have arranged Rs. 5,000 or so. I should like your advice in the matter.

Yours,

Jawaharlal

The Hon'ble Sardar Vallabhbhai Patel

New Delhi"

Sardar Patel *vide* his letter dated 29.8.1950 informed Nehru that like political sufferers, the widow of Shri Bardoloi can be granted Ex-gratia pension in the manner to be settled by the Governor and the Chief Minister of Assam. It reads as under:

220

New Delhi
29 August, 1950

My dear Jawaharlal,

Thank you for your letter of 24 August, 1950 about Bardoloi's family.

I think it would be proper on the part of the Government of Assam to award an *ex-gratia* pension to Bardoloi's widow. Some of the State Governments have a scheme for grant of pension to political sufferers. Bardoloi's family will certainly come in this category. How this can be done and what amount should be given could be settled by the Governor and the Chief Minister in the first instance. They could be asked to let us know what their proposals are and we could then give our opinion.

I think the Government of Assam would make an initial grant also and take that into consideration while fixing the amount of pension. In other words, the initial grant should be by way of partial commutation of the pension.

If you agree, you might write to Jairamdas, since he has already written to you also.

Yours,
Vallabhbhai Patel

The Hon'ble Pandit Jawaharlal Nehru
New Delhi"

The Governor informed Sardar Patel vide letter dated 26th September,1950 that *Shri Bardoloi used to draw only a sum of Rs.1500 out of his salary of Rs.2000 per month and the remaining amount of Rs.500, he used to surrender to the Government.* This letter, also in original, reads as under:

221

Shillong
26 September, 1950

My dear Sardar,

I wrote to you yesterday in connection with the question of pension for Mrs. Bardoloi. After that Shri Medhi informed me of the latest development. Your suggestion of a lump sum amount has been taken. It seems that Shri Bardoloi, though his pay was Rs. 2,000, drew only Rs. 1,500 and surrendered the remaining Rs. 500 to the Government. The total amount of all these surrendered sums comes to nearly Rs. 10,000, and so in consultation with party members, it has been decided to give to Mrs. Bardoloi a lump sum of Rs. 10,000 which would mean the payment to her of what otherwise Bardoloi would have drawn for his expenses. Shri Medhi feels that a precedent of a biggish amount as family pension would be awkward. It appears that on the occasion of the death of another Minister some time ago, no steps were taken to sanction any family pension. On the whole, I feel that the payment of this lump sum which was, as it were, Shri Bardoloi's money, is a better way of meeting the situation. So, with the Prime Minister's liberal donation of Rs. 5,000 and this lump sum of Rs. 10,000 and scholarships for the children, the question of appropriately helping Bardoloi's family will have been satisfactorily settled. Mrs. Bardoloi has started moving about and I expect will be gradually taking some part in public work. The Assembly opened today and I addressed the House. I am sending you a copy of my speech. I have not unfortunately been able to get proper time today for sending you the note in regard to the question of Part B Tribal Areas's representation in the Assam Legislature. I hope to send it to you tomorrow.

Yours sincerely,
Jairamdas Doulatram

The Hon'ble Sardar Vallabhbhai Patel

New Delhi"

Even such like used to be the Chief Ministers after independence. The present day scenario is dismal as would be reflected in the judgments reproduced in this book.

Now coming to the role of Judiciary after independence of our country. To start with, I reproduce a letter in original written by Sardar Patel to Nehru along with the enclosure (9th Volume of SARDAR PATEL's CORRESPONDENCE 1945-1950). The order was passed by the Chief Justice of India, Federal Court, prior to the enforcement of the Constitution of India, although the correspondence took place thereafter. It shows how forcefully the Chief Justice of India objected to the interference by the Executive in the independence of Judiciary. It reads

319

New Delhi
16 February, 1950

My dear Jawaharlal,

I have seen your letter of 14 February to the Chief Justice of India [See enclosure]. I do not know what provoked you to raise this issue so many months after the judgment was delivered. I would, however, be interested to know what [H.J.] Kania says in reply. I myself felt it rather strange that the judges should have commented on what you and Pantji did in this connection when it was, as far as I know, the unanimous wish and hope of every judge, with whom this matter came to be discussed, that it was in the fitness of things that Shiva Prasad Sinha should himself resign and quit. This is precisely what you and Pantji advised him to do.

Yours sincerely,
Vallabhbhai Patel

The Hon'ble Pandit Jawaharlal Nehru
Prime Minister
New Delhi"

"ENCLOSURE

New Delhi
14 February, 1950

My dear Chief Justice,

You will remember that the Federal Court considered the case of a judge of the Allahabad High Court, Shiva Prasad Sinha, last year. In the report made by the Federal Court, the last paragraph contained an observation. I quote the last paragraph:

> "Before parting with the case we wish to make an observation. In the course of the enquiry it was stated that before the commencement of these proceedings Mr. Justice Sinha was called upon to appear before certain executive authorities and was asked to resign his office or face an enquiry into his alleged misconduct. If the statement is true, the procedure adopted is hardly consistent with the great dignity and prestige associated with the office of judge of a High Court and is calculated to undermine the independence of the Judiciary. If, on the information available to it, the appropriate Executive authority is satisfied that there are sufficient grounds for the removal of a judge, the procedure laid down by the Constitution Act has to be followed, as it was, in fact, eventually followed in this case. It cannot be too often emphasised that in the adherence by all who wield the power of Government to the basic principle of independence of the judiciary lies a great safeguard of a free, progressive and democratic society."

When I read it at the time, I wanted to address you on the subject then. But I refrained from doing so, as I did not wish to interfere in any way with further proceedings in that particular case. Now that some time has elapsed, I am writing to you on this subject.

I do not know exactly what the reference "to certain executive authorities" is. But I presume that this was meant for me and for the Premier of the UP. I shall be glad to know exactly what, in the opinion of the Federal Court judges, was inconsistent with propriety, dignity or prestige, or how what was done interfered with, the independence of the judiciary.

Further (presuming that the reference was to me and Premier Pant) I should like to know whether it would not have been desirable for some reference to be made to us before a comment was made, in a matter affecting us.

I write this because I am totally unaware of having done anything which, in the slightest degree, was lacking in propriety. I seek your advice therefore because unless I know this, I am likely to act in a similar manner in the future.

Yours sincerely,
Jawaharlal Nehru

The Hon'ble Mr. Justice Harilal J. Kania
Chief Justice of India
New Delhi

Copy to: The Hon'ble Sardar Vallabhbhai Patel"

Jawahar Lal Nehru sent the reply to Sardar Patel vide his letter dated 26.2.1950 along with the reply received from the Chief Justice of India to Nehru and further letter sent by Nehru to the Chief Justice. These are reproduced in original as under:

320

New Delhi
26 February, 1950

My dear Vallabhbhai,

I am sending you a copy of a letter from the Chief Justice of India to me and my reply to him.

Yours,
Jawaharlal

The Hon'ble Sardar Vallabhbhai Patel
New Delhi"

"ENCLOSURE I

New Delhi
23 February, 1950

My dear Pandit Nehru,

Your letter of the 14th instant to hand. It is in three parts:

(1) A quotation from the last para of the report of the Federal Court in the matter of the inquiry on Mr. Justice Sinha.

You are right in thinking that the reference therein is to you and to the Chief Minister of Uttar Pradesh.

(2) A question whether it would not have been desirable for some reference to be made to you before a comment was made; and

(3) A desire to know what was the suggested lack in propriety, so that such a thing may not happen again.

Only because I understand the gist of your letter to be in part (3) I am sending this reply. Otherwise, the inquiry would be to know why the Report of the Court was so made, and that would not have been proper.

In the course of the inquiry, the following statements made on oath by Mr. Sinha were noticed.

"In the end I may be permitted to submit that gross injustice has been done to me. I had been summoned by the Prime Minister of India at his residence on 13 December 1947 and he saw me only at about 11 p.m. With him was sitting the Premier of the UP. I was confronted with the alternative of resignation forthwith or facing an enquiry. It was with great difficulty that two weeks were allowed to me to make up my mind. Before the expiration of the period I was humiliated by stopping all work with effect from 19 December 1947. I do not know what passed between the Chief Justice and the Premier of the UP... Whether the Chief Justice did it on his own account or only as a mouthpiece of the Hon'ble the Premier, the result was the same. It was nothing but a threat and I mentioned it the very next day to Mr. Bannerjee, the Advocate-General of the UP.

"On the evening of 17 February, 1948 the Chief Justice called me again and told me that the Hon'ble the Premier of the UP had sent for him on 12 February, the day of the immersion of the ashes of Mahatma Gandhi or the next day, and he had asked him to impress upon me to resign otherwise I shall have to suffer the humiliation of facing an inquiry. I took a week's time. I decided not to resign, as resigning after the utter humiliation to which I had been subjected had lost all grace.

"The inquiry was conducted by the Chief Justice at the suggestion or under the orders of the Prime Minister of India or Dr. K.N. Katju, the then Minister of Justice."

In the counter-affidavits filed on behalf of the Governor-General, these statements were not denied. On the other hand the following statements were found therein.

Mr. K.K. Verma (the ex-Chief Justice of Allahabad) *inter alia,* stated in writing as follows:

"The circumstances which have led to this inquiry against Mr. Justice Sinha are as follows:

> Complaints against the conduct of Mr. Justice Sinha appear to have reached the ears of the Prime Minister of India, Pandit Jawaharlal Nehru. He paid a visit to Allahabad on 11 August 1947 and I received a telephonic message from Swaraj Bhawan or Anand Bhawan asking me to see the Prime Minister after the party given to him that afternoon at Swaraj Bhawan, as the Prime Minister wanted to talk to me. Accordingly I met the Prime Minister. He asked me to make inquiries about certain complaints which he had heard about Mr. Justice Sinha. I pointed out to him how difficult and delicate a matter it was to make such inquiries about a brother judge. He then gave me a letter asking me to make such inquiries. Dr. Katju had also written a similar letter to me. Even upon the receipt of these letters I hesitated and did not do anything for some time."

Mr. Justice B. Malik (the Chief Justice of Allahabad) stated:

> "I have already stated that the Premier asked me on the telephone to have the charges framed and to give a copy of the same to Mr. Justice Sinha. The Premier had made that request as Mr. Justice Sinha in his letter dated 25 December 1947 addressed

to him wanted that he must be in possession of definite charges to enable him to decide upon the alternative suggested to him at the interview.

"I have already said that I had sent for Mr. Justice Sinha at the Premier's request and when Mr. Justice Sinha saw me on 17 February he took a week's time to consider his position and on 24 February wrote to me that he did not see any reason to reconsider his decision."

Mr. Justice B. Malik in reply affidavit:

"That I came to know that on the night of 13 December, 1947 Mr. Justice Sinha had been asked to a private interview by the Prime Minister of India and the Premier of this province and had been asked to resign or face an inquiry. I had not been informed of this interview nor, to the best of my knowledge, had my predecessor been informed of it nor did we know anything about it at the time.

"That soon after I took over charge reports started circulating about what had happened at the interview and the matter became public and a local paper came out with a short report.

"That on 16 December, 1947 Mr. Justice Sinha came to me and told me that at the interview with the Prime Minister two police reports were mentioned and he asked me to get copies of these so that he might be able to make up his mind within the two weeks that had been given to him by the Prime Minister whether he would resign or face an inquiry.

"In his letter to the UP Premier Mr. Sinha further asked for information as to the charges against him. The Premier telephoned to me and asked me to frame charges and to give Mr. Justice Sinha a copy thereof. The charges were framed on 27 December 1947."

During the arguments, it was strenuously urged on behalf of Mr. Sinha that the whole evidence was massed against him because of the interest taken by the UP Premier and you in the matter. Although this argument was repeated about four times in the course of discussion, the Advocate-General, appearing on behalf of the Governor-General did not contradict it.

These personal interviews and what was alleged to have taken place at those interviews in the absence of the Chief Justice, even before intimation of any specific charge was given to Mr. Sinha, were considered improper and gave occasion for the comment found in the Report.

As to part (2), this inquiry had started on the complaint of the U.P. Government. The Governor-General made the reference to the Federal Court on that complaint. The persons sponsoring the inquiry were therefore the Government of India, at the instance of the U.P. Government. They were thus both in the position of [complainants]. It was considered that the parties (the Government of India and the UP Government, who were both conversant with the proceedings) would have put in replies to these allegations if they wanted to contradict the same, as they had done in respect of other allegations. There was thus no occasion for the Federal Court to inquire of you why you had acted, as you were alleged to have acted in the affidavits. In this connection I may draw your attention to the first two sentences of the passage from the Report quoted in your letter.

I may inform you that soon after the Report reached H.E. the Governor-General, before passing this order, he thought of giving Mr. Sinha, a chance to resign and in that connection asked me to see him. The passage from the Report quoted in your letter was noticed during the discussion. H.E. the Governor-General and the Hon'ble Sardar Vallabhbhai Patel, who was also present at the interview, were informed of the above-mentioned facts. So far as I remember, you were not then in India.

Yours sincerely,
H.J. Kania

The Hon'ble Pandit Jawaharlal Nehru
Prime Minister of India
New Delhi"

"ENCLOSURE II

New Delhi
26 February, 1950

My dear Chief Justice,

I thank you for your letter of 23 February.

Till I received your letter, my knowledge of what took place in the course of the enquiry into the conduct of the Allahabad High Court Judge, Mr. Sinha, was limited to the fact that an enquiry was taking place, and that a certain order had been passed. I knew nothing as to what was said in the course of the enquiry or what statements were made on affidavit or otherwise. I did not even know that our Advocate-General was participating in this enquiry on behalf of the Governor-General, though presumably I should have known this. The matter was being dealt with by the Home Ministry and no reference was made to me. Naturally, the Premier of the United Provinces, Pandit Govind Ballabh Pant, knew as little as I did about the enquiry.

You have drawn my attention to various statements made in the course of the enquiry. I do not know if it was necessary for the Advocate-General to draw my attention to these statements. In any event he did not do so and I knew nothing about them. Perhaps if you or your brother judges had suggested this to him, he would no doubt have drawn my attention and the UP Premier's attention to them. Neither of us thought that we were in a sense concerned with this matter and the Advocate-General may have thought so too. If any indication had been given to him that you considered any conduct of ours improper, the obvious course for him would have been to draw our attention to it and to such statements as had been made relating to it. Apparently the only suggestion that there was some impropriety in what we did came when your report was made to His Excellency the Governor-General.

The facts, so far as I can recollect them, and I have a fairly vivid recollection of this matter, are as follows:

The then Chief Justice of the Allahabad High Court, Shri Kamala Kant Verma, wrote to me that he wanted to see me urgently. I gave him an appointment and he came to see me in Delhi. I believe he also saw the Home Minister. He informed me that Mr. Justice Sinha's record was a very bad one and he was accused of grave offences. He said that this had become a public scandal and mentioned names of respected leaders of the Bar like Sir Tej Bahadur Sapru in this connection, saying that they thoroughly disapproved of Mr. Justice Sinha's conduct. I told the Chief Justice that this was none of my concern and as Chief Justice, he should take such steps as he thought proper. I gathered from him that he had reported the matter also to the Premier of the U.P.

As far as I can remember, the Chief Justice of Allahabad came to see me again and said that the position was becoming intolerable. He mentioned that he had consulted some of his brother judges also. I again told him that whatever the procedure was should be followed. He suggested that the alternatives were for Justice Sinha to resign or to face an enquiry. I told the Chief Justice that he should deal with the matter himself and tell Justice Sinha of the charges.

I remember mentioning this matter to the Home Minister who was of the same opinion, that is, that the Chief Justice should inform Justice Sinha of the charges. Thereupon there should be an enquiry unless Justice Sinha resigned.

I happened to go to Allahabad some time later and the Chief Justice of Allahabad again reminded me of this and asked me to speak to Justice Sinha on this subject. It was on his instance that Justice Sinha was invited to see me.' I forget whether Justice Sinha was sent for by the Chief Justice to me or whether a telephone message was sent to him to come and see me. The Premier of the UP was also present. I had the briefest of conversation with him though I think that the Premier had a slightly longer conversation. The purport of what I said to Justice Sinha was that the Chief Justice had brought these matters to our notice and they appeared to be serious charges. I could not say anything about them, but the normal course would presumably be an enquiry if the Chief Justice so desired. If on the other hand he chose to resign, possibly the necessity for a further enquiry might not arise. In answer he said that he would like to think over this matter. I never saw him again, nor had I any kind of communication with him.

You will notice that this account is somewhat different from the accounts you received in the course of the enquiry. It may be that people's memories are different or fail them. The Chief Justice appears to say in his statement that I took the initiative in this matter. As a matter of fact it was he who came to me twice on this subject. On each occasion I told him that it was up to him to deal with the matter after enquiry. I had received no other complaints except through the Chief Justice, though perhaps I might have heard some vague rumours.

I shall be glad to know if you think that there was any impropriety in what I did, as referred to above. I confess I do not see it. I had no desire at all to interfere in this matter and it was no concern of mine. It was only on the insistence of the Chief Justice that I took the step that I did.

Yours sincerely,
Jawaharlal Nehru

The Hon'ble Mr. Justice Harilal J. Kania
Chief Justice of India
New Delhi"

There is no further correspondence. Either Hon'ble Mr. Justice Kania might not have replied or it might not have been printed in the 9th Volume of SARDAR PATEL'S CORRESONDENCE.

After the Constitution of India became applicable with effect from 26th January, 1950, it was amended by the Parliament for the first time by the Constitution (First Amendment) Act, 1951 by which Articles 31-A, 31-B and Ninth Schedule were added. Article 31-B provided immunity to the laws included in the Ninth Schedule from the challenge on the ground of contravention of Article 13 of the Constitution. Article 13 prohibited the State from enacting any law which takes away or abridges the fundamental rights provided in Part III of the Constitution. The constitutional validity of the first amendment was upheld by the Supreme Court in *Sankari Prasad Singh Deo* v. *Union of India*, AIR 1951 SC 458: 1952 SCR 89.

However while determining the legality and validity of the detention order passed under section 3(1) of the Preventive Detention Act, 1950, the Supreme Court held in *A. K. Gopalan* v. *State of Madras,* AIR 1950 SC 27 that article 32 being kept in Part III, it is the fundamental right of a citizen to resort to this remedy and the

Supreme Court has the right to determine the Legislative limits *qua* the fundamental rights.

The Constitution was amended for a number of times thereafter.

By the Constitution (Seventeenth Amendment) Act 1964, certain laws were again kept in the Ninth Schedule, the legality and validity of which was challenged but the Supreme Court in the Judgment *Sajjan Singh* v. *State of Rajasthan*, AIR 1965 SC 845: (1965)1 SCR 933 upheld the amendment and re-iterated the law laid down in *Sankari's* case.

The Supreme Court by 11 Judge-Bench judgment in *Golak Nath v. State of Punjab A*IR1967 SC 1643: (1967) 2 SCR 762 overruled the judgments in *Sankari's* case and *Sajjan Singh's* case by a majority of 6 to 5. It was held that the Constitution amendment was a law within the meaning of article 13 of the Constitution and it was declared that the Parliament will have no power from the date of that decision (27.2.1967) to amend any of the provisions of Part III of the Constitution so as to take away or abridge the fundamental rights incorporated therein.

The Parliament by the Constitution (Twenty-fourth Amendment) Act,1971 amended article 13 of the Constitution by adding clause 4 as under:

> "13. (4) Nothing in this Article shall apply to any amendment of this Constitution made under Article 368."

By the same Amendment Act 1971, article 368 was also amended and in article 368(1) the words, "in exercise of its constituent power" were inserted.

Thereafter the Constitution was amended by the Parliament for a number of times. These amendments were challenged and the Supreme Court in the 13 Judge-Bench judgment in *Kesavananda Bharati v. State of Kerala* (1973) 4 SCC 225: 1973 Supp SCR 1 rendered on 24.4.1973 overruled *Golak Nath's* case by a majority of 7 to 6 and it was held that article 368 did not empower the Parliament to alter the basic structure of the Constitution and any such amendment brought after the date of that decision (24.4.1973) would be examined by the law laid down in this judgment.

After the election of Mrs. Indira Gandhi Prime Minister was set aside in June, 1975 on the ground of alleged corrupt practices, the Parliament amended the Constitution by the Constitution (Thirty-ninth Amendment) Act, 1975. By clause 4 of this amendment, article 329-A was inserted and by clause 5, Entries 87 to 124 were included in the Ninth Schedule of the Constitution. These amendments were challenged and the Supreme Court by judgment in *Indira Nehru Gandhi v. Raj Narain* 1975 (Supp) SCC 1 struck down both these clauses being violative of the basic structure of the Constitution.

Prime Minister Indira Gandhi had declared internal emergency on 26.6.1975 which continued up to March, 1977. During this period, the Parliament passed the Constitution (Fortieth Amendment) Act 1976 and by clause 3 of this amendment, Entries 125 to 188 were included in the Ninth Schedule. The Constitution was again amended by the Constitution (Forty second Amendment) Act 1976 by which clauses 4 and 5 were added in article 368. However, after the emergency was lifted, the Constitution was again amended by the Constitution (Forty fourth

Amendment) Act, 1978 to undo some of the wrongs committed in the Constitution during the emergency.

In *Maneka Gandhi* v. *Union of India* (1978) 1 SCC 248 a Bench of 7 Judges of the Supreme Court held that the words "procedure established by law" in article 21 of the Constitution had to be reasonable and not violative of article 14 of the Constitution. In *Minerva Mills Ltd.* v. *Union of India,* (1980) 3 SCC 625, the Supreme Court struck down clauses (4) and (5) of article 368 holding that these provisions violated the basic structure of the Constitution. In *Waman Rao* v. *Union of India,* (1981) 2 SCC 362 and *Bhim Singhji* v. *Union of India* (1981)1 SCC 166 also, the Supreme Court examined the law from the point of view of basic structure of the Constitution.

Then comes the significant judgment of the Supreme Court in *L. Chandra Kumar* v. *Union of India* (1997) 3 SCC 261: 1997 SCC (L&S) 577 in which it was held that power of judicial review is an integral and essential feature of the Constitution. It was also held that the jurisdiction conferred on the High Courts and the Supreme Court were a part of the basic structure of the Constitution and it was also held as inviolable.

Nine Judge-Bench Judgment of the Supreme Court in *I.R.Coelho (dead) by LRs* .v. *State of T.N.,* (2007) 2 SCC 1 considered the ratio of law laid down in all the previous judgments on this subject and it was concluded as under:

(i) A law that abrogates or abridges rights guaranteed by Part III of the Constitution may violate the basic structure doctrine or it may not. If former is the consequence of the law, whether by amendment of any Article of Part III or by an insertion in the Ninth Schedule, such law will have to be invalidated in exercise of judicial review power of the Court. The validity or invalidity would be tested on the principles laid down in this judgment.

(ii) The majority judgment in *Kesavananda Bharti* case (1973) 4 SCC 225 read with *Indira Gandhi* case 1975 (Supp) SCC1 requires the validity of each new constitutional amendment to be judged on its own merits. The actual effect and impact of the law on the rights guaranteed under Part III has to be taken into account for determining whether or not it destroys basic structure. The impact test would determine the validity of the challenge.

(iii) All amendments of the Constitution made on or after 24.4.1973 by which the Ninth Schedule is amended by inclusion of various laws therein shall have to be tested on the touchstone of the basic or essential features of the Constitution as reflected in Article 21 read with article 14, article 19 and the principles underlying them. To put it differently even though an Act is put in the Ninth Schedule by a constitutional amendment, its provisions would be open to attack on the ground that they destroy or damage the basic structure if the fundamental right or rights taken away or abrogated pertains to or pertain to the basic structure.

(iv) Justification for conferring protection, not blanket protection, on the laws included in the Ninth Schedule by constitutional amendments shall be a matter of constitutional adjudication by examining the nature and extent of infraction of a fundamental right by a statute, sought to be constitutionally protected, and on the touchstone of the basic structure doctrine *as reflected in article 21 read with article 14 and article 19* by application of the "rights test" and the "essence of the right" test taking the synoptic view of the articles in Part III as held in *Indira Gandhi* case 1975 (Supp) SCC 1. Applying the above tests to the Ninth Schedule laws, if the infraction affects the basic structure then such law(s) will not get the protection of the Ninth Schedule.

(v) If the validity of any Ninth Schedule law has already been upheld by this Court, then it would not be open to challenge such law again on the principles declared by this judgment. However, if a law held to be violative of any rights in Part III is subsequently incorporated in the Ninth Schedule after 24.4.1973, such a violative/infraction shall be open to challenge on the ground that it destroys or damages the basic structure as indicated in article 21 read with article 14, article 19 and the principles underlying thereunder.

(vi) Action taken and transactions finalized as a result of the impugned Acts shall not be open to challenge.

After answering the reference the matter was again sent for hearing before a three Judge Bench.

Therefore from the law laid down by the Hon'ble Supreme Court, it stands settled that the Supreme Court has the right and duty under the Constitution to ensure that the laws passed by the Legislature or the decisions taken by the Executive must be in accordance with the provisions of the Constitution and to set aside those enactments or decisions which violate the Constitutional provisions.

This power was exercised by the Hon'ble Supreme Court for a number of times, whenever it found that the enactment passed by the Legislature or the decisions taken by the Executive were not in accordance with the Constitution of India.

The judgments reproduced in this book are indicative of it.

QUESTION OF LAW RELATING TO THE EXERCISE OF POWER UNDER ARTICLE 356 OF THE CONSTITUTION OF INDIA WAS CONSIDERED IN THIS CASE

Rameshwar Prasad
v.
Union of India[1]

SUPREME COURT OF INDIA

Writ Petition (Civil) 257 of 2005

with

[With W.P. (C) No. 255 of 2005, W.P. (C) No. 258 of 2005 and W.P. (C) No. 353 of 2005]

Decided on 24-1-2006

BENCH

Y.K. Sabharwal, C.J.I., K.G. Balakrishnan, B.N. Agrawal, Ashok Bhan and Arijit Pasayat, JJs.

JUDGMENT

Y.K. Sabharwal, CJI (For himself and on behalf of B.N. Agrawal and Ashok Bhan JJ.)

The challenge in these petitions is to the constitutional validity of Notification dated 23rd May, 2005 ordering dissolution of the Legislative Assembly of the State of Bihar. It is a unique case. Earlier cases that came up before this Court were those where the dissolutions of Assemblies were ordered on the ground that the parties in power had lost the confidence of the House. The present case is of its own kind where before even the first meeting of the Legislative Assembly, its dissolution has been ordered on the ground that attempts are being made to cobble a majority by illegal means and lay claim to form the Government in the State and if these attempts continue, it would amount to tampering with constitutional provisions.

2. One of the questions of far reaching consequence that arises is whether the dissolution of Assembly under article 356(1) of the Constitution of India can be ordered to prevent the staking of claim by a political party on the ground that the majority has been obtained by illegal means. We would first note the circumstances which led to the issue of impugned notification.

FACTUAL BACKGROUND

3. Election to the State of Bihar was notified by the Election Commission on 17th December, 2004. Polling for the said elections were held in three phases, *i.e.*, 3rd February, 2005, 5th February, 2005 and 13th February, 2005. Counting of votes took place on 27th February, 2005. Results of the said elections were declared by the Election Commission. On 4th March, 2005, Notification was issued by the Election Commission in pursuance of section 73 of Representation of People Act, 1951 (for short 'the RP Act, 1951') duly notifying the names of the members elected for all the constituencies along with party affiliation.

---

1. AIR 2006 SC 980: 2006 AIR SCW 494: (2006) 2 SCC 1.

4. Bihar Legislative Assembly comprises of 243 members and to secure an absolute majority support of 122 Members of Legislative Assembly (in short 'MLAs'), is required. National Democratic Alliance (for short 'NDA'), a political coalition of parties comprising of the Bharatiya Janata Party (for short 'BJP') and the Janata Dal (United) (for short 'JD(U)') was the largest pre-poll combination having the support of 92 MLAs. The party-wise strength in the Assembly was as under:

"1.	NDA	:	92
2.	RJD	:	75
3.	LJP	:	29
4.	Congress (I)	:	10
5.	CPI (ML)	:	07
6.	Samajwadi Party	:	04
7.	NCP	:	03
8.	Bahujan Samaj Party	:	02
9.	Independents	:	17
10.	Others	:	09"

REPORT OF THE GOVERNOR OF BIHAR (SARDAR BUTA SINGH) DATED 6-3-2005 FOR KEEPING THE ASSEMBLY IN SUSPENDED ANIMATION

5. Report dated 6th March, 2005 sent by the Governor to the President, recommending newly constituted Assembly to be kept in suspended animation for the present reads as under:

"Respected Rashtrapati Jee,

The present Bihar Legislative Assembly has come to an end on 6th March, 2005. The Election Commission's notification with reference to the recent elections in regard to constitution of the new Assembly issued *vide* No. 308/ B.R.-L.A./2005 dated 4th March, 2005 and 464/Bihar-LA/2005, dated the 4th March, 2005 is enclosed (Annexure-I)

2. Based on the results that have come up, the following is the party-wise position:

1.	RJD	:	75
2.	JD (U)	:	55
3.	BJP	:	37
4.	Cong (I)	:	10
5.	BSP	:	02
6.	LJP	:	29
7.	CPI	:	03
8.	CPI (M)	:	01
9.	CPI (ML)	:	07
10.	NCP	:	03
11.	SP	:	04
12.	Independent	:	17
	Total	:	243

The R.J.D. and its alliance position is as follows:

1.	RJD	:	75
2.	Cong.(I)	:	10
3.	CPI	:	03
	(support letter not recd.)		
4.	CPI (M)	:	01
5.	NCP	:	03
	Total	:	92

The N.D.A. alliance position is as follows:

1.	BJP	:	37
2.	JD (U)	:	55
	Total	:	92

3. The present C.M., Bihar, Smt. Rabri Devi met me on 28.2.2005 and submitted her resignation along with her Council of Ministers. I have accepted the same and asked her to continue till an alternative arrangement is made.

4. A delegation of members of LJP met me in the afternoon of 28.2.2005 and they submitted a letter (Annexure II) signed by Shri Ram Vilas Paswan, President of the Party, stating therein that they will neither support the RJD nor the BJP in the formation of Government. The State President of Congress Party, Shri Ram Jatan Sinha, also met in the evening of 28.2.2005.

5. The State President of BJP, Shri Gopal Narayan Singh along with supporters met me on 1.3.2005. They have submitted a letter (Annexure III) stating that apart from combined alliance strength of 92 [BJP and JD(U)] they have support of another 10 to 12 Independents. The request in the letter is not to allow the RJD to form a Government.

6. Shri Dadan Singh, State President of Samajwadi Party, has sent a letter (Annexure IV) indicating their decision not to support the RJD or NDA in the formation of the government. He also met me on 2.3.2005.

7. Shri Ram Naresh Ram, Leader of the CPI (ML-Lib.), Legislature Party along with 4 others met me and submitted a letter (Annexure V) that they would not support any group in the formation of Government.

8. Shri Ram Vilas Paswan, National President of LJP, along with 15 others met me and submitted another letter (Annexure VI). They have reiterated their earlier stand.

9. The RJD met me on 5.3.2005 in the forenoon and they staked claim to form a Government indicating the support from the following parties:

1.	Cong(I)	:	10
2.	NCP	:	03
3.	CPI(M)	:	01
4.	BSP	:	02

(Copy enclosed as Annexure VII)

The RJD with the above will have only 91. They have further claimed that some of the Independent members may support the RJD. However, it has not been disclosed as to the number of Independent MLAs from whom they expect support nor their names.

Even if we assume the entire Independents totalling 17 to extend support to RJD alliance, which has a combined strength of 91, the total would be 108, which is still short of the minimum requirement of 122 in a House of 243.

10. The NDA delegation led by Shri Sushil Kumar Modi, MP, met me in the evening of 5.3.2005. They have not submitted any further letter. However, they stated that apart from their pre-election alliance of 92, another 10 Independents will also support them and they further stated that they would be submitting letters separately. This has not been received so far. Even assuming that they have support of 10 Independents, their strength will be only 102, which is short of the minimum requirement of 122.

11. Six Independent MLAs met me on 5.3.2005 and submitted a letter in which they have claimed that they may be called to form a Government and they will be able to get support of others (Annexure VIII). They have not submitted any authorisation letter supporting their claim.

12. I have also consulted the legal experts and the case laws particularly the case reported in AIR 1994 SC 1918 where the Supreme Court in para 365 of the report summarised the conclusion. The relevant part is para 2, *i.e.,* the recommendation of the Sarkaria Commission do merit serious consideration at the hands of all concerned. Sarkaria Commission in its report has said that Governor while going through the process of selection should select a leader who in his judgment is most likely to command a majority in the Assembly. The Book "Constitution of India" written by Shri V.N. Shukla (10th Edition) while dealing with article 75 and article 164 of the Constitution of India has dealt with this subject wherein it has quoted the manner of selection by the Governor in the following words:

> "In normal circumstances the Governor have no doubt as to who is the proper person to be appointed; it is leader of majority party in the Legislative Assembly, but circumstances can arise when it may be doubtful who that leader is and the Governor may have to exercise his personal judgment in selecting the C.M. Under the Constitutional Scheme which envisages that a person who enjoys the confidence of the Legislature should alone be appointed as C.M."

In *Bommai's* case referred to above in para 153, Supreme Court has stated with regard to the position where, I quote:

> "After the General Elections held, no political party or coalition of parties or group is able to secure absolute majority in the Legislative Assembly and despite the Governor's exploring the alternatives, the situation has arisen in which no political party is able to form stable government, it would be case of completely demonstrable inability of any political party to form a stable government commanding the confidence of the majority members of the Legislature. It would be a case of failure of constitutional machinery."

13. I explored all possibilities and from the facts stated above, I am fully satisfied that no political party or coalition of parties or groups is able to substantiate a claim of majority in the Legislative Assembly, and having explored the alternatives with all the political parties and groups and Independents MLAs, a situation has emerged in which no political party or groups appear to be able to form a government commanding a majority in the House. Thus, it is a case of complete inability of any political party to form a stable government commanding the confidence of the majority members. This is a case of failure of constitutional machinery.

14. I, as Governor of Bihar, am not able to form a popular government in Bihar, because of the situation created by the election results mentioned above.

15. I, therefore, recommend that the present newly constituted Assembly be kept in suspended animation for the present, and the President of India is requested to take such appropriate action/decision, as required."

PRESIDENT'S RULE IMPOSED ON 7.3.2005

6. Since no political party was in a position to form a government, a notification was issued on 7th March, 2005 under article 356 of the Constitution imposing President's Rule over the State of Bihar and the Assembly was kept in suspended animation. Another notification of the same date was also issued, *inter alia,* stating that the powers exercisable by the President shall, subject to the superintendence, direction and control of the President be exercisable also by the Governor of Bihar.

OBJECT OF THE PRESIDENT RULE IS TO GIVE TIME TO EXPLORE THE POSSIBILITY OF FORMATION OF POPULAR GOVERNMENT

7. The object of the proclamation imposing President's Rule was to give time and space to the political process to explore the possibility of forming a majority government in the State through a process of political realignment as is reflected in the speech of Home Minister Shri Shivraj V. Patil in the Rajya Sabha on 21st March, 2005 when the Bihar Appropriation (Vote on Account) Bill, 2005 was discussed. The Home Minister said

"But, I would like to make one point very clear. We are not very happy to impose President's Rule on the State of Bihar. Let there be no doubt in the minds of any Members of the House; were not happy. After the elections we would have been happy if government would have been formed by the elected representatives. That was not possible and that is why, President's Rule was imposed. But we cannot take pleasure in saying "Look we did this". We are not happy about it. I would ensure that the President's Rule is not continued for a long time. The sooner it disappear, the better it would be for Bihar, for democracy and for the system we are following in our country. But, who have to take steps in this respect. The governor can and, I would like to request in this House that elected representatives should talk to each other and create a situation in which it becomes possible for them to form a Government. Even if it is minority government with a slight margin, there is no problem."

HOME MINISTER'S ASSURANCE TO THE NATION

8. The Home Minister gave a solemn assurance to the nation that the imposition of President's rule was temporary and transient and was intended to explore the possibility of forming a popular Government.

VERSION OF THE PETITIONERS

9. According to the petitioners, process of realignment of forces was set in motion and several political parties and independent MLAs re-considered their position in terms of their commitment to provide a majority government in deference to the popular wishes of the people and announced support to the NDA led by Shri Nitish Kumar. First such announcement was made by the entire group of 17 independent MLAs on 8th April, 2005. The signed declaration was released by these MLAs to the media. With the support of 17 independent MLAs the support base of the NDA rose to 109 MLAs. Later on, it rose to 115 MLAs with the declaration of support by the Samajwadi Party (SP), the Bahujan Samaj Party (BSP) and the Nationalist Congress Party (NCP).

BIHAR GOVERNOR'S REPORT DATED 27.4.2005

10. Governor of Bihar sent a report on 27th April, 2005 to the President of India, *inter alia,* stating that the newspaper reports and other reports gathered through meeting with various party functionaries/leaders and also intelligence reports received, indicated a trend to gain over elected representatives of the people and various elements within the party and also outside the party being approached through various allurements like money, caste, posts etc., which was a disturbing feature. According to the said report, the situation was fast approaching a scenario wherein if the trend is not arrested immediately the consequent political instability will further give rise to horse trading being practiced by various political parties/groups trying to allure elected MLAs. That it would not be possible to contain the situation without giving the people another opportunity to give their mandate through a fresh poll. The report is reproduced below in its entirety.

> "Respected Rashtrapati Jee,
>
> I invite a reference to my D.O. No. 33/GB dated the 6th March, 2005 through which a detailed analysis of the results of the Assembly elections were made and a recommendation was also made to keep the newly constituted Assembly (constituted *Vide* Election Commission's notification No. 308/BRL. A./2005 dated the 4th March, 2005 and 464/Bihar-LA/2005, dated the 4th March, 2005) in a suspended animation and also to issue appropriate direction/ decision. In the light of the same, the President was pleased to issue a proclamation under article 356 of the Constitution of India *vide* notification No. G.S.R. 162(E), dated 7th March, 2005, and the proclamation has been approved and assented by the Parliament.
>
> 2. As none of the parties either individually or with the then pre-election combination or with post-election alliance combination could stake a claim to form a popular government wherein they could claim a support of a simple majority of 122 in a House of 243, I had no alternative but to send the above mentioned report with the said recommendation.

3. I am given to understand that serious attempts are being made by JDU and BJP to cobble a majority and lay claim to form the government in the State. Contacts in JD-U and BJP have informed that 16-17 LJP MLAs have been won over by various means and attempt is being made to win over others. The JD-U is also targeting Congress for creating a split. It is felt in JD-U circle that in case LJP does not split then it can still form the government with the support of Independent, NCP, BSP and SP MLAs and two-third of Congress MLAs after it splits from the main Congress party. The JD-U and BJP MLAs are quite convinced that by the end of this month or latest by the first week of May JD-U will be in a position to form the government. The high pressure moves of JD-U/BJP is also affecting the RJD MLAs who have become restive. According to a report there is a lot of pressure by the RJD MLAs on Lalu Prasad Yadav to either form the Government in Bihar on UPA pattern in the Centre, with the support of Congress, LJP and others or he should at least ensure the continuance of President's Rule in the State.

4. The National Commission to review the working of the Constitution has also noticed that the reasons for increasing instability of elected governments was attributable to unprincipled and opportunistic political realignment from time to time. A reasonable degree of stability of government and a strong government is important. It has also noticed that the changing alignment of the members of political parties so openly really makes a mockery of our democracy. Under the Constitutional Scheme a political party goes before the electorate with a particular programme and it sets up candidates at the election on the basis of such programmes. The 10th Schedule of the Constitution was introduced on the premise that political propriety and morality demands that if such persons after the elections changes his affiliation, that should be discouraged. This is on the basis that the loyalty to a party is a norm, being based on shared beliefs. A divided party is looked on with suspicion by the electorate.

5. Newspaper reports in the recent time and other reports gathered through meeting with various party functionaries/leaders and also intelligence reports received by me, indicate a trend to gain over elected representatives of the people and various elements within the party and also outside the party being approached through various allurements like money, caste, posts etc., which is a disturbing feature. This would affect the constitutional provisions and safeguards built therein. Any such move may also distort the verdict of the people as shown by results of the recent elections. If these attempts are allowed to continue then it would be amounting to tampering with constitutional provisions.

6. Keeping in view the above mentioned circumstances the present situation is fast approaching a scenario wherein if the trend is not arrested immediately, the consequent political instability will further give rise to horse trading being practiced by various political parties/groups trying to allure elected MLAs. Consequently, it may not be possible to contain the situation without giving the people another opportunity to give their mandate through a fresh poll.

7. I am submitting these facts before the Hon'ble President for taking such action as deemed appropriate."

VERSION OF THE PETITIONERS

11. According to the petitioners, Lok Janashakti Party (LJP) had contested elections on the plank of opposing the then government led by Rashtriya Janata Dal (RJD), which again is a constituent of United Progressive Alliance (UPA) in the Centre. It had a strength of 29 MLAs in the new assembly. The leader of LJP Shri Ram Vilas Paswan had taken the stand that he was opposed to RJD as well as NDA led by the BJP. MLAs belonging to LJP were in a rebellious mood. About 22 MLAs belonging to the LJP assembled on or around 21st May, 2005 and started working towards a major political realignment in the stand of the said party. According to them, 22 LJP members of the Legislative wing supported by members of the original political party reached a consensus subsequently to merge their party with the JD(U). That, with this the repolarisation of political forces was complete. According to them the proposed merger between two political formations was in consonance with the principles enumerated in para 4 of the Tenth Schedule to the Constitution. It provides that on a merger of the political party, all the members of the new political party with which the merger has taken place if and only if not less than two-third of the members of the said party have agreed to the said merger.

ANOTHER REPORT OF GOVERNOR DATED 21.5.2005 FROM CAMP OFFICE, DELHI

It is their allegation that in order to thwart the formation of a government led by JD(U), the Governor of Bihar sent another report from its Camp Office in Delhi on 21st May, 2005 to the President of India. It was reiterated in the report that from the information gathered through reports from media, meeting with various political functionaries, as also intelligence reports, a trend was indicated to win over elected representatives of the people. In his view a situation had arisen in the State wherein it would be desirable in the interest of State that Assembly which has been kept in suspended animation be dissolved so that the people/electorate could be provided with one more opportunity to seek the mandate of the people at an appropriate time to be decided in due course. The report dated 21st May, 2005 is reproduced in its entirety as follows:

"Respected Rashtrapati Jee,

I invite a reference to my D.O. letter No. 52/GB dated 27th April, 2005 through which I had given a detailed account of the attempts made by some of the parties notably the JD(U) and BJP to cobble a majority and lay a claim to form a government in the State. I had informed that around 16-17 MLAs belonging to LJP were being wooed by various means so that a split could be effected in the LJP. Attention was also drawn to the fact that the RJD MLAs had also become restive in the light of the above moves made by the JD(U). As you are aware after the Assembly Elections in February, this year, none of the political parties either individually or with the then pre-election combination or with post-election alliance combination could stake a claim to form a popular government since they could not claim a support of a simple majority of 122 in a House of 243 and hence the President was pleased to issue a proclamation under article 356 of the Constitution *vide* Notification No. GSR/026 162(E), dated 7th March, 2005 and the Assembly was kept in suspended animation. The reports received by me in the recent past through the media and also through meeting with various political functionaries, as also intelligence reports, indicate a trend to win over elected representatives of the people. Report has also been received of one of the LJP MLA, who is General Secretary of the party having resigned today and also 17-18 more perhaps are moving towards the JD(U) clearly indicating that various allurements have been offered which is very disturbing and alarming feature. Any move by the breakaway faction to align with any other party to cobble a majority and stake claim to form a government would positively affect the Constitutional provisions and safeguards built therein and distort the verdict of the people as shown by the results in the recent Elections. If these attempts are allowed it would be amounting to tampering with Constitutional provisions. Keeping the abovementioned circumstances, I am of the considered view that if the trend is not arrested immediately, it may not be possible to contain the situation. Hence, in my view a situation has arisen in the State wherein it would be desirable in the interest of the State that the Assembly presently kept in suspended animation is dissolved, so that the people/electorate can be provided with one more opportunity to seek the mandate of the people at an appropriate time to be decided in due course."

UNION CABINET MET IN THE NIGHT AT 11 P.M., TOOK THE DECISION FOR DISSOLVING THE BIHAR ASSEMBLY AND REPORT WAS SENT TO THE PRESIDENT IN MOSCOW BY FAX FOR GETTING HIS APPROVAL

12. The report of the Governor was received by Union of India and on 22nd May, 2005 and on the same day, the Union cabinet met at about 11.00 P.M. and decided to accept the report of the Governor and sent the fax message to the President of India, who had already left for Moscow, recommending the dissolution of the Legislative Assembly of Bihar.

PRESIDENT RECEIVED THE MESSAGE IN MOSCOW IN MIDNIGHT AND SIGNED THE SAME AT 1:52 HOURS

This message was received by the President of India at his Camp office in Moscow at 01:52 hrs. (IST). President of India accorded his approval and sent the same through the fax message which was received at 03:50 hrs. (IST) on 23rd May, 2005.

EVEN NOTIFICATION OF DISSOLUTION OF BIHAR ASSEMBLY WAS ISSUED BY THE CENTRAL GOVERNMENT IN MIDNIGHT AT 2.30 A.M. ON 23.5.2005

After due process the notification was issued formally at 14:30 hrs. (IST) on 23rd May, 2005 dissolving the Bihar Assembly which has been impugned in these writ petitions.

WRIT PETITION FILED

13. Challenging proclamation dated 23rd May, 2005 issued under article 356 of the Constitution, ordering dissolution of Bihar Legislative Assembly, petitioners have also prayed for restoration of Election Commission notification dated 4th May, 2005 issued under section 73 of the RP Act of 1951.

NDA CONSTITUENTS WERE ABOUT TO FORM THE GOVERNMENT AS PER THE VERSION OF THE PETITIONERS

14. According to the petitioners, the condition precedent for dissolving the Assembly is that there must be satisfaction of the President that a situation has arisen in which the Government of a State cannot be carried on in accordance with the provisions of the Constitution. That this satisfaction has to be based on cogent material. Power of dissolution cannot be used to prevent the staking of claim for the formation of a government by a political party with support of others. That the Assembly as placed under suspended animation with the intention of providing time and space to political parties to explore the possibility of providing a majority government in the State. No sooner the process of realignment was complete ensuring that the NDA led by Shri Nitish Kumar had the support of over 135 MLAs, report was sent by the Governor. The midnight meeting of the Cabinet was hurriedly called in order to prevent the formation of a government. It was incumbent upon the Governor to make a meaningful and real effort for securing the possibility of a majority government in the State. According to them the intention of the Governor was to prevent the formation of a Government led by Shri Nitish Kumar. That there was no material available or in existence to indicate that any political defection was being attempted through the use of money or muscle power. In the absence of any such material the exercise of power under article 356 was a clear fraud on the exercise of power.

15. That allegations in the Governor's report of horse trading was factually incorrect and fictional. It was incumbent upon the Governor to verify the facts personally from the MLAs. That under the Scheme of the Constitution the decision with regard to mergers and disqualifications on the ground of defection or horse trading is vested in the Speaker. The Governor could not have attempted to act on that basis and arrogated to himself such an authority. Relying heavily on the Nine-Judge Bench judgment of this Court in *S.R. Bommai* v. *Union of India*, (1994) 3 SCC 1, it was contended that action of the Governor is *mala fide* in law; irrational, without any cogent material to support the conclusion arrived at and is based on mere *ipse dixit* and, thus, was not sustainable in law. It was contended that in exercise of judicial review this Court should quash the impugned notification and as a consequence restore the Legislative Assembly constituted by the Election Commission notification dated 4th March, 2005.

SUBMISSION IN SUPPORT OF THIS CONTENTION

16. Mr. Soli Sorabjee led the arguments in support of the challenge to the validity of the impugned notification contending that the dissolution of the Assembly when examined in the light of law laid down in *Bommai's* case (*supra*) is clearly unconstitutional and deserves to be set aside and the *status quo ante* at least as on 7th March, 2005 may be directed.

17. Mr. Viplav Sharma, advocate, appearing in person in Writ Petition No. 258 of 2005 adopting the arguments of Mr. Sorabjee further contended that before even elected candidates making and subscribing oath or affirmation, as contemplated by article 188 of the Constitution, even the Assembly could not be placed under suspended animation and *status quo* as on the date of issue of notification under section 73 of the RP Act of 1951 deserves to be directed.

18. Mr. Narasimha, appearing in Writ Petition (C) No. 353 for the petitioner, also adopted the arguments of Mr. Sorabjee but at the same time further contended that it is not legally permissible to order the dissolution of Assembly before its meeting even once and the MLAs being administered the oath as contemplated by the Constitution. This was also the submission of Mr. Viplav Sharma. Arguments on behalf of respondent 026 Union of India were led by learned Attorney General, Mr. Milon Banerjee, followed by learned Solicitor General and Additional Solicitor General, Mr. Gulam Vahanavati and Mr. Gopal Subramaniam respectively. Mr. P.P. Rao, learned senior advocate argued for State of Bihar. We place on record our appreciation for excellent and very able assistance rendered by all the advocates.

GOVERNOR IS NOT ACCOUNTABLE AS A PERSON HELD BY THE SUPREME COURT *VIDE* INTERIM ORDER DATED 8.9.2005

19. After hearing arguments on the question of the Governor not being answerable to any Court in view of immunity granted by article 361(1) of the Constitution. Supreme Court accepted the submission of the government in terms of order dated 8th September, 2005 that notice may not be issued to the Governor, giving brief reason in order to be followed by detailed reasons later. The said order reads as under:

> "On the question whether the Governor could be impleaded in his capacity as the Governor and whether notice could be issued to him on the writ petitions in the context of averments made and the prayers contained in the petitions and other aspects highlighted in the order dated 31st August, 2005, we have heard Mr. Soli J. Sorabjee, learned senior counsel appearing in Writ Petition (C) No. 257 of 2005, and Mr. Viplav Sharma, petitioner-in-person in Writ Petition (C) No.258 of 2005. We have also heard the submissions made by Mr. Milon K. Banerji, Attorney-General for India, and Mr. Gopal Subramaniam, learned Additional Solicitor-General. The Constitution of India grants immunity to the Governor as provided in article 361. Article 361(1), *inter alia*, provides that the Governor shall not be answerable to any Court for the exercise and performance of the powers and duties of his office or for any act done or purporting to be done by him in exercise and performance of those powers and duties. It is submitted by learned Attorney-General and Additional Solicitor-General that in view of article 361(1), this Court may not issue notice to the Governor. While we accept the submission but, at the same time, it is also necessary to note that the immunity granted to the Governor does not affect the power of the Court to judicially scrutinize the attack made to the proclamation issued under article 356(1) of the Constitution of India on the ground of *mala fides* or it being *ultra vires*. It would be for the Government to satisfy the Court and adequately meet such ground of challenge. A *mala fide* act is wholly outside the scope of the power and has no existence in the eyes

of law. Even, the expression purporting to be done in article 361 does not cover acts which are *mala fide* or *ultra vires* and, thus, the Government supporting the proclamation under article 356(1) shall have to meet the challenge. The immunity granted under article 361 does not mean that in the absence of Governor, the ground of *mala fides* or proclamation being *ultra vires* would not be examined by the Court. At this stage, we have not examined the question whether the exercise of power by the Governor was *mala fide* or *ultra vires* or not. That is a question still to be argued.

These are our brief reasons. We will give detailed reason later."

QUESTIONS CONSIDERED BY THE SUPREME COURT

20. Under the aforesaid factual background, the points that fall for our determination are:

1. Is it permissible to dissolve the Legislative Assembly under article 174(2)(b) of the Constitution without its first meeting taking place?
2. Whether the proclamation dated 23rd May, 2005 dissolving the Assembly of Bihar is illegal and unconstitutional?
3. If the answer to the aforesaid question is in affirmative, is it necessary to direct *status quo ante* as on 7th March, 2005 or 4th March, 2005?
4. What is the scope of article 361 granting immunity to the Governor?

BRIEF ORDER PASSED BY THE SUPREME COURT ON 7.10.2005

21. After hearing elaborate arguments, by a brief order dated 7th October, 2005, the notification dated 23rd May, 2005 was held to be unconstitutional but having regard to the facts and circumstances of the case, relief directing *status quo ante* to restore the Legislative Assembly as it stood on 7th March, 2005, was declined. The Order dated 7th October reads as under: (SCC pp. 625-626, paras 1 to 9)

"1. The General Elections to the Legislative Assembly of Bihar were held in the month of February, 2005. The Election Commission of India, in pursuance of section 73 of the Representation of the People Act, 1951 in terms of Notification dated 4th March, 2005 notified the names of the elected members.

2. As no party or coalition of the parties was in a position to secure 122 seats so as to have majority in the Assembly, the Governor of Bihar made a report dated 6th March, 2005 to the President of India, whereupon in terms of Notification G.S.R. 162(E), dated 7th March, 2005, issued in exercise of powers under article 356 of the Constitution of India, the State was brought under President's Rule and the Assembly was kept in suspended animation. By another Notification G.S.R. 163(E) of the same date, 7th March, 2005, it was notified that all powers which have been assumed by the President of India, shall, subject to the superintendence direction and control of the President, be exercisable also by the Governor of the State. The Home Minister in a speech made on 21st March, 2005 when the Bihar Appropriation (Vote on Account) Bill, 2005 was being discussed in the Rajya Sabha said that the Government was not happy to impose President's Rule in Bihar and would have been happy if government would have been formed by the elected representatives after the election. That was, however, not possible and, therefore, President's

Rule was imposed. It was also said that the Government would not like to see that President's Rule is continued for a long time but it is for elected representatives to take steps in this respect; the Governor can ask them and request them and he would also request that the elected representatives should talk to each other and create a situation in which it becomes possible for them to form a government. The Presidential Proclamation dated 7th March, 2005 was approved by the Lok Sabha at its sitting held on 19th March, 2005 and Rajya Sabha at its sitting held on 21st March, 2005.

3. The Governor of Bihar made two reports to the President of India, one dated 27th April, 2005 and the other dated 21st May, 2005. On consideration of these reports, Notification dated 23rd May, 2005 was issued in exercise of the powers conferred by sub-clause (b) of clause (2) of article 174 of the Constitution, read with clause (a) of the Notification G.S.R. 162(E) dated 7th March, 2005 issued under article 356 of the Constitution and the Legislative Assembly of the State of Bihar was dissolved with immediate effect.

4. These writ petitions have been filed challenging constitutional validity of the aforesaid Proclamation dated 23rd May, 2005. Mr. Soli J. Sorabjee, Senior Advocate and Mr. P.S. Narasimha, Advocate and Mr. Viplav Sharma, Advocate appearing-in-person have made elaborate submissions in support of the challenge to the impugned action of dismissing the Assembly.

5. On the other hand, Mr. Milon K. Banerjee, Attorney-General for India, Mr. Goolam E. Vahanavati, Solicitor-General and Mr. Gopal Subramaniam, Additional-Solicitor-General appearing for Union of India and Mr. P.P. Rao, Senior Advocate appearing for the State of Bihar also made elaborate submissions supporting the impugned Proclamation dated 23rd May, 2005.

6. Many intricate and important questions of law having far reaching impact have been addressed from both sides. After the conclusion of the hearing of oral arguments, written submissions have also been filed by learned counsel.

7. Fresh elections in State of Bihar have been notified. As per press note dated 3rd September, 2005 issued by Election Commission of India, the schedule for general elections to the Legislative Assembly of Bihar has been announced. According to it, the polling is to take place in four phases commencing from 18th October, 2005 and ending with the fourth phase voting on 19th November, 2005. As per the said press note, the date of Notification for first and second phase of poll was 23rd September and 28th September, 2005, date of poll being 18th October, 2005 and 26th October, 2005 respectively. Notifications for third and fourth phases of poll are to be issued on 19th and 26th October, 2005 respectively.

8. Keeping in view the questions involved, the pronouncement of judgment with detailed reasons is likely to take some time and, therefore, at this stage, we are pronouncing this brief order as the order of the Court to be followed by detailed reasons later.

9. Accordingly, as per majority opinion, this court orders as under:

1. The Proclamation dated 23rd May, 2005 dissolving the Legislative Assembly of the State of Bihar is unconstitutional.

2. Despite unconstitutionality of the impugned Proclamation, but having regard to the facts and circumstances of the case, the present is not a case where in exercise of discretionary jurisdiction the *status quo ante* deserves to be ordered to restore the Legislative Assembly as it stood on the date of Proclamation dated 7th March, 2005 whereunder it was kept under suspended animation."

ANSWER GIVEN BY THE SUPREME COURT TO POINT NO. 1

Point No. 1—Is it Permissible to Dissolve the Legislative Assembly under Article 174(2)(b) of the Constitution without its First Meeting taking place?

22. Article 174 of the Constitution deals with the power of the Governor to summon the House, prorogue the House and dissolve the Legislative Assembly. This Court never had the occasion to consider the question of legality of dissolution of a Legislative Assembly even before its first meeting contemplated under article 172 of the Constitution. It has been contended on behalf of the petitioners by Mr. Narsimha and Mr. Viplav Sharma, appearing-in-person, that a Legislative Assembly can be dissolved under article 174(2)(b) only after its first meeting is held as postulated by article 172 of the Constitution. The argument is that there cannot be any dissolution without even members taking oath and the Legislative Assembly coming into existence. What does not exist, cannot be dissolved, is the submission. In this regard, the question to be considered also is whether the date for first meeting of the Legislative Assembly can be fixed without anyone being in a position to form the Government.

23. Let us first examine the relevant constitutional and statutory provisions.

24. Part VI of the Constitution dealing with the States has six chapters but relevant for our purpose are Chapter II and Chapter III. Chapter II comprising article 153 to article 167 relates to the Executive, Chapter III comprising article 168 to article 212 relates to the State Legislature.

25. The federal structure under our Constitution contemplates that there shall be a Legislature for every State which shall consist of a Governor and one or two Houses, as provided in article 168. Article 170 prescribes that the Legislative Assembly of each State shall consist of members chosen by direct election from territorial constituencies in the States. Article 170, therefore, brings in the democratic process of election.

26. Article 164 puts into place an Executive Government. It enjoins upon the Governor to appoint the Chief Minister and other Ministers on the advice of the Chief Minister. The Council of Ministers (article 163) exercises the Executive power of the State as provided under article 154. Article 164(2) provides that the Council of Ministers shall be collectively responsible to the Legislative Assembly of the State.

27. As provided in article 172, every Legislative Assembly of every State, unless sooner dissolved, shall continue for five years from the date appointed for its first meeting and no longer and the expiration of the said period of five years shall operate as a dissolution of the Assembly. Article 174(1) provides that the Governor shall from time to time summon the House to meet at such time and place as he thinks fit, but six months shall not intervene between its last sitting in one session and the date appointed for its first sitting in the next session. Article 174(2)(b) provides that the Governor may from time to time dissolve the Legislative Assembly.

28. Every member of the Legislative Assembly of the State shall, before taking his seat, make and subscribe before the Governor, an oath or affirmation, as provided in article 188 of the Constitution.

29. The contention urged is that the function of the Governor in summoning the House and administering the oath or affirmation to the members of the Legislative Assembly are not the matters of privilege, prerogative or discretion of the Governor but are his primary and fundamental constitutional obligations on which the principles of Parliamentary democracy, federalism and even 'separation of power' are dependent. Further contention is that another constitutional obligation of the Governor is to constitute the Executive Government.

30. According to Mr. Narasimha, the Governor failed to fulfil these constitutional obligations. Neither the Executive Government nor the Legislative Assembly has been constituted by the Governor. On the other hand, the Governor has frustrated the very object of exercise of his constitutional obligation by dissolving the Legislative Assembly under article 174(2)(b) without the Legislative Assembly being even constituted. When the Legislative Assembly is not even constituted, where is the question of its dissolution, is the contention urged. The submission is that under the Scheme of Indian Constitution, it is impermissible to dissolve a Legislative Assembly before its first meeting and members making oath or affirmation as required by article 188. According to the petitioners, under Indian Constitution, the Legislative Assembly is duly constituted only upon the House being summoned and from the date appointed for its first meeting. Article 172 which provides for duration of State Legislatures reads as under:

ARTICLE 172 OF THE CONSTITUTION OF INDIA AND ITS EFFECT

"172. *Duration of State Legislatures.*—(1) Every Legislative Assembly of every State, unless sooner dissolved shall continue for (five years) from the date appointed for its first meeting and no longer and the expiration of the said period of (five years) shall operate as a dissolution of the Assembly:

Provided that the said period, may while a proclamation of Emergency is in operation, be extended by Parliament by law for a period not exceeding one year at a time and not extending in any case beyond a period of six months after the Proclamation has ceased to operate.

(2) The Legislative Council of a State shall not be subject to dissolution, but as nearly as possible one-third of the members thereof shall retire as soon as may be on the expiration of every second year in accordance with the provisions made in that behalf by Parliament by law."

31. The aforesaid constitutional provision stipulates that five years term of a Legislative Assembly shall be reckoned from the date appointed for its first meeting and on the expiry of five years commencing from the date of the first meeting, the Assembly automatically stands dissolved by afflux of time. The duration of the Legislative Assembly beyond five years is impermissible in view of the mandate of the aforesaid provision that the Legislative Assembly shall continue for five years and 'no longer'. Relying upon these provisions, it is contended that the due constitution of the Legislative Assembly can only be after its first meeting when the members subscribe oath or affirmation under article 188. The statutory deemed constitution of the Assembly under section 73 of the RP Act, 1951, according to the petitioners, has no relevance for determining due constitution of Legislative Assembly for the purpose of Constitution of India.

32. Reference on behalf of the petitioners has also been made to law existing prior to the enforcement of the Constitution of India contemplating the commencement of the Council of State and Legislative Assembly from the date of its first meeting. It was pointed out that section 63(d) in the Government of India Act, 1915 which dealt with Indian Legislature provided that every Council of State shall continue for five years and every Legislative Assembly for three years from the date of its first meeting. Likewise, section 72(b) provided that every Governor's Legislative Council shall continue for three years from its first meeting. The Government of India Act, 1919, repealing 1915 Act, provided in section 8(1) that every Governor's Legislative Council shall continue for three years from its first meeting and in section 21 provided that every Council of State shall continue for five years and every Legislative Assembly for three years from its first meeting. Likewise, the Government of India Act, 1935 repealing 1919 Act, had provision identical to article 172 of the Constitution.

SECTION 73 OF THE REPRESENTATION OF THE PEOPLE ACT, 1951

33. Section 73 of the RP Act, 1951, insofar as relevant for our purposes, is as under:

> "*73. Publication of results of general elections to the House of the People and the State Legislative Assemblies.*—Where a general election is held for the purpose of constituting a new House of the People or a new State Legislative Assembly, there shall be notified by the Election Commission in the Official Gazette, as soon as may be after the results of the elections in all the constituencies other than these in which the poll could not be taken for any reason on the date originally fixed under clause (d) of section 30 or for which the time for completion of the election has been extended under the provisions of section 153 have been declared by the returning officer under the provisions of section 53 or, as the case may be section 66, the names of the members elected for those constituencies and upon the issue of such notification that House or Assembly shall be deemed to be duly constituted."

34. In the present case, Notification under section 73 of the RP Act, 1951 was issued on 4th March, 2005. The deemed constitution of the Legislative Assembly took place under section 73 on the issue of the said notification. The question is whether this deemed constitution of Legislative Assembly is only for the purpose of the RP Act, 1951 and not for the constitutional provisions so as to invoke power of dissolution under article 174(2)(b). The stand of the government is that in view of aforesaid legal fiction, the constitution of the Legislative Assembly takes place for all purposes and, thus, the Legislative Assembly is deemed to have been 'duly constituted' on 4th March, 2005 and, therefore, the Governor could exercise the power of dissolution under article 174(2)(b).

35. Section 73 of the RP Act, 1951 enjoins upon the Election Commission to issue notification after declaration of results of the elections in all the constituencies. The superintendence, direction and control of elections to Parliament and to the Legislature of every State vests in Election Commission under article 324 of the Constitution. Article 327 provides that Parliament may make provision with respect to all matters relating to, or in connection with, elections to the Legislative Assembly of a State and all other matters necessary for securing the 'due constitution' of the House of the Legislature. Article 329 bars the interference by courts in electoral matters except by an election petition presented to such authority and in such manner as may be provided for by or under any law made by the appropriate Legislature. Article 327 read with section 73 of the RP Act, 1951 provide for as to when the House or Assembly shall be 'duly constituted'. No provision, constitutional or statutory, stipulates that the 'due constitution' is only for the purposes of articles 324, 327 and 329 and not for the purpose of enabling the Governor to exercise power under article 174(2)(b) of the Constitution. Insofar as the argument based on article 172 is concerned, it seems clear that the due constitution of the Legislative Assembly is different than its duration which is five years — to be computed from the date appointed for its first meeting and no longer. There is no restriction under article 174(2)(b) stipulating that the power to dissolve the Legislative Assembly can be exercised only after its first meeting. Clause (b) of proviso to section 73 of the RP Act, 1951 also does not limit the deemed constitution of the Assembly for only specific purpose of the said Act or articles 324, 327 and 329 of the Constitution. The said clause provides that the issue of notification under section 73 shall not be deemed to affect the duration of the State Legislative Assembly, if any, functioning immediately before the issue of the said notification. In fact, clause (b) further fortifies the conclusion that the duration of the Legislative Assembly is different than the due constitution thereof. In the present case, we are not concerned with the question of duration of the Assembly but with the question whether the Assembly had been duly constituted or not so as to enable the Governor to exercise the power of dissolution under article 174(2)(b). The Constitution of India does not postulate one 'due constitution' for the purposes of elections under Part XV and another for the purposes of the Executive and the State Legislature under Chapters II and III of Part VI. The aforenoted provisions existing prior to the enforcement of Constitution of India are also of no relevance for determining the effect of deemed constitution of Assembly under section 73 of the RP Act, 1951 to exercise power of dissolution under article 274(2)(b).

PRIOR LAW ON THE SUBJECT DISCUSSED

36. In *K.K. Abu* v. *Union of India*, AIR 1965 Ker 229, a learned Single Judge of the High Court of Kerala rightly came to the conclusion that neither article 172 nor article 174 prescribe that dissolution of a State Legislature can only be after commencement of its term or after the date fixed for its first meeting. Once the Assembly is constituted, it becomes capable of dissolution. This decision has been referred to by one of us (Arijit Pasayat, J.) in *Special Reference No. 1 of 2002 (popularly known as Gujarat Assembly Election matter)*, (2002) 8 SCC 237. No provision of the

Constitution stipulates that the dissolution can only be after the first meeting of the State Legislature.

37. The acceptance of the contention of the petitioners can also lead to a breakdown of the Constitution. In a given case, none may come forth to stake claim to form the government, for want of requisite strength to provide a stable government. If petitioners' contention is accepted, in such an eventuality, the Governor will neither be able to appoint Executive Government nor would he be able to exercise power of dissolution under article 174(2)(b). The Constitution does not postulate a live Assembly without the Executive Government.

38. On behalf of the petitioners, reliance has, however, been placed upon a decision of a Division Bench of Allahabad High Court in the case of *Udai Narain Sinha* v. *State of Uttar Pradesh,* AIR 1987 All 203. Disagreeing with the Kerala High Court, it was held that in the absence of the appointment of a date for the first meeting of the Assembly in accordance with article 172(1), its life did not commence for the purposes of that article, even though it might have been constituted by virtue of notification under section 73 of the RP Act, 1951 so as to entitle the Governor to dissolve it by exercising power under article 174(2). It was held by the Division Bench that section 73 of the RP Act, 1951 only created a fiction for limited purpose for paving the way for the Governor to appoint a date for first meeting of either House or the Assembly so as to enable them to function after being summoned to meet under article 174 of the Constitution. We are unable to read any such limitation. In our view, the Assembly, for all intends and purposes, is deemed to be duly constituted on issue of notification under section 73 and the duration thereof is distinct from its due constitution. The interpretation which may lead to a situation of constitutional breakdown deserves to be avoided, unless the provisions are so clear as not to call for any other interpretation. This case does not fall in the later category.

39. In *Gujarat Assembly Election Matter,*[1] the issue before the Constitution Bench was whether six months' period contemplated by article 174(1) applies to a dissolved Legislative Assembly. While dealing with that question and holding that the said provision applies only to subsisting Legislative Assembly and not to a dissolved Legislative Assembly, *it was held that the constitution of any Assembly can only be under section 73 of the RP Act, 1951 and the requirement of article 188 of Constitution suggests that the Assembly comes into existence even before its first sitting commences.* (Emphasis supplied by us).

40. In view of the above, the first point is answered against the petitioners.

ANSWER GIVEN BY THE SUPREME COURT ON POINT NUMBER 2

Point No. 2: Whether the Proclamation dated 23rd May, 2005 Dissolving the Assembly of Bihar is Illegal and Unconstitutional?

41. This point is the heart of the matter. The answer to the constitutional validity of the impugned notification depends upon the scope and extent of judicial review in such matters as determined by a Nine-Judge Bench decision in *Bommai's* case. Learned counsel appearing for both sides have made elaborate submissions on the question as to what is the ratio decidendi of *Bommai's* case.

1. *Special Reference No. 1 of 2002,* (2002) 8 SCC 237.

42. According to the petitioners, the notification dissolving the Assembly is illegal as it is based on the reports of the Governor which suffered from serious legal and factual infirmities and are tainted with pervasive *mala fides* which is evident from the record. It is contended that the object of the reports of the Governor was to prevent political party led by Mr. Nitish Kumar to form the government. The submission is that such being the object, the consequent notification of dissolution accepting the recommendation deserves to be annulled.

43. Under article 356 of the Constitution, the dissolution of an Assembly can be ordered on the satisfaction that a situation has arisen in which the Government of the State cannot be carried on in accordance with the Constitution. Such a satisfaction can be reached by the President on receipt of report from the Governor of a State or otherwise. It is permissible to arrive at the satisfaction on receipt of the report from Governor and on other material. Such a satisfaction can also be reached only on the report of the Governor. It is also permissible to reach such a conclusion even without the report of the Governor in case the President has other relevant material for reaching the satisfaction contemplated by article 356. The expression 'or otherwise' is of wide amplitude.

44. In the present case, it is not in dispute that the satisfaction that a situation has arisen in which the Government of State cannot be carried on in accordance with the provisions of the Constitution has been arrived at only on the basis of the reports of the Governor. It is not the case of the Union of India that it has relied upon any material other than the reports of the Governor which have been earlier reproduced *in extenso*.

45. The Governor in the report dated 6th March, 2005 has referred to *Bommai's* case as also to the recommendations of Sarkaria Commission. Sarkaria Commission Report in Chapter IV deals extensively with the role of the Governors. Since in this case, the dissolution of the Assembly is based solely on the reports of the Governor and the issue also is as to the role played by the Governor and submissions also having been made on role which is expected from a high constitutional functionary like Governor, it would be useful to first examine that aspect.

ROLE OF THE GOVERNOR OF A STATE

Role of the Governor

46. The role of the Governor has been a key issue in the matters of Central-State relations. The Constitution of India envisages three tiers of Government — the Union, State and the Local Self-Government. From the functional standpoint, it is stated that such a Constitution "is not a static format, but a dynamic process" [Report of the Sarkaria Commission on Centre-State Relations (1988)]. In the context of Union-State relations it has been noted that "the very dynamism of the system with all its checks and balances brings in its wake problems and conflicts in the working of Union-State relations."

47. In the light of a volatile system prevailing today, it is pertinent to recognise the crucial role played by the Governors in the working of the democratic framework. Addressing the Conference of Governors in June, 2005, the President of India Dr. A.P.J. Abdul Kalam stressed the relevance of recommendations of the

Sarkaria Commission and observed that "While there are many checks and balances provided by the Constitution, the office of the Governor has been bestowed with the independence to rise above the day-to-day politics and override compulsions either emanating from the Central system or the State system." The Prime Minister Dr. Manmohan Singh on the same occasion noted that "you are the representatives of the Center in States and hence, you bring a national perspective to State level actions and activities."

GOVERNOR IS NOT AN EMPLOYEE OF THE CENTRAL GOVERNMENT

48. In *Hargovind Pant* v. *Dr. Raghukul Tilak*, (1979) 3 SCC 458, observing on the issue as to whether a Governor could be considered as an "employee" of the Government of India, this Court said "it is no doubt true that the Governor is appointed by the President which means in effect and substance the Government of India, but that is only a mode of appointment and it does not make the Governor an employee or servant of the Government of India."

49. Referring to article 356 of the Constitution, the Court reasoned that "one highly significant role which he (Governor) has to play under the Constitution is of making a report where he finds that a situation has arisen in which the Government of the State cannot be carried on in accordance with the provisions of the Constitution" and further added that the Governor "is not amenable to the directions of the Government of India, nor is he accountable to them for the manner in which he carries out his functions and duties. He is an independent constitutional office which is not subject to the control of the Government of India."

50. Fortifying the same, Justice V.R. Krishna Iyer has observed that the mode of appointment can never legitimize any form of interference in the working of the Governor, else the concept of "judicial independence" would not be tenable, as even the judges of the High Courts and the Supreme Court are appointed by the President; *V.R. Krisnha Iyer, A Constitutional Miscellany,* 2nd Edn., Lucknow: Eastern Book Co., 2003, at p. 44.

51. The then Vice-President of India, Shri G.S. Pathak, had remarked in 1970 that "in the sphere which is bound by the advice of the Council of Ministers, for obvious reasons, the Governor must be independent of the Centre" as there may be cases "where the advice of the Centre may clash with advice of the State Council of Ministers" and that "in such cases the Governor must ignore the Centre's "advice" and act on the advice of his Council of Ministers."

52. Relevant for the present controversy, very significant observations were made in *Bommai's* case, (1994) 3 SCC 1 when it was said—

> "He (Governor) is as much bound to exercise this power in a situation contemplated by article 356 as *he is bound not to use it where such a situation has not really arisen*" (SCC p. 215 para 272, per Jeevan Reddy J.)
>
> (Emphasis supplied by us).

53. The role of the Governor has come in for considerable criticism on the ground that some Governors have failed to display the qualities of impartiality expected of them. The Sarkaria Commission Report has noted that "many have traced this mainly to the fact that the Governor is appointed by, and holds office during the pleasure of the President, *i.e.*, in effect, the Union Council of Ministers."

GOVERNOR SHOULD BE APPOINTED AFTER CONSULTING THE STATE GOVERNMENT

54. Rejecting the suggestion of an elected Governor, the Constituent Assembly repeatedly stressed on consultation with the Provincial/State Government prior to the appointment of the Governor. Sir Alladi Krishnaswamy Ayyar is quoted to have stated that "a convention of consulting the provincial cabinet might easily grow up" as was said to be the case in Canada (White Paper on the Office of the Governor, Government of Karnataka (22nd September, 1983) *c.f. V.R. Krishna Iyer, A Constitutional Miscellany* (2nd Edn., Lucknow: Eastern Book Co., 2003) at p. 45). Shri Jawaharlal Nehru had also observed in the debate on the appointment of Governor in the Constituent Assembly that a Governor "must be acceptable to the Province, he must be acceptable to the Government of the Province and yet he must not be known to be a part of the party machine of that province." He was of the opinion that a nominated Governor shall have "far fewer common links with the Centre."

55. Querying as to what could be an objective and representative body which will fit into our Constitutional framework to facilitate the appointment of Governors on meritorious basis, the Sarkaria Commission has observed that:

> "There is no gainsaying that a procedure must be devised which can ensure objectivity in selection and adherence to the criteria for selection and insulate the system from political pressures. Also, the new procedure must not only be fair but should be seen to be fair." (Chapter IV "Role of the Governor", Report of the Sarkaria Commission on Centre-State Relations (1988) at para 4.6.30). Recommending that the Vice-President of India and the Speaker of the Lok Sabha should be consulted by the Prime Minister in selecting a Governor, the Sarkaria Commission has noted that "such consultation will greatly enhance the credibility of the selection process."

56. The other related issue of debate was regarding the extent of discretionary powers to be allowed to the Governor. Following the decision to have a nominated Governor, references in the various articles of the Draft Constitution relating to the exercise of specified functions by the Governor 'in his discretion' were deleted. (Chapter IV "Role of the Governor", Report of the Sarkaria Commission on Centre-State Relations (1988) at para 4.2.07). Article 163 of the Constitution (then Draft article 143) generated considerable discussion, and Dr. Ambedkar is stated to have "maintained that vesting the Governor with certain discretionary powers was not contrary to responsible Government." [Constituent Assembly Debates (Volume VIII, Revised Edition) at pp. 00-502].

GOVERNOR MUST ACT OBJECTIVELY

57. The expression "required" found in article 163(1) is stated to signify that the Governor can exercise his discretionary powers only if there is a compelling necessity to do so. It has been reasoned that the expression "by or under the Constitution" means that the necessity to exercise such powers may arise from any express provision of the Constitution or by necessary implication. The Sarkaria Commission Report further adds that such necessity may arise even from rules and orders made "under" the Constitution.

58. Observing that the Governor needs to discharge "dual responsibility"– to the Union and the State – the Sarkaria Commission has sought to evaluate the róle of the Governors in certain controversial circumstances, such as, in appointing the Chief Minister, in ascertaining the majority, in dismissal of the Chief Minister, in dissolving the Legislative Assembly, in recommending President's Rule and in reserving Bills for President's consideration.

59. Finding that the position of the Governor is indispensable for the successful working of the Constitutional Scheme of governance, the Sarkaria Commission has noted that [Chapter IV "Role of the Governor", Report of the Sarkaria Commission on Centre-State Relations (1988) at para 4.5.07]

> "most of the safeguards will be such as cannot be reduced to a set of precise rules of procedure or practice. This is so because of the very nature of the office and the role of the Governor. The safeguards have mostly to be in the nature of conventions and practices, to be understood in their proper perspective and faithfully adhered to, not only by the Union and the State Governments but also by the political parties."

It was further added that

> "the fact that it will be impossible to lay down a concrete set of standards and norms for the functioning of a Governor will make it difficult for a Parliamentary Committee or the Supreme Court to inquire into a specific charge against a Governor."

Instrument of Instruction:

60. The Constituent Assembly, pursuant to the Report of the Provincial Constitution Committee, had decided to insert an Instrument of Instructions to the Governors in the form of a Schedule to the Constitution. Such an instrument was found to be necessary, "because of the mode of appointment and the injunction to act upon the advice of Ministers were not contained in the Constitution itself." [The framing of India's Constitution – Select Documents (Volume IV, B. Shiva Rao (ed.), New Delhi: (Universal Law Publishing Co., 2004) at p. 86. The complete test of the suggested Instructions is reproduced in pp. 88-90]. In the Government of India Act, 1935, the Instrument of Instructions appeared as instructions from the Sovereign.

61. The suggested list of instructions considered by the Constituent Assembly included value based standards that are expected of a Governor in discharging his duties *vis-a-vis* appointment of the Chief Minister after ascertaining a "stable majority"; appointments of Council of Ministers who "will best be in a position collectively to command the confidence of the Legislature"; to constitute an Advisory Board comprising of duly elected members of the Legislature, including the Leader of the Opposition,

> "to aid the Governor in the matter of making appointments under the Constitution" such as that of the Auditor-in-Chief for the State, Chairman of the State Public Services Commission; and mandating the Governor to do "all that in him lies to maintain standards of good administration, to promote all measures making for moral, social and economic welfare and tending to fit all

classes of the population to take their due share in the public life and government of the State, and to secure amongst all classes and creeds co-operation, goodwill and mutual respect for religious beliefs and sentiments."

62. The instructions were proposed as a Schedule to the Constitution as the Assembly felt that "it is preferable not to put them into the body of the Constitution, because they are conventions rather than legal rules." However, the same was not appended to the Constitution and lamenting about it, Shri A.G. Noorani has stated that the Instrument of Instructions could have codified conventions between the President and the Governors if allowed to exist. [A.G. Noorani, Constitutional Questions in India – The President, Parliament and the States (New Delhi: Oxford University Press, 2000) at p. 11.]

63. The P.V. Rajamannar Committee (1969), Inquiry Committee constituted by the Government of Tamil Nadu to report on the Centre-State relations, and the Study Team of the Administrative Reforms Commission (1967) headed by Shri M.C. Setalvad, have been quoted to have opined that:

> "A specific provision should be inserted in the Constitution enabling the President to issue Instruments of Instructions to the Governors. The Instruments of Instructions should lay down guidelines indicating the matters in respect of which the Governor should consult the Central Government or in relation to which the Central Government could issue directions to him." [White Paper on the Office of the Governor, Government of Karnataka (22nd September, 1983) c.f. *V.R. Krishna Iyer, A Constitutional Miscellany* (2nd Edn., Lucknow: Eastern Book Co., 2003 at p. 47].

Justice Krishna Iyer has stated that a "Handbook" setting out the guidelines for Governors must be prepared officially by the Law Commission and approved by the Parliament to be kept as a reference in the same status as that of an Instrument of Instructions. However, the Sarkaria Commission has observed that:

> "Considering the multifaceted role of the Governor and the nature of his functions and duties, we are of the view that it would be neither feasible nor desirable to formulate a comprehensive set of guidelines for the exercise by him of his discretionary powers. No two situations which may require a Governor to use his discretion, are likely to be identical."

DISCRETIONARY POWERS OF THE GOVERNOR

64. The Expounding in detail on the exercise of discretionary powers by the Governor, the Sarkaria Commission has mainly recommended the following:

> "Appointment of the Chief Minister – It is clear that the leader of the party which has an absolute majority in the Legislative Assembly should invariably be called upon by the Governor to form a Government. However, if there is a fractured mandate, then the Commission recommends an elaborate step-by-step approach and has further emphasized that:
>
> "the Governor, while going through the process of selection as described, should select a leader who, in his (Governor's) judgment, is most likely to command a majority in the Assembly. The Governor's subjective judgment will play an important role."

Upon being faced by several contesting claims, the Commission suggests that the most prudent measure on part of the Governor would be to test the claims on the floor of the House.

"Dismissal of the Chief Minister — Recommending a test of majority on the floor of the House to ascertain whether an incumbent Chief Minister continues to enjoy the majority, the Commission clearly dissuades the Governor from dismissing the Ministry based only on his "subjective satisfaction".

Dissolution of the Assembly – Despite best efforts, if ultimately a viable Ministry fails to emerge, a Governor is faced with two alternatives – he may either dissolve the Assembly or recommend President's Rule under article 356, leaving it to the Union Government to decide the question of dissolution. The Commission expressed its firm view that the proper course would be "to allow the people of the State to settle matters themselves". The Commission recommended that:

> "the Governor should first consider dissolving the Assembly and arranging for a fresh election and before taking a decision, he should consult the leaders of the political parties concerned and the Chief Election Commissioner."

WHERE NO SINGLE PARTY GETS MAJORITY THE COURSE TO BE ADOPTED BY THE GOVERNOR

65. Para 4.11.04 of Sarkaria Commission Report specifically deals with the situation where no single party obtains absolute majority and provides the order of preference the Governor should follow in selecting a Chief Minister. The order of preference suggested is:

1. An alliance of parties that was formed prior to the Elections.
2. The largest single party staking a claim to form the government with the support of others, including "independents".
3. A post-electoral coalition of parties, with all the partners in the coalition joining the government.
4. A post-electoral alliance of parties, with some of the parties in the alliance forming a government and the remaining parties, including "independents" supporting the government from outside.

66. The Sarkaria Commission has noticed that in a number of situations of political instability in States, the Governors recommended President's Rule under article 356 without exhausting all possible steps under the Constitution to induct or maintain a stable government. The Governors concerned neither gave a fair chance to contending parties to form a Ministry, nor allowed a fresh appeal to the electorate after dissolving the Legislative Assembly. Almost all these cases have been criticized on the ground that the Governors, while making their recommendations to the President behaved in a partisan manner. The report further states that there has been no uniformity of approach in such situations and that these aspects have been dealt with in Chapter VI 'Emergency Provisions'.

EMERGENCY PROVISIONS

67. In Chapter VI, Sarkaria Commission dealt with the emergency provisions noting the concern of framers of the Constitution of need for such provision in a country of our dimensions, diversities, disparities and "multitudinous people, with possibly divided loyalties". They took care to provide that, in a situation of such emergency, the Union shall have overriding powers to control and direct all aspects of administration and legislation throughout the country. They realised that a failure or breakdown of the constitutional machinery in a State could not be ruled out as an impossibility and a situation may arise in which the Government of the State cannot be carried on in accordance with the provisions of the Constitution.

68. The common thread in all the emergency provisions is that the resort to such provision has to be in exceptional circumstances when there be the real and grave situation calling for the drastic action.

ARTICLE 356 OF THE CONSTITUTION OF INDIA IS MOSTLY ABUSED TO SERVE POLITICAL PURPOSE

69. Sarkaria Commission as also this Court has noted the persistent criticism in ever-mounting intensity, both in regard to the frequency and the manner of the use of the power under article 356. The Sarkaria Commission has noticed that gravemen of the criticism is that, more often than not, these provisions have been misused, to promote the political interests of the party in power at the Centre. Some examples have been noted of situations in which the power of article 356 was invoked improperly if not illegally. It is noted that the constitutional framers did not intend that this power should be exercised for the purpose of securing good government. It also notices that this power cannot be invoked, merely on the ground that there are serious allegations of corruption against the Ministry.

70. Whether it is a case of existing government losing the majority support or of installation of new government after fresh elections, the act of the Governor in recommending dissolution of Assembly should be only with sole object of preservation of the Constitution and not promotion of political interest of one or the other party.

WHO SHOULD BE APPOINTED AS A GOVERNOR?

71. In the present context of fractured verdicts in elections, the aforesaid discussion assumes great importance and relevance. The criteria suggested in Sarkaria Commission Report for appointment of a person as a Governor is:

(i) He should be eminent in some walk of life;

(ii) He should be a person from outside the State;

(iii) He should be a detached figure and not too intimately connected with the local politics of the State; and

(iv) He should be a person who has not taken too great a part in politics generally and particularly in the recent past.

72. It has not been seriously disputed by learned counsel appearing for the parties that, unfortunately, the criteria has been observed in almost total breach by all political parties. It is seen that one day a person is in active politics in as much as he holds the office of the Chief Minister or Minister or a party post and almost on the following day or, in any case, soon thereafter, the same person is appointed as the Governor in another State with hardly any cooling period. Ordinarily, it is difficult to expect detachment from party politics from such a person while performing the constitutional functions as Governor.

73. On this issue, we would like to say no more and leave this aspect to the wisdom of the political parties and their leaders to discuss and debate and arrive at, if possible, a national policy with some common minimum parameters applicable and acceptable to all major political parties.

Defections

74. At this stage, we may consider another side issue, namely, defections being a great evil.

75. Undoubtedly, defection is a great evil. It was contended for the government that the unprincipled defections induced by allurements of office, monetary consideration, pressure, etc., were destroying the democratic fabric. With a view to control this evil, Tenth Schedule was added by the Constitution (Fifty-Second Amendment) Act, 1985. Since the desired goal to check defection by the legislative measure could not be achieved, law was further strengthened by the Constitution (Ninety-first Amendment) Act, 2003. The contention is that the Governor's action was directed to check this evil, so that a government based on such defections is not formed.

76. Reliance has been placed on the decision in the case of *Kihoto Hollohan* v. *Zachillhu*, 1992 Supp (2) SCC 651, to bring home the point that defections undermine the cherished values of democracy and Tenth Schedule was added to the Constitution to combat this evil. It is also correct that to further strengthen the law in this direction, as the existing provisions of the Tenth Schedule were not able to achieve the desired goal of checking defection, by 91st Amendment, defection was made more difficult by deleting provision which did not treat mass shifting of loyalty by 1/3 as defection and by making the defection, altogether impermissible and only permitting merger of the parties in the manner provided in the Tenth Schedule as amended by 91st Amendment.

77. In *Kihoto's* case, 1992 Supp (2) SCC 651, the challenge was to validity of the Tenth Schedule, as it stood then. Argument was that this law was destructive of the basic structure of the Constitution as it is violative of the fundamental Principle of Parliamentary Democracy, a basic feature of the Indian Constitutionalism and is destructive of the freedom of speech, right to dissent and freedom of conscience as the provisions seek to penalize and disqualify elected representatives for the exercise of these rights and freedoms which are essential to the sustenance of the system of Parliamentary democracy. It was also urged that unprincipled political defections may be an evil, but it will be the beginning of much greater evils if the remedies, graver than the decease itself, are adopted. It was said that the Tenth Schedule seeks to throw away the baby with the bath water.

78. Dealing with aforesaid submissions, the Court noted that, in fact, the real question was whether under the Indian Constitutional Scheme, is there any immunity from constitutional correctives against a legislatively perceived political evil of unprincipled defections induced by the lure of office and monetary inducements. It was noted that (SCC p. 679 paras 33 and 34):

> "33. The points raised in the petition are, indeed, far reaching and of no small importance-invoking the 'sense of relevance and constitutionally stated principles of unfamiliar settings'. On the one hand there was the real and imminent threat to the very fabric of Indian democracy posed by certain level of political behaviour conspicuous by their utter and total disregard of well recognised political proprieties and morality. These trends tend to degrade the tone of political life and, in their wider propensities, are dangerous to and undermine the very survival of the cherished values of democracy. There is the legislative determination through experimental constitutional processes to combat that evil.
>
> 34. On the other hand, there may be certain side-effects and fall-out which might affect and hurt even honest dissenters and conscientious objectors."

While dealing with the argument that the constitutional remedy was violative of basic features of the Constitution, it was observed that the argument ignores" (SCC p. 680 para 38)

> "the essential organic and evolutionary character of a Constitution and its flexibility as a living entity to provide for the demands and compulsions of the changing times and needs. The people of this country were not beguiled into believing that the menace of unethical and unprincipled changes of political affiliations is something which the law is helpless against and is to be endured as a necessary concomitant of freedom of conscience."

The unethical political defections was described as a 'canker' eating into the vitals of those values that make democracy a living and worthwhile faith.

79. It was contended that the Governor was only trying to prevent members from crossing the floor as the concept of the freedom of its members to vote as they please independently of the political party's declared policies will not only embarrass its public image and popularity but would also undermine public confidence in it which, in the ultimate analysis, is its source of sustenance – nay, indeed, its very survival. The contention is based on para 144 of the judgment in *Kihoto's* case, [1992 Supp (2) SCC 651] which reads thus:

> "44. But a political party functions on the strength of shared beliefs. Its own political stability and social utility depends on such shared beliefs and concerted action of its Members in furtherance of those commonly held principles. Any freedom of its Members to vote as they please independently of the political party's declared policies will not only embarrass its public image and popularity but also undermine public confidence in it which, in the ultimate analysis, is its source of sustenance — nay, indeed, its very survival. Intra-party debates are of course a different thing. But a public image of disparate stands by Members of the same political party is not looked upon, in political tradition, as a desirable state of things. Griffith and Ryle on "Parliament, Functions, Practice and Procedure" (1989 Edn., p. 119) say:
>
> "Loyalty to party is the norm, being based on shared beliefs. A divided party is looked on with suspicion by the electorate. It is natural for members to accept the opinion of their Leaders and Spokesmen on the wide variety of matters on which those Members have no specialist knowledge. Generally,

Members will accept majority decisions in the party even when they disagree. It is understandable therefore that a Member who rejects the party whip even on a single occasion will attract attention and more criticism than sympathy. To abstain from voting when required by party to vote is to suggest a degree of unreliability. To vote against party is disloyalty. To join with others in abstention or voting with the other side smacks of conspiracy."

Clause (b) of sub-para (1) of paragraph 2 of the Tenth Schedule gives effect to this principle and sentiment by imposing a disqualification on a Member who votes or abstains from voting contrary to "any directions" issued by the political party. The provision, however, recognises two exceptions: one when the Member obtains from the political party prior permission to vote or abstain from voting and the other when the Member has voted without obtaining such permission but his action has been condoned by the political party. This provision itself accommodates the possibility that there may be occasions when a Member may vote or abstain from voting contrary to the direction of the party to which he belongs. This, in itself again, may provide a clue to the proper understanding and construction of the expression "Any Direction" in clause (b) of paragraph 2(1) whether really all directions or whips from the party entail the statutory consequences or whether having regard to the extra-ordinary nature and sweep of the power and the very serious consequences that flow including the extreme penalty of disqualification the expression should be given a meaning confining its operation to the contexts indicated by the objects and purposes of the Tenth Schedule. We shall deal with this aspect separately."

ANTI-DEFECTION LAW

80. Our attention was also drawn to the objects and reasons for the 91st Constitutional Amendment. It states that demands were made from time to time in certain quarters for strengthening and amending the Anti-defection law as contained in the Tenth Schedule to the Constitution of India, on the ground that these provisions had not been able to achieve the desired goals of checking defections. The Tenth Schedule was also criticized on the ground that it allowed bulk defections while declaring individual defections as illegal. The provision for exemption from disqualification in case of splits as provided in paragraph 3 of the Tenth Schedule to the Constitution of India had, in particular, come under severe criticism on account of its destabilising effect on the Government.

81. Reliance has also been placed to the exposition of Lord Diplock in a decision of House of Lords in the case of *Council of Civil Service Unions* v. *Minister for the Civil Service,* (1984) 3 All ER 935 on the aspect of irrationality to the effect that: (All ER p. 951a)

> "it applies to a decision may be so outrageous or in defiance of logic or of accepted moral standards that no sensible person who had applied his 'mind to the question to be decided, could have arrived at it".

It is contended that the Governor has many sources information wherefrom led him to conclude that the process that was going on in the State of Bihar was destroying the very fabric of democracy and, therefore, such approach cannot be described as outrageous or in defiance of logic, particularly, when proof in such cases is difficult if not impossible as bribery takes place in the cover of darkness and deals are made in secrecy. It is, thus, contended that Governor's view is permissible and legitimate view.

82. Almost similar contention has been rejected in *Bommai's* case *S.R. Bommai* v. *Union of India,* (1994) 3 SCC 1.

83. The other decision of House of Lords in *Puhlhofer* v. *Hillingdon, London Borough Council,* (1986) 1 All ER 467 (474) relied upon by the respondents, has been considered by Justice Sawant in *Bommai's* case, (1994) 3 SCC 1. The reliance was to the proposition that where the existence or non-existence of a fact is left to the judgment and discretion of a public body and that fact involves a broad spectrum ranging from the 'obvious' to the 'debatable' to the 'just conceivable', it is the duty of the Court to leave the decision of that fact to the public body to whom Parliament has entrusted the decision-making power save in a case where it is obvious that the public body, consciously or unconsciously, are acting perversely. But in the present case, the inference sought to be drawn by the Governor without any relevant material, cannot fall in the category of 'debatable' or 'just conceivable', it would fall in the category of 'obviously perverse'. On facts, the inescapable inference is that the sole object of the Governor was to prevent the claim being made to form the Government and the case would fall under the category of 'bad faith'.

THE SITUATION IN THE PRESENT CASE WAS NOT DEFECTION

84. The question in the present case is not about MLAs voting in violation of provisions of Tenth Schedule as amended by the Constitution (91st Amendment), as we would presently show.

85. Certainly, there can be no quarrel with the principles laid in *Kihoto's* case about evil effects of defections but the same have no relevance for determination of point in issue. The stage of preventing members to vote against declared policies of the political party to which they belonged had not reached. If MLAs vote in a manner so as to run the risk of getting disqualified, it is for them to face the legal consequences. That stage had not reached. In fact, the reports of the Governor intended to forestall any voting and staking of claim to form the Government.

THE REPORTS OF THE GOVERNOR DATED 27.4.2005 AND 21.5.2005 HAD NO LEGS TO STAND AND WERE NOT *BONA FIDE*

86. Undisputedly, a Governor is charged with the duty to preserve, protect and defend the Constitution and the laws, has a concomitant duty and obligation to preserve democracy and not to permit the 'canker' of political defections to tear into the vitals of the Indian democracy. But on facts of the present case, we are unable to accept that the Governor by reports dated 27th April and 21st May, 2005 sought to achieve the aforesaid objective. There was no material, let alone relevant, with the Governor to assume that there were no legitimate realignment of political parties and there was blatant distortion of democracy by induced defections through unfair, illegal, unethical and unconstitutional means.

IN THE PRESENT CASE THE GOVERNOR ACTED TO STOP THE FORMATION OF STATE GOVERNMENT OF NDA CONSTITUENTS

87. The report dated 27th April, 2005 refers to:

1. serious attempt to cobble a majority;
2. winning over MLAs by various means;
3. targeting parties for a split;
4. high pressure moves;
5. offering various allurements like castes, posts, money etc.; and
6. Horse-trading.

Almost similar report was sent by the Governors of Karnataka and Nagaland leading to the dissolution of the Assembly of Karnataka and Nagaland, invalidated in *Bommai's* case. Further, the contention that the Central Government did not act upon the report dated 27th April, 2005 is of no relevance and cannot be considered in isolation since the question is about the manner in which the Governor moved, very swiftly and with undue haste, finding that one political party may be close to getting majority and the situation had reached where claim may be staked to form the Government which led to the report dated 21st May, 2005. It is in this context that the Governor says that instead of installing a Government based on a majority achieved by a distortion of the system, it would be preferable that the people/electorate could be provided with one more opportunity to seek the mandate of the people. This approach makes it evident that the object was to prevent a particular political party from staking a claim and not the professed object of anxiety not to permit the distortion of the political system, as sought to be urged. Such a course is nothing but wholly illegal and irregular and has to be described as *mala fide*. The recommendation for dissolution of the Assembly to prevent the staking of claim to form the Government purportedly on the ground that the majority was achieved by distortion of system by allurement, corruption and bribery was based on such general assumptions without any material which are quite easy to be made if any political party not gaining absolute majority is to be kept out of governance. No assumption without any basis whatever could be drawn that the reason for a group to support the claim to form the Government by Nitish Kumar, was only the aforesaid distortions. That stage had not reached. It was not allowed to be reached. If such majority had been presented and the Governor forms a legitimate opinion that the party staking claim would not be able to provide stable Government to the State, that may be a different situation. Under no circumstances, the action of Governor can be held to be *bona fide* when it is intended to prevent a political party to stake claim for formation of the Government. After elections, every genuine attempt is to be made which helps in installation of a popular Government, whichever be the political party.

Interpretation of a Constitution and Importance of Political Parties

88. For principles relevant for interpretation of a Constitution, our attention was drawn to what Justice Aharon Barak, President of Supreme Court of Israel says in Harvard Law Review, Vol. 116 (2002-2003) dealing particularly with the aspect of purposive interpretation of Constitution. Learned Judge has noticed as under:

"The task of expounding a constitution is crucially different from that of construing a statute. A statute defines present rights and obligations. It is easily enacted and as easily repealed. A constitution, by contrast, is drafted with an eye to the future. Its function is to provide a continuing framework for the legitimate exercise of governmental power and, when joined by a Bill or Charter of rights, for the unremitting protection of individual rights and liberties. Once enacted, its provisions cannot easily be repealed or amended. It must, therefore, be capable of growth and development over time to meet new social, political and historical realities often unimagined by its framers. The judiciary is the guardian of the constitution and must, in interpreting its provisions, bear these considerations in mind."

89. It is further said that the political question doctrine, in particular, remits entire areas of public life to Congress and the President, on the grounds that the Constitution assigns responsibility for these areas to the other branches, or that their resolution will involve discretionary, polycentric decisions that lack discrete criteria for adjudication and thus are better handled by the more democratic branches.

90. In fact, the scope of judicial review as enunciated in *Bommai's* case is in tune with the principles sought to be relied upon.

91. In support of the proposition that in Parliament Democracy there is importance of political parties and that interpretation of the constitutional provisions should advance the said basic structure based on political parties, our attention was drawn to write up Designing Federalism – A Theory of Self-Sustainable Federal Institution and what is said about political parties in a Federal State which is as under:

"Political parties created democracy and modern democracy is unthinkable save in terms of parties.

Schattschneider 1942:

I here is a factor in the organisation of Federal Government which is of primary importance but which cannot be ensured or provided for in a Constitution – a good party system.

Wheare 1953: 86

Whatever the general social conditions, if any, that sustain the federal bargain, there is one institutional condition that controls the nature of the bargain in all Instances... with which I am familiar. This is the structure of the party system, which may be regarded as the main variable intervening between the background social conditions and the specific nature of the federal bargain.

Riker 1964: 136

In a country which was always to be in need of the cohesive force of institutions, the national parties, for all their faults, were to become at an early hour primary and necessary parts of the machinery of government, essential vehicles to convey men's loyalties to the State.

Hofstadter 1969: 70-I"

92. It is contended that the political parties are the main means not only whereby provincial grievances are aired but also whereby centralised and decentralized trends are legitimised. This contention is made in connection with the alleged stand of two-third MLAs of LJP against the professed stand of that political party.

93. We are afraid that on facts of present case, the aforesaid concept and relevance of political parties is not quite relevant for our purpose to decide why and how the members of political parties had allegedly decided to adopt the course which they did, to allegedly support the claim for formation of the Government.

MORALITY

94. We may also deal with the aspect of morality sought to be urged. The question of morality is of course very serious and important matter. It has been engaging the attention of many constitutional experts, legal luminaries, jurists and political leaders. The concept of morality has also been changing from time to time also having regard to the ground realities and the compulsion of the situation including the aspect and relevance of coalition governance as opposed to a single party Government. Even in the economic field, the concept of morality has been a matter of policy and priorities of the Government. The Government may give incentive, which ideally may be considered unethical and immoral, but insofar as Government is concerned, it may become necessary to give incentive to unearth black money; *R.K. Garg* v. *Union of India*, (1981) 4 SCC 675 (paras 18 and 31). It may be difficult to leave such aspects to be determined by high constitutional functionaries, on case to case basis, depending upon the facts of the case, and personal mould of the constitutional functionaries. With all these imponderables, the Constitution does not contemplate the dissolution of Assemblies based on the assumption of such immoralities for formation of the satisfaction that situation has arisen in which the government cannot be of the Constitution of India.

Article 356 and *Bommai's* Case

95. Article 356(1) of the Constitution is as follows:

"356(1) Provisions in case of failure of constitutional machinery in State.—

(1) If the President, on receipt of report from the Governor of the State or otherwise, is satisfied that a situation has arisen in which the Government of the State cannot be carried on in accordance with the provisions of this Constitution, the President may by Proclamation—

(a) assume to himself all or any of the functions of the Government of the State and all or any of the powers vested in or exercisable by the Governor or any body or authority in the State other than the Legislature of the State;

(b) declare that the powers of the Legislature of the State shall be exercisable by or under the authority of Parliament;

(c) make such incidental and consequential provisions as appear to the President to be necessary or desirable for giving effect to the objects of the Proclamation, including provisions for suspending in whole or in part the operation of any provisions of this Constitution relating to any body or authority in the State:

Provided that nothing in this clause shall authorise the President to assume to himself any of the powers vested in or exercisable by a High Court, or to suspend in whole or in part the operation of any provision of this Constitution relating to High Courts."

96. Power under article 356(1) is an emergency power but it is not an absolute power. Emergency means a situation which is not normal, a situation which calls for urgent remedial action. Article 356 confers a power to be exercised by the President in exceptional circumstances to discharge the obligation cast upon him by article 355. It is a measure to protect and preserve the Constitution. The Governor takes the oath, prescribed by article 159 to preserve, protect and defend the Constitution and the laws to the best of his ability. Power under article 356 is conditional, condition being formation of satisfaction of the President as contemplated by article 356(1). The satisfaction of the President is the satisfaction of Council of Ministers. As provided in article 74(1), the President acts on the aid and advice of Council of Ministers. The plain reading of article 74(2) stating that the question whether any, and if so what, advice was tendered by Ministers to the President shall not be inquired into in any Court, may seem to convey that the Court is debarred from inquiring into such advice but *Bommai* has held that article 74(2) is not a bar against scrutiny of the material on the basis of which the President has issued the proclamation under article 356. Justice Sawant, in para 86 states that:

"What is further, although article 74(2) bars judicial review so far as the advice given by the Ministers is concerned, it does not bar scrutiny of the material on the basis of which the advice is given. The Courts are not interested in either the advice given by the Ministers to the President or the reasons for such advice. The Courts are, however, justified in probing as to whether there was any material on the basis of which the advice was given, and whether it was relevant for such advice and the President could have acted on it. Hence, when the Courts undertake an enquiry into the existence of such material, the prohibition contained in article 74(2) does not negate their right to know about the factual existence of any such material."

97. It was further said that the Parliament would be entitled to go into the material on basis of what the Council of Ministers tendered the advice and, therefore, secrecy in respect of material cannot remain inviolable. It was said that: (SCC pp. 109-110 para 87)

"When the Proclamation is challenged by making out a *prima facie* case with regard to its invalidity, the burden would be on the Union Government to satisfy that there exists material which showed that the Government could not be carried on in accordance with the provisions of the Constitution. Since such material would be exclusively within the knowledge of the Union Government, in view of the provisions of section 106 of the Evidence Act, the burden of proving the existence of such material would be on the Union Government."

98. On the similar lines, is the opinion of Jeevan Reddy, J.: (SCC pp. 241-242-243 paras 321 & 324)

"321. Clause (2) of article 74, understood in its proper perspective, is thus confined to a limited aspect. It protects and preserves the secrecy of the deliberations between the President and his Council of Ministers. In fact, clause (2) is a reproduction of sub-section (4) of section 10 of the Government of India Act, 1935. (The Government of India Act did not contain a provision corresponding to article 74(1) as it stood before or after the Amendments aforementioned). The scope of clause (2) should not be extended beyond its legitimate fields. In any event, it cannot be read or understood as conferring an immunity upon the Council of Ministers or the Minister/Ministry concerned to explain, defend and justify the orders and acts of the President done in exercise of his functions. The limited provision contained in article 74(2) cannot override the basic provisions in the Constitution relating to judicial review. If and when any action taken by the President in exercise of his functions is questioned in a Court of Law, it is for the Council of Ministers to justify the same, since the action or order of the President is presumed to have been taken in accordance with article 74(1). As to which Minister or which official of which Ministry comes forward to defend the order/action is for them to decide and for the Court to be satisfied about it. Where, of course, the act/order questioned is one pertaining to the Executive power of the Government of India, the position is much simpler. It does not represent the act/order of the President done/taken in exercise of his functions and hence there is no occasion for any aid or advice by the Ministers to him. It is the act/order of Government of India, though expressed in the name of the President. It is for the concerned Minister or Ministry, to whom the function is allocated under the Rules of Business to defend and justify such action/order.

* * * * *

324. In our respectful opinion, the above obligation cannot be evaded by seeking refuge under article 74(2). The argument that the advice tendered to the President comprises material as well and, therefore, calling upon the Union of India to disclose the material would amount to compelling the disclosure of the advice is, if we can say so respectfully, to indulge in sophistry. The material placed before the President by the Minister/Council of Ministers does not thereby become part of advice. Advice is what is based upon the said material. Material is not advice. The material may be placed before the President to acquaint him — and if need be to satisfy him — that the advice being tendered to him is the proper one. But it cannot mean that such material, by dint of being placed before the President in support of the advice, becomes advice itself. One can understand if the advice is tendered in writing; in such a case that writing is the advice and is covered by the protection provided by article 74(2). But it is difficult to appreciate how does the supporting material, become part of advice. The respondents cannot say that whatever the President sees – or whatever is placed before the President becomes prohibited material and cannot be seen or summoned by the Court.

Article 74(2) must be interpreted and understood in the context of entire constitutional system. Undue emphasis and expansion of its parameters would engulf valuable constitutional guarantees. For these reasons, we find it difficult to agree with the reasoning in *State of Rajasthan* on this score, insofar as it runs contrary to our holding."

99. The scope of judicial review has been expanded by *Bommai,* (1994) 3 SCC 1 and dissent has been expressed from the view taken in *State of Rajasthan's* case, (1977) 3 SCC 592.

100. The above approach shows objectivity even in subjectivity. The constitutionalism or constitutional system of Government abhors absolutism — it is premised on the Rule of Law in which subjective satisfaction is substituted by objectivity provided by the provisions of the Constitution itself. This line is clear also from *Maru Ram* v. *Union of India,* (1981) 1 SCC 107. It would also be clear on in depth examination of *Bommai* that declared the dissolution of three Assemblies illegal but before we further revert to that decision, a brief historical background including the apprehension of its abuse expressed by our founding fathers may be noted.

101. Articles 355 and 356 of the Constitution set the tenor for the precedence of the Union over the States. It has been explained that the rationale for introducing article 355 was to distinctly demarcate the functioning of the State and Union Governments and to prevent any form of unprincipled invasions by the Union into the affairs of the State. It was felt that through the unambiguous language of articles 355 and 356, the Union shall be constitutionally obliged to interfere only under certain limited circumstances as laid down in the provisions.

102. Referring to what is now article 355, Dr. Ambedkar had reasoned that T.K. Thope, Dr. Ambedkar and article 356 of the Constitution [(1993) 4 SCC (Jour) 1 "in view of the fact that we are endowing the Provinces with plenary powers and making them sovereign within their own fields it is necessary to provide that if any invasion of the provincial field is done, it is in virtue of this obligation." Pursuant to this reasoning, Dr. Ambedkar further explained that before resorting to article 356

> "the first thing the President will do would be to issue warning to a province that has erred, that things were not happening in the way in which they were intended to happen in the Constitution. If the warning fails the second thing for him to do will be to order an election allowing the people of the province to settle matters by themselves. It is only when those two remedies fail that he would resort to this article."

Dr. Ambedkar admitted that these articles were "liable to be abused" and that he cannot "altogether deny that there is a possibility of these articles being employed for political purposes." But he reasoned that such an "objection applies to every part of the Constitution which gives power to the Centre to override the Provinces" and added that the "proper thing we ought to expect is that such articles will never be called into operation and they would remain a dead letter." Constituent Assembly Debates (Volume IX, Revised Edition) at pp.175-177.

Scope of Judicial Review under Article 356

State of Rajasthan v. *Union of India*, (1977) 3 SCC 592

103. In *State of Rajasthan's* case, there was a broad consensus among five of the seven Judges that the Court can interfere if it is satisfied that the power has been exercised *mala fide* or on "wholly extraneous or irrelevant grounds". Some learned Judges have stated the rule in narrow terms and some others in a little less narrow terms but not a single learned Judge held that the proclamation is immune from judicial scrutiny. It must be remembered that at that time clause (5) was there barring judicial review of the proclamation and yet they said that Court can interfere on the ground of *mala fides*. Surely, the deletion of clause (5) has not restricted the scope of judicial review but has widened it.

104. Justice Reddy in *Bommai's* case has noticed, insofar as it was relevant, the ratio underlying each of the six opinions delivered by Seven-Judge Bench in the case of *State of Rajasthan* (supra) as under:

"Beg, C.J.—The opinion of Beg, C.J. contains several strands of thought. They may be stated briefly thus:

(i) The language of article 356 and the practice since 1950 shows that the Central Government can enforce its will against the State Governments with respect to the question how the State Governments should function and who should hold reins of power.

(ii) By virtue of article 365(5) and article 74(2), it is impossible for the Court to question the satisfaction of the President. It has to decide the case on the basis of only those facts as may have been admitted by or placed by the President before the Court.

(iii) The language of article 356(1) is very wide. It is desirable that conventions are developed channelising the exercise of this power. The Court can interfere only when the power is used in a grossly perverse and unreasonable manner so as to constitute patent misuse of the provisions or to an abuse of power. The same idea is expressed at another place saying that if "a constitutionally or legally prohibited or extraneous or collateral purpose is sought to be achieved" by the proclamation, it would be liable to be struck down. The question whether the majority party in the Legislative Assembly of a State has become totally estranged from the electorate is not a matter for the Court to determine.

(iv) The assessment of the Central Government that a fresh chance should be given to the electorate in certain States as well as the question when to dissolve the Legislative Assemblies are not matters alien to article 356. It cannot be said that the reasons assigned by the Central Government for the steps taken by them are not relevant to the purposes underlying article 356.

We may say at once that we are in respectful disagreement with propositions (i), (ii) and (iv) altogether. So far as proposition (iii) is concerned, it is not far off the mark and in substance accords with our view, as we shall presently show.

Y.V. Chandrachud, J.—On the scope of judicial review, the learned Judge held that where the reasons disclosed by the Union of India are wholly extraneous, the Court can interfere on the ground of *mala fides*. Judicial scrutiny, said the learned Judge, is available "for the limited purpose of seeing whether the reasons bear any rational nexus with the action proposed". The Court cannot sit in judgment over the satisfaction of the President for determining whether any other view of the situation is reasonably possible, opined the learned Judge. Turning to the facts of the case before him, the learned Judge observed that the grounds assigned by the Central Government in its counter-affidavit cannot be said to be irrelevant to article 356. The Court cannot go deeper into the matter nor shall the Court enquire whether there were any other reasons besides those disclosed in the counter-affidavit.

P.N. Bhagwati and A.C. Gupta, JJ.—The learned Judges enunciated the following propositions in their opinion:

The action under article 356 has to be taken on the subjective satisfaction of the President. The satisfaction is not objective. There are no judicially discoverable and manageable standards by which the Court can examine the correctness of the satisfaction of the President. The satisfaction to be arrived at is largely political in nature, based on an assessment of various and varied facts and factors besides several imponderables and fast changing situations. The Court is not a fit body to enquire into or determine the correctness of the said satisfaction or assessment, as it may be called. However, if the power is exercised *mala fide* or is based upon wholly extraneous or irrelevant grounds, the Court would have jurisdiction to examine it. Even clause (5) is not a bar when the contention is that there was no satisfaction at all.

The scope of judicial review of the action under article 356, — the learned Judges held — is confined to a "narrow minimal area: May be that in most cases, it would be difficult, if not impossible, to challenge the exercise of power under article 356(1) on the aforesaid limited ground, because the facts and circumstances on which the satisfaction is based, would not be known. However, where it is possible, the existence of satisfaction can always be challenged on the ground that it is *mala fide* or based on wholly extraneous and irrelevant grounds."

We may say with great respect that we find it difficult to agree with the above formulations *in toto*. We agree only with the statements regarding the permissible grounds of interference by Court and the effect of clause (5), as it then obtained. We also agree broadly with the first proposition, though not in the absolute terms indicated therein.

Goswami and Untwalia, JJ.—The separate opinions of Goswami and Untwalia, JJ. emphasise one single fact, namely, that inasmuch as the facts stated in the counter-affidavit filed by the Home Minister cannot be said to be "*mala fide*, extraneous or irrelevant", the action impugned cannot be assailed in the Court.

Fazal Ali, J.—The learned Judge held that:

(i) the action under article 356 is immune from judicial scrutiny unless the action is "guided by extraneous consideration" or "personal considerations".

(ii) the inference drawn by the Central Government following the 1977 elections to the Lok Sabha cannot be said to be unreasonable. It cannot be said that the inference drawn had no nexus with article 356."

(Emphasis in Original)

Bommai's Case, (1994) 3 SCC 1

105. The Nine Judge Bench considered the validity of dissolution of Legislative Assembly of States of Karnataka, Meghalaya, Nagaland, Madhya Pradesh, Himachal Pradesh and Rajasthan. Out of six States, the majority held as unconstitutional the dissolution of Assemblies of Karnataka, Nagaland and Meghalaya as well. Six opinions have been expressed. There is unanimity on some issues, likewise there is diversity amongst several opinions on various issues.

Karnataka Facts

106. In the case of Karnataka, the facts were that the Janta Party being the majority party in the State Legislature had formed the Government under the leadership of Shri S.R. Bommai on August 30, 1988 following the resignation on August 1, 1988 of the earlier Chief Minister Shri Hegde who headed the Ministry from March 1985 till his resignation. On 17th April, 1989 one legislator presented a letter to the Governor withdrawing his support to the Ministry. On the next day he presented to the Governor 19 letters allegedly written by 17 Janta Dal legislators, one independent but associate legislator and one legislator belonging to the BJP which was supporting the Ministry, withdrawing their support to the Ministry. On receipt of these letters, the Governor is said to have called the Secretary of the Legislature Department and got the authenticity of the signatures on the said letters verified. On April 19, 1989, the Governor sent a report to the President stating therein that there were dissensions in the Janta Party which had led to the resignation of Shri Hegde and even after the formation of the new party *viz.*, Janta Dal, there were dissensions and defections. In support, the Governor referred to the 19 letters received by him. He further stated that in view of the withdrawal of the support by the said legislators, the Chief Minister Shri Bommai did not command a majority in the Assembly and hence it was inappropriate under the Constitution, to have the State administered by an Executive consisting of Council of Ministers which did not command the majority in the House. He also added that no other political party was in a position to form the Government. He, therefore, recommended to the President that he should exercise power under article 356(1). The Governor did not ascertain the view of Shri Bommai either after the receipt of the 19 letters or before making his report to the President. On the next day *i.e.*, April 20, 1989, 7 out of the 19 legislators who had allegedly sent the letters to the Governor complained that their signatures were 'obtained on the earlier letters by misrepresentation and affirmed their support to the Ministry. The State Cabinet met on the same day and decided to convene the Session of the Assembly within a week *i.e.*, on April 21, 1989. The Chief Minister and his Law Minister met the

Governor on the same day and informed him about the decision to summon the Assembly Session. The Chief Minister offered to prove his majority on the floor of the House, even by pre-poning the Assembly Session, if needed. To the same effect, the Governor however, sent yet another report to the President on the same day *i.e.*, April 20, 1989, in particular, referring to the letters of seven Members pledging their support to the Ministry and withdrawing their earlier letters. He however opined in the report that the letters from the 7 legislators were obtained by the Chief Minister by pressurising them and added that horse-trading was going on and atmosphere was getting vitiated. In the end, he reiterated his opinion that the Chief Minister had lost the confidence of the majority in the House and repeated his earlier request for action under article 356(1) of the Constitution. On that very day, the President issued the Proclamation dissolving the House. The Proclamation was thereafter approved by the Parliament as required by article 356(3).

107. A writ petition filed in the High Court challenging the validity of dissolution was dismissed by a three Judge Bench, *inter alia* holding that the facts stated in the Governor's report cannot be held to be irrelevant and that the Governor's satisfaction that no other party was in a position to form the Government had to be accepted since his personal *bona fides* were not questioned and his satisfaction was based upon reasonable assessment of all the relevant facts. The High Court relied upon the test laid down in the *State of Rajasthan* case and held that on the basis of materials disclosed, the satisfaction arrived at by the President could not be faulted.

Nagaland Facts

108. In the case of Nagaland, the Presidential Proclamation dated August 7, 1988 was issued under article 356(1) imposing President's rule. At the relevant time in the Nagaland Assembly there were 60 legislators, 34 belonging to Congress (I), 18 to Naga National Democratic Party and 1 to Naga Peoples' Party and seven were independent legislators. On July 28, 1988, 13 out of the 34 MLAs of the ruling Congress (I) party informed the Speaker of the Assembly that they have formed a separate party and requested him for allotment of separate seats for them in the House. The Session was to commence on August 28, 1988. By decision dated July 30, 1988 the Speaker held that there was a split in the party within the meaning of the Tenth Schedule of the Constitution. On July 31, 1988, Shri Vamuzo, one of the 13 defecting MLAs who had formed a separate party, informed the Governor that he commanded the support of 35 out of the then 59 Members in the Assembly and was in a position to form the Government. On August 3, 1988, the Chief Secretary of the State wrote to Shri Vamuzo that according to his information, Shri Vamuzo had wrongfully confined the MLAs who had formed the new party. The allegations were denied by Shri Vamuzo and he asked the Chief Secretary to verify the truth from the Members themselves. On verification, the Members told the Chief Secretary that none of them was confined as alleged. On August 6, 1988 the Governor sent a report to the President of India about the formation of a new party by the 13 MLAs. He also stated that the said MLAs were allured by money. He further stated that the said MLAs were kept in forcible confinement by Mr. Vamuzo and one other person, and that the story of split in the ruling party was not true.

He added that the Speaker was hasty in according recognition to the new group of the 13 members and commented that horse-trading was going on, in the State. He made a special reference to the insurgency in Nagaland and also stated that some or the Members of the Assembly were having contacts with the insurgents. He expressed the apprehension that if the affairs were .allowed to continue as they were, it would affect the stability of the State. In the meantime the Chief Minister submitted his resignation to the Governor and recommended the imposition of the President's rule. The President thereafter issued the impugned Proclamation and dismissed the Government and dissolved the Assembly. Shri Vamuzo, the leader of the new group challenged the validity of the Proclamation in the Gauhati High Court. The Petition was heard by a Division Bench. The Bench differed on the effective operation of article 74(2) and hence the matter was referred to the third Judge. But before the third learned Judge could hear the matter, the Union of India moved this Court for grant of Special Leave which was granted and the proceedings in the High Court were stayed.

109. Dealing with the implications of article 74(2) of the Constitution Justice Sawant speaking for himself and Justice Kuldip Singh came to the conclusion that although the advice given by the Council of Ministers is free from the gaze of the Court, the material on the basis of which the advice is given cannot be kept away from it and is open to judicial scrutiny. On the facts, Justice Sawant expressed the view that the Governor should have allowed Shri Vamuzo to test his strength on the floor of the House notwithstanding the fact that the Governor in his report has stated that during the preceding 25 years, no less than 11 Governments, had been formed and according to his information, the Congress (I) MLAs were allured by the monetary benefits and that amounted to incredible lack of political morality and complete disregard of the wishes of the electorate.

Meghalaya

110. Insofar as the Proclamation in respect of the Meghalaya is concerned, that was also held to be invalid. The ground on which dissolution was invalidated was the constitutional functionary had failed to realize the binding legal consequences of the orders of this Court and the constitutional obligation to give effect to the said order.

Facts of Madhya Pradesh, Rajasthan and Himachal Pradesh

111. Insofar as the cases of States of Madhya Pradesh, Rajasthan and Himachal Pradesh are concerned the dismissal of the Governments was a consequence of violent reactions in India and abroad as well as in the neighbouring countries where some temples were destroyed, as a result of demolition of Babri Masjid structure on 6th December, 1992.The Union of India is said to have tried to cope up the situation by taking several steps including banning of some organizations which had along with BJP given a call for Kar sevaks to march towards Ayodhya on December 6, 1992. The Proclamation in respect of these States was issued on January 15, 1993. The Proclamations dissolving the assemblies were issued on arriving at satisfaction as contemplated by article 356(1) on the basis of Governor's report. It was held that the Governor's reports are based on relevant materials and are made *bona fide* and after due verification.

112. The Conclusion Nos. I, II, IV, VI, VII, IX and X in the opinion of Justice Sawant are as under: (SCC pp. 148-50 para 153)

"153. I. The validity of the Proclamation issued by the President under article 356(1) is judicially reviewable to the extent of examining whether it was issued on the basis of any material at all or whether the material was relevant or whether the Proclamation was issued in the *mala fide* exercise of the power. When a *prima facie* case is made out in the challenge to the Proclamation, the burden is on the Union Government to prove that the relevant material did in fact exist. Such material may be either the report of the Governor or other than the report.

II. Article 74(2) is not a bar against the scrutiny of the material on the basis of which the President had arrived at his satisfaction.

IV. Since the provisions contained in clause (3) of article 356 are intended to be a, check on the powers of the President under clause (1) thereof, it will not be permissible for the President to exercise powers under sub-clauses (a), (b) and (c) of the latter clause, to take irreversible actions till at least both the Houses of Parliament have approved of the Proclamation. It is for this reason that the President will not be justified in the Governor under article 174(2)(b) read with article 356(1)(a) till at least both the Houses of Parliament approve of the Proclamation.

VI. In appropriate cases, the Court will have power by an interim injunction, to restrain the holding of fresh elections to the Legislative Assembly pending the final disposal of the challenge to the validity of the Proclamation to avoid the *fait accompli* and the remedy of judicial review being rendered fruitless. However, the Court will not interdict the issuance of the Proclamation or the exercise of any other power under the Proclamation.

VII. While restoring the *status quo ante*, it will be open for the Court to mould the relief suitably and declare as valid actions taken by the President till that date. It will also be open for the Parliament and the Legislature of the State to validate the said actions of the President.

IX. The Proclamations dated April 21, 1989 and October 11, 1991 and the action taken by the President in removing the respective Ministries and the Legislative Assemblies of the State of Karnataka and the State of Meghalaya challenged in Civil Appeal No. 3645 of 1989 and Transfer Case Nos. 5 and 7 of 1992 respectively are unconstitutional. The Proclamation dated August 7, 1988 in respect of State of Nagaland is also held unconstitutional. However, in view of the fact that fresh elections have since taken place and the new Legislative Assemblies and Ministries have been constituted in all the three States, no relief is granted consequent upon the above declarations. However, it is declared that all actions which might have been taken during the period the Proclamation operated, are valid. The Civil Appeal No. 3645 of 1989 and Transfer case Nos. 5 and 7 of 1992 are allowed accordingly with no order as to costs. Civil Appeal Nos. 193-194 of 1989 are disposed of by allowing the writ petitions filed in the Gauhati High Court accordingly but without costs.

X. The Proclamations dated 15th December, 1992 and the actions taken by the President removing the Ministries and dissolving the Legislative Assemblies in the States of Madhya Pradesh, Rajasthan and Himachal Pradesh pursuant to the said proclamations are not unconstitutional. Civil Appeals Nos. 1692, 1692A-1692C, 4627-30 of 1993 are accordingly allowed and Transfer case Nos. 8 and 9 of 1993 are dismissed with no order as to costs."

THE OPINION OF JEEVAN REDDY, J. AND AGRAWAL, J.

113. Justice Jeevan Reddy has expressed opinion for himself and Justice Agrawal. The conclusions Nos. 2, 3, 7, 8 and 12 in paragraph 434 are relevant for our purpose and the same read as under: (SCC pp. 296-99)

"434(2) The power conferred by article 356 upon the President is a conditioned power. It is not an absolute power. The existence of material — which may comprise of or include the report(s) of the Governor – is a pre-condition. The satisfaction must be formed on relevant material. The recommendations of the Sarkaria Commission with respect to the exercise of power under article 356 do merit serious consideration at the hands of all concerned.

(3) Though the power of dissolving of the Legislative Assembly can be said to be implicit in clause (1) of article 356, it must be held, having regard to the overall constitutional scheme that the President shall exercise it only after the proclamation is approved by both Houses of Parliament under clause (3) and not before. Until such approval, the President can only suspend the Legislative Assembly by suspending the provisions of Constitution relating to the Legislative Assembly under sub-clause (c) of clause (1). The dissolution of Legislative Assembly is not a matter of course. It should be resorted to only where it is found necessary for achieving the purposes of the proclamation.

* * * * *

(7) The proclamation under article 356(1) is not immune from judicial review. The Supreme Court or the High Court can strike down the proclamation if it is found to be *mala fide* or based on wholly irrelevant or extraneous grounds. Then deletion of clause (5) (which was introduced by 38th (Amendment) Act) by the 44th (Amendment) Act, removes the cloud on the reviewability of the action. When called upon, the Union of India has to produce the material on the basis of which action was taken. It cannot refuse to do so, if it seeks to defend the action. The Court will not go into the correctness of the material or its adequacy. Its enquiry is limited to see whether the material was relevant to the action. Even if part of the material is irrelevant, the court cannot interfere so long as, there is some material which is relevant to the action taken.

(8) If the Court strikes down the proclamation, it has the power to restore the dismissed Government to office and revive and reactivate the Legislative Assembly wherever it may have been dissolved or kept under suspension. In such a case, the Court has the power to declare that acts done, orders passed and laws made during the period the proclamation was in force shall remain

unaffected and be treated as valid. Such declaration, however, shall not preclude the Government/Legislative Assembly or other competent authority to review, repeal or modify such Act, orders and laws.

* * * * *

(12) The proclamations dated January 15, 1993 in respect of Madhya Pradesh, Rajasthan and Himachal Pradesh concerned in Civil Appeals Nos. 1692, 1692A-1692C of 1993, 4627-4630 of 1990, Transferred Case (C) No. 9 of 1993 and Transferred Case No. 8 of 1993 respectively are not unconstitutional. The Civil Appeals are allowed and the judgment of the High Court of Madhya Pradesh in M.P. (C) No. 237 of 1993 is set aside. The Transferred Cases are dismissed."

114. Justice Jeevan Reddy has also expressed agreement with the conclusions I, II and IV to VII in the judgment of Justice Sawant delivered on behalf of himself and Justice Kuldip Singh.

OPINION OF PANDIAN, J.

115. Justice Pandian has expressed agreement with the opinion of Justice P.B. Sawant on his conclusions I, II and IV to VIII but so far as the reasoning and other conclusions are concerned, the learned Judge has agreed with the judgment of Justice Reddy.

116. For determining the scope of judicial review in terms of law enunciated by *Bommai*, it is vital to keep in view that majority opinion in that case declared as illegal the dissolution of Assemblies of Karnataka and Nagaland. At an appropriate place later, we will note the reason that led to this declaration.

117. Some observations made in the minority opinion of Justice K. Ramaswamy are also very significant. Learned Judge has said that the motivating factor for action under article 356(1) should never be for political gain to the party in power at the Centre, rather it must be only when it is satisfied that the constitutional machinery has failed. It has been further observed that the frequent elections would belie the people's belief and faith in Parliamentary form of government, apart from enormous election expenditure to the State and the candidates. The Court, if upon the material placed before it, finds that satisfaction reached by the President is unconstitutional, highly irrational or without any nexus, then the Court would consider the contents of the Proclamation or reasons disclosed therein and in extreme cases the material produced pursuant to discovery order nisi to find the action is wholly irrelevant or bears no nexus between purpose of the action and the satisfaction reached by the President or does not bear any rationale to the proximate purpose of the Proclamation. In that event, the Court may declare that the satisfaction reached by the President was either on wholly irrelevant grounds or colourable exercise of power and consequently, Proclamation issued under article 356 would be declared unconstitutional.

OPINION OF AHMADI AND RAMASWAMY, JJ.

118. It is apparent that Justice Ahmadi and Justice Ramaswamy though in minority, yet learned Judges have frowned upon the highly irrational action.

OPINION OF SAWANT AND KULDEEP SINGH, JJ.

119. Now, let us see the opinion of Justice Sawant, who spoke for himself and Justice Kuldip Singh and with whom Justice Pandian, Justice Jeevan Reddy and Justice Agrawal agreed, to reach the conclusion as to the invalidity of Proclamation dissolving Assemblies of Karnataka and Nagaland.

120. Learned Judge has opined that the President's satisfaction has to be based on objective material. That material may be available in the report sent to the President by the Governor or otherwise or both from the report and other sources. Further opines Justice Sawant that the objective material, so available must indicate that the Government of State cannot be carried on in accordance with the provisions of the Constitution. The existence of the objective material showing that the Government of the State cannot be carried on in accordance with the provisions of the Constitution is a condition precedent before the issue of the Proclamation.

121. Reference has been made to a decision of the Supreme Court of Pakistan on the same subject, although the language of the provisions of the relevant articles of Pakistan Constitution is not couched in the same terms. In *Muhammad Sharif* v. *Federation of Pakistan*, PLD 1988 (LAH) 725, the question was whether the order of the President dissolving the National Assembly on 29th May, 1988 was in accordance with the powers conferred on him under article 58(2)(b) of the Pakistan Constitution. It was held in that case that it is not quite right to contend that since it was the discretion of the President, on the basis of his opinion, the President could dissolve the National Assembly but he has to have the reasons which are justifiable in the eyes of the people and supportable by law in a court of justice.

He could not rely upon the reasons which have no nexus to the action, are bald, vague, general or such as can always be given and have been given with disastrous effects (Emphasis supplied by us). It would be instructive to note as to what was stated by the learned Chief Justice and Justice R.S. Sidhwa, as reproduced in the opinion of Justice Sawant: (*Bommai* case SCC pp. 97-98, para 69)

> "Whether it is 'subjective' or 'objective' satisfaction of the President or it is his 'discretion' or 'opinion', this much is quite clear that the President cannot exercise his powers under the Constitution on wish or whim. He has to have facts, circumstances which can lead a person of his status to form an intelligent opinion requiring exercise of discretion of such a grave nature that the representatives of the people who are primarily entrusted with the duty of running the affairs of the State are removed with a stroke of the pen. His action must appear to be called for and justifiable under the Constitution if challenged in a Court of Law. No doubt, the Courts will be chary to interfere in his 'discretion' or formation of the 'opinion' about the 'situation' but if there be no basis or justification for the order under the Constitution, the Courts will have to perform their duty cast on them under the Constitution. While doing so, they will not be entering in the political arena for which appeal to electorate is provided for."

122. Dealing with the second argument, the learned Chief Justice held: (*Bommai* case SCC p. 98, para 69)

"If the argument be correct then the provision 'Notwithstanding anything contained in clause (2) of article 48' would be rendered redundant as if it was no part of the Constitution. It is obvious and patent that no letter or part of a provision of the Constitution can be said to be redundant or non-existent under any principle of construction of Constitutions. The argument may be correct in exercise of other discretionary powers but it cannot be employed with reference to the dissolution of National Assembly. Blanket coverage of validity and unquestionability of discretion under article 48(2) was given up when it was provided under article 58(2) that 'Notwithstanding clause (2) of article 48.... the discretion can be exercised in the given circumstances. Specific provision will govern the situation. This will also avoid expressly stated; otherwise it is presumed to be there in Courts of record. Therefore, it is not quite right to contend that since it was in his 'discretion', on the basis of his 'opinion' the President could dissolve the National Assembly. He has to have reasons which are justifiable in the eyes of the people and supportable by law in a Court of Justice..... It is understandable that if the President has any justifiable reason to exercise his 'discretion' in his 'opinion' but does not wish to disclose, he may say so and may be believed or if called upon to explain the reason he may take the Court in confidence without disclosing the reason in public, may be for reason of security of State. After all patriotism is not confined to the office holder for the time being. He cannot simply say like Caesar it is my will, opinion or discretion. Nor give reasons which have no nexus to the action, are bald, vague, general or such as can always be given and have been given with disastrous effects......".

123. Dealing with the same arguments, R.S. Sidhwa, J. stated as follows: (*Bommai* case SCC p. 98, para 69)

".....I have no doubt that both the Governments are not compelled to disclose all the reasons they may have when dissolving the Assemblies under articles 58(2)(b) and 112(2)(b). If they do not choose to disclose all the material, but only some, it is their pigeon, for the case will be decided on a judicial scrutiny of the limited material placed before the Court and if it happens to be totally irrelevant or extraneous, they must suffer."

124. It is well-settled that if the satisfaction is *mala fide* or is based on wholly extraneous or irrelevant grounds, the court would have the jurisdiction to examine it because in that case there would be no satisfaction of the President in regard to the matter on which he is required to be satisfied. On consideration of these observations made in the case of *State of Rajasthan* as also the other decisions *Kehar Singh* v. *Union of India*, (1989) 1 SCC 204 and *Maru Ram* v. *Union of India*, (1981) 1 SCC 107, Justice Sawant concluded that: (SCC p. 102, para 74)

"The exercise of power to issue proclamation under article 356(1) is subject to judicial review at least to the extent of examining whether the conditions precedent to the issue of Proclamation have been satisfied or not. *This examination will necessarily involve the scrutiny as to whether there existed material for the satisfaction of the President that the situation had arisen in which the Government of the State could not be carried on in accordance with the provisions of the Constitution.*"

While considering the question of material, it was held that: (SCC p. 102, para 74)

> *"It is not the personal whim, wish, view or opinion or the* ipse dixit *of the President* de hors *the material but a legitimate inference drawn from the material placed before him which is relevant for the purpose. In other words, the President has to be convinced of or has to have sufficient proof of information with regard to or has to be free from doubt or uncertainty about the state of things indicating that the situation in question has arisen.* (Emphasis supplied by us). Although, therefore, the sufficiency or otherwise of the material cannot be questioned, the legitimacy of inference drawn from material is certainly open to judicial review."

125. It has been further held that: (SCC pp. 109-110 para 87)

> "When the Proclamation is challenged by making a *prima facie* case with regard to its invalidity, the burden would be on the Union Government to satisfy that there exists material which showed that the Government could not be carried on in accordance with the provisions of the Constitution. Since such material would be exclusively within the knowledge of the Union Government in view of the provisions of section 106 of the Evidence Act, the burden of proof would be on the Union Government."

SATISFACTION OF THE GOVERNOR CANNOT BE BASED ON HIS PERSONAL WHIMS OR ON *MALA FIDE* BASIS

126. Thus having reached the aforesaid conclusions as to the parameters of the judicial review that the satisfaction cannot be based on the personal whim, wish, view, opinion or *ipse dixit de hors* the legitimate inference from the relevant material and that the legitimacy of the inference drawn was open to judicial review, the report on basis whereof Proclamation dissolving the Assembly of Karnataka had been issued was subjected to a close scrutiny, as is evident from paragraphs 118, 119 and 120 of the opinion of Justice Sawant which read as under: (SCC pp. 127-28)

> "118. In view of the conclusions that we have reached with regard to the parameters of the judicial review, *it is clear that the High Court had committed an error in ignoring the most relevant fact that in view of the conflicting letters of the seven legislators, it was improper on the part of the Governor to have arrogated to himself the task of holding,* firstly, *that the earlier nineteen letters were genuine and were written by the said legislators of their free will and volition. He had not even cared to interview the said legislators, but had merely got the authenticity of the signatures verified through the Legislature Secretariat.* Secondly, *he also took upon himself the task of deciding that the seven out of the nineteen legislators had written the subsequent letters on account of the pressure from the Chief Minister and not out of their free will. Again he had not cared even to interview the said legislators.* Thirdly, *it is not known from where the Governor got the information that there was horse trading going on between the legislators. Even assuming that it was so, the correct and the proper course for him to adopt was to await the test on the floor of the House* which test the Chief Minister had willingly undertaken to go through on any day that the Governor chose. In fact, the State Cabinet had itself taken an initiative to convene the meeting of the Assembly on April 27, 1989, *i.e.*, only

a week ahead of the date on which the Governor chose to send his report to the President. *Lastly*, what is important to note in connection with this episode is that the Governor at no time asked the Chief Minister even to produce the legislators before him who were supporting the Chief Minister, if the Governor thought that the situation posed such grave threat to the governance of the State that he could not await the result of the floor-test in the House. We are of the view that *this is a case where all canons of propriety were thrown to wind and the undue haste made by the Governor in inviting the President to issue the Proclamation under article 356(1) clearly smacked of* mala fides. The Proclamation issued by the President on the basis of the said report of the Governor and in the circumstances so obtaining, therefore, equally suffered from *mala fides*. A duly constituted Ministry was dismissed on the basis of material which was neither tested nor allowed to be tested and was no more than the *ipse dixit* of the Governor. The action of the Governor was more objectionable since as a high constitutional functionary, he was expected to conduct himself more firmly, cautiously and circumspectly. Instead, *it appears that the Governor was in a hurry to dismiss the Ministry and dissolve the Assembly. The Proclamation having been based on the said report and so-called other information which is not disclosed was, therefore, liable to be struck down.* (Emphasis supplied by us).

119. In this connection, it is necessary to stress that in all cases where the support to the Ministry is claimed to have been withdrawn by some Legislators, the proper course for testing the strength of the Ministry is holding the test on the floor of the House. That alone is the constitutionally ordained forum for seeking openly and objectively the claims and counter-claims in that behalf. *The assessment of the strength of the Ministry is not a matter of private opinion of any individual, be he the Governor or the President*. It is capable of being demonstrated and ascertained publicly in the House. Hence, when such demonstration is possible, it is not open to bypass it and instead depend upon the subjective satisfaction of the Governor or the President. Such private assessment is an anathema to the democratic principle, apart from being open to serious objections of personal *mala fides*. It is possible that on some rare occasions, the floor-test may be impossible, although it is difficult to envisage such situation. Even assuming that there arises one, it should be obligatory on the Governor in such circumstances, to state in writing, the reasons for not holding the floor-test. The High Court was, therefore, wrong in holding that the floor test was neither compulsory nor obligatory or that it was not a pre-requisite to sending the report to the President recommending action under article 356(1). Since we have already referred to the recommendations of the Sarkaria Commission in this connection, it is not necessary to repeat them here. (Emphasis supplied by us).

120. The High Court was further wrong in taking the view that the facts stated in the Governor's report were not irrelevant when the Governor without ascertaining either from the Chief Minister or from the seven MLAs whether their retraction was genuine or not, proceeded to give his unverified opinion in the matter. What was further forgotten by the High Court was that assuming that the support was withdrawn to the Ministry by the 19 MLAs, it was

incumbent upon the Governor to ascertain whether any other Ministry could be formed. The question of personal *bona fides* of the Governor is irrelevant in such matters. What is to be ascertained is whether the Governor had proceeded legally and explored all possibilities of ensuring a constitutional Government in the State before reporting that the constitutional machinery had broken down. Even if this meant installing the Government belonging to a minority party, the Governor was duty bound to opt for it so long as the Government could enjoy the confidence of the House. That is also the recommendation of the Five-member Committee of the Governors appointed by the President pursuant to the decision taken at the Conference of Governors held in New Delhi in November, 1970, and of the Sarkaria Commission quoted above. It is also obvious that beyond the report of the Governor, there was no other material before the President before he issued the Proclamation. Since the *"facts" stated by the Governor in his report, as pointed out above contained his own opinion based on unascertained material, in the circumstances, they could hardly be said to form an objective material on which the President could have acted. The Proclamation issued was, therefore, invalid."* (Emphasis supplied by us).

127. The view of the High Court that the facts stated in the Governor's report had to be accepted was not upheld despite the fact that the Governor had got the authenticity of the signatures of 19 MLAs on letters verified from the Legislature Secretariat, on the ground that he had not cared to interview the legislators and that there were conflicting letters from the seven legislators. The conclusion drawn by the Governor that those seven legislators had written the subsequent letters on account of the pressure from the Chief Minister and not out of their own free will was frowned upon, particularly when they had not been interviewed by the Governor. It was further observed that it is not known from where the Governor got the information about the horse-trading going on between the legislators. Further conclusion reached was that the Governor had thrown all cannons of propriety to the winds and showed undue haste in inviting the President to issue Proclamation under article 356(1) which clearly smacked of *mala fides*. It was noticed that the facts stated by the Governor in his report were his own opinion based on unascertained material and in the circumstances they could hardly be said to form the objective material on which the President could have acted.

GOVERNOR'S REPORT WAS MOTIVATED

128. When the facts of the present case are examined in light of the scope of the judicial review as is clear from the aforesaid which represents *ratio decidendi* of majority opinion of *Bommai's* case, it becomes evident that the challenge to the impugned Proclamation must succeed.

129. The case in hand is squarely covered against the Government by the *dicta* laid down in *Bommai's* case. There cannot be any presumption of allurement or horse trading only for the reason that some MLAs, expressed the view which was opposed to the public posture of their leader and decided to support the formation of the Government by the leader of another political party. The minority Governments are not unknown. It is also not unknown that the Governor, in a given circumstance, may not accept the claim to form the Government, if satisfied that the party or the group staking claim would not be able to provide to the State a stable Government. It is also not unknown that despite various differences of perception, the party, group or MLAs may still not opt to take a step which may lead to the fall of the Government for various reasons including their being not prepared to face the elections. These and many other imponderables can result in MLAs belonging to even different political parties to come together. It does not necessarily lead to assumption of allurement and horse-trading.

130. As opposed to the cases of dissolution of Karnataka and Nagaland, while considering the cases of dissolution of assemblies of Madhya Pradesh, Rajasthan and Himachal Pradesh, it was held in *Bommai*, (1994) 3 SCC 1 that the reports of the Governors disclosed that the State Governments had miserably failed to protect the citizens and property of the State against internal disturbances, it was found that the Governor's reports are based on relevant material and are made *bona fide* and after due verification. It is in the light of these findings that the validity of the Proclamation was unanimously upheld in respect of these three States.

THE VIEW OF B.P. JEEVAN REDDY AND AGRAWAL, JJ IN *S.R. BOMMAI'S* CASE ANALYSED

131. Now, let us revert to the reasoning given in the opinion of Justice B.P. Jeevan Reddy, speaking for himself and Justice Agrawal.

132. As already noticed, Justice Reddy to the extent stated in para 324 [of *Bommai* case, (1994) 3 SCC 1] expressed his dissent with the reasoning of *State of Rajasthan* case, (1977) 3 SCC 592.

133. Before we examine paragraph 389, wherein Justice Reddy has noticed, in brief, eight reasons given by the Special Bench of the High Court in dismissing the writ petition and the opinion of learned Judge as contained in para 391, we feel that to fully appreciate *Bommai's* case which reversed Full Bench decision of Karnataka High Court, it would be quite useful to note what exactly was stated by the High Court in Paragraphs 28 to 34 of its judgment reported in *S.R. Bommai* v. *Union of India*, AIR 1990 Kant 5. The said paragraphs read as under: (AIR pp. 22-24 paras 28-33)

> "28. Coming to the second facet of the contention of Mr. Soli Sorabjee, we find that the criticism levelled is that the inference drawn by the Governor that there is no other party which is in a position to form the Government, is not only vague but factually incorrect and hence the President had no relevant material to arrive at his satisfaction for proclamation issued by him.
>
> The aforesaid contention again is without any merit for the reasons:
>
> (i) that the Governor formed the said satisfaction which can necessarily be the result of his own impressions. Narration of events in no way advances the case of satisfaction because the very satisfaction of the Governor is an integral part of the material relevant fact. It may also be that the Governor would have met several MLAs and enquired of them. But what transpired between them cannot be a matter of record. In the context where the Governor's personal *bona fides* are not in question, his satisfaction expressed is to be assumed as part of the relevant material

facts in the sense that the very satisfaction stated therein comprehends within itself the idea of all the other necessary factors.

(ii) the report of 19th April, 1989 has to be read with the second report of 20th April, 1989 wherein 'atmosphere getting vitiated' and 'horse-trading' were referred. 'Pressurisation of MLAs', 'Horse-trading' and 'vitiating atmosphere' referred to in the report necessarily indicate the existence of facts for the satisfaction that no other party was in a position to form the government in accordance with the Constitution: The report could have been more explicit and, not adopting such a course by itself cannot nullify the essence of the report. If the President had any reason to doubt the veracity of those statements it was for him to seek a clarification or further report. However, if the President chose to accept the statement of the Governor as to the satisfaction that none else was in a position to form the government it is because the President found it to be a sufficient and acceptable statement as to the existence of factual situation, this statement in para 3 of the first report may also be weighed and understood in the background of the principle that in case the existing Ministry was found to have lost the majority in the House, it is left to the discretion of the Governor to call upon someone else to form the Ministry, whom he thinks is in a position to command majority in the House. Further, absolutely no material has been placed before us to show that any other party or individual staked his or her claim to form a stable Ministry; rather, through out, the petitioners' case has been that the existing Ministry headed by Sri S.R. Bommai continued to enjoy the support of the majority in the House. This premise was held to be not correct for which material facts were given in both the reports made by the Governor.

29. It may be emphasised that a person holding majority does not require time to prove that majority. Instead of telling the Governor that he would prove majority on the floor of the House, the Chief Minister could have as well obtained the signatures of 113 MLAs and placed before the Governor to demonstrate his strength. Moreover, the second report of the Governor also conveys certain material facts; some of the MLAs who withdrew their support to Sri S.R. Bommai wrote again withdrawing the earlier letters with oscillation and fickle-mindedness. Fluctuating loyalties leading to unhealthy practice are pointed out in the report. The democratic culture was being vulgarised. Vitiation of the atmosphere was felt by the Governor. In the context of the prevailing situation the Governor was certainly entitled to report to the President the aforesaid facts. We are, therefore, of the firm view that the two reports of the Governor conveyed to the President the essential and relevant facts from which the President could assess the situation for an action under article 356 of the Constitution.

30. Another major attack levelled against the reports of the Governor by Mr. Soli Sorabjee was that nowhere in the report's it is stated that the State Government cannot be carried on in accordance with the Constitution. In other words, there is no material on the record to show that there has been Constitutional breakdown of the machinery in the State. In support of his

argument the learned counsel drew our attention to the statement in the report which reads:

'It is not appropriate under the circumstances to have the State administered by an Executive consisting of Council of Ministers who do not command the majority in the House.'

What was sought to be argued by the learned counsel was to say that it is not appropriate is quite different from saying that there is a constitutional breakdown, and as the Governor only feels that it is not appropriate, there was no legal justification for taking the impugned action.

Again we find ourselves unable to agree with Mr. Soli Sorabjee. The words "it is not appropriate under the circumstances" have to be understood in the context of the report, especially the next sentence, so as to convey the meaning that the Executive which does not command the support of the majority in the House cannot administer the State in accordance with the Constitution. 'Inappropriateness' stated here is referable to the meaning 'is not in accordance with law'. Reference to any dictionary would show that 'appropriateness' and 'compatibility' are interchangeable and, therefore, when something is said to be not appropriate it conveys the meaning that it is not compatible or not in accordance with law. Hence, the statement of the Governor in this sentence clearly asserts his understanding of the true principle that an Executive having no majority support in the Legislature, if carries on the Government, will be administering the State not in accordance with the Constitution.

31. In view of the aforesaid discussion, we find no escape from the conclusion that the grounds stated and material supplied in the reports of the Governor are neither irrelevant nor vague, that the reasons disclosed bear a reasonable nexus with the exercise of the particular power and hence the satisfaction of the President must be treated as conclusive, and that there is no scope at all for a finding that the action of the President is in flagrant violation of the very words of article 356(1).

32. Mr. Soli Sorabjee also contended that the factors like the alleged 'unethical methods adopted during the formation of Janata Dal' 'expansion of cabinet', 'horse-trading' and 'atmosphere getting vitiated' are not only vague but have no nexus at all with the question of failure of Constitutional machinery. The learned counsel also laid great stress by contending that the Governor by acting upon the letters given by 19 legislators had circumvented the Anti Defection legislation, the primary aim of which is to discourage the toppling game by legislators by changing their loyalties, and by acting upon those letters the legislators were permitted, in substance, to play the game of toppling the ruling Ministry without incurring the consequences of Anti-Defection Law because, if these legislators had withdrawn their support in the House and voted against the Ministry, they would have incurred disqualification under Anti-Defection Law. Reliance upon these letters is contrary to the underlying purpose and the essence of Anti-Defection legislation and therefore illegitimate and prohibited. The learned counsel buttressed his arguments by contending that if the floor test had been held the

legislators who had written letters might have changed their mind for several valid reasons *e.g.*,

(i) change in the style of functioning of leadership,

(ii) change in the leadership,

(iii) realization for maintaining party unity,

(iv) unwillingness to incur disqualification under Anti-Defection legislation and

(v) not giving a pretext for imposition of President's Rule. In support of the contention that the floor test has always been recognised as the legitimate and relevant method, Sri Soli Sorabjee relied on the judgment of the Orissa High Court in *Bijayananda* v. *President of India*, AIR 1974 Ori 52 (61, 69, 70), *Sarkaria Commission Report*, page 173 para 6.5.01, the judgment of Gauhati High Court in *Vamuzo* v. *Union of India*, (1988) 2 Gau LJ 468 (483), Report of the Committee of Governors dated 1-10-1971, pages 208, 209, 210, 217-219, 221-219, 221- 223 and 234, and Address by Speaker of Lok Sabha on the occasion of Speakers' Conference on 16-7-1970 paras 13 and 14.

33. In our view, the aforesaid contentions/points urged by the learned counsel do not in any way destroy the effect of the two material grounds on the basis of which the subjective satisfaction was arrived at by the President. The Governor honestly and truly has stated all the facts. They are not vague at all and are narrative in nature. What was happening in the State, the Governor has disclosed in the report. The Governor was assessing whether the first petitioner was commanding majority and he (Governor) was entitled to take into consideration the behaviour of the MLAs one way or the other.

It is expected that a Government to be effective should not only command a majority in the House but should also be backed by the majority members outside the house so that the Government would not be under a perennial pressure of being dislodged whenever the House meets again.

We have gone through the judgments of the Orissa and Gauhati High Courts mentioned above and find that the same are distinguishable. In *Bijayanand's* case, 1974 Ori 52 (61, 69, 70) the main fact was that the Leader of the Opposition who had shown his majority in the House was not tailed upon to form the Ministry not because he had no majority but because the Governor expected that the majority might fall at any moment and there may be no stable Ministry, and on this aspect G.K. Misra, C.J. observed that the Governor is not concerned whether the Ministry could be stable in future. If the Ministry which would have been formed by the Leader of the Opposition would have fallen afterwards, the Governor would have been justified to recommend for the President's Rule if at that time no other person was in a position to from an alternative Ministry by having majority support. But, in the instant case, the position is entirely different as at the initial stage itself the Governor has in unequivocal terms stated in his report that he is also satisfied that there is no other party which is in a position to form the Government."

THE FACTS OF *VAMUZO'S* CASE

Coming to the case of *Vamuzo*, 1988 (2) Gau LJ 468 the facts were: [*S.R. Bommai* case, AIR 1990 Kant 5 (24-25), para 33-34]

> "33. ...Hokishe Sema formed the Government in 1987. Chishi attempted to bring down and destabilise the Government. To achieve that end he offered money and lured the separated group of 13 to step out from the ruling party. The Governor called the episode 'incredible lack of political morality and complete disregard of the wishes of the electorates on the part of the breakway congressmen'. That none of them therefore had ever expressed any grievances to the Chief Minister at any time in the past. The 13 persons are kept under forcible confinement by K.L. Chishi and Vamuzo. The split of the party is not true. It is obvious that what may be called a political group of the darkest hue has been stated in his absence contrary to the, noble Naga character and democratic traditions'. The recognition by the Speaker was done in haste. The entire incident manifests political horse trading and machinations. He added there is proof that they are the group of 13 persons have not separated from the ruling party voluntarily ....."

If we look at those facts, again we find that there is absolutely no similarity of the aforesaid facts to the two material facts in the case on hand. In the said case, as found on those facts, the Governor was held to have exceeded his jurisdiction and the facts stated therein were found to be irrelevant to the provisions of article 356(1), by the Gauhati High Court.

SARKARIA COMMISSION REPORT

So far as Sarkaria Commission Report, the report of the Committee of Governors and the Address of the Speaker of Lok Sabha are concerned, the views expressed therein are really commendable and it is expected that wherever any such drastic action, like the exercise of power under article 356(1), is taken, it should be ensured that the subjective satisfaction of the President is not based on any irrelevant, irrational or perverse ground. But, in the view we have taken on the facts of this case, the views expressed in those reports are of no assistance to the petitioners. Moreover these recommendations are to alter the existing laws, which implies that till these recommendations are moulded into constitutionally enforceable norms the existing law would prevail.

ANTI-DEFECTION LAW NOT APPLICABLE

134. Mr. Soli Sorabjee had made pointed reference to the Tenth Schedule *i.e.*, Anti-Defection Law, for bringing home his point that the factum of the withdrawal of the support by 19 legislators was wholly irrelevant. This argument was advanced to prove his point that in the context of Anti-Defection Legislation, floor test was the most relevant, legitimate and surest method to determine whether the Council of Ministers headed by Sri S.R. Bommai commanded the majority in the House or not. We are afraid, we are unable to agree with this submission of the learned counsel. The introduction of Tenth Schedule in the Constitution has not in any way affected the exercise of power under article 356 nor has it amended article 356 in any manner. The amending body which inserted the Tenth Schedule to the Constitution had before it several decisions [specially the *Rajasthan* case,

(1977) 3 SCC 592] as to the scope of article 356. There is a presumption that the law-making body was aware of the existing interpretation given by the Supreme Court on a provision of law or of a Constitutional provision. If the said Constitutional provision (article 356) was untouched while adding a new Schedule to the Constitution elsewhere without reference to the existing provision (article 356), we have to presume that the existing interpretation of the said provision continues to govern the situation. It is not possible to hold that the interpretation given to article 356 in *Rajasthan* case, (1977) 3 SCC 592 if continued to govern it, would destroy the efficacy of the Tenth Schedule. Tenth Schedule to the Constitution is applicable to the transaction of business inside the House of Legislature. The anti-defection activity outside the House is not penalised in any manner by Tenth Schedule. Concept of the failure of the Constitutional machinery of the Government is not confined to the loss of majority by a ministry in the House; it may be due to several reasons. Therefore, if meeting of the Legislature, was contemplated as a mandatory requirement preceding a report of the Governor for an action under article 356 and floor test was impliedly made the sole and exclusive test to judge the stability of the Ministry (after the Tenth Schedule was added to the Constitution), the Tenth Schedule would have been suitably worded, or article 356 would have been altered."

135. In para 389, [of *Bommai* case, (1994) 3 SCC 1] Justice Reddy states that the High Court has dismissed the writ petition giving following reasoning: (*Bommai* case SCC pp. 275-76)

"389(1) The proclamation under article 356(1) is not immune from judicial scrutiny. The court can examine whether the satisfaction has been formed on wholly extraneous material or whether there is a rational nexus between the material and the satisfaction.

(2) In article 356, the President means the Union Council of Ministers. The satisfaction referred to therein is subjective satisfaction. This satisfaction has no doubt to be formed on a consideration of all the facts and circumstances.

(3) The two reports of the Governor conveyed to the President essential and relevant facts which were relevant for the purpose of article 356. The facts stated in the Governor's report cannot be stated to be irrelevant. They are perfectly relevant.

(4) Where the Governor's "personal *bona fides*" are not questioned, his satisfaction that no other party is in a position to form the government has to be accepted as true and is based upon a reasonable assessment of all the relevant facts.

(5) Recourse to floor test was neither compulsory nor obligatory. It was not a prerequisite to sending up a report recommending action under article 356(1).

(6) The introduction of Xth Schedule to the Constitution has not affected in any manner the content of the power under article 356.

(7) Since the proclamation has to be issued on the satisfaction of the Union Council of Ministers the Governor's report cannot be faulted on the ground of legal *mala fides*.

(8) Applying the test indicated in the *State of Rajasthan* v. *Union of India*, (1977) 3 SCC 592 the court must hold, on the basis of material disclosed, that the subjective satisfaction arrived at by the President is conclusive and cannot be faulted. The proclamation, therefore, is unobjectionable."

136. Except for aforesaid reasons 1 and 2, other reasons were not accepted by Justice Reddy. Learned Judge did not accept the reasoning of the High Court that where Governor's personal *bona fides* are not questioned, his satisfaction that no party is in a position to form the government has to be accepted as true as it is based on reasonable assessment of all the relevant facts. The Court also did not accept the reasoning that the Governor's report cannot be faulted on the ground of *mala fides*. Learned Judge has stated that the question whether government has lost the confidence of the House is not a matter to be determined by the Governor or for that matter anywhere else except the floor of the House. The House is the place where the democracy is in action. It is not a question of subjective satisfaction of the Governor. It would be useful to note what has been observed in paragraph 391 which reads thus: [*Bommai* case, (1944) 3 SCC 1 (276)]

"391. We must also say that the observation under point (7) is equally misplaced. It is true that action under article 356 is taken on the basis of satisfaction of the Union Council of Ministers but on that score it cannot be said that 'legal *mala fides*' of the Governor is irrelevant. When the article speaks of the satisfaction being formed on the basis of the Governor's report, the legal *mala fides*, if any, of the Governor cannot be said to be irrelevant. The Governor's report may not be conclusive but its relevance is undeniable. Action under article 356 can be based only and exclusively upon such report. Governor is a very high constitutional functionary. He is supposed to act fairly and honestly consistent with his oath. He is actually reporting against his own government. It is for this reason that article 356 places such implicit faith on his report. If, however, in a given case his report is vitiated by legal *mala fides*, it is bound to vitiate the President's action as well. Regarding the other points made in the judgment of the High Court, we must say that the High Court went wrong in law in approving and upholding the Governor's report and the action of the President under article 356. The Governor's report is vitiated by more than one assumption totally unsustainable in law. The Constitution does not create an obligation that the political party forming the Ministry should necessarily have a majority in the Legislature. Minority Governments are not unknown. What is necessary is that that government should enjoy the confidence of the House. This aspect does not appear to have been kept in mind by the Governor. *Secondly* and more importantly whether the council of ministers have lost the confidence of the House is not a matter to be determined by the Governor or for that matter anywhere else except the floor of the House. The principle of democracy underlying our Constitution necessarily means that any such question should be decided on the floor of the House. The House is the place where the democracy is in action. It is not for the Governor to determine the said question on his own or on his own verification. This is not a matter within his subjective satisfaction. It is an objective fact capable of being established on the floor of the House. It is gratifying to note that Sri R. Venkataraman, the former President of India has affirmed this view in his Rajaji Memorial Lecture (Hindustan Times dated February 24, 1994).

137. The substantial reasons given by the High Court in paragraphs 28 to 34 for dismissing the writ petition did not find favour with this Court. Dealing with the report of the Governor in respect of Karnataka, it was held that in the circumstances it cannot be said that the Governor's report contained or was based upon relevant material. There could be no question of the Governor making an assumption of his own.

BOMMAI'S JUDGMENT EXPANDED THE SCOPE OF JUDICIAL REVIEW OF THE REPORT OF THE GOVERNOR IF IT IS BASED ON RELEVANT MATERIAL OR NOT, IN *BONA FIDE* OR NOT

138. Clearly, *Bommai's* case, (1994) 3 SCC 1 expanded the scope of judicial review. True, observations by Justice Reddy were made in the context of a situation where the incumbent Chief Minister is alleged to have lost the majority support or the confidence of the House and not in the context of a situation arisen after a general election in respect whereof no opinion was expressed, but, in our view the principles of scope of judicial review in such matters cannot be any different. By and large, same principles will apply when making recommendation for dissolution of a newly elected Assembly and again plunging the State to elections.

139. Justice Reddy, for upholding the dissolution of the State Legislatures of Madhya Pradesh, Rajasthan and Himachal Pradesh also came to the conclusion that the reports of the Governor disclosed that the State Government had miserably failed to protect the citizens and the property of the State against the internal disturbances and on the basis of the said report, the President formed the requisite satisfaction. Dealing with the circumstances in the State of Madhya Pradesh, it was held that '*Governor's reports are based upon relevant material and are made bona fide and after due verification*'. (Emphasis supplied by us)

140. Thus, it is open to the Court, in exercise of judicial review, to examine the question whether the Governor's report is based upon relevant material or not; whether it is made *bona fide* or not; and whether the facts have been duly verified or not. The absence of these factors resulted in the majority declaring the dissolution of State Legislatures of Karnataka and Nagaland as invalid.

THE VIEW OF THE CENTRAL GOVERNMENT REJECTED:

141. In view of the above, we are unable to accept the contention urged by the learned Attorney-General for India, Solicitor General of India and Additional Solicitor General, appearing for the government that the report of the Governor itself is the material and that it is not permissible within the scope of judicial review to go into the material on which the report of the Governor may be based and the question whether the same was duly verified by the Governor or not. In the present case, we have nothing except the reports of the Governor. In absence of the relevant material much less due verification, the report of the Governor has to be treated as the personal *ipse dixit* of the Governor. The drastic and extreme action under article 356 cannot be justified on mere *ipse dixit*, suspicion, whims and fancies of the Governor. This Court cannot remain a silent spectator watching the subversion of the Constitution. It is to be remembered that this Court is the sentinel on the *qui vive*. In the facts and circumstances of this case, the Governor may be main player, but Council of Ministers should have verified facts stated in the report of the Governor before hurriedly accepting it as a gospel truth as to what Governor stated. Clearly, the Governor has mislead the Council of Ministers which lead to aid and advice being given by the Council of Ministers to the President leading to the issue of the impugned Proclamation.

142. Regarding the argument urged on behalf of the Government of lack of judicially manageable standards and, therefore, the court should leave such complex questions to be determined by the President, Union Council of Ministers and the Governor, as the situation like the one in Bihar, is full of many imponderables, nuances, implications and intricacies and there are too many ifs and buts not susceptible of judicial scrutiny, the un-tenability of the argument becomes evident when it is examined in the light of decision in *Bommai's* case upholding the challenge made to dissolution of the Assemblies of Karnataka and Nagaland. Similar argument defending the dissolution of these two Assemblies having not found favour before a Nine-Judge Bench, cannot be accepted by us. There too, argument was that there were no judicially manageable standards for judging Horse-trading, Pressure, Atmosphere being vitiated, wrongful confinement, Allurement by money, contacts with insurgents in Nagaland. The argument was rejected.

THE POSITION IN DISSOLUTION OF M.P., H.P. AND RAJASTHAN GOVERNMENTS OF BJP WAS DIFFERENT

143. The position was different when Court considered validity of dissolution of Assemblies of Madhya Pradesh, Rajasthan and Himachal Pradesh.

144. In paragraphs 432 and 433 of the opinion of Justice Jeevan Reddy in *Bommai's* case, (1994) 3 SCC 1 after noticing the events that led to demolition of Babri Masjid on 6th December, 1992, the assurances that had been given prior to the said date, the extraordinary situation that had arisen after demolition, the prevailing tense communal situation, the learned Judge came to the conclusion that on material placed before the Court including the reports of the Governors, it was not possible to say that the President had no relevant material before him on the basis of which he could form satisfaction that BJP Governments of Madhya Pradesh, Rajasthan and Himachal Pradesh cannot disassociate themselves from the action and its consequences and that these governments, controlled by one and the same party, whose leading lights were actively campaigning for the demolition of structure, cannot be disassociated from the acts and deeds of the leaders of BJP. It was further held that if the President was satisfied that the faith of these BJP Governments in the concept of secularism was suspected in view of the acts and conduct of the party controlling these governments and that in the volatile situation that developed pursuant to the demolition, the Government of these States cannot be carried on in accordance with the provisions of the Constitution, the Court is not able to say that there was no relevant material upon which he could be so satisfied. Under these circumstances, it was observed that the Court cannot question the correctness of the material produced and that even if part of it is not relevant to the action the Court cannot interfere so long as there is some relevant material to sustain the action. For appreciating this line of reasoning, it has to be borne in mind that the same learned Judge, while examining the validity of dissolution of Karnataka and Nagaland Assemblies, agreeing with the reasoning and conclusions given in the opinion of Justice Sawant which held that the material relied upon by the Governor was nothing but his *ipse dixit* came to the conclusion that the said dissolutions were illegal. The majority opinion and the correct ratio thereof can only be appreciated if it is kept in view that the majority has declared invalid the dissolution of Assemblies of Karnataka and Nagaland and held as valid the dissolution of the Assemblies of Madhya Pradesh, Rajasthan and Himachal Pradesh. Once this factor is kept in full focus, it becomes absolutely clear that the plea of perception of the same facts or the argument of lack of any judicially manageable standards would have no legs to stand on.

IN THE PRESENT CASE THERE WAS NO BASIS OR JUSTIFICATION FOR THE GOVERNOR TO RECOMMEND DISSOLUTION OF BIHAR ASSEMBLY

145. In the present case, like in *Bommai's* case, (1994) 3 SCC 1 there is no material whatsoever except the *ipse dixit* of the Governor. The action which results in preventing a political party from staking claim to form a Government after election, on such fanciful assumptions, if allowed to stand, would be destructive of the democratic fabric. It is one thing to come to the conclusion that the majority staking claim to form the government, would not be able to provide stable government to the State but it is altogether different thing to say that they have garnered majority by illegal means and, therefore, their claim to form the government cannot be accepted. In the latter case, the matter may have to be left to the wisdom and will of the people, either in the same House it being taken up by the opposition or left to be determined by the people in the elections to follow. Without highly cogent material, it would be wholly irrational for constitutional authority to deny the claim made by a majority to form the government only on the ground that the majority has been obtained by offering allurements and bribe which deals have taken place in the cover of darkness but his undisclosed sources have confirmed such deals. The extra-ordinary emergency power of recommending dissolution of a Legislative Assembly is not a matter of course to be resorted to for good governance or cleansing of the politics for the stated reasons without any authentic material. These are the matters better left to the wisdom of others including opposition and electorate.

146. It was also contended that the present is not a case of undue haste. The Governor was concerned to see the trend and could legitimately come to the conclusion that ultimately, people would decide whether there was an 'ideological realignment", then their verdict will prevail and such realigned group would win elections, to be held as a consequence of dissolution. It is urged that given a choice between going back to the electorate and accepting a majority obtained improperly, only the former is the real alternative. The proposition is too broad and wide to merit acceptance. Acceptance of such a proposition as a relevant consideration to invoke exceptional power under article 356 may open a floodgate of dissolutions and has far reaching alarming and dangerous consequences. It may also be a handle to reject post-election alignments and realignments on the ground of same being unethical, plunging the country or the State to another election. This aspect assumes great significance in situation of fractured verdicts and in the formation of coalition governments. If, after polls two or more parties come together, it may be difficult to deny their claim of majority on the stated ground of such illegality. These are the aspects better left to be determined by the political parties which, of course, must set healthy and ethical standards for themselves, but, in any case, the ultimate judgment has to be left to the electorate and the Legislature comprising also of members of opposition.

147. To illustrate the aforesaid point, we may give two examples in a situation where none of the political party was able to secure majority on its own:

1. After polls, two or more political parties come together to form the majority and stake claim on that basis for formation of the government. There may be reports in the media about bribe having been offered to the elected members of one of the political parties for its consenting to become part of majority. If the contention of the respondents is to be accepted, then the constitutional functionary can decline the formation of the government by such majority or dissolve the House or recommend its dissolution on the ground that such a group has to be prevented to stake claim to form the government and, therefore, a situation has arisen in which the government of the State cannot be carried on in accordance with the provisions of the Constitution.
2. A political party stakes claim to form the government with the support of independent elected candidates so as to make the deficient number for getting majority. According to the media reports, under cover of darkness, large sums of bribe were paid by the particular party to independent elected candidates to get their support for formation of government. The acceptance of the contention of the respondents would mean that without any cogent material the constitutional functionary can decline the formation of the government or recommend its dissolution even before such a claim is made so as to prevent staking of claim to form the government.

THE POWER UNDER ARTICLE 356(1) OF THE CONSTITUTION OF INDIA WAS CLEARLY ABUSED

148. We are afraid that resort to action under article 356(1) under the aforesaid or similar eventualities would be clearly impermissible. These are not the matters of perception or of the inference being drawn and assumptions being made on the basis whereof it could be argued that there are no judicial manageable standards and, therefore, the Court must keep its hands off from examining these matters in its power of judicial review. In fact, these matters, particularly without very cogent material, are outside the purview of the constitutional functionary for coming to the conclusion that a situation has arisen in which the Government of the State cannot be carried on in accordance with the provisions of the Constitution.

149. The contention that the installation of the government is different than removal of an existing government as a consequence of dissolution as was the factual situation before the Nine-Judge Bench in *Bommai's* case and, therefore, same parameters cannot be applied in these different situations, has already been dealt with hereinbefore. Further, it is to be remembered that a political party *prima facie* having majority has to be permitted to continue with the government or permitted to form the government, as the case may be. In both categories, ultimately the majority shall have to be proved on the floor of the House. The contention also overlooks the basic issue. It being that a party even, *prima facie,* having majority can be prevented to continue to run the government or claim to form the government declined on the purported assumption of the said majority having been obtained by illegal means. There is no question of such basic issues allegedly falling in the category of "political thicket" being closed on the ground that there are many imponderables for which there is no judicially manageable standards and, thus, outside the scope of judicial review.

150. The further contention that the expression 'situation has arisen in which the Government of the State cannot be carried on in accordance with the provisions of the Constitution' in article 356 shows that the power is both preventive and/or curative and, therefore, a constitutional functionary would be well within his rights to deny formation of the government to a group of parties or elected candidates on the ground of purity of political process is of no avail on the facts and circumstances of this case, in view of what we have already stated. Even if preventive, power cannot be abused.

151. Another contention urged is that the power under article 356 is legislative in character and, therefore, the parameters relevant for examining the validity of a legislative action alone are required to be considered and in that light of the expressions such as '*mala fide*' or 'irrational' or 'extraneous' have to be seen with a view to ultimately find out whether the action is *ultra vires* or not. The contention is that the concept of *mala fides* as generally understood in the context of Executive action is unavailable while deciding the validity of legislative action. The submission is that that the *mala fides* or extraneous consideration cannot be attributed to a legislative act which when challenged the scope of inquiry is very limited.

152. For more than one reason, we are unable to accept the contention of the proclamation of the nature in question being a legislative act. *Firstly,* if the contention was to be accepted, *Bommai's* case would not have held the proclamation in case of Karnataka and Nagaland as illegal and invalid. *Secondly,* the contention was specifically rejected in the majority opinion of Justice Jeevan Reddy in paragraph 377. The contention was that the proclamation of the present nature assumes the character of legislation and that it can be struck down only on the ground on which a legislation can be struck down. Rejecting the contention, it was held that every act of Parliament does not amount to and does not result in legislation and that the Parliament performs many other functions. One of such functions is the approval of the proclamation under clause (3) of article 356. Such approval can, by no stretch of imagination, be called 'legislation'. Its legal character is wholly different. It is a constitutional function, a check upon the exercise of power under clause (1) of article 356. It is a safeguard conceived in the interest of ensuring proper exercise of power under clause (1). It is certainly not legislation nor legislative in character.

153. Mr. Subramaniam, learned Additional Solicitor General, however, contended that *Bommai's* case proceeded on the assumption that the proclamation under article 356(1) is not legislative but when that issue is examined in depth with reference to earlier decisions in the cases of In Re: The Delhi Laws Act, 1912, *the Ajmer-Merwara (Extension of Laws) Act, 1947 and the Part C States (Laws) Act, 1950,* 1951 SCR 747 (SCR at pp. 970-971); *Jayantilal Amrit Lal Shodhan* v. *F.N. Rana*, (1964) 5 SCR 294 (SCC at pp. 205-206); *Rameshchandra Kachardas Porwal* v. *State of Maharashtra*, (1981) 2 SCC 722; and *A.K. Roy* v. *Union of India*, (1982) 1 SCC 271, it would be clear that the conclusion of Justice Reddy in para 377 requires re-look in the light of these decisions. We are unable to accept the contention. The decision of Nine-Judge Bench is binding on us.

SCOPE OF JUDICIAL REVIEW

154. Though *Bommai*, (1994) 3 SCC 1 has widened the scope of judicial review, but going even by principles laid in *State of Rajasthan's* case, (1977) 3 SCC 592 the existence of the satisfaction can always be challenged on the ground that it is *mala fide* or based on wholly extraneous and irrelevant grounds. Apart from the fact that the narrow minimal area of judicial review as advocated in *State of Rajasthan's* case is no longer the law of the land in view of its extension in *Bommai's* case but the present case even when considered by applying limited judicial review, cannot stand judicial scrutiny as the satisfaction herein is based on wholly extraneous and irrelevant ground. The main ground being to prevent a party to stake claim to form the government.

155. In *State of Rajasthan's* case, (1977) 3 SCC 592 in para 185, (SCC p. 673) Justice Untwalia observed that this Court is not powerless to interfere with such an order which is *ultra vires*, wholly illegal or *mala fide* as in such a situation it will tantamount in law to be no order at all. Further observing that it is incompetent and hazardous for the Court to draw conclusions by investigation of facts by entering into the prohibited area but at the same time it would be equally untenable to say that the Court would be powerless to strike down the order, if on its face, or, by going round the circumference of the prohibited area, the Court finds the order as a mere pretence or colourable exercise of the extraordinary powers given under certain articles of the Constitution and thus in a given case it may be possible to conclude that it is a fraud on the exercise of the power. In the present case, we have reached the conclusion that the action of the Governor was a mere pretence, the real object being to keep away a political party from staking a claim to form the government.

156. Referring to the opinion of Justice Reddy, in *Bommai's* case, (1994) 3 SCC 1 it was contended for the respondents that the approach adopted in *Barium Chemicals Ltd.* v. *Company Law Board*, (1966) Supp SCR 311] and other cases where action under challenge is taken by statutory or administrative authorities, is not applicable when testing the validity of the constitutional action like the present one. For proper appreciation of the contention, it may be useful to reproduce in full paragraphs 372 and 373 from which certain observations were relied upon. The same read as under: [*Bommai* case, (1994) 3 SCC 1 (266)]

"372. Having noticed various decisions projecting different points of view, we may now proceed to examine what should be the scope and reach of judicial review when a proclamation under article 356(1) is questioned. While answering this question, we should be, and we are, aware that the power conferred by article 356(1) upon the President is of an exceptional character designed to ensure that the government of the States is carried on in accordance with the Constitution. *We are equally aware that any misuse or abuse of this power is bound to play havoc with our constitutional system.* Having regard to the form of Government we have adopted, the power is really that of the Union Council of Ministers with the Prime Minister at its head. In a sense, it is not really a power but an obligation cast upon the President in the interest of preservation of constitutional Government in the States. *It is not a power conceived to preserve or promote the interests of the political party in power at the Centre for the time being nor is it supposed to be a weapon with which to strike your political opponent.* The very enormity of this power—undoing the will of the people of a State by dismissing the duly constituted government and dissolving the duly elected Legislative Assembly — must itself act as a warning against its frequent use or misuse, as the case may be. Every misuse of this power has its consequences which may not be evident immediately but surface in a vicious form a few years later. Sow a wind and you will reap the whirlwind. Wisdom lies in moderation and not in excess."

(Emphasis supplied by us)

157. Further, learned Judge states that: [*Bommai* case, (1994) 3 SCC 1 (266-67) para 373]

"373. Whenever a proclamation under article 356 is questioned, the court will no doubt start with the presumption that it was validly issued but it will not and it should not hesitate to interfere if the invalidity or unconstitutionality of the proclamation is clearly made out. Refusal to interfere in such a case would amount to abdication of the duty cast upon the court—Supreme Court and High Courts—by the Constitution. Now, what are the grounds upon which the court can interfere and strike down the proclamation? While discussing the decisions herein above, we have indicated the unacceptability of the approach adopted by the Privy Council in *Bhagat Singh* v. *Emperor,* AIR 1931 PC 111 and *King Emperor* v. *Bengari Lal Sarma,* AIR 1945 PC 48. That was in the years 1931 and 1944, long before the concept of judicial review had acquired its present efficacy. As stated by the Pakistan Supreme Court, that view is totally unsuited to a democratic polity. Even the Privy Council has not stuck to that view, as is evident from its decision in the case from *Malaysia Stephen Kalong Ningkan* v. *Government of Malaysia,* (1970 AC 379). In this case, the Privy Council proceeded on the assumption that such a proclamation is amenable to judicial review. On facts and circumstances of this case, it found the action justified. Now, coming to the approach adopted by the Pakistan Supreme Court, it must be said – as indicated hereinbefore— that it is coloured by the nature of the power conferred upon the President by section 58(2)(b) of the Pakistani Constitution. The power to dismiss the federal Government and the National Assembly is vested in the President and

President alone. He has to exercise that power in his personal discretion and judgment. One man against the entire system, so to speak—even though that man too is elected by the representatives of the people. That is not true of our Constitution. Here the President acts on the aid and advice of the Union Council of Ministers and not in his personal capacity. Moreover, there is the check of approval by Parliament which contains members from that State (against the Government/Legislative Assembly of which State, action is taken) as well. So far as the approach adopted by this Court in *Barium Chemicals* (1966 Supp SCR 311) is concerned, it is a decision concerning subjective satisfaction of an authority created by a statute. The principles evolved then cannot *ipso facto* be extended to the exercise of a constitutional power under article 356. Having regard to the fact that this is a high constitutional power exercised by the highest constitutional functionary of the Nation, it may not be appropriate to adopt the tests applicable in the case of action taken by statutory or administrative authorities—nor at any rate, in their entirety. We would rather adopt the formulation evolved by this Court in *State of Rajasthan* as we shall presently elaborate. We also recognise, as did the House of Lords in *C.C.S.U.* v. *Minister*, 1985 AC 374, for the Civil Service that there are certain areas including those elaborated therein where the court would leave the matter almost entirely to the President/Union Government. The court would desist from entering those arenas, because of the very nature of those functions. They are not the matters which the court is equipped to deal with. The court has never interfered in those matters because they do not admit of judicial review by their very nature. Matters concerning foreign policy, relations with other countries, defence policy, power to enter into treaties with foreign powers, issues relating to war and peace are some of the matters where the court would decline to entertain any petition for judicial review. But the same cannot be said of the power under article 356. It is another matter that in a given case the court may not interfere. It is necessary to affirm that the proclamation under article 356(1) is not immune from judicial review, though the parameters thereof may vary from an ordinary case of subjective satisfaction."

158. The aforesaid paragraphs cannot be read in isolation and have to be seen while bearing in mind that learned Judge invalidated dissolution of Assembly of Karnataka and Nagaland. Be that as it may, in the present case, the validity of the impugned notification is not being judged on application of principles available for judging the validity of administrative actions.

159. Further, para 376 of the opinion of Justice Jeevan Reddy is very instructive and it may be reproduced as under: (SCC p. 269)

"376. We recognise that judicial process has certain inherent limitations. It is suited more for adjudication of disputes rather than for administering the country. The task of governance is the job of the Executive. The Executive is supposed to know how to administer the country, while the function of the Judiciary is limited to ensure that the government is carried on in accordance with the Constitution and the Laws. *Judiciary accords, as it should, due weight to the opinion of the Executive in such matters but that is not to say, it defers to the opinion of Executive altogether. What ultimately determines the scope of judicial review is the facts and circumstances of the given case. A case may be a clear one—like Meghalaya and Karnataka cases—where the court can find unhesitatingly that the proclamation is bad. There may also be cases – like those relating to Madhya Pradesh, Rajasthan and Himachal Pradesh—where the situation is so complex, full of imponderables and a fast-evolving one that the court finds it not a matter which admits of judicial prognosis, that it is a matter which should be left to the judgment of and to be handled by the Executive and may be in the ultimate analysis by the people themselves. The best way of demonstrating what we say is by dealing with the concrete cases before us.* (Emphasis supplied by us).

FACTS OF EACH CASE DETERMINE THE LEGALITY OR OTHERWISE OF THE POWER EXERCISED UNDER ARTICLE 356 OF THE CONSTITUTION OF INDIA

160. It is evident from the above that what ultimately determines the scope of judicial review is the facts and circumstances of the given case and it is for this reason that the Proclamations in respect of Karnataka and Nagaland were held to be bad and not those relating to Madhya Pradesh, Rajasthan and Himachal Pradesh.

ALLEGED INCURRING OF DISQUALIFICATION WAS WHOLLY EXTRANEOUS CONSIDERATION AT THAT STAGE

161. We are not impressed with the argument based on a possible disqualification under Tenth Schedule if the MLAs belonging to LJP party had supported the claim of Nitish Kumar to form the government. At that stage, it was a wholly extraneous to take into consideration that some of the members would incur the disqualification if they supported a particular party against the professed stand of the political party to which they belong. The intricate question as to whether the case would fall within the permissible category of merger or not could not be taken into consideration. Assuming it did not fall in the permissible arena of merger and the MLAs would earn the risk of disqualification, it is for the MLAs or the appropriate functionary to decide and not for the Governor to assume disqualification and thereby prevent staking of claim by recommending dissolution. It is not necessary for us to examine, for the present purpose, para 4 of the Tenth Schedule dealing with merger and/or deemed merger. In this view the question sought to be raised that there cannot be merger of legislative party without the first merger of the original party is not necessary to be examined. The contention sought to be raised was that even if two-third legislators of LJP legislative party had agreed to merge, in law there cannot be any merger without merger of original party and even in that situation those two-third MLAs would have earned disqualification. Presently, it is not necessary to decide this question. It could not have been gone into by the Governor for recommending dissolution.

CORRUPT PRACTICE, ELECTORAL OFFENCES WERE IRRELEVANT AT THAT STAGE

162. The provision of the Tenth Schedule dealing with defections, those of RP Act of 1951 dealing with corrupt practice, electoral offences and disqualification and the provisions of Prevention of Corruption Act, 1988 are legal safeguards available for ensuring purity of public life in a democracy. But, insofar as the present case is concerned, these had no relevance at the stage when the dissolution of the Assembly was recommended without existence of any material whatsoever. There was no material for the assumption that claim may be staked based not on democratic principles and based on manipulations by breaking political parties.

GOVERNOR WAS DUTY BOUND TO ACT AS PER THE CONSTITUTIONAL PROVISIONS BUT HIS ACT WAS TOTALY UNCONSTITUTIONAL

163. There cannot be any doubt that the oath prescribed under article 159 requires the Governor to faithfully perform duties of his office and to the best of his ability preserve, protect and defend the Constitution and the laws. The Governor cannot, in the exercise of his discretion or otherwise, do anything what is prohibited to be done. The Constitution enjoins upon the Governor that after the conclusion of elections, every possible attempt is made for formation of a popular Government representing the will of the people expressed through the electoral process. If the Governor acts to the contrary by creating a situation whereby a party is prevented even to stake a claim and recommends dissolution to achieve that object, the only inescapable inference to be drawn is that the exercise of jurisdiction is wholly illegal and unconstitutional. We have already referred to the Governor report dated 21st May, 2005, *inter alia*, stating that 17-18 MLAs belonging to LJP party are moving towards JDU which would mean JDU may be in a position to stake claim to form the government. The further assumption that the move of the said members was itself indicative of various allurements having been offered to them and on that basis drawing an assumption that the claim that may be staked to form a government would affect the constitutional provisions and safeguards built therein and distort the verdict of the people, would be arbitrary. This shows that the approach was to stall JDU from staking a claim to form the government. At that stage, such a view cannot be said to be consistent with the provisions of Tenth Schedule. In fact, the provisions of the said Schedule at that stage had no relevance. It is not a case of 'assumption', or 'perception' as to the provisions of Constitution by the Governor. It is a clear case where attempt was to somehow or the other prevent the formation of a government by a political party – an area wholly prohibited insofar as the functions, duties and obligations of the Governor are concerned. It was thus a wholly unconstitutional act.

164. It is true as has been repeatedly opined in various reports and by various constitutional experts that the defections have been a bane of the Indian Democracy but, at the same time, it is to be remembered that the defections have to be dealt with in the manner permissible in law.

IF ONE POLITICAL PARTY STAKES CLAIM OF MAJORITY AND SATISFIES THE GOVERNOR HE CANNOT OVERRIDE THE CLAIM UNDER THE CONSTITUTION

165. If a political party with the support of other political party or other MLA's stakes claim to form a government and satisfies the Governor about its majority to form a stable government, the Governor cannot refuse formation of government and override the majority claim because of his subjective assessment that the majority was cobbled by illegal and unethical means. No such power has been vested with the Governor. Such a power would be against the democratic principles of majority rule. Governor is not an autocratic political Ombudsman. If such a power is vested in the Governor and/or the President, the consequences can be horrendous. The ground of mal-administration by a State Government enjoying majority is not available for invoking power under article 356. The remedy for corruption or similar ills and evils lies elsewhere and not in article 356(1). In the same vein, it has to be held that the power under Tenth Schedule for defection lies with the Speaker of the House and not with the Governor. The power exercised by the Speaker under the Tenth Schedule is of judicial nature. Dealing with the question whether power of disqualification of members of the House vests exclusively with the House to the exclusion of Judiciary which in Britain was based on certain British Legislature practices, as far as India is concerned, it was said in *Kihoto's* case that: (SCC p. 705 para 94)[1]"

> "94. It is, therefore, inappropriate to claim that the determinative jurisdiction of the Speaker or the Chairman in the Tenth Schedule is not a judicial power and is within the non-justiciable legislative area."

GOVERNOR CANNOT ASSUME JUDICIAL POWER TO HIMSELF

166. The Governor cannot assume to himself aforesaid judicial power and based on that assumption come to the conclusion that there would be violation of Tenth Schedule and use it as a reason for recommending dissolution of Assembly.

THE PROCLAMATION OF DISSOLUTION DATED 23.5.2005 WAS UNCOSTITUTIONAL

167. The Governor, a high constitutional functionary is required to be kept out from the controversies like disqualification of members of a Legislative Assembly and, therefore, there are provisions like article 192(2) in the Constitution providing for Governor obtaining the opinion of the Election Commission and acting according to such opinion, in the Constitutional Scheme of things. Similar provision, insofar as, member of Parliament is concerned being in article 103(2) of the Constitution; [*Brundaban Nayak* v. *Election Commission of India*, (1965) 3 SCR 53 and *Election Commission of India* v. *Dr. Subramaniam Swamy*, (1996) 4 SCC 104.]

168. For all the aforesaid reasons, the Proclamation dated 23rd May, 2005 is held to be unconstitutional.

STATUS QUO ANTE CANNOT BE RESTORED AS NOTIFICATIONS FOR FRESH ELECTIONS WERE ALREADY ISSUED

Point No. 3: If the Answer to the Aforesaid Questions is in Affirmative, is it Necessary to Direct *status quo ante* as on 7th March, 2005 or 4th March, 2005?

169. As a consequence of the aforesaid view on point No. 2, we could have made an order of *status quo ante* as prevailing before dissolution of Assembly. However, having regard to the facts and the circumstances of the case, in terms of order of this Court dated 7th October, 2005, such a relief was declined. Reasons are the larger public interest, keeping in view the ground realities and taking a pragmatic view. As a result of the impugned Proclamation, the Election Commission of India had not only made preparations for the four phase election

1. *Kihoto Hollohan* v. *Zachillhu*, 1992 Supp (2) SCC 651.

to be conducted in the State of Bihar but had also issued Notification in regard to first two phases before conclusion of arguments. Further, in regard to these two phases, before 7th October, 2005, even the last date for making nominations and scrutiny thereof was also over. In respect of 1st phase of election, even the last date for withdrawal of nominations also expired and polling was fixed for 18th October, 2005. The election process had been set in motion and was at an advanced stage. Judicial notice could be taken of the fact that considerable amount must have been spent; enormous preparations made and ground works done in the process of election and that too for election in a State like the one under consideration. Having regard to these subsequent developments coupled with numbers belonging to different political parties, it was thought fit not to put the State in another spell of uncertainty. Having regard to the peculiar facts, despite unconstitutionality of the Proclamation, the relief was moulded by not directing *status quo ante* and consequently permitting the completion of the ongoing election process with the fond hope that the electorate may again not give fractured verdict and may give a clear majority to one or other political party — the Indian electorate possessing utmost intelligence and having risen to the occasion on various such occasions in the past.

Point No. 4: What is the Scope of Article 361 Granting Immunity to the Governor?

170. By order dated 8th September, 2005, we held that the Constitution of India grants immunity to the Governor as provided in article 361. Article 361(1), *inter alia*, provides that the Governor shall not be answerable to any Court for the exercise and performance of the powers and duties of his office or for any act done or purported to be done by him in the exercise and performance of those powers and duties. We accepted the submissions made on behalf of the respondents that in view of this article notice could not be issued to the Governor, at the same time, further noticing that the immunity granted does not affect the power of this Court to judicial scrutinising attack made on the Proclamation issued under article 356(1) of the Constitution of India on the ground of *mala fides* or it being *ultra vires* and that it would be for the government to satisfy the Court and adequately meet such ground of challenge. A *mala fide* act is wholly outside the scope of the power and has no existence in the eyes of the law. We, further held that the expression 'purported to be done' in article 361 does not cover acts which are *mala fide* or *ultra vires* and thus, the government supporting the Proclamation under article 356(1) shall have to meet the challenge. The immunity granted under article 361 does not mean that in the absence of Governor, the grounds of *mala fide* or being *ultra vires* would not be examined by the Court. This order was made at the stage when we had not examined the question whether the exercise of power by the Governor was *mala fide* or *ultra vires* or not. This question was argued later.

171. In our order dated 8th September, 2005 while giving the brief reasons we stated that detailed reasons will be given later.

172. Article 361(1) which grants protection to the President and the Governor reads as under:

"*361. Protection of President and Governors and Rajpramukhs.*—(1) The President, or the Governor or Rajpramukh of a State, shall not be answerable to any court for the exercise and performance of the powers and duties of his office or for any act done or purporting to be done by him in the exercise and performance of those powers and duties:

Provided that the conduct of the President may be brought under review by any court, tribunal or body appointed or designated by either House of Parliament for the investigation of a charge under article 61:

Provided further that nothing in this clause shall be construed as restricting the right of any person to bring appropriate proceedings against the Government of India or the Government of a State.

(2) No criminal proceedings whatsoever shall be instituted or continued against the President, or the Governor of a State, in any court during his term of office.

(3) No process for the arrest or imprisonment of the President, or the Governor of a State, shall issue from any court during his term of office.

(4) No civil proceedings in which relief is claimed against the President, or the Governor of a State, shall be instituted during his term of office in any court in respect of any act done or purporting to be done by him in his personal capacity, whether before or after he entered upon his office as President, or as Governor of such State, until the expiration of two months next after notice in writing has been delivered to the President or the Governor, as the case may be, or left at his office stating the nature of the proceedings, the cause of action therefor, the name, description and place of residence of the party by whom such proceedings are to be instituted and the relief which he claims."

173. A plain reading of the aforesaid article shows that there is a complete bar to the impleading and issue of notice to the President or the Governor inasmuch as they are not answerable to any Court for the exercise and performance of their powers and duties. Most of the actions are taken on aid and advice of Council of Ministers. The personal immunity from answerability provided in article 361 does not bar the challenge that may be made to their actions. Under law, such actions including those actions where the challenge may be based on the allegations of *mala fides* are required to be defended by Union of India or the State, as the case may be. Even in cases where the personal *mala fides* are alleged and established, it would not be open to the Governments to urge that the same cannot be satisfactorily answered because of the immunity granted. In such an eventuality, it is for the respondent defending the action to satisfy the Court either on the basis of the material on record or even filing the affidavit of the person against whom such allegation of personal *mala fides* are made. Article 361 does not bar filing of an affidavit if one wants to file on his own. The bar is only against the power of the Court to issue notice or making the President or the Governor answerable. In view of the bar, the Court cannot issue direction to President or Governor for even filing of affidavit to assist the Court. Filing of an affidavit on one's own volition is one thing than issue of direction by the Court to file an affidavit. The personal immunity under article 361(1) is complete and, therefore, there is no question of the President or the Governor being made answerable to the Court in respect of even charges of *mala fides*.

UNION CARBIDE CORPORATION'S CASE

174. In *Union Carbide Corporation* v. *Union of India*, (1991) 4 SCC 584, dealing with article 361(2) of the Constitution, Justice Venkatahalliah referred to the famous case of *Richard Nixon*, (1982) 457 US 731 about theoretical basis for the need for such immunity. It was said:

> "101. Article 361(2) of the Constitution confers on the President and the Governors immunity even in respect of their personal acts and enjoins that no criminal proceedings shall be instituted against them during their term of office. As to the theoretical basis for the need for such immunity, the Supreme Court of the United States in a case concerning immunity from civil liability; *Richard Nixon* v. *Ernest Fitzgerald*, 457 US 731: 73 Law Ed 2d 349 said: (L Ed pp. 362-363)
>
> ".....This Court necessarily also has weighed concerns of public policy, especially as illuminated by our history and the structure of our Government....."
>
> ".....In the case of the President the inquiries into history and policy though mandated independently by our case, tend to converge. Because the Presidency did not exist through most of the development of common law, any historical analysis must draw its evidence primarily from our constitutional heritage and structure. Historical inquiry thus merges almost at its inception with the kind of "public policy" analysis appropriately undertaken by a federal court. This inquiry involves policies and principles that may be considered implicit in the nature of the President's office in a system structured to achieve effective Government under, a constitutionally mandated separation" of powers." (L Ed p. 367)
>
> ".....In view of the special nature of the President's constitutional office and functions, we think it appropriate to recognise absolute Presidential immunity from damages liability for acts within the "outer perimeter" of his official responsibility. Under the Constitution and laws of the United States the President has discretionary responsibilities in a broad variety of areas, many of them highly sensitive. In many cases it would be difficult to determine which of the President's innumerable "functions" encompassed a particular action.."

GOVERNOR IS NOT ANSWERABLE TO THE COURT BUT THE VALIDITY OF HIS ACTION CAN BE EXAMINED BY THE COURT

175. A division Bench of the Bombay High Court in the case of *Shri Pratapsing Raojirao Rane* v. *The Governor of Goa*, AIR 1999 Bom 53, has correctly held that in respect of his official acts, the Governor is not answerable to the Court even in respect of charge of *mala fide* and that in such an eventuality the Governor cannot be said to be under the duty to deal with the allegations of *mala fide*. *The Constitutional Law of India*, 4th Edn. by H.M. Seervai has been rightly relied upon in the said judgment. The observations made by full Bench of the Madras High

Court in *K.A. Mathialagan* v. *The Governor of Tamil Nadu,* AIR 1973 Mad 198, that the Governor would be under duty to deal with allegations of *mala fide* in order to assist the Court has been rightly described in Seervai's commentary being in direct conflict with the complete personal immunity of the Governor.

176. The words 'purported to be done' are of wide amplitude. In *Biman Chandra* v. *Governor, West Bengal,* AIR 1952 Cal 799, it was held that article 361 affords immunity in respect of its exercise and performance of the power and duties of the office and any act done or purported to be done by him in exercise and performance of those powers and duties.

177. In *G.D. Karkare* v. *T.L. Shevde,* AIR 1952 Nag 330 construing the expression 'purporting to be done' it was held that any act, though not done in pursuance of the Constitution, may nevertheless be accorded this protection if the act professes or purports to be done in pursuance of the Constitution. It was further explained that though the Governor is not amenable to the process of the Court but it cannot be said that the High Court cannot examine his action and grant relief in the absence of authority making the decision.

178. In *State* v. *Kawas Manekshaw Nanavati,* AIR 1960 Bom 502 full Bench of the High Court held that article 361 only gives personal protection to the Governor. It is not necessary that the Governor should be a party to the proceeding. Validity of actions can be considered and decided in the absence of the Governor. In *The State of West Bengal* v. *Sailendra Nath Bose,* AIR 1964 Cal 184 it was held that a citizen is not without redress even though he cannot implead the Governor as a party but can be given relief.

179. The position in law, therefore, is that the Governor enjoys complete immunity. Governor is not answerable to any Court for the exercise and performance of the powers and duties of his office or for any act done or purporting to be done by him in the exercise and performance of those powers and duties. The immunity granted by article 361(1) does not, however, take away the power of the Court to examine the validity of the action including on the ground of *mala fides*.

DISSOLUTION OF BIHAR ASSEMBLY WAS UNCONSTITUTIONAL BUT *STATUS QUO ANTE* DECLINED

180. In view of the above, while holding the impugned Proclamation dated 23rd May, 2005 unconstitutional, we have moulded the relief and declined to grant *status quo-ante* and consequentially permitted the completion of ongoing election process.

181. All petitions are disposed of accordingly.

Justice K.G. Balakrishnan and Justice Arijit Pasayat gave dissenting judgments separately on point No. 2. Since the majority judgment is to prevail therefore the dissenting views have not been reproduced.

However in view of the majority judgment, the proclamation of dissolution of Bihar Assembly was held to be unconstitutional but *status quo ante* was not restored because the notification for fresh elections was already issued.

CONSTITUTIONALITY OF THE PROVISO TO SUB-SECTION (11A) OF SECTION 11 MADE BY THE ALL INDIA INSTITUTE OF MEDICAL SCIENCES (AMENDMENT) ACT, 2007 WAS CHALLENGED AND DECIDED IN THIS CASE

P. Venugopal

v.

Union of India[1]

SUPREME COURT OF INDIA

CIVIL ORIGINAL JURISDICTION

Writ Petition (Civil) No. 656 of 2007

Decided on 8-5-2008

BENCH

Tarun Chatterjee and Harjit Singh, JJ.

FACTS IN THE BACKGROUND OF THIS JUDGMENT

Author's Note: In paras 9, 24 to 28 and 31 of the judgment dated 8.5.2008, the Hon'ble Supreme Court has referred to the orders passed by the Hon'ble Delhi High Court on 7.7.2006 and 18.10.2006 in W.P. (Civil) No. 10687 of 2006 and to the order dated 29.3.2007 passed by the Division Bench in appeal against the order dated 18.10.2006. Those matters also related to Dr. P. Venugopal. The facts in brief of those cases before the Delhi High Court are given for the benefit of the readers.

Dr. P. Venugopal Professor in the All India Institute of Medical Sciences in the department of Cardiovascular and Thoracic Surgery was appointed as Director of the All India Institute of Medical Sciences (in short AIIMS) by the Appointments Committee of the Cabinet, Government of India *vide* letter, dated 3rd July, 2003 for a period of five years from the date he assumed the charge of the post and until further orders. He was also allowed to continue as Professor in the department in which he was already working. He joined his duties on the same day and his term of five years was to come to an end on 2nd July, 2008.

7.2.2005. The Health Minister of the Government of India (Shri Ambumani Ramadoss) was appointed as President of the All India Institute of Medical Sciences after being nominated as a member of the Governing body of AIIMS under section 4(e) of the All India Institute of Medical Sciences Act, 1956.

5.7.2006. An extra-ordinary meeting of the Institute was held and a decision was taken to terminate the 5 year tenure of the Director Dr. P. Venugopal. The note placed in the meeting of the governing body was that Dr. P. Venugopal had gathered faculty, students and outsiders in the AIIMS's auditorium and spoke openly criticizing the Government for allegedly interfering in the affairs of AIIMS.

---

1. AIR 2008 SC (Supp) 969: (2008) 8 SCR 1: (2008) 5 SCC 1: (2008) 2 SCALE 255.

It led to considerable tension in the Institute. It has brought indiscipline and bad name to the Institute. Therefore, Rule 9 of the CCS Conduct Rules was attracted and it was in public interest to terminate the term of Dr. P. Venugopal as Director of AIIMS with immediate effect after giving him 3 month's salary in lieu of the notice period as per Regulation 31. It was publicly announced and a copy of the decision was given to Dr. Venugopal. It was also sent for approval to the Cabinet Committee.

6.7.2006. Dr. P. Venugopal challenged this decision in the Delhi High Court by filing writ Petition (civil) No. 10687 of 2006 along with misc. application (CM) No. 8169 of 2006 seeking stay order against the implementation of the decision dated 5.7.2006.

7.7.2006. The Delhi High Court stayed the order dated 5.7.2006 and further restrained the respondents from passing any further order on the basis of the impugned decision of the Governing Body of the AIIMS till all the allegations and counter allegations are considered and in order to nullify the probability of any irreparable loss to any of the parties. The High Court had held that the speech was made by Dr. P. Venugopal during the strike on the question of reservation which was alleged as criticism of the Government. It was held by the High Court that if the students and the faculty were on strike, it could not be said that the Director had gathered and assembled them.

The text of the address of the petitioner to the faculty and students was as under:

"My dear colleagues and friends,

Today I am talking to you as a faculty and as a part of the AIIMS family.

Three years back I reluctantly accepted the post of Director of AIIMS which I had earlier declined in 1996. This I did with the hope that with the support of all of you, we together will take AIIMS to new heights of excellence and achievement, thereby adding further milestones to the achievements of my predecessors.

This institute is a temple of learning, research and patient care. During the last about 2 years there has been a systematic undermining of institute and the authority of its Director. I being the Director, am disturbed with the humiliation to the respect and dignity of my faculty, officers, residents, students and staff. As the head of the AIIMS family, it is my bounden duty to either ensure that legitimate interests of the Institute and its functionaries are maintained or to seek justice from appropriate authorities. And I know in this country of great Parliamentarians, academicians and enlightened citizens, it would be difficult for anyone to trample upon this great institute for vested interest.

I stand here to seek a decision from all of you and your blessings to maintain the sanctity of this temple of learning. I assure you my friends that in case I fail in my duties to deliver as Director and to prevent the destruction of the dignity and autonomy of AIIMS, I would not hesitate in leaving this coveted chair for one of you to take over and continue the effort.

Thank you and God bless you."

The High Court took the view that this speech could not be termed as criticism of the Government to entail action under Rule 9 of the Code. Although the Government took the plea that there were other grounds for taking action against Dr. P. Venugopal but admittedly the other grounds were not made a part of the agenda placed before the governing body which took decision only on the agenda placed before it.

25.7.2006. LPA No. 1674 of 2006 was filed against this order by the respondents but it was got dismissed as withdrawn.

21.9.2006. The President of the Governing Body of the Institute (Health Minsiter of the Government of India) asked the Director, Dr. Venugopal member secretary of the governing body to call the meeting of the Governing Body for 10.10.2006 at 11.00 a.m. at Nirman Bhawan, New Delhi. 23rd September was Saturday and 24th September was Sunday.

25.9.2006. The Director informed the President that regulation 4(3) of the Regulations required to send the notice of the meeting of the Institute body along with the agenda and requested that the officials be directed to make the agenda available to him for necessary compliance of the orders of the President.

28.9.2006. The President wrote back that the agenda could be sent later on and directed the Director to call the Extra-ordinary meeting on the said date, time and place and the agenda would be sent later on and the compliance be sent by 29th September, 2006. The Director complied with the said orders and informed the members that the agenda would be sent later on.

6.10.2006. Apprehending that the President of the governing body of the Institute wanted to circumvent the order dated 7.7.2006 firstly by calling a meeting for 10.10.2006 without providing the agenda and thereafter by converting the said meeting in to an extra-ordinary meeting for the same date, time and place, even then without supplying the agenda, filed an application (C.M.) No. 12471 of 2006 in W.P. (Civil) No. 10687 of 2006 seeking stay of notice dated 29.9.2006. It was also prayed that the issue regarding the continuation of the petitioner as Director of the Institute be not taken up in the meeting on 10.10.2006 and in any subsequent meeting of the Governing Body. It came up for hearing on 6.10.2006.

10.10.2006. The respondents appeared. They demanded copies of the application and the documents. These were supplied but the case was adjourned to 16.10.2006.

10.10.2006. The meeting fixed for 10.10.2006 was postponed to 18.10.2006 due to serious spreading of dengue problem in AIIMS even as per the version of the Union of India.

18.10.2006. The Court passed the order in C.M. No. 12471 of 2006 that it will be appropriate to allow the Institute's Body to consider everything but not to allow the implementation of any adverse order, decision or resolution against the petitioner till further orders regarding his tenure appointment and his functioning as Director of the All India Institute of Medical Sciences and any such resolution and decision would be subject to the outcome of this writ petition.

The All India Institute of Medical Sciences filed LPA No. 2046 of 2006 against the order dated 18.10.2006. One self created body also filed writ petition (civil) No. 8485 of 2006 in the name of Centre for Public Interest Litigation against the Union of India and others for the removal of Dr. P. Venugopal from the post of Director of AIIMS. Both these matters namely LPA and the Writ Petition were heard together by the Division Bench of Delhi High Court.

29.3.2007. The Division Bench of the Delhi High Court directed that the Institute can proceed against the Director in accordance with law, but without in any way violating the orders of the Court dated 7.7.2006. The order dated 18.10.2006 was modified to the extent aforesaid.

Having failed to proceed against Dr. P. Venugopal, Director AIIMS within the framework of the existing laws and the terms and conditions of his appointment as Director AIIMS before the expiry of his 5 year term of appointment as Director, Government of India got section 11 of the All India Institute of Medical Sciences amended through Parliament by getting passed the AIIMS (Amendment) Act, 2007 by which section (11A) with its Proviso to section 11 of the AIIMS Act was introduced under which his term of appointment could be reduced even earlier.

8.5.2008: Dr. P. Venugopal, Director AIIMS filed writ petition (civil) No. 656 of 2007 in the Supreme Court. Hence, the judgment dated 8.5.2008.

JUDGMENT

1. In this writ application under article 32 of the Constitution moved at the instance of Dr. P. Venugopal, a renowned and internationally famed Cardio Vascular Surgeon, calls in question the constitutional validity of the proviso to sub-section (1A) of section 11 of the All India Institute of Medical Sciences (Amendment) Act, 2007.

2. The writ petitioner was admittedly the Director of All India Institute of Medical Sciences (in short the "AIIMS") immediately prior to the commencement of the added provisions and by virtue of the legislative command contained in the added provision he had been made to demit his office as Director of the said Institute from the date of coming into force of this added provision.

3. The writ petitioner claims and it does not appear to be disputed that he was a Gold Medalist in his batch of MBBS, passed out from the AIIMS itself and thereafter he acquired qualification of MS and MCH in cardio vascular surgery and that he served the Institute for about three/four decades with honesty and respect without any blemish. It is also not in dispute that the writ petitioner was to complete his five-year term in the Office of the Director on 2nd of July, 2008, but due to this added provision in the Act, had to suffer a pre-mature termination and consequent removal from the office of the Director on 30th of November, 2007. It is alleged that this adverse affectation has been brought about directly by the added provision.

STATEMENT OF OBJECTS AND REASONS FOR THE AMENDMENT

4. In the Statement of Objects and Reasons of the Amendment Act of 1987 being Act XXX of 1987, as stated herein above, AIIMS and the Post Graduate Institute of Medical Education and Research, Chandigarh, are statutory autonomous bodies wholly financed by the Government of India. Sub-section (2) of section 3 of the All

India Institute of Medical Sciences Act, 1956, provides for the incorporation of the Institute and declares:

> "that the Institute shall be a body corporate by the name aforesaid having perpetual succession and a common seal with a power to acquire, hold and dispose of property, both movable and immovable, and to contract, and shall by the said name sue and be sued".

Section 5 of the Parent Act declares "that the Institute shall be an Institute of National Importance." Section 4 of the Act deals with the composition of the Institute and the Director of the Institute has been made an *ex-officio* Member of the Institute and under sub-section 2 of section 6, he is to continue as such so long as he holds office in virtue of which, he is such a Member.

5. The Act provides for Constitution of a Governing Body by the Institute from amongst its members in such manner as may be prescribed by the Regulations to exercise such power and discharge such functions as the Institute may, by Regulation, make in this behalf confer or impose upon it. Under regulation 25, the Institute is required to carry out such directions as may be issued to it from time to time by the Central Government for the efficient administration under the Act. Section 26 deals with the dispute between the Institute and the Central Government in the matter of exercise of its power and discharge of its function under the Act and makes the decision of the Central Government final. Thus the Act designed the Institute to be an autonomous statutory body of national importance subject to limited control in respect of specified matters. Amendment of section 11 of the AIIMS Act made sub-section (1A) with its proviso added to section 11 of the AIIMS (Amendment) Act, 2007 reads as follows:—

> "(1A) The Director shall hold office for a term of five years from the date on which he enters upon his office or until he attains the age of sixty-five years, whichever is earlier:
>
> Provided that any person holding office as a Director immediately before the commencement of the All India Institute of Medical Sciences and the Post-Graduate Institute of Medical Education and Research (Amendment) Act, 2007, shall insofar as his appointment is inconsistent with the provisions of this sub-section, cease to hold office on such commencement as such Director and shall be entitled to claim compensation not exceeding three months' pay and allowances for the premature termination of his office or of any contract of service..."

SIGNIFICANT CHANGE MADE BY THE PROVISO TO SUB-SECTION (1A) OF SECTION 11 IN THE AIIMS ACT

6. As noted herein earlier in this writ petition, the challenge has been confined only to the proviso of the added sub-section (1A) of section 11 of the Act. Mr. Arun Jaitley, learned senior counsel appearing on behalf of the writ petitioner submitted at the first instance that the provisions, no doubt, acquire their operational significance from the added sub-section but manifestly, it makes a significant departure from the substantive part and proceeds to deal only with the particular Director holding office immediately prior to its coming into force and is not concerned with any other officer or member of the Institute, nor to any other person who may be coming to hold the same office of Director in future.

POINTS OF CHALLENGE

7. We have carefully examined the proviso to the added sub-section (1A) to section 11 of the Act. Reading the proviso in the manner as aforesaid, the writ petitioner has challenged its constitutional validity mainly on the following grounds:

(i) The proviso is patently a single-man legislation and intended to affect the writ petitioner only and none else thus introduces a "naked discrimination" to deprive the writ petitioner of the constitutional protection under article 14 of the Constitution.

(ii) The writ petitioner has been singled out to be deprived of the two protective conditions in respect of curtailment of his tenure. The benefit of notice and justifiable reasons being the two such conditions will continue to be available to all future Directors but the proviso makes them non-available to the writ petitioner being the Director presently in office and requires him to move out of the office under the legislative command.

(iii) In the facts and circumstances of the case and in view of the pending proceedings with different orders passed therein, such calculated steps to force the writ petitioner out of his office offend the constitutional scheme envisaging fair, reasonable and equal treatment on the part of the State in its dealing with the individual in general and with people in public employment in particular.

(iv) The writ petitioner claims the protection of articles 14 and 16 of the Constitution of India.

(v) In the factual context of the case, there has been a violation of the orders issued in favour of the writ petitioner passed by the learned Single Judge of the High Court of Delhi in W.P. No. 10687/2006 in connection with interim applications CMP Nos. 8169/2006 and 12471/2006 and by the Division Bench in W.P.) No. 8485/2006 and LPA Nos. 2045-46/2006.

AGE OF SUPERANNUATION CAN BE ALTERED

8. It is true that in establishments like AIIMS, there is an age of superannuation governing the length of service of its officers and employees. Such age of superannuation may be suitably altered by way of reducing the age so as to affect even the serving employees under appropriate circumstances and no exception can be taken to such course of action. Similarly under the Service Rules, there may be provision for extension of service after the attainment of the age of superannuation and it is well-settled that in the event of refusal by an employer to grant an extension, the employee cannot justifiably claim to be deprived of any right or privilege. The view taken is that the employer has a discretion to grant or not to grant such extension having regard to the interest of the employer or the establishment. This view is expressed by this Court in the case of *State Bank of*

Bikaner and Jaipur v. *Jag Mohan Lal*, AIR 1989 SC 75. In this case, at para 12, this Court observed as follows: (SCC p. 226 para 13)

> "13. ...The Bank has no obligation to extend the services of all officers even if they are found suitable in every respect. The interest of the Bank is the primary consideration for giving extension of service. With due regard to exigencies of service, the Bank in one year may give extension to all suitable retiring officers. In another year, it may give extension to some and not to all. In a subsequent year, it may not give extension to any one of the officers. The Bank may have a lot of fresh recruits in one year. The Bank may not need the services of all retired persons in another year. The Bank may have lesser workload in a succeeding year. The retiring persons cannot in any year demand that "extension to all or none". If we concede that right to retiring persons, then the very purpose of giving extension in the interest of the Bank would be defeated. We are, therefore, of opinion that there is no scope for complaining arbitrariness in the matter of giving extension of service to retiring persons."

FACTS IN THE BACKGROUND

9. In the instant case, the material facts and circumstances bring into focus other consideration. In the case of the writ petitioner, a Division Bench of the Delhi High Court by its judgment and order dated 29th of March, 2007 (Pages 119 to 181 of Volume I of Writ Petition No. 656 of 2007) has considered the right of the writ petitioner to hold the office of the Director for five years from the age of 61 years to 66 years.

VERSION OF THE CENTRAL GOVERNMENT

There can be no dispute with regard to the contentions raised by Mr. K.A. Parasaran, learned senior counsel appearing for the respondent, that a person appointed in Government service acquires a status and his service conditions will be determined by the Service Rules or Statutory Rules and not by the contrary or inconsistent terms of the contract, and such terms and conditions of service may be unilaterally altered by the Government.

PRIOR LAW RELIED UPON BY THE CENTRAL GOVERNMENT

This view has been candidly expressed in paragraph 6 of a decision of this Court, namely, *Roshan Lal Tandon* v. *Union of India*, AIR 1967 SC 1889 which, in our view, should be required to be reproduced. Accordingly, we reproduce para 6 of the aforesaid decision which is as under: (AIR pp. 1894-95)

> "6. We pass on to consider the next contention of the petitioner that there was a contractual right as regards the condition of service applicable to the petitioner at the time he entered Grade 'D' and the condition of service could not be altered to his disadvantage afterwards by the notification issued by the Railway Board. It was said that the order of the Railway Board dated January 25, 1958, Annexure 'B', laid down that promotion to Grade 'C' from Grade 'D' was to be based on seniority-cum-suitability and this condition of service was contractual and could not be altered thereafter to the prejudice of the petitioner.

In our opinion, there is no warrant for this argument. It is true that the origin of Government service is contractual. There is an offer and acceptance in every case. But once appointed to his post or office the Government servant acquires a status and his rights and obligations are no longer determined by consent of both parties, but by statute or statutory rules which may be framed and altered unilaterally by the Government. In other words, the legal position of a Government servant is more one of status than of contract. The hall-mark of status is the attachment to a legal relationship of rights and duties imposed by the public law and not by mere agreement of the parties. The emolument of the Government servant and his terms of service are governed by statute or statutory rules which may be unilaterally altered by the Government without the consent of the employee. It is true that article 311 imposes constitutional restrictions upon the power of removal granted to the President and the Governor under article 310. But it is obvious that the relationship between the Government and its servant is not like an ordinary contract of service between a master and servant. The legal relationship is something entirely different, something in the nature of status. It is much more than a purely contractual relationship voluntarily entered into between the parties. The duties of status are fixed by the law and in the enforcement of these duties society has an interest. In the language of jurisprudence status is a condition of membership of a group of which powers and duties are exclusively determined by law and not by agreement between the parties concerned. The matter is clearly stated by *Salmond and Williams on Contracts* as follows:

"So we may find both contractual and status-obligations produced by the same transaction. The one transaction may result in the creation not only of obligations defined by the parties and so pertaining to the sphere of contract but also and concurrently of obligations defined by the law itself, and so pertaining to the sphere of status. A contract of service between employer and employee, while for the most part pertaining exclusively to the sphere of contract, pertains also to that of status so far as the law itself has been fit to attach to this relation compulsory incidents, such as liability to pay compensation for accidents. The extent to which the law is content to leave matters within the domain of contract to be determined by the exercise of the autonomous authority of the parties themselves, or thinks fit to bring the matter within the sphere of status by authoritatively determining for itself the contents of the relationship, is a matter depending on considerations of public policy. In such contracts as those of service the tendency in modern times is to withdraw the matter more and more from the domain of contract into that of status."

10. Similarly in *N. Lakshmana Rao* v. *State of Karnataka*, (1976) 2 SCC 502 in paras 20 and 21, it was observed as follows (SCC p. 508):—

"20. As a result of the exercise of option by the teachers of the local bodies they became Government servants. The term that the service conditions would not be varied to their disadvantage would mean that they would be like all other Government servants subject to article 310(1) of the Constitution. This could mean that under the law these teachers would be entitled to continue in service up to the age of superannuation. The exercise of option does not mean that there was a contract whereby a limitation was put on prescribing an age of superannuation. It has been held by this Court that prescribing an age of superannuation does not amount to an action under article 311 of the Constitution. Article 309 confers legislative power to provide conditions of service. The Legislature can regulate conditions of service by Law which can impair conditions or terms of service.

21. This Court in *Roshan Lal Tandon* v. *Union of India*, AIR 1967 SC 1889 said that there is no vested contractual right in regard to the terms of service. The legal position of a Government servant is one of status than of contract. The duties of status are fixed by law. The terms of service are governed by statute or statutory rules which may be unilaterally altered by the Government without the consent of the employee."

11. A further decision relied upon in this connection by Mr. Parasaran, learned senior counsel appearing for the respondent, is the decision of this Court reported in *Union of India* v. *Dr. S. Baliar Singh*, (1998) 2 SCC 208, particularly learned senior counsel has relied on paragraph 12 of the said decision in support of his contention. Relying on this decision of this Court, it was contended that the rules which were in force on the date of retirement would govern the employee concerned. On this aspect of the matter, there cannot be any dispute as such aspect is well-settled by a series of decisions of this Court as referred to herein above. But the problem arises when the constitutional validity of the statutory provisions is called in question on the ground of violation of fundamental rights. A person entering into a Government service is no doubt liable to be dealt with by the relevant Act or the Rules but it ceases to be so in the event of his success in challenging the constitutional validity of the same.

12. A government servant entering into a Government service does not forego his fundamental rights. On the other hand, because of his status as a person in public employment, he acquires additional rights constitutionally protected. The State or other public authorities are not, therefore, entitled to make and impose laws governing the service conditions of an employee which manifestly deprive him of the privileges of that status. A person in public employment is endowed with a status not merely subjecting him to liabilities and obligation but also protecting him against any arbitrary, unreasonable and unequal treatment. Such a person is also entitled to constitutional remedies whether under article 32 or under article 226 of the Constitution.

13. The next contention on behalf of the respondent is that the constitutionality of law cannot be judged on the basis of its peculiar operation in special or individual cases and it must be judged on the basis of its ordinary effect and use of operation. It was pointed out that a few freak instances of hardship may arise at a time or at different times but the same cannot invalidate the order or the policy. In this connection, Mr. Parasaran, learned senior counsel appearing on behalf of the respondent, had placed reliance on a decision of the Federal Court reported in AIR 1939 Federal Court P1 (*Central Provinces and Berar Sales of Motor Spirit and Lubricants Taxation Act, 1938.*) While examining the legality of Central Provinces and Berar Sales of Motor Spirit and Lubricants Taxation Act, 1938, Justice

Sulaiman, as His Lordship then was, in a concurring judgment referred to the observations of Lord Herschell in *Attorney General for Canada* v. *Attorney General for Ontario,* (1898) AC 700 (PC) to the following effect:—

"The Supreme Legislative power in relation to any subject-matter is always capable of abuse, but it is not to be assumed that it will be improperly used, if it is, the only remedy is an appeal to those by whom the Legislature is elected." (*See* C.P. Motor Spirit Act, AIR 1939 FC 1 AIR p. 30).

14. Reliance can also be placed in this connection on the case of *R.S. Joshi, Sales Tax Officer, Gujarat* v. *Ajit Mills Ltd.,* (1977) 4 SCC 98]. Mr. Parasaran, learned senior counsel had also relied on another decision reported in *Tamil Nadu Education Department Ministerial and General Subordinate Services Association* v. *State of Tamil Nadu,* (1980) 3 SCC 97. Reliance was also placed by the learned senior counsel for the respondent on the decision in the matter of *State of Himachal Pradesh* v. *Kailash Chand Mahajan,* (1992 Supp 2 SCC 351) and *Virender Singh Hooda* v. *State of Haryana,* (2004) 12 SCC 588.

JUDGMENTS RELIED UPON BY THE UNION OF INDIA ARE NOT APPLICABLE TO THE FACTS OF THIS CASE

15. On a close examination of the aforesaid decisions, it appears that the questions involved in the aforesaid decisions were significantly different. So far as *Central Provinces and Berar Sales of Motor Spirit and Lubricants Taxation Act 1938,* AIR 1939 FC 1 is concerned, the question of constitutional invalidity, as in the present case, was not in issue. In *R.S. Joshi's* case, (1977) 4 SCC 98 the law in question did not lack in generality in respect of its operation. But exception was sought to be taken on the basis of the hardship or injustice in particular cases. So far as (1980) 3 SCC 197 (*Tamil Nadu Education Department* case) is concerned, the law was general in its operation and freak instances of hardship were held not relevant to determine its validity.

16. So far as the last decision of this Court, as referred to by Mr. Parasaran, namely, *State of Himachal Pradesh* v. *Kailash Chand Mahajan,* 1992 Supp 2 SCC 351 is concerned, the impugned law in the decision being the Ordinance of 1990 was a law of general application and it applied not only to the Chairman-cum-Managing Director of Himachal Pradesh State Electricity Board, but also to all members of the Electricity Board. This Court, accordingly, held that this was not a one-man legislation and consequently upheld it on merit. Therefore, the respective contentions are to be examined in the context of the Constitutional Scheme of India having a written Constitution with guaranteed fundamental rights.

17. In India, under article 13(2) of the Constitution

13(2) "The State shall not make any law which takes away or abridges the rights conferred by this part and any law made in contravention of this clause shall, to the extent of the contravention, be void."

Thus, in India, a law cannot be accepted merely because it purports to be a law falling within the legislative field of the maker thereof. Each such provision of law is required to stand the test of article 13(2) of the Constitution and survive.

PRIOR LAW RELIED UPON BY THE PETITIONER

18. Mr. Arun Jaitley, learned senior counsel appearing on behalf of the writ petitioner laid stress on the following three judgments of this Court. The first decision is the case of *Ram Prasad Narayan Sahi* v. *The State of Bihar*, AIR 1953 SC 215. Mr. Jaitley had drawn our attention to a passage of this judgment rendered by the former Chief Justice of this Court, Justice Patanjali Sastri, in which the Chief Justice, after referring to the facts of the earlier case of *Ameerunissa Begum* v. *Mahboob Begum*, AIR 1953 SC 91, in which the Legislature intervened in a private dispute in respect of succession to an estate, observed:—

> "Legislation based upon mis-management or other misconduct as the differentia and made applicable to a specified individual or corporate body is not far removed from the notorious parliamentary procedure formerly employed in Britain of punishing individual delinquents by passing bills of attainder, and should not, I think, receive judicial encouragement." (*See* Page 217 AIR para 6 of this decision).

19. Chief Justice Patanjali Sastri further referred to his own dissenting judgment in *Charanjit Lal Chowdhury* v. *Union of India*, AIR 1951 SC 41 and observed that similar view was taken in *Ameerunnissa Begum's* case (Supra). The former Chief Justice Patanjali Sastri, in the same decision proceeded to observe (*Ram Prasad Narayan Sahi* case, AIR 1953 SC 215, AIR p. 217, para 7):

> "7. ...Whenever, then, a section of the people in a locality, in assertion of an adverse claim, disturb a person in the quiet enjoyment of his property, the Bihar Government would seem to think that it is not necessary for the police to step in to protect him in his enjoyment until he is evicted in due course of law, but the Legislature could intervene by making a 'Law' to oust the person from his possession. Legislation such as we have now before us is calculated to draw the vitality from the Rules of Law which our Constitution so unmistakably proclaims, and it is to be hoped that the democratic process in the country will not function along these lines."

20. In *Ameerunnissa Begum's* case (supra), the former Chief Justice of India, Mr. Justice Bijon Kumar Mukherjee, as His Lordship then was, also applied the principles laid down in the case of *Ram Prasad Narayan Sahi's* case (supra) and at page 220 para 19 observed as follows:—

> "19. ...What the Legislature has done is to single out these two individuals and deny them the right which every Indian citizen possesses to have his rights adjudicated upon by a judicial tribunal in accordance with law which applied to his case. The meanest of citizens has a right of access to a court of law for the redress of his just grievances and it is from his right that the appellants have been deprived, by this Act. It is impossible to conceive of a worse form of discrimination than the one which differentiates a particular individual from all his fellow subjects and visits him with a disability which is not imposed upon anybody else and against which even the right of complaint is taken away. The learned attorney general who placed his case with his usual fairness and ability, could not put forward any convincing or

satisfactory reason upon which this legislation could be justified." (*See* AIR page 220 para 19 of this decision).

The observation made by His Lordship in the aforesaid decision is also material and therefore we reproduce the same: [*Ram Prasad Narayan Sahi's* case (*supra*)].

"19. ...It is true that the presumption is in favour of the constitutionality of a legislative enactment and it has to be presumed that a legislature understands and correctly appreciates the needs of its own people. But when on the face of a statute, there is no classification at all and no attempt has been made to select any individual or group with reference to any differentiating attribute peculiar to that individual or group and not possessed by others, this presumption is of little or no assistance to the State."

DISCUSSION BY THE SUPREME COURT ON THE AMENDMENT MADE

21. Let us now look into the facts of the case in hand. In the instant case it was submitted that the impugned proviso was manifestly designed to apply and was in fact applied only against the writ petitioner and was not intended to and could not apply even, in principle or otherwise, to anybody else because there was only one AIIMS in the country, there was only one Director of the AIIMS on the date of commencement of the Amending Act, and there could be none else who could conceivably be effected by its operation. It is claimed that reference to a similar proviso introduced in the PGI Chandigarh Act, 1956, is somewhat misleading as the term of appointment of the present Director of PGI Chandigarh was only upto the age of 68 years and accordingly there was no question under the PGI Chandigarh Act as the proviso is affecting the present incumbent or his successor.

22. It was further submitted on behalf of the writ petitioner that the proviso itself declares that "any person holding office as a Director immediately before the commencement of the All India Institute of Medical Sciences and the Post Graduate Institute of Medial Education and Research (Amendment) Act of 2007 shall in so far as his appointment is inconsistent with the provisions of this sub-section ceases to hold office on such commencement as such Director and *shall be entitled to claim compensation not exceeding three months' pay and allowances for the premature termination of his office or of any contract of service.*"

(Emphasis supplied).

23. This submission, as advanced by Mr. Jaitley, learned senior counsel appearing on behalf of the writ petitioner, in our view, has merit that the impugned proviso does not at all deal with the alteration of the age of superannuation. On the contrary, it really modifies the initial appointment on the ground of alleged inconsistency with a subsequent enactment and makes him entitled to compensation for premature termination of his office. To equate the impugned proviso with the simple alteration of the age of superannuation is to ignore the clear language of the proviso itself. The proviso brings about a premature termination and provides for compensation. A superannuation in usual course gives rise to ordinary retiral benefits and not to any compensation. Again it is impossible to ignore the force in the submission of Mr. Jaitley, learned senior counsel appearing on behalf of the writ petitioner, that a person is being singled out for premature termination without any question of his being justifiably treated as a Member of a separate and distinct class on any rational basis, any question of intelligible differentia having a nexus to the object of classification cannot arise. It was contended by Mr. Jaitley that in reality there is no legislation in respect of any class but there is legislation in respect of an individual, a living human being requiring him to move out of office.

DISCUSSION ON THE PREVIOUS JUDGMENTS OF DELHI HIGH COURT

24. The Delhi High Court in its judgment dated 29th of March, 2007 has held that the writ petitioner was entitled to continue as a Director upto 2nd of July, 2008 and issued a Writ of *Mandamus* that premature termination could only be made for justifiable reasons and in compliance with the principles of natural justice. By a Writ in the nature of Prohibition issued by the High Court, the respondent was prohibited from implementing any adverse decision against the writ petitioner without giving him a period of two weeks for approaching the High Court. It would be appropriate at this stage to refer to the Statement of Objects and Reasons of the Amendment Act of 2007. It declares that with a view to comply with the directions of the High Court of Delhi in the judgment dated 29th of March, 2007, the amendments are being introduced. It is difficult to conceive how the amendments are in compliance or in consonance with the directions of the High Court. On behalf of the writ petitioner, it was contended and not without reason, that the amendments were made precisely to frustrate the judgment of the High Court reducing his search for justice to an exercise in futility.

25. It appears that the direction No. 13 in the judgment of the Delhi High Court was not confined or related to the particular case of the writ petitioner as regards his right to continue as a Director until he attains the age of 66 years, *i.e.*, upto 2nd of July, 2008. It was otherwise and independently upheld in the same judgment. It is also true that the impugned proviso does not lay down any policy or principle at all, but deals only with the case of the writ petitioner and seeks to affect him in isolation.

26. After the order of the Delhi High Court dated 29th of November, 2002, in *Health India (Registered)* v. *Union of India*, (2003) 102 DLT 19, the writ petitioner was appointed with the approval of the ACC as the Director at the age of 61 years on 3rd of July, 2003 for a term of five years expiring on 2nd of July, 2008, *i.e.*, on attainment of the age of 66 years. Shri R.L. Malhotra, Under Secretary to the Government of India, in fact, by a letter to the Director, All India Institute of Medical Sciences, Ansari Nagar, New Delhi, conveyed the approval of the Appointments Committee of the Cabinet for appointment of Prof. P. Venugopal as Director, All India Institute of Medical Sciences, New Delhi in the pay scale of Rs. 26,000 with Non-Practicing Allowance for a period of five years from the date he assumes charge of the post and until further orders. He will also continue as Professor in the Department of Cardiovascular and Thoracic Surgery, AIIMS, New Delhi. The appointment of the Director, PGI, Chandigarh, was restricted upto the age of 62 years and his appointment does not bear any comparison with the instant case.

27. The learned Single Judge of the Delhi High Court in the writ petition being W.P. [C] No. 10687/2006 on 7th of July, 2006, *inter alia*, observed that "*the petitioner has not been given any notice and according to him his tenure of five years could not be curtailed on the grounds which are not justifiable...*" and then proceeded to injunct the respondent against premature termination of the term of the writ petitioner. The learned Single Judge reiterated and re-emphasized the prohibition against the respondent by subsequent order dated 18th of October, 2006 (*See* pages 89-118 of Vol. 1).

28. The Division Bench of the Delhi High Court by its judgment dated 29th of March, 2007 has rendered an effective and binding determination of the right of the writ petitioner to continue as Director for five years upto 2nd of July, 2008. In the said judgment (at P. 127 of Vol. I), the learned Judge of the High Court has referred to the AIIMS Regulations and particularly to clause 5 thereof which provides for fixed tenure of five years for the Member of the Governing Body as the Director being full fledged Member of the Governing Body and not an *ex officio* Member and was entitled to the benefit of his tenure as a Member, and could not justifiably be deprived of the same.

PETITIONER WAS BEING SINGLED OUT BY THIS AMENDMENT

The writ petitioner is, however, being singled out and treated differently from other members of the Governing Body. In this connection, reference can be made to sections 4, 6 and 10 of the AIIMS Act, 1956 which are relevant for our purpose.

Accordingly, we quote relevant provisions as indicated herein above:—

"*Section 4. Composition of the Institute.*—The Institute shall consist of the following members, namely:

(a) the Vice-Chancellor of the Delhi University, *ex officio*;

(b) the Director-General of Health Services, Government of India, *ex officio*;

(c) the Director of the Institute, *ex officio*;

(d) two representatives of the Central Government to be nominated by that Government, one from the Ministry of Finance and one from the Ministry of Education;

(e) five persons of whom one shall be a non-medical scientist representing the Indian Science Congress Association, to be nominated by the Central Government;

(f) four representatives of the medical faculties of Indian Universities to be nominated by the Central Government in the manner prescribed by rules; and

(g) three members of Parliament of whom two shall be elected from among themselves by the members of the House of the People and one from among themselves by the members of the Council of States.

Section 6. Term of office of, and vacancies among, members—

(1) Save as otherwise provided in the section, the term of office of a member shall be five years from the date of his nomination or election:

Provided that the term of office of a member elected under clause (g) of section 4 shall come to an end as soon as he [becomes a Minister or

Minister of State or Deputy Minister, or the Speaker or the Deputy Speaker of the House of the People, or the Deputy Chairman of the Council of States or] ceases to be a member of the House from which he was elected.

(2) The term of office of an *ex officio* member shall continue so long as he holds the office in virtue of which he is such a member.

(3) The term of office of a member nominated or elected to fill a casual vacancy shall continue for the remainder of the term of the member in whose place he is nominated or elected.

(4) An outgoing member shall, unless the Central Government otherwise directs, continue in office until another person is nominated or elected as a member in his place.

(5) An outgoing member shall be eligible for re-nomination or re-election.

(6) A member may resign his office by writing under his hand addressed to the Central Government but he shall continue in office until his resignation is accepted by that Government.

(7) The manner of filling vacancies among members shall be such as may be prescribed by rules.

Section 10. Governing Body and other Committees of the Institute—

(1) There shall be a Governing Body of the Institute which shall be constituted by the Institute from among its members in such manner as may be prescribed by regulations.

(2) The Governing Body shall be the Executive Committee of the Institute and shall exercise such powers and discharge such functions as the Institute may, by regulations made in this behalf, confer or impose upon it.

(3) The President of the Institute shall be the Chairman of the Governing Body and as Chairman thereof shall exercise such powers and discharge such functions as may be prescribed by regulations.

(4) The procedure to be followed in the exercise of its powers and discharge of its functions by the Governing Body, and the term of office of, and the manner of filling vacancies among, the members of the Governing Body shall be such as may be prescribed by regulations.

(5) Subject to such control and restrictions as may be prescribed by rules, the Institute may constitute as many Standing Committees and as many *ad hoc* Committees as it thinks fit for exercising any power or discharging any function of the Institute or for inquiring into or reporting or advising upon, any matter which the Institute may refer to them.

(6) A Standing Committee shall consist exclusively of members of the Institute; but an *ad hoc* Committee may include persons who are not members of the Institute but the number of such persons shall not exceed one-half of its total membership.

(7) The Chairman and members of the Governing Body and the Chairman and members of a Standing Committee or an *ad hoc* Committee shall receive such allowances, if any, as may be prescribed by regulations."

DISCUSSION BY THE SUPREME COURT ON THE LEGALITY OF THE AMENDMENT IN THE LIGHT OF SECTIONS 4, 6 AND 10 OF THE AIIMS ACT

29. Keeping the provisions, as noted herein above, in our mind, we now proceed to take up the question in hand. The tenure of the writ petitioner as a Director to act as a Member of the Governing Body is for five years which expires on 2nd of July, 2008 on the basis of his initial appointment and, therefore, it is not in dispute that it was a tenure appointment which could not be otherwise dealt with. It was seriously contended by Mr. Parasaran, learned senior counsel appearing on behalf of the respondent, that reliance on the Delhi High Court's judgment and orders particularly those of the learned Single Judge dated 7th of July, 2006 and 18th of October, 2006 and the order dated 29th of March, 2007 of the Division Bench was wholly misconceived as the two orders of the Single Judge were interim orders and the special leave petition against the orders of the Division Bench was pending before this Court. It was also contended by Mr. Parasaran, learned senior counsel for the respondent that the writ petition filed by the writ petitioner in the Delhi High Court is still pending before the learned Single Judge and therefore, it was pointed out on behalf of the respondent that in such view of the matter, no reliance could be placed upon the decision in *Madan Mohan Pathak* v. *Union of India,* (1978) 2 SCC 50, and in the case of *A.V. Nachane* v. *Union of India,* (1982) 1 SCC 205.

30. It is true that respondent has, no doubt, raised the plea that the judgment of the Division Bench is under challenge before this Court and, therefore, it has not yet attained the kind of finality which was there in *Madan Mohan Pathak's* case. In *Madan Mohan Pathak's* case (Supra), the question of finality was taken into consideration only for the purpose of enforceability of the direction of the Calcutta High Court in respect of payment of bonus under the settlement of Class III and Class IV employees and it was held that irrespective of the question of Constitutionality of the Amendment Act, the Calcutta High Court judgment operating inter parties and becoming final was enforceable. In this connection, Para 8 of the decision in *Madan Mohan Pathak's* case is important for the purpose of the present case. Accordingly, we reproduce the said paragraph which runs as under: (SCC pp. 64-65, para 8)—

> "8. It is significant to note that there was no reference to the judgment of the Calcutta High Court in the Statement of Objects and Reasons, nor any *non-obstante* clause referring to a judgment of a court in section 3 of the impugned Act. The attention of Parliament does not appear to have been drawn to the fact that the Calcutta High Court has already issued a writ of *Mandamus* commanding the Life Insurance Corporation to pay the amount of bonus for the year 1st April, 1975 to 31st March, 1976. It appears that unfortunately the judgment of the Calcutta High Court remained almost unnoticed and the impugned Act was passed in ignorance of that judgment. Section 3 of the impugned Act provided that the provisions of the Settlement insofar as they relate to payment of annual cash bonus to Class III and Class IV employees shall not have any force or effect and shall not be deemed to have had any force or effect from 1st April, 1975. But the writ of *Mandamus* issued by the

Calcutta High Court directing the Life Insurance Corporation to pay the amount of bonus for the year 1st April, 1975 to 31st March, 1976 remained untouched by the impugned Act. So far as the right of Class III and Class IV employees to annual cash bonus for the year 1st April, 1975 to 31st March, 1976 was concerned, it became crystallised in the judgment and thereafter they became entitled to enforce the writ of *Mandamus* granted by the judgment and not any right to annual cash bonus under the settlement. This right under the judgment was not sought to be taken away by the impugned Act. The judgment continued to subsist and the Life Insurance Corporation was bound to pay annual cash bonus to Class III and Class IV employees for the year 1st April, 1975 to 31st March, 1976 in obedience to the writ of *Mandamus*. The error committed by the Life Insurance Corporation was that it withdrew the Letters Patent Appeal and allowed the judgment of the learned Single Judge to become final. By the time the Letters Patent Appeal came up for hearing, the impugned Act had already come into force and the Life Insurance Corporation could, therefore, have successfully contended in the Letters Patent Appeal that, since the Settlement, in as far as it provided for payment of annual cash bonus, was annihilated by the impugned Act with effect from 1st April, 1975, Class III and Class IV employees were not entitled to annual cash bonus for the year 1st April, 1975 to 31st March, 1976 and hence no writ of *Mandamus* could issue directing the Life Insurance Corporation to make payment of such bonus. If such contention had been raised, there is little doubt, subject of course to any constitutional challenge to the validity of the impugned Act, that the judgment of the learned Single Judge would have been upturned and the Writ petition dismissed. But on account of some inexplicable reason, which is difficult to appreciate, the Life Insurance Corporation did not press the Letters Patent Appeal and the result was that the judgment of the learned Single Judge granting writ of *Mandamus* became final and binding on the parties. It is difficult to see how in these circumstances the Life Insurance Corporation could claim to be absolved from the obligation imposed by the judgment to carry out the Writ of *Mandamus* by relying on the impugned Act."

Mr. Justice P.N. Bhagwati, former Chief Justice of India in that decision at Para 8 pointed out that Life Insurance Corporation (Modification and Settlement) Act, 1976 was enacted apparently in ignorance of the Calcutta High Court judgment and the attention of the Parliament was not drawn to that judgment at all. It was also pointed out in that decision at para 8 that there was no reference to the said judgment in the Statement of Objects and Reasons nor any non-obstante clause incorporating in section 3 of the impugned Act in that case to override the judgment. This Court has been moved by the respondent in the writ application challenging the propriety of certain directions issued by the Delhi High Court requiring the respondent to take approval of ACC for any adverse decision against the writ petitioner and for giving the writ petitioner two weeks' time against any such adverse decision. This Court has, however, declined to pass any interim order in the SLP filed by the respondent. Therefore, the interim order or final order of the Delhi High Court would remain binding upon the parties for the time being and they cannot be ignored or disregarded unless they are modified or leave is granted to take any step contrary thereto.

31. It may not be out of place to mention that the SLP of the respondent indicates that the term of office of five years of the writ petitioner as Director was not really in dispute. In the Statement of Objects and Reasons of the Act introducing the impugned proviso, it is stated that the same is being introduced with a view to comply with the direction of the High Court in the judgment and order dated 29th of March, 2007. It, however, appears that the Division Bench of the Delhi High Court has determined the question of tenure of the writ petitioner to be five years and there are writs in the nature of *Mandamus* and Prohibition issued by the Delhi High Court directing the right of the writ petitioner indicated in the respective orders. As in *Madan Mohan Pathak's* case (para 8), as quoted herein above, in the instant case also the Parliament does not seem to have been apprised about the pendency of the proceedings before the Delhi High Court and this Court and declaration made and directions issued by the Delhi High Court at different stages. In the impugned amendment, there is no *non-obstante* clause. The impugned amendment introducing the proviso, therefore, cannot be treated to be a validating Act. This Court in the case of *Dr. L.P. Agarwal* v. *Union of India*, (1992) 3 SCC 526 (Para 16) observed as follows (SCC pp. 533-34 para 16):—

> "16. We have given our thoughtful consideration to the reasoning and the conclusions reached by the High Court. We are not inclined to agree with the same. Under the Recruitment Rules the post of Director of the AIIMS is a tenure post. The said rules further provide the method of direct recruitment for filling the post. These service-conditions make the post of Director a tenure post and as such the question of superannuating or prematurely retiring the incumbent of the said post does not arise. The age of 62 years provided under Proviso to Regulation 30(2) of the Regulations only shows that no employee of the AIIMS can be given extension beyond that age. This has obviously been done for maintaining efficiency in the Institute-Services. We do not agree that simply because the appointment order of the appellant mentions that "he is appointed for a period of five years or till he attains the age of 62 years", the appointment ceases to be to a tenure-post. Even an outsider (not an existing employee of the AIIMS) can be selected and appointed to the post of Director. Can such person be retired prematurely curtailing his tenure of five years? Obviously not. The appointment of the appellant was on a Five Years Tenure but it could be curtailed in the event of his attaining the age of 62 years before completing the said tenure. The High Court failed to appreciate the simple alphabet of the service jurisprudence. The High Court's reasoning is against the clear and unambiguous language of the Recruitment Rules. The said rules provide "Tenure for five years inclusive of one year probation" and the post is to be filled "by direct recruitment". Tenure means a term during which an office is held. It is a condition of holding the office. Once a person is appointed to a tenure post, his appointment to the said office begins when he joins and it comes to an end on the completion of the tenure unless curtailed on justifiable grounds. Such a person does not superannuate, he only goes out of the office on completion of his tenure. The question of prematurely retiring him does not arise. The appointment order gave a clear tenure to the appellant. The High Court fell into error in reading "the concept of superannuation" in the said

order. Concept of superannuation which is well-understood in the service jurisprudence is alien to tenure appointments which have a fixed life span. The appellant could not therefore have been prematurely retired and that too without being put on any notice whatsoever. Under what circumstances can an appointment for a tenure be cut short is not a matter which requires our immediate consideration in this case because the order impugned before the High Court concerned itself only with premature retirement and the High Court also dealt with that aspect of the matter only. This Court's judgment in *Dr. Bool Chand* v. *The Chancellor Kurukshetra University*, AIR 1968 SC 292 relied upon by the High Court is not on the point involved in this case. In that case the tenure of Dr. Bool Chand was curtailed as he was found unfit to continue as Vice-Chancellor having regard to his antecedents which were not disclosed by him at the time of his appointment as Vice-Chancellor. Similarly the judgment in *Dr. D.C. Saxena* v. *State of Haryana*, (1987) 3 SCC 251 has no relevance to the facts of this case".

PETITIONER HAD TENURE POST AND THE QUESTION OF HIS PREMATURE RETIREMENT OR SUPERANNUATION DID NOT ARISE

32. From the above quotation, as made in para 16 of the said decision of this Court, it is evident that this Court has laid down that the term of 5 years for a Director of AIIMS is a permanent term. Service Conditions make the post of Director, a tenure post and as such the question of superannuating or prematurely retiring the incumbent of the said post does not arise at all. Even an outsider (not an existing employee of the AIIMS) can be selected and appointed to the post of Director. The appointment is for a tenure to which principle of superannuation does not apply. "Tenure" means a term during which the office is held. It is a condition of holding the office. Once a person is appointed to a tenure post, his appointment to the said post begins when he joins and it comes to an end on the completion of tenure unless curtailed on justifiable grounds. Such a person does not superannuate, he only goes out of the office on completion of his tenure.

33. It was in 1958 that AIIMS had framed its regulations under section 29 of the Act. Regulation 30A was brought into AIIMS Regulation by an amendment dated 25th of July, 1981 notified in the Gazette on 10th of October, 1981 coming into force w.e.f. 1st of August, 1981. The provision of regulation 30A was very much in existence when this Court had decided the case of *Dr. L.P. Agarwal* on 21st of July, 1992. It is the same provision of regulation 30A which was brought into force w.e.f. 1st of August, 1981 in the AIIMS Regulations and had been renumbered as Regulation 31, when the AIIMS 1958 Regulations had been substituted by AIIMS Regulations, 1999. Therefore, it is incorrect on the part of the respondent to contend that regulation 31 was introduced in the AIIMS Regulations only after the judgment of this Court in *Dr. L.P. Agarwal's* case, (1992) 3 SCC 526.

34. This question was specifically deliberated upon by Justice Kuldip Singh, as His Lordship then was, in *Dr. L.P. Agarwal's* case *(supra)* and a question was formulated on this aspect at page 530 of the said decision. After formulating the aforesaid question, a submission on behalf of the respondent was also considered by this Court in the aforesaid decision at SCC paragraph 13 page 532 of the said decision which is as follows:—

"13. The respondent argued before the High Court that the appellant was retired by the AIIMS under regulation 30(3) of the Regulations in public interest after he attained the age of 55 years. It was further contended that fundamental rule 56(j) was also applicable to the AIIMS employees by virtue of regulation 35 of the Regulations. It was argued that even if regulation 30(3) was not attracted the Institute had the power to prematurely retire the appellant, in public interest, under fundamental rule 56(j) applicable to the Central Government employees. It was contended that despite the fact that the appellant was on a tenure post there was no bar to prematurely retire him by invoking either regulation 30(3) or Fundamental rule 56(j)."

35. After formulating the question and after considering the submission made on behalf of the parties, this Court in that decision at SCC para 16 of pages 533-34 concluded in the same manner: (Para 31)—

THIS AMENDMENT WAS VOID AND UNCONSTITUTIONAL – THE CURTAILMENT OF THE TENURE OF THE PETITIONER WAS NOT MADE FOR JUSTIFIABLE REASONS AND IT WAS NAKED DISCRIMINATION

36. From the aforesaid discussion, the principle of law stipulated by this Court that curtailment of the term of five years can only be made for justifiable reasons and compliance with principles of natural justice for premature termination of the term of a Director of AIIMS – squarely applied also to the case of the writ petitioner as well and will also apply to any future Director of AIIMS. Thus, there was never any permissibility for any artificial and impermissible classification between the writ petitioner on the one hand and any future Director of AIIMS on the other when it relates to the premature termination of the term of office of the Director. Such an impermissible over classification through a one man legislation clearly falls foul of article 14 of the Constitution being an apparent case of "naked discrimination" in our democratic civilized society governed by Rule of Law and renders the impugned proviso as void, *ab initio* and unconstitutional.

37. Such being our discussion and conclusion, on the constitutionality of the proviso to section 11A, we must, therefore, come to this conclusion without any hesitation in mind, that the instant case is squarely covered by the principles of law laid down by this Court in the various pronouncements as noted herein above including in the case of *D.S. Reddy* v. *Chancellor, Osmania University*, (1967) 2 SCR 214.

38. In the case of *D.S. Reddy* (supra), the facts of that case are somewhat similar to that of the writ petitioner. In that decision, D.S. Reddy was already a Vice-Chancellor for the past seven years and had not challenged the fixation of term from five years to three years. He was aggrieved by the second amendment in the University Act whereby section 13A was introduced to make the provision of section 12(2) providing for inquiry by an Hon. Judge of High Court/Supreme Court and hearing before premature termination of the term of the Vice-Chancellor inapplicable to the incumbent to the office of the Vice-Chancellor on the commencement of the 2nd Amendment. The core contention of D.S. Reddy was that this amendment was only for his removal and therefore was a case of "naked discrimination" as it also deprived the protection of section 12(2) to him when section 12(2) was applicable to all other Vice-Chancellors and there being no distinction in this regard between the Vice-Chancellor in office and the Vice-Chancellors to be appointed. In that situation, the plea of the respondent-Government was that the provision similar to section 13A was also incorporated in two other enactments relating to Andhra University and Shri Venkateswara and was, therefore, not a one man legislation. It was further contended by the State that it was always open and permissible to the State Legislature to treat the Vice-Chancellor in office as a class in itself and make provisions in that regard. All the contentions on behalf of the State Government were rejected by the Constitution Bench judgment of this Court in the case of *D.S. Reddy* (supra) and it was held that it was a clear case of "naked discrimination" for removal of one man and by depriving him of the protection under section 12(2) of the Act without there being any rationality of creating a classification between the Vice-Chancellor in office and the Vice-Chancellor to be appointed in future.

39. It was further held in the case of *D.S. Reddy* that such a classification was not founded on an intelligible differentia and was held to be violative of article 14 of the Constitution of India. Accordingly, the provision of section 13A was held to be *ultra vires* and unconstitutional and hit by article 14 of the Constitution. Similarly in the present case, the impugned proviso to section 11(1A) itself states that it is carrying out premature termination of the tenure of the writ petitioner. It is also admitted that such a premature termination is without following the safeguards of justifiable reasons and notice. It is thus a case similar to the case of *D.S. Reddy* and other decisions cited above that the impugned legislation is hit by article 14 as it creates an unreasonable classification between the writ petitioner and the future Directors and deprives the writ petitioner of the principles of natural justice without there being any intelligible differentia.

WRIT PETITION ALLOWED, PETITIONER REINSTATED AND HELD ENTITLED TO WHAT HE WAS GETTING PRIOR TO HIS PREMATURE TERMINATION

40. In view of our discussion made hereinabove and for the reasons aforesaid, we are of the view that this writ petition is covered by the decisions of this Court in the cases of *D.S. Reddy* and *L.P. Agarwal* and the impugned proviso to section 11A of the AIIMS Act is, therefore, hit by article 14 of the Constitution. Accordingly, we hold that the proviso is *ultra vires* and unconstitutional and accordingly it is struck down. The writ petition under article 32 of the Constitution is allowed. In view of our order passed in the writ petition, the writ petitioner shall serve the nation for some more period, *i.e.*, upto 2nd of July, 2008. We direct the AIIMS Authorities to restore the writ petitioner in his office as Director of AIIMS till his period comes to an end on 2nd of July, 2008. The writ petitioner is also entitled to his pay and other emoluments as he was getting before premature termination of his office from the date of his order of termination. Considering the facts and circumstances of the present case, there will be no order as to costs.

Petition allowed.

....J.

[Tarun Chatterjee]

New Delhi: ....J.

May 8, 2008 [Harjit Singh Bedi]

Author's Note: A person against whom, a criminal case under the Prevention of corruption case was pending and against whom the previous Central Vigilance Commissioner had recommended the initiation of Major Penalty Proceedings was selected as Central Vigilance Commissioner by the High Powered Committee headed by Dr. Manmohan Singh, Prime Minister and of which Shri P. Chidambaram, Home Minister and Smt. Sushma Swaraj Leader of Opposition were the members. Smt. Sushma Swaraj had opposed the appointment of Shri P.J. Thomas as CVC on the plea that a tainted person should not be appointed as CVC because the main function of the CVC was to check corruption and the background of Shri Thomas was such which disentitled him for such a job. Inspite of the dissent note of Smt. Sushma Swaraj, Leader of the Opposition, Dr. Manmohan Singh, PM and Shri P. Chidambaram, HM selected Shri P.J. Thomas as CVC and got him appointed as such. His appointment was challenged by way of PIL. The judgment is reproduced below:

LEGALITY OF APPOINTMENT OF P.J. THOMAS AS CVC WAS CONSIDERED BY THE SUPREME COURT IN THESE CASES

Centre for PIL

v.

Union of India[1]

SUPREME COURT OF INDIA

CIVIL ORIGINAL JURISDICTION

Writ Petition (C) No. 348 of 2010
with
Writ Petition (C) No. 355 of 2010

Dediced on 3-3-2011

JUDGMENT

S.H. Kapadia, CJI

1. The two writ petitions filed in this Court under article 32 of the Constitution of India give rise to a substantial question of law and of public importance as to the legality of the appointment of Shri P.J. Thomas (respondent No. 2 in W.P. (C) No. 348 of 2010) as Central Vigilance Commissioner under section 4(1) of the Central Vigilance Commission Act, 2003 ("2003 Act" for short).

GOVERNMENT MAY NOT BE ACCOUNTABLE FOR THE POLICY DECISIONS BUT IS ACCOUNTABLE FOR THE LEGALITY OF THE DECISIONS TAKEN

2. Government is not accountable to the courts in respect of policy decisions. However, they are accountable for the legality of such decisions. While deciding this case, we must keep in mind the difference between legality and merit as also between judicial review and merit review. On 3rd September, 2010, the High

1. AIR 2011 SC 1267: (2011) 4 SCC 1: 2011 (3) MLJ 355.

Powered Committee ("HPC" for short), duly constituted under the proviso to section 4(1) of the 2003 Act, had recommended the name of Shri P.J. Thomas for appointment to the post of Central Vigilance Commissioner. The validity of this recommendation falls for judicial scrutiny in this case. If a duty is cast under the proviso to section 4(1) on the HPC to recommend to the President the name of the selected candidate, the integrity of that decision-making process is got to ensure that the powers are exercised for the purposes and in the manner envisaged by the said Act, otherwise such recommendation will have no existence in the eye of law.

CRIMINAL CASE PENDING AGAINST P.J. THOMAS

Clarification

3. At the very outset we wish to clarify that in this case our judgment is strictly confined to the legality of the recommendation dated 3rd September, 2010 and the appointment based thereon. As of date, Shri P.J. Thomas is Accused No. 8 in criminal case CC 6 of 2003 pending in the Court of Special Judge, Thiruvananthapuram with respect to the offences under section 13(2) read with section 13(1)(d) of the Prevention of Corruption Act, 1988 and under section 120B of the Indian Penal Code ("IPC" for short) [hereinafter referred to as the "Palmolein case"]. According to the petitioners herein, Shri P.J. Thomas allegedly has played a big part in the cover-up of the 2G spectrum allocation which matter is subjudice. Therefore, we make it clear that we do not wish to comment in this case on the pending cases and our judgment herein should be strictly understood to be under judicial review on the legality of the appointment of respondent No. 2 and any reference in our judgment to the Palmolein case should not be understood as our observations on merits of that case.

Shri P.J. Thomas was Secretary DOFCS in Kerala Government when Palmolein Oil was Purchased

Facts

4. Shri P.J. Thomas was appointed to the Indian Administrative Service (Kerala Cadre), 1973 batch where he served in different capacities with the State Government including as Secretary, Department of Food and Civil Supplies. State of Kerala in the year 1991. During that period itself, the State of Kerala decided to import 30,000 MT of palmolein. The Chief Minister of Kerala, on 5th October, 1991, wrote a letter to the Prime Minister stating that the State was intending to import Palmolein oil and that necessary permission should be given by the concerned Ministries. On 6th November, 1991, the Government of India issued a scheme for direct import of edible oil for Public Distribution System (PDS) on the condition that an ESCROW account be opened and import clearance be granted as per the rules.

5. Respondent No. 2 wrote letters to the Secretary, Government of India stating that against its earlier demand for import of 30,000 MT of Palmolein oil, the present minimum need was 15,000 MT and the same was to meet the heavy ensuing demand during the festivals of Christmas and *Sankranti*, in the middle of January, 1992, therefore, the State was proposing to immediately import the said quantity of Palmolein on obtaining requisite permission. The price for the same was fixed on 24th January, 1992, *i.e.*, 56 days after the execution of the agreement. The Kerala

State Civil Supplies Corporation Ltd., was to act as an agent of the State Government for import of Palmolein. The value of the Palmolein was to be paid to the suppliers only in Indian rupees. Further, the terms governing the ESCROW account were to be as approved by the Ministry of Finance. This letter contained various other stipulations as well.

6. This was responded to by the Joint Secretary, Government of India, Ministry of Civil Supplies and Public Distribution, New Delhi *vide* letter dated 26th November, 1991 wherein it was stated that it had been decided to permit the State to import 15,000 MT of Palmolein on the terms and conditions stipulated in the Ministry's circular of even number dated 6th November, 1991. It was specifically stated that the service charges up to a maximum of 15% in Indian rupees may be paid. After some further correspondence, the order of the State of Kerala is stated to have been approved by the Cabinet on 27th November, 1991, and the State of Kerala actually imported Palmolein by opening an ESCROW account and getting the import clearance at the rate of US $ 405 per MT in January, 1992.

COMPTROLLER AND AUDITOR GENERAL OF INDIA AND COMMITTEE ON PUBLIC UNDERTAKINGS RAISED OBJECTIONS TO THE PROCEDURE ADOPTED

7. The Comptroller and Auditor General ('CAG'), in its report dated 2nd February, 1994 for the year ended 31st March, 1993 took exception to the procedure adopted for import of Palmolein by the State Government. While mentioning some alleged irregularities, the CAG observed, "therefore, the agreement entered into did not contain adequate safeguards to ensure that imported product would satisfy all the standards laid down in Prevention of Food Adulteration Rules, 1956".

8. This report of the CAG was placed before the Public Undertaking Committee of the Kerala Assembly. The 38th Report of the Kerala Legislative Assembly – Committee on Public Undertakings dated 19th March, 1996, *inter alia,* referred to the alleged following irregularities:—

(a) That the service fee of 15% to meet the fluctuation in exchange rate was not negotiated and hence was excessive. Even the price of the import product ought not to have been settled in US Dollars.

(b) That the concerned department of the State of Kerala had not invited tenders and had appointed M/s. Mala Export Corporation, an associate company of M/s. Power and Energy Pvt. Ltd., the company upon which the import order was placed as handling agent for the import.

(c) That the delay in opening of ESCROW accounts and in fixation of price, which were not in conformity with the circular issued by the Central Government had incurred a loss of more than Rs. 4 crores to the Exchequer.

The Committee also alleged that under the pretext of plea of urgency, the deal was conducted without inviting global tenders and if the material was procured by providing ample time by inviting global tenders, other competitors would have emerged with lesser rates for the import of the item, which in turn, would have been more beneficial.

WRIT PETITION FILED FOR REGISTRATION OF F.I.R. BUT DISMISSED – APPEAL FILED – ALSO DISMISSED

9. The Chief Editor of the *Gulf India Times* even filed a writ petition being O.P. No. 3813 of 1994 in the Kerala High Court praying that directions be issued to the State to register an FIR on the ground that import of Palmolein was made in violation of the Government of India Guidelines. However, it came to be dismissed by the learned Single Judge of the Kerala High Court on 4th April, 1994. Still another writ petition came to be filed by one Shri M. Vijay Kumar, who was MLA of the Opposition in the Kerala Assembly praying for somewhat similar relief. This writ petition was dismissed by a learned Single Judge of the Kerala High Court and even appeal against that order was also dismissed by the Division Bench of that Court *vide* order dated 27th September, 1994.

F.I.R. REGISTERED UNDER THE PREVENTION OF CORRUPTION ACT AGAINST SHRI KARUNAKARAN, FORMER CHIEF MINISTER AND OTHERS

10. Elections were held in the State of Kerala on 20th May, 1996 and the Left Democratic Front formed the government. An FIR was registered against Shri Karunakaran, former Chief Minister and six others in relation to an offence under section 13(2) read with section 13(1)(d) of the Prevention of Corruption Act, 1988 and section 120B of the IPC. The State of Kerala accorded its sanction to prosecute the then Chief Minister Shri Karunakaran and various officers in the State hierarchy, who were involved in the import of Palmolein, including respondent No. 2 on 30th November, 1999.

FORMER CHIEF MINISTER FILED WRIT PETITION FOR QUASHING THE F.I.R. – DISMISSED

11. Shri Karunakaran, the then Chief Minister filed a petition before the High Court being Criminal Miscellaneous No. 1353/1997 praying for quashing of the said FIR registered against him and the other officers. Shri P.J. Thomas herein was not a party in that petition. However, the High Court dismissed the said writ petition declining to quash the FIR registered against the said persons. In the meanwhile, a challan (report under section 173 of the Code of Criminal Procedure) had also been filed before the Court of Special Judge, Thiruvananthapuram and in this background the State of Kerala, *vide* its letter dated 31st December, 1999 wrote to the Department of Personnel and Training (DoPT) seeking sanction to prosecute the said person before the Court of competent jurisdiction.

P.J. THOMAS WAS ADDED AS AN ACCUSED

Keeping in view the investigation of the case conducted by the agency, two other persons including Shri P.J. Thomas were added as accused Nos. 7 and 8.

FORMER CHIEF MINISTER FILED SLP AGAINST THE JUDGMENT OF THE HIGH COURT FOR QUASHING THE F.I.R.

12. Shri Karunakaran challenged the order before this Court by filing a Petition for Special Leave to Appeal, being Criminal Appeal No. 86 of 1998, which also came to be dismissed by this Court on 29th March, 2000. *K. Karunakaran* v. *State of Kerala*, (2000) 3 SCC 761. This Court held that "after going through the pleadings of the parties and keeping in view the rival submissions made before us, we are of the opinion that the registration of the FIR against the appellants and others cannot be held to be the result of *mala fides* or actuated by extraneous considerations. The menace of corruption cannot be permitted to be hidden under the carpet of the legal technicalities...".

13. The Government Order granting sanction (Annexure R-I in that petition) was also upheld by this Court and it was further held that "our observations with respect to the legality of the Government Order are not conclusive regarding its constitutionality but are restricted so far as its applicability to the registration of the FIR against the appellant is concerned. We are, therefore, of the opinion that the aforesaid Government Order has not been shown to be in any way illegal or unconstitutional so far as the rights of the appellants are concerned...". Granting liberty to the parties to raise all pleas before the Trial Court, the appeal was dismissed.

IN THE CHARGE-SHEET DEFINITE ROLE WAS ATTRIBUTED TO P.J. THOMAS

In the charge-sheet filed before the Trial Court, in paragraph 7, definite role was attributed to Accused No. 8 (respondent No. 2 herein) and allegations were made against him.

SANCTION FOR PROSECUTION OF SHRI P.J. THOMAS NOT GRANTED FOR 5 YEARS BY THE CENTRAL GOVERNMENT – ONLY DEPARTMENTAL ENQUIRY SUGGESTED

14. For a period of 5 years, the matter remained pending with the Central Government and *vide* letter dated 20th December, 2004, the Central Government asked the State Government to send a copy of the report which had been filed before the Court of competent jurisdiction. After receiving the request of the State Government, it appears that the file was processed by various authorities and as early as on 18th January, 2001, a note was put up by the concerned under Secretary that a regular departmental enquiry should be held against Shri P.J. Thomas and Shri Jiji Thomson for imposing a major penalty. According to this note, it was felt that because of lack of evidence, the prosecution may not succeed against Shri P.J. Thomas but sanction should be accorded for prosecution of Shri Jiji Thomson.

15. On 18th February, 2003, the DoPT had made a reference to the Central Vigilance Commission ("CVC" for short) on the cited subject, which was responded to by the CVC *vide* their letter dated 3rd June, 2003 and it conveyed its opinion as follows:—

> "Department of Personnel and Training may refer to their DO letter No. 107/1/2000-AVD.I dated 18.2.2003 on the subject cited above."
>
> 2. Keeping in view the facts and circumstances of the case, the Commission would advise the Department of Personnel and Training to initiate major penalty proceedings against Shri P.J. Thomas, IAS (KL:73) and Shri Jiji Thomson, IAS (KL:80) and completion of proceedings thereof by appointing departmental IO.
>
> 3. Receipt of the Commission's advice may be acknowledged."

Despite receipt of the above opinion of CVC, the matter was still kept pending, though a note was again put up on 24th February, 2004 on similar lines as that of 18th January, 2001.

STATE GOVERNMENT WITHDREW THE REQUEST FOR PROSECUTION OF P.J. THOMAS

16. In the meanwhile, the State of Kerala, *vide* its letter dated 24th January, 2005 wrote to the DoPT that for reasons recorded in the letter, they wish to withdraw their request for according the sanction for prosecution of the officers, including respondent No. 2, as made *vide* their letter dated 31st December, 1999. The matter which was pending for all this period attained a quietus in view of the letter of the State of Kerala and the PMO had been informed accordingly. In its letter dated 4th November, 2005, the State took the position that the allegations made by the Investigating Agency were invalid and the cases and request for sanction against Shri P.J. Thomas should be withdrawn.

STATE GOVERNMENT RE-ITERATED ITS DEMAND FOR SANCTION FOR THE PROSECUTION OF SHRI P.J. THOMAS

17. On 18th May, 2006 again, the Left Democratic Front formed the Government in the State of Kerala with Mr. Achuthanandan as the Chief Minister. This time the Government of Kerala filed an affidavit in this Court disassociating itself from the contents of the earlier affidavit. *Vide* letter dated 10th October, 2006, the Chief Secretary to the Government of Kerala again wrote a letter to the Government of India informing them that the State Government had decided to continue the prosecution launched by it and as such it sought to withdraw its above letter dated 24th January, 2005. In other words, it reiterated its request for grant of sanction by the Central Government. *Vide* letter dated 25th November, 2006, the Additional Secretary to the DoPT wrote to the State of Kerala asking them for the reasons for change in stand, in response to the letter of the State of Kerala dated 10th October, 2006.

FORMER CHIEF MINISTER FILED WRIT PETITION BUT DISMISSED – NOT CHALLENGED BY SHRI THOMAS

18. This action of the State Government reviving its sanction and continuing prosecution against Shri Karunakaran and others, including Respondent No. 2, was challenged by Shri Karunakaran by filing Criminal Revision Petition No. 430 of 2001 in the High Court of Kerala on the ground that the Government Order was liable to be set aside on the ground of *mala fide* and arbitrariness. This petition was dismissed by the High Court. In its judgment, the High Court referred to the alleged role of Shri P.J. Thomas in the Palmolein case. The action of the State Government or pendency of proceedings before the Special Judge at Thiruvananthapuram was never challenged by Shri P.J. Thomas before any court of competent jurisdiction.

CENTRAL GOVERNMENT WITHOUT GIVING REPLY TO THE STATE GOVERNMENT SOUGHT THE OPINION OF THE CVC IF P.J. THOMAS CAN BE CONSIDERED FOR A HIGHER POST

19. The request of the State Government for sanction by the Central Government was considered by different persons in the Ministry and *vide* its noting dated 10th May, 2007, a query was raised upon the CVC as to whether pendency of a reply to Ministry's letter, from State Government in power, on a matter already settled by the previous State Government should come in the way of empanelment of these officers for appointment to higher post in the Government. Rather than rendering the advice asked for, the CVC *vide* its letter dated 25th June, 2007 informed the Ministry as follows:

> "Department of Personnel and Training may refer to their note dated 17.5.2007, in file No. 107/1/2000-AVD-I, on the above subject.
>
> 2. The case has been re-examined and Commission has observed that no case is made out against S/Shri P.J. Thomas and Jiji Thomson in connection with alleged conspiracy with other public servants and private persons in the matter of import of Palmolein through a private firm. The abovesaid officers acted in accordance with a legitimately taken Cabinet decision and no loss has been caused to the State Government and most important, no case is made out that they had derived any benefit from the transaction.
>
> (Emphasis supplied)
>
> 3. In view of the above, Commission advises that the case against S/Shri P.J. Thomas and Jiji Thomson may be dropped and matter be referred once again thereafter to the Commission so that Vigilance Clearance as sought for now can be recorded.

4. DOPT's file No. 107/1/2000-AVD-I along with the records of the case, is returned herewith. Its receipt may be acknowledged. Action taken in pursuance of Commission's advice may be intimated to the Commission early."

CENTRAL GOVERNMENT KEPT THE OPINION OF CVC PENDING

20. It may be noticed that neither in the above reply nor on the file any reasons are available as to why CVC had changed its earlier opinion/stand as conveyed to the Ministry vide its letter dated 3rd June, 2003. After receiving the above advice of CVC, the Ministry on 6th July, 2007 had recorded a note in the file that as far as CVC's advice regarding dropping all proceedings is concerned, the Ministry should await the action to be taken by the Government of Kerala *and the relevant courts*.

SUPREME COURT DISMISSED THE APPEAL OF FORMER CHIEF MINISTER

21. The legality and correctness of the order of the Kerala High Court dated 19th February, 2003 was questioned by Shri Karunakaran by filing a petition before this Court on which leave was granted and it came to be registered as Criminal Appeal No. 801 of 2003. This appeal was also dismissed by this Court *vide* its order dated 6th December, 2006. However, the parties were given liberty to raise the plea of *mala fides* before the High Court.

FORMER CHIEF MINISTER FILED WRIT PETITION IN THE HIGH COURT ALLEGING *MALA FIDE* – DISMISSED – APPEAL ABATED

Even on reconsideration, the High Court dismissed the petition filed by Shri Karunakaran raising the plea of *mala fides* vide its order dated 6th July, 2007. The High Court had, thus, declined to accept that action of the State Government in prosecuting the persons stated therein was actuated by *mala fides*. The order of the

High Court was again challenged by Shri Karunakaran by preferring a Petition for Special Leave to Appeal before this Court. This Court had stayed further proceedings before the Trial Court. This appeal remained pending till 23rd December, 2010 when it abated because of unfortunate demise of Shri Karunakaran.

P.J. THOMAS APPOINTED AS CHIEF SECRETARY

22. *Vide* order dated 18th September, 2007, the Government of Kerala appointed Shri P.J. Thomas as the Chief Secretary.

VIGILANCE CLEARANCE GIVEN TO P.J. THOMAS FOR TOP POST WITHOUT EXPLAINING THE EARLIER NOTING RECOMMENDING PENALTY PROCEEDING

Thereafter, on 6th October, 2008 CVC accorded vigilance clearance to all officers except Smt. Parminder M. Singh. We have perused the files submitted by the learned Attorney General for India. From the said files we find that there are at least six notings of DoPT between 26th June, 2000 and 2nd November, 2004 which has recommended initiation of penalty proceedings against Shri P.J. Thomas and yet in the clearance given by CVC on 6th October, 2008 and in the Brief prepared by DoPT dated 1st September, 2010 and placed before HPC there is no reference to the earlier notings of the then DoPT and nor any reason has been given as to why CVC had changed its views while granting vigilance clearance on 6th October, 2008. On 23rd January, 2009, Shri P.J. Thomas was appointed as Secretary, Parliamentary Affairs to the Government of India.

MATTER PLACED BEFORE THE HIGH POWERED COMMITTEE

23. The DoPT empanelled three officers *vide* its note dated 1st September, 2010. *Vide* the same note along with the Brief the matter was put up to the HPC for selecting one candidate out of the empanelled officers for the post of Central Vigilance Commissioner. The meeting of the HPC consisting of the Prime Minister, the Home Minister and the Leader of the Opposition was held on 3rd September, 2010.

LEADER OF OPPOSITION RECORDED DISAGREEMENT TO THE RECOMMENDATION OF THE NAME OF P.J. THOMAS BUT RECOMMENDED BY P.M. AND H.M. AND APPOINTED

In the meeting, disagreement was recorded by the Leader of the Opposition, despite which, name of Shri P.J. Thomas was recommended for appointment to the post of Central Vigilance Commissioner by majority. A note was thereafter put up with the recommendation of the HPC and placed before the Prime Minister which was approved on the same day. On 4th September, 2010, the same note was submitted to the President who also approved it on the same day. Consequently, Shri P.J. Thomas was appointed as Central Vigilance Commissioner and he took oath of his office.

CVC IS AN INTEGRITY INSTITUTION SET UP IN 1964

Setting up of the CVC

24. Vigilance is an integral part of all government institutions. Anti-corruption measures are the responsibility of the Central Government. Towards this end the Government set up the following departments:

(i) CBI;

(ii) Administrative Vigilance Division in DoPT;

(iii) Domestic Vigilance Units in the Ministries/Departments, Government companies, Government Corporations, nationalized banks and PSUs;

(iv) CVC.

25. Thus, CVC as an *integrity institution* was set up by the Government of India in 1964 *vide* Government Resolution pursuant to the recommendations of Santhanam Committee. However, it was not a statutory body at that time. According to the recommendations of the Santhanam Committee, CVC, in its functions, was supposed to be independent of the Executive. The sole purpose behind setting up of the CVC was to improve the *vigilance administration* of the country.

REVIEW COMMITTEE RECOMMENDED STATUTORY STATUS FOR CVC

26. In September, 1997, the Government of India established the Independent Review Committee to monitor the functioning of CVC and to examine the working of CBI and the Enforcement Directorate. Independent Review Committee *vide* its report of December, 1997 suggested that CVC be given a *statutory status*. It also recommended that the selection of Central Vigilance Commissioner shall be made by a High Powered Committee comprising of the Prime Minister, the Home Minister and the Leader of Opposition in Lok Sabha. It also recommended that the appointment shall be made by the President of India on the specific recommendations made by the HPC. That, the CVC shall be responsible for the efficient functioning of CBI; CBI shall report to CVC about cases taken up for investigations; the appointment of CBI Director shall be by a Committee headed by the Central Vigilance Commissioner; the Central Vigilance Commissioner shall have a minimum fixed tenure and that a Committee headed by the Central Vigilance Commissioner shall prepare a panel for appointment of Director of Enforcement.

SUPREME COURT DIRECTED FOR STATUTORY STATUS FOR CVC – BY 2003 ACT, CVC WAS GIVEN STATUTORY STATUS, AUTONOMY AND WAS MADE FREE FROM EXTERNAL INFLUENCES

27. On 18th December, 1997 the judgment in the case of *Vineet Narain* v. *Union of India*, (1998) 1 SCC 226 came to be delivered. Exercising authority under article 32 read with article 142, this Court in order to implement an important constitutional principle of the rule of law ordered that CVC shall be given a statutory status as recommended by Independent Review Committee. All the above recommendations of Independent Review Committee were ordered to be given a statutory status.

28. The judgment in *Vineet Narain's* case (supra) was followed by the 1999 Ordinance under which CVC became a multi-member Commission headed by Central Vigilance Commissioner. The 1999 Ordinance conferred statutory status on CVC. The said Ordinance incorporated the directions given by this Court in *Vineet Narain's* case. Suffice it to state, that, the 1999 Ordinance stood promulgated to improve the *vigilance administration* and to create a culture of *integrity* as far as government administration is concerned. The said 1999 Ordinance was ultimately replaced by the enactment of the 2003 Act which came into force with effect from 11th September, 2003.

BY THE ACT 2003 CVC WAS MADE AN INTEGRITY INSTITUTION

Analysis of the 2003 Act

29. The 2003 Act has been enacted to provide for the constitution of a Central Vigilance Commission as an institution to inquire or cause inquiries to be conducted into offences alleged to have been committed under the Prevention of Corruption Act, 1988 by certain categories of public servants of the Central Government, corporations established by or under any Central Act, Government companies, societies and local authorities owned or controlled by the Central Government and for matters connected therewith or incidental thereto (*see* Preamble). By way of an aside, we may point out that in Australia, US, UK and Canada there exists a concept of *integrity institutions*. In Hongkong we have an Independent Commission against corruption. In Western Australia there exists a statutory Corruption Commission. In Queensland, we have Misconduct Commission. In New South Wales there is Police Integrity Commission. All these come within the category of *integrity institutions*.

30. In our opinion, CVC is an *integrity institution*. This is clear from the scope and ambit (including the functions of the Central Vigilance Commissioner) of the 2003 Act. It is an Institution which is statutorily created under the Act. It is to supervise *vigilance administration*. The 2003 Act provides for a mechanism by which the CVC retains control over CBI. That is the reason why it is given autonomy and insulation from external influences under the 2003 Act.

RELEVANT PROVISIONS OF 2003 ACT

31. For the purposes of deciding this case, we need to quote the relevant provisions of the 2003 Act:

> *3.* ***Constitution of Central Vigilance Commission.***—(2) The Commission shall consist of—
>
> (a) a Central Vigilance Commissioner – Chairperson;
>
> (b) not more than two Vigilance Commissioners – Members.
>
> (3) The Central Vigilance Commissioner and the Vigilance Commissioners shall be appointed from amongst persons—
>
> (a) who have been or are in an All-India Service or in any civil service of the Union or in a civil post under the Union having knowledge and experience in the matters relating to vigilance, policy making and administration including police administration;
>
> *4.* ***Appointment of Central Vigilance Commissioner and Vigilance Commissioners.***—(1) The Central Vigilance Commissioner and the Vigilance Commissioners shall be appointed by the President by warrant under his hand and seal:
>
> Provided that every appointment under this sub-section shall be made after obtaining the recommendation of a Committee consisting of—

(a) the Prime Minister – Chairperson;

(b) the Minister of Home Affairs – Member;

(c) the Leader of the Opposition in the House of the People – Member.

Explanation.—For the purposes of this sub-section, "the Leader of the Opposition in the House of the People" shall, when no such Leader has been so recognised, include the Leader of the single largest group in opposition of the Government in the House of the People.

(2) No appointment of a Central Vigilance Commissioner or a Vigilance Commissioner shall be invalid merely by reason of any vacancy in the Committee.

5. Terms and other conditions of service of Central Vigilance Commissioner.—(1) Subject to the provisions of sub-sections (3) and (4), the Central Vigilance Commissioner shall hold office for a term of four years from the date on which he enters upon his office or till he attains the age of sixty-five years, whichever is earlier. The Central Vigilance Commissioner, on ceasing to hold the office, shall be ineligible for reappointment in the Commission.

(3) The Central Vigilance Commissioner or a Vigilance Commissioner shall, before he enters upon his office, make and subscribe before the President, or some other person appointed in that behalf by him, an oath or affirmation according to the form set out for the purpose in Schedule to this Act.

(6) *On ceasing to hold office, the Central Vigilance Commissioner and every other Vigilance Commissioner shall be ineligible for*—

(a) any diplomatic assignment, appointment as administrator of a Union Territory and such other assignment or appointment which is required by law to be made by the President by warrant under his hand and seal.

(b) further employment to any office of profit under the Government of India or the Government of a State.

6. Removal of Central Vigilance Commissioner and Vigilance Commissioner.—(1) Subject to the provisions of sub-section (3), the Central Vigilance Commissioner or any Vigilance Commissioner shall be removed from his office only by order of the President on the ground of proved misbehaviour or incapacity after the Supreme Court, on a reference made to it by the President, has, on inquiry, reported that the Central Vigilance Commissioner or any Vigilance Commissioner, as the case may be, ought on such ground be removed.

(3) Notwithstanding anything contained in sub-section (1), the President may by order remove from office the Central Vigilance Commissioner or any Vigilance Commissioner if the Central Vigilance Commissioner or such Vigilance Commissioner, as the case may be,—

(a) is adjudged an insolvent; or

(b) has been convicted of an offence which, in the opinion of the Central Government, involves moral turpitude; or

(c) engages during his term of office in any paid employment outside the duties of his office; or

(d) is, in the opinion of the President, unfit to continue in office by reason of infirmity of mind or body; or

(e) has acquired such financial or other interest as is likely to affect prejudicially his functions as a Central Vigilance Commissioner or a Vigilance Commissioner.

*8. **Functions and powers of Central Vigilance Commission.***—(1) The functions and powers of the Commission shall be to—

(a) exercise superintendence over the functioning of the Delhi Special Police Establishment insofar as it relates to the investigation of offences alleged to have been committed under the Prevention of Corruption Act, 1988 or an offence with which a public servant specified in sub-section (2) may, under the Code of Criminal Procedure, 1973, be charged at the same trial;

(b) give directions to the Delhi Special Police Establishment for the purpose of discharging the responsibility entrusted to it under sub-section (1) of section 4 of the Delhi Special Police Establishment Act, 1946;

[***]

(e) review the progress of investigations conducted by the Delhi Special Police Establishment into offences alleged to have been committed under the Prevention of Corruption Act, 1988 or the public servant may, under the Code of Criminal Procedure, 1973, be charged at the same trial;

(f) review the progress of applications pending with the competent authorities for sanction of prosecution under the Prevention of Corruption Act, 1988;

(h) exercise superintendence over the vigilance administration of the various Ministries of the Central Government or corporations established by or under any Central Act, Government companies, societies and local authorities owned or controlled by that Government:

(2) The persons referred to in clause (d) of sub-section (1) are as follows:—

(a) members of All-India Services serving in connection with the affairs of the Union and Group 'A' officers of the Central Government;

(b) such level of officers of the corporations established by or under any Central Act, Government companies, societies and other local authorities, owned or controlled by the Central Government, as that Government may, by notification in the Official Gazette, specify in this behalf:

Provided that till such time a notification is issued under this clause, all officers of the said corporations, companies, societies and local authorities shall be deemed to be the persons referred to in clause (d) of sub-section (1).

11. Power relating to inquiries.—The Commission shall, while conducting any inquiry referred to in clauses (c) and (d) of sub-section (1) of section 8, have all the powers of a civil court trying a suit under the Code of Civil Procedure, 1908 and in particular, in respect of the following matters, namely:—

(a) summoning and enforcing the attendance of any person from any part of India and examining him on oath;

(b) requiring the discovery and production of any document;

(c) receiving evidence on affidavits;

(d) requisitioning any public record or copy thereof from any court or office;

(e) issuing commissions for the examination of witnesses or other documents; and

(f) any other matter which may be prescribed.

OATH OF OFFICE WHICH CVC IS TO SUBSCRIBE

THE SCHEDULE

[*See* section 5(3)]

Form of oath or affirmation to be made by the Central Vigilance Commissioner or Vigilance Commissioner:—

'I, A.B., having been appointed Central Vigilance Commissioner (or Vigilance Commissioner) of the Central Vigilance Commission do swear in the name of God/ solemnly affirm that I will bear true faith and allegiance to the Constitution of India as by law established, that I will uphold the sovereignty and integrity of India, that I will duly and faithfully and to the best of my ability, knowledge and judgment perform the duties of my office without fear or favour, affection or ill-will and that I will uphold the Constitution and the laws.'.

CVC IS AN INSTITUTION – INCUMBENT SHOULD BE WITHOUT ANY BLEMISH

32. On analysis of the 2003 Act, the following are the salient features. CVC is given a statutory status. It stands established as an Institution. CVC stands established to inquire into offences alleged to have been committed under the Prevention of Corruption Act, 1988 by certain categories of public servants enumerated above. Under section 3(3)(a) the Central Vigilance Commissioner and the Vigilance Commissioners are to be appointed from amongst persons who have been or are in All India Service or in any civil service of the Union or who are in a civil post under the Union having knowledge and experience in the matters relating to vigilance, policy-making and administration including police administration.

33. The underlined words "who have been or who are" in section 3(3)(a) refer to the person holding office of a civil servant or who has held such office. These underlined words came up for consideration by this Court in the case of *N. Kannadasan* v. *Ajoy Khose*, (2009) 7 SCC 1 in which it has been held that the said words indicate the eligibility criteria and further they indicate that such past or present eligible persons should be without any *blemish* whatsoever and that they should not be appointed merely because they are eligible to be considered for the post.

34. One more aspect needs to be highlighted. The constitution of CVC as a statutory body under section 3 shows that CVC is an Institution. The key word is Institution. We are emphasizing the key word for the simple reason that in the present case the recommending authority (High Powered Committee) has gone by personal integrity of the officers empanelled and not by institutional integrity.

35. Section 4 refers to appointment of Central Vigilance Commissioner and Vigilance Commissioners. Under section 4(1) they are to be appointed by the President by warrant under her hand and seal. Section 4(1) indicates the importance of the post. Section 4(1) has a proviso. Every appointment under section 4(1) is to be made after obtaining the *recommendation* of a Committee consisting of—

(a) The Prime Minister – Chairperson;

(b) The Minister of Home Affairs – Member;

(c) The Leader of the Opposition in the House of the People – Member.

HIGH POWERED COMMITTEE DUTY BOUND TO RECOMMEND A MAN OF INTEGRITY AND WITHOUT ANY BLEMISH

36. For the sake of brevity, we may refer to the Selection Committee as High Powered Committee. The key word in the proviso is the word *"recommendation"*. While making the recommendation, the HPC performs a statutory duty. The impugned recommendation dated 3rd September, 2010 is in exercise of the statutory power vested in the HPC under the proviso to section 4(1). The post of Central Vigilance Commissioner is a statutory post. The Commissioner performs statutory functions as enumerated in section 8. The word 'recommendation' in the proviso stands for an informed decision to be taken by the HPC on the basis of a consideration of relevant material keeping in mind the purpose, object and policy of the 2003 Act. As stated, the object and purpose of the 2003 Act is to have an integrity Institution like CVC which is in charge of *vigilance administration* and which constitutes an anti-corruption mechanism. In its functions, the CVC is similar to Election Commission, Comptroller and Auditor General, Parliamentary Committees etc. Thus, while making the recommendations, the service conditions of the candidate being a public servant or civil servant in the past is not the sole criteria. The HPC must also take into consideration the question of institutional competency into account. If the selection adversely affects institutional competency and functioning then it shall be the duty of the HPC not to recommend such a candidate. Thus, the institutional integrity is the primary consideration which the HPC is required to consider while making recommendation under section 4 for appointment of Central Vigilance Commissioner.

37. In the present case, this vital aspect has not been taken into account by the HPC while recommending the name of Shri P.J. Thomas for appointment as Central Vigilance Commissioner. We do not wish to discount personal integrity of the candidate. What we are emphasizing is that institutional integrity of an institution like CVC has got to be kept in mind while recommending the name of the candidate. Whether the incumbent would or would not be able to function?

Whether the working of the Institution would suffer? If so, would it not be the duty of the HPC not to recommend the person. In this connection the HPC has also to keep in mind the object and the policy behind enactment of the 2003 Act.

38. Under section 5(1) the Central Vigilance Commissioner shall hold the office for a term of 4 years. Under section 5(3) the Central Vigilance Commissioner shall, before he enters upon his office, makes and subscribes before the President an oath or affirmation according to the form set out in the Schedule to the Act. Under section 6(1) the Central Vigilance Commissioner shall be removed from his office only by order of the President and that too on the ground of proved misbehaviour or incapacity after the Supreme Court, on a reference made to it by the President, has on inquiry reported that the Central Vigilance Commissioner be removed.

39. These provisions indicate that the office of the Central Vigilance Commissioner is not only given independence and insulation from external influences, it also indicates that such protections are given in order to enable the Institution of CVC to work in a free and fair environment. The prescribed form of oath under section 5(3) requires Central Vigilance Commissioner to uphold the sovereignty and integrity of the country and to perform his duties without *fear or favour*. All these provisions indicate that CVC is an *integrity institution.* The HPC has, therefore, to take into consideration the values independence and impartiality of the Institution. The said Committee has to consider the institutional competence. It has to take an informed decision keeping in mind the abovementioned vital aspects indicated by the purpose and policy of the 2003 Act.

FUNCTIONS AND POWERS OF CVC

40. Chapter III refers to functions and powers of the Central Vigilance Commission. CVC exercises superintendence over the functioning of the Delhi Special Police Establishment insofar as it relates to investigation of offences alleged to have been committed under the Prevention of Corruption Act, 1988, or an offence with which a public servant specified in sub-section (2) may, under the Code of Criminal Procedure, 1973 be charged with at the trial. Thus, CVC is empowered to exercise superintendence over the functioning of CBI. It is also empowered to give directions to CBI. It is also empowered to review the progress of investigations conducted by CBI into offences alleged to have been committed under the Prevention of Corruption Act, 1988 or under the Code of Criminal Procedure by a public servant. CVC is also empowered to exercise superintendence over the vigilance administration of various Ministries of the Central Government, PSUs, Government companies etc. The powers and functions discharged by CVC is the sole reason for giving the institution the administrative autonomy, independence and insulation from external influences.

HPC HAS TO KEEP IN MIND AND THE POLICY PURPOSE OF 2003 ACT

Validity of the Recommendation dated 3rd September, 2010

41. One of the main contentions advanced on behalf of Union of India and Shri P.J. Thomas before us was that once the CVC clearance had been granted on 6th October, 2008 and once the candidate stood empanelled for appointment at the Centre and in fact stood appointed as Secretary, Parliamentary Affairs and, thereafter, Secretary Telecom, it was legitimate for the HPC to proceed on the basis that there was no impediment in the way of appointment of respondent No. 2 on the basis of the pending case which had been found to be without any substance.

42. We find no merit in the above submissions. Judicial review seeks to ensure that the statutory duty of the HPC to recommend under the proviso to section 4(1) is performed keeping in mind the policy and the purpose of the 2003 Act. We are not sitting in appeal over the opinion of the HPC. What we have to see is whether relevant material and vital aspects having nexus to the object of the 2003 Act were taken into account when the decision to recommend took place on 3rd September, 2010.

HPC CANNOT ADOPT OFFICIAL ARBITRARINESS

43. Appointment to the post of the Central Vigilance Commissioner must satisfy not only the eligibility criteria of the candidate but also the decision making process of the recommendation [*see* para 88 of *N. Kannadasan* (supra)]. The decision to recommend has got to be an informed decision keeping in mind the fact that CVC as an institution has to perform an important function of vigilance administration. If a statutory body like HPC, for any reason whatsoever, fails to look into the relevant material having nexus to the object and purpose of the 2003 Act or takes into account irrelevant circumstances then its decision would stand vitiated on the ground of official arbitrariness; see *State of Andhra Pradesh* v. *Nalla Raja Reddy*, (1967) 3 SCR 28. Under the proviso to section 4(1), the HPC had to take into consideration what is good for the institution and not what is good for the candidate; *see* para 93 of *N. Kannadasan* (supra).

PERSONAL INTEGRITY HAS CO-RELATIONSHIP WITH INSTITUTIONAL INTEGRITY AND PUBLIC INTEREST SHOULD BE THE TOUCHSTONE

When institutional integrity is in question, the touchstone should be "public interest" which has got to be taken into consideration by the HPC and in such cases the HPC may not insist upon proof; *see* SCC para 103 of *N. Kannadasan* (supra).

44. *We should not be understood to mean that the personal integrity is not relevant. It certainly has a co-relationship with institutional integrity.* The point to be noted is that in the present case the entire emphasis has been placed by the CVC, the DoPT and the HPC only on the bio-data of the empanelled candidates. None of these authorities have looked at the matter from the larger perspective of institutional integrity including institutional competence and functioning of CVC.

NOTINGS RECOMMENDING MAJOR PENALTY AGAINST P.J. THOMAS IGNORED WHILE GIVING CVC CLEARANCE

Moreover, we are surprised to find that between 2000 and 2004 the notings of DoPT dated 26th June, 2000, 18th January, 2001, 20th June, 2003, 24th February, 2004, 18th October, 2004 and 2nd November, 2004 have all observed that penalty proceedings may be initiated against Shri P.J. Thomas. Whether State should initiate such proceedings or the Centre should initiate such proceedings was not relevant. What is relevant is that such notings were not considered in juxtaposition with the clearance of CVC granted on 6th October, 2008. Even in the Brief submitted to the HPC by DoPT, there is no reference to the said notings between the years 2000 and 2004. Even in the C.V. of Shri P.J. Thomas, there is no reference to the earlier notings of DoPT recommending initiation of penalty proceedings against Shri P.J. Thomas.

HPC FAILED TO CONSIDER THE ENTIRE SERVICE RECORD OF P.J. THOMAS AND OBJECT OF THE ACT, 2003

Therefore, even on personal integrity, the HPC has not considered the relevant material. The learned Attorney General, in his usual fairness, stated at the Bar that only the Curriculum Vitae of each of the empanelled candidates stood annexed to the agenda for the meeting of the HPC. The fact remains that the HPC, for whatsoever reason, has failed to consider the relevant material keeping in mind the purpose and policy of the 2003 Act.

INDEPENDENCE AND IMPARTIALITY OF CVC INSTITUTION HAS TO BE MAINTAINED

45. The system governance established by the Constitution is based on distribution of powers and functions amongst the three organs of the State, one of them being the Executive whose duty is to enforce the laws made by the Parliament and administer the country through various statutory bodies like CVC which is empowered to perform the function of vigilance administration. Thus, we are concerned with the institution and its integrity including institutional competence and functioning and not the desirability of the candidate alone who is going to be the Central Vigilance Commissioner, though personal integrity is an important quality, it is the independence and impartiality of the institution like CVC which has to be maintained and preserved in larger interest of the rule of law; see *Vineet Narain* (supra).

HPC PERFORMS STATUTORY DUTY – HAS TO CONSIDER RELEVANT MATERIAL

46. While making recommendations, the HPC performs a statutory duty. Its duty is to recommend. While making recommendations, the criteria of the candidate being a public servant or a civil servant in the past is not the sole consideration. The HPC has to look at the record and take into consideration whether the candidate would or would not be able to function as a Central Vigilance Commissioner. Whether the institutional competency would be adversely affected by pending proceedings and if by that touchstone the candidate stands disqualified then it shall be the duty of the HPC not to recommend such a candidate. In the present case apart from the pending criminal proceedings, as stated above, between the period 2000 and 2004 various notings of DoPT recommended disciplinary proceedings against Shri P.J. Thomas in respect of Palmolein case. Those notings have not been considered by the HPC. As stated above, the 2003 Act confers autonomy and independence to the institution of CVC. Autonomy has been conferred so that the Central Vigilance Commissioner could act without fear or favour.

INSTITUTION IS MORE IMPORTANT THAN AN INDIVIDUAL

47. We may reiterate that *institution is more important than an individual*. This is the test laid down in para 93 of *N. Kannadasan's* case (supra). In the present case, the HPC has failed to take this test into consideration. The recommendation dated

3rd September, 2010 of HPC is entirely premised on the blanket clearance given by CVC on 6th October, 2008 and on the fact of respondent No. 2 being appointed as Chief Secretary of Kerala on 18th September, 2007; his appointment as Secretary of Parliamentary Affairs and his subsequent appointment as Secretary, Telecom. In the process, the HPC, for whatever reasons, has failed to take into consideration the pendency of Palmolein case before the Special Judge, Thiruvananthapuram being case CC 6 of 2003; the sanction accorded by the Government of Kerala on 30th November, 1999 under section 197 Cr. P.C. for prosecuting *inter alia* Shri P.J. Thomas for having committed alleged offence under section 120B, IPC read with section 13(1)(d) of the Prevention of Corruption Act; the judgment of the Supreme Court dated 29th March, 2000 in the case of *K. Karunakaran* v. *State of Kerala,* (2000) 3 SCC 761 in which this Court observed that: SCC p. 767, para 8

> "8. ...the registration of the FIR against Shri Karunakaran and others cannot be held to be the result of *mala fides* or actuated by extraneous considerations. The menace of corruption cannot be permitted to be hidden under the carpet of legal technicalities and in such cases probes conducted are required to be determined on facts and in accordance with law".

Further, even the judgment of the Kerala High Court in Criminal Revision Petition No. 430 of 2001 has not been considered.

RECOMMENDATIONS OF HPC ARE *NON-EST*

48. It may be noted that the clearance of CVC dated 6th October, 2008 was not binding on the HPC. However, the aforestated judgment of the Supreme Court dated 29th March, 2000 in the case of *K. Karunakaran* v. *State of Kerala* in Criminal Appeal No. 86 of 1998 was certainly binding on the HPC and, in any event, required due weightage to be given while making recommendation, particularly when the said judgment had emphasized the importance of probity in high offices. This is what we have repeatedly emphasized in our judgment – *institution is more important than individual(s).*

49. For the above reasons, it is declared that the recommendation made by the HPC on 3rd September, 2010 is *non-est* in law.

WRIT OF *QUO WARRANTO* MAINTAINABLE AND INVOCABLE – DECLARATORY RELIEF ALSO SOUGHT

Is Writ of *Quo Warranto* invocable?

50. Shri K.K. Venugopal, learned senior counsel appearing on behalf of respondent No. 2, submitted that the present case is neither a case of infringement of the statutory provisions of the 2003 Act nor of the appointment being contrary to any procedure or rules. According to the learned counsel, it is well-settled that a writ of *quo warranto* applies in a case when a person usurps an office and the allegation is that he has no title to it or a legal authority to hold it. According to the learned counsel for a writ of *quo warranto* to be issued there must be a clear infringement of the law. That, in the instant case there has been no infringement of any law in the matter of appointment of respondent No. 2.

51. The procedure of *quo warranto* confers jurisdiction and authority on the Judiciary to control Executive action in the matter of making appointments to public offices against the relevant statutory provisions. Before a citizen can claim a writ of *quo warranto* he must satisfy the court *inter alia* that the office in question is a public office and it is held by a person without legal authority and that leads to the inquiry as to whether the appointment of the said person has been in accordance with law or not. A writ of *quo warranto* is issued to prevent a continued exercise of unlawful authority.

52. One more aspect needs to be mentioned. In the present petition, as rightly pointed by Shri Prashant Bhushan, learned counsel appearing on behalf of the petitioner, a declaratory relief is also sought besides seeking a writ of *quo warranto.*

53. At the outset it may be stated that in the main writ petition the petitioner has prayed for issuance of any other writ, direction or order which this Court may deem fit and proper in the facts and circumstances of this Case. Thus, nothing prevents this Court, if so satisfied, from issuing a writ of declaration. Further, as held hereinabove, recommendation of the HPC and, consequently, the appointment of Shri P.J. Thomas was in contravention of the provisions of the 2003 Act, hence, we find no merit in the submissions advanced on behalf of respondent No. 2 on non-maintainability of the writ petition. If public duties are to be enforced and rights and interests are to be protected, then the court may, in furtherance of public interest, consider it necessary to inquire into the state of affairs of the subject matter of litigation in the interest of justice; see *Ashok Lanka* v. *Rishi Dixit*, (2005) 5 SCC 598.

PRIOR LAW RELIED UPON BY RESPONDENT NO. 2 – CONSIDERED AND DISTINGUISHED

54. Keeping in mind the above parameters, we may now consider some of the judgments on which reliance has been placed by the learned counsel for respondent No. 2."

55. In *Ashok Kumar Yadav* v. *State of Haryana,* (1985) 4 SCC 417, the Division Bench of the Punjab and Haryana Court had quashed and set aside selections made by the Haryana Public Service Commission to the Haryana Civil Service and other Allied Services.

In that case some candidates who had obtained very high marks at the written examination failed to qualify as they had obtained poor marks in the *viva voce* test. Consequently, they were not selected. They were aggrieved by the selections made by Haryana Public Service Commission. Accordingly, Civil Writ Petition 2495 of 1983 was filed in the High Court challenging the validity of the selections and seeking a writ for quashing and setting aside the same. There were several grounds on which the validity of the selection made by the Commission was assailed. A declaration was also sought that they were entitled to be selected. A collateral attack was launched. It was alleged that the Chairperson and members of Public Service Commission were not men of high integrity, calibre and qualification and they were appointed solely as a matter of political patronage and hence the selections made by them were invalid. This ground of challenge was sought to be repelled on behalf of the State of Haryana who contended that not only was it not competent to the Court on the existing set of pleadings to examine whether the Chairman and members of the Commission were men of high integrity, caliber and qualification but also there was no material at all on the basis of which the Court could come to the conclusion that they were men lacking in integrity, calibre or qualification.

56. The writ petition came to be heard by a Division Bench of the High Court of Punjab and Haryana. The Division Bench held that the Chairperson and members of the Commission had been appointed purely on the basis of political considerations and that they did not satisfy the test of high integrity, calibre and qualification. The Division Bench went to the length of alleging corruption against the Chairperson and members of the Commission and observed that they were not competent to validly wield the golden scale of *viva voce* test for entrance into the public service.

57. This Court in *Ashok Kumar Yadav's* case, (1985) 4 SCC 417 *vide* para 9 observed that it was difficult to see how the Division Bench of the High Court could have possibly undertaken an inquiry into the question whether Chairman and members of the Commission were men of integrity, calibre and qualification; that such an inquiry was totally irrelevant inquiry because even if they were men lacking in integrity, calibre and qualification, it would not make their appointments invalid so long as the constitutional and legal requirement in regard to appointment are fulfilled. *It was held that none of the constitutional provisions namely, Article 316 and 319 stood violated in making appointments of the Chairperson and members of the Commission nor was any legal provision breached.* Therefore, the appointments of the Chairperson and members of the Commission were made in conformity with the constitutional and legal requirements, and if that be so, it was beyond the jurisdiction of the High Court to hold that such appointments were invalid on the ground that the Chairman and the members of the Commission lacked integrity, calibre and qualification. The Supreme Court observed that it passed their comprehension as to how the appointments of the Chairman and members of the Commission could be regarded as suffering from infirmity merely on the ground that in the opinion of the Division Bench of the High Court the Chairperson and the members of the Commission were not men of integrity or caliber. In the present case, there is a breach/violation of the proviso to section 4(1) of the 2003 Act.

58. In *R.K. Jain* v. *Union of India,* [(1993) 4 SCC 119] Shrj Harish Chandra was a Senior Vice-President when the question of filling up the vacancy of the President came up for consideration. He was qualified for the post under the Rules. No challenge was made on that account. Under rule 10(1) the Central Government was conferred the power to appoint one of the members to be the President. The validity of the Rule was not questioned. Thus, the Central Government was entitled to appoint Shri Harish Chandra as the President. It was stated that the track record of Shri Harish Chandra was poor. He was hardly fit to hold the post of the President. It was averred that Shri Harish Chandra has been in .the past proposed for appointment as a Judge of the Delhi High Court.

His appointment, however, did not materialize due to certain adverse reports.

59. It was held by this Court in *R.K. Jain's* case (supra) that judicial review is concerned with whether the incumbent possessed requisite qualification for appointment and the manner in which the appointment came to be made or the procedure adopted was fair, just and reasonable. When a candidate was found qualified and eligible and is accordingly appointed by the Executive to hold an office as a Member or Vice President or President of a Tribunal, in judicial review the Court cannot sit over the choice of the selection. It is for the Executive to select the personnel as per law or procedure: Shri Harish Chandra was the Senior Vice-President at the relevant time. The question of comparative merit which was the key contention of the petitioner could not be gone into in a PIL; that the writ petition was not a writ of *quo warranto* and in the circumstances the writ petition came to be dismissed.

60. It was held in *R.K. Jain's* case (supra) that even assuming for the sake of arguments that the allegations made by the petitioner were factually accurate, still, this Court cannot sit in judgment over the choice of the person made by the Central Government for appointment as a President of CEGAT so long as the person chosen possesses the prescribed qualification and is otherwise eligible for appointment. It was held that this court cannot interfere with the appointment of Shri Harish Chandra as the President of CEGAT on the ground that his track record was poor or because of adverse reports on which account his appointment as a High Court Judge had not materialized.

61. In the case of *Hari Bansh Lal* v. *Sahodar Prasad Mahto*, (2010)9 SCC 655, the appointment of Shri Hari Bansh Lal as Chairman, Jharkhand State Electricity Board stood challenged on the ground that the Board had been constituted in an arbitrary manner; that Shri Hari Bansh Lal was a person of doubtful integrity; that he was appointed as a Chairman without following the rules and procedure and in the circumstances the appointment stood challenged. On the question of maintainability, the Division Bench of this Court held that a writ of *quo warranto* lies only when the appointment is contrary to a statutory provision.

62. It was further held in *Hari Bansh Lal's* case (supra) that "suitability" of a candidate for appointment to a post is to be judged, by the appointing authority and not by the court unless the appointment is contrary to the statutory rules/ provisions. It is important to note that this Court went into the merits of the case and came to the conclusion that there was no adequate material to doubt the integrity of Shri Hari Bansh Lal who was appointed as the Chairperson of Jharkhand State Electricity Board. This Court further observed that in the writ petition there was no averment saying that the appointment was contrary to statutory provisions.

DISTINCTION BETWEEN JUDICIAL REVIEW AND MERIT REVIEW

63. As stated above, we need to keep in mind the difference between judicial review and merit review. As stated above, in this case the judicial determination is confined to the integrity of the decision-making process undertaken by the HPC in terms of the proviso to section 4(1) of the 2003 Act. If one carefully examines the judgment of this Court in *Ashok Kumar Yadav's* case (supra) the facts indicate that the High Court had sat in appeal over the personal integrity of the Chairman and Members of the Haryana Public Service Commission in support of the collateral attack on the selections made by the State Public Service Commission. In that case, the High Court had failed to keep in mind the difference between judicial and merit review. Further, this Court found that the appointments of the Chairperson and Members of Haryana Public Service Commission was in accordance with the provisions of the Constitution. In that case, there was no issue as to the legality of the decision-making process. On the contrary the last sentence of para 9 supports our above reasoning when it says that it is always open to the Court to set aside the decision (selection) of the Haryana Public Service Commission if such decision is vitiated by the influence of extraneous considerations or if such selection is made in breach of the statute or the rules.

GOVERNMENT IS NOT ACCOUNTABLE FOR THE CHOICE MADE BUT FOR THE LEGALITY OF THE DECISION TAKEN

64. Even in *R.K. Jain's* case (*supra*), this Court observed *vide* para 73 that judicial review is concerned with whether the incumbent possessed qualifications for the appointment and the manner in which the appointment came to be made or whether procedure adopted was fair, just and reasonable. We reiterate that Government is not accountable to the courts for the choice made but Government is accountable to the courts in respect of the lawfulness/legality of its decisions when impugned under the judicial review jurisdiction. We do not wish to multiply the authorities on this point.

APPOINTMENT OF CVC IS AT THE DISCRETION OF THE PRESIDENT—SUBMITTED P.J. THOMAS

Appointment of Central Vigilance Commissioner at the President's discretion

65. On behalf of respondent No. 2 it was submitted that though under section 4(1) of the 2003 Act, the appointment of Central Vigilance Commissioner is made on the basis of the *recommendation* of a High Powered Committee, the President of India is not to act on the *advice* of the Council of Ministers as is provided in article 74 of the Constitution. In this connection, it was submitted that the exercise of powers by the President in appointing respondent No. 2 has not been put in issue in the PIL, nor is there any pleading in regard to the exercise of powers by the President and in the circumstances it is not open to the petitioner to urge that the appointment is invalid.

RECOMMENDATIONS BINDING ON THE PRESIDENT—SUBMITTED CENTRAL GOVERNMENT

66. Shri G.E. Vahanvati, learned Attorney General appearing on behalf of Union of India, however, submitted that the proposal sent after obtaining and accepting the recommendations of the High Powered Committee under section 4(1) was binding on the President. Learned counsel submitted that under article 74 of the Constitution the President acts in exercise of her function on the aid and advice of the Council of Ministers headed by the Prime Minister which advice is binding on the President subject to the proviso to article 74.

67. According to the learned counsel article 77 of the Constitution *inter alia* provides for conduct of Government Business. Under article 77(3), the President makes rules for transaction of Government Business and for allocation of business among the Ministers. On facts, learned Attorney General submitted that under Government of India (Transaction of Business) Rules, 1961 the Prime Minister had taken a decision on 3rd September, 2010 to propose the name of respondent No. 2 for appointment as Central Vigilance Commissioner after the recommendation of the High Powered Committee.

68. It was accordingly submitted on behalf of Union of India that this advice of the Prime Minister under article 77(3), read with article 74 of the Constitution is binding on the President. That, although the recommendation of the High Powered Committee under section 4(1) of the 2003 Act may not be binding on the President *proprio vigore*, however, if such recommendation has been accepted by the Prime Minister, who is the concerned authority under article 77(3), and if such recommendation is then forwarded to the President under article 74, then the President is bound to act in accordance with the advice tendered. That, the intention behind article 77(3) is that it is physically impossible that every decision is taken by the Council of Ministers. The Constitution does not use the term "Cabinet". Rules have been framed for convenient transaction and allocation of such business. Under the Rules of Business, the concerned authority is the Prime Minister. The advice tendered to the President by the Prime Minister regarding the appointment of the Central Vigilance Commissioner would be thus binding on the President.

69. Lastly, it was submitted that unless the Constitution expressly permits the exercise of discretion by the President, every decision of the President has to be on the aid and advice of Council of Ministers.

P.J. THOMAS REFERRED TO THE PRIOR LAW—CONSIDERED AND DISTINGUISHED

70. Shri Venugopal, learned counsel appearing on behalf of respondent No. 2 submitted that though the President has an area of discretion in regard to exercise of certain powers under the Constitution, the Constitution is silent about the exercise of powers by the President/Governor where a Statute confers such powers.

71. In this connection learned counsel placed reliance on the judgment of this Court in *Bhuri Nath* v. *State of Jammu and Kashmir,* (1997) 2 SCC 745. In that case, the appellants-Baridars challenged the constitutionality of Jammu and Kashmir Shri Mata Vaishno Devi Shrine Act, 1988 which was enacted to provide for better management, administration and governance of Shri Mata Vaishno Devi Shrine and its endowments including the land and buildings attached to the Shrine. By operation of that Act the administration, management and governance of the Shrine and its Funds stood vested in the Board. Consequently, all rights of Baridars stood extinguished from the date of the commencement of the Act by operation of section 19(1) of the Act.

72. One of the questions which came up for consideration in that case was that when the Governor discharges the functions under the Act, is it with the aid and advice of the Council of Ministers or whether he discharges those functions in his official capacity as the Governor. This question arose because by an order dated 16th January, 1995, this Court had directed the Board to frame a scheme for rehabilitation of persons engaged in the performance of Pooja at Shri Mata Vaishno Devi Shrine. When that matter came up for hearing on 20th March, 1995, the Baridars stated that they did not want rehabilitation. Instead, they preferred to receive compensation to be determined under section 20 of the impugned Act 1988. This Court noticed that in the absence of guidelines for determination of the compensation by the Tribunal to be appointed under section 20 it was not possible to award compensation to the Baridars. Consequently, the Supreme Court ordered that the issue of compensation be left to the Governor to make appropriate guidelines to determine the compensation. Pursuant thereto, guidelines were framed by the Governor which were published in the State Gazette and placed on record on 8th May, 1995. It is in this context that the question arose that when the Legislature entrusted the powers under the Act to the Governor whether the Governor discharges the functions under the Act with the aid and advice of the Council of Ministers or whether he acts in his official capacity as a Governor under the Act.

73. After examining the Scheme of the 1988 Act, the Division Bench of this Court in *Bhuri Nath's* case (supra) held that the Legislature of Jammu and Kashmir, while making the Act was aware that similar provisions in the Endowments Act, 1966 gives power of the State Government to dissolve the Board of Trustees of Tirupati Devasthanams and the Board of Trustees of other institutions. Thus, it is clear that the Legislature entrusted the powers under the Act to the Governor in his official capacity.

74. On examination of the 1988 Act in *Bhuri Nath's* case (supra) this Court found that the Governor is to preside over the meetings of the Board and in his absence his nominee, a qualified Hindu, shall preside over the functions. That, under the 1988 Act no distinction was made between the Governor and the Executive Government. That, under the Scheme of the 1988 Act there was nothing to indicate that the power was given to the Council of Ministers and the Governor was to act on its advice as Executive Head of the State. It is in these circumstances that this Court held that while discharging the functions under the 1988 Act the Governor acts in his official capacity.

75. In the same judgment in *Bhuri Nath's* case (supra) this Court has also referred to the judgment of the Full Bench of the Punjab and Haryana High Court in *Hardwari Lal* v. *G.D. Tapase,* AIR 1982 P&H 439, in which a similar question arose as to whether the Governor in his capacity as the Chancellor of Maharshi Dayanand University acts under the 1975 Act in his official capacity as Chancellor or with the aid and advice of the Council of Ministers. The Full Bench of the High Court, after elaborate consideration of the provisions of the Act, observed that under the Maharshi Dayanand University Act, 1975, the State Government would not interfere in the affairs of the University. Under that Act, the State Government is an Authority different and distinct from the authority of the Chancellor. Under that Act the State Government was not authorised to advise the Chancellor to act in a particular manner. Under that Act the University was a statutory body, autonomous in character and it had been given powers exercisable by the Chancellor in his absolute discretion. In the circumstances, under the Scheme of that Act it was held that while discharging the functions as a Chancellor, the Governor does everything in his discretion as a Chancellor and he does not act on the aid and advice of his Council of Ministers.

THIS JUDGMENT NOT APPLICABLE TO THE FACTS OF THIS CASE

76. This judgment in *Hardwari Lal* case (supra) has no application to the Scheme of the 2003 Act. As stated hereinabove, the CVC is constituted under section 3(1) of the 2003 Act. The Central Vigilance Commissioner is appointed under section 4(1) of the 2003 Act by the President by warrant under her hand and seal after obtaining the recommendation of a Committee consisting of the Prime Minister as the Chairperson and two other Members. As submitted by the learned Attorney General although under the 2003 Act the Central Vigilance Commissioner is appointed after obtaining the recommendation of the High Powered Committee, such recommendation has got to be accepted by the Prime Minister, who is the concerned authority under article 77(3), and if such recommendation is forwarded to the President under article 74, then the President is bound to act in accordance with the advice tendered. Further under the Rules of Business the concerned authority is the Prime Minister. Therefore, the advice tendered to the President by the Prime Minister regarding appointment of the Central Vigilance Commissioner will be binding on the President.

77. It may be noted that the above submissions of the Attorney General find support even in the judgment of the Division Bench of this Court in *Bhuri Nath's* case (*supra*) which in turn has placed reliance on the judgment of this Court in *Samsher Singh* v. *State of Punjab*, (1974) 2 SCC 831 in which a Bench of 7 Judges of this Court held that under the Cabinet system of Government, as embodied in our Constitution, the Governor is the formal Head of the State. He exercises all his powers and functions conferred on him by or under the Constitution with the aid and advice of his Council of Ministers. That, the real Executive power is vested in the Council of Ministers of the Cabinet. The same view is reiterated in *R.K. Jain's* case (*supra*). However, in *Bhuri Nath's* case (*supra*) it has been clarified that: (SCC p. 764 para 20)

> "20. The Governor being the constitutional head of the State, unless he is required to perform the function under the Constitution in his individual discretion, the performance of the Executive power, which is coextensive with the Legislative power, is with the aid and advice of the Council of Ministers headed by the Chief Minister."

78. Thus, we conclude that the judgment in *Bhuri Nath's* case has no application as the Scheme of the Jammu and Kashmir Shri Mata Vaishno Devi Shrine Act, 1988 as well as the Scheme of Maharshi Dayanand University Act, 1975 as well as the Scheme of the various Endowment Acts is quite different from the Scheme of the 2003 Act. Hence, there is no merit in the contention advanced on behalf of respondent No. 2 that in the matter of appointment of Central Vigilance Commissioner under section 4(1) of the 2003 Act, the President is not to act on the advice of the Council of Ministers as is provided in article 74 of the Constitution.

EACH MEMBER TO ACT IN PUBLIC INTEREST – OPINION MAY NOT BE UNANIMOUS

Unanimity or consensus under section 4(2) of the 2003 Act

79. One of the arguments advanced on behalf of the petitioner before us was that the recommendation of the High Powered Committee under the proviso to section 4(1) has to be unanimous. It was submitted that CVC was set up under the Resolution dated 11th February, 1964. Under that Resolution the appointment of Central Vigilance Commissioner was to be initiated by the Cabinet Secretary and approved by the Prime Minister. However, the provision made in section 4 of the 2003 Act was with a purpose, namely, to introduce an element of bipartisanship and political neutrality in the process of appointment of the head of the CVC. The provision made in section 4 for including the Leader of Opposition in the High Powered Committee made a significant change from the procedure obtaining before the enactment of the said Act. It was further submitted that if unanimity is ruled out then the very purpose of inducting the Leader of Opposition in the process of selection will stand defeated because if the recommendation of the Committee were to be arrived at by majority it would always exclude the Leader of Opposition since the Prime Minister and the Home Minister will always be *ad idem*.

80. It was submitted that one must give a purposive interpretation to the scheme of the Act. It was submitted that under section 9 it has been *inter alia* stated that all business of the Commission shall, as far as possible, be transacted unanimously. It was submitted that since in *Vineet Narain's* case (*supra*) this Court had observed that CVC would be selected by a three member Committee, including the Leader of the Opposition it was patently obvious that the said Committee would decide by unanimity or consensus. That, it was no where stated that the Committee would decide by majority.

A MEMBER OF HPC CANNOT BE GIVEN THE VETO POWER

81. We find no merit in these submissions. To accept the contentions advanced on behalf of the petitioners would mean conferment of a "veto right" on one of the members of the HPC. To confer such a power on one of the members would amount to judicial legislation. Under the proviso to section 4(1) Parliament has put its faith in the High Powered Committee consisting of the Prime Minister, the Minister for Home Affairs and the Leader of the Opposition in the House of the People. It is presumed that such High Powered Committee entrusted with wide discretion to make a choice will exercise its powers in accordance with the 2003 Act, objectively and in a fair and reasonable manner. It is well-settled that mere conferment of wide discretionary powers *per se* will not violate the doctrine of reasonableness or equality. The 2003 Act is enacted with the intention that such High Powered Committee will act in a bipartisan manner and shall perform its statutory duties keeping in view the larger national interest. Each of the Members is presumed by the Legislature to act in public interest. On the other hand, if veto power is given to one of the three Members, the working of the Act would become unworkable.

EVEN VACANCY IN THE COMMITTEE DOES NOT INVALIDATE THE APPOINTMENT OF CVC

82. One more aspect needs to be mentioned. Under section 4(2) of the 2003 Act it has been stipulated that the vacancy in the Committee shall not invalidate the appointment. This provision militates against the argument of the petitioner that the recommendation under section 4 has to be unanimous.

83. Before concluding, we would like to quote the observations from the judgment in *Grindley* v. *Barker*, 1 Bos & Pul 229, which reads as under:

> "I think it is now pretty well-established, that where a number of persons are entrusted with the powers not of mere private confidence, but in some respects of a general nature and all of them are regularly assembled, **the majority will conclude the minority, and their act will be the act of the whole.**"
>
> (Emphasis supplied)

84. The Court in Grindley, (1798) 1 Bos and Pau 229: 126 ER 875 while explaining the *raison d'etre* behind the principle, observed (ER p. 880):

> "...It is impossible that bodies of men should always be brought to think alike. There is often a degree of coercion, and the majority is governed by the minority, and *vice versa*, according to the strength of opinions, tempers, prejudices, and even interests. We shall not therefore think ourselves bound in this case by the rule which holds in that. I lay no great stress on the clause of the Act which appoints a majority to act in certain cases, because that appears to have been done for particular reasons which do not apply to the ultimate trial: it relates only to the assembling the searchers; now *there is no doubt that all the six triers must assemble; and the only question, is what they must do when assembled*? We have no light to direct us in this part, except the argument from the nature of the subject. The leather being subject to seizure in every stage of the manufacture, the tribunal ought to be composed of persons skilful in every branch of the manufacture. And I cannot say there is no weight in the argument, drawn from the necessity of persons concurring in the judgments, who are possessed of different branches of knowledge, but standing alone it is not so conclusive as to oblige us to break through the general rule; besides, *it is very much obviated by this consideration when all have assembled and communicated to each other the necessary information, it is fitter that the majority should decide than that all should be pressed to a concurrence*. If this be so, then the reasons drawn from the act and which have been supposed to demand, that the whole body should unite in the judgment, have no sufficient avail, and consequently the general rule of law will take place; *viz.* that the judgment of four out of six being the whole body to which the authority is delegated regularly assemble and acting, *is the judgment of the all.*"
>
> (Emphasis supplied)

85. Similarly, we would like to quote *Halsbury's Laws of England* (4th Ed. Re-issue), on this aspect, which states as under:

> "Where a power of a public nature is committed to several persons, in the absence of statutory provision or implication to the contrary the act of the majority is binding upon the minority."

86. In the circumstances, we find no merit in the submission made on behalf of the petitioner on this point that the recommendation/decision dated 3rd September, 2010 stood vitiated on the ground that it was not unanimous.

GUIDELINES FOR THE APPOINTMENT OF CVC

Guidelines/Directions of this Court

87. The 2003 Act came into force on and from 11th September, 2003. In the present case we find non-compliance of some of the provisions of the 2003 Act. Under section 3(3), the Central Vigilance Commissioner and the Vigilance Commissioners are to be appointed from amongst persons—

(a) who have been or who are in All-India Service or in any civil service of the Union or in a civil post under the Union having requisite knowledge and experience as indicated in section 3(3)(a); or

(b) who have held office or are holding office in a corporation established by or under any Central Act or a Central Government company and persons who have experience in finance including insurance and banking, law, vigilance and investigations.

ZONE OF CONSIDERATION CANNOT BE RESTRICTED TO CIVIL SERVICE ONLY

88. No reason has been given as to why in the present case the zone of consideration stood restricted only to the civil service. We therefore direct that:

(i) In our judgment we have held that there is no prescription of unanimity or consensus under section 4(2) of the 2003 Act. However, the question still remains as to what should be done in cases of difference of opinion amongst the Members of the High Powered Committee. As in the present case, if one Member of the Committee dissents that Member should give reasons for the dissent and if the majority disagrees with the dissent, the majority shall give reasons for overruling the dissent. This will bring about fairness-in-action. Since we have held that legality of the choice or selection is open to judicial review we are of the view that if the above methodology is followed transparency would emerge which would also maintain the integrity of the decision-making process.

(ii) In future the zone of consideration should be in terms of section 3(3) of the 2003 Act. It shall not be restricted to civil servants.

(iii) All the civil servants and other persons empanelled shall be outstanding civil servants or persons of impeccable integrity.

(iv) The empanelment shall be carried out on the basis of rational criteria, which is to be reflected by recording of reasons and/or noting akin to reasons by the empanelling authority.

(v) The empanelment shall be carried out by a person not below the rank of Secretary to the Government of India in the concerned Ministry.

(vi) The empanelling authority, while forwarding the names of the empanelled officers/persons, shall enclose complete information, material and data of the concerned officer/person, whether favourable or adverse. Nothing relevant or material should be withheld from the Selection Committee. It will not only be useful but would also serve larger public interest and enhance public confidence if the contemporaneous service record and acts of outstanding performance of the officer under consideration, even with adverse remarks is specifically brought to the notice of the Selection Committee.

(vii) The Selection Committee may adopt a fair and transparent process of consideration of the empanelled officers.

RECOMMENDATION AND APPOINTMENT OF P.J. THOMAS *NON-EST* IN LAW – HENCE QUASHED – WRIT PETITION ALLOWED

89. For the above reasons, it is declared that the recommendation dated 3rd September, 2010 of the High Powered Committee recommending the name of Shri P.J. Thomas as Central Vigilance Commissioner under the proviso to section 4(1) of the 2003 Act is *non-est* in law and, consequently, the impugned appointment of Shri P.J. Thomas as Central Vigilance Commissioner is quashed.

90. The writ petitions are accordingly allowed with no order as to costs.

……….…………………….…CJI
(S.H. Kapadia)
……..……………………………..J.
(K.S. Panicker Radhakrishnan)
……..……………………………..J.
(Swatanter Kumar)

New Delhi
March 3, 2011

Author's Note: The Countrymen who have deposited their BLACK MONEY secretly in the Banks of Foreign Countries are traitors. It is not a matter of avoiding the payment of Income-tax, it is a crime against the Nation including danger to the security of our country. Those persons deserve to be prosecuted and BLACK MONEY needs be brought back and confiscated to the State and utilized for National Growth. Such a matter had come up for consideration before the Hon'ble SUPREME COURT in this judgment.

Ram Jethmalani

v.

Union of India[1]

SUPREME COURT OF INDIA

CIVIL ORIGINAL JURISDICTION

Writ Petition (Civil) No. 176 of 2009, with I.A. No. 1 of 2009

SLP (C) 11032 of 2009, WPs (C) 37 of 2010 and 136 of 2011

Decided on 4-7-2011

BENCH

B. Sudershan Reddy and Surinder Singh Nijjar, JJ.

ORDER

PART I

Money Controls the Economy

1. "Follow the money" was the short and simple advice given by the secret informant, within the American Government, to Bob Woodward, the journalist from Washington Post, in aid of his investigations of the Watergate Hotel break-in. Money has often been claimed, by economists, to only be a veil that covers the real value and the economy. As a medium of exchange, money is vital for the smooth functioning of exchange in the market place. However, increasing monetization of most social transactions has been viewed as potentially problematic for the social order, in as much as it signifies a move to evaluating value, and ethical desirability, of most areas of social interaction only in terms of price obtained in the market place.

2. Price based notions of value and values, as propounded by some extreme neo-liberal doctrines, implies that the values that ought to be promoted, in societies, are the ones for which people are willing to pay a price for. Values, and social actions, for which an effective demand is not expressed in the market, are neglected, even if lip service is paid to their essentiality. However, it cannot be denied that not everything that can be, and is transacted, in the market for a price

1. (2011) 8 SCC 1.

is necessarily good, and enhances social welfare. Moreover, some activities, even if costly and without being directly measurable in terms of exchange value, are to be rightly viewed as essential.

STATE IS DUTY-BOUND TO CHECK THE ACTIVITIES HARMFUL TO THE SOCIETY

3. It is a well-established proposition, of political economy, and of Statecraft, that the State has a necessary interest in determining, and influencing, the kinds of transactions, and social actions, that occur within a legal order. From prevention of certain kinds of harmful activities, that may range from outright crimes, to regulating or controlling, and consequently mitigating, socially harmful modes of social and economic production, to promotion of activities that are deemed to be of higher priority, than other activities which may have a lower priority, howsoever evaluated in terms of social utility, are all the responsibilities of the State. Whether such activities by the State result in directly measurable benefits or not is often not the most important factor in determining their desirability; their absence, or their substantial evisceration, are to be viewed as socially destructive.

EXCHANGE OF MONEY CAN PLAY A MAJOR ROLE IN THE COMMISSION OF CRIME

4. The scrutiny, and control, of activities, whether in the economic, social or political contexts, by the State, in the public interest as posited by modern constitutionalism, is substantially effectuated by the State "following the money." In modern societies very little gets accomplished without transfer of money. The incidence of crime, petty and grand, like any other social phenomena is often linked to transfers of monies, small or large. Money, in that sense, can both power, and also reward, crime. As noted by many scholars, with increasing globalization, an ideological and social construct, in which transactions across borders are accomplished with little or no control over the quantum, and mode of transfers of money in exchange for various services and value rendered, both legal and illegal, nation-States also have begun to confront complex problems of cross-border crimes of all kinds. Whether this complex web of flows of funds, instantaneously, and in large sums is good or bad, from the perspective of lawful and desired transactions is not at issue in the context of the matters before this Court.

COURT IS CONCERNED IN THIS CASE ABOUT UNACCOUNTED MONEY DEPOSITED IN FOREIGN COUNTRIES AND ITS SERIOUS CONSEQUENCES

5. The worries of this Court that arise, in the context of the matters placed before us, are with respect to transfers of monies, and accumulation of monies, which are unaccounted for by many individuals and other legal entities in the country, in foreign banks. The worries of this Court relate not merely to the quantum of monies said to have been secreted away in foreign banks, but also the manner in which they may have been taken away from the country, and with the nature of activities that may have engendered the accumulation of such monies. The worries of this Court are also with regard to the nature of activities that such monies may engender, both in terms of the concentration of economic power, and also the fact that such monies may be transferred to groups and individuals who may use them for unlawful activities that are extremely dangerous to the nation, including actions against the State. The worries of this Court also relate to whether the activities of engendering such unaccounted monies, transferring them abroad, and the routing them back to India may not actually be creating a culture that extols the virtue of such cycles, and the activities that engender such cycles are viewed as desirable modes of individual and group action.

6. The worries of this Court also relate to the manner, and the extent to which such cycles are damaging to both national and international attempts to combat the extent, nature and intensity of cross-border criminal activity. Finally, the worries of this Court are also with respect to the extent of incapacities, system wide, in terms of institutional resources, skills, and knowledge, as well as about incapacities of ethical nature, in keeping an account of the monies generated by various facets of social action in the country, and thereby developing effective mechanisms of control.

FAILURE TO CONTROL THE UNACCOUNTED MONEY GOING ABROAD IS FAILURE OF GOVERNANCE AS PER CONSTITUTIONAL IMPERATIVES

These incapacities go to the very heart of constitutional imperatives of governance. Whether such incapacities are on account of not having devoted enough resources towards building such capacities, or on account of a broader culture of venality in the wider spheres of social and political action, they run afoul of constitutional imperatives.

UNACCOUNTED MONEY IS UNLAWFUL IN ORIGIN AND ANTE-NATIONAL WHEN STASHED IN FOREIGN BANKS

7. Large amounts of unaccounted monies, stashed away in banks located in jurisdictions that thrive on strong privacy laws protecting bearers of those accounts to avoid scrutiny, raise each and every worry delineated above. First and foremost, such large monies stashed abroad, and unaccounted for by individuals and entities of a country, would suggest the necessity of suspecting that they have been generated in activities that have been deemed to be unlawful. In addition, such large amounts of unaccounted monies would also lead to a natural suspicion that they have been transferred out of the country in order to evade payment of taxes, thereby depleting the capacity of the nation to undertake many tasks that are in public interest.

PRIMARY FUNCTIONS OF A STATE

8. Many schools of thought exist with regard to the primary functions of the State, and the normative expectations of what the role of the State ought to be. The questions regarding which of those schools provide the absolutely correct view cannot be the criteria to choose or reject any specific school of thought as an aid in constitutional adjudication. Charged with the responsibility of having to make decisions in the present, within the constraints of epistemic frailties of human knowledge, constitutional adjudicators willy-nilly are compelled to choose those that seem to provide a reasoned basis for framing of questions relevant, both with respect to law, and to facts.

PROVIDING PUBLIC GOOD IS DUTY OF A STATE

9. Institutional economics gives one such perspective which may be a useful guide for us here. Viewed from a functional perspective, the State, and Governments, may be seen as coming into existence in order to solve, what institutional economists have come to refer to as, the coordination problems in providing public goods, and prevent the disutility that emerges from the moral hazard of a short run utility maximizer, who may desire the benefits of goods and services that are to be provided in common to the public, and yet have the interest of not paying for their production.

STATE BOUND TO STOP ACTIVITIES THAT STOP SOCIAL GOOD

10. Security of the nation, infrastructure of governance, including those that relate to law making and law keeping functions, crime prevention, detection and punishment, coordination of the economy, and ensuring minimal levels of material, and cultural goods for those who may not be in a position to fend for themselves or who have been left by the wayside by the operation of the economy and society, may all be cited as some examples of the kinds of public goods that the State is expected to provide for, or enable the provision of. In as much as the market is primarily expected to cater to purely self-centered activities of individuals and groups, markets and the domain of purely private social action significantly fail to provide such goods. Consequently, the State, and government, emerges to rectify the coordination problem, and provide the public goods.

NON-CONTROLLING OF STASHING OF ILLEGAL MONEY IN TAX HAVENS BY THE CITIZENS IS A CONSTITUTIONAL FAILURE OF THE GOVERNMENT

11. Unaccounted monies, especially large sums held by nationals and entities with a legal presence in the nation, in banks abroad, especially in tax havens or in jurisdictions with a known history of silence about sources of monies, clearly indicate a compromise of the ability of the State to manage its affairs in consonance with what is required from a constitutional perspective. This is so in two respects. The quantum of such monies by itself, along with the numbers of individuals or other legal entities who hold such monies, may indicate in the first instance that a large volume of activities, in the social and the economic spheres within the country are unlawful and causing great social damage, both at the individual and the collective levels. Secondly, large quanta of monies stashed abroad, would also indicate a substantial weakness in the capacity of the State in collection of taxes on incomes generated by individuals and other legal entities within the country. The generation of such revenues is essential for the State to undertake the various public goods and services that it is constitutionally mandated, and normatively expected by its citizenry, to provide. A substantial degree of incapacity, in the above respect, would be an indicia of the degree of failure of the State; and beyond a particular point, the State may spin into a vicious cycle of declining moral authority, thereby causing the incidence of unlawful activities in which wealth is sought to be generated, as well as instances of tax evasion, to increase in volume and in intensity.

STASHING OF ILLEGAL MONEY IN TAX HAVENS LIKELIHOOD OF UNHOLY NEXUS BETWEEN LAW MAKERS, LAW KEEPERS AND LAW BREAKERS – ARE INDICATIONS OF A SOFT STATE

12. Consequently, the issue of unaccounted monies held by nationals, and other legal entities, in foreign banks, is of primordial importance to the welfare of the citizens. The quantum of such monies may be rough indicators of the weakness of the State, in terms of both crime prevention, and also of tax collection. Depending on the volume of such monies, and the number of incidents through which such monies are generated and secreted away, it may very well reveal the degree of "softness of the State."

13. The concept of a "soft State" was famously articulated by the Nobel Laureate, Gunnar Myrdal. It is a broad based assessment of the degree to which the State, and its machinery, is equipped to deal with its responsibilities of governance. The more soft the State is, greater the likelihood that there is an unholy nexus between the law-maker, the law-keeper, and the law breaker.

STASHING OF ILLEGAL MONEY IN TAX HAVENS IS A BIGGER CRIME THAT THREATENS NATIONAL SECURITY

14. When a catch-all word like "crimes" is used, it is common for people, and the popular culture to assume that it is "petty crime," or crimes of passion committed by individuals. That would be a gross mischaracterization of the seriousness of the issues involved. Far more dangerous are the crimes that threaten national security, and national interest. For instance, with globalization, nation States are also confronted by the dark worlds of international arms dealers, drug peddlers, and various kinds of criminal networks, including networks of terror. International criminal networks that extend support to home-grown terror or extremist groups, or those that have been nurtured and sustained in hostile countries, depend on networks of formal and informal, lawful and unlawful mechanisms of transfer of monies across boundaries of nation-States. They work in the interstices of the micro-structures of financial transfers across the globe, and thrive in the lacunae, the gaps in law and of effort. The loosening of control over those mechanisms of transfers, guided by an extreme neo-liberal thirst to create a global market that is free of the friction of law and its enforcement, by nation-States, may have also contributed to an increase in the volume, extent and intensity of activities by criminal and terror networks across the globe.

STATE IS THEN CONTROLLED BY SUCH BLACK MONEY MAFIAS

15. Increasingly, on account of "greed is good" culture that has been promoted by neo-liberal ideologues, many countries face the situation where the model of capitalism that the State is compelled to institute, and the markets it spawns, is predatory in nature. From mining mafias to political operators who, all too willingly, bend policies of the State to suit particular individuals or groups in the social and economic sphere, the *raison d'etre* for weakening the capacities and intent to enforce the laws is the lure of the lucre. Even as the State provides violent support to those who benefit from such predatory capitalism, often violating the human rights of its citizens, particularly it's poor, the market begins to function like a bureaucratic machine dominated by big business; and the State begins to function like the market, where everything is available for sale at a price.

REDUCTION OF TAXES MAY POSSIBLY CHECK THE TREND OF BLACK MONEY

16. The paradigm of governance that has emerged, over the past three decades, prioritizes the market, and its natural course, over any degree of control of it by the State. The role for the State is visualized by votaries of the neo-liberal paradigm as that of a night watchman; and moreover it is also expected to take its hands out of the till of the wealth generating machinery. Based on the theories of Arthur Laffer, and pushed by the Washington Consensus, the prevailing wisdom of the elite, and of the policy makers, is that reduction of tax rates, thereby making tax regimes regressive, would incentivise the supposed genius of entrepreneurial souls of individuals, actuated by pursuit of self-interest and desire to accumulate great economic power. It was expected that this would enable the generation of more wealth, at a more rapid pace, thereby enabling the State to generate appropriate tax revenues even with lowered tax rates. Further, benefits were also expected in moral terms – that the lowering of tax rates would reduce the incentivise of wealth generators to hide their monies, thereby saving them from the guilt of tax evasion. Whether that is an appropriate model of social organisation or not, and from the perspective of constitutional adjudication, whether it meets the requirements of constitutionalism as embedded in the texts of various Constitutions, is not a question that we want to enter in this matter.

STATE MUST FOLLOW THE MONEY TO SAVE THE NATION FROM DISASTROUS RESULTS AND SHOULD NOT LOOK THE OTHER WAY

17. Nevertheless, it would be necessary to note that there is a fly in the ointment of the above story of friction free markets that would always clear, and always work to the benefit of the society. The strength of tax collection machinery can, and ought to be, expected to have a direct bearing on the revenues collected by the State. If the machinery is weak, understaffed, ideologically motivated to look the other way, or the agents motivated by not so salubrious motives, the amount of revenue collected by the State would decline, stagnate, or may not generate the revenue for the State that is consonant with its responsibilities. From within the neo-liberal paradigm, also emerged the under-girding current of thought that revenues for the State implies a big government, and hence a strong tax collecting machinery itself would be undesirable. Where the elite lose out in democratic politics of achieving ever decreasing tax rates, it would appear that State machineries in the hands of the Executive, all too willing to promote the extreme versions of the neo-liberal paradigm and co-opt itself in the enterprises of the elite, may also become all too willing to not develop substantial capacities to monitor and follow the money, collect the lawfully mandated taxes, and even look the other way. The results, as may be expected, have been disastrous across many nations.

FAILURE TO CONTROL ILLEGAL MONEY AMOUNTS TO IGNORING SCAMs

18. In addition, it would also appear that in this miasmic cultural environment in which greed is extolled, conspicuous consumption viewed as both necessary and socially valuable, and the wealthy viewed as demi-Gods, the agents of the

State may have also succumbed to the notions of the neo-liberal paradigm that the role of the State ought to only be an enabling one, and not exercise significant control. This attitude would have a significant impact on exercise of discretion, especially in the context of regulating economic activities, including keeping an account of the monies generated in various activities, both legal and illegal. Carried away by the ideology of neo-liberalism, it is entirely possible that the agents of the State entrusted with the task of supervising the economic and social activities may err more on the side of extreme caution, whereby signals of wrong doing may be ignored even when they are strong. Instances of the powers that be ignoring publicly visible stock market scams, or turning a blind eye to large scale illegal mining have become all too familiar, and may be readily cited. That such activities are allowed to continue to occur, with weak, or non-existent, responses from the State may, at best, be charitably ascribed to this broader culture of permissibility of all manner of private activities in search of ever more lucre. Ethical compromises, by the elite – those who wield the powers of the State, and those who fatten themselves in an ever more exploitative economic sphere – can be expected to thrive in an environment marked by such a permissive attitude, of weakened laws, and of weakened law enforcement machineries and attitudes.

FAILURE ON THIS FRONT REVEALS LACK OF WILL BETWEEN VARIOUS GOVERNMENTAL DEPARTMENTS TO CONTROL IT

19. To the above, we must also add the fragmentation of administration. Even as the range of economic, and social activities have expanded, and their sophistication increased by leaps and bounds, the response in terms of administration by the State has been to create ever more specialized agencies, and departments. To some degree this has been unavoidable. Nevertheless, it would also appear that there is a need to build internal capacities to share information across such departments, lessen the informational asymmetries between, and friction to flow of information across the boundaries of departments and agencies, and reduce the levels of consequent problems in achieving coordination. Life, and social action within which human life becomes possible, do not proceed on the basis of specialized fiefdoms of expertise. They cut across the boundaries erected as a consequence of an inherent tendency of experts to specialize. The result, often, is a system-wide blindness, while yet being lured by the dazzle of ever greater specialization. Many dots of information, now collected in ever increasing volume by development of sophisticated information technologies, get ignored on account of lack of coordination across agencies, and departments, and tendency within bureaucracy to jealously guard their own turfs. In some instances, the failure to properly investigate, or to prevent, unlawful activities could be the result of such over-specialization, frictions in sharing of information, and coordination across departmental and specialized agency boundaries.

SOFT STATE LOOSES MORAL AUTHORITY

20. If the State is soft to a large extent, especially in terms of the unholy nexus between the law makers, the law-keepers, and the law-breakers, the moral authority, and also the moral incentives, to exercise suitable control over the economy and the society would vanish. Large unaccounted monies are generally an indication of that.

RULERS BECOME RICH BUT SOCIETY DEGENERATES (BECOMES POORER)

21. In a recent book, Prof. Rotberg states, after evaluating many failed and collapsed States over the past few decades:

> *"...Failed States offer unparalleled economic opportunity – but only for a privileged few. Those around the ruler or ruling oligarchy grow richer while their less fortunate brethren starve. Immense profits are available from an awareness of regulatory advantages and currency speculation and arbitrage. But the privilege of making real money when everything else is deteriorating is confined to clients of the ruling elite.... The nation State's responsibility to maximize the well-being and prosperity of all its citizens is conspicuously absent, if it ever existed.... Corruption flourishes in many States, but in failed States it often does so on an unusually destructive scale. There is widespread petty or lubricating corruption as a matter of course, but escalating levels of venal corruption mark failed States."* ["The Failure and Collapse of Nation-States – Breakdown, Prevention and Repair" in Rofferg, Robert I., Ed. "When State Fail: Causes And Consequences, Princeton University Press (2004).]

INDIANS HAVE STASHED ILLEGAL MONEY IN TAX HAVEN COUNTRIES AT AN ASTRONOMICAL LEVEL

22. India finds itself in a peculiar situation. Often celebrated, in popular culture, as an emerging economy that is rapidly growing, and expected to be a future economic and political giant on the global stage, it is also popularly perceived, and apparently even in some responsible and scholarly circles, and official quarters, that some of its nationals and other legal entities have stashed the largest quantum of unaccounted monies in foreign banks, especially in tax havens, and in other jurisdictions with strong laws of secrecy. There are also apparently reports, and analyses, generated by Government of India itself, which place the amounts of such unaccounted monies at astronomical levels.

THERE SHOULD BE SERIOUS AND PURPOSEFUL DEBATE ON THE ILLEGAL MONEY DEPOSITED IN FOREIGN BANKS

23. We do not wish to engage in any speculation as to what such analyses, reports, and factuality imply with respect to the state of the nation. The citizens of our country can make, and ought to be making, rational assessments of the situation. We fervently hope that it leads to responsible, reasoned and reasonable debate, thereby exerting the appropriate democratic pressure on the State, and its agents, within the constitutional framework, to bring about the necessary changes without sacrificing cherished, and inherently invaluable social goals and values enshrined in the Constitution.

FAULT LIES NOT IN THE CONSTITUTION BUT IN POLITICO-BUREAUCRATIC POWER WIELDING PEOPLE

24. The failures are discernible when viewed against the vision of the constitutional project, and as forewarned by Dr. Ambedkar, have been on account of the fact that man has been vile, and not the defects of a Constitution forged in the fires of wisdom gathered over eons of human experience. If the politico-bureaucratic, power wielding, and business classes bear a large part of the blame, at least some part of blame ought to be apportioned to those portions of the citizenry that is well informed, or is expected to be informed. Much of that citizenry has disengaged itself with the political process, and with the masses.

ELITE GAINS AT THE COST OF DOWN-TRODDEN AND POOR PEOPLE – CITIZENRY SHOULD WAKE-UP

Informed by contempt for the poor and the down trodden, the elite classes that have benefited the most, or expects to benefit substantially from the neo-liberal policies that would wish away the hordes, has also chosen to forget that constitutional mandate is as much the responsibility of the citizenry, and through their constant vigilance, of all the organs of the State, and national institutions including political parties. To not be engaged in the process, is to ensure the evisceration of constitutional content. Knee jerk reactions, and ill-advised tinkering with the constitutional framework are not the solutions. The road is always long, and needs the constant march of the citizenry on it. There is no other way. To expect instant solutions, because this law or that body is formed, without striving to solve system wide, and systemic, problems that have emerged is to not understand the demands of a responsible citizenry in modern constitutional republican democracies.

NAMED OR UNNAMED COUNTRYMEN WHO HAVE DEPOSITED MONEY IN TAX HAVEN COUNTRIES ARE NOT BEING INVESTIGATED

25. These matters before us relate to issues of large sums of unaccounted monies, allegedly held by certain named individuals, and loose associations of them; consequently we have to express our serious concerns from a constitutional perspective. The amount of unaccounted monies, as alleged by the Government of India itself is massive. The show cause notices were issued a substantial length of time ago. The named individuals were very much present in the country. Yet, for unknown, and possibly unknowable, though easily surmisable, reasons the investigations into the matter proceeded at a laggardly pace. Even the named individuals had not yet been questioned with any degree of seriousness. These are serious lapses, especially when viewed from the perspective of larger issues of security, both internal and external, of the country.

SIGNIFICANT QUESTIONS CONSIDERED BY THE SUPREME COURT

26. It is in light of the above, that we heard some significant elements of the instant writ petitions filed in this Court, and at this stage it is necessary that appropriate orders be issued. There are two issues we deal with below:

(i) the appointment of a Special Investigation Team; and

(ii) disclosure, to the Petitioners, of certain documents relied upon by the Union of India in its response.

PART II

PETITIONERS ARE HIGH STATUS WHO THINK SERIOUSLY ABOUT THE NATION AND ITS PEOPLE

27. The instant writ petition was filed, in 2009, by Shri Ram Jethmalani, Shri Gopal Sharman, Smt. Jalbala Vaidya, Shri K.P.S. Gill, Prof. B.B. Dutta, and

Shri Subhash Kashyap, all well-known professionals, social activists, former bureaucrats or those who have held responsible positions in the society. They have also formed an organization called Citizen India, the stated objective of which is said to be to bring about changes and betterment in the quality of governance, and functioning of all public institutions.

PETITONERS ALLEGE ILLEGAL AND UNACCOUNTED MONEY DEPOSITED IN TAX HEVEN COUNTRIES

28. The Petitioners state that there have been a slew of reports, in the media, and also in scholarly publications that various individuals, mostly citizens, but may also include non-citizens, and other entities with presence in India, have generated, and secreted away large sums of monies, through their activities in India or relating to India, in various foreign banks, especially in tax havens, and jurisdictions that have strong secrecy laws with respect to the contents of bank accounts and the identities of individuals holding such accounts. The Petitioners allege that most of such monies are unaccounted, and in all probability have been generated through unlawful activities, whether in India or outside India, but relating to India. Further, the Petitioners also allege that a large part of such monies may have been generated within India, and have been taken away from India, breaking various laws, including but not limited to evasion of taxes.

WEAK GOVERNMENT IS THE REASON – PETITIONERS ALLEGE

29. The Petitioners contend:

(i) that the sheer volume of such monies points to grave weaknesses in the governance of the nation, because they indicate a significant lack of control over unlawful activities through which such monies are generated, evasion of taxes, and use of unlawful means of transfer of funds;

(ii) that these funds are then laundered and brought back into India, to be used in both legal and illegal activities;

(iii) that the use of various unlawful modes of transfer of funds across borders, gives support to such unlawful networks of international finance; and

(iv) that in as much as such unlawful networks are widely acknowledged to also effectuate transfer of funds across borders in aid of various crimes committed against persons and the State, including but not limited to activities that may be classifiable as terrorist, extremist, or unlawful narcotic trade, the prevailing situation also has very serious connotations for the security and integrity of India.

BLACK MONEY MAY BE OF POWERFUL PERSONS – GOVERNMENT NOT INVESTIGATING – ALLEGE PETITIONERS

30. The Petitioners also further contend that a significant part of such large unaccounted monies include the monies of powerful persons in India, including leaders of many political parties. It was also contended that the Government of India, and its agencies, have been very lax in terms of keeping an eye on the various unlawful activities generating unaccounted monies, the consequent tax evasion; and that such laxity extends to efforts to curtail the flow of such funds out, and into, India. Further, the Petitioners also contend that the efforts to prosecute the individuals, and other entities, who have secreted such monies in foreign banks, have been weak or non-existent. It was strongly argued that the efforts at identification of such monies in various bank accounts in many jurisdictions across the globe, attempts to bring back such monies, and efforts to strengthen the governance framework to prevent further outflows of such funds, have been sorely lacking.

DERELICTION OF DUTY BY CENTRAL GOVERNMENT – ALLEGE PETITIONERS

31. The Petitioners also made allegations about certain specific incidents and patterns of dereliction of duty, wherein the Government of India, and its various agencies, even though in possession of specific knowledge about the monies in certain bank accounts, and having estimated that such monies run into many scores of thousands of crores, and upon issuance of show cause notices to the said individual, surprisingly have not proceeded to initiate, and carry out suitable investigations, and prosecute the individuals.

HASSAN ALI AND TAPURIAS DEPOSITED BLACK MONEY IN TAX HAVEN COUNTRIES – NO ACTION TAKEN – ALLEGE PETITIONERS

The individual specifically named is one Hassan Ali Khan. The Petitioners also contended that Kashinath Tapuria, and his wife Chandrika Tapuria, are also party to the illegal activities of Hassan Ali Khan.

32. Specifically, it was alleged that Hassan Ali Khan was served with an Income-tax demand for Rs. 40,000.00 Crores (Rupees Forty Thousand Crores), and that the Tapurias were served an Income-tax demand notice of Rs. 20,580.00 Crores (Rupees Twenty Thousand and Five Hundred and Eighty Crores). The Enforcement Directorate, in 2007, disclosed that Hassan Ali Khan had "dealings amounting to 1.6 billion US dollars" in the period 2001-2005. In January 2007, upon raiding Hassan Ali's residence in Pune, certain documents and evidence had been discovered regarding deposits of 8.04 billion dollars with UBS bank in Zurich.

33. It is the contention of the Petitioners that, even though such evidence was secured nearly four and half years ago,

(i) a proper investigation had not been launched to obtain the right facts from abroad;

(ii) the individuals concerned, though present in India, and subject to its jurisdiction, and easily available for its exercise, had not even been interrogated appropriately;

(iii) that the Union of India, and its various departments, had even been refusing to divulge the details and information that would reveal the actual status of the investigation, whether in fact it was being conducted at all, or with any degree of seriousness;

(iv) given the magnitude of amounts in question, especially of the demand notice of Income-tax, the laxity of investigation indicates multiple problems of serious non-governance, and weaknesses in the system, including pressure from political quarters to hinder, or scuttle, the investigation, prosecution, and ultimately securing the return of such monies; and

(v) given the broadly accepted fact that within the political class corruption is rampant, ill-begotten wealth has begun to be amassed in massive quantities by many members in that class, it may be reasonable to suspect, or even conclude, that investigation was being deliberately hindered because Hassan Ali Khan, and the Tapurias, had or were continuing to handle the monies of such a class. The fact that both Income-tax Department, and the Enforcement Directorate routinely, and with alacrity, seek the powers for long stretches of custodial interrogation of even those suspected of having engaged in money laundering, or evaded taxes, with respect to very small amounts, ought to raise the reasonable suspicion that inaction in the matters concerning Hassan Ali Khan, and Tapurias, was deliberately engineered, for nefarious reasons.

USA SUCCEEDED TO GET BACK ILLEGAL MONEY DEPOSITED BY THEIR CITIZENS IN TAX HAVEN COUNTRIES – BUT INACTION OF UNION OF INDIA IS SHOCKING ALLEGE PETITIONERS

34. In addition, the Petitioners also state that in as much as the bank in which the monies had been stashed by Hassan Ali Khan was UBS Zurich, the needle of suspicion has to inexorably turn to high level political interference and hindrance to the investigations. The said bank, it was submitted, is the biggest or one of the biggest wealth management companies in the world. The Petitioners also narrated the mode, and the manner, in which the United States had dealt with UBS, with respect to monies of American citizens secreted away with the said bank. It was also alleged that UBS had not cooperated with the U.S. authorities. Contrasting the relative alacrity, and vigour, with which the United States Government had pursued the matters, the Petitioners contend the inaction of Union of India is shocking.

UBS BANK DEALS IN SHADDY TRANSACTIONS – GOVERNMENT ALLOWED IT TO OPEN ITS BRANCH IN INDIA – ALLEGE PETITIONERS

35. The Petitioners further allege that in 2007, the Reserve Bank of India had obtained some "knowledge of the dubious character" of UBS Security India Private Limited, a branch of UBS, and consequently stopped this bank from extending its business in India by refusing to approve its takeover of Standard Chartered Mutual Funds business in India. It was also claimed by the Petitioners that the SEBI had alleged that UBS played a role in the stock market crash of 2004. The said UBS Bank has apparently applied for a retail banking license in India, which was approved in principle by RBI initially. In 2008, this license was withheld on the ground that "investigation of its unsavoury role in the Hassan Ali Khan case was pending investigation in the Enforcement Directorate." However, it seems that the RBI reversed its decision in 2009, and no good reasons seem to be forthcoming for the reversal of the decision of 2008.

BLACK MONEY WOULD NEVER BE UNEARTHED TILL S.I.T. IS APPOINTED BY SUPREME COURT UNDER ITS CONTROL – ALLEGE PETITIONERS

The Petitioners contend that such a reversal of decision could only have been accomplished through high level intervention, and that it is further evidence of linkages between members of the political class, and possibly even members of the bureaucracy, and such banking operations, and the illegal activities of Hassan Ali Khan and the Tapurias. Hence, the Petitioners argued, in the circumstances it would have to be necessarily concluded that the investigations into the affairs of Hassan Ali Khan, and the Tapurias, would be severely compromised if the Court does not intervene, and monitor the investigative processes by appointing a special investigation team reporting directly to the Court.

FAILURE OF THE GOVERNMENT HITS THE FUNDAMENTAL RIGHTS OF ITS PEOPLE – ALLEGE PETITIONERS

36. The learned senior counsel for the Petitioners sought that this Court intervene, order proper investigations, and monitor continuously, the actions of the Union of India, and any and all governmental departments and agencies, in these matters. It was submitted that their filing of this Writ Petition under article 32 is proper, as the inaction of the Union of India, as described above, violates the fundamental rights – to proper governance, in as much as article 14 provides for equality before the law and equal protection of the law, and article 21 promises dignity of life to all citizens.

DISCUSSION BY SUPREME COURT

37. We have heard the learned senior counsel for the Petitioners, Shri Anil B. Divan, the learned senior counsel for interveners, Shri K.K. Venugopal, and the learned senior counsel for the petitioners in the connected Writ Petition, Shri Shanti Bhushan. We have also heard the learned Solicitor General, Shri Gopal Subramaniam, on behalf of the respondents.

38. Shri Divan, specifically argued that, having regard to the nature of the investigation, its slow pace so far, and the non-seriousness on the part of the respondents, there is a need to constitute a Special Investigation Team ("SIT") headed by a former judge or two of this Court.

GOVERNMENT OPPOSES IT BUT RELUCTANTLY AGREES TO IT

However, this particular plea has been vociferously resisted by the Solicitor General. Relying on the status reports submitted from time to time, the learned Solicitor General stated that all possible steps were being taken to bring back the monies stashed in foreign banks, and that the investigations in cases registered were proceeding in an appropriate manner. He expressed his willingness for a Court monitored investigation. He also further submitted that the Respondents, in principle, have no objections whatsoever against the main submissions of the Petitioners.

REAL POINT AT ISSUE SAYS SUPREME COURT

39. The real point of controversy is, given above, as to whether there is a need to constitute a SIT to be headed by a judge or two, of this court, to supervise the investigation.

ACTION OF THE CENTRAL GOVERNMENT WAS VERY POOR, SLOW AND CASUAL – NO SATISFACTORY EXPLANATION

40. We must express our serious reservations about the responses of the Union of India. In the first instance, during the earlier phases of hearing before us, the attempts were clearly evasive, confused, or originating in the denial mode. It was only upon being repeatedly pressed by us did the Union of India begin to admit that indeed the investigation was proceeding very slowly. It also became clear to us that in fact the investigation had completely stalled, in as much as custodial interrogation of Hassan Ali Khan had not even been sought for, even though he was very much resident in India. Further, it also now appears that even though his passport had been impounded, he was able to secure another passport from the RPO in Patna, possibly with the help or aid of a politician.

BREACH OF CONSTITUTIONAL DUTY BY THE CENTRAL GOVERNMENT

41. During the course of the hearings the Union of India repeatedly insisted that the matter involves many jurisdictions, across the globe, and a proper investigation could be accomplished only through the concerted efforts by different law enforcement agencies, both within the Central Government, and also various State Governments. However, the absence of any satisfactory explanation of the slowness of the pace of investigation, and lack of any credible answers as to why the respondents did not act with respect to those actions that were feasible, and within the ambit of powers of the Enforcement Directorate itself, such as custodial investigation, leads us to conclude that the lack of seriousness in the efforts of the respondents are contrary to the requirements of laws and constitutional obligations of the Union of India. It was only upon the insistence and intervention of this Court has the Enforcement Directorate initiated and secured custodial interrogation over Hassan Ali Khan.

UNION OF INDIA ADMITTED – MUCH WAS DESIRED TO BE DONE

42. The Union of India has explicitly acknowledged that there was much to be desired with the manner in which the investigation had proceeded prior to the intervention of this Court.

HASSAN ALI AND TAPURIAS INTERROGATED AT THE INSISTENCE OF SUPREME COURT – MANY NAMES OF POLITICALLY POWERFUL PERSONS CROPPED UP

From the more recent reports, it would appear that the Union of India, on account of its more recent efforts to conduct the investigation with seriousness, on account of the gravitas brought by this Court, has led to the securing of additional information, and leads, which could aid in further investigation. For instance, during the continuing interrogation of Hassan Ali Khan and the Tapurias, undertaken for the first time at the behest of this Court, many names of important persons, including leaders of some corporate giants, politically powerful people, and international arms dealers have cropped up. So far, no significant attempt has been made to investigate and verify the same.

THIS NECESSITATES THE CONSTITUTION OF S.I.T. MONITORED BY THE SUPREME COURT

This is a further cause for the grave concerns of this Court, and points to the need for continued, effective and day to day monitoring by a S.I.T. constituted by this Court, and acting on behalf, behest and direction of this Court.

CENTRAL GOVERNMENT CLAIMS TO HAVE CONSTITUTED HIGH LEVEL COMMITTEE

43. In light of the fact that the issues are complex, requiring expertise and knowledge of different departments, and the necessity of coordination of efforts across various agencies and departments, it was submitted to us that the Union of India has recently formed a High Level Committee, under the aegis of the Department of Revenue in the Ministry of Finance, which is the nodal agency responsible for all economic offences. The composition of the High Level Committee ("HLC") is said to be as follows:

(i) Secretary, Department of Revenue, as the Chairman;
(ii) Deputy Governor, Reserve Bank of India;
(iii) Director (IB);
(iv) Director, Enforcement;
(v) Director, CBI;
(vi) Chairman, CBDT;
(vii) DG, Narcotics Control Bureau;
(viii) DG, Revenue Intelligence;
(ix) Director, Financial Intelligence Unit; and
(x) JS (FT & TRI), CBDT.

It was also submitted that the HLC may co-opt, as necessary, representation not below the rank of Joint Secretary from the Home Secretary, Foreign Secretary, Defense Secretary and the Secretary, Cabinet Secretariat.

UNION OF INDIA CLAIMS THIS COMMITTEE WOULD UNEARTH BLACK MONEY

The Union of India claims that such a multi-disciplinary group and Committee would now enable the conducting of an efficient and a systematic investigation into the matters concerning allegations against Hassan Ali Khan and the Tapurias; and further that such a Committee would also enable the taking of appropriate steps to bring back the monies stashed in foreign banks, for which purposes a need may arise to register further cases. The Union of India also claims that the formation of such a Committee indicates the seriousness with which it is viewing the entire matter.

EVEN THEN CENTRAL GOVERNMENT MOVING EXTREMELY SLOW – NO URGENCY, NO SINCERE EFFORTS SHOWN

44. While it would appear, from the Status Reports submitted to this Court, that the Enforcement Directorate has moved in some small measure, the actual facts are not comforting to an appropriate extent. In fact we are not convinced that the situation has changed to the extent that it ought to so as to accept that the investigation would now be conducted with the degree of seriousness that is warranted. According to the Union of India the HLC was formed in order to take charge of and direct the entire investigation, and subsequently, the prosecution. In the meanwhile a charge sheet has been filed against Hassan Ali Khan. Upon inquiry by us as to whether the charge-sheet had been vetted by the HLC, and its inputs secured, the counsel for Union of India were flummoxed. The fact was that the charge-sheet had not been given even for the perusal of the HLC, let alone securing its inputs, guidance and direction. We are not satisfied by the explanation offered by the Directorate of Enforcement by way of affidavit after the orders were reserved. Be it noted that a nodal agency was set up, pursuant to directions of this Court in *Vineet Narain* case given many years ago. Yet the same was not involved and these matters were never placed before it. Why?

45. From the status reports, it is clear that the problem is extremely complex, and many agencies and departments spread across the country have not responded with the alacrity, and urgency, that one would desire.

LICENCE GRANTED TO UBS AFTER REVERSING EARLIER ORDER AT THE COST OF CONSTITUTIONAL CONCERN – PLEA TAKEN BY THE CENTRAL GOVERNMENT FICTITIOUS

Moreover, the Union of India has been unable to answer any of the questions regarding its past actions, and their implications, such as the slowness of the investigation, or about grant of license to conduct retail banking by UBS, by reversing the decision taken earlier to withhold such a license on the grounds that the said bank's credentials were suspect. To this latter query, the stance of the Union of India has been that entry of UBS would facilitate flow of foreign investments into India.

NO NEED TO COMMENT ON THE SO CALLED SINCERE EFFORTS OF UNION OF INDIA

46. The question that arises is whether the task of bringing foreign funds into India override all other constitutional concerns and obligations?

47. The predominant theme in the responses of Union of India before this Court has been that it is doing all that it can to bring back the unaccounted monies stashed in various banks abroad. To this is added the qualifier that it is an extremely complex problem, requiring the cooperation of many different jurisdictions, and an internationally coordinated effort. Indeed they are complex. We do not wish to go into the details of arguments about whether the Union of India is, or is not, doing necessary things to achieve such goals. That is not necessary for the matters at hand.

UNION OF INDIA KNEW THAT HASSAN ALI HAS CONNECTIONS WITH INTERNATIONAL ARMS-DEALERS

48. What is important is that the Union of India had obtained knowledge, documents and information that indicated possible connections between Hassan Ali Khan, and his alleged co-conspirators and known international arms dealers. Further, the Union of India was also in possession of information that suggested that because the international arms dealing network, and a very prominent dealer in it, could not open a bank account even in a jurisdiction that is generally acknowledged to lay great emphasis on not asking sources of money being deposited into its banks, Hassan Ali Khan may have played a crucial role in opening an account with the branch of the same bank in another jurisdiction.

HASSAN ALI AND TAPURIAS LIABLE TO PAY THOUSANDS OF CRORES OF RUPEES AS INCOME TAX EVEN WHEN THEY HAVE NO KNOWN SOURCES OF INCOME

The volume of alleged Income-taxes owed to the country, as demanded by the Union of India itself, and the volume of monies, by some accounts US $8.04 billion, and some other accounts in excess of Rs. 70,000 crores, that are said to have been routed through various bank accounts of Hassan Ali Khan, and Tapurias. Further, from all accounts it has been acknowledged that none of the named individuals have any known and lawful sources for such huge quantities of monies.

NOT ONLY INCOME TAX, NATIONAL SECURITY INVOLVED

49. All of these factors, either individually or combined, ought to have immediately raised questions regarding the sources being unlawful activities, national security, and transfer of funds into India for other illegal activities, including acts against the State. It was only at the repeated insistence by us that such matters have equal, if not even greater importance than issues of tax collection, has the Union of India belatedly concluded that such aspects also ought to be investigated with thoroughness. However, there is still no evidence of a really serious investigation into these other matters from the national security perspective.

STEPS TAKEN BY CENTRAL GOVERNMENT BY CONSTITUTING HPC – NOT INSUFFICIENT

50. The fact remains that the Union of India has struggled in conducting a proper investigation into the affairs of Hassan Ali Khan and the Tapurias. While some individuals, whose names have come to the adverse knowledge of the Union of India, through the more recent investigations, have been interrogated, many more are yet to be investigated. This highly complex investigation has in fact just begun. It is still too early to conclude that the Union of India has indeed placed all the necessary machinery to conduct a proper investigation. The formation of the HLC was a necessary step, and may even be characterized as a welcome step. Nevertheless, it is an insufficient step.

NOTHING ACHIEVED IN 4 YEARS BY HIGH LEVEL COMMITTEE – CONVERTED INTO S.I.T. HEADED BY TWO SUPREME COURT JUDGES (RETD.) – GOVERNMENT OPPOSES IT – BUT NO REASON

51. In light of the above, we had proposed to the Union of India that the same HLC constituted by it be converted into a Special Investigation Team, headed by two retired judges of the Supreme Court of India. The Union of India opposes the same, but provides no principle as to why that would be undesirable, especially in light of the many lapses and lacunae in its actions in these matters spread over the past four years.

MONITORING BY SUPREME COURT IS ITS CONSTITUTIONAL OBLIGATION – BUT ON DAY TO DAY BASIS NOT POSSIBLE – HENCE TWO RETIRED SUPREME COURT JUDGES

52. We are of the firm opinion that in these matters fragmentation of government, and expertise and knowledge, across many departments, agencies and across various jurisdictions, both within the country, and across the globe, is a serious impediment to the conduct of a proper investigation. We hold that it is in fact necessary to create a body that coordinates, directs, and where necessary orders timely and urgent action by various institutions of the State. We also hold that the continued involvement of this Court in these matters, in a broad oversight capacity, is necessary for upholding the rule of law, and achievement of constitutional values. However, it would be impossible for this Court to be involved in day to day investigations, or to constantly monitor each and every aspect of the investigation.

53. The resources of this Court are scarce, and it is overburdened with the task of rendering justice in well over a lakh of cases every year. Nevertheless, this Court is bound to uphold the Constitution, and its own burdens, excessive as they already are, cannot become an excuse for it to not perform that task. In a country where most of its people are uneducated and illiterate, suffering from hunger and squalor, the retraction of the monitoring of these matters by this Court would be unconscionable.

CENTRAL GOVERNMENT UNDER CONSTITUTIONAL OBLIGATION TO BRING BACK BLACK MONEY STASHED IN FOREIGN BANKS

54. The issue is not merely whether the Union of India is making the necessary effort to bring back all or some significant part of the alleged monies. The fact that there is some information and knowledge that such vast amounts may have been stashed away in foreign banks, implies that the State has the primordial responsibility, under the Constitution, to make every effort to trace the sources of such monies, punish the guilty where such monies have been generated and/or taken abroad through unlawful activities, and bring back the monies owed to the Country. We do recognise that the degree of success, measured in terms of the amounts of monies brought back, is dependent on a number of factors, including aspects that relate to international political economy and relations, which may or may not be under our control.

CRIMINAL NEXUS – THREAT TO NATIONAL SECURITY – NOT EVEN EXAMINED

The fact remains that with respect to those factors that were within the powers of the Union of India, such as investigation of possible criminal nexus, threats to national security etc., were not even attempted.

SAFETY OF MORALITY, INTEGRITY AND CONSTITUTIONAL PROJECTS – BOUNDEN DUTY OF CENTRAL GOVERNMENT

Fealty to the Constitution is not a matter of mere material success; but, and probably more importantly from the perspective of the moral authority of the State, a matter of integrity of effort on all the dimensions that inform a problem that threatens the constitutional projects. Further, the degree of seriousness with which efforts are made with respect to those various dimensions can also be expected to bear fruit in terms of building capacities, and the development of necessary attitudes to take the law enforcement part of accounting or following the money seriously in the future.

BLACK MONEY WHEN BROUGHT BACK WOULD MAKE EVEN THE POOR CHEERFUL

55. The merits of vigour of investigations, and attempts at law enforcement, cannot be measured merely on the scale of what we accomplish with respect to what has happened in the past. It would necessarily also have to be appreciated from the benefits that are likely to accrue to the country in preventing such activities in the future. Our people may be poor, and may be suffering from all manner of deprivation. However, the same poor and suffering masses are rich, morally and from a humanistic point of view. Their forbearance of the many foibles and failures of those who wield power, no less in their name and behalf than of the rich and the empowered, is itself indicative of their great qualities, of humanity, trust and tolerance. That greatness can only be matched by exercise of every sinew, and every resource, in the broad goal of our constitutional project of bringing to their lives dignity. The efforts that this Court makes in this regard, and will make in this respect and these matters, can only be conceived as a small and minor, though nevertheless necessary, part. Ultimately, the protection of the Constitution and striving to promote its vision and values is an elemental mode of service to our people.

S.I.Ts. CONSTITUTED EARLIER ALSO IN OTHER CASES

56. We note that in many instances, in the past, when issues referred to the Court have been very complex in nature, and yet required the intervention of the Court, Special Investigation Teams have been ordered and constituted in order to enable the Court, and the Union of India and/or other organs of the State, to fulfil their constitutional obligations. The following instances may be noted: *Vineet Narain* v. *Union of India*, (1996) 2 SCC 199.

NHRC v. *State of Gujarat*, (2004) 8 SCC 610;

Sanjiv Kumar v. *State of Haryana*, (2005) 5 SCC 517; and

Centre for PIL v. *Union of India*, (2011) 1 SCC 560.

NOW S.I.T WITH TWO RETIRED SUPREME COURT JUDGES AS CHAIRMAN AND VICE-CHAIRMAN WILL CONSIST AS UNDER

57. In light of the above we herewith order:

(i) That the High Level Committee constituted by the Union of India, comprising of:

(a) Secretary, Department of Revenue;

(b) Deputy Governor, Reserve Bank of India;

(c) Director (IB);

(d) Director, Enforcement;

(e) Director, CBI;

(f) Chairman, CBDT;

(g) DG, Narcotics Control Bureau;

(h) DG, Revenue Intelligence;

(i) Director, Financial Intelligence Unit; and

(j) JS (FT & TR-I), CBDT be forthwith appointed with immediate effect as a Special Investigation Team;

(ii) That the Special Investigation Team, so constituted, also include Director, Research and Analysis Wing;

(iii) That the above Special Investigation Team, so constituted, be headed by and include the following former eminent judges of this Court:

(a) Hon'ble Mr. Justice B.P. Jeevan Reddy as Chairman; and

(b) Hon'ble Mr. Justice M.B. Shah as Vice-Chairman;

and that the Special Investigation Team function under their guidance and direction;

(iv) That the Special Investigation Team, so constituted, shall be charged with the responsibilities and duties of investigation, initiation of proceedings, and prosecution, whether in the context of appropriate criminal or civil proceedings of:

(a) all issues relating to the matters concerning and arising from unaccounted monies of Hassan Ali Khan and the Tapurias;

(b) all other investigations already commenced and are pending, or awaiting to be initiated, with respect to any other known instances of the stashing of unaccounted monies in foreign bank accounts by Indians or other entities operating in India; and

(c) all other matters with respect to unaccounted monies being stashed in foreign banks by Indians or other entities operating in India that may arise in the course of such investigations and proceedings.

It is clarified here that within the ambit of responsibilities described above, also lie the responsibilities to ensure that the matters are also investigated, proceedings initiated and prosecutions conducted with regard to criminality and/or unlawfulness of activities that may have been the source for such monies, as well as the criminal and/or unlawful means that are used to take such unaccounted monies out of and/or bring such monies back into the country, and use of such monies in India or abroad. The Special Investigation Team shall also be charged with the responsibility of preparing a comprehensive action plan, including the creation of necessary institutional structures that can enable and strengthen the country's battle against generation of unaccounted monies, and their stashing away in foreign banks or in various forms domestically.

(v) That the Special Investigation Team so constituted report and be responsible to this Court, and that it shall be charged with the duty to keep this Court informed of all major developments by the filing of periodic status reports, and following of any special orders that this Court may issue from time to time;

(vi) That all organs, agencies, departments and agents of the State, whether at the level of the Union of India, or the State Government, including but not limited to all statutorily formed individual bodies, and other constitutional bodies, extend all the cooperation necessary for the Special Investigation Team so constituted and functioning;

(vii) That the Union of India, and where needed even the State Governments, are directed to facilitate the conduct of the investigations, in their fullest measure, by the Special Investigation Team so constituted and functioning, by extending all the necessary financial, material, legal, diplomatic and intelligence resources, whether such investigations or portions of such investigations occur inside the country or abroad.

(viii) That the Special Investigation Team also be empowered to further investigate even where charge-sheets have been previously filed; and that the Special Investigation Team may register further cases, and conduct appropriate investigations and initiate proceedings, for the purpose of bringing back unaccounted monies unlawfully kept in bank accounts abroad.

CENTRAL GOVERNMENT DIRECTED TO ISSUE NOTIFICATION OF THE CONSTITUTION OF S.I.T.

58. We accordingly direct the Union of India to issue appropriate notification and publish the same forthwith. It is needless to clarify that the former judges of this Court so appointed to supervise the Special Investigation Team are entitled to their remuneration, allowances, perks, facilities as that of the judges of the Supreme Court. The Ministry of Finance, Union of India, shall be responsible for creating the appropriate infrastructure and other facilities for proper and effective functioning of the Special Investigation Team at once.

PART III

PRINCIPALITY OF LIECHTENSTEIN IS A TAX HAVEN

59. We now turn our attention to the matter of disclosure of various documents referenced by the Union of India, as sought by the Petitioners. These documents, including names and bank particulars, relate to various bank accounts, of Indian citizens, in the Principality of Liechtenstein ("Liechtenstein"), a small landlocked sovereign nation-State in Europe. It is generally acknowledged that Liechtenstein is a tax haven.

FEDERAL REPUBLIC OF GERMANY GOT THE LIST OF ITS CITIZENS WHO HAD DEPOSITED MONEY IN THIS TAX HAVEN

60. Apparently, as alleged by the Petitioners, a former employee of a bank or banks in Liechtenstein secured the names of some 1400 bank account holders, along with the particulars of such accounts, and offered the information to various entities. The same was secured by the Federal Republic of Germany ("Germany"), which in turn, apart from initiating tax proceedings against some 600 individuals, also offered the information regarding nationals and citizens of other countries to such countries.

NUMEROUS INDIANS HAVE ALSO DEPOSITED MONEY IN THAT TAX HAVEN COUNTRY BUT INDIAN GOVERNMENT IS NOT SERIOUS TO GET BACK THAT BLACK MONEY – SUBMIT PETITIONERS

It is the contention of the Petitioners that even though the Union of India was informed about the presence of the names of a large number of Indian citizens in the list of names revealed by the former bank employee, the Union of India never made a serious attempt to secure such information and proceed to investigate such individuals.

61. It is the contention of the Petitioners that such names include the identities of prominent and powerful Indians, or the identities of individuals, who may or may not be Indian citizens, but who could lead to information about various powerful Indians holding unaccounted monies in bank accounts abroad. It is also the contention of the Petitioners that, even though they had sought the information under the Right to Information Act (2005), the Respondents had not revealed the names nor divulged the relevant documents. The Petitioners argue that such a reluctance is only on account of the Union of India not having initiated suitable steps to recover such monies, and punish the named individuals, and also because revelation of names of individuals on the list would lead to discovery of powerful persons engaged in various unlawful activities, both in generation of unlawful and unaccounted monies, and their stashing away in banks abroad.

GERMANY OFFERED INFORMATION WITHOUT ANY CONDITION BUT CENTRAL GOVERNMENT CONCEALED IT – ALLEGE PETITIONERS

62. It was also alleged by the Petitioners that in fact Germany had offered such information, freely and generally to any country that requests the same, and did not specify that the names and other information pertaining to such names ought to be requested only pursuant to any double taxation agreements it has with other countries. The Petitioners also alleged that Union of India has chosen to proceed under the assumption that it could have requested such information only pursuant to the double taxation agreement it has with Germany. The Petitioners contend that the Government of India took such a step primarily to conceal the information from public gaze.

CENTRAL GOVERNMENT PLEADS SIX OBJECTIONS TO IT

63. The response of the Union of India may be summed up briefly:

(i) that they secured the names of individuals with bank accounts in banks in Liechtenstein, and other details with respect to such bank accounts, pursuant to an agreement of India with Germany for avoidance of double taxation and prevention of fiscal evasion;

(ii) that the said agreement proscribes the Union of India from disclosing such names, and other documents and information with respect to such bank accounts, to the Petitioners, even in the context of these ongoing proceedings before this court;

(iii) that the disclosure of such names, and other documents and information, secured from Germany, would jeopardize the relations of India with a foreign State;

(iv) that the disclosure of such names, and other documents and information, would violate the right to privacy of those individuals who may have only deposited monies in a lawful manner;

(v) that disclosure of names, and other documents and information can be made with respect to those individuals with regard to whom investigations are completed, and proceedings initiated; and

(vi) that contrary to assertions by the Petitioners, it was Germany which had asked the Union of India to seek the information under double taxation agreement, and that this was in response to an earlier request by Union of India for the said information.

VERACITY OF THE CLAIM OF THE GOVERNMENT TO BE EXAMINED

64. For the purposes of the instant order, the issue of whether the Union of India could have sought and secured the names, and other documents and information, without having to take recourse to the double taxation agreement is not relevant. For the purposes of determining whether Union of India is obligated to disclose the information that it obtained, from Germany, with respect to accounts of Indian citizens in a bank in the Principality of Liechtenstein, we need only examine the claims of the Union of India as to whether it is proscribed by the double taxation agreement with Germany from disclosing such information. Further, and most importantly, we would also have to examine whether in the context of article 32 proceedings before this Court, wherein this Court has exercised jurisdiction, the Union of India can claim exemption from providing such information to the Petitioners, and also with respect to issues of right to privacy of individuals who hold such accounts, and with respect of whom no investigations have yet been commenced, or only partially conducted, so that the State has not yet issued a show cause and initiated proceedings.

AGREEMENT WITH GERMANY DOES NOT PROSCRIBE THE DISCLOSURE OF NAMES

65. We have perused the said agreement with Germany. We are convinced that the said agreement, by itself, does not proscribe the disclosure of the relevant documents and details of the same, including the names of various bank account holders in Liechtenstein. In the first instance, we note that the names of the individuals are with respect to bank accounts in the Liechtenstein, which though populated by largely German speaking people, is an independent and sovereign nation state. The agreement between Germany and India is with regard to various issues that crop up with respect to German and Indian citizens' liability to pay taxes to Germany and/or India. It does not even remotely touch upon information regarding Indian citizens' bank accounts in Liechtenstein that Germany secures and shares that have no bearing upon the matters that are covered by the double taxation agreement between the two countries.

66. In fact, the "information" that is referred to in article 26 is that which is "necessary for carrying out the purposes of this agreement", *i.e.* the Indo-German

DTAA. Therefore, the information sought does not fall within the ambit of this provision. It is disingenuous for the Union of India, under these circumstances, to repeatedly claim that it is unable to reveal the documents and names as sought by the Petitioners on the ground that the same is proscribed by the said agreement.

COURTS CAN EXAMINE IN DETAIL THE TERMS OF AGREEMENT

It does not matter that Germany itself may have asked India to treat the information shared as being subject to the confidentiality and secrecy clause of the double taxation agreement. It is for the Union of India, and the courts, in appropriate proceedings, to determine whether such information concerns matters that are covered by the double taxation agreement or not. In any event, we also proceed to examine the provisions of the double taxation agreement below, to also examine whether they proscribe the disclosure of such names, and other documents and information, even in the context of these instant proceedings.

TERMS OF THE DOUBLE TAXATION AGREEMENT WITH GERMANY AND ITS INTERPRETATION

67. Relevant portions of article 26 of the double taxation agreement with Germany, a copy of which was submitted by Union of India, reads as follows:

"1. The competent authorities of the Contracting States shall exchange such information as is necessary for carrying out the purposes of this Agreement. Any information received by a Contracting State shall be treated as secret in the same manner as information obtained under the domestic laws of that State and shall be disclosed only to persons or authorities (including courts and administrative bodies) involved in the assessment or collection of, the enforcement or prosecution in respect of, or the determination of appeals in relation to, the taxes covered by this Agreement. They may disclose the information in public court proceedings or in judicial proceedings.

2. In no case shall the provisions of paragraph 1 be construed so as to impose on a Contracting State the obligation:

   (a) to carry out administrative measures at variance with the laws and administrative practice of that or of the other Contracting State;

   (b) to supply information which is not obtainable under the laws or in the normal course of the administration of that or of the other Contracting State;

   (c) to supply information which would disclose any trade, business, industrial, commercial or professional secret or trade process, or information, the disclosure of which would be contrary to public policy (order public)."

PLEA OF CENTRAL GOVERNMENT FALSE – COULD BE DISCLOSED IN COURT PROCEEDINGS AS ARE THESE

The above clause in the relevant agreement with Germany would indicate that, contrary to the assertions of Union of India, there is no absolute bar of secrecy. Instead the agreement specifically provides that the information may be disclosed in public court proceedings, which the instant proceedings are. The proceedings in this matter before this Court, relate both to the issue of tax collection with respect to unaccounted monies deposited into foreign bank accounts, as well as with issues relating to the manner in which such monies were generated, which may include activities that are criminal in nature also. Comity of nations cannot be predicated upon clauses of secrecy that could hinder constitutional proceedings such as these, or criminal proceedings.

PUBLIC COURT PROCEEDINGS MEANS TAXATION PROCEEDINGS – SUBMITS UNION OF INDIA – BUT NO MATERIAL TO SUPPORT IT

68. The claim of Union of India is that the phrase "public court proceedings", in the last sentence in article 26(1) of the double taxation agreement only relates to proceedings relating to tax matters. The Union of India claims that such an understanding comports with how it is understood internationally. In this regard Union of India cites a few treatises. However, the Union of India did not provide any evidence that Germany specifically requested it to not reveal the details with respect to accounts in the Liechtenstein even in the context of proceedings before this court.

RULE OF INTERPRETATION IN VIENNA CONVENTION

69. Article 31, "General Rule of Interpretation", of the Vienna Convention of the Law of Treaties, 1969 provides that a "treaty shall be interpreted in good faith in accordance with the ordinary meaning to be given to the terms of the treaty in their context and in the light of its object and purpose." While India is not a party to the Vienna Convention, it contains many principles of customary international law, and the principle of interpretation, of article 31 of the Vienna Convention, provides a broad guideline as to what could be an appropriate manner of interpreting a treaty in the Indian context also.

TREATIES ARE TO BE GIVEN A NORMAL MEANING

70. This Court in *Union of India* v. *Azadi Bachao Andolan*, (2004) 10 SCC 1 approvingly noted Frank Bennion's observations that a treaty is really an indirect enactment, instead of a substantive legislation, and that drafting of treaties is notoriously sloppy, whereby inconveniences obtain. In this regard this Court further noted the dictum of Lord Widgery, C.J. that the words "are to be given their general meaning, general to lawyer and layman alike.... The meaning of the diplomat rather than the lawyer." The broad principle of interpretation, with respect to treaties, and provisions therein, would be that ordinary meanings of words be given effect to, unless the context requires or otherwise. However, the fact that such treaties are drafted by diplomats, and not lawyers, leading to sloppiness in drafting also implies that care has to be taken to not render any word, phrase, or sentence redundant, especially where rendering of such word, phrase or sentence redundant would lead to a manifestly absurd situation, particularly from a constitutional perspective.

CENTRAL GOVERNMENT HAS NO RIGHT TO BIND THE COUNTRY CONTRARY TO THE CONSTITUTIONAL PROVISIONS

The government cannot bind India in a manner that derogates from Constitutional provisions, values and imperatives.

LAST PART OF ARTICLE 26(1) OF THE AGREEMENT AUTHORISES THE DISCLOSURE IN PUBLIC COURT PROCEEDINGS

71. The last sentence of article 26(1) of the double taxation agreement with Germany, "[T]hey may disclose this information in public court proceedings or in judicial decisions," is revelatory in this regard. It stands out as an additional aspect or provision, and an exception, to the preceding portion of the said article. It is located after the specification that information shared between contracting parties may be revealed only to "persons or authorities (including courts and administrative bodies) involved in the assessment or collection of, the enforcement or prosecution in respect of, or the determination of appeals in relation to taxes covered by this Agreement." Consequently, it has to be understood that the phrase "public court proceedings" specified in the last sentence in article 26(1) of the double taxation agreement with Germany refers to court proceedings other than those in connection with tax assessment, enforcement, prosecution etc., with respect to tax matters. If it were otherwise, as argued by Union of India, then there would have been no need to have that last sentence in article 26(1) of the double taxation agreement at all. The last sentence would become redundant if the interpretation pressed by Union of India is accepted. Thus, notwithstanding the alleged convention of interpreting the last sentence only as referring to proceedings in tax matters, the rubric of common law jurisprudence, and fealty to its principles, leads us inexorably to the conclusion that the language in this specific treaty, and under these circumstances cannot be interpreted in the manner sought by Union of India.

72. While we agree that the language could have been tighter, and may be deemed to be sloppy, to use Frank Bennion's characterization, negotiation of such treaties are conducted and secured at very high levels of government, with awareness of general principles of interpretation used in various jurisdictions. It is fairly well-known, at least in Common Law Jurisdictions, that legal instruments and statutes are interpreted in a manner whereby redundancy of expressions and phrases is sought to be avoided. Germany would have been well aware of it.

REDUNDANT CLAUSE OF AN AGREEMENT CANNOT AMEND THE BASIC STRUCTURE OF OUR CONSTITUTION

73. The redundancy that would have to be ascribed to the said last sentence of article 26(1) of the double taxation agreement with Germany, if the position of Union of India were to be accepted, also leads to a manifest absurdity, in the context of the Indian Constitution. Such a redundancy would mean that constitutional imperatives themselves are to be set aside. Modern constitutionalism, to which Germany is a major contributor too, especially in terms of the basic structure doctrine, specifies that powers vested in any organ of the State have to be exercised within the four corners of the Constitution, and further that organs created by a Constitution cannot change the identity of the Constitution itself.

BASIC STRUCTURE OF THE CONSTITUTION OF INDIA CANNOT BE AMENDED EVEN BY THE AMENDING POWER OF PARLIAMENT

74. The basic structure of the Constitution cannot be amended even by the amending power of the Legislature. Our Constitution guarantees the right, pursuant to clause (1) of article 32, to petition this Court on the ground that the rights guaranteed under Part III of the Constitution have been violated. This provision is a part of the basic structure of the Constitution. Clause (2) of article 32 empowers this Court to issue "directions or orders or writs, including writs in the nature of *habeas corpus, mandamus, prohibition, quo warranto and certiorari,* whichever may be appropriate for the enforcement of any of the rights conferred by" Part III. This is also a part of the basic structure of the Constitution.

NON-SUPPLY OF INFORMATION DEMANDED BY THE PETITIONERS WOULD BE COUNTER TO ARTICLE 32(1) OF THE CONSTITUTION

75. In order that the right guaranteed by clause (1) of article 32 be meaningful, and particularly because such petitions seek the protection of fundamental rights, it is imperative that in such proceedings the petitioners are not denied the information necessary for them to properly articulate the case and be heard, especially where such information is in the possession of the State. To deny access to such information, without citing any constitutional principle or enumerated grounds of constitutional prohibition, would be to thwart the right guaranteed by clause (1) of article 32.

GOVERNMENT IS EQUALLY BOUND TO PLACE RELEVANT INFORMATION BEFORE THE COURT

76. Further, in as much as, by history and tradition of common law, judicial proceedings are substantively, though not necessarily fully, adversarial, both parties bear the responsibility of placing all the relevant information, analyses, and facts before this court as completely as possible. In most situations, it is the State which may have more comprehensive information that is relevant to the matters at hand in such proceedings. However, some agents of the State may perceive that because these proceedings are adversarial in nature, the duty and burden to furnish all the necessary information rests upon the Petitioners, and hence the State has no obligation to fully furnish such information. Some agents of the State may also seek to cast the events and facts in a light that is favourable to the government in the immediate context of the proceedings, even though such actions do not lead to rendering of complete justice in the task of protection of fundamental rights. To that extent, both the petitioners and this Court would be handicapped in proceedings under clause (1) of article 32.

STATE IS BOUND TO PROTECT FUNDAMENTAL RIGHTS

77. It is necessary for us to note that the burden of asserting, and proving, by relevant evidence a claim in judicial proceedings would ordinarily be placed upon the proponent of such a claim; however, the burden of protection of fundamental rights is primarily the duty of the State.

STATE SHOULD NOT ACT TO STOP THE COURT FROM RENDERING COMPLETE JUSTICE

Consequently, unless constitutional grounds exist, the State may not act in a manner that hinders this Court from rendering complete justice in such proceedings. Withholding of information from the petitioners, or seeking to cast the relevant events and facts in a light favourable to the State in the context of the proceedings, even though ultimately detrimental to the essential task of protecting fundamental rights, would be destructive to the guarantee in clause (1) of article 32, and substantially eviscerate the capacity of this Court in exercising its powers contained in clause (2) of article 32, and those traceable to other provisions of the Constitution and broader jurisprudence of constitutionalism, in upholding fundamental rights enshrined in Part III.

78. In the task of upholding of fundamental rights, the State cannot be an adversary. The State has the duty, generally, to reveal all the facts and information in its possession to the Court, and also provide the same to the petitioners. This is so, because the petitioners would also then be enabled to bring to light facts and the law that may be relevant for the Court in rendering its decision. In proceedings such as those under article 32, both the petitioner and the State, have to necessarily be the eyes and ears of the Court. Blinding the petitioner would substantially detract from the integrity of the process of judicial decision making in article 32 proceedings, especially where the issue is of upholding of fundamental rights.

THERE IS CO-RELATION BETWEEN ARTICLE 32 AND ARTICLE 19 OF THE CONSTITUTION

79. Furthermore, we hold that there is a special relationship between clause (1) of article 32 and sub-clause (a) of clause (1) of article 19, which guarantees citizens the freedom of speech and expression. The very genesis, and the normative desirability of such a freedom, lies in historical experiences of the entire humanity: unless accountable, the State would turn tyrannical. A proceeding under clause (1) of article 32, and invocation of the powers granted by clause (2) of article 32, is a primordial constitutional feature of ensuring such accountability. The very promise, and existence, of a constitutional democracy rests substantially on such proceedings.

CENTRAL GOVERNMENT CANNOT VIOLATE FUNDAMENTAL RIGHTS OF CITIZENS UNLESS THE CASE FALLS IN EXCEPTION

80. Withholding of information from the petitioners by the State, thereby constraining their freedom of speech and expression before this Court, may be premised only on the *Exceptions* carved out, in clause (2) of article 19, "in the interests of sovereignty and integrity of India, security of the State, friendly relations with foreign States, public order, decency or morality, or in relation to contempt of court, defamation or incitement to an offence" or by law that demarcate *Exceptions*, provided that such a law comports with the enumerated grounds in clause (2) of article 19, or that may be provided for elsewhere in the Constitution.

STATE CANNOT SIGN TREATIES WITH OTHER COUNTRIES WHICH HIT CONSTITUTIONAL PROVISIONS

81. It is now a well-recognized proposition that we are increasingly being entwined in a global network of events and social action. Considerable care has to be exercised in this process, particularly where governments which come into being on account of a constitutive document, enter into treaties. The actions of governments can only be lawful when exercised within the four corners of constitutional permissibility. No treaty can be entered into, or interpreted, such that constitutional fealty is derogated from. The redundancy, that the Union of India presses, with respect to the last sentence of article 26(1) of the double taxation agreement with Germany, necessarily transgresses upon the boundaries erected by our Constitution. It cannot be permitted.

AGREEMENT WITH GERMANY IS NO OBSTACLE IN DISCLOSING THE NAMES – HELD SUPREME COURT

82. We have perused the documents in question, and heard the arguments of Union of India with respect to the double taxation agreement with Germany as an obstacle to disclosure. We do not find merit in its arguments flowing from the provisions of double taxation agreement with Germany. However, one major constitutional issue, and concern remains. This is with regard to whether the names of individuals, and details of their bank accounts, with respect to whom there has been no completed investigations that reveal wrong doing and proceedings initiated, and there is no other credible information and evidence currently available with the Petitioners that there has been any wrong doing, may be disclosed to the Petitioners.

RIGHT OF PRIVACY AND RIGHT UNDER ARTICLE 32 HAVE TO BE BALANCED

83. Right to privacy is an integral part of right to life. This is a cherished constitutional value, and it is important that human beings be allowed domains of freedom that are free of public scrutiny unless they act in an unlawful manner. We understand and appreciate the fact that the situation with respect to unaccounted monies is extremely grave. Nevertheless, as constitutional adjudicators we always have to be mindful of preserving the sanctity of constitutional values, and hasty steps that derogate from fundamental rights, whether urged by governments or private citizens, howsoever well meaning they may be, have to be necessarily very carefully scrutinised. The solution for the problem of abrogation of one zone of constitutional values cannot be the creation of another zone of abrogation of constitutional values.

84. The rights of citizens, to effectively seek the protection of fundamental rights, under clause (1) of article 32 have to be balanced against the rights of citizens and persons under article 21. The latter cannot be sacrificed on the anvil of fervid desire to find instantaneous solutions to systemic problems such as unaccounted monies, for it would lead to dangerous circumstances, in which vigilant investigations, inquisitions and rabble rousing, by masses of other citizens could become the order of the day. The right of citizens to petition this Court for upholding of fundamental rights is granted in order that citizens, *inter alia*, are ever vigilant about the functioning of the State in order to protect the constitutional project. That right cannot be extended to being inquisitors of fellow citizens. An inquisitorial order, where citizens' fundamental right to privacy is breached by fellow citizens is destructive of social order. The notion of fundamental rights, such as a right to privacy as part of right to life, is not merely that the State is enjoined from derogating from them. It also includes the responsibility of the State to uphold them against the actions of others in the society, even in the context of exercise of fundamental rights by those others.

RIGHT OF PRIVACY OF LAWFUL TRANSACTIONS CANNOT BE SACRIFICED MERELY BECAUSE THE STATE HAS FAILED TO IDENTIFY UNLAWFUL TRANSACTIONS

85. An argument can be made that this Court can make exceptions under the peculiar circumstances of this case, wherein the State has acknowledged that it has not acted with the requisite speed and vigour in the case of large volumes of suspected unaccounted monies of certain individuals. There is an inherent danger in making exceptions to fundamental principles and rights on the fly. Those exceptions, bit by bit, would then eviscerate the content of the main right itself. Undesirable lapses in upholding of fundamental rights by the Legislature, or the Executive, can be rectified by assertion of constitutional principles by this Court. However, a decision by this Court that an exception could be carved out remains permanently as a part of judicial canon, and becomes a part of the constitutional interpretation itself. It can be used in the future in a manner and form that may far exceed what this Court intended or what the Constitutional text and values can bear. We are not proposing that Constitutions cannot be interpreted in a manner that allows the nation-State to tackle the problems it faces. The principle is that *Exceptions* cannot be carved out willy-nilly, and without forethought as to the damage they may cause.

86. One of the chief dangers of making exceptions to principles that have become a part of constitutional law, through aeons of human experience, is that the logic, and ease of seeing exceptions, would become entrenched as a part of the constitutional order. Such logic would then lead to seeking exceptions, from protective walls of all fundamental rights, on grounds of expediency and claims that there are no solutions to problems that the society is confronting without the evisceration of fundamental rights. That same logic could then be used by the State in demanding exceptions to a slew of other fundamental rights, leading to violation of human rights of citizens on a massive scale.

INFORMATION SHARED WITH GERMANY HAS INDIAN NAMES

87. It is indeed true that the information shared by Germany, with regard to certain bank accounts in Liechtenstein, also contains names of individuals who appear to be Indians. The Petitioners have also claimed that names of all the individuals have been made public by certain segments of the media. However, while some of the accounts, and the individuals holding those accounts, are claimed to have been investigated, others have not been. No conclusion can be drawn as to whether those who have not been investigated, or only partially investigated and proceedings not initiated have committed any wrong doing. There is no presumption that every account holder in banks of Liechtenstein has acted unlawfully. In these circumstances, it would be inappropriate for this Court to order the disclosure of such names, even in the context of proceedings under clause (1) of article 32.

SOME OF THESE NAMES MAY BE OF PERSONS HAVING LAWFUL TRANSACTIONS

88. The revelation of details of bank accounts of individuals, without establishment of *prima facie* grounds to accuse them of wrong doing, would be a violation of their rights to privacy. Details of bank accounts can be used by those who want to harass, or otherwise cause damage, to individuals. We cannot remain blind to such possibilities, and indeed experience reveals that public dissemination of banking details, or availability to unauthorized persons, has led to abuse. The mere fact that a citizen has a bank account in a bank located in a particular jurisdiction cannot be a ground for revelation of details of his or her account that the State has acquired. Innocent citizens, including those actively working towards the betterment of the society and the nation, could fall prey to the machinations of those who might wish to damage the prospects of smooth functioning of society. Whether the State itself can access details of citizen's bank accounts is a separate matter. However, the State cannot compel citizens to reveal, or itself reveal details of their bank accounts to the public at large, either to receive benefits from the State or to facilitate investigations, and prosecutions of such individuals, unless the State itself has, through properly conducted investigations, within the four corners of constitutional permissibility, been able to establish *prima facie* grounds to accuse the individuals of wrong doing.

GOVERNMENT TO FIRST IDENTIFY ILLEGAL TRANSACTIONS AND THEN DISCLOSE THE SAME TO THE PUBLIC FAILING WHICH THE COURTS CAN ALWAYS INTERVENE

It is only after the State has been able to arrive at a *prima facie* conclusion of wrong doing, based on material evidence, would the rights of others in the nation to be informed, enter the picture. In the event citizens, other persons and entities have credible information that a wrong doing could be associated with a bank account, it is needless to state that they have the right, and in fact the moral duty, to inform the State, and consequently the State would have the obligation to investigate the same, within the boundaries of constitutional permissibility. If the State fails to do so, the appropriate Courts can always intervene.

INACTION OF THE CENTRAL GOVERNMENT WITH REGARD TO HASSAN ALI AND TAPURIAS, IS A MAJOR FAILURE WHICH AMOUNTS TO PARALLEL ECONOMY AND CAUSE OF GENERATING BLACK MONEY

89. The major problem, in the matters before us, has been the inaction of the State. This is so, both with regard to the specific instances of Hassan Ali Khan and the Tapurias, and also with respect to the issues regarding parallel economy, generation of black money etc. The failure is not of the Constitutional values or of the powers available to the State; the failure has been of human agency. The response cannot be the promotion of vigilantism, and thereby violate other constitutional values.

COUNTRYMEN SHOULD WAKE UP SO THAT AGENTS OF THE STATE SHOULD NOT WEEKEN THE INVESTIGATING MACHINERY

The response has to necessarily be a more emphatic assertion of those values, both in terms of protection of an individual's right to privacy and also the protection of individual's right to petition this Court, under clause (1) of article 32, to protect fundamental rights from evisceration of content because of failures of the State. The balancing leads only to one conclusion: strengthening of the machinery of investigations, and vigil by broader citizenry in ensuring that the agents of State do not weaken such machinery.

FOLLOWING DIRECTIONS WERE GIVEN IN THE INTEREST OF JUSTICE

90. In light of the above we order that:

(i) The Union of India shall forthwith disclose to the Petitioners all those documents and information which they have secured from Germany, in connection with the matters discussed above, subject to the conditions specified in (ii) below;

(ii) That the Union of India is exempted from revealing the names of those individuals who have accounts in banks of Liechtenstein, and revealed to it by Germany, with respect of whom investigations/enquiries are still in progress and no information or evidence of wrongdoing is yet available;

(iii) That the names of those individuals with bank accounts in Liechtenstein, as revealed by Germany, with respect of whom investigations have been concluded, either partially or wholly, and show cause notices issued and proceedings initiated may be disclosed; and

(iv) That the Special Investigation Team, constituted pursuant to the orders of today by this Court, shall take over the matter of investigation of the individuals whose names have been disclosed by Germany as having accounts in banks in Liechtenstein, and expeditiously conduct the same. The Special Investigation Team shall review the concluded matters also in this regard to assess whether investigations have been thoroughly and properly conducted or not, and on coming to the conclusion that there is a need for further investigation shall proceed further in the matter. After conclusion of such investigations by the Special Investigation Team, the Respondents may disclose the names with regard to whom show cause notices have been issued and proceedings initiated.

CENTRAL GOVERNMENT WAS DIRECTED TO FILE THE COMPLIANCE REPORT

91. Compliance reports shall be filed by Respondents, with respect of all the orders issued by this Court today. List for further directions in the week following the Independence Day, August 15, of 2011.

Ordered accordingly.

....J.

(B. Sudershan Reddy)

New Delhi, ...J.

July 4, 2011. (Surinder Singh Nijjar

Author's Note: The Government of India should have no reason to object to the Constitution of S.I.T. under the supervision of two retired Judges of the Supreme Court to identify the persons who have deposited black money in Tax haven countries. However, this order so much bothered the authorities that immediately thereafter the Union of India filed the Review Petition in the Supreme Court. Hence this judgment.

Ram Jethmalani

v.

Union of India[1]

SUPREME COURT OF INDIA

ORIGINAL CIVIL JURISDICTION

I.A. No. 8 of 2011 in Writ Petition (Civil) No. 176 of 2009

Decided on 23-9-2011

BENCH

Altamas Kabir and S.S. Nijjar, JJ.

FACT IN THE BACKGROUND OF REVIEW APPLICATION – ALTAMAS KABIR J.

ORDER

1. Writ Petition (Civil) No. 176 of 2009 was filed by Shri Ram Jethmalani and five others against the Union of India, the Reserve Bank of India, the Securities Exchange Board of India, the Director, Directorate of Enforcement and the Chairman, Central Board of Direct Taxes, Department of Revenue, Ministry of Finance, Government of India, against the purported inaction of the Government to arrange for recovery of large sums of money deposited by Indian citizens in foreign banks and, in particular, in Swiss Banks. In that context the Petitioners, *inter alia*, prayed for the following reliefs:—

> "(a) that this Hon'ble Court may be pleased to issue notice to all the Respondents calling upon them to disclose all the facts which have come to their knowledge so far pertaining to the aforementioned issues and the steps taken by them in this regard;
>
> (b) to make orders from time to time to ensure that the outcome of the investigations are not suppressed or even unduly delayed;
>
> (c) the suitable directions be issued to the Respondent No. 1 to apply to the Foreign Banks, more particularly the UBS Bank for freezing the amounts in the said foreign banks, particularly, the UBS Bank which as stated above is holding, *inter alia*, the Khan and Tapurias' assets."

SUPREME COURT *VIDE* ORDER DATED 4TH JULY, 2011 PASSED IN I.A. NO. 1 OF 2009 IN WRIT PETITION (CIVIL) NO. 176 OF 2009

2. On 4th July, 2011, on I.A. No. 1 of 2009 in the Writ Petition several directions were given. In fact, the said order was divided into three parts. The *first* part of

1. (2011) 9 SCC 751.

the order dealt with the alleged failure of the Central Government to recover the large sums of money kept in such foreign banks and in tax havens having strong secrecy laws with regard to deposits made by individuals.

3. The *second* part dealt with the unlawful activities allegedly funded out of such deposits and accounts which were a threat to the security and integrity of India. The amounts deposited in such tax havens in respect of one Shri Hassan Ali Khan and Shri Kashinath Tapuria and his wife Chandrika Tapuria were alleged to be in billions of dollars in UBS Bank in Zurich alone. Income-tax demands were made to Shri Hassan Ali Khan for Rs. 40,000 crores and a similar demand was served on the Tapurias amounting to Rs. 20,580 crores. On being convinced that, in the absence of any known source of income, the large sums of money involved in the various transactions by Hassan Ali Khan and the Tapurias were the proceeds of crime, which required a thorough investigation, this Court felt the necessity of appointing a Special Investigation Team to act on behalf and at the behest of the directions of this Court

4. It was noted by this Court that the issues involved were complex and would require expertise and knowledge of different departments and the coordination of efforts between various agencies and departments. It was also recorded that on behalf of the Union of India, it had been submitted that a High Level Committee had recently been formed under the initiative of the Department of Revenue in the Ministry of Finance, composed of:

(i) Secretary, Department of Revenue, as the Chairman;

(ii) Deputy Governor, Reserve Bank of India;

(iii) Director (IB);

(iv) Director, Enforcement;

(v) Director, CBI;

(vi) Chairman, CBDT;

(vii) DG, Narcotics Control Bureau;

(viii) DG, Revenue Intelligence;

(ix) Director, Financial Intelligence Unit; and

(x) JS (FT & TR-I), CBDT.

with powers to co-opt, as necessary, representatives not below the rank of Joint Secretary such as the Home Secretary, Foreign Secretary, Defence Secretary and the Secretary, Cabinet Secretariat.

5. It was further recorded that the Union of India had claimed that such a multi-disciplinary group and Committee would enable the conducting of an efficient and a systematic investigation into the matters concerning allegations against Hassan Ali Khan and the Tapurias and would also be able to take appropriate steps to bring back the monies deposited in foreign banks.

6. In the light of such submission made on behalf of Union of India and citing the judgments of this Court in (1) *Vineet Narain* v. *Union of India*, (1996) 2 SCC 199, (2) *NHRC* v. *State of Gujarat*, (2004) 8 SCC 610, (3) *Sanjiv Kumar* v. *State of Haryana*, (2005) 5 SCC 517 and (4) *Centre for PIL* v. *Union of India*, (2011) 1 SCC 560, this

Court completed the second part of the order by directing as follows: [*Ram Jethmalani* case, (2011) 8 SCC 1. [SCC pp. 27-28 para 57]—

"57. In light of the above we herewith order:

(i) That the High Level Committee constituted by the Union of India, comprising of

(a) Secretary, Department of Revenue;

(b) Deputy Governor, Reserve Bank of India;

(c) Director (IB);

(d) Director, Enforcement;

(e) Director, CBI;

(f) Chairman, CBDT;

(g) DG, Narcotics Control Bureau;

(h) DG, Revenue Intelligence;

(i) Director, Financial Intelligence Unit; and

(j) JS (FT &TR-I), CBDT be forthwith appointed with immediate effect as a Special Investigation Team;

(ii) That the Special Investigation Team, so constituted, also include Director, Research and Analysis Wing;

(iii) That the above Special Investigation Team, so constituted, be headed by and include the following former eminent judges of this Court:

(a) Hon'ble Mr. Justice B.P. Jeevan Reddy as Chairman; and

(b) Hon'ble Mr. Justice M.B. Shah as Vice-Chairman;

and that the Special Investigation Team function under their guidance and direction;

(iv) That the Special Investigation Team, so constituted, shall be charged with the responsibilities and duties of investigation, initiation of proceedings, and prosecution, whether in the context of appropriate criminal or civil proceedings of:

(a) all issues relating to the matters concerning and arising from unaccounted monies of Hassan Ali Khan and the Tapurias;

(b) all other investigations already commenced and are pending, or awaiting to be initiated, with respect to any other known instances of the stashing of unaccounted monies in foreign bank accounts by Indians or other entities operating in India; and

(c) all other matters with respect to unaccounted monies being stashed in foreign banks by Indians or other entities operating in India that may arise in the course of such investigations and proceedings. It is clarified here that within the ambit of responsibilities described above, also lie the responsibilities to ensure that the matters are also investigated, proceedings initiated and prosecutions conducted with regard to criminality and/or unlawfulness of activities that may have been the source for such monies, as well as the criminal and/or unlawful means that are used to take such unaccounted monies out of and/or bring such monies back into the country, and use of such monies in India or abroad. The Special Investigation Team shall also be charged with the responsibility of preparing a comprehensive action plan, including the creation of necessary institutional structures that can enable and strengthen the country's battle against generation of unaccounted monies, and their stashing away in foreign banks or in various forms domestically.

(v) That the Special Investigation Team so constituted report and be responsible to this Court, and that it shall be charged with the duty to keep this Court informed of all major developments by the filing of periodic status reports, and following of any special orders that this Court may issue from time to time;

(vi) That all organs, agencies, departments and agents of the State, whether at the level of the Union of India, or the State Government, including but not limited to all statutorily formed individual bodies, and other constitutional bodies, extend all the cooperation necessary for the Special Investigation Team so constituted and functioning;

(vii) That the Union of India, and where needed even the State Governments, are directed to facilitate the conduct of the investigations, in their fullest measure, by the Special Investigation Team so constituted and functioning, by extending all the necessary financial, material, legal, diplomatic and intelligence resources, whether such investigations or portions of such investigations occur inside the country or abroad.

(viii) That the Special Investigation Team also be empowered to further investigate even where charge-sheets have been previously filed; and that the Special Investigation Team may register further cases, and conduct appropriate investigations and initiate proceedings, for the purpose of bringing back unaccounted monies unlawfully kept in bank accounts abroad."

7. The third part of the order deals with the disclosure of various documents referred to by the Union of India in relation to the names and particulars of various bank accounts of Indian citizens in the Principality of Liechtenstein, a small landlocked sovereign nation-State in Europe, which is generally acknowledged as a tax haven.

PETITION FILED BY THE CENTRAL GOVERNMENT SEEKING MODIFICATION AGAINST CONVERTING H.L.C. INTO S.I.T.

8. The third part of the order is not of relevance at this stage, since an application, being I..A. No. 8 of 2011, has been filed by the Union of India in the Writ Petition, purporting to be an application under article 142 of the Constitution read with Order XLVII, rule 6 of the Supreme Court Rules, 1966, seeking modification of the aforesaid order dated 4th July, 2011.

OBJECTION TAKEN BY THE PETITIONERS AGAINST THE MAINTAINABILITY OF THE PETITION FOR MODIFICATION

9. Before the application could be moved by the learned Attorney General, Mr. Anil B. Divan, learned Senior Advocate appearing for the Writ Petitioners, took a preliminary objection that the interlocutory application was not maintainable on several counts. It was firstly urged that in effect, in the guise of an application for modification, the Respondents/Applicants were wanting either a re-hearing and/or review of the order passed on 4th July, 2011, disposing of I.A. No. 1 of 2009.

10. Mr. Divan pointed out that it was the Government itself which had set up a High Level Committee consisting of senior officers of different departments to take steps for retrieving the black money which had been deposited in banks in tax havens all over the world and, in particular, in Swiss Banks and it did not, therefore, lie in the mouth of the Government to take a different stand when the same Committee had been converted into a Special Investigation Team with two former Judges of the Supreme Court to monitor the progress of the recovery proceedings.

11. Mr. Divan also contended that the formation of a Special Investigation Team to monitor the investigation is not a new concept and has been resorted to on different occasions in order that justice is done between the parties and the rule of law is not obstructed either by the investigating agency or otherwise. Mr. Divan urged that once the matter had been decided on merits and a direction had been given for the formation of a Special Investigation Team composed of the very officers who had been appointed as members of the High Level Committee for the very same purpose, the Government is not justified in objecting to the investigation being monitored by such Committee headed by two retired Judges of the Supreme Court with impeccable credentials.

12. Mr. Divan submitted that the contention of the Respondents in I.A. No. 8 of 2011 was as if by appointing a Special Investigation Team, the Supreme Court had taken over the Executive powers of the Union. It was submitted that although a case against the accused was pending since 2007, no attempt had been made to interrogate the accused in regard to the allegations made against them.

13. Mr. Divan submitted that possibly other fora were available to the Respondents, but the present I.A. would not provide any remedy to the Respondents. Mr. Divan urged that it was on account of the complete inertia of the investigating authority that in spite of huge sums of unaccounted money deposited in tax havens abroad, little or no action was taken to proceed with the investigation or even to interrogate the persons accused of having been involved in money laundering and acting against the interests of the country and its citizens. Mr. Divan submitted that the remedy available to the Respondents lay in a review petition under the provisions of Order XLVII of the Supreme Court Rules, 1966, and not by an interlocutory application and that too in a disposed of matter.

14. Mr. Shekhar Naphade, learned Senior Advocate who appeared for the Petitioner in Writ Petition (Civil) No. 136 of 2011, supported the submissions made by Mr. Anil Divan with regard to the maintainability of the Interlocutory Application No. 8 of 2011 filed by the Union of India. It was contended that neither the provisions of article 142 of the Constitution nor Order XLVII, rule 6 of the Supreme Court Rules were attracted in the facts of this case, inasmuch as, the said provisions conferred power and not jurisdiction on this Court in respect of a matter which was pending before it. Mr. Naphade submitted that article 142 very clearly vested the Supreme Court with jurisdiction to pass such decree or make such order as is necessary for doing complete justice in any case or matter pending before it.

15. Mr. Naphade also contended that, as had been held by this Court, in *Saurav Chaudhary* v. *Union of India*, (2004) 5 SCC 618, this Court could exercise its jurisdiction under article 142 of the Constitution at the time of rendition of the judgment and not thereafter. It was further observed that once judgment had been delivered by the Court, it could not recall the same and could only exercise its power of review in case it intended to take a different view from the one rendered in the main judgment. Mr. Naphade also urged that even the provisions of Order XLVII, rule 6 of the Supreme Court Rules were of no assistance to the Union of India. It was submitted that the Rules framed under article 145(1) of the Constitution only empowered the Supreme Court to frame Rules to regulate its practice and procedure and does not take in its sweep the power to create a new jurisdiction to entertain a cause or matter.

16. Reference was also made to the decision of this Court in *Raja Soap Factory* v. *S.P. Shantharaj*, (1965) 2 SCR 800, wherein it was observed that by jurisdiction what is meant is the extent of power which is conferred upon a Court by its Constitution to try a matter or a cause. Such power is not capable of being enlarged because an extraordinary situation requires the Court to exercise it.

17. Mr. Naphade submitted that by virtue of this application, the Union of India was seeking to review a final order passed by this Court, treating the same to be an application for recalling the order. Mr. Naphade repeated and reiterated his submissions that the application filed on behalf of the Union of India and its authorities was not maintainable and could only be dismissed.

REPLY ON BEHALF OF THE UNION OF INDIA

18. Replying to the submissions made by Mr. Divan and Mr. Naphade, the learned Attorney General submitted that in earlier cases also this question had been raised and considered by this Court. Referring to the decision of a Bench of Seven Judges in the case of *A.R. Antulay* v. *R.S. Nayak*, (1988) 2 SCC 602, the learned Attorney General submitted that by a majority judgment this Court held that directions, if given in violation of the principles of natural justice, if subsequently questioned in another appeal instead of by way of a Review Petition under article 137, the same could be set aside by another Bench of the Court *ex debito justitiae* in exercise of its inherent powers. The majority amongst the Judges held that the want of jurisdiction could be addressed solely by a superior Court and, in practice, no decision could be reviewed collaterally by any inferior Court, but the superior Court could always correct its error either by way of a petition or *ex debito justitiae.* In fact, it was also observed that in certain situations, the Supreme Court could always invoke its power of review in exercise of its inherent jurisdiction in any proceeding pending before it, without insisting on the formalities of a review application.

19. The learned Attorney General submitted that by appointing two retired Judges of the Supreme Court, Justice B.P. Jeevan Reddy as the Chairman and Justice M.B. Shah as the Vice-Chairman, and directing that the Special Investigation Team would function under their guidance and directions, would amount to interference with the Executive authority of the different officials representing different sections of the administration which would lead to a chaotic situation. The direction given to include the Director, Research and Analysis Wing, was also improper, since the said authority functioned under strict rules of secrecy, which could be jeopardized if its Director were to be included in the Special Investigation Team.

20. The learned Attorney General submitted that, in the event there was any doubt as to whether the powers of the Supreme Court under article 142 of the Constitution could be invoked for doing complete justice in a matter which was not pending before it, the present application could always be treated as a Review Petition under article 137 of the Constitution read with Order XLVII, Rule 6 of the Supreme Court Rules, 1966.

21. The learned Attorney General submitted that in view of the magnitude of the transactions involved and that too without any accounting of the monies used, this Court should cut across technicalities and consider the matter pragmatically. The learned Attorney General submitted that the present application may, therefore, be treated as a Review Petition under article 137 of the Constitution read with Order XLVII, rule 6 of the Supreme Court Rules, 1966 and be proceeded with accordingly, notwithstanding the objection taken on behalf of the Petitioners in regard to the different procedure to be adopted in respect of a review application. It was also submitted that as indicated in *A.R. Antulay's* case (*supra*), the Supreme Court can grant relief in exercise of its inherent powers as the guardian of the Constitution.

PRIOR LAW RELIED UPON BY THE CENTRAL GOVERNMENT BESIDES THE LAW REFERRED TO IN ABOVE PARAGRAPHS

22. Reference was also made by the learned Attorney General to the decision of this Court in *S. Nagaraj* v. *State of Karnataka*, (1993) Supp 4 SCC 595, which was heard along with several other cases by a Bench of three Judges. In the said cases an order had been passed on orally mentioning which ultimately resulted in several contempt petitions being filed. Two of the Hon'ble Judges, after considering the anomalous circumstances which had resulted from the passing of the order on oral mentioning, held that justice is a virtue which transcends all barriers and neither the rules of procedure nor technicalities of law can stand in its way. It was further observed that the order of the Court should not be prejudicial to anyone and if the Court found that the order was passed under a mistake and it would not have exercised the jurisdiction, but for the erroneous assumption which in fact did not exist, and its perpetration would result in miscarriage of justice, then it would not on any principle be precluded from rectifying the order. Mistake is accepted as a valid reason to recall an order.

23. Their Lordships in *S. Nagaraj* case (supra) emphasized the fact that rectification of an order stems from the fundamental principles that justice is above all. It is exercised to remove the error and not for disturbing finality. In the judgment it was also observed that the Supreme Court has the inherent power to make such orders as may be necessary for the interest of justice or to prevent the abuse of process of court. The Court is, therefore, not precluded from recalling or reviewing its own order, if it is satisfied that it is necessary to do so for the sake of justice. It was pointed out that even the learned third Judge held that while the government was mainly responsible for the unfortunate state of affairs that should not desist the Supreme Court from revising or reviewing the said orders which had serious consequences. The learned third Judge also observed that it is the duty of the Court to rectify, revise and recall its orders as and when it is brought to its notice that certain of its orders were passed on a wrong or mistaken assumption of facts and that implementation of those orders will have serious consequences.

PETITION FOR MODIFICATION WAS HELD AS MAINTAINABLE BY ONE HON'BLE JUDGE OF THE HON'BLE DIVISION BENCH

24. On a careful consideration of the submissions made on behalf of the respective parties in regard to the maintainability of I.A. No. 8 of 2011 filed on behalf of the Union of India, wherein, *inter alia,* a prayer has been made to modify the order dated 4th July, 2011 and to delete the directions relating to the Special Investigation Team in paragraphs 49 and 50 of the said order, it appears that the I.A. is maintainable. In view of the preliminary objection relating to the maintainability of the interlocutory application filed on behalf of the Union of India, the said issue regarding the maintainability of I.A. No. 8 of 2011 has been taken up first.

DISCUSSION

25. From the arguments advanced on behalf of the respective parties, it appears at first blush that Mr. Anil B. Divan is technically correct in submitting that since there was no matter pending before this Court, the provisions of article 142 of the Constitution would not be attracted and that even the inherent powers of this Court preserved under Order XLVII, rule 6 of the Rules framed by the Supreme Court in exercise of its powers under article 145 of the Constitution would not be applicable. However, this Court has preserved its inherent powers to make such orders as may be necessary for the ends of justice in Order XLVII, rule 6 of the Supreme Court Rules, 1966, framed under article 145 of the Constitution.

26. As has been held in *A.R. Antulay's* case (*supra*) and in *S. Nagaraj's* case (*supra*), such a power was not only inherent in the Supreme Court, but the Supreme Court was also entitled to and under an obligation to do justice to exercise such powers as the guardian of the Constitution. Justice transcends all barriers and neither rules of procedure nor technicalities can stand in its way, particularly if its implementation would result in injustice.

27. In addition to the decision rendered by this Court in *A.R. Antulay's* case (*supra*) and in *S. Nagaraj's* case (supra), reference may also be made to another equally important pronouncement of this Court in *Vineet Narain's* case (supra), wherein the concept of continuing *mandamus* was introduced in order to maintain the credibility of the investigation being conducted.

28. Reference may also be made to the decision of this Court in *Manganese Ore (India) Ltd.* v. *Chandi Lal Saha*, (1991) Supp 2 SCC 465, wherein this Court extended the benefit of its judgment to persons who were not even in appeal before it.

29. Even if the present application was to be dismissed as being not maintainable under article 142 of the Constitution read with Order XLVII, rule 6 of the Supreme Court Rules, 1966, it would not preclude the Applicants from filing an application for review under article 137 of the Constitution. As the very working of the Special Investigation Team appointed under the Order of 4th July, 2011, is in question, it is necessary to cut across the technical tapes sought to be invoked on behalf of the Petitioners and hold that in view of the inherent powers vested in the Supreme Court of India, preserved in Order XLVII, rule 6 of the Supreme Court Rules, 1966, and having regard to the fact that the Supreme Court is the guardian of the Constitution, I.A. No. 8 of 2011, even in its present form is maintainable in the facts and circumstances of the case, which include threats to the security of the country.

OBJECTION TAKEN ABOUT MAINTAINABILITY OF THE REVIEW PETITION REJECTED

30. The objections raised by Mr. Anil B. Divan and supported by Mr. Shekhar Naphade, regarding the maintainability of I.A. No. 8 of 2011, are, therefore, rejected and the said application may therefore be proceeded with for hearing.

....J.

(ALTAMAS KABIR)

New Delhi,

Dated: 23.9.2011.

VIEW OF THE OTHER HON'BLE JUDGE OF THE HON'BLE SUPREME COURT S.S. NIJJAR, J. (DISAGREEING)

31. I have had the opportunity, and the benefit of reading, in draft, the learned opinion of Hon'ble Mr. Justice Altamas Kabir. However, with all humility and with due respect, I would not be able to concur with the view taken by my Learned Brother. My Learned Brother has rejected the preliminary objections raised by Mr. Anil Divan and Mr. Shekhar Naphade, appearing for the writ petitioners and directed the application to proceed for hearing. In my opinion, the application is not maintainable for a number of reasons.

HON'BLE JUDGE GIVES IN DETAIL THE FACTS STATED IN THE APPLICATION FOR MODIFICATION OF THE ORDER DATED 4TH JULY, 2011

32. The application clearly states that the order passed by this Court in I.A. No. 1 on 4th July, 2011 impinges upon the doctrine of separation of powers. The application thereafter sets out the facts leading to the filing of the writ petition invoking article 32 of the Constitution of India. The application sets out the prayers made in the writ petition. Thereafter, it is stated that the writ petition, as originally filed, did not contain any prayer for appointment of a Special Investigation Team. The application also points out that in the counter affidavit filed on behalf of the Union of India, it had been clearly stated that the Central Government had been alive to the need to be able to retrieve information about the alleged money lying deposited in the foreign accounts and highlighting steps taken by it in this behalf.

33. It further points out that it was on account of such an initiative, tax haven countries, including countries like Switzerland, made solemn attempts to enter into effective tax information exchange agreements with various countries. The application proceeds to delineate the steps taken and the strategy formulated to eradicate the menace of "Black Money". It states that the government had joined the global crusade against Black Money. It had decided to create an appropriate legislative framework by incorporating various tax evasion measures in existing Acts. Thereafter, the application gives the details of the proposed new legislation for unearthing Black Money.

34. After enumerating all the efforts made by the Government at national and international level, it is stated that above all the Government has constituted a Committee on 27th May, 2011 under the Chairman, C.B.D.T. to examine ways to strengthen laws to stop the generation of Black Money in the country, its illegal transfer abroad and its recovery. The Committee also examined various other issues which are enumerated in the application. The application further proceeds to tabulate the efforts to create further legislative and administrative framework to obtain information about illicit money of Indian citizens already parked outside the country. Thereafter, the application sets out the efforts already made and the results thereof. On the basis of that, it is stated that the government has achieved substantial success not only in getting information on illicit money parked outside the country but also in stopping the transfer of illicit money outside the country. Thereafter, the details are given of the illicit money detected. It is stated that in the Order dated 4th July, 2011, [*Ram Jethmalani* v. *Union of India,* (2011) 8 SCC 1] these efforts have neither been adverted to nor evaluated before rendering the finding in Paragraph 54 of the judgment.

35. The application thereafter sets out various efforts made in the matter of investigation of the case of *Hassan Ali Khan* and *Kashinath Tapuriah*. The application thereafter reproduces the directions sought in I.A. No. 1 of 2009, which was filed on 8th September, 2009. Thereafter, it is submitted that even in this application, no prayer was made for appointment of a Special Investigation Team [S.I.T.]. It is further submitted that such a prayer ought not to have been granted on the basis of written submissions of the learned counsel for the petitioners in the absence of requisite pleadings in the writ petition or in the absence of a formal prayer. The application further proceeds to state that it is filed invoking the inherent power of this Court under article 142(1) of the Constitution of India for doing complete justice in any case or matter pending before it.

CONSTITUTION OF S.I.T. DOES NOT IMPINGE ON THE POLICY DECISIONS

36. In the grounds of the application, it is stated that this Court while exercising its jurisdiction would not be pleased to attain to itself, the task entrusted to the Executive. It is emphatically submitted in the application that the order is without jurisdiction since the constitution of the High Level Committee is within the realm of a decision on policy matters. It is also submitted that formation of a S.I.T. headed by two former Judges of this Court not only impinges on the policy decision of the Government but also impinges upon the doctrine of separation of powers. This, according to the application, would be beyond the jurisdiction conferred on this Court under article 32 of the Constitution of India, which can be exercised for the enforcement of the rights conferred by Part III and for no other purpose.

37. It is further submitted that the judgment proceeds on admissions, concessions, submissions and acknowledgments attributed to the counsel appearing for the Union of India. It is pointed out that such concessions and admissions do not appear to have been made. On the basis of the facts pleaded, the prayer is made for modification of the Order dated 4th July, 2011 and deletion of the directions relating to S.I.T. in Paragraphs 49 and 50. Since the directions given in these paragraphs have been reproduced verbatim by His Lordship, Justice Kabir, the same are not necessary to be reproduced herein again.

THIS PETITION SEEKS TO REOPEN THE WHOLE ISSUE ON MERITS – DESERVES DISMISSAL AT THE THRESHOLD

38. The aforesaid facts have been stated merely to indicate that the application would not be maintainable, in its present form, as in substance, it is more in the nature of a Memorandum of Appeal. In my opinion, the application seeks to reopen the whole matter on merits which would not be permissible in an application for modification. Therefore, in my opinion, the application deserves to be dismissed at the threshold.

39. As the submissions made by the learned counsel for the parties have been succinctly noticed by my Learned Brother Altamas Kabir, J. in His Lordship's order, the same need not be repeated herein.

THIS PETITION FOR CLARIFICATION/MODIFICATION TOUCHING MERITS NOT MAINTAINABLE

40. In my opinion, an application for clarification/modification touching the merits of the matter is not maintainable. The Court can consider the matter, if at all, only upon a review application on limited grounds. In considering the application for review, the procedure laid down under Order XL of the Supreme Court Rules, 1966 read with article 137 would have to be followed. Review of a judgment is a serious matter and is, therefore, governed by constitutional and statutory provisions. This view of mine will find support from a number of earlier decisions of this Court. It would, at this stage, be appropriate to make a reference to some of the observations made.

41. In the case of *Ram Chandra Singh* v. *Savitri Devi*, (2004) 12 SCC 713 this Court considered the issue as to whether an application for clarification/ modification would be maintainable in the face of the provisions contained in article 137 and Order XL, rule 1 of Supreme Court Rules. Upon consideration of the entire issue, it was observed as follows: (SCC p. 717 paras 13-14)

"13. It is now well-settled that an application for clarification or modification touching the merit of the matter would not be maintainable. A Court can rehear the matter upon review of its judgment but, therefore, the procedure laid down in Order XL, rules 3 and 5 of the Supreme Court Rules, 1966 as also article 137 of the Constitution are required to be complied with as review of a judgment is governed by the constitutional as well as statutory provisions.

14. ... The prayer of the applicant is that apart from the corrections which are required to be made in the judgment, as noticed hereinbefore, the merit of the matter may also be considered, inter alia, with reference to the pleadings of (2004) 12 SCC 713 the parties. Such a course of action, in our opinion, is not contemplated in law. If there exist errors apparent on the face of the record, an application for review would be maintainable but an application for clarification and/or modification cannot be entertained unless it is shown that the same is necessary in the interest of justice. An application which is in effect and substance an application for review cannot be entertained dehors the statutory embargo contained in Order XL, rules 3 and 5 of the Supreme Court Rules, 1966."

THIS PETITION IS AN ABUSE OF THE PROCESS OF THE COURT

42. I am of the considered opinion that the present application would be an abuse of the process of the Court as it seeks to camouflage an application for Review as an application for modification. In my opinion, such a course ought not to be encouraged. It would be relevant to notice the observations made by this Court in paragraph 16 of the judgment in the case of *Delhi Administration* v. *Gurdip Singh Uban*, (2000) 7 SCC 296: (SCC pp. 308-09 para 16)

"16. At the outset, we have to refer to the practice of filing review applications in large numbers in undeserving cases without properly examining whether the cases strictly come within the narrow confines of rule XL of the Supreme Court Rules. In several cases, it has become almost everyday experience that review applications are filed mechanically as a matter of routine and the grounds for review are a mere reproduction of the grounds of special leave and there is no indication as to which ground strictly falls within the narrow limits of Rule XL of the Rules. We seriously deprecate this practice. If parties file review petitions indiscriminately, the time of the Court is unnecessarily wasted, even it be in chambers where the review petitions are listed. Greater care, seriousness and restraint is needed in filing review applications."

IT HAS BECOME PRACTICE TO FILE SUCH APPLICATIONS FOR CLARIFICATION/MODIFICATION

43. In my opinion, ten years down the line, the situation is even worst than what is depicted by the aforesaid observations. Now we are facing an almost daily practice of having to consider applications for "modification and clarification".

In the aforesaid judgment, this Court also considered the nature and scope of the jurisdiction to review its own order/judgment. Since the application herein has been described as an application for "modification", it would be necessary to notice the observations made by this Court in Paragraphs 17 and 18 of the judgment.

44. The observations of this Court are as under: [*Gurdip Singh Uban* case, (2000) 7 SCC 296, SCC p. 309]

> "17. We next come to applications described as applications for "clarification", "modification" or "recall" of judgments or orders finally passed. We may point out that under the relevant Rule XL of the Supreme Court Rules, 1966 a review application has first to go before the learned Judges in circulation and it will be for the Court to consider whether the application is to be rejected without giving an oral hearing or whether notice is to be issued.
>
> Order XL, rule 3 states as follows:
>
> > "3. Unless otherwise ordered by the Court, an application for review shall be disposed of by circulation without any oral arguments, but the petitioner may supplement his petition by additional written arguments. The Court may either dismiss the petition or direct notice to the opposite party...."
>
> In case notice is issued, the review petition will be listed for hearing, after notice is served. This procedure is meant to save the time of the Court and to preclude frivolous review petitions being filed and heard in open court. However, with a view to avoid this procedure of "no hearing", we find that sometimes applications are filed for "clarification", "modification" or "recall" etc. not because any such clarification, modification is indeed necessary but because the applicant in reality wants a review and also wants a hearing, thus avoiding listing of the same in chambers by way of circulation. Such applications, if they are in substance review applications, deserve to be rejected straight away inasmuch as the attempt is obviously to bypass Order XL, rule 3 relating to circulation of the application in chambers for consideration without oral hearing. By describing an application as one for "clarification" or "modification", — though it is really one of review — a party cannot be permitted to circumvent or bypass the circulation procedure and indirectly obtain a hearing in the open Court. What cannot be done directly cannot be permitted to be done indirectly. [See in this connection a detailed order of the then Registrar of this Court in *Sone Lal* v. *State of Uttar Pradesh*, (1982) 2 SCC 398 deprecating a similar practice.]
>
> 18. We, therefore, agree with the learned Solicitor General that the Court should not permit hearing of such an application for "clarification", "modification" or "recall" if the application is in substance one for review. In that event, the Court could either reject the application straight away with or without costs or permit withdrawal with leave to file a review application to be listed initially in chambers."

These observations leave no manner of doubt that the Court should not permit hearing of such an application for "clarification", "modification" or "recall" if the application is in substance one for review. It is clearly indicated that in those circumstances the Court could either reject the application straight away or permit withdrawal with leave to file a review application to be listed initially in chambers.

THIS PETITION FOR MODIFICATION OF THE ORDER DATED 4.7.2011 IS IN THE NATURE OF AN APPEAL OR AT THE BEST FOR REVIEW

45. Examined on the touch stone of the observations made above, I am of the considered opinion that the application herein though described as an application for modification is in substance more in the nature of a Memorandum of Appeal. At best, it could be said to be in substance an Application for Review. It certainly does not lie within the very narrow limits within which this Court would entertain an application for modification.

46. In yet another case of *Zahira Habibullah Sheikh* v. *State of Gujarat*, (2004) 5 SCC 353 this Court, faced with a similar situation, had this to say: (SCC p. 358, para 4)

> "4. The petition is in essence and substance seeking for a review under the guise of making an application for direction and modification apparently being fully aware of the normal procedure that such applications for review are not, unless the Court directs, listed for open hearing in Court, at the initial stage at least, before ordering notice to the other side and could be summarily rejected, if found to be of no *prima facie* merit. The move adopted in itself is unjustified, and could not be countenanced also either by way of review or in the form of the present application as well. The nature of relief sought, and the reasons assigned are such that even under the pretext of filing a review such an exercise cannot be undertaken, virtually for rehearing and alteration of the judgment because it is not to the liking of the party, when there is no apparent error on record whatsoever to call for even a review. The said move is clearly misconceived and nothing but sheer abuse of process, which of late is found to be on the increase, more for selfish reasons than to further or strengthen the cause of justice. The device thus adopted, being otherwise an impermissible move by mere change in nomenclature of the applications does not change the basic nature of the petition. Wishful thinking virtually based on surmises too, at any rate is no justification to adopt such undesirable practices. If at all, it should be for weighty and substantial reasons and not to exhibit the might or weight or even the affluence of the party concerned or those who represent such parties when they happen to be public authorities and institutions."

This Court approved the observations made in the case of *Gurdip Singh Uban* (supra) and observed that what cannot be done directly cannot be permitted to be done indirectly. The Court should not permit hearing of such an application for "clarification", "modification" or "recall" if the application is in substance a clever move for review.

47. These observations were reiterated in the case of *A.P. SRTC* v. *Abdul Kareem*, (2007) 2 SCC 466. This Court observed that the petition was in essence and substance seeking for a review under the guise of making an application for direction and modification apparently being fully aware of the normal procedure that such applications for review are not, unless the Court directs, listed for open hearing in Court, at the initial stage at least, before ordering notice to the other side and could be summarily rejected, if found to be of no *prima facie* merit. The Court further observed that such a move ought not to be countenanced. The move was clearly misconceived and nothing but sheer abuse of process, which of late is found to be on the increase, more for selfish reasons than to further or strengthen the cause of justice.

LAW RELIED UPON BY THE CENTRAL GOVERNMENT NOT APPLICABLE TO THE FACTS OF THIS CASE

48. To be fair, it must be noticed that the learned Attorney General appearing for the Union of India had relied on a number of judgments in support of his submissions that the Court would have inherent powers to modify its own order/judgment. The primary judgment relied upon by the learned Attorney General is in the case of *S. Nagaraj* v. *State of Karnataka*, 1993 Supp (4) SCC 595. I am of the considered opinion that the aforesaid judgment would be of no assistance to the submissions made by the learned Attorney General. The aforesaid judgment was rendered in the background of very peculiar facts. It would appear that this Court 1993 (Supp) 4 SCC 595 had passed an order having far reaching consequences and pre-judicially affecting the rights of other groups of employees under articles 14 and 16 of the Constitution of India. The order had permitted backdoor entry of thousands of stipendiary graduates because of the negligence of the State in putting correct facts before the Court. The government seemed to have woken up after considerable damage had already been done and moved an application for modification/clarification of the order dated 30th October, 1991 [*S. Nagaraj* v. *State of Karnataka* CPs Nos. 142 and 166 of 1991 WP(c) No. 1249 of 1989 order dated 30.10.1991 (SC)]. The learned Attorney General placed strong reliance on the observations made by this Court in paragraphs 18, 19 and 36 of the judgment in support of the submission that the Court should not decline to review its orders when it is brought to the notice of the Court that it would be in the interest of justice to modify the same.

49. In order to appreciate the submission of learned Attorney-General, it would be appropriate to notice the observations made by this Court in paragraphs 18, 19 and 36 of the judgment, which are as under: [*S. Nagaraj* case, 1993 Supp (4) SCC 595 SCC pp. 618-20 & 630-631]

> "18. Justice is a virtue which transcends all barriers. Neither the rules of procedure nor technicalities of law can stand in its way. The order of the Court should not be prejudicial to anyone. Rule of *stare decisis* is adhered for consistency but it is not as inflexible in Administrative Law as in Public Law. Even the law bends before justice. Entire concept of writ jurisdiction exercised by the higher courts is founded on equity and fairness. If the Court finds that the order was passed under a mistake and it would not have exercised the jurisdiction but for the erroneous assumption which in fact did not exist and its perpetration shall result in miscarriage of justice then it cannot on any principle be precluded from rectifying the error. Mistake is accepted as valid reason to recall an order. Difference lies in the nature of mistake and scope of rectification, depending on if it is of fact or law. But the root from which the power flows is the anxiety to avoid injustice. It is either statutory or inherent. The latter is available where the mistake is of the Court. In Administrative Law the scope is still wider. Technicalities apart if the Court is satisfied of the injustice then it is its constitutional and legal obligation to set it right by

recalling its order. Here as explained, the Bench of which one of us (Sahai, J.) was a member did commit an error in placing all the stipendiary graduates in the scale of First Division Assistants due to State's failure to bring correct facts on record. But that obviously cannot stand in the way of the Court correcting its mistake. Such inequitable consequences as have surfaced now due to vague affidavit filed by the State cannot be permitted to continue.

WHAT REVIEW MEANS

19. Review literally and even judicially means re-examination or re-consideration. Basic philosophy inherent in it is the universal acceptance of human fallibility. Yet in the realm of law the courts and even the statutes lean strongly in favour of finality of decision legally and properly made. Exceptions both statutorily and judicially have been carved out to correct accidental mistakes or miscarriage of justice. Even when there was no statutory provision and no rules were framed by the highest court indicating the circumstances in which it could rectify its order the courts culled out such power to avoid abuse of process or miscarriage of justice. In *Raja Prithwi Chand Lal Choudhury* v. *Sukhraj Rai,* AIR 1941 PC 1 the Court observed that even though no rules had been framed permitting the highest Court to review its order yet it was available on the limited and narrow ground developed by the Privy Council and the House of Lords. The Court approved the principle laid down by the Privy Council in *Rajunder Narain Rae* v. *Bijai Govind Singh,* (1837-1841) 2 MIA 181 that an order made by the Court was final and could not be altered:

> "... nevertheless, if by misprision in embodying the judgments, by errors have been introduced, these Courts possess, by Common law, the same power which the Courts of record and statute have of rectifying the mistakes which have crept in .... The House of Lords exercises a similar power of rectifying mistakes made in drawing up its own judgments, and this Court must possess the same authority. The Lords have however gone a step further, and have corrected mistakes introduced through inadvertence in the details of judgments; or have supplied manifest defects in order to enable the decrees to be enforced, or have added explanatory matter, or have reconciled inconsistencies."

Basis for exercise of the power was stated in the same decision as under:

> "It is impossible to doubt that the indulgence extended in such cases is mainly owing to the natural desire prevailing to prevent irremediable injustice being done by a Court of last resort, where by some accident, without any blame, the party has not been heard and an order has been inadvertently made as if the party had been heard."

RECTIFICATION OF AN ORDER IS BASED ON THE FUNDAMENTAL PRINCIPLE THAT JUSTICE SHOULD BE DONE

Rectification of an order thus stems from the fundamental principle that justice is above all. It is exercised to remove the error and not for disturbing finality. When the Constitution was framed the substantive power to rectify or recall the order passed by this Court was specifically provided by article 137 of the Constitution. Our Constitution-makers who had the practical wisdom to visualise the efficacy of such provision expressly conferred the substantive power to review any judgment or order by article 137 of the Constitution. And clause (c) of article 145 permitted this Court to frame rules as to the conditions subject to which any judgment or order may be reviewed. In exercise of this power Order XL had been framed empowering this Court to review an order in civil proceedings on grounds analogous to Order XLVII, rule 1 of the Civil Procedure Code. The expression, 'for any other sufficient reason' in the clause has been given an expanded meaning and a decree or order passed under misapprehension of true state of circumstances has been held to be sufficient ground to exercise the power. Apart from Order XL, rule 1 of the Supreme Court Rules this Court has the inherent power to make such orders as may be necessary in the interest of justice or to prevent the abuse of process of Court. The Court is thus not precluded from recalling or reviewing its own order if it is satisfied that it is necessary to do so for sake of justice.

37. There is yet another circumstance. The question is, whether this Court should enforce the 1982 Rules as amended in 1987. The 1987 amendments have the effect of smuggling in thousands of persons into Government service by a back-door — without complying with the requirements of articles 14 and 16. One can understand the rules as framed in 1982, but it is extremely difficult to appreciate or understand the reasons for which the 1987 amendment was brought in. The question, to repeat, is whether this Court should extend its arm — its discretionary power under articles 136 and 32, as the case may be, to implement such unconstitutional rules and help these persons to gain a back-door entry into Government service — that too at the highest level in group 'C' services straightaway. It is true that no one has questioned the 1987 amendments. The petitioners do not question them because they are advantageous to them; they want them to be implemented. The Government cannot and does not question them because it has itself made them. The parties who are affected namely the persons awaiting employment under the Government probably do not even know what is happening. But where an unconstitutional provision of such vast impact is brought to the notice of this Court and it is asked to enforce it, it is the constitutional duty of this Court to refuse to do so. I am, therefore, of the firm opinion that this Court should refuse to make any orders directing implementation of the rules as amended in 1987. The proper direction would be to direct the absorption of the S.Gs. in accordance with the 1982 Rules as originally framed (*i.e.*, without reference to the 1987 amendments) and to the extent provided therein. Of course those S.Gs. who have been absorbed already into group 'C' service in accordance with the said rules will remain unaffected since disturbing them, without notice to them and in view of all the circumstances of this case, may not be advisable. All those S.Gs. who have not so far been absorbed in group 'C' service shall continue in the present status, drawing Rs. 960 per month. They will be entitled for absorption in group 'C' posts only in accordance with the 1982 Rules, without reference to the 1987 amendments."

(Emphasis in original)

Relying on these observations, learned Attorney General, submits that the Court should regardless of any technical objections proceed to hear the present application without insisting that the applicant should seek its relief in an application for review.

S. NAGARAJ'S CASE NOT APPLICABLE TO THE FACTS OF THIS CASE

50. I am of the considered opinion that the facts and circumstances highlighted in the present application would not enable the applicant to satisfy the conditions under which this Court exercised its inherent jurisdiction in the *S. Nagaraj's* case (supra). A perusal of the judgment would clearly show that the Court was anxious to "even the balance". On the one side, there were orders of the Court passed on vague and incomplete affidavit, creating rights and hopes in favour of five thousand stipendiary graduates to be absorbed as First Division Assistant, and on the other hand, there were others, the likely injustice to whom had been highlighted in the affidavit filed by the Government and in the writ petition filed by different sections of the employees. The Court in fact emphasised the principle of finality of orders and binding nature of directions issued by the Court which could only be overridden, if there is injustice inherent in the situation (*see* Page 615, para 14(e) and (f).

51. A little later in the judgment, in Paragraph 16, the Court observed as follows: [*S. Nagaraj* case (supra) SCC p. 617]—

> "16. "Mere eligibility was not sufficient unless availability of posts was also established. In absence of posts and due to equitable considerations arising in favour of other employees the practical difficulty in appointing all the five thousand stipendiary graduates as First Division Assistants appears to be insurmountable. *Even so we have no hesitation in saying that we would have refused to modify our order dated October 30, 1991 at the instance of the Government but the Court cannot be unjust to other employees."* (emphasis supplied)

These observations make it abundantly clear that the Court was dealing with a particularly unsavory situation created by the Government which had led to insurmountable difficulties and possible injustice to both the stipendiary Magistrates and other employees. The Court, therefore, observed that but for this unique situation, it would have refused to modify the order dated 30th October, 1991. In Paragraph 18, the Court makes it clear that the order was passed under a mistake. The Court would not have exercised its jurisdiction but for the erroneous assumption, which in fact did not exist. In Paragraph 36, again, it is reiterated by the Court that it would be the duty of the Court to rectify, revise and recall its orders as and when it is brought to its notice and certain of its orders were based on wrong or mistaken assumption of facts and that implementation of those orders would have serious consequences.

THERE WAS NO QUESTION OF MISTAKEN FACTS IN THIS CASE NOR MISCARRIAGE OF JUSTICE

52. In my opinion, in the present case, there is no question of mistaken facts, being presented by anyone to the Court. The application also fails to indicate any miscarriage of justice or injustice which would be caused to any particular class. The other authorities cited by the learned Attorney General followed the judgment in *S. Nagaraj's* case (supra) and would not advance the cause of the applicant or Union of India any further.

53. The judgment in *Gurdip Singh Uban's* case (supra) rather supports the writ petitioner as noticed in the earlier part of this order. The learned Attorney-General further submitted that this Court would be fully justified in passing the orders in exercise of its inherent jurisdiction under article 142 of the Constitution of India. It can always correct its non-errors brought to its notice either by way of a review petition or *ex debito justitiae.* In support of the submission, the learned Attorney-General has relied on judgment of this Court in the case of *A.R. Antulay* v. *R.S. Nayak*, (1988) 2 SCC 602.

54. In my opinion, the aforesaid judgment was also delivered in view of the peculiar circumstances of the case. The Court therein set out the circumstances in which this Court can pass the appropriate orders unhindered by technical rules. The observations made in paragraph 48, which are of relevance, are as under: [*AR Antulay* case, (1988) 2 SCC 602 SCC p. 654]

> "48. According to Shri Jethmalani, the doctrine of *per incuriam* has no application in the same proceedings. We are unable to accept this contention. We are of the opinion that this Court is not powerless to correct its error which has the effect of depriving a citizen of his fundamental rights and moreso, the right to life and liberty. It can do so in exercise of its inherent jurisdiction in any proceeding pending before it without insisting on the formalities of a review application. Powers of review can be exercised in a petition filed under article 136 or article 32 or under any other provision of the Constitution if the court is satisfied that its directions have resulted in the deprivation of the fundamental rights of a citizen or any legal right of the petitioner. *See* the observations in *Prem Chand Garg* v. *Excise Commissioner*, AIR 1963 SC 996."

In my opinion, the aforesaid observations would not be applicable in the facts and circumstances of the present case.

THIS PETITION IS NOT FILED BY AN INDIVIDUAL ALLEGING THE INFRINGEMENT OF HIS FUNDAMENTAL RIGHT BUT BY UNION OF INDIA

55. The application herein is not moved by an individual, who had been deprived of his fundamental rights by an order dated 4th July, 2011. The application is filed by the Union of India challenging the order on various legal and factual issues. In *Antulay's* case (supra), one of the grounds taken was that the directions have been issued by the Court without following the principle of *audi alteram partem*. In the present case, the directions had been issued after hearing the learned counsel for the parties at length and on numerous dates.

PETITION FOR MODIFICATION CANNOT BE CONSIDERED AS REVIEW PETITION

These directions, in my opinion, cannot be recalled in an application seeking only modification of the order. At this stage, it would also not be possible to treat the present application for modification as an application for review.

WITH UTMOST RESPECT – NOT POSSIBLE TO AGREE WITH BROTHER JUDGE

25. In view of the above, with utmost respect, it would not be possible to agree with the order passed by Hon'ble Mr. Justice Altamas Kabir. In my opinion, the applicant. Union of India has failed to make out a case to enable this Court to treat the modification application as application for review and proceed to hear the same in open Court.

THIS PETITION IS WHOLLY MISCONCEIVED—DISMISSED

In my opinion, the present application is wholly misconceived. It is, therefore, dismissed. Union of India is, however, at liberty to take recourse to any other legal remedy that may be available to it.

....................................J.
[Surinder Singh Nijjar]

New Delhi;
September 23, 2011.

DISSENTING OPINION REFERRED TO CHIEF JUSTICE

Ram Jethmalani

v.

Union of India

I.A. No. 8 of 2011 in Writ Petition (Civil) No. 176 of 2009

ORDER

Since we have differed in our views regarding the maintainability of I.A. No. 8 of 2011 filed in W.P. No. 176 of 2009, let the matter be placed before Hon'ble the Chief Justice of India, for reference to a third Judge.

......................J.
(ALTAMAS KABIR)
......................J.
(SURINDER SINGH NIJJAR)

New Delhi:
September 23, 2011.

Author's Note: Dr. Subramanian Swami had filed an application to the Prime Minister for giving permission to prosecute the Minister C & IT (A. Raja) Government of India for causing loss to the Nation worth thousands of crores of rupees. That application remained pending in the PMO for more than 16 months. Thereafter a reply was received by Dr. Subramanian Swami from the department of Personnel that CBI has already registered the case. Dr. Swami filed a Writ Petition in the Delhi High Court which was dismissed. Hence, Dr. Swami filed the appeal in the Hon'ble Supreme Court. Hence this judgment.

SUPREME COURT CONSIDERED QUESTION OF LAW – CAN A PRIVATE CITIZEN SEEK PERMISSION FROM COMPETENT AUTHORITY FOR PROSECUTING A PUBLIC SERVANT?

Dr. Subramanian Swamy

v.

Dr. Manmohan Singh[1]

SUPREME COURT OF INDIA

CIVIL APPELLATE JURISDICTION

Civil Appeal No. 1193 of 2012

Decided on 31-1-2012

[Arising out of SLP(C) No. 27535 of 2010][1]

BENCH

G.S. Singhvi and Asok Kumar Ganguly, JJ.

JUDGMENT

G.S. Singhvi, J. (For himself and Ganguly, J.; Ganguly, J. Supplementary)

1. Leave granted. Whether a complaint can be filed by a citizen for prosecuting a public servant for an offence under the Prevention of Corruption Act, 1988 (for short, 'the 1988 Act') and whether the authority competent to sanction prosecution of a public servant for offences under the 1988 Act is required to take an appropriate decision within the time specified in clause I(15) of the directions contained in paragraph 58 of the judgment of this Court in *Vineet Narain* v. *Union of India*, (1998) 1 SCC 226 and the guidelines issued by the Central Government, Department of Personnel and Training and the Central Vigilance Commission (CVC) are the questions which require consideration in this appeal.

LOSS OF THOUSANDS OF CRORES OF RUPEES CAUSED TO THE NATION BY ARBITRARY AND ILLEGAL GRANT OF LICENCES – ALLEGES APPELLANT

2. For the last more than three years, the appellant has been vigorously pursuing, in public interest, the cases allegedly involving loss of thousands of crores of rupees to the Public Exchequer due to arbitrary and illegal grant of

1. (2012) 3 SCC 64.

licences at the behest of Mr. A. Raja (respondent No. 2) who was appointed as Minister for Communication and Information Technology on 16.5.2007 by the President on the advice of Dr. Manmohan Singh (respondent No. 1).

REPRESENTATION DATED 29-11-2008 FILED BY THE APPELLANT TO THE PM (RESPONDENT NO. 1) FOR SANCTION TO PROSECUTE RESPONDENT NO. 2, A. RAJA, MINISTER C&IT FOR CAUSING LOSS TO THE NATION OF THOUSANDS OF CRORES OF RUPEES – ALLEGES APPELLANT

3. After collecting information about the grant of licences, the appellant made detailed representation dated 29.11.2008 to respondent No. 1 to accord sanction for prosecution of respondent No. 2 for offences under the 1988 Act. In his representation, the appellant pointed out that respondent No. 2 had allotted new licences in 2G mobile services on 'first-come-first-served' basis to novice telecom companies, *viz.*, Swan Telecom and Unitech, which was in clear violation of clause 8 of the Guidelines for United Access Services Licence issued by the Ministry of Communication and Information Technology *vide* letter No. 10-21/2005-BS.I. (Vol. II)/49 dated 14.12.2005 and, thereby, caused loss of over Rs. 50,000 crores to the Government. The appellant gave details of the violation of clause 8 and pointed out that the two officers, *viz.*, R.J.S. Kushwaha and D. Jha of the Department of Telecom, who had opposed the showing of undue favour to Swan Telecom, were transferred just before the grant of licences and Bharat Sanchar Nigam Limited (BSNL) which had never entered into a roaming agreement with any operator, was forced to enter into such an agreement with Swan Telecom.

LICENCEES WHO GOT THE LICENCES ILLEGALLY SOLD A SHARE OF THE LICENCE TO FOREIGN COMPANIES AND EARNED THOUSANDS OF CRORES OF RUPEES – ALLEGES APPELLANT

4. The appellant further pointed out that immediately after acquiring 2G spectrum licences, Swan Telecom and Unitech sold their stakes to foreign companies, *i.e.*, Etisalat, a telecom operator from UAE and Telenor of Norway respectively and, thereby, made huge profits at the expense of public revenue. He claimed that by 2G spectrum allocation under respondent No. 2, the Government received only one-sixth of what it would have received if it had opted for an auction. The appellant pointed out how respondent No. 2 ignored the recommendations of the Telecom Regulatory Authority of India (TRAI) and gave totally unwarranted benefits to the two companies and thereby caused loss to the Public Exchequer.

EXCERPTS FROM THE REPRESENTATION MADE BY THE APPELLANT TO THE PRIME MINISTER

5. Some of the portions of the appellant's representation are extracted below:

> "Clause 8 has been violated as follows: While Anil Dhirubhai Ambani Group (ADAG), the promoters of Reliance Communications (R Com), had more than 10 per cent. stake in Swan Telecom, the figures were manipulated and showed as 9.99 per cent. holding to beat the said Clause. The documents available disclose that on March 2, 2007, when Swan Telecom applied for United Access Services Licences, it was owned 100 per cent. by Reliance

Communications and its associates *viz.*, Reliance Telecom, and by Tiger Trustees Limited, Swan Infonet Services Private Limited, and Swan Advisory Services Private Limited (*see* Annexure I). At one or the other point of time, employees of ADAG (Himanshu Agarwal, Ashish Karyekar, Paresh Rathod) or its associate companies have been acquiring the shares of Swan Telecom itself. But still the ADAG manipulated the holdings in Swan to reduce it to only 9.99 per cent. Ambani has now quietly sold his shares in Swan to Delphi Investments, a Mauritius based company owned by Ahmed O. Alfi, specializing in automobile spare parts. In turn, Swan has sold 45% of its shares to UAE's Emirates Telecom Corporation (Etisalat) for Rs. 9000 crores! All this is highly suspicious and not normal business transactions. Swan company got 60% of the 22 Telecom licenced areas at a throw away price of Rs. 1650 crores, when it was worth Rs. 60,000 crores total.

Room has operations in the same circles where the application for Swan Telecom was filed. Therefore, under clause 8 of the Guidelines, Swan should not have been allotted spectrum by the Telecommunication Ministry. But the company did get it on Minister's direction, which is an undue favour from him (Raja). There was obviously a *quid pro quo* which only a CBI enquiry can reveal, after an FIR is registered. There is no need for a P/E, because the CVC has already done the preliminary enquiry.

Quite surprisingly, the 2G spectrum licences were priced at 2001 levels to benefit these private players. That was when there were only 4 million cellphone subscribers; now it is 350 million. Hence, 2001 price is not applicable today.

Immediately after acquiring 2G spectrum licences both Swan and Unitech sold their stakes to foreign companies at a huge profits. While Swan Telecom sold its stakes to UAE telecom operator Etisalat, Unitech signed a deal with Telenor of Norway for selling its share at huge premium.

In the process of this 2G spectrum allocation, the government received only one-sixth of what it would have got had it gone through a fresh auction route. The total loss to the exchequer of giving away 2G GSM spectrum in this way – including to the CDMA operators – is over Rs. 50,000 crores and is said to be one of the biggest financial scams of all times in the country.

While approving the 2G licences, Minister Raja turned a blind eye to the fact that these two companies do not have any infrastructure to launch their services falsely claiming that the Telecom Regulatory Authority of India had approved the first-cum-first-served rule, Raja went ahead with the 2G spectrum allocation to two debutants in the Telecom sector. In fact earlier TRAI had discussed the spectrum allocation issue with existing services providers and suggested to the Telecom Ministry that spectrum allocation be made through a transparent tender and auction process. This is confirmed by what the TRAI Chairman N. Misra told the CII organised conference on November 28, 2008 (Annexure 2). But Raja did not bother to listen to the TRAI either and pursued the process on 'first come, first served' basis, benefiting those who had inside information, causing a loss of Rs. 50,000 crores to the Government. His dubious move has been to ensure benefit to others at the cost of the national exchequer."

PRAYER MADE IN THE REPRESENTATION OF THE APPELLANT TO THE PRIME MINISTER

6. The request made in the representation, which was relied upon by the learned Attorney-General for showing that the below:

> "According to an uncontradicted report in CNN-IBN news channel of November 26, 2008, you are said to be "very upset with A. Raja over the spectrum allocation issue". This confirms that an investigation is necessary, for which I may be given sanction so that the process of law can be initiated. I, therefore, writ to demand the grant of sanction to prosecute Mr. A. Raja, Minister for Telecom of the Union of India for offences under the Prevention of Corruption Act. The charges in brief are annexed herewith (Annexure 3)."

NO REPLY RECEIVED FROM THE PM ON WHICH REMINDERS WERE SENT BY THE APPELLANT

7. Since the appellant did not receive any response from respondent No. 1, he sent letters dated 30.5.2009, 23.10.2009, 31.10.2009, 8.3.2010 and 13.3.2010 and reiterated his request/demand for grant of sanction to prosecute respondent No. 2. In his letter dated 31.10.2009, the appellant referred to the fact that on being directed by the CVÇ, the Central Bureau of Investigation (CBI) had registered a first information report, and claimed that *prima facie* case is established against respondent No. 2 for his prosecution under sections 11 and 13(1)(d) of the 1988 Act. The appellant also claimed that according to various Supreme Court judgments it was not necessary to carry out a detailed inquiry, and he had produced sufficient evidence for grant of sanction to initiate criminal prosecution against respondent No. 2 for the misuse of authority and pecuniary gains from corrupt practices.

IN REMINDERS THE LOSS TO THE NATION WAS PLACED AT RUPEES 65,000 CRORES

8. In his subsequent letters, the appellant again asserted that the nation had suffered loss of nearly Rs. 65,000 crores due to arbitrary, unreasonable and *mala fide* action of respondent No. 2. In letter dated 13.3.2010, the appellant referred to the proceedings of the case in which this Court refused to interfere with the order of the Delhi High Court declaring that the decision of respondent No. 2 to change the cut-off date fixed for consideration of applications made for grant of licences was arbitrary and *mala fide*.

REPLY RECEIVED AFTER MORE THAN 16 MONTHS, THAT TOO, VAGUE AND FROM THE MINISTRY OF PERSONNEL

9. After 1 year and 4-1/2 months of the first letter written by him, Secretary, Department of Personnel and Training, Ministry of Personnel sent letter dated 19.3.2010 to the appellant mentioning therein that the CBI had registered a case on 21.10.2009 against unknown officers of the Department of Telecommunications (DoT), unknown private persons/companies and others and that the issue of grant of sanction for prosecution would arise only after perusal of the evidence collected by the investigating agency and other material provided to the Competent Authority and that it would be premature to consider sanction for prosecution at that stage.

APPELLANT FILED WRIT PETITION IN DELHI HIGH COURT – DISMISSED

10. On receipt of the aforesaid communication, the appellant filed Civil Writ Petition No. 2442/2010 in the Delhi High Court and prayed for issue of a *mandamus* to respondent No. 1 to pass an order for grant of sanction for prosecution of respondent No. 2.

11. The Division Bench of the Delhi High Court referred to the submission of the learned Solicitor-General that when respondent No. 1 has directed investigation by the CBI and the investigation is in progress, it is not permissible to take a decision on the application of the appellant either to grant or refuse the sanction because that may affect the investigation, and dismissed the writ petition by recording the following observations:[1]

> "The question that emanates for consideration is whether, at this stage, when the investigation by the CBI is in progress and this Court had earlier declined to monitor the same by order dated 25th May, 2010, which has been pressed into service by the learned Solicitor-General of India, it would be appropriate to direct the respondent No. 1 to take a decision as regards the application submitted by the petitioner seeking sanction to prosecute.

In our considered opinion, when the matter is being investigated by the CBI, and the investigation is in progress, it would not be in fitness of things to issue a *mandamus* to the first respondent to take a decision on the application of the petitioner."

SLP FILED IN THE SUPREME COURT BY THE APPELLANT

12. The special leave petition filed by the appellant, out of which this appeal arises, was initially taken up for consideration along with SLP(C) No. 24873/2010 filed by the Center for Public Interest Litigation against order dated 25.5.2010 (Del.) passed by the Division Bench of the High Court in *Centre for Public Interest Litigation* v. *Union of India,* Writ Petition (Civil) No. 3522/2010 order dated 25.5.2010 (Del) to which reference had been made in the impugned order.

SUPREME COURT CALLED FOR AFFIDAVIT OF RESPONDENT NO. 1

13. During the course of hearing of the special leave petition filed by the appellant, the learned Solicitor-General, who had appeared on behalf of respondent No. 1, made a statement that he has got the record and is prepared to place the same before the Court. However, keeping in view the fact that the record sought to be produced by the learned Solicitor-General may not be readily available to the appellant, the Court passed order dated 18.11.2010 requiring the filing of an affidavit on behalf of respondent No. 1.

THE DIRECTOR IN THE PMO FILED THE AFFIDAVIT – ITS CONTENTS

14. Hereafter, Shri V. Vidyavati, Director in the PMO filed affidavit dated 20.11.2010, which reveals the following facts:

"(i) On 1.12.2008, the Prime Minister perused the letter and noted "Please examine and let me know the facts of this case". This was marked to the

---

1. *Subramanian Swamy* v. *Manmohan Singh,* WP(C) No. 2442 of 2010 Order dated 18-8-2010 (Del).

Principal Secretary to the Prime Minister who in turn marked it to the Secretary. The Secretary marked it to me as Director in the PMO. I prepared a note dated 5.12.2008 factually summarizing the allegations and seeking approval to obtain the factual position from the sectorial side (in the PMO dealing with Telecommunications).

(ii) On 11.12.2008, a copy of appellant's letter dated 29.11.2008 was sent to the Secretary, Department of Telecommunication for submitting a factual report. The Department of Telecommunication sent reply dated 13.2.2009 incorporating his comments.

(iii) In the meanwhile, letters dated 10.11.2008 and 22.11.2008 were received from Shri Gurudas Gupta and Shri Suravaran Sudhakar Reddy respectively (copies of these letters have not been produced before the Court). The same were forwarded to the Department of Telecommunication on 25.3.2009 for sending an appropriate reply to the appellant.

(iv) On 1.6.2009, letter dated 30.5.2009 received from the appellant was placed before respondent No.1, who recorded the following endorsement "please examine and discuss".

(v) On 19.6.2009, the Director of the concerned Sector in the PMO recorded that the Minister of Telecommunications and Information Technology has sent D.O. letter dated 18.6.2009 to the appellant. When letter dated 23.10.2009 of the appellant was placed before respondent No. 1, he recorded an endorsement on 27.10.2009 "please discuss".

(vi) In response to letter dated 31.10.2009 of the appellant, respondent No. 1 made an endorsement "please examine".

(vii) On 18.11.2009, respondent No. 1 stated that Ministry of Law and Justice should examine and advice. The advice of Ministry of Law and Justice was received on 8.2.2010. Para 7 thereof was as follows:

"From the perusal of letters dated 23.10.2009 and 31.10.2009, it is noticed that Shri Swamy wants to rely upon the action and investigation of the CBI to collaborate and strengthen the said allegation levelled by him against Shri A. Raja, Minister for Communication and Information Technology. It is specifically mentioned in Para 2 of the letter dated 31.10.2009 of Shri Swamy that the FIR was registered by the CBI and "the substance of the allegation made by me in the above cited letters to you are already under investigation". If it is so, then it may be stated that decision to accord of sanction of prosecution may be determined only after the perusal of the evidence (oral or documentary) collected by the investigation agency, *i.e.*, CBI and other materials to be provided to the competent authority."

(viii) On 5.3.2010, the deponent prepared a note that an appropriate reply be sent to the appellant in the light of the advice given by the Law Department and final reply was sent to the appellant after respondent No. 1 had approved note dated 17.3.2010."

THE APPELLANT FILED REJOINDER

15. The appellant filed rejoinder affidavit on 22.11.2010 along with a copy of letter dated 18.6.2009 written to him by respondent No. 2 in the context of representation dated 29.11.2008 submitted by him to respondent No. 1.

A. RAJA, MINISTER C& IT RESIGNED ON 14.11.2010

16. Although, respondent No. 2 resigned from the Council of Ministers on 14.11.2010, the appellant submitted that the issues relating to his right to file a complaint for prosecution of respondent No. 2 and grant of sanction within the time specified in the judgment in *Vineet Narain's* case, (1998) 1 SCC 226 should be decided.

WRITTEN SUBMISSIONS FILED BY THE ATTORNEY GENERAL STATING THAT SANCTION FOR PROSECUTION WAS AWAITED IN 126 CASES

17. During the course of hearing, the learned Attorney-General filed written submissions. After the hearing concluded, the learned Attorney-General filed supplementary written submissions along with a compilation of 126 cases in which the sanction for prosecution is awaited for periods ranging from more than one year to few months.

HOWEVER NO OBSTACLE IN DECIDING 2G CASE

18. Final order in this case was deferred because it was felt that the directions given by this Court in *Vineet Narain's* case may require further elaboration in the light of the order passed in Civil Appeal No. 10660/2010 (arising out of SLP(C) No. 24873/2010) and the fact that decision on the question of grant of sanction under the 1988 Act and other statutes is pending for a sufficiently long time in 126 cases. However, as the investigation with regard to some of the facets of what has come to be termed as 2G case is yet to be completed, we have considered it appropriate to pass final order in the matter.

SUBMISSIONS OF THE APPELLANT

19. Appellant Dr. Subramanian Swamy argued that the embargo contained in section 19(1) of the 1988 Act operates only against the taking of cognizance by the Court in respect of offences punishable under sections 7, 10, 11, 13 and 15 committed by a public servant, but there is no bar to the filing of a private complaint for prosecution of the concerned public servant and grant of sanction by the Competent Authority, and that respondent No. 1 was duty bound to take appropriate decision on his representation within the time specified in clause I(15) of the directions contained in paragraph 58 of *Vineet Narain's* case (supra), moreso because he had placed sufficient evidence to show that respondent No. 2 had committed offences under the 1988 Act.

SEEKING SANCTION PREMATURELY – SUBMISSIONS ON BEHALF OF THE UNION OF INDIA

20. The learned Attorney-General argued that the question of grant of sanction for prosecution of a public servant charged with any of the offences enumerated in section 19(1) arises only at the stage when the Court decides to take cognizance and any request made prior to that is premature. He submitted that the embargo contained in section 19(1) of the Act is applicable to the Court which is competent to take cognizance of an offence punishable under sections 7, 10, 11, 13 and 15 alleged to have been committed by a public servant and there is no provision for grant of sanction at a stage before the competent Court applies its mind to the issue of taking cognizance.

JUDGMENTS RELIED UPON BY THE RESPONDENTS

21. Learned Attorney-General relied upon the judgment of the Calcutta High Court in *Superintendent and Remembrancer of Legal Affairs* v. *Abani Kumar Banerjee*, AIR 1950 Cal 437 as also the judgments of this Court in *R.R. Chari* v. *State of Uttar Pradesh*, 1951 SCR 312; *Devarapalli Lakshminarayana Reddy* v. *V. Narayana Reddy*, (1976) 3 SCC 252; *Ram Kumar* v. *State of Haryana*, (1987) 1 SCC 476; *Krishna Pillai* v. *T.A. Rajendran*, 1990 (Supp) SCC 121; *State of West Bengal* v. *Mohd. Khalid*, (1995) 1 SCC 684; *State through C.B.I.* v. *Raj Kumar Jain*, (1998) 6 SCC 551; *K. Kalimuthu* v. *State*, (2005) 4 SCC 512; *Centre for Public Interest Litigation* v. *Union of India*, (2005) 8 SCC 202 and *State of Karnataka* v. *Pastor P. Raju*, (2006) 6 SCC 728 neither PM committed any offence in not granting the sanction nor appellant has any right to prosecute A. Raja – submits AG and argued that letter dated 29.11.2008 sent by the appellant for grant of sanction to prosecute respondent No. 2 for the alleged offences under the 1988 Act was wholly misconceived and respondent No. 1 did not commit any illegality or constitutional impropriety by not entertaining his prayer, moreso because the appellant had himself asked for an investigation into the alleged illegal grant of licences at the behest of respondent No. 2.

22. Learned Attorney-General further argued that the appellant does not have the *locus standi* to file a complaint for prosecuting respondent No. 2 because the CBI is already investigating the allegations of irregularity committed in the grant of licences for 2G spectrum and the loss, if any, suffered by the Public Exchequer.

DISCUSSION BY THE HON'BLE SUPREME COURT – SECTION 19 OF PC ACT, 1988

23. We have considered the respective submissions.

24. Section 19 of the 1988 Act reads as under:

> "***19. Previous sanction necessary for prosecution.***—(1) No court shall take cognizance of an offence punishable under sections 7, 10, 11, 13 and 15 alleged to have been committed by a public servant, except with the previous sanction,—
>
> (a) in the case of a person who is employed in connection with the affairs of the Union and is not removable from his office save by or with the sanction of the Central Government, of that Government;
>
> (b) in the case of a person who is employed in connection with the affairs of a State and is not removable from his office save by or with the sanction of the State Government, of that Government;
>
> (c) in the case of any other person, of the authority competent to remove him from his office.
>
> (2) Where for any reason whatsoever any doubt arises as to whether the previous sanction as required under sub-section (1) should be given by the

Central Government or the State Government or any other authority, such sanction shall be given by that Government or authority which would have been competent to remove the public servant from his office at the time when the offence was alleged to have been committed.

(3) Notwithstanding anything contained in the Code of Criminal Procedure, 1973 (2 of 1974),—

(a) no finding, sentence or order passed by a special Judge shall be reversed or altered by a court in appeal, confirmation or revision on the ground of the absence of, or any error, omission or irregularity in, the sanction required under sub-section (1), unless in the opinion of that court, a failure of justice has in fact been occasioned thereby;

(b) no court shall stay the proceedings under this Act on the ground of any error, omission or irregularity in the sanction granted by the authority, unless it is satisfied that such error, omission or irregularity has resulted in a failure of justice;

(c) no court shall stay the proceedings under this Act on any other ground and no court shall exercise the powers of revision in relation to any interlocutory order passed in any inquiry, trial, appeal or other proceedings.

(4) In determining under sub-section (3) whether the absence of, or any error, omission or irregularity in, such sanction has occasioned or resulted in a failure of justice the court shall have regard to the fact whether the objection could and should have been raised at any earlier stage in the proceedings.

Explanation.—For the purposes of this section, (a) error includes competency of the authority to grant sanction;

(b) a sanction required for prosecution includes reference to any requirement that the prosecution shall be at the instance of a specified authority or with the sanction of a specified person or any requirement of a similar nature."

SINCE A. RAJA HAD RESIGNED AS A MINISTER, NO SANCTION WAS REQUIRED EVEN THOUGH HE WAS M.P. AS HE COMMITTED THE OFFENCE AS A MINSTER AND NOT AS AN M.P.

25. The question whether sanction for prosecution of respondent No. 2 for the offences allegedly committed by him under the 1988 Act is required even after he resigned from the Council of Ministers, though he continues to be a Member of Parliament, need not detain us because the same has already been answered by the Constitution Bench in *R.S. Nayak* v. *A.R. Antulay*, (1984) 2 SCC 183 the relevant portions of which are extracted below: (SCC pp. 206-08 paras 24-25)

"24. Now if the public servant holds two offices and he is accused of having abused one and from which he is removed but continues to hold the other which is neither alleged to have been used (*sic* misused) nor abused, is a sanction of the authority competent to remove him from the office which is neither alleged or shown to have been abused or misused necessary? The submission is that if the harassment of the public servant by a frivolous prosecution and criminal waste of his time in law courts keeping him away from discharging public duty, are the objects underlying section 6, the same would be defeated if it is held that the sanction of the latter authority is not necessary. The submission does not commend to us. We fail to see how the competent authority entitled to remove the public servant from an office which is neither alleged to have been used (*sic* misused) or abused would be able to decide whether the prosecution is frivolous or tendentious. An illustration was posed to the learned counsel that a minister who is indisputably a public servant greased his palms by abusing his office as minister, and then ceased to hold the office before the court was called upon to take cognizance of the offence against him and therefore, sanction as contemplated by section 6 would not be necessary; but if after committing the offence and before the date of taking of cognizance of the offence, he was elected as a Municipal President in which capacity he was a public servant under the relevant municipal law, and was holding that office on the date on which court proceeded to take cognizance of the offence committed by him as a minister, would a sanction be necessary and that too of that authority competent to remove him from the office of the Municipal President. The answer was in affirmative. But the very illustration would show that such cannot be the law. Such an interpretation of section 6 would render it as a shield to an unscrupulous public servant. Someone interested in protecting may shift him from one office of public servant to another and thereby defeat the process of law. One can legitimately envisage a situation wherein a person may hold a dozen different offices, each one clothing him with the status of a public servant under section 21 IPC and even if he has abused only one office for which either there is a valid sanction to prosecute him or he has ceased to hold that office by the time court was called upon to take cognizance, yet on this assumption, sanction of 11 different competent authorities each of which was entitled to remove him from 11 different public offices would be necessary before the court can take cognizance of the offence committed by such public servant, while abusing one office which he may have ceased to hold. Such an interpretation is contrary to all canons of construction and leads to an absurd end product which of necessity must be avoided. Legislation must at all costs be interpreted in such a way that it would not operate as a rogue's charter.

25. ...We would however, like to make it abundantly clear that if the two decisions purport to lay down that even if a public servant has ceased to hold that office as public servant which he is alleged to have abused or misused for corrupt motives, but on the date of taking cognizance of an offence alleged to have been committed by him as a public servant which he ceased to be and holds an entirely different public office which he is neither alleged to have misused or abused for corrupt motives, yet the sanction of authority competent to remove him from such latter office would be necessary before taking cognizance of the offence alleged to have been committed by the public servant while holding an office which he is alleged to have abused or misused and which he has ceased to hold, the decision in our opinion, do not lay down the correct law and cannot be accepted as making a correct interpretation of section 6."

The same view has been taken in *Habibullsa Khan* v. *State of Orissa*, (1995) 2 SCC 437 (para 12); *State of Himachal Pradesh* v. *M. P. Gupta*, (2004) 2 SCC 349 (paras 17 and 19); *Parkash Singh Badal* v. *State of Punjab*, (2007) 1 SCC 1 and *Balakrishnan Ravi Menon* v. *Union of India*, (2007) 1 SCC 45.

26. In *Balakrishnan Ravi Menon's* case (supra), it was argued that the observations made in para 25 of the judgment in *Antulay's* case are obiter. While negating this submission, the Court observed; *Balakrishnan Ravi Menon's* case, (2002) 2 SCC 45 (SCC pages 47-48 paras 5-7).

"5. Hence, it is difficult to accept the contention raised by Mr. U.R. Lalit, the learned Senior Counsel for the petitioner that the aforesaid finding given by this Court in *Antulay* case is obiter.

6. Further, under section 19 of the PC Act, sanction is to be given by the Government or the authority which would have been competent to remove the public servant from his office at the time when the offence was alleged to have been committed. The question of obtaining sanction would arise in a case where the offence has been committed by a public servant who is holding the office and by misusing or abusing the powers of the office, he has committed the offence. The word "office" repeatedly used in section 19 would mean the "office" which the public servant misuses or abuses by corrupt motive for which he is to be prosecuted. Sub-sections (1) and (2) of section 19 are as under:

"19. *Previous sanction necessary for prosecution.*—(1) No court shall take cognizance of an offence punishable under sections 7, 10, 11, 13 and 15 alleged to have been committed by a public servant, except with the previous sanction,—

(a) in the case of a person who is employed in connection with the affairs of the Union and is not removable from his office save by or with the sanction of the Central Government, of that Government;

(b) in the case of a person who is employed in connection with the affairs of a State and is not removable from his office save by or with the sanction of the State Government, of that Government;

(c) in the case of any other person, of the authority competent to remove him from his office.

(2) Where for any reason whatsoever any doubt arises as to whether the previous sanction as required under sub-section (1) should be given by the Central Government or the State Government or any other authority, such sanction shall be given by that Government *or authority which would have been competent to remove the public servant from his office at the time when the offence was alleged to have been committed.*" (Emphasis supplied)

7. Clauses (a) and (b) of sub-section (1) specifically provide that in case of a person who is employed and is not removable from his office by the Central Government or the State Government, as the case may be, sanction to prosecute is required to be obtained either from the Central Government or the State Government. The emphasis is on the words "who is employed" in connection with the affairs of the Union or the

State Government. If he is not employed then section 19 nowhere provides for obtaining such sanction. Further, under sub-section (2), the question of obtaining sanction is relatable to the time of holding the office when the offence was alleged to have been committed. In case where the person is not holding the said office as he might have retired, superannuated, be discharged or dismissed then the question of removing would not arise. Admittedly, when the alleged offence was committed, the petitioner was appointed by the Central Government. He demitted his office after completion of five years' tenure. Therefore, at the relevant time when the charge-sheet was filed, the petitioner was not holding the office of the Chairman of Goa Shipyard Ltd. Hence, there is no question of obtaining any previous sanction of the Central Government." (Emphasis supplied)

The same view was reiterated in *Parkash Singh Badal's* case, (2007) 1 SCC 1 and the argument that even though some of the accused persons had ceased to be Ministers, they continued to be the Members of the Legislative Assembly and one of them was a Member of Parliament and as such cognizance could not be taken against them without prior sanction, was rejected.

PRIVATE COMPLAINT NOT MAINTAINABLE – SUBMISSION OF AG – REJECTED

27. The next question which requires consideration is whether the appellant has the *locus standi* to file a complaint for prosecution of respondent No. 2 for the offences allegedly committed by him under the 1988 Act.

28. There is no provision either in the 1988 Act or the Code of Criminal Procedure, 1973 (CrPC) which bars a citizen from filing a complaint for prosecution of a public servant who is alleged to have committed an offence.

Therefore, the argument of the learned Attorney-General that the appellant cannot file a complaint for prosecuting respondent No. 2 merits rejection. A similar argument was negatived by the Constitution Bench in *A.R. Antulay* v. *Ramdas Sriniwas Nayak*, (1984) 2 SCC 500.

29. The facts of that case (*A.R. Antulay's* case) (supra) show that on a private complaint filed by the respondent, the Special Judge took cognizance of the offences allegedly committed by the appellant. The latter objected to the jurisdiction of the Special Judge on two counts, including the one that the Court set-up under section 6 of the Criminal Law Amendment Act, 1952 (for short, 'the 1952 Act') was not competent to take cognizance of any of the offences enumerated in section 6(1)(a) and (b) upon a private complaint. His objections were rejected by the Special Judge. The revision filed by the appellant was heard by the Division Bench of the High Court which ruled that a Special Judge is competent and is entitled to take cognizance of offences under section 6(1)(a) and (b) on a private complaint of the facts constituting the offence. The High Court was of the opinion that a prior investigation under section 5A of the Prevention of Corruption Act, 1947 (for short, 'the 1947 Act') by a police officer of the designated rank is not *sine qua non* for taking cognizance of an offence under section 8(1) of the 1952 Act. Before the Supreme Court, the argument against the *locus standi* of the respondent was reiterated and it was submitted that section 5A of the 1947 Act is mandatory and an investigation by the designated officer is a condition precedent to the taking of cognizance by the Special Judge of an offence or offences committed by a public servant.

30. While dealing with the issue relating to maintainability of a private complaint, the Constitution Bench observed: (*A.R. Antulay's* case, SCC pp . 508-09 para 6)

"6. It is a well-recognised principle of criminal jurisprudence that anyone can set or put the criminal law into motion except where the statute enacting or creating an offence indicates to the contrary. The Scheme of the Code of Criminal Procedure envisages two parallel and independent agencies for taking criminal offences to court. Even for the most serious offence of murder, it was not disputed that a private complaint cannot only be filed but can be entertained and proceeded with according to law. *Locus standi of the complainant is a concept foreign to criminal jurisprudence save and except that where the statute creating an offence provides for the eligibility of the complainant, by necessary implication the general principle gets excluded by such statutory provision.* Numerous statutory provisions, can be referred to in support of this legal position such as (i) section 187A of Sea Customs Act, 1878; (ii) section 97 of Gold Control Act, 1968;(iii) Section 6 of Import and Export Control Act, 1947; (iv) section 271 and section 279 of the Income-tax Act, 1961; (v) section 61 of the Foreign Exchange Regulation Act, 1973; (vi) section 621 of the Companies Act, 1956; and (vii) Section 77 of the Electricity Supply Act. This list is only illustrative and not exhaustive. *While section 190 of the Code of Criminal Procedure permits anyone to approach the Magistrate with a complaint, it does not prescribe any qualification the complainant is required to fulfil to be eligible to file a complaint.* But where an eligibility criterion for a complainant is contemplated specific provisions have been made such as to be found in sections 195 to 199 of the Cr. P.C. These specific provisions clearly indicate that in the absence of any such statutory provision, a *locus standi* of a complainant is a concept foreign to criminal jurisprudence. *In other words, the principle that anyone can set or put the criminal law in motion remains intact unless contra-indicated by a statutory provision. This general principle of nearly universal application is founded on a policy that an offence i.e., an act or omission made punishable by any law for the time being in force is not merely an offence committed in relation to the person who suffers harm but is also an offence against society. The society for its orderly and peaceful development is interested in the punishment of the offender. Therefore, prosecution for serious offences is undertaken in the name of the State representing the people which would exclude any element of private vendetta or vengeance. If such is the public policy underlying penal statutes, who brings an act or omission made punishable by law to the notice of the authority competent to deal with it, is immaterial and irrelevant unless the statute indicates to the contrary. Punishment of the offender in the interest of the society being one of the objects behind penal statutes enacted for larger good of the society, right to initiate proceedings cannot be whittled down, circumscribed or fettered by putting it into a straitjacket formula of* locus standi *unknown to criminal jurisprudence, save and except specific statutory exception.* To hold that such an exception exists that a private complaint for offences of corruption committed by public servant is not maintainable, the court would require an unambiguous statutory provision and a tangled web of argument for drawing a far fetched implication, cannot be a substitute for an express statutory provision." (Emphasis supplied)

31. The Constitution Bench then considered whether the Special Judge can take cognizance only on the basis of a police report and answered the same in negative in the following words: (*A.R. Antulay's* case, SCC p. 509 para 6)

> "6. In the matter of initiation of proceeding before a Special Judge under section 8(1), the Legislature while conferring power to take cognizance had three opportunities to unambiguously state its mind whether the cognizance can be taken on a private complaint or not. The first one was an opportunity to provide in section 8(1) itself by merely stating that the Special Judge may take cognizance of an offence on a police report submitted to it by an investigating officer conducting investigation as contemplated by section 5A. While providing for investigation by designated police officers of superior rank, the Legislature did not fetter the power of Special Judge to take cognizance in a manner otherwise than on police report. The second opportunity was when by section 8(3) a status of a deemed public prosecutor was conferred on a private complainant if he chooses to conduct the prosecution. The Legislature being aware of a provision like the one contained in section 225 of the Cr. P.C., could have as well provided that in every trial before a Special Judge the prosecution shall be conducted by a Public Prosecutor, though that itself would not have been decisive of the matter. And the third opportunity was when the Legislature while prescribing the procedure prescribed for warrant cases to be followed by Special Judge did not exclude by a specific provision that the only procedure which the Special Judge can follow is the one prescribed for trial of warrant cases on a police report. *The disinclination of the Legislature to so provide points to the contrary and no canon of construction permits the court to go in search of a hidden or implied limitation on the power of the Special Judge to take cognizance unfettered by such requirement of its being done on a police report alone.* In our opinion, it is no answer to this fairly well-established legal position that for the last 32 years no case has come to the notice of the court in which cognizance was taken by a Special Judge on a private complaint for offences punishable under the 1947 Act." (Emphasis supplied)

32. The Court then referred to section 5A of the 1947 Act, the provisions of the 1952 Act, the judgments in *H.N. Rishbud and Inder Singh* v. *State of Delhi,* (1955) 1 SCR 1150; *State of Madhya Pradesh* v. *Mubarak Ali,* 1959 Supp (2) SCR 201; *Union of India* v. *Mahesh Chandra,* AIR 1957 MB 43 and held: (*A.R. Antulay's* case pp. 522-524 paras 21-24)

> "21. ...Having carefully examined these judgments in the light of the submissions made, the only conclusion that unquestionably emerges is that section 5A is a safeguard against investigation of offences committed by public servants, by petty or lower rank police officer. It has nothing to do directly or indirectly with the mode and method of taking cognizance of offences by the Court of Special Judge. *It also follows as a necessary corollary that provision of section 5A is not a condition precedent to initiation of proceedings before the Special*

Judge who acquires power under section 8(1) to take cognizance of offences enumerated in section 6(1)(a) and (b), with this limitation alone that it shall not be upon commitment to him by the Magistrate.

22. Once the contention on behalf of the appellant that investigation under section 5A is a condition precedent to the initiation of proceedings before a Special Judge and therefore cognizance of an offence cannot be taken except upon a police report, does not commend to us and has no foundation in law, it is unnecessary to refer to the long line of decisions commencing from Taylor *v.* Taylor, *(1876) 1 Ch D 426;* Nazir Ahmad *v.* King Emperor, *(1935-36) 63 IA 372 and ending with* Chettiam Veettil Ammad *v.* Taluk Land Board, *(1980) 1 SCC 499, laying down hitherto uncontroverted legal principle that where a statute requires to do a certain thing in a certain way, the thing must be done in that way or not at all. Other methods of performance are necessarily forbidden.*

23. Once section 5A is out of the way in the matter of taking cognizance of offences committed by public servants by a Special Judge, the power of the Special Judge to take cognizance of such offences conferred by section 8(1) with only one limitation, in any one of the known methods of taking cognizance of offences by courts of original jurisdiction remains indented. One such statutorily recognised well-known method of taking cognizance of offences by a court competent to take cognizance is upon receiving a complaint of facts which constitutes the offence. And section 8(1) says that the Special Judge has the power to take cognizance of offences enumerated in section 6(1)(a) and (b) and the only mode of taking cognizance excluded by the provision is upon commitment. It, therefore, follows that the Special Judge can take cognizance of offences committed by public servants upon receiving a complaint of facts constituting such offences.

24. It was, however, submitted that even if it be held that the Special Judge is entitled to entertain a private complaint, no further steps can be taken by him without directing an investigation under section 5A so that the safeguard of section 5A is not whittled down. This is the selfsame argument under a different apparel. Accepting such a submission would tantamount to saying that on receipt of the complaint the Special Judge must direct an investigation under section 5A. There is no warrant for such an approach. Astounding as it appeared to us, in all solemnity it was submitted that investigation of an offence by a superior police officer affords a more solid safeguard compared to a court. Myopic as this is, it would topsy turvy the fundamental belief that to a person accused of an offence there is no better safeguard than a court. And this is constitutionally epitomised in article 22 that upon arrest by police, the arrested person must be produced before the nearest Magistrate within twenty-four hours of the arrest. Further, numerous provisions of the Code of Criminal Procedure such as section 161, section 164, and section 25 of the Indian Evidence Act would show the Legislature's hesitation in placing confidence on police officers away from court's gaze. And the very fact that power is conferred on a Presidency Magistrate or Magistrate of the first class to permit police officers of lower rank to investigate these offences would speak for the mind of the Legislature that the court is a more reliable safeguard than even superior police officers."

(Emphasis supplied)

33. In view of the aforesaid judgment of the Constitution Bench, it must be held that the appellant has the right to file a complaint for prosecution of respondent No. 2 in respect of the offences allegedly committed by him under the 1988 Act.

QUESTION OF GRANTING SANCTION TO BE CONSIDERED AT THE TIME OF TAKING COGNIZANCE BY THE COURT – NOT BEFORE – REJECTED

34. The argument of the learned Attorney-General that the question of granting sanction for prosecution of a public servant charged with an offence under the 1988 Act arises only at the stage of taking cognizance and not before that is neither supported by the plain language of the section nor the judicial precedents relied upon by him. Though, the term 'cognizance' has not been defined either in the 1988 Act or the Cr. P.C., the same has acquired a definite meaning and connotation from various judicial precedents. In legal parlance cognizance is "taking judicial notice by the court of law, possessing jurisdiction, on a cause or matter presented before it so as to decide whether there is any basis for initiating proceedings and determination of the cause or matter judicially".

COGNIZANCE IS TAKEN WHEN THE COURT APPLIES ITS MIND

35. In *R.R. Chari* v. *State of Uttar Pradesh,* (1951) SCR 312, the three-Judge Bench approved the following observations made by the Calcutta High Court in *Superintendent and Remembrancer of Legal Affairs, West Bengal* v. *Abni Kumar Banerjee (supra)*: (AIR p. 438 para 7)

> "...What is taking cognizance has not been defined in the Criminal Procedure Code and I have no desire to attempt to define it. It seems to me clear however that before it can be said that any magistrate has taken cognizance of any offence under section 190(1)(a), Criminal Procedure Code, he must not only have applied his mind to the contents of the petition but he must have done so for the purpose of proceeding in a particular way as indicated in the subsequent provisions of this Chapter – proceeding under section 200 and thereafter sending it for inquiry and report under section 202. When the Magistrate applies his mind not for the purpose of proceeding under the subsequent sections of this Chapter, but for taking action of some other kind, *e.g.*, ordering investigation under section 156(3), or issuing a search warrant for the purpose of the investigation, he cannot be said to have taken cognizance of the offence."

36. In *State of West Bengal* v. *Mohd. Khalid*, (1995) 1 SCC 684 the Court referred to section 190 of the Cr.P.C. and observed:

> "In its broad and literal sense, it means taking notice of an offence. This would include the intention of initiating judicial proceedings against the offender in respect of that offence or taking steps to see whether there is any basis for initiating judicial proceedings or for other purposes. The word 'cognizance' indicates the point when a Magistrate or a Judge first takes judicial notice of an offence. It is entirely a different thing from initiation of proceedings; rather it is the condition precedent to the initiation of proceedings by the Magistrate or the Judge. Cognizance is taken of cases and not of persons."

37. In *Pastor P. Raju's* case, (2006) 6 SCC 278, this Court referred to the provisions of Chapter XIV and sections 190 and 196 (1A) of the Cr.P.C. and observed (SCC p. 732 para 8)

> "8. There is no bar against registration of a criminal case or investigation by the police agency or submission of a report by the police on completion of investigation, as contemplated by section 173 Cr.P.C. If a criminal case is registered, investigation of the offence is done and the police submits a report as a result of such investigation before a Magistrate without the previous sanction of the Central Government or of the State Government or of the District Magistrate, there will be no violation of section 196(1A) Cr.P.C. and no illegality of any kind would be committed."

38. The Court then referred to some of the precedents including the judgment in *Mohd. Khalid's* case, (1995) 1 SCC 684 and observed: [*Pastor P. Raju's* case (supra) SCC p. 734 para 13]

> "13. It is necessary to mention here that taking cognizance of an offence is not the same thing as issuance of process. Cognizance is taken at the initial stage when the Magistrate applies his judicial mind to the facts mentioned in a complaint or to a police report or upon information received from any other person that an offence has been committed. The issuance of process is at a subsequent stage when after considering the material placed before it the court decides to proceed against the offenders against whom a *prima facie* case is made out."

CBI CAN SUBMIT THE REPORT IN THE COURT AFTER OBTAINING SANCTION OF THE COMPETENT AUTHORITY, IF A CASE IS MADE OUT

39. In *Kalimuthu's* case, (2005) 4 SCC 512, the only question considered by this Court was whether in the absence of requisite sanction under section 197, Cr.P.C., the Special Judge for CBI cases, Chennai did not have the jurisdiction to take cognizance of the alleged offences. The High Court had taken the view that section 197 was not applicable to the appellant's case. Affirming the view taken by the High Court, this Court observed: (SCC p. 521 para 15)

> "15. The question relating to the need of sanction under section 197 of the Code is not necessarily to be considered as soon as the complaint is lodged and on the allegations contained therein. This question may arise at any stage of the proceeding. The question whether sanction is necessary or not may have to be determined from stage to stage. Further, in cases where offences under the Act are concerned, the effect of section 197, dealing with the question of prejudice has also to be noted."

40. In *State through CBI* v. *Raj Kumar Jain*, (1998) 6 SCC 551, this Court considered the question whether the CBI was required to obtain sanction from the prosecuting authority before approaching the Court for accepting the report under section 173(2) of the Cr.P.C. This question was considered in the backdrop of the fact that the CBI, which had investigated the case registered against the respondent under section 5(2) read with section 5(1)(e) of the 1947 Act found that the allegation made against the respondent could not be substantiated. The Special Judge declined to accept the report submitted under section 173(2) Cr.P.C. by observing that the CBI was required to place materials collected during investigation before the sanctioning authority and it was for the concerned authority to grant or refuse sanction. The Special Judge opined that only after the decision of the sanctioning authority, the CBI could submit the report under section 173(2). The High Court dismissed the petition filed by the CBI and confirmed the order of the Special Judge.

41. This Court referred to section 6(1) of the 1947 Act and observed: (*Raj Kumar Jain's* case, SCC pp. 552-53 para 5)

> "5. From a plain reading of the above section it is evidently clear that a court cannot take cognizance of the offences mentioned therein without sanction of the appropriate authority. In enacting the above section, the legislature thought of providing a reasonable protection to public servants in the discharge of their official functions so that they may perform their duties and obligations undeterred by vexatious and unnecessary prosecutions. Viewed in that context, the CBI was under no obligation to place the materials collected during investigation before the sanctioning authority, when they found that no case was made out against the respondent. To put it differently, if the CBI had found on investigation that a *prima facie* case was made out against the respondent to place him on trial and accordingly prepared a charge-sheet (challan) against him, then only the question of obtaining sanction of the authority under section 6(1) of the Act would have arisen for without that the Court would not be competent to take cognizance of the charge-sheet. It must, therefore, be said that both the Special Judge and the High Court were patently wrong in observing that the CBI was required to obtain sanction from the prosecuting authority before approaching the Court for accepting the report under section 173(2) Cr.P.C."

JUDGMENTS RELIED UPON BY THE RESPONDENTS REGARDING GRANT OF SANCTION – NOT APPLICABLE

42. In our view, the decisions relied upon by the learned Attorney-General do not have any bearing on the moot question whether respondent No. 1, being the Competent Authority to sanction prosecution of respondent No. 2, was required to take appropriate decision in the light of the direction contained in *Vineet Narain's* case, (1998) 1 SCC 226.

COURT DOES NOT ANALYSE EVIDENCE ON THE PRESENTATION OF CHALLAN, IT JUST EXAMINES THE AVERMENTS MADE

43. Before proceeding further, we would like to add that at the time of taking cognizance of the offence, the Court is required to consider the averments made in the complaint or the charge sheet filed under section 173. It is not open for the Court to analyse the evidence produced at that stage and come to the conclusion that no *prima facie* case is made out for proceeding further in the matter. However, before issuing the process, it is open to the Court to record the evidence and on consideration of the averments made in the complaint and the evidence thus adduced, find out whether an offence has been made out. On finding that such an offence has been made out the Court may direct the issue of process to the respondent and take further steps in the matter. If it is a charge sheet filed under section 173, Cr.P.C., the facts stated by the prosecution in the charge-sheet, on the basis of the evidence collected during investigation, would disclose the offence for which cognizance would be taken by the Court. Thus, it is not the province of the Court at that stage to embark upon and sift the evidence to come to the conclusion whether or not an offence has been made out.

AT THE TIME OF GRANT OF SANCTION FOR PROSECUTION, ACCUSED NEED NOT BE HEARD

44. We may also observe that grant or refusal of sanction is not a *quasi*-judicial function and the person for whose prosecution the sanction is sought is not required to be heard by the Competent Authority before it takes a decision in the matter. What is required to be seen by the Competent Authority is whether the facts placed before it which, in a given case, may include the material collected by the complainant or the investigating agency *prima facie* disclose commission of an offence by a public servant. If the Competent Authority is satisfied that the material placed before it is sufficient for prosecution of the public servant, then it is required to grant sanction. If the satisfaction of the Competent Authority is otherwise, then it can refuse sanction. In either case, the decision taken on the complaint made by a citizen is required to be communicated to him and if he feels aggrieved by such decision, then he can avail appropriate legal remedy.

VINEET NARAIN'S CASE ALSO KNOWN AS HAWALA CASE OR JAIN DIARIES CASE – PRINCIPLES LAID DOWN – DIRECTIONS

45. In *Vineet Narain's* case, (1998) 1 SCC 226, the Court entertained the writ petitions filed in public interest for ensuring investigation into what came to be known as 'Hawala case'. The writ petition remained pending for almost four years. During that period, several interim orders were passed which are reported as *Vineet Narain* v. *Union of India*, (1996) 2 SCC 199: (1996) 1 SCALE (SP) 42; *Vineet Narain* v. *Union of India*, (1996) 2 SCC 199; *Vineet Narain* v. *Union of India*, (1997) 4 SCC 778: (1997) 5 SCALE 254. The final order was passed in *Vineet Narain* v. *Union of India*, (1998) 1 SCC 226.

46. In *Vineet Narain's* case, (1996) 2 SCC 199: (1996) 1 SCALE (SP) 42, the Court referred to the allegations made in the writ petition that Government agencies like the CBI and the revenue authorities have failed to perform their duties and legal obligations inasmuch as they did not investigate into the matters arising out of seizure of the so-called "Jain Diaries" in certain raids conducted by the CBI. The Court took note of the allegation that the arrest of some terrorists led to the discovery of financial support to them by clandestine and illegal means and a nexus between several important politicians, bureaucrats and criminals, who were recipients of money from unlawful sources, and proceeded to observe:

> "The facts and circumstances of the present case do indicate that it is of utmost public importance that this matter is examined thoroughly by this Court to ensure that all government agencies, entrusted with the duty to discharge their functions and obligations in accordance with law, do so, bearing in mind constantly the concept of equality enshrined in the Constitution and the basic tenet of rule of law: "Be you ever so high, the law is above you." Investigation into every accusation made against each and every person on a reasonable basis, irrespective of the position and status of

that person, must be conducted and completed expeditiously. This is imperative to retain public confidence in the impartial working of the government agencies."

HOLDERS OF PUBLIC OFFICE MUST DISCHARGE THEIR FUNCTIONS IN PUBLIC INTEREST OF WHOM THEY ARE THE TRUSTEES – CORRUPTION IN PUBLIC LIFE HAS ADVERSE EFFECT ON THE COUNTRY AS A WHOLE

47. After examining various facets of the matter in detail, the three-Judge Bench in its final order in *Vineet Narain's* case reported in (1998) 1 SCC 226 observed (SCC page 268 paras 55-56):

"55. These principles of public life are of general application in every democracy and one is expected to bear them in mind while scrutinising the conduct of every holder of a public office. It is trite that the holders of public offices are entrusted with certain powers to be exercised in public interest alone and, therefore, the office is held by them in trust for the people. Any deviation from the path of rectitude by any of them amounts to a breach of trust and must be severely dealt with instead of being pushed under the carpet. If the conduct amounts to an offence, it must be promptly investigated and the offender against whom a *prima facie* case is made out should be prosecuted expeditiously so that the majesty of law is upheld and the rule of law vindicated. It is the duty of the Judiciary to enforce the rule of law and, therefore, to guard against erosion of the rule of law.

56. The adverse impact of lack of probity in public life leading to a high degree of corruption is manifold. It also has adverse effect on foreign investment and funding from the International Monetary Fund and the World Bank who have warned that future aid to underdeveloped countries may be subject to the requisite steps being taken to eradicate corruption, which prevents international aid from reaching those for whom it is meant. Increasing corruption has led to investigative journalism which is of value to a free society. The need to highlight corruption in public life through the medium of public interest litigation invoking judicial review may be frequent in India but is not unknown in other countries: "*R.* v. *Secy. of State for Foreign and Commonwealth Affairs*," (1995) 1 WLR 386.

48. In paragraph 58 of the judgment, the Court gave several directions in relation to the CBI, the CVC and the Enforcement Directorate. In para 58(1)(15), the Court gave the following direction: "Time-limit of three months for grant of sanction for prosecution must be strictly adhered to. However, additional time of one month may be allowed where consultation is required with the Attorney-General (AG) or any other law officer in the AG's office."

DIRECTIONS ISSUED BY THE CVC IN ACCORDANCE WITH THE JUDGMENTS OF VARIOUS HIGH COURTS

49. The CVC, after taking note of the judgment of the Punjab and Haryana High Court in *Jagjit Singh* v. *State of Punjab*, (1996) Cr LJ 2962; *State of Bihar* v. *P.P. Sharma*, 1991 Supp 1 SCC 222; *Superintendent of Police (CBI)* v. *Deepak Chowdhary*, (1995) 6 SCC 225, framed guidelines which were circulated *vide* office order No. 31/5/05 dated 12.5.2005. The relevant clauses of the guidelines are extracted below:

"2(i) Grant of sanction is an administrative act. The purpose is to protect the public servant from harassment by frivolous or vexatious prosecution and not to shield the corrupt. The question of giving opportunity to the public servant at that stage does not arise. The sanctioning authority has only to see whether the facts would *prima facie* constitute the offence.

(ii) The competent authority cannot embark upon an inquiry to judge the truth of the allegations on the basis of representation which may be filed by the accused person before the Sanctioning Authority, by asking the I.O. to offer his comments or to further investigate the matter in the light of representation made by the accused person or by otherwise holding a parallel investigation/ enquiry by calling for the record/report of his department.

* * * * * * *

(vii) However, if in any case, the Sanctioning Authority after consideration of the entire material placed before it, entertains any doubt on any point the competent authority may specify the doubt with sufficient particulars and may request the Authority who has sought sanction to clear the doubt. But that would be only to clear the doubt in order that the authority may apply its mind proper, and not for the purpose of considering the representations of the accused which may be filed while the matter is pending sanction.

(viii) If the Sanctioning Authority seeks the comments of the IO while the matter is pending before it for sanction, it will almost be impossible for the Sanctioning Authority to adhere to the time limit allowed by the Supreme Court in *Vineet Narain's* case, (1998) 1 SCC 226.

NO DETAILED ENQUIRY IS REQUIRED WHILE GRANTING SANCTION

50. The aforementioned guidelines are in conformity with the law laid down by this Court that while considering the issue regarding grant or refusal of sanction, the only thing which the Competent Authority is required to see is whether the material placed by the complainant or the investigating agency *prima facie* discloses commission of an offence. The Competent Authority cannot undertake a detailed inquiry to decide whether or not the allegations made against the public servant are true.

DELHI HIGH COURT ADOPTED ERRONEOUS ASSUMPTION

51. In the light of the above discussion, we shall now consider whether the High Court was justified in refusing to entertain the writ petition filed by the appellant.

52. In this context, it is apposite to observe that the High Court had proceeded under a wholly erroneous assumption that respondent No. 1 had directed investigation by the CBI into the allegations of grave irregularities in the grant of licences. As a matter of fact, on receipt of representation dated 4.5.2009 that the grant of licences by respondent No. 2 had resulted in huge loss to the Public Exchequer, the CVC got conducted an inquiry under section 8(d) of the Central Vigilance Commission Act, 2003 and forwarded a copy of the report to the Director, CBI for making an investigation into the matter to establish the criminal conspiracy in the allocation of 2G spectrum under the UASL policy of the DoT and to bring to book all the wrongdoers. Thereupon, the CBI registered FIR No. RC-DI-2009-A-

0045 dated 21.10.2009 against unknown officials of the DoT, unknown private persons/companies and others for offences under section 120B, IPC read with sections 13(2) and 13(1)(d) of the 1988 Act.

CBI REMAINED SLEEPING TILL SHAKEN BY THE SUPREME COURT.

53. For the next about one year, the matter remained dormant and the CBI took steps for vigorous investigation only when this Court intervened in the matter. The material placed on record does not show that the CBI had registered a case or started investigation at the instance of respondent No. 1.

APPELLANT SUBMITTED THE REPRESENTATION TO THE PM ABOUT ONE YEAR BEFORE THE REGISTRATION OF THE F.I.R.

On his part, the appellant had submitted representation to respondent No. 1 almost one year prior to the registration of the first information report by the CBI and highlighted the grave irregularities committed in the grant of licences resulting in the loss of thousands of crores of rupees to the Public Exchequer. He continuously pursued the matter by sending letters to respondent No. 1 at regular intervals.

PMO SENT THE REPRESENTATION TO DoPT UNDER A. RAJA

The affidavit filed by Shri V. Vidyawati, Director in the PMO shows that the matter was placed before respondent No. 1 on 1.12.2008, who directed the concerned officer to examine and apprise him with the facts of the case. Surprisingly, instead of complying with the direction given by respondent No. 1 the concerned officer sent the appellant's representation to the DoT which was headed by none other than respondent No. 2 against whom the appellant had made serious allegations of irregularities in the grant of licences. It was natural for respondent No. 2 to have seized this opportunity, and he promptly sent letter dated 18.6.2009 to the appellant justifying the grant of licences. The concerned officer in the PMO then referred the matter to the Ministry of Law and Justice for advice.

DELAY OF MORE THAN ONE YEAR IN THE PMO IN SUCH A SERIOUS MATTER, WHERE THOUSANDS OF CRORES OF RUPEES OF LOSS TO THE NATION WAS INVOLVED, WAS CLEARLY UNUNDERSTANDABLE

54. It is not possible to appreciate that even though the appellant repeatedly wrote letters to respondent No. 1 highlighting the seriousness of the allegations made in his first representation and the fact that he had already supplied the facts and documents which could be made basis for grant of sanction to prosecute respondent No. 2 and also pointed out that as per the judgments of this Court, detailed inquiry was not required to be made into the allegations, the concerned officers in the PMO kept the matter pending and then took the shelter of the fact that the CBI had registered the case and the investigation was pending.

IT WAS THE BOUNDEN DUTY OF THE OFFICERS IN THE PMO AND THE MINISTRY OF LAW AND JUSTICE TO INFORM THE PM ABOUT SERIOUSNESS OF THE MATTER

In our view, the officers in the PMO and the Ministry of Law and Justice, were duty bound to apprise respondent No. 1 about seriousness of allegations made by the appellant and the judgments of this Court including the directions contained in paragraph 58(I) of the judgment in *Vineet Narain's* case as also the guidelines framed by the CVC so as to enable him to take appropriate decision in the matter.

55. By the very nature of the office held by him, respondent No. 1 is not expected to personally look into the minute details of each and every case placed before him and has to depend on his advisers and other officers. Unfortunately, those who were expected to give proper advice to respondent No. 1 and place full facts and legal position before him failed to do so. We have no doubt that if respondent No. 1 had been apprised of the true factual and legal position regarding the representation made by the appellant, he would have surely taken appropriate decision and would not have allowed the matter to linger for a period of more than one year.

APPEAL ACCEPTED – NECESSARY DIRECTIONS GIVEN

56. In the result, the appeal is allowed. The impugned order is set aside. It is declared that the appellant had the right to file a complaint for prosecuting respondent No. 2. However, keeping in view the fact that the Court of Special Judge, CBI has already taken cognizance of the offences allegedly committed by respondent No. 2 under the 1988 Act, we do not consider it necessary to give any other direction in the matter. At the same time, we deem it proper to observe that in future every Competent Authority shall take appropriate action on the representation made by a citizen for sanction of the prosecution of a public servant strictly in accordance with the direction contained in *Vineet Narain* v. *Union of India,* (1998) 1 SCC 226 and the guidelines framed by the CVC.

……………………………………J.
[G.S. Singhvi]
……………………………………J.
[Asok Kumar Ganguly]

New Delhi,
January 31, 2012.

A.K. GANGULY, J. (Supplementing)

57. After going through the judgment rendered by my learned brother G.S. Singhvi, J., I am in agreement with the various conclusions reached by His Lordship. However, I have added my own views on certain important facts of the questions raised in this case.

58. Brother Singhvi, J., has come to a finding that having regard to the very nature of the office held by respondent No. 1, it may not be expected of respondent No. 1 to personally look into the minute details of each and every matter and the respondent No. 1, having regard to the burden of his very onerous office, has to depend on the officers advising him. At the same time it may be noted that in the course of submission, the appellant, who argued in person, did not ever allege any *mala fide* or lack of good faith against the respondent No. 1. The delay which had taken place in the office of the respondent No. 1 is unfortunate but it has not even been alleged by the appellant that there was any deliberate action on the part of the respondent No. 1 in causing the delay. The position of respondent No.1 in our democratic polity seems to have been summed up in the words of Shakespeare "Uneasy lies the head that wears a crown" (Henry, The Fourth, Part 2 Act 3, scene 1).

APPELLANT COULD FILE COMPLAINT PROSECUTING RESPONDENT NO. 2

59. I also agree with the conclusions of brother Singhvi, J., that the appellant has the *locus* to file the complaint for prosecution of the respondent No. 2 in respect of the offences alleged to have been committed by him under the 1988 Act. Therefore, I agree with the finding of brother Singhvi, J., that the argument of the learned Attorney General to the contrary cannot be accepted.

SECTION 197 Cr.P.C. AND SECTION 19 P.C. ACT OPERATE DIFFERENTLY

60. Apart from that the learned Attorney-General in the course of his submission proceeded on the basis that the question of sanction has to be considered with reference to section 19 of the Prevention of Corruption Act (hereinafter "the P.C. Act") or with reference to section 197 of the Code of Criminal Procedure, 1973 (hereinafter "the Code"), and the Scheme of both the sections being similar (*Vide* paragraph 3 of the supplementary written submission filed by the learned Attorney-General). In fact, the entire submission of the learned Attorney General is structured on the aforesaid assumption. I fail to appreciate the aforesaid argument as the same is contrary to the Scheme of section 19 of the P.C. Act and also section 197 of the Code.

61. In *Kalicharan Mahapatra* v. *State of Orissa*, (1998) 6 SCC 411, this Court compared section 19 of P.C. Act with section 197 of the Code. After considering several decisions on the point and also considering section 6 of the old P.C. Act, 1947 which is almost identical with section 19 of the P.C. Act, 1988 and also noting Law Commission's Report, this Court in paragraph 13 of *Kalicharan* (supra) came to the following conclusions: (SCC pp. 415-416)

> "13. The sanction contemplated in section 197 of the Code concerns a public servant who "is accused of any offence alleged to have been committed by him while acting or purporting to act in the discharge of his official duty", whereas the offences contemplated in the PC Act are those which cannot be treated as acts either directly or even purportedly done in the discharge of his official duties. Parliament must have desired to maintain the distinction and hence the wording in the corresponding provision in the former PC Act was materially imported in the new PC Act, 1988 without any change in spite of the change made in section 197 of the Code."

62. The above passage in *Kalicharan* (supra) has been quoted with approval subsequently by this Court in *Lalu Prasad* v. *State of Bihar*, reported in (2007) 1 SCC 49 at paragraph 9, page 54. In paragraph 10, (page 54 of the report) this Court held in *Lalu Prasad* (supra) that: (SCC p. 54)

> "10. ...section 197 of the Code and section 19 of the Act operate in conceptually different fields".

63. In view of such consistent view by this Court the basic submission of the learned Attorney General to the contrary is, with respect, untenable.

SANCTION FOR PROSECUTION IS REQUIRED AT THE INITIAL STAGE

64. I also entirely agree with the conclusion of learned brother Singhvi, J., that the argument of the learned Attorney General that question for granting sanction for prosecution of a public servant charged with offences under the 1988 Act arises only at the stage of cognizance is also not acceptable. In formulating this submission, the learned Attorney-General substantially advanced two contentions. The first contention is that an order granting sanction is not required to be filed along with a complaint in connection with a prosecution under section 19 of the P.C. Act. The aforesaid submission is contrary to the settled law laid down by this Court in various judgments.

64.1 Recently, a unanimous three-judge Bench decision of this Court in the case of *State of Uttar Pradesh* v. *Paras Nath Singh*, (2009) 6 SCC 372, speaking through Justice Pasayat and construing the requirement of sanction, held that without sanction: (SCC p. 375, para 6)

> "6. ....The very cognizance is barred. That is, the complaint cannot be taken notice of. According to *Black's Law Dictionary* the word 'cognizance' means 'jurisdiction' or 'the exercise of jurisdiction' or 'power to try and determine causes'. In common parlance, it means taking notice of. *A court, therefore, is precluded from entertaining a complaint or taking notice of it or exercising jurisdiction if it is in respect of a public servant who is accused of an offence alleged to have been committed* during discharge of his official duty."
>
> (Emphasis supplied)

64.2 The other contention of the learned Attorney-General is that in taking cognizance under the P.C. Act the Court is guided by the provisions under section 190 of the Code and in support of that contention the learned Attorney-General relied on several judgments.

65. However, the aforesaid submissions were made without noticing the judgment of this Court in the case of *Dilawar Singh* v. *Parvinder Singh* alias *Iqbal Singh*, (2005) 12 SCC 709. Dealing with section 19 of P.C. Act and section 190 of the Code, this Court held in paragraph 8 at page 713 of the report as follows:

> "8. ......The Prevention of Corruption Act is a special statute and as the preamble shows, this Act has been enacted to consolidate and amend the law relating to the prevention of corruption and for matters connected therewith. Here, the principle expressed in the maxim *generalia specialibus non derogant* would apply which means that if a special provision has been made on a certain matter, that matter is excluded from the general provisions. [See *Godde Venkateswara Rao* v. *Government of Andhra Pradesh*, AIR 1966 SC 828; *State of Bihar* v. *Dr. Yogendra Singh*, (1982) 1 SCC 664 and *Maharashtra State Board of Secondary and Higher Secondary Education* v. *Paritosh Bhupeshkumar Sheth*, (1984) 4 SCC 27.] Therefore, the provisions of section 19 of the Act will have an overriding effect over the general provisions contained in section 190......"

66. Therefore, concurring with brother Singhvi, J., I am unable to uphold the submission of the learned Attorney-General.

CORRUPTION THREATENS EVEN THE VERY FOUNDATION OF INDIAN DEMOCRACY AND RULE OF LAW

67. As I am of the humble opinion that the questions raised and argued in this case are of considerable constitutional and legal importance, I wish to add my own reasoning on the same.

68. Today, corruption in our country not only poses a grave danger to the concept of constitutional governance, it also threatens the very foundation of Indian democracy and the Rule of Law. The magnitude of corruption in our public life is incompatible with the concept of a socialist, secular democratic republic. It cannot be disputed that where corruption begins all rights end. Corruption devalues human rights, chokes development and undermines justice, liberty, equality, fraternity which are the core values in our Preambular vision.

IT IS COURT'S DUTY TO FIGHT AGAINST CORRUPTION

Therefore, the duty of the Court is that any anti-corruption law has to be interpreted and worked out in such a fashion as to strengthen the fight against corruption. That is to say in a situation where two constructions are eminently reasonable, the Court has to accept the one that seeks to eradicate corruption to the one which seeks to perpetuate it.

69. Time and again this Court has expressed its dismay and shock at the ever growing tentacles of corruption in our society but even then situations have not improved much; [See *Sanjiv Kumar* v. *State of Haryana*, (2005) 5 SCC 517; *State of Andhra Pradesh* v. *V. Vasudeva Rao*, (2004) 9 SCC 319; *Shobha Suresh Jumani* v. *Appellate Tribunal Forfeited Property*, (2001) 5 SCC 755; *State of Madhya Pradesh* v. *Ram Singh*, (2000) 5 SCC 88; *J. Jayalalitha* v. *Union of India*, (1999) 5 SCC 138; *Major S.K. Kale* v. *State of Maharashtra*, (1977) 2 SCC 394.]

OUT OF 319 REQUESTS FOR PROSECUTION, SANCTION IS AWAITED IN 126 CASES

70. Learned Attorney-General in the course of his submission fairly admitted before us that out of total 319 requests for sanction, in respect of 126 of such requests, sanction is awaited. Therefore, in more than 1/3rd cases of request for prosecution in corruption cases against public servants, sanctions have not been accorded.

THIS SCENARIO RAISES QUESTIONS OF NATIONAL IMPORTANCE FOR THE JUDICIARY

The aforesaid scenario raises very important constitutional issues as well as some questions relating to interpretation of such sanctioning provision and also the role that an independent Judiciary has to play in maintaining rule of law and common man's faith in the justice delivering system.

ROLE OF JUDICIARY UNDER THE CONSTITUTION IS VERY IMPORTANT TO OVERSEE THE EXECUTIVE ACTIONS THAT THREATEN THE BASIC HUMAN RIGHTS AND RULE OF LAW

Both rule of law and equality before law are cardinal questions in our Constitutional Laws as also in International law and in this context the role of the Judiciary is very vital. In his famous treatise on Administrative Law, Professor

Wade while elaborating the concept of rule of law referred to the opinion of Lord Griffith's which runs as follows:

> "...the judiciary accept a responsibility for the maintenance of the rule of law that embraces a willingness to oversee executive action and to refuse to countenance behaviour that threatens either basic human rights or the rule of law;" [See *R.* v. *Horseferry Road Magistrates' Court ex p. Bennett*, (1994) 1 AC 42 at p. 62A]

I am in respectful agreement with the aforesaid principle.

71. In this connection we might remind ourselves that courts while maintaining rule of law must structure its jurisprudence on the famous formulation of Lord Coke where the learned Law Lord made a comparison between "the golden and straight metwand of law" as opposed to "the uncertain and crooked cord of discretion".

72. The right of private citizen to file a complaint against a corrupt public servant must be equated with his right to access the Court in order to set the criminal law in motion against a corrupt public official. This right of access, a Constitutional right should not be burdened with unreasonable fetters. When a private citizen approaches a court of law against a corrupt public servant who is highly placed, what is at stake is not only a vindication of personal grievance of that citizen but also the question of bringing orderliness in society and maintaining equal balance in the rule of law.

73. It was pointed out by the Constitution Bench of this Court in *Sheonandan Paswan* v. *State of Bihar*, (1987) 1 SCC 288 (315): (SCC para 14)

> "14. ......It is now settled law that a criminal proceeding is not a proceeding for vindication of a private grievance but it is a proceeding initiated for the purpose of punishment to the offender in the interest of the society. It is for maintaining stability and orderliness in the society that certain acts are constituted offences and the right is given to any citizen to set the machinery of the criminal law in motion for the purpose of bringing the offender to book. It is for this reason that in *A.R. Antulay* v. *R.S. Nayak* this Court pointed out that (SCC p. 509, para 6)
>
> "6. punishment of the offender in the interest of the society being one of the objects behind penal statutes enacted for larger good of the society, right to initiate proceedings cannot be whittled down, circumscribed or fettered by putting it into a strait-jacket formula of *locus standi......*"

IT APPEARS THAT SECTION 19 PROTECTS THE CORRUPT PUBLIC SERVANTS

74. Keeping those principles in mind, as we must, if we look at section 19 of the P.C. Act which bars a Court from taking cognizance of cases of corruption against a public servant under sections 7, 10, 11, 13 and 15 of the Act, unless the Central or the State Government, as the case may be, has accorded sanction, virtually imposes fetters on private citizens and also on prosecutors from approaching Court against corrupt public servants. These protections are not available to other citizens. Public servants are treated as a special class of persons enjoying the said protection so that they can perform their duties without fear and favour and without threats of malicious prosecution. However, the said protection against malicious prosecution which was extended in public interest cannot become a shield to protect corrupt officials. These provisions being exceptions to the equality provision of article 14 are analogous to provisions of protective discrimination and these protections must be construed very narrowly. These procedural provisions relating to sanction must be construed in such a manner as to advance the causes of honesty and justice and good governance as opposed to escalation of corruption.

SANCTION FOR PROSECUTION BE GIVEN PROMPTLY TO MAINTAIN RULE OF LAW

75. Therefore, in every case where an application is made to an appropriate authority for grant of prosecution in connection with an offence under the P.C. Act it is the bounden duty of such authority to apply its mind urgently to the situation and decide the issue without being influenced by any extraneous consideration. In doing so, the authority must make a conscious effort to ensure the rule of law and cause of justice is advanced. In considering the question of granting or refusing such sanction, the authority is answerable to law and law alone. Therefore, the requirement to take the decision with a reasonable dispatch is of the essence in such a situation. Delay in granting sanction proposal thwarts a very valid social purpose, namely, the purpose of a speedy trial with the requirement to bring the culprit to book. Therefore, in this case the right of the sanctioning authority, while either sanctioning or refusing to grant sanction, is coupled with a duty.

76. The sanctioning authority must bear in mind that what is at stake is the public confidence in the maintenance of rule of law which is fundamental in the administration of justice. Delay in granting such sanction has spoilt many valid prosecution and is adversely viewed in public mind that in the name of considering a prayer for sanction, a protection is given to a corrupt public official as a *quid pro quo* for services rendered by the public official in the past or may be in the future and the sanctioning authority and the corrupt officials were or are partners in the same misdeeds. I may hasten to add that this may not be factual position in this but the general demoralizing effect of such a popular perception is profound and pernicious.

77. By causing delay in considering the request for sanction, the sanctioning authority stultifies judicial scrutiny and determination of the allegations against corrupt official and thus the legitimacy of the judicial institutions is eroded. It, thus, deprives a citizen of his legitimate and fundamental right to get justice by setting the criminal law in motion and thereby frustrates his right to access judicial remedy which is a constitutionally protected right. In this connection, if we look at section 19 of the P.C. Act, we find that no time limit is mentioned therein. This has virtually armed the sanctioning authority with unbridled power which has often resulted in protecting the guilty and perpetuating criminality and injustice in society.

SANCTION FOR PROSECUTION GRANTED AFTER 13 YEARS – IT IS BLATANT SUBVERSION OF THE RULE OF LAW

78. There are instances where as a result of delayed grant of sanction prosecutions under the P.C. Act against a public servant has been quashed. See *Mahendra Lal Das* v. *State of Bihar*, (2002) 1 SCC 149, wherein this Court quashed the prosecution as the sanctioning authority granted sanction after 13 years. Similarly, in the case of *Santosh De* v. *Archna Guha*, (1994) Supp 3 SCC 735, this Court quashed prosecution in a case where grant of sanction was unduly delayed. There are several such cases. The aforesaid instances show a blatant subversion of the rule of law. Thus, in many cases public servants whose sanction proposals are pending before authorities for long periods of time are being allowed to escape criminal prosecution.

79. Article 14 must be construed as a guarantee against uncanalized and arbitrary power. Therefore, the absence of any time limit in granting sanction in section 19 of the P.C. Act is not in consonance with the requirement of the due process of law which has been read into our Constitution by the Constitution Bench decision of this Court in *Maneka Gandhi* v. *Union of India*, (1978) 1 SCC 248.

80. I may not be understood to have expressed any doubt about the constitutional validity of section 19 of the P.C. Act, but in my judgment the power under section 19 of the P.C. Act must be reasonably exercised. In my judgment the Parliament and the appropriate authority must consider restructuring section 19 of the P.C. Act in such a manner as to make it consonant with reason, justice and fairplay.

GUIDELINES FOR SANCTION TO BE GRANTED WITHIN THREE MONTHS

81. In my view, the Parliament should consider the Constitutional imperative of article 14 enshrining the rule of law wherein 'due process of law' has been read into by introducing a time limit in section 19 of the P.C. Act, 1988 for its working in a reasonable manner. The Parliament may, in my opinion, consider the following guidelines:

(a) All proposals for sanction placed before any Sanctioning Authority, empowered to grant sanction for the prosecution of a public servant under section 19 of the P.C. Act must be decided within a period of three months of the receipt of the proposal by the concerned authority.

(b) Where consultation is required with the Attorney-General or the Solicitor General or the Advocate-General of the State, as the case may be, and the same is not possible within the three months mentioned in clause (a) above, an extension of one month period may be allowed, but the request for consultation is to be sent in writing within the three months mentioned in (a) above. A copy of the said request will be sent to the prosecuting agency or the private complainant to intimate them about the extension of the time limit.

(c) At the end of the extended period of time limit, if no decision is taken, sanction will be deemed to have been granted to the proposal for prosecution, and the prosecuting agency or the private complainant will proceed to file the charge-sheet/complaint in the court to commence prosecution within 15 days of the expiry of the aforementioned time limit.

AGREED WITH BROTHER JUDGE – APPEAL ALLOWED

82. With these additional reasons, as indicated, I agree with Brother Singhvi, J., and allow the appeal and the judgment of the High Court is set aside. No costs.

......................J.
(ASHOK KUMAR GANGULY)
New Delhi
January 31, 2012

Author's Note: The Minister for Communication and Information Technology had allotted the UAS licences arbitrarily by changing the cut-off date on the price-rate of 2001 obviously to his choice persons. One of the persons who had applied for such licence was not considered because of the change in the cut-off date. He had filed writ petition in the Delhi High Court which was accepted and the change in the cut-off date was held as illegal. The Union of India including the Ministry of Tele-communication had filed an appeal before the Division Bench but the appeal was also dismissed. The Union of India had filed SLP in the Supreme Court. It was pending when two writ petitions were filed in the Supreme Court by the good-intentioned citizens of our country to challenge the whole process adopted by the Ministry of Tele-communications in the allocation of spectrum which is well-known by the name of 2G scam.

THE VALIDITY OF THE ALLOCATION OF SPECTRUM KNOWN AS 2G WAS CONSIDERED IN THIS CASE

SUPREME COURT OF INDIA
CIVIL ORIGINAL JURISDICTION

Centre for Public Interest Litigation

v.

Union of India[1]

Writ Petition (Civil) No. 423 of 2010 with

Dr. Subramanian Swamy

v.

Union of India

Writ Petition (Civil) No. 10 of 2011

JUDGMENT

G.S. Singhvi, J.

1. The important questions which arise for consideration in these petitions, one of which has been filed by Centre for Public Interest Litigation, a registered Society formed by Shri V.M. Tarkunde (former Judge of the Bombay High Court) for taking up causes of public interest and conducting public interest litigation in an organised manner, Lok Satta, a registered Society dedicated to political governance, reforms and fight against corruption, Telecom Watchdog and Common Cause, both Non-Governmental Organisations registered as Societies for taking up issues of public importance and national interest, Sarva Shri J.M. Lingdoh, T.S. Krishnamurthi and N. Gopalasamy, all former Chief Election Commissioners, P. Shanker, former Central Vigilance Commissioner, Julio F. Ribero, former member of the Indian Police Service, who served as Director General

---

1. (2012) 3 SCC 1: AIR 2012 Sc 3725: 2012 (2) SCALE 180.

of Police, Gujarat, Punjab and C.R.P.F. and Commissioner of Police, Mumbai, P.G. Thakurta, an eminent Senior Journalist and visiting faculty member of various institutions including IIMs, IIT, FTII, IIFT, Delhi University, Jawaharlal Nehru University and Jamia Milia Islamia University and Admiral R.H. Tahiliyani, former Chief of Naval Staff, former Governor and former Chairman of Transparency International India and the other has been filed by Dr. Subramanian Swami, a political and social activist, are:

(i) Whether the Government has the right to alienate, transfer or distribute natural resources/national assets otherwise than by following a fair and transparent method consistent with the fundamentals of the equality clause enshrined in the Constitution?

(ii) Whether the recommendations made by the Telecom Regulatory Authority of India (TRAI) on 28.8.2007 for grant of Unified Access Service Licence (for short 'UAS Licence') with 2G spectrum in 800, 900 and 1800 MHz at the price fixed in 2001, which were approved by the Department of Telecommunications (DoT), were contrary to the decision taken by the Council of Ministers on 31.10.2003?

(iii) Whether the exercise undertaken by the DoT from September, 2007 to March, 2008 for grant of UAS Licences to the private respondents in terms of the recommendations made by TRAI is vitiated due to arbitrariness and *mala fides* and is contrary to public interest?

(iv) Whether the policy of first-come-first-served followed by the DoT for grant of licences is *ultra vires* the provisions of article 14 of the Constitution and whether the said policy was arbitrarily changed by the Minister of Communications and Information Technology (hereinafter referred to as 'the Minister of C&IT'), without consulting TRAI, with a view to favour some of the applicants?

(v) Whether the licences granted to ineligible applicants and those who failed to fulfil the terms and conditions of the licence are liable to be quashed?

HISTORY OF GROWTH OF TELECOMMUNICATIONS IN THE COUNTRY

2. For detailed examination of the issues raised by the petitioners, it will be useful to briefly notice the history of the growth of telecommunications in the country and the reforms introduced 1984 onwards.

3. In 1839, the first telegraph link was experimented between Calcutta and Diamond Harbour covering 21 miles. In 1851, the telegraph line was opened for traffic, mostly for the official work of the East India Company. In course of time, telegraphy service was made available for public traffic. The Indian Telegraph Act was enacted in 1885. It gave the exclusive privilege of establishing, maintaining and working of "telegraphs" to the Central Government. It also empowered the Government to grant licences on such conditions and in consideration of such payments as it thought fit, to any person to establish, maintain or work a telegraph in any part of India.

4. After independence, Government of India took complete control of the telecom sector and brought it under the Post and Telegraph Department. One major step taken for improving telecommunication services in the country was the establishment of a modern telecommunication manufacturing facility at Bangalore under the Public Sector, in the name of "Indian Telephone Industries Ltd." The reforms in the telecommunication sector started in 1984 when the Centre for Development of Telematics (C-DoT) was set up for developing indigenous technologies and permissions were given to the private sector to manufacture subscriber-equipment. In 1986, *Mahanagar Telephone Nigam Ltd., (MTNL) and Videsh Sanchar Nigam Ltd.,* (*VSNL*) were set up.

NEW ECONOMIC POLICY OF INDIA

5. The New Economic Policy of India was announced on 24.7.1991. It was aimed at meeting India's competitiveness in the global market; rapid growth of exports, attracting foreign direct investment; and stimulating domestic investments. With a view to achieve standards comparable to international facilities, the sub-sector of Value Added Services was opened up to private investment in July, 1992 for the following services: (a) Electronic Mail; (b) Voice Mail; (c) Data Services; (d) Audio Text Services; (e) Video Text Services; (f) Video Conferencing; (g) Radio Paging; and (h) Cellular Mobile Telephone. In respect of services (a) to (f), the companies registered in India were permitted to operate under a licence on non-exclusive basis. For services covered by (g) and (h) mentioned above, keeping in view the constraints on the number of companies that could be allowed to operate, a policy of selection through a system of tendering was followed for grant of licences.

National Telecom Policy, 1994

6. National Telecom Policy, 1994 (NTP, 1994) was announced on 13.5.1994.

This was the first major step towards deregulation, liberalization and private sector participation. The objectives of the policy were:

- (i) affording telecommunication for all and ensuring the availability of telephone on demand;
- (ii) providing certain basic telecom services at affordable and reasonable prices to all people and covering all villages;
- (iii) giving world standard telecom services; addressing consumer complaints, dispute resolution and public interface to receive special attention and providing widest permissible range of services to meet the customers' demand and at the same time at a reasonable price;
- (iv) creating a major manufacturing base and major export of telecom equipment having regard to country's size and development; and
- (v) protecting the defence and security interest of the country.

7. In furtherance of NTP, 1994, licences were granted to eight Cellular Mobile Telephone Service (CMTS) operators, two in each of the four metropolitan cities of Delhi, Mumbai (Bombay), Kolkata (Calcutta) and Chennai (Madras). In the second phase, in December, 1995, after following a competitive bidding process, 14 CMTS licences were awarded in 18 State circles, 6 Basic Telephone Services (BTS) licences were awarded in 6 State circles and paging licences were awarded in 27 cities and 18 state circles. However, this did not yield the intended results apparently because revenue realised by the cellular and basic operators was less than the projections and the operators were unable to arrange finances for their projects.

New Telecom Policy, 1999

8. On the directions of the Prime Minister, a high level Group on Telecommunications (GoT) was constituted on 20.11.1998 to review the existing telecom policy and suggest further reforms. On the basis of the report of the GoT, a draft New Telecom Policy 1999 (NTP, 1999) was formulated. After its approval by the Cabinet, NTP, 1999 was announced to be effective from 1.4.1999. NTP, 1999 had the following objectives:

(i) to make available affordable and effective communications for the citizens, considering access to telecommunications as utmost important for achievement of the country's social and economic goals;

(ii) to provide universal service to all uncovered areas including the rural areas and also provide high level services capable of meeting the needs of the country's economy by striking a balance between the two;

(iii) to encourage development of telecommunication in remote, hilly and tribal areas of the country;

(iv) to create a modern and efficient telecommunications infrastructure taking into account the convergence of IT, media, telecom and consumer electronics which will in turn propel India to become an IT superpower;.

(v) to convert PCOs wherever justified into Public Teleinfo centres having multimedia capability such as Integrated Services Digital Network (ISDN) services, remote database access, government and community information systems, etc.;

(vi) to transform, in a time bound manner, the telecommunications sector in both urban and rural areas into a greater competitive environment providing equal opportunities and level playing field for all players;

(vii) to strengthen research and development efforts in the country and provide an impetus to build world class manufacturing capabilities;

(viii) to achieve efficiency and transparency in spectrum management;

(ix) to protect defence and security interests of the country; and

(x) to enable Indian Telecom Companies to become truly global players.

9. NTP, 1999 categorized 8 services in the telecom sector, namely;

(i) Cellular Mobile Service Providers (CMSPs), Fixed Service Providers (FSPs) and Cable Service Providers, collectively referred as 'Access Providers';

(ii) Radio Paging Service Providers;

(iii) Public Mobile Radio Trunking Service Providers;

(iv) National Long Distance Operators;

(v) International Long Distance Operators;

(vi) Other Service Providers,

(vii) Global Mobile Personal Communication by Satellite (GMPCS) Service Providers;

(viii) V-SAT based Service Providers. NTP, 1999 dealt with, and provided the framework for, all these categories of telecom service providers.

POLICY ON SPECTRUM MANAGEMENT

10. The policy on spectrum management as enumerated in NTP 1999 was as under:

(i) Proliferation of new technologies and the growing demand for telecommunication services has led to manifold increase in demand for spectrum and consequently it is essential that the spectrum is utilized efficiently, economically, rationally and optimally.

(ii) *There is a need for a transparent process of allocation of frequency spectrum for use by a service provider and making it available to various users under specific conditions.*

(iii) With the proliferation of new technologies it is essential to revise the National Frequency Allocation Plan (NFAP) in its entirety so that it becomes the basis for development, manufacturing and spectrum utilization activities in the country amongst all users. NFAP was under review and the revised NFAP was to be made public by the end of 1999 detailing information regarding allocation of frequency bands for various services, without including security information.

(iv) NFAP would be reviewed no later than every two years and would be in line with radio regulations of the International Telecommunication Union (ITU).

(v) Adequate spectrum is to be made available to meet the growing need of telecommunication services. Efforts would be made for relocating frequency bands assigned earlier to defence and others. Compensation for relocation may be provided out of spectrum fee and revenue share.

(vi) There is a need to review the spectrum allocation in a planned manner so that required frequency bands are available to the service providers.

(vii) *There is a need to have a transparent process of allocation of frequency spectrum which is effective and efficient and the same would be further examined in the light of ITU guidelines. In this regard the following course of action shall be adopted viz.:*

(a) spectrum usage fee shall be charged;

(b) an Inter-Ministerial Group to be called Wireless Planning Coordination Committee, as a part of the Ministry of Communications for periodical review of spectrum availability and broad allocation policy, should be set up; and

(c) massive computerization in WPC Wing would be started in the next three months so as to achieve the objective of making all operations completely computerized by the end of the year 2000.

(emphasis supplied)

Establishment of the Telecommunication Commission (for short, 'the Telecom Commission') and the Telecom Regulatory Authority of India

11. On 11.4.1989, the Council of Ministers passed a resolution and decided to establish the Telecom Commission. The relevant portions of that resolution are extracted below:

"CABINET SECRETARIAT
New Delhi the 11th April, 1989
RESOLUTION
CONSTITUTION OF TELECOM COMMISSION

No. 15/1/2/87-Cab. 1. Telecommunication service is an essential infrastructure for national development. It has impact on social and economic activities. Besides, business, industry and administration depends heavily on information and telecom for productivity, efficiency and their day-to-day operations. Its development, therefore, is vital for nation building.

In order to promote rapid development in all aspects of telecommunications including technology, production and services, the Government of India consider it necessary to set up an organisation, which will have responsibility in the entire field of telecommunications.

After careful consideration, the Government of India have decided to establish a Telecommunication Commission with full executive and financial powers modelled on the lines of the Atomic Energy Commission.

2. Constitution of the Commission

(a) The Commission will consist of full-time and part-time Members;

(b) The Secretary to the Government of India in the Department of Telecommunications shall be the *ex-officio* Chairman of the Commission;

(c) The full time Members of the Commission shall be *ex-officio* Secretary to the Government of India in the Department of Telecommunications. One of these Members shall be Member for Finance; and

(d) The Secretary and the full-time Members of the Commission shall be drawn from the best persons available, including from within the Department of Telecommunications.

FUNCTIONS OF THE TELECOM COMMISSION

"3. Functions: The Telecom Commission shall be responsible:

(a) For formulating the policy of the Department of Telecommunications for approval of the Government;

(b) For preparing the budget for the Department of Telecommunications for each financial year and getting it approved by the Government; and

(c) implementation of the Government's policy in all matters concerning telecommunication.

4. Within the limits of the budget provision, approval by the Parliament, the Commission shall have the powers of the Government of India, both administrative and financial, for carrying out the work of the Department of Telecommunications.

5. Chairman

(a) The Chairman, in his capacity as Secretary to the Government of India in the Department of Telecommunications, shall be responsible under the Minister of Communications for arriving at decisions on technical questions and advising Government on policy and allied matters of telecommunication. All recommendations of the Commission on policy and allied matters shall be put to the Minister of Communications through the Chairman.

(b) In case of any difference of opinion in the meetings of the Commission, the decision of the Chairman shall be final, but in financial matters, Member (Finance) of the Commission will have access to Finance Minister.

(c) The Chairman may authorise any Member of the Commission to exercise on his behalf, subject to such general or special orders as he may issue from time to time, such of his powers and responsibilities as he may decide.

6. Member Finance

The Member of Finance shall exercise powers of the Government of India in financial matters concerning the Department of Telecommunications except insofar as such powers have been, or may in future be conferred on or delegated to the Department.

7. The Commission shall have power to frame its own rules and procedures. The Commission shall meet at such time and places as fixed by the Chairman.

8. The Telecom Commission shall take over all legal and statutory authority vested with the Telecom Board."

RULES OF BUSINESS FOR TELECOM COMMUNICATION ALSO FRAMED

12. The Rules of Business for the Telecom Commission were also framed in 1989. In terms of para 2 of the Rules of Business read with item 1 of Annexure 'A' appended thereto, all important matters of policy relating to Telecommunications are required to be brought before the Telecom Commission.

TELECOM REGULATORY AUTHORITY OF INDIA ACT PASSED IN 1997

13. In 1997, Parliament enacted the Telecom Regulatory Authority of India Act, 1997 (for short, 'the 1997 Act') to provide for the establishment of TRAI. By Act No. 2 of 2000, the 1997 Act was amended and provision was made for establishment of the Telecom Disputes Settlement and Appellate Tribunal (TDSAT).

14. Sections 11 and 13, which have bearing on the decision of these petitions read as under:

"11. *Functions of Authority.*—(1) Notwithstanding anything contained in the Indian Telegraph Act, 1885 (13 of 1885), the functions of the Authority shall be to—

(a) to make recommendations, either *suo motu* or on a request from the licensor, on the following matters, namely:—

(i) need and timing for introduction of new service provider;

(ii) terms and conditions of licence to a service provider;

(iii) revocation of licence for non-compliance of terms and conditions of licence;

(iv) measures to facilitate competition and promote efficiency in the operation of telecommunication services so as to facilitate growth in such services;

(v) technological improvements in the services provided by the service providers;

(vi) type of equipment to be used after inspection of equipment used in the network;

(vii) measures for the development of telecommunication technology and any other matter relatable to telecommunication industry in general;

(viii) efficient management of available spectrum;

(b) discharge the following functions, namely:—

(i) ensure compliance of terms and conditions of licence;

(ii) notwithstanding anything contained in the terms and conditions of the licence granted before the commencement of the Telecom Regulatory Authority of India (Amendment) Act, 2000, fix the terms and conditions of inter-connectivity between the service providers;

(iii) ensure technical compatibility and effective interconnection between different service providers;

(iv) regulate arrangement amongst service providers of sharing their revenue derived from providing telecommunication services;

(v) lay-down the standards of quality of service to be provided by the service providers and ensure the quality of service and conduct the periodical survey of such service provided by the service providers so as to protect interest of the consumers of telecommunication service;

(vi) lay-down and ensure the time period for providing local and long distance circuits of telecommunication between different service providers;

(vii) maintain register of interconnect agreements and of all such other matters as may be provided in the regulations;

(viii) keep register maintained under clause (vii) open for inspection to any member of public on payment of such fee and compliance of such other requirement as may be provided in the regulations;

(ix) ensure effective compliance of universal service obligations;

(c) levy fees and other charges at such rates and in respect of such services as may be determined by regulations;

(d) perform such other functions including such administrative and financial functions as may be entrusted to it by the Central Government or as may be necessary to carry out the provisions of this Act:

Provided that the recommendations of the Authority specified in clause (a) of this sub-section shall not be binding upon the Central Government:

Provided further that the Central Government shall seek the recommendations of the Authority in respect of matters specified in sub-clauses (i) and (ii) of clause (a) of this sub-section in respect of new licence to be issued to a service provider and the Authority shall forward its recommendations within a period of sixty days from the date on which that Government sought the recommendations:

Provided also that the Authority may request the Central Government to furnish such information or documents as may be necessary for the purpose of making recommendations under sub-clauses (i) and (ii) of clause (a) of this sub-section and that Government shall supply such information within a period of seven days from receipt of such request:

Provided also that the Central Government may issue a licence to a service provider if no recommendations are received from the Authority within the period specified in the second proviso or within such period as may be mutually agreed upon between the Central Government and the Authority:

Provided also that if the Central Government having considered that recommendation of the Authority, comes to a *prima facie* conclusion that such recommendation cannot be accepted or needs modifications, it shall, refer the recommendation back to the Authority for its reconsideration, and the Authority may within fifteen days from the date of receipt of such reference, forward to the Central Government its recommendation after considering the reference made by that Government. After receipt of further recommendation if any, the Central Government shall take a final decision.

(2) Notwithstanding anything contained in the Indian Telegraph Act, 1885 (13 of 1885), the Authority may, from time to time, by order, notify in the Official Gazette the rates at which the telecommunication services within India and outside India shall be provided under this Act including the rates at which messages shall be transmitted to any country outside India:

Provided that the Authority may notify different rates for different persons or class of persons for similar telecommunication services and where different rates are fixed as aforesaid the Authority shall record the reasons therefor.

(3) While discharging its functions under sub-section (1) or sub-section (2) the Authority shall not act against the interest of the sovereignty and integrity of India, the security of the State, friendly relations with foreign States, public order, decency or morality.

(4) The Authority shall ensure transparency while exercising its powers and discharging its functions.

13. *Power of Authority to issue directions.*—The Authority may, for the discharge of its functions under sub-section (1) of section 11, issue such directions from time to time to the service providers, as it may consider necessary:

Provided that no direction under sub-section (4) of section 12 or under this section shall be issued except on the matters specified in clause (b) of sub-section (1) of section 11."

RECOMMENDATIONS MADE BY TELECOM REGULATORY AUTHORITY OF INDIA ON 23.6.2000

15. After its establishment, TRAI made various recommendations either *suo motu* or on the request of the licensor, *i.e.*, the Central Government or the Telegraph Authority. On a reference made by the Ministry of Communications and Information Technology on four issues including the issues of appropriate level of entry fee, basis of selection of new operators and entry of 4th cellular operator, TRAI made its recommendations, which were communicated to Secretary, DoT *vide* D.O. No. 250-14/2000-Fin (DF) (Vol. II) dated 23.6.2000. Paragraphs 4.1 to 4.3, 4.5 to 4.6 and 4.11 to 4.15 of that letter are extracted below:

"4. For the purposes of clarity each issue on which TRAI's recommendation has been sought has been stated separately and recommendations have been given therefor.

4.1(A) Appropriate level of entry fee, basis for selection of new operators and entry of fourth operator. The issues under this head can be broken under three main sub-heads. These are:

(i) Level of entry fee;

(ii) Basis for selection of new operation;

(iii) Entry of the fourth operator.

We take these issues sequentially.

4.2(1) Level of Entry Fee: – New operators are to be licensed in the following vacant circles/slots:

(a) Jammu and Kashmir – Andamans and Nicobar Islands;

(b) Assam and West Bengal;

(c) DOT/MTNL as the third operator.

(d) Fourth operator in circles where migration has been permitted.

4.3 DOT/MTNL wherever they come in as the third operator as also the fourth operator to be introduced will be required to pay as licence fee the same percentage share of their revenue as recommended by TRAI for the existing CMSPs who are being allowed to migrate to revenue sharing arrangement in accordance with NTP, 1999. The fourth operator will also pay an entry fee which will be fixed through a process of bidding.

4.5 (ii) Selection of new operators: The TRAI recommends that all new operators barring DOT/MTNL be selected through a competitive process. This is recommended to be a multi-stage bidding process preceded by a pre-qualification round.

4.6 Pre-qualification Prospective operators would be required to meet pre-determined criteria in order to qualify to bid for the licence. Pre-qualifications will mainly be on the following grounds:—

- Financial strength and experience as Telecom Service Provider
- Minimum roll out obligation
- Technical Plan

- Business Plan
- Payment terms and other commercial conditions

It is recommended that prospective bidders who meet the pre-determined threshold as set out in the pre-qualification criteria be short-listed for bidding for entry fee in the next stage. No weightages need be attached to the pre-qualification criteria. The criteria for pre-qualification could be developed on the following lines:—

4.11 The Structure of the Bidding Process Selection from amongst all those who pass the pre-qualification round will be by a process of bidding. The bids will be carefully structured so as to guard against the possible misuses of the process such as preemptive over-bidding or cartelisation. For this purpose, a bid structure involving "Multi Stage Informed Ascending Bids" is recommended. It is also recommended that such bids be invited for the entry fee for selection of operations and issuing licenses to them. Although, as recommended earlier in the case of NLDO, TRAI is primarily of the opinion that because of its greater relevance, direct impact on operations and being equitable, revenue sharing is a better basis on which to invite bids for licenses, in the case of CMSPs this choice is not available except in two vacant circles/ slots. The 34 incumbent operators have already been given licenses through a process of bidding and it would not be correct to subject them to yet another process of bidding, this time concerning revenue sharing. They have already been asked to pay as license fee, albeit on a provisional basis a fixed amount of the revenue share *viz.* 15%. It is, therefore, recommended that a fixed percentage of revenue share be paid by all operators as the license fee and this percentage be the same for all the operators barring the exceptions specifically mentioned in the paragraph 5.9 below.

4.12 While, the detailed bid structure can be prepared at the time bids are being called and assistance/advise of experts may be taken in doing so, based on the experience of such successful bids elsewhere, the basic outlines of the proposed structure can be given. Bids can be invited for more than one licence at a time. The total number of rounds in which the bids will be finalised will be pre-determined and all bidders should be eligible to bid for all licenses on offer in each of the rounds. The licensor, may, however, if it so desires, stipulate beforehand the total number of licences that can be finally allotted to a single bidder. The TRAI's recommendation in this regard is that the number of licences that can go to a single bidder need not be restricted. This will favour the serious and techno-financially strong bidders and will help keep the bids at operationally feasible optimal levels.

4.13 *After each stage of bidding, bids received will be made public and all bidders (those lower than the highest bidder as well as the highest bidder) will be permitted to raise their bids in the subsequent rounds of bidding. The process will be deemed complete only on the completion of the pre-determined number of bid rounds at the end of which the highest bidder for each licence will have the claim to the license in question. Licences will become effective on payment of the amount of the winning bid for the entry fee within a period specified in the tender document.*

4.14 The same process of bidding will also enable selection of operators where two slots in the same circle are vacant *viz.*, Jammu and Kashmir and Andaman and Nicobar where no operators exist. In these circles, two bidders may be selected and it is recommended in this regard that while the second highest bidder in these circles may be considered for the second slot available, he need not be asked to match the bid of the highest bidder. It may be provided though that if the difference between the first and the second highest bids is substantial, say more than 25%, fresh bids for the second slot will be invited. Such an arrangement while being equitable will act as a good incentive for attracting bids for these circles which have not proved to be attractive in the past.

(III). Entry of the Fourth Operator:

4.15 DOT/MTNL, the incumbent in basic services, are to enter the field of cellular mobile services as the third operator in terms of NTP, 1999 with the existing availability of spectrum. TRAI, however, has no information about the availability of spectrum either for the third or the fourth operator. The financial analysis conducted by the TRAI for the purpose of studying the revenue share which the operators can part with as licence fee assumes entry of the third operator in the sixth year of licence *i.e.*, in the current year and of another *i.e.*, the fourth operator two years later in accordance with NTP, 1999. The analysis reveals that even if the business in each of these metropolitan areas and circles is required to produce a reasonable IRR say 16-18% and a decent return on the capital say around 20%, it would still enable the operators to share upto about 25% of the Gross (adjusted) revenue as the licence fee. In the circumstances, it would be reasonable to assume that on purely economic grounds, in most circles there is even at present, a fair case for the entry of the fourth operator. In this context, however, more than the market, the determining factor has to be the availability of a spectrum and its optimal utilisation. Moreover, it is also a matter for careful consideration that even when additional spectrum is released, whether it should be utilised to augment the number of service providers or for improving the quality and coverage of the already available services. In the GSM 900 band the maximum frequency spectrum made available to the operators in a large number of countries is a pair of 12.5 MHz. Against this in India the circle operators have been given a pair of less than 5 MHz and the metro operators of less than 7 MHz. It is learnt that in a number of metros and circles, no further expansion of services is possible unless additional spectrum is made available to the existing operators. Paucity of frequency spectrum is also adversely affecting the quality of service in a number of service areas. In the circumstances a fair balance between the two objectives of increasing competition on the one hand and improving the quality, coverage and price-efficiency of the service on the other will have to be struck so that the larger objective of providing quality services at affordable prices is not jeopardised. A sub-optimal cost structure and quality of service may finally turn out to be detrimental to the growth of tele-density notwithstanding a higher number of service providers. Similar views were expressed also by the BICP in their report on Cellular Mobile

Services (para 20 page V) of the report). Accordingly, TRAI *is of the opinion that a view can be taken in this matter only after getting a full report from the DOT on the quantum of spectrum being made available for the CMSPs, existing as well as the proposed new entrants and its location* i.e., *whether it is going to be in the 900 MHz or in 1800MHz bands."* (emphasis supplied)

GUIDELINES ISSUED BY THE GOVERNMENT OF INDIA ON 5.1.2001

16. On 5.1.2001, the Government of India issued guidelines for issue of licence for CMTS. These guidelines envisaged a detailed bidding process for selection of the new service providers.

RECOMMENDATIONS MADE BY THE TELECOM REGULATORY AUTHORITY OF INDIA ON 27.10.2003

17. On 27.10.2003, TRAI made recommendations under section 11(1)(a)(i), (ii), (iv) and (vii) of the 1997 Act on Unified Licensing. TRAI referred to international practices, NTP, 1994 and NTP, 1999 and growth of telephone density – national objective and priority. Para 7.2 of those recommendations read as under:

> "7.2 The Guidelines would be notified by the licensor based on TRAI recommendations to include nominal entry fee, USO, etc. The charges for spectrum shall be determined separately. The operator shall be required to approach the licensor mainly for spectrum allocation. Since, spectrum is a scarce resource, it needs to be regulated separately. Spectrum should be distributed using such a mechanism that it is allocated optimally to the most efficient user."

18. Paragraphs 7.15 to 7.19 of the 2003 recommendations contained various alternatives for deciding the benchmark for the entry fee for Unified Access Licensing Regime. In paragraph 7.30, TRAI laid emphasis on efficient utilization of spectrum by all service providers and indicated that it would make further recommendations on efficient utilization of spectrum, spectrum pricing, availability and spectrum allocation procedure shortly, and the DoT may like to issue spectrum related guidelines based on its recommendations.

GROUP OF MINISTERS CONSTITUTED ON 10.9.2003

19. In the meanwhile, a Group of Ministers was constituted on 10.9.2003 with the approval of the Prime Minister to consider the following matters:

(i) To recommend how to ensure release of adequate spectrum needed for the growth of the telecom sector;

(ii) To recommend measures for ensuring adequate resources for the realization of the NTP targets of rural telephony;

(iii) To resolve issues relating to the enactment of the Convergence Bill;

(iv) To chart the course to a Universal Licence;

(v) To review adequacy of steps and enforcing limited mobility within the SDCA for WLL(M) services of basic operators, and recommend the future course of action;

(vi) To appraise FDI limits in the telecom sector and give recommendations thereon;

(vii) To identify issues relating to mergers and acquisitions in the telecom sector and recommend the way forward; and

(viii) To consider issues relating to imposition of trade-tax on telecom services by the State Governments.

RECOMMENDATIONS MADE BY GROUP OF MINISTERS ON 30.10.2003 AND ACCEPTED BY THE COUNCIL OF MINISTERS ON 31.10.2003

20. After considering the entire matter, the Group of Ministers made detailed recommendations on 30.10.2003, the relevant portions of which are extracted below:

"2.1 1st Term of Reference: to recommend how to ensure release of adequate spectrum needed for the growth of the telecom sector.

2.1.1 The GOM was informed that the availability of adequate spectrum in appropriate frequency bands, *i.e.*, 1800 MHz in a timely manner is crucial, for the growth of mobile telephone services. The growth of mobile services and resultant spectrum needs are mainly in metro, major and main cities having population above 1 million. However, the frequency bands of 1800 MHz are extensively used by Defence services, thus severely limiting their availability for the mobile telecom operators.

2.1.2 In the above context, GoM recommended the following:

(1) Adequate spectrum be made available for the unimpeded growth of telecom services, modalities for which will be jointly worked out by Wireless Planning and Coordination (WPC) Wing of Department of Telecom and Defence Services. The Ministry of Defence would coordinate release additional spectrum in a number of cities for which requirements have been projected within a month.

(2) The Ministry of Finance will provide necessary budgetary support to Ministry of Defence for modernization of their existing equipment to facilitate release of required spectrum. The actual fund requirements including its phasing will be worked out between the Ministry of Defence Ministry of Finance and the Department of Telecom in a time bound manner.

(3) *The Department of Telecom and Ministry of Finance would discuss and finalise spectrum pricing formula which will include incentive for efficient use of spectrum as well as disincentive for sub-optimal usages.*

(4) *The allotment of additional spectrum be transparent fair and equitable, avoiding monopolistic situation regarding spectrum allotment usage.*

(5) The long term 15-20 years, spectrum requirements along with time frames would also be worked out by Department of Telecom.

(6) As per the directions of GoM, a Task Force has been constituted under the Chairmanship of Wireless Adviser to the Government of India with representatives from Department of Telecom, Ministry of Defence and Ministry of Finance. The terms of reference of the Task Force and the progress of its work so far are given in Annexures II and III. (Page 17-18).

2.4 4th Term of Reference:—To chart the course to a Universal Licence:

2.4.1 The GoM took note of the exercise that had already been indicated by Telecom Regulatory Authority of India (TRAI), in regard to Unified Licensing Regime in the Telecom Sector Chairman, TRAI and Chairman HDFC were specially invited made presentations before the GoM.

2.4.2 TRAI submitted its recommendations to the Government on this matter on 27.10.2003. TRAI has recommended that the present system of licensing in the Telecom Sector should be replaced by Unified Licensing/Automatic Authorisation Regime. The Unified Licensing/Automatic Authorisation Regime has been recommended to be achieved in a two stage process with the Unified Access Regime for basic and cellular services in the first phase to be implemented immediately. This is to be followed by a process of consultation to define the guidelines and rules for achieving a fully Unified Licensing/ Authorisation Regime. TRAI has recommended that it will enter into a consultation process so that the replacement of the existing licensing regime by a Unified Licensing Regime gets initiated within 6 months. Broad rationale key recommendations and some key policy issues that have been addressed by TRAI are listed in the Annexure IV (pages 19-21).

2.4.3 The salient points of TRAI recommendations in regard to the Unified Access Licensing (basic and cellular mobile), are as under:

(i) Unification of licenses to be done in two stages:

   (a) Unified access regime for basic and cellular services in the first phase immediately;

   (b) Unified authorisation regime encompassing all telecom services in the second phase.

(ii) Fee paid by fourth cellular operator to be benchmark for migration of basic players to the new access regime.

(iii) Cellular operators not to pay any entry fee for migration to the unified access regime while basic operators to pay the differences between fourth cellular operators licence fee and the BSO fee already paid by them.

(iv) Reliance Infocom required to pay Rs. 1096 crores for migration in addition to penalty of Rs. 485 crores for offering cellular type services.

(v) Process of migration to the new regime to be voluntary.

(vi) The existing BSOs after migration to Unified Access Licensing Regime may offer full mobility however WLL(M) operators after migration will be required to offer limited mobility service to such customers who so desire.

(vii) No additional fee to be paid for any of the circles where there is no fourth cellular operator.

2.4.4 Enhancing the scope of current Telecom Policy (NTF-99) to provide category of Unified License and Unified Access Service License NTP-99 recognises access service providers as a distinct class. For the purpose of licensing, this has been sub-divided into cellular fixed and cable service providers. NTP-99 also states that convergence of both markets and technologies is a reality that is forcing realignment of the industry. This convergence now allows operators to use their facilities to deliver some services reserved for other operators necessitating a re-look at NTP-94 policy framework. For bringing into effect the regime of Unified Access Service for basic and cellular service licenses and Unified Licensing comprising all telecom services, it would be necessary to enhance the scope of NTP-99 to include these as distinct categories of licenses as pet of NTP-99.

2.4.5 TRAI recommendations on entry fee of WLL(M) based on TDSAT judgment: TRAI has also submitted its recommendations in regard to additional entry fee payable by basic service operators for providing WLL(M) services on which Government had sought its recommendations based on the judgment of TDSAT dated 8.8.2003 in the WLL(M) case. TRAI has given detailed reasoning on this matter and has recommended additional entry fee for such of the Basic Service Operators who provide WLL(M) service. The salient features are in Annexure V (page 22).

2.4.6 Based on the above the GoM has recommended the following course of action:

(i) The scope of NTP-99 may be enhanced to provide for licensing of Unified Access Service for basic and cellular license services and Unified Licensing comprising all telecom services. Department of Telecommunications may be authorised to issue necessary addendum to NTP-99 to this effect.

(ii) The recommendations of TRAI with regard to implementation of the Unified Access Licensing Regime for basic and cellular services may be accepted. DoT may be authorized to finalise the details of implementation with the approval of the Minister of Communication and IT in this regard including the calculation of the entry fee depending upon the date of payment based on the principles given by TRAI in its recommendations.

(iii) The recommendations of TRAI in this regard to the course of action to be adopted subsequently in regard to the implementation of the fully Unified License Authorisation Regime may be approved. DoT may be authorised to finalise the details of implementation with the approval of the Minister of Communications and IT on receipt of recommendations of TRAI in this behalf.

(iv) The recommendations of TRAI in regard to additional entry fee payable by basic service operators for providing WLL(M) service on which Government sought its recommendations based on the judgment of TDSAT dated 8.8.2003 in the WLL(M) case may be accepted.

(v) While there appears to be no case for giving any compensation package to them, because of the perception that the finances of the cellular operators are strained and because of the effect these may have on financial institutions. Finance Ministry would address the difficulties of the cellular operators, if any, separately and appropriately.

(vi) If new services are introduced as a result of technological advancements which require additional spectrum over and above the spectrum already allotted/contracted allocation of such spectrum will be considered on payment of additional fee or charges, these will be determined as per guidelines to be evolved in consultation with TRAI."

(emphasis supplied)

21. The recommendations of the Group of Ministers were accepted by the Council of Ministers on 31.10.2003.

OFFICE MEMO DATED 11.11.2003 ISSUED

Thereafter, DoT issued Office Memorandum dated 11.11.2003 and made some additions to NTP, 1999. The same day, DoT issued new guidelines for UAS Licences. Two salient features of these guidelines were that the existing operators would have an option to continue under the existing licensing regime or to migrate to new UAS Licence and the licence fee, service area, rollout obligations and performance bank guarantee under UAS Licence was to be the same as the 4th CMTS.

RECOMMENDATIONS MADE BY THE CHAIRMAN TRAI ON 14.11.2003 WERE ACCEPTED BY THE MINISTER C. AND I.T. ON 24.11.2003

22. *Vide* letter dated 14.11.2003, the Chairman, TRAI, on his own, made recommendation regarding entry fee to be charged from the new UAS Licensees. On 24.11.2003, the Minister of C&IT accepted the recommendation that entry fee for new UAS Licensees will be the entry fee of 4th cellular operator and where there is no 4th cellular operator, it will be the entry fee fixed by the Government for the basic operator. A decision was also taken by him in F. No. 20-231/2003-BS-III (LOIs for UASL) at 4/N that,

> "As regards the point raised about the grant of new licences on first-come-first-served basis, the announced guidelines have made it open for new licences to be issued on continuous basis at any time. However, the spectrum is to be allotted subject to availability. This in effect would imply that an applicant who comes first will be granted the spectrum first so it will result in grant of licence on first-come-first-served basis."

Although, in terms of the decision taken by the Minister of C&IT, the applications for grant of UAS Licence could be made on continuous basis and were required to be processed within 30 days, some applications were made in 2004 and 2006 and the same were kept pending.

TRAI MADE COMPREHENSIVE RECOMMENDATIONS ON 13.5.2005 ON PRICING OF SPECTRUM

23. On 13.5.2005, TRAI made comprehensive recommendations on various issues relating to spectrum policy, *i.e.*, efficient utilisation of spectrum, spectrum allocation, spectrum pricing, spectrum charging and allocation for other terrestrial wireless links. These recommendations were not placed before the Telecom Commission. Though, the then Secretary, DoT submitted the file to the then Minister of C&IT on 16.8.2005 for information with a note that he will go through the recommendations and put up the file to the Minister for policy decision, the file was returned on 12.9.2006, *i.e.*, after one year and no further action appears to have been taken.

PRIME MINISTER CONSTITUTED GROUP OF MINISTERS ON 23.2.2006 TO CONSIDER THE SPECTRUM PRICING POLICY

24. In the meanwhile, on 23.2.2006, the Prime Minister approved constitution of a Group of Ministers, consisting of the Ministers of Defence, Home Affairs, Finance, Parliamentary Affairs, Information and Broadcasting and C&IT, to look into issues relating to vacation of spectrum. Deputy Chairman, Planning Commission was special invitee. The Terms of Reference of the Group of Ministers, among other things, included suggesting a Spectrum Pricing Policy and examining the possibility of creation of a spectrum relocation fund. After five days, the Minister C&IT wrote letter dated 28.2.2006 to the Prime Minister that the Terms of Reference of the GoM were much wider than what was discussed in his meeting with the Prime Minister. He appears to have protested that the Terms of Reference would impinge upon the work of his Ministry and requested that the Terms of Reference be modified in accordance with the draft enclosed with the letter. Interestingly, the Minister's draft did not include the important issue relating to Spectrum Pricing. Thereafter, *vide* letter 7.12.2006, the Cabinet Secretary conveyed the Prime Minister's approval to the modification of the Terms of Reference. The revised Terms of Reference did not include the issue relating to Spectrum Pricing.

DOT ISSUED REVISED GUIDELINES ON 14.12.2005

25. On 14.12.2005, the DoT issued revised guidelines for UAS Licence. Paragraph 11 of the new guidelines reads as under:

> "The licences shall be issued without any restriction on the number of entrants for provision of unified access services in a Service Area."

26. In terms of paragraph 14 of the guidelines, the licensee was required to pay annual licence fee at 10/8/6% of Adjusted Gross Revenue (AGR) for category A/B/C service areas, respectively excluding spectrum charges. This was in addition to the non-refundable entry fee. In terms of paragraph 19 the licensee was required to pay spectrum charges in addition to the licence fee on revenue share basis. However, while calculating AGR for limited purpose of levying spectrum charges, revenue from wireless subscribers was not to be taken into account.

DOT REQUESTED TRAI *VIDE* LETTER DATED 13.4.2007 TO MAKE RECOMMENDATIONS UNDER SECTION 11(1)(A) OF 1997 ACT

27. After one year and about six months, the DoT *vide* its letter dated 13.4.2007, requested TRAI to furnish its recommendations under section 11(1) (a) of the 1997 Act on the issues of limiting the number of access providers in each service area and review of the terms and conditions in the access provider licence mentioned in the letter. Paragraph 2 of that letter is extracted below:

> "2. Fast changes are happening in the Telecommunication sector. In order to ensure that the policies keep pace with the changes/developments in the Telecommunication sector, the government is contemplating to review the following terms and conditions in the Access provider (CMTS/UAS/Basic) license:
>
> (i) Substantial equity holding by a company/legal person in more than one licensee company in the same service area (clause 1.4 of UASL agreement).

(ii) Transfer of licences (clause 6 of the UASL).

(iii) Guidelines dated 21.02.2004 on Mergers and Acquisitions. TRAI in its recommendations dated 30.1.2004 had opined that the guidelines may be reviewed after one year.

(iv) Permit service providers to, offer access services using combination of technologies (CDMA, GSM and/or any other) under the same license.

(v) Roll-out obligations (clause 34 of UASL).

(vi) Requirement to publish printed telephone directory."

TRAI MADE RECOMMENDATIONS ON 28.8.2007 MAINLY FOR FAIR COMPETITION

28. In furtherance of the aforesaid communication, TRAI made recommendations dated 28.8.2007. The main emphasis of these recommendations was the principles of fair competition, no restriction on the number of access service providers in any service area, need for spectrum management, measures to increase spectrum efficiency, allocation of spectrum and compliance of roll out obligations by the service providers. It was also recommended that in future all spectrum excluding the spectrum in 800, 900 and 1800 MHz bands in 2G services should be auctioned. In paragraphs 2.33, 2.39, 2.41, 2.54 and 2.63, TRAI repeatedly mentioned about scarce availability of spectrum.

29. Paragraphs 2.37, 2.40, 2.69 and 2.73 to 2.79 of the TRAI's recommendations dated 28.8.2007 are extracted below:

"2.37 Accordingly, the Authority recommends that no cap be placed on the number of access service providers in any service area.

2.40 The present spectrum allocation criteria, pricing methodology and the management system suffer from a number of deficiencies and therefore the Authority recommends that this whole issue is not to be dealt with in piecemeal but should be taken up as a long term policy issue. There is an urgent need to address the issues linked with spectrum efficiency and its management.

2.69 The Entry fee for acquiring a UASL license enables the licensee to become eligible for spectrum allocation in certain specified bands without any additional fee for acquisition of spectrum which means that allocation of spectrum follows the grant of license subject however to availability of spectrum. There is only one direct cost to the operator for spectrum *i.e.*, spectrum charge in the form of royalty.

2.73 The allocation of spectrum is after the payment of entry fee and grant of license. The entry fee as it exists today is, in fact, a result of the price discovered through a markets based mechanism applicable for the grant of license to the 4th cellular operator. In today's dynamism and unprecedented growth of telecom sector, the entry fee determined then is also not the realistic price for obtaining a license. Perhaps, it needs to be reassessed through a market mechanism. On the other hand spectrum usage charge is in the form of a royalty which is linked to the revenue earned by the operators and to that extent it captures the economic value of the spectrum that is used. Some stakeholders have viewed the charges/fee as a hybrid model of extracting economic rent for the acquisition and also meet the criterion of efficiency in the utilization of this scarce resource. The Authority in the context of 800, 900 and 1800 MHz is conscious of the legacy *i.e., prevailing practice and the overriding consideration of level playing field. Though the dual charge in present form does not reflect the present value of spectrum it needed to be continued for treating already specified bands for 2G services* i.e., *800, 900 and 1800 MHz. It is in this background that the Authority is not recommending the standard options pricing of spectrum, however, it has elsewhere in there commendation made a strong case for adopting auction procedure in the allocation of all other spectrum bands except 800, 900 and 1800 MHz.*

2.74 Some of the existing service providers have already been allocated spectrum beyond 6.2 MHz in GSM and 5 MHz in CDMA as specified in the license agreements without charging any extra one time spectrum charges. The maximum spectrum allocated to a service provider is 10 MHz so far. However, the spectrum usage charge is being increased with increased allocation of spectrum. The details are available at Table 8.

2.75 The Authority has noted that the allocation beyond 6.2 MHz for GSM and 5 MHz for CDMA at enhanced spectrum usage charge has already been implemented. Different licensees are at different levels of operations in terms of the quantum of spectrum. Imposition of additional acquisition fee for the quantum beyond these thresholds may not be legally feasible in view of the fact that higher levels of usage charges have been agreed to and are being collected by the Government. Further, the Authority is conscious of the fact that further penetration of wireless services is to happen in semi-urban and rural areas where affordability of services to the common man is the key to further expansion.

2.76 However, the Authority is of the view that the approach needs to be different for allocating and pricing spectrum beyond 10 MHz in these bands *i.e.*, 800, 900 and 1800 MHz. In this matter, the Authority is guided by the need to ensure sustainable competition in the market keeping in view the fact that there are new entrants whose subscriber acquisition costs will be far higher than the incumbent wireless operators. Further, the technological progress enables the operators to adopt a number of technological solutions towards improving the efficiency of the radio spectrum assigned to them. A cost- benefit analysis of allocating additional spectrum beyond 10 MHz to existing wireless operators and the cost of deploying additional CAPEX towards technical improvements in the networks would show that there is either a need to place a cap on the maximum allocable spectrum at 10 MHz or to impose framework of pricing through additional acquisition fee beyond 10 MHz.

The Authority feels it appropriate to go in for additional acquisition fee of spectrum instead of placing a cap on the amount of spectrum that can be allocated to any wireless operator. In any case, the Authority is recommending a far stricter norm of subscriber base for allocation of additional spectrum beyond the initial allotment of spectrum. The additional acquisition fee beyond 10 MHz could be decided either administratively or through an auction method from amongst the eligible wireless service providers. In this matter, the Authority has taken note of submissions of a number of stakeholders who have cited evidences of the fulfilment of the quality of service benchmarks of the existing wireless operators at 10 MHz and even below in almost all the licensed service areas. Such an approach would also be consistent with the Recommendation of the Authority in keeping the door open for new entrant without putting a limit on the number of access service providers.

2.77 The Authority in its recommendation on "Allocation and pricing of spectrum for 3G and broadband wireless access services" had recommended certain reserve price for 5 MHz of spectrum in different service areas. The recommended price are as below:

Service Areas Price (Rs. in million) for 2X5 MHz Mumbai, Delhi and Category A 800; Chennai, Kolkatta and Category B 400; Category C 150.

The Authority recommends that any licensee who seeks to get additional spectrum beyond 10 MHz in the existing 2G bands *i.e.*, 800, 900 and 1800 MHz after reaching the specified subscriber numbers shall have to pay a onetime spectrum charge at the above mentioned rate on prorata basis for allotment of each MHz or part thereof of spectrum beyond 10 MHz. For one MHz allotment in Mumbai, Delhi and Category A service areas, the service provider will have to pay Rs. 160 million as one time spectrum acquisition charge.

2.78 As far as a new entrant is concerned, the question arises whether there is any need for change in the pricing methodology for allocation of spectrum in the 800, 900 and 1800 MHz bands. *Keeping in view the objective of growth, affordability, penetration of wireless services in semi-urban and rural areas, the Authority is not in favour of changing the spectrum fee regime for a new entrant. Opportunity for equal competition has always been one of the prime principles of the Authority in suggesting a regulatory framework in telecom services. Any differential treatment to a new entrant vis-a-vis incumbents in the wireless sector will go against the principle of level playing field.* This is specific and restricted to 2G bands only *i.e.*, 800, 900 and 1800 MHz. This approach assumes more significance particularly in the context where subscriber acquisition cost for a new entrant is likely to be much higher than for the incumbent wireless operators.

2.79 In the case of spectrum in bands other than 800, 900 and 1800 MHz *i.e.* bands that are yet to be allocated, the Authority examined various possible approaches for pricing and has come to the conclusion that it would be appropriate in future for a market based price discovery systems. In response to the consultation paper, a number of stakeholders have also strongly recommended that the allocation of spectrum should be immediately de-linked from the license and the future allocation should be based on auction. The Authority in its recommendation on "Allocation and pricing of spectrum for 3G and broadband wireless access services" has also favoured auction methodology for allocation of spectrum for 3G and BWA services. *It is, therefore, recommended that in future all spectrum excluding the spectrum in 800, 900 and 1800 bands should be auctioned so as to ensure efficient utilization of this scarce resource. In the 2G bands (800 MHz/900 MHz/1800 MHz), the allocation through auction may not be possible as the service providers were allocated spectrum at different times of their license and the amount of spectrum with them varies from 2X4.4 MHz to 2X10 MHz for GSM technology and 2X2.5 MHz to 2X5 MHz in CDMA technology. Therefore, to decide the cut-off after which the spectrum is auctioned will be difficult and might raise the issue of level playing field."*

(Emphasis supplied)

RECOMMENDATIONS OF TRAI WERE NOT CONSIDERED BY TELECOM COMMISSION IN ALL PERSPECTIVE NOR ALL MEMBERS OF COMMISSION WERE INVITED – THE MINISTER C&IT ACCEPTED THE RECOMMENDATIONS

30. The aforesaid recommendations of TRAI were first considered by an Internal Committee of the DoT constituted *vide* letter dated 21.9.2007 under the Chairmanship of Member, Telecommunication. The report of the Committee was placed before the Telecom Commission on 10.10.2007. However, the four non-permanent members, *i.e.*, Finance Secretary; Secretary, Department of Industrial Policy and Promotion; Secretary, Department of Information Technology and Secretary, Planning Commission were not even informed about the meeting. In this meeting of the Telecom Commission, which was attended by the officials of the DoT only, the report of the Internal Committee was approved. On 17.10.2007, the Minister of C&IT accepted the recommendations of the Telecom Commission and thereby approved the recommendations made by TRAI. However, neither the Internal Committee of the DoT and the Telecom Commission nor the Minister of C&IT took any action in terms of paragraph 2.40 of the recommendations wherein it was emphasised that the existing spectrum allocation criteria, pricing methodology and the management system suffer from a number of deficiencies and the whole issue should be addressed keeping in view issues linked with spectrum efficiency and its management. The DoT also did not get in touch with the Ministry of Finance to discuss and finalise the spectrum pricing formula which had to include incentive for efficient use of spectrum as well as disincentive for sub-optimal usage in terms of the Cabinet decision of 2003.

ON 24.9.2007 DDG(AS) SUGGESTED THE CUT-OFF DATE AS 10.10.2007 BUT MINISTER C&IT (A. RAJA) MADE IT AS 1.10.2007 AND PRESS NOTE WAS ISSUED ON 24.9.2007 ACCORDINGLY

31. In the meanwhile, on 24.9.2007, Shri A.K. Srivastava, DDG (AS), DoT prepared a note mentioning therein that as on that date, 167 applications had been received from 12 companies for 22 service areas and opined that it may be difficult to handle such a large number of applications at any point of time. He suggested that 10.10.2007 may be announced as the cut-off date for receipt of new UAS Licence applications. Shri A. Raja who was, at the relevant time, Minister of C&IT did not agree with the suggestion and ordered that 1.10.2007 be fixed as the cut-off date for receipt of applications for new UAS Licence. Accordingly, press note dated 24.9.2007 was issued by the DoT stating that no new application for UAS Licence will be accepted after 1.10.2007.

LARGE NUMBER OF APPLICANTS – LEGAL OPINION WAS SOUGHT

It is borne out from the record that Vodafone Essar Spacetel Ltd. (respondent No. 12) had made an application for UAS Licence in 2004 and 3 others, namely, Idea Cellular Ltd. (respondent No. 8), Tata Teleservices Ltd. (respondent No. 9) and M/s. Aircel Ltd. (respondent No. 11) had made similar applications in 2006. However, the same were not disposed of by the DoT and they were included in the figure of 167.

32. Between 24.9.2007 and 1.10.2007, over 300 applications were received for grant of UAS Licences. Member (Technology), Telecom Commission and *ex-officio* Secretary to Government of India sent a letter dated 26.10.2007 to Secretary, Department of Legal Affairs, Ministry of Law and Justice seeking the opinion of the Attorney-General of India/Solicitor-General of India on the issue of the mechanism to deal with what he termed as an unprecedented situation created due to receipt of large number of applications for grant of UAS Licence. The statement of case accompanying the letter of Member (Technology) contained as many as 14 paragraphs. Paragraph 11 outlined the following four alternatives:

(I) The applications may be processed on first-come-first-served basis in chronological order of receipt of applications in each service area as per existing procedure. LoI may be issued simultaneously to applicants (the numbers will vary based on availability of spectrum to be ascertained from WPC Wing) who fulfil the eligibility conditions of the existing UASL Guidelines and are senior most in the queue. The time limit for compliance should be 7 days as per the existing provision of LoI and 15 days for submission of PBG, FBG, entry fee, etc. as per the existing procedure. However, those who fulfil the conditions of LoI within stipulated time, their seniority of license/spectrum will be on the basis of their application date. The compliance of eligibility conditions as on the date of issue of LoI may be accepted. No relaxation of this time limit will be given and LoI shall stand terminated after the stipulated time period (however, the applicant may have the right to apply for new UAS Licence again as and when the window for submission of new UAS Licence is opened again). Subsequent applications may be considered for issue of LoI if the spectrum is available.

(II) LoIs to all those who applied by 25.9.2007 (date on which the cut-off date for receipt of applications were made public through press) may be issued in each service area as it is expected that only serious players will deposit the entry fee and seniority for license/spectrum be based on (i) the date of application, or (ii) the date/time of fulfilment of all LoI conditions.

(III) DoT may issue LoIs to all eligible applications simultaneously received up to cut-off date. Since LoIs will clearly stipulate that spectrum allocation is subject to availability and is not guaranteed, the LoI holders are supposed to pay the entry fee if their business case permits them top wait for spectrum allocation subject to availability an initial roll out using wireline technology.

(IV) Any other better approach which may be legally tenable and sustainable for issue of new licences.

33. Paragraph 13 of the statement of case is extracted below:

"Issue of LoIs to M/s. TATA and others for usage of Dual Technology spectrum based on their applications received after 18.10.2007. Whether

(i) To treat their request prior to existing applicants; or

(ii) To treat their request after processing all 575 applications."

LAW MINISTER SUGGESTED CONSTITUTION OF GROUP OF MINISTERS

34. The Law Secretary placed the papers before the Minister of Law and Justice on 1.11.2007, who recorded the following note:

"I agree. In view of the importance of the case and various options indicated in the statement of the case, it is necessary that whole issue is first considered by an empowered Group of Ministers and in that process legal opinion of Attorney-General can be obtained."

MINISTER C&IT (A. RAJA) CHANGED CUT-OFF DATE TO 25.9.2007. REJECTED RECOMMENDATIONS OF LAW MINISTER AND WROTE TO THE PRIME MINISTER SUGGESTING FIRST-COME-FIRST-SERVED AS ON 25.9.2007

35. When the note of the Law Minister was placed before the Minister of C&IT, he recorded the following note on 2.11.2007 – "Discuss please". On the same day, *i.e.*, 2.11.2007 the Minister of C&IT did two things. He approved the note prepared by Director (AS-1) containing the following issues:

(i) Issuing of LoIs to new applicants as per the existing policy,

(ii) Number of LoIs to be issued in each circle,

(iii) Approval of draft LoI,

(iv) Considering application of TATAs for dual technology after the decision of TDSAT on dual technology, and

(v) Authorising Shri R.K. Gupta, ADG (AS-1) for signing the LoIs on behalf of President of India.

36. While approving the note, the Minister of C&IT on his own recorded the following – "LoI may be issued to the applicants received upto 25th Sept. 2007". Simultaneously, he sent D.O. No. 20/100/2007-AS.I dated 2.11.2007 to the Prime Minister and criticised the suggestion made by the Law Minister by describing it as totally out of context. He also gave an indication of what was to come in the future by mentioning that the DoT has decided to continue with the existing policy of first-come-first-served for processing of applications received up to 25.9.2007 and the procedure for processing the remaining applications will be decided at a later date, if any spectrum is left available after processing the applications received up to 25.9.2007.

37. Paragraphs 3 and 4 of the letter of the Minister of C&IT are extracted below:

"3. The Department wanted to examine the possibility of any other procedure in addition to the current procedure of allotment of Licences to process the huge number of applications. A few alternative procedures as debated in the Department and also opined by few legal experts were suggested by the Department of Telecom to Ministry of Law and Justice to examine its legal tenability to avoid future legal complications, if any. Ministry of Law and Justice, instead of examining the legal tenability of these alternative procedures, suggested referring the matter to empowered Group of Ministers. Since, generally new major policy decisions of a Department or inter-departmental issues are referred to GoM, and, needless to say that the present issue relates to procedures, the suggestion of Law Ministry is totally out of context.

4. Now, the Department has decided to continue with the existing policy (first-come-first-served) for processing of applications received up to 25th September 2007, *i.e.*, the date when the news-item on announcement of cut-off date appeared in the newspapers. The procedure for processing the remaining applications will be decided at a later date, if any spectrum is left available after processing the applications received up to 25th September, 2007.

5. As the Department is not deviating from the existing procedure, I hope this will satisfy the Industry."

PRIME MINISTER OF HIS OWN *VIDE* LETTER DATED 2.11.2007 SUGGESTED TO ADOPT FAIR AND TRANSPARENT POLICY

38. In the meanwhile, the Prime Minister who had received representations from telecom sector companies and had read reports appearing in a section of media sent letter dated 2.11.2007 to the Minister of C&IT and suggested that a fair and transparent method should be adopted for grant of fresh licences. That letter reads as under:

"Prime Minister

New Delhi
2 November, 2007

Dear Shri Raja,

A number of issues relating to allocation of spectrum have been raised by telecom sector companies as well as in sections of the media. Broadly, the issues relate to enhancement of subscriber linked spectrum allocation criteria, permission to CDMA service providers to also provide services on the GSM standard and be eligible for spectrum in the GSM service band, and the processing of a large number of applications received for fresh licenses against the backdrop of *inadequate spectrum to cater to overall demand*. Besides these, there are some other issues recommended by TRAI that require early decision. The key issues are summarized in the annexed note.

I would request you to give urgent consideration to the issues being raised with a view to ensuring fairness and transparency and let me know of the position before you take any further action in this regard.

With regards,

Yours sincerely,
Sd/-
(Manmohan Singh)

Shri A. Raja
Minister of Communications and IT
New Delhi.

Annexure

1. Enhancement of subscriber linked spectrum allocation criteria.

In August, 2007, the TRAI has recommended interim enhancement of subscriber linked spectrum allocation criteria. Service providers have objected to these recommendations, alleging errors in estimation/assumptions as well as due procedure not having been followed by the TRAI while arriving at the recommendations.

2. Permission to CDMA service providers to also provide services on the GSM standard and be eligible for spectrum in the GSM service band.

Based on media reports, it is understood that the DoT has allowed 'cross technology' provision of services by CDMA service providers and three such companies have already paid the license fee. With the deposit of the fee, they would be eligible for GSM spectrum, for which old incumbent operators have been waiting since last several years. The Cellular Operators Association of India (COAI), being the association of GSM service providers, has represented against this. It is understood that the COAI has also approached the TDSAT against this.

3. Processing of a large number of applications received for fresh licenses against the backdrop of inadequate spectrum to cater to overall demand.

The DoT has received a large number of applications for new licenses in various telecom circles. Since spectrum is very limited, even in the next several years all these licensees may never be able to get spectrum. The Telecom Policy that had been approved by the Union Cabinet in 1999 specifically stated that new licenses would be given subject to availability of spectrum.

4. *In order that spectrum use efficiency gets directly linked with correct pricing of spectrum, consider:*

(i) *introduction of a transparent methodology of auction, wherever legally and technically feasible, and*

(ii) *revision of entry fee, which is currently benchmarked on old spectrum auction figures*

5. Early decision on issues like rural telephony, infrastructure sharing, 3G, Broadband, Number Portability and Broadband Wireless Access, on which the TRAI has already given recommendations." (emphasis supplied)

A. RAJA BRUSHED ASIDE THE SUGGESTIONS OF THE PRIME MINISTER AND INFORMED HIM ACCORDINGLY

39. The Minister of C&IT did not bother to consider the suggestion made by the Prime Minister, which was consistent with the constitutional principle of equality, that keeping in view the inadequate availability of spectrum, fairness and transparency should be maintained in the allocation of spectrum, and within few hours of the receipt of the letter from the Prime Minister, he sent a reply wherein he brushed aside the suggestion made by the Prime Minister by saying that it will be unfair, discriminatory, arbitrary and capricious to auction the spectrum to new applicants as it will not give them a level playing field. The relevant portions of paragraph 3 of the Minister's letter are extracted below:

"3. Processing of a large number of applications received for fresh licenses against the backdrop of inadequate spectrum to cater to overall demand.

The issue of auction of spectrum was considered by the TRAI and the Telecom Commission and was not recommended as the existing licence holders who are already having spectrum upto 10 MHz per Circle have got it without any spectrum charge. It will be unfair, discriminatory, arbitrary and capricious to auction the spectrum to new applicants as it will not give them level playing field.

I would like to bring it to your notice that DoT has earmarked totally 800 MHz in 900 MHz and 1800 MHz bands for 2G mobile services. Out of this, so for a maximum of about 35 to 40 MHz per Circle has been allotted to different operators and being used by them. The remaining 60 to 65 MHz, including spectrum likely to be vacated by Defence Services, is still available for 2G services.

Therefore, there is enough scope for allotment of spectrum to few new operators even after meeting the requirements of existing operators and licensees. An increase in number of operators will certainly bring real competition which will lead to better services and increased teledensity at lower tariff. Waiting for spectrum for long after getting licence is not unknown to the Industry and even at present Aircel, Vodafone, Idea and Dishnet are waiting for initial spectrum in some Circles since December, 2006."

FINANCE SECRETARY *VIDE* LETTER DATED 22.11.2007 QUESTIONED THE APPLICATION OF 2001 FORMULA IN 2007

40. On 20.11.2007, the Secretary, DoT had made a presentation on the spectrum policy to the Cabinet Secretary. The Finance Secretary, who appears to have witnessed the presentation, dispatched letter dated 22.11.2007 to the Secretary, DoT and expressed his doubt as to how the rate of Rs. 1600 crores determined in 2001, could be applied without any indexation for a licence to be given in 2007. He also emphasized that in view of the financial implications, the Ministry of Finance should have been consulted before the matter was finalised at the level of the DoT. Secretary, DoT promptly replied to the Finance Secretary by sending letter dated 29.11.2007 in which he mentioned that as per the Cabinet decision dated 31.10.2003, the DoT had been authorised to finalise the details of implementation of the recommendations of TRAI and in its recommendations dated 28.8.2007, TRAI had not suggested any change in the entry fee/licence fee.

DOT SUBMITTED NOTE DATED 22.11.2007 SUGGESTING REVISION OF RATES. A. RAJA, MINISTER (C & IT) REJECTED IT

In the context of letter dated 22.11.2007 sent by the Finance Secretary, Member (Finance), DoT submitted note dated 30.11.2007 suggesting that the issue of revision of rates should be examined in depth before any final decision is taken in the matter. When the note was placed before the Minister of C&IT, he observed that the matter of entry fee has been deliberated in the department several times in light of various guidelines and the TRAI recommendations and accordingly decision was taken not to revise the entry fee and that the Secretary, DoT had also replied to the Finance Secretary's letter on the above lines.

A. RAJA, MINISTER (C&IT) ON 26.11.2007 DISTORTED AND PROPAGATED THAT THE POLICY OF FIRST-COME-FIRST-SERVED HAS THE APPROVAL OF THE PRIME MINISTER

41. Although, the record produced before this Court does not show as to when the policy of first-come-first-served was distorted by the Minister of C&IT, in an apparent bid to show that he had secured the Prime Minister's approval to this act of his, the Minister C&IT sent letter dated 26.12.2007 to the Prime Minister, paragraphs 1 and 2 of which are extracted below:

> "1. Issue of Letter of Intent (LoI): DoT follows a policy of First-cum-First Served for granting LoI to the applicants for UAS licence, which means, an application received first will be processed first and if found eligible will be granted LoI.
>
> 2. Issue of Licence: The First-cum-First Served policy is also applicable for grant of licence on compliance of LoI conditions. Therefore, any applicant who complies with the conditions of LoI will be granted UAS licence first. This issue never arose in the past as at one point of time only one application was processed and LoI was granted and enough time was given to him for compliance of conditions of LoI. However, since the Government has adopted a policy of "No Cap" on number of UAS Licence, a large number of LoI's are proposed to be issued simultaneously. *In these circumstances, an applicant who fulfils the conditions of LoI first will be granted licence first, although several applicants will be issued LoI simultaneously. The same has been concurred by the Solicitor-General of India during the discussions."* (emphasis supplied)

WITHOUT WAITING FOR THE REPLY, A. RAJA, MINISTER (C&IT) CHANGED THE POLICY

42. After 12 days, DDG (AS), DoT prepared a note incorporating therein the changed first-come-first-served policy to which reference had been made by the Minister of C&IT in letter dated 26.12.2007 sent to the Prime Minister. On the same day the Minister of C&IT approved the change.

MEETING OF FULL TELECOM COMMISSION FIXED FOR 9.1.2008 WAS POSTPONED TO 15.1.2008

43. The meeting of the full Telecom Commission, which was scheduled to be held on 9.1.2008 to consider two important issues *i.e.,* performance of telecom sector and pricing of spectrum was postponed to 15.1.2008.

PRESS RELEASE ISSUED ON 10.1.2008 THAT THE POLICY OF FIRST COME FIRST SERVED SHALL BE APPLICABLE WITH CUT-OFF DATE AS 25.09.2007

On 10.1.2008 *i.e.,* after three days of postponement of the meeting of the Telecom Commission, a press release was issued by the DoT under the signature of Shri A.K. Srivastava, DDG (AS), DoT. The same reads as under:

> "In the light of Unified Access Services Licence (UASL) guidelines issued on 14th December 2005 by the department regarding number of Licenses in a Service Area, a reference was made to TRAI on 13-4-2007. The TRAI on 28-08-2007 recommended that No cap be placed on the number of access

service providers in any service area. The government accepted this recommendation of TRAI. Hon'ble Prime Minister also emphasized on increased competition while inaugurating India Telecom 2007. Accordingly, DoT has decided to issue LoI to all the eligible applicants on the date of application who applied upto 25-09-2007.

UAS licence authorises licencee to rollout telecom access services using any digital technology which includes wire-line and/or wireless (GSM and/or CDMA) services. They can also provide Internet Telephony, Internet Services and Broadband services. UAS licence in broader terms is an umbrella licence and does not automatically authorise UAS licencees usage of spectrum to rollout Mobile (GSM and/or CDMA) services. For this, UAS licencee has to obtain another licence, *i.e.* Wireless Operating Licence which is granted on first-come-first-served basis subject to availability of spectrum in particular service area.

DoT has been implementing a policy of First-cum-First Served for grant of UAS licences under which initially an application which is received first will be processed first and thereafter if found eligible will be granted LOI and then who so ever complied with the conditions of LoI first will be granted UAS licence.

Department of Telecom

(AS Cell)

10-01-2008" (emphasis supplied)

ANOTHER PRESS RELEASE ISSUED ON THE SAME DAY ASKING THE APPLICANTS TO COLLECT THE LICENCES WITHIN 45 MINUTES

44. On the same day, another press release was issued asking all the applicants to assemble at the departmental headquarters within 45 minutes to collect the response(s) of the DoT. They were also asked to submit compliance of the terms of LoIs within the prescribed period. The second press release is also reproduced below:

"Department of Telecommunications

Press Release

Date: 10th January, 2008

Sub: UASL applicants to depute their authorised representative to collect responses of DOT on 10.1.2008.

The applicant companies who have submitted applications to DOT for grant of UAS licences in various service areas on or before 25.9.2007 are requested to depute their Authorised signatory/Company Secretary/authorised representative with authority letter to collect response(s) of DOT. They are requested to bring the company's rubber stamp for receiving these documents to collect letters from DoT in response to their UASL applications. Only one representative of the Company/group Company will be allowed. Similarly, the companies who have applied for usage of dual technology spectrum are also requested to collect the DoT's response.

All above are requested to assemble at 3:30 pm on 10.1.2008 at Committee Room, 2nd Floor, Sanchar Bhawan, New Delhi. The companies which fail to report before 4:30 P.M. on 10.1.2008, the responses of DoT will be dispatched by post.

All eligible LoI holders for UASL may submit compliance to DoT to the terms of LoIs within the prescribed period during the office hours *i.e.,* 9:00 A.M. to 5:30 P.M. on working days.

File No. 20-100/2007-AS-I

Dated 10.1.2008

(A.K. Srivastava)

DDG(AS)

Department of Telecom

DDG (C&A): The above Press Release may kindly be uploaded on DoT website immediately."

EVEN INELIGIBLE APPLICANTS WERE GRANTED UAS LICENCE

45. All the applicants including those who were not even eligible for UAS Licence collected their LoIs on 10.1.2008. The acceptance of 120 applications and compliance with the terms and conditions of the LoIs for 78 applications was also received on the same day.

3 GRANTEES OF LOIS PARTLY SOLD THEIR STAKES WITH BENEFIT OF THOUSANDS OF CRORES OF RUPEES

Soon after obtaining the LoIs, 3 of the successful applicants off-loaded their stakes for thousands of crores in the name of infusing equity, their details are as under:

(i) Swan Telecom Capital Pvt. Ltd. (now known as Etisalat DB Telecom Pvt. Ltd.) which was incorporated on 13.7.2006 and got UAS Licence by paying licence fee of Rs. 1537 crores transferred its 45% (approximate) equity in favour of Etisalat Mauritius Limited, a wholly owned subsidiary of Emirates Telecommunications Corporation of UAE for over Rs. 3,544 crores.

(ii) Unitech which had obtained licence for Rs. 1651 crores transferred its stake 60% equity in favour of Telenor Asia Pte. Ltd., a part of Telenor Group (Norway) in the name of issue of fresh equity shares for Rs. 6120 crores between March, 2009 and February, 2010.

(iii) Tata Tele Services transferred 27.31% of equity worth Rs. 12,924 crores in favour of NTT DOCOMO.

(iv) Tata Tele Services (Maharashtra) transferred 20.25% of equity worth Rs. 949 crores in favour of NTT DOCOMO.

WRIT FILED IN DELHI HIGH COURT CHALLENGING THE ARBITRARY CHANGE IN THE CUT-OFF DATE – ACCEPTED

46. S. Tel Ltd., who had applied for grant of licence pursuant to press note dated 24.9.2007, but was ousted from the zone of consideration because of the cut-off date fixed by the Minister of C&IT, filed Writ Petition No. 636 of 2008 in the Delhi High Court with the prayer that the first press release dated 10.1.2008 may be quashed. After hearing the parties, the learned Single Judge *vide* his order dated 1.7.2009 declared that the cut-off date, *i.e.,* 25.9.2007 was totally arbitrary and directed the respondents in the writ petition to consider the offer made by the writ petitioner to pay Rs. 17.752 crores towards additional revenue share over and above the applicable spectrum revenue share.

47. The observations made by the learned Single Judge on the justification of fixing 25.9.2007 as the cut-off date read as under:

> "Thus on the one hand the respondent has accepted the recommendation of the TRAI in the impugned press note, but acted contrary thereto by amending the cut-off date and thus placed a cap on the number of service providers. The stand taken by respondent and the justification sought to be given for fixing a cutoff date retrospectively is on account of large volume of applications, is without any force in view of the fact that neither any justification was rendered during the course of argument, nor any justification has been rendered in the counter-affidavit as to what is the effect of receipt of large number of applications in view of the fact that a recommendation of the TRAI suggests no cap on the number of access service providers in any service area. This recommendation was duly accepted and published in the newspaper. Further as per the counter affidavit 232 UASL applications were received till 25.9.2007 from 22 companies. Assuming there was increase in the volume of applications, the respondent has failed to answer the crucial question as to date. Even otherwise, admittedly 232 applications were made by 25.9.2007 and between 25.9.2007 and 1.10.2007 only 76 were applications were received. It was only on 1.10.2007 that 267 applications were made. Thus, on 28.09.2007 it cannot be said that large number of applications were received.
>
> Thus taking into consideration the opinion of the expert body, which as per the press note of the respondent itself was accepted by the respondent, certainly the respondent cannot be allowed to change the rules of the game after the game had begun, to put it in the words of the Apex Court especially when the respondent has failed to give any plausible justification or the rationale for fixing the cut-off date by merely a week. Taking into consideration that on 13.4.2007 the Government of India had recommended TRAI to furnish its recommendation in terms of 11(e) of the TRAI Act, 1997 on the issue as to whether a limit should be put on the number of access service providers in each service area. The TRAI having given its recommendations on 28.8.2007 which were duly accepted by the Government, the respondent cannot be allowed to arbitrarily change the cut-off date and that too without any justifiable reasons."

APPEAL DISMISSED ON 24.11.2009

48. The letters patent appeal filed against the order of the learned Single Judge was dismissed by the Division Bench of the High Court *vide* judgment dated 24.11.2009, paragraphs 13 and 14 whereof are reproduced below:

> "13. We are unable to agree with the submission of the learned Attorney General that the parameters that would apply to revising a cut-off date that has been earlier fixed prior to the receipt of the applications would be no different from fixing a cut-off date in the first place. While the decision in

D.S. Nakara which has subsequently been distinguished in N. Subbarayudu is about fixing a cut-off date which might be an exercise in the discretion of the Appellant, those decisions are not helpful in deciding the revision of a cut-off date after applications have been received in terms of the previous cut-off date, is amenable to judicial review on administrative and constitutional law parameters. We are of the view that the two situations cannot be equated. The Government would have to justify its decision to revise a cut-off date already fixed, after applications have been received from persons acting on the basis of the earlier cut-off date. It would be for the court to be satisfied when a challenge is made, that the decision to revise a cut-off date after receiving applications on the basis of the cut-off date earlier fixed was based on some rational basis and was not intended to benefit a few applicants while discriminating against the rest. In the present case, for the reasons pointed out by the learned Single Judge, with which we concur, the Appellant has been unable to show that its decision to revise the cut-off date after receiving the application of the Respondent was based on some rational criteria. It is vulnerable to being labelled arbitrary and irrational.

14. We are not able to appreciate, in the instant case, the submission of the learned Attorney-General that the mere advancing of the cut-off date would not tantamount to changing the rules after the game has begun. In a sense it does. It makes ineligible for consideration the applicants who had applied, after 25th September, 2007 but on or before 1st October, 2007. Further this ineligibility is announced after the applications have been made. In other words, while at the time of making the application there was no such ineligibility, it is introduced later and that too for a select category of applicants. This cannot but be a change in the rule after the game has begun. We do not think that the decisions relied upon by the learned Attorney-General contemplate such a situation. On the other hand the decisions in *Monarch Infrastructure (P) Ltd.* and *K. Manjushree* fully support the Respondent's case for invalidation of the Appellant's impugned decision revise the cut-off date from 1st October 2007 to 25th September 2007, long after receiving the application from the Respondent."

SLP FILED BY UOI DISPOSED OF AS COMPROMISED BUT FINDING OF DELHI HIGH COURT APPROVED

49. The Union of India challenged the judgment of the Division Bench in SLP(C) No. 33406/2009. During the pendency of the special leave petition, some compromise appears to have been reached between the writ petitioner and the authorities and, therefore, an additional affidavit was filed along with agreed minutes of order before this Court on 12.3.2010. In view of this development, the Court disposed of the appeal arising out of the special leave petition but specifically approved the findings recorded by the High Court with regard to the cut-off date by making the following observations:

"Taking the additional affidavit and the suggestions made by the learned Attorney-General, this appeal is disposed of as requiring no further adjudication.

However, we make it clear that the findings recorded by the High Court with regard to the cut-off date is not interfered with and disturbed by this Court in the present case."

GRANT OF LoIS AND UAS LICENCES WAS ILLEGAL – SUBMIT THE PETITIONERS

Grounds of Challenge

50. The petitioners have questioned the grant of UAS Licences to the private respondents by contending that the procedure adopted by the DoT was arbitrary, illegal and in complete violation of article 14 of the Constitution. They have relied upon the order passed by the learned Single Judge of the Delhi High Court as also the judgment of the Division Bench, which was approved by this Court and pleaded that once the Court has held that the cut-off date, *i.e.*, 25.9.2007 fixed for consideration of the applications was arbitrary and unconstitutional, the entire procedure adopted by the DoT for grant of UAS Licences with the approval of the Minister of C&IT is liable to be declared illegal and quashed. Another plea taken by the petitioners is that the DoT violated the recommendations made by TRAI that there should be no cap on the number of Access Service Providers in any service area and this was in complete violation of section 11(1) of the 1997 Act.

51. The petitioners have relied upon the report of the Comptroller and Auditor-General (CAG) and pleaded that the consideration of large number of ineligible applicants and grant of LoIs and licenses to them is *ex facie* illegal and arbitrary. The petitioners have also pleaded that the entire method adopted by the DoT for grant of licence is flawed because the recommendations made by TRAI for grant of licences at the entry fee determined in 2001 was wholly arbitrary, unconstitutional and contrary to public interest.

52. Yet another plea of the petitioners is that while deciding to grant licences, which are bundled with spectrum, at the price fixed in 2001 the DoT did not bother to consult the Finance Ministry and, thereby, violated the mandate of the decision taken by the Council of Ministers in 2003. The petitioners have also pleaded that the policy of first-come-first-served is by itself violative of article 14 of the Constitution and in any case distortion thereof by the Minister of C&IT and the consequential grant of licences is liable to be annulled.

53. Another ground taken by the petitioners is that even though a number of licensees failed to fulfil the rollout obligations and violated conditions of the licence, the Government of India did not take any action to cancel the licences.

Counter-affidavits of the Respondents

54. Most of the respondents have filed separate but similar counter-affidavits in both the petitions. The main points raised by the respondents are:

(i) The petitioners are not entitled to challenge the recommendations made by TRAI and the policy decisions taken by the Government for grant of UAS Licences.

(ii) The Court cannot review and nullify the recommendations made by TRAI in the matter of allocation of spectrum in 800, 900 and 1800 MHz bands at the rates fixed in 2001.

(iii) The report prepared by the CAG cannot be relied upon for the purpose of recording a finding that the procedure adopted for the grant of UAS Licences is contrary to article 14 of the Constitution. The private respondents have also claimed that the observations made by the CAG and the conclusions recorded by him are seriously flawed and are based on totally unfounded assumptions.

(iv) The UAS Licences were given strictly in accordance with the modified first-come-first-served policy. That the respondents were able to fulfil LoI conditions because newspapers had already published stories about the possible grant of licences in the month of January, 2008.

(v) That those who had made applications in 2004 and 2006 cannot be clubbed with those who had applied in the month of August and September, 2007 because in terms of the existing UASL guidelines they were entitled to licences.

(vi) That private respondents have made huge investments for creating infrastructure to provide services in different parts of the country and if the licences granted to them are cancelled at this stage, public interest would be adversely affected.

(vii) That the private respondents have been able to secure foreign direct investment of thousands of crores for providing better telecom services in remote areas of the country and any intervention by the Court would result in depriving the people living in those areas of telecom services.

(viii) The Government and TRAI have already initiated action for levy of penalty/liquidated damages for non-compliance of the roll out obligations and violation of conditions of the license. That the licensees have not violated any conditions of the license and that the notices issued by TRAI alleging the same have already been challenged before TDSAT and in most cases, interim orders have been passed. That the remedy, if any, available to the petitioners is to approach the TDSAT.

(ix) Some of the respondents have also questioned the application of the policy of first-come-first-served by asserting that even though they had applied in 2004 and 2006, and licences had been granted to them before 25.9.2007, the allocation of spectrum was delayed till 2008 and those who had applied in 2007 were placed above them because they could fulfil the conditions of LoI in terms of the distorted version of the policy first-come-first-served.

REJOINDER FILED BY THE PETITIONERS

55. The petitioners have filed rejoinder affidavit and reiterated the assertions made in the main petition that the grant of UAS Licences is fundamentally flawed and is violative of the Constitutional principles. They have also placed on record report dated 31.1.2011 submitted by the One Man Committee, (hereinafter referred to as 'One-Man Committee Report'), comprising *Justice Shivaraj V. Patil* (former Judge of this Court), which was constituted by the Government of India *vide* Office Memorandum dated 13.12.2010 to examine the appropriateness of the procedure followed by the DoT in issuance of licences and allocation of spectrum during the period 2001 to 2009. They have also placed on record photostat copies of the notings recorded on the files of the DoT.

SUBMISSIONS BY THE PETITIONERS

Arguments

56. Shri Prashant Bhushan, learned counsel for the petitioners in Writ Petition (C) No. 423 of 2010 and Dr. Subramanian Swamy, who is petitioner-in-person in Writ Petition (C) No. 10 of 2011 made the following submissions:

(i) The spectrum, which is a national asset, cannot be distributed by adopting the policy of first-come-first-served on the basis of the application received by the DoT without any advertisement and without holding auction.

(ii) The grant of licences bundled with spectrum is *ex facie* arbitrary illegal and violative of article 14 of the Constitution.

(iii) The decision of the Minister of C&IT to pre-pone the cut-off date from 1.10.2007 to 25.9.2007, which eliminated large number of applications, is violative of article 14 of the Constitution and the entire exercise undertaken with reference to this cut-off date has resulted in discrimination *vis-à-vis* other eligible applicants.

(iv) Once the cut-off date fixed by the Minister of C&IT for consideration of the applications received in the light of the earlier press release fixing the last date as 1.10.2007 has been declared to be arbitrary and unconstitutional by the High Court, the consequential actions taken by the DoT on that basis are liable to be annulled.

(v) The first-come-first-served policy suffers from a fundamental flaw inasmuch as there is no defined criterion for operating that policy. There is no provision for issue of advertisement notifying obligations for grant of licence and allocation of spectrum and any person who makes an application becomes entitled to get licence and spectrum.

(vi) The first-come-first-served policy was manipulated by the Minister of C&IT to favour some of the applicants including those who were not even eligible. Shri Bhushan pointed out that, out of 122 applications, 85 were found to be ineligible and those who could obtain information either from the concerned Minister or the officers of DoT about the change of the criteria for implementing the first-come-first-served policy got advantage and acquired priority over those who had applied earlier.

(vii) The meeting of the Telecom Commission scheduled for 9.1.2008 was deliberately postponed because *vide* letter dated 22.11.2007 the Finance Secretary had strongly objected to the charging of entry fee fixed in 2001.

(viii) Shri Bhushan pointed out that the recommendations made by TRAI on 28.8.2007 were contrary to public interest as well as financial interest of the nation because at the time of entry of 4th cellular operator the same TRAI had suggested multi-stage bidding and even for allocation of 3G spectrum the methodology of auction was suggested but, for no ostensible reason, the so-called theory of level playing field was innovated for grant of UAS Licences in 2007 on the basis of the entry fee fixed in 2001.

Learned counsel emphasized that the transfer of equity by three of the licensees immediately after issue of licences for gain of many thousand crores shows that if the policy of auction had been followed, the nation would have been enriched by many thousand crores.

(ix) Both, Shri Prashant Bhushan and Dr. Subramanian Swamy pointed out that although the Prime Minister had suggested that a fair and transparent method be adopted for grant of UAS Licences through the process of auction, the Minister of C&IT casually and arbitrarily brushed aside the suggestion and granted licence to the applicants for extraneous reasons.

(x) Shri Prashant Bhushan also questioned the grant of the benefit of the policy of dual technology to Tata Teleservices Ltd. By contending that this was a result of manipulation made by the service provider. Dr. Subramanian Swamy also raised a concern regarding the national security and pointed out that some of the applicants who have trans-border connections have received licences and they may ultimately prove to be dangerous for the nation.

ARGUMENTS OF UNION OF INDIA, MINISTER (C&IT) AND OTHER RESPONDENTS

57. Shri G.E. Vahanvati, learned Attorney-General referred to NTP 1994 and NTP 1999 and submitted that the policy decision taken by the Government of India for private sector participation, which could bring in the funds required for expansion of telecommunication services in different parts of the country, cannot be scrutinized by the Court. He submitted that in the last more than 20 years, the telecom services have expanded beyond anybody's expectation because of private sector participation and it cannot be said that granting UAS Licences by charging the entry fee determined at 2001 prices is unconstitutional. Learned counsel referred to the history of development in the field of telecommunications and the concept of spectrum, and submitted that the policy decision taken by the DoT for migration of CDMA service providers was neither illegal nor unconstitutional.

58. Shri Salve, learned senior counsel appearing for respondent No. 9, pointed out that Tata Teleservices had sent an application through fax for grant of GSM for the existing licences which were issued on 19.10.2007 and no exception can be taken to this because Reliance Telecom, which had applied for GSM on 6.2.2006, was given the benefit of migration to dual technology on 18.10.2007, *i.e.*, even before the policy was made public.

59. Learned senior counsel argued that the decision not to auction UAS Licences was based on the recommendations of TRAI and as the petitioners have not challenged the recommendations for two years, the exercise undertaken by the DoT for grant of UAS Licences in 2008 and subsequent allotment of spectrum should not be nullified. Shri Salve argued that the question of institutional integrity is involved in the matter and if the Court comes to the conclusion that auction is the only method for grant of licences and allocation of spectrum then everything should be annulled right from 2001.

60. Learned senior counsel submitted that multi-stage bidding was done only for the purpose of entry of 4th cellular operator but, thereafter, no auction was held. He submitted that if the spectrum was allotted free of charge till 2007, there could be no justification for auction of licences or spectrum in 2007.

61. Shri C.A. Sundaram, learned counsel appearing for respondent Nos. 2 and 4, heavily relied on paragraphs 7.2, 7.4, 7.12, 7.29, 7.30, 7.37 and 7.39 of TRAI's recommendations dated 27.10.2003 and argued that the recommendations made in 2007 were nothing but a continuation of the old policy and, therefore, the petitioners are not entitled to question the method adopted for grant of UAS Licences pursuant to the 2007 recommendations.

62. Learned senior counsel submitted that the policy for grant of UAS Licences and allocation of spectrum cannot be said to be *per se* arbitrary because the same was decided after great deliberations and consideration of international practices. He also relied upon the speech made by the Prime Minister on 2.11.2007 and submitted that the action of the DoT should not be nullified because that will have a far-reaching adverse impact on the availability of telecommunication services in the country.

63. Shri Vikas Singh, learned senior counsel appearing for respondent No. 10, argued that the recommendations made by TRAI in 2007, which were approved by the Minister of C&IT are in national interest because the same would attract investment by foreign players and would benefit the people at large. Learned counsel emphasised that his client has already invested Rs. 6,000 crores and it would be totally unjust if the licence granted in 2008 is cancelled.

64. Shri Vikas Singh also submitted that after the grant of licences and allocation of spectrum the people have been hugely benefited inasmuch as the telecom services have become competitive with the international market and even cheaper than that.

65. Shri C.S. Vaidyanathan, learned senior counsel appearing for respondent No. 8, argued that the application made by his client was pending since June, 2006 and its priority was pushed down due to the application of the distorted version of the first-come-first-served policy. Shri Vaidyanathan pointed out that when the Minister of C&IT announced that applications will not be received after 1.10.2007, there was a huge rush of applications and a large number of players who had no experience in the field of telecom made applications and got the licences.

66. Dr. Abhishek Manu Singhvi, learned senior counsel appearing for respondent Nos. 11 and 12, argued that his clients had made applications much prior to 2007 but they were unfairly clubbed with those who had applied in 2007 and in this manner the principle of equality was violated. Dr. Singhvi submitted that if the applications made prior to 2007 had been processed as per the existing policy, respondent Nos. 11 and 12 would have received licences bundled with spectrum without competition/objection from anyone.

67. Shri Dayan Krishnan, learned counsel for respondent No. 6, adopted the arguments of other learned counsel and submitted that the licences granted in 2007 should not be quashed at this belated stage.

68. Shri Rakesh Dwivedi, learned senior counsel for TRAI, referred to TRAI's written submissions to justify why it had not recommended auction of licences. Learned senior counsel extensively referred to the recommendations made by TRAI in 2007 and submitted that even though it was specifically suggested that the DoT should take a comprehensive decision on the allocation of spectrum, no effort was made in that direction and the licences were granted without determining availability of spectrum. Shri Dwivedi also submitted that TRAI has already initiated action for cancellation of licences of those respondents who have violated the terms of licence and/or failed to fulfil rollout obligations.

JUDGMENTS RELIED UPON BY THE PARTIES

69. Learned counsel for both the sides relied upon a large number of decisions. Shri Prashant Bhushan and Dr. Subramanian Swamy relied upon the following judgments: *K. Manjusree* v. *State of Andhra Pradesh*, (2008) 3 SCC 512; *Monarch Infrastructure (P) Ltd.* v. *Commissioner, Ulhasnagar Municipal Corpn.*, (2000) 5 SCC 287; *Home Communication Ltd.* v. *Union of India*, 52 (1993) DLT 168; *Jamshed Hormusji Wadia* v. *Board of Trustees, Port of Mumbai*, (2004) 3 SCC 214; *Chaitanya Kumar* v. *State of Karnataka*, (1986) 2 SCC 594; *Shivsagar Tiwari* v. *Union of India*, (1996) 6 SCC 558; *Common Cause, A Registered Society (Petrol Pumps Matter)* v. *Union of India*, (1996) 6 SCC 530; *Nagar Nigam* v. *Al Faheem Meat Exports (P) Ltd.*, (2006) 13 SCC 382.

70. Learned Attorney-General and learned counsel appearing for the private respondents relied upon *Delhi Science Forum* v. *Union of India*, (1996) 2 SCC 405, *BALCO Employees' Union (Regd.)* v. *Union of India*, (2002) 2 SCC 333; *Villianur Iyarkkai Padukappu Maiyam* v. *Union of India*, (2009) 7 SCC 561; *Ministry of Labour and Rehabilitation* v. *Tiffin's Barytes Asbestos and Paints Ltd.*, (1985) 3 SCC 594; *United India Fire and General Insurance Co. Ltd.* v. *K.S. Vishwanathan*, (1985) 3 SCC 686; *State of Tamil Nadu* v. *M.N. Sundararajan*, (1980) 4 SCC 592; *Sunil Pannalal Banthia* v. *City and Industrial Development Corporation of Maharashtra Ltd.*, (2007) 10 SCC 674; *Bombay Dyeing and Mfg. Co. Ltd. (3)* v. *Bombay Environmental Action Group*, (2006) 3 SCC 434; *Prem Chand Somchand Shah* v. *Union of India*, (1991) 2 SCC 48 and *Sanjeev Coke Mfg. Co.* v. *Bharat Coking Coal Ltd.*, (1983) 1 SCC 147.

CAG REPORT AND REPORT OF ONE MAN COMMITTEE

71. Before dealing with the arguments of the learned counsel for the parties and adverting to some of the precedents, we consider it necessary to mention that during the course of hearing, Shri Prashant Bhushan and Dr. Subramanian Swamy heavily relied upon the CAG report as also the One-Man Committee Report. Learned Attorney-General and learned senior counsel appearing for some of the private respondents also referred to the One-Man Committee Report. However, as the CAG report is being examined by the Public Accounts Committee and Joint Parliamentary Committee of Parliament we do not consider it proper to refer to the findings and conclusions contained therein.

72. Likewise, we do not consider it necessary to advert to the observations made, and the suggestions given by the One-Man Committee because the Government of India has already taken a decision to segregate spectrum from licence and allot the same by auction. This is evident from the following extracts of the press statement dated 29.1.2011 issued by the present Minister of C&IT:

"In future, the spectrum will not be bundled with licence. The licence to be issued to telecom operators will be in the nature of 'unified licence' and the licence holder will be free to offer any of the multifarious telecom services. In the event the licence holder would like to offer wireless services, it will have to obtain spectrum through a market driven process. In future, there will be no concept of contracted spectrum and, therefore, no concept of initial or start-up spectrum. Spectrum will be made available only through market driven process.

While moving towards a new policy dispensation, it is necessary to ensure a level playing field between all players. Hence, going forward, any new policy of pricing would need to be applied to equally to all players. Additionally, assignment of balance of contracted spectrum may need to be ensured for the existing licensees who have so far been allocated only the start up spectrum of 4.4 MHz. It may be recalled that show cause notices have been issued to certain licensees for cancellation. Only in respect of the licences that will be found valid after the process is completed, the additional 1.8 MHz will be assigned on their becoming eligible, but the spectrum will be assigned to them at a price determined under the new policy.

We need to seriously consider the adoption of an auction process for allocation and pricing of spectrum beyond 6.2 MHz while ensuring that there is adequate competition in the auction process.

TRAI had made recommendations in May, 2010 and indicated that it would apprise the Government of the findings of a study on the question of pricing of 2G spectrum in future. This is expected shortly. We would examine their recommendations speedily as soon as they are received, keeping the perspectives that I have outlined, while finalizing our new policy. I am confident that we will be able to design a policy that ensures that existing licence holders get the spectrum they need and are entitled to, while simultaneously, ensuring that the Government also receives revenues commensurate with the current market value of spectrum."

DISCUSSION BY THE SUPREME COURT

73. We shall now consider the questions enumerated in the opening paragraph of the judgment.

74. Question No. 1

At the outset, we consider it proper to observe that even though there is no universally accepted definition of natural resources, they are generally understood as elements having intrinsic utility to mankind. They may be renewable or non renewable. They are thought of as the individual elements of the natural environment that provide economic and social services to human society and are considered valuable in their relatively unmodified, natural, form. A natural resource's value rests in the amount of the material available and the demand for it. The latter is determined by its usefulness to production. Natural resources belong to the people but the State legally owns them on behalf of its people and from that point of view natural resources are considered as national assets, moreso because the State benefits immensely from their value.

75. The State is empowered to distribute natural resources. However, as they constitute public property/national asset, while distributing natural resources, the State is bound to act in consonance with the principles of equality and public trust and ensure that no action is taken which may be detrimental to public interest. Like any other State action, constitutionalism must be reflected at every stage of the distribution of natural resources. In article 39(b) of the Constitution it has been provided that the ownership and control of the material resources of the community should be so distributed so as to best sub-serve the common good, but no comprehensive legislation has been enacted to generally define natural resources and a framework for their protection. Ofcourse, environment laws enacted by Parliament and State Legislatures deal with specific natural resources, *i.e.*, Forest, Air, Water, Costal Zones, etc.

76. The ownership regime relating to natural resources can also be ascertained from international conventions and customary international law, common law and national constitutions. In international law, it rests upon the concept of sovereignty and seeks to respect the principle of permanent sovereignty (of peoples and nations) over (their) natural resources as asserted in the 17th Session of the United Nations General Assembly and then affirmed as a customary international norm by the International Court of Justice in the case of *Democratic Republic of Congo* v. *Uganda*. Common Law recognises States as having the authority to protect natural resources insofar as the resources are within the interests of the general public. The State is deemed to have a proprietary interest in natural resources and must act as guardian and trustee in relation to the same. Constitutions across the world focus on establishing natural resources as owned by, and for the benefit of, the country. In most instances where constitutions specifically address ownership of natural resources, the Sovereign State, or, as it is more commonly expressed, 'the people', is designated as the owner of the natural resource.

SPECTRUM IS A SCARE, FINITE AND RENEWABLE NATURAL RESOURCE

77. Spectrum has been internationally accepted as a scarce, finite and renewable natural resource which is susceptible to degradation in case of inefficient utilisation. It has a high economic value in the light of the demand for it on account of the tremendous growth in the telecom sector. Although it does not belong to a particular State, right of use has been granted to States as per international norms.

NATURAL RESOURCES ARE A TRUST IN THE HANDS OF UNION OF INDIA – DISPOSAL MUST BE GUIDED BY CONSTITUTIONAL PRINCIPLES, DOCTRINE OF EQUALITY AND PUBLIC GOOD

78. In India, the Courts have given an expansive interpretation to the concept of natural resources and have from time to time issued directions, by relying upon the provisions contained in articles 38, 39, 48, 48A and 51A(g), for protection and proper allocation/distribution of natural resources and have repeatedly insisted on compliance of the constitutional principles in the process of distribution, transfer and alienation to private persons.

79. The doctrine of public trust, which was evolved in *Illinois Central Railroad Co.* v. *People of the State of Illinois*, 146 US 387 (1892), has been held by this Court to be a part of the Indian jurisprudence in *M.C. Mehta* v. *Kamal Nath*, (1997) 1 SCC 388 and has been applied in *Jamshed Hormusji Wadia* v. *Board of Trustee, Port of Mumbai*, (2002) 3 SCC 214; *Intellectuals Forum, Tirupathi* v. *State of Andhra Pradesh*, (2006) 3 SCC 549 and *Fomento Resorts and Hotels Limited* v. *Minguel Martins*, (2009) 3 SCC 571.

80. In *Jamshed Hormusji Wadia's* case (supra), this Court held that the State's actions and the actions of its agencies/instrumentalities must be for the public good, achieving the objects for which they exist and should not be arbitrary or capricious. In the field of contracts, the State and its instrumentalities should design their activities in a manner which would ensure competition and non-discrimination. They can augment their resources but the object should be to serve the public cause and to do public good by resorting to fair and reasonable methods.

81. In *Fomento Resorts* and *Hotels Limited* case (supra), the Court referred to the article of Prof. Joseph L. Sax and made the following observations: (SCC pp. 614-15 paras 53-55)

> "53. The public trust doctrine enjoins upon the Government to protect the resources for the enjoyment of the general public rather than to permit their use for private ownership or commercial purposes. This doctrine puts an implicit embargo on the right of the State to transfer public properties to private party if such transfer affects public interest, mandates affirmative State action for effective management of natural resources and empowers the citizens to question ineffective management thereof.
>
> 54. The heart of the public trust doctrine is that it imposes limits and obligations upon government agencies and their administrators on behalf of all the people and especially future generations. For example, renewable and non-renewable resources, associated uses, ecological values or objects in which the public has a special interest (*i.e.*, public lands, waters, etc.) are held subject to the duty of the State not to impair such resources, uses or values, even if private interests are involved. The same obligations apply to managers of forests, monuments, parks, the public domain and other public assets. Professor Joseph L. Sax in his classic article, "The Public Trust Doctrine in Natural Resources Law: Effective Judicial Intervention" (1970), indicates that the public trust doctrine, of all concepts known to law, constitutes the best practical and philosophical premise and legal tool for protecting public rights and for protecting and managing resources, ecological values or objects held in trust.
>
> 55. The public trust doctrine is a tool for exerting long-established public rights over short-term public rights and private gain. Today every person exercising his or her right to use the air, water, or land and associated natural ecosystems has the obligation to secure for the rest of us the right to live or otherwise use that same resource or property for the long-term and enjoyment by future generations. To say it another way, a landowner or lessee and a water right holder has an obligation to use such resources in a manner as not to impair or diminish the people's rights and the people's long-term interest

in that property or resource, including down slope lands, waters and resources."

82. In *Secretary, Ministry of Information and Broadcasting, Government of India* v. *Cricket Association of Bengal*, (1995) 2 SCC 161, the Court was dealing with the right of organizers of an event, such as a sport tournament, to its live audiovisual broadcast, universally, through an agency of their choice, national or foreign. In paragraph 78, the Court described the airwaves/frequencies as public property in the following words: (SCC p. 226)

> "78. There is no doubt that since the airwaves/frequencies are a public property and are also limited, they have to be used in the best interest of the society and this can be done either by a central authority by establishing its own broadcasting network or regulating the grant of licences to other agencies, including the private agencies."

83. In *Reliance Natural Resources Limited* v. *Reliance Industries Limited*, (2010) 7 SCC 1, P. Sathasivam J., with whom Balakrishnan, C.J., agreed, made the following observations: (SCC p. 64, para 114)

> "114. It must be noted that the constitutional mandate is that the natural resources belong to the people of this country. The nature of the word "vest" must be seen in the context of the public trust doctrine (PTD). Even though this doctrine has been applied in cases dealing with environmental jurisprudence, it has its broader application."

84. The Learned Judge then referred to the judgments, *In re Special Reference No. 1 of 2001*, (2004) 4 SCC 489, *M.C. Mehta* v. *Kamal Nath*, (1997) 1 SCC 388 and observed: (SCC p. 65, para 116)

> "116. ...This doctrine is part of Indian law and finds application in the present case as well. It is thus the duty of the Government to provide complete protection to the natural resources as a trustee of the people at large."

The Court also held that natural resources are vested with the Government as a matter of trust in the name of the people of India, thus it is the solemn duty of the State to protect the national interest and natural resources must always be used in the interests of the country and not private interests.

85. As natural resources are public goods, the doctrine of equality, which emerges from the concepts of justice and fairness, must guide the State in determining the actual mechanism for distribution of natural resources. In this regard, the doctrine of equality has two aspects: *first*, it regulates the rights and obligations of the State *vis-à-vis* its people and demands that the people be granted equitable access to natural resources and/or its products and that they are adequately compensated for the transfer of the resource to the private domain; and *second*, it regulates the rights and obligations of the State *vis-à-vis* private parties seeking to acquire/use the resource and demands that the procedure adopted for distribution is just, non-arbitrary and transparent and that it does not discriminate between similarly placed private parties.

86. In *Akhil Bharatiya Upbhokta Congress* v. *State of Madhya Pradesh*, (2011) 5 SCC 29, this Court examined the legality of the action taken by the Government of Madhya Pradesh to allot 20 acres land to an institute established in the name of Kushabhau Thakre on the basis of an application made by the Trust. One of the grounds on which the appellant challenged the allotment of land was that the State Government had not adopted any rational method consistent with the doctrine of equality. The High Court negatived the appellant's challenge. Before this Court, learned senior counsel appearing for the State relied upon the judgments in *Ugar Sugar Works Ltd.* v. *Delhi Administration*, (2001) 3 SCC 635; *State of Uttar Pradesh* v. *Choudhary Rambeer Singh*, (2008) 5 SCC 550; *State of Orissa* v. *Gopinath Dash*, (2005) 13 SCC 495 and *Meerut Development Authority* v. *Association of Management Studies*, (2009) 6 SCC 171 and argued that the Court cannot exercise the power of judicial review to nullify the policy framed by the State Government to allot Nazul land without advertisement.

87. This Court rejected the argument, referred to the judgments in *Ramanna Dayaram Shetty* v. *International Airports Authority of India*, (1979) 3 SCC 489; *S.G. Jaisinghani* v. *Union of India*, AIR 1967 SC 1427; *Kasturilal Lakshmi Reddy* v. *State of Jammu and Kashmir*, (1980) 4 SCC 1; *Common Cause* v. *Union of India*, (supra); *Shrilekha Vidyarthy* v. *State of Uttar Pradesh*, (1991) 1 SCC 212; *LIC* v. *Consumer Education and Research Centre*, (1995) 5 SCC 482; *New India Public School* v. *HUDA*, (1996) 5 SCC 510 and held: (SCC p. 60 para 65)

> "65. What needs to be emphasised is that the State and/or its agencies/instrumentalities cannot give largesse to any person according to the sweet will and whims of the political entities and/or officers of the State. Every action/decision of the State and/or its agencies/instrumentalities to give largesse or confer benefit must be founded on a sound, transparent, discernible and well-defined policy, which shall be made known to the public by publication in the Official Gazette and other recognised modes of publicity and such policy must be implemented/executed by adopting a non-discriminatory and non-arbitrary method irrespective of the class or category of persons proposed to be benefited by the policy. The distribution of largesse like allotment of land, grant of quota, permit licence, etc. by the State and its agencies/instrumentalities should always be done in a fair and equitable manner and the element of favouritism or nepotism shall not influence the exercise of discretion, if any, conferred upon the particular functionary or officer of the State."

88. In *Sachidanand Pandey* v. *State of West Bengal*, (1987) 2 SCC 295, the Court referred to some of the precedents and laid down the following propositions: (SCC p. 330, para 40)

> "40. ...State-owned or public-owned property is not to be dealt with at the absolute discretion of the Executive. Certain precepts and principles have to be observed. Public interest is the paramount consideration. One of the methods of securing the public interest, when it is considered necessary to dispose of a property, is to sell the property by public auction or by inviting tenders. Though that is the ordinary rule, it is not an invariable rule. There may be situations where there are compelling reasons necessitating departure from the rule but then the reasons for the departure must be rational and should not be suggestive of discrimination. Appearance of public justice is as

important as doing justice. Nothing should be done which gives an appearance of bias, jobbery or nepotism."

89. In conclusion, we hold that the State is the legal owner of the natural resources as a trustee of the people and although it is empowered to distribute the same, the process of distribution must be guided by the constitutional principles including the doctrine of equality and larger public good.

2G SPECTRUM ALLOCATED IN 2007-2008 AT THE PRICE FIXED IN 2001

Question No. 2

90. Although, while making recommendations on 28.8.2007, TRAI itself had recognised that spectrum was a scarce commodity, it made recommendation for allocation of 2G spectrum on the basis of 2001 price by invoking the theory of level playing field. Paragraph 2.40 of the recommendations dated 28.8.2007 shows that as per TRAI's own assessment the existing system of spectrum allocation criteria, pricing methodology and the management system suffered from number of deficiencies and there was an urgent need to address the issues linked with spectrum efficiency and its management and yet it decided to recommend the allocation of spectrum at the price determined in 2001. All this was done in the name of growth, affordability, penetration of wireless services in semi-urban and rural areas, etc.

TRAI COMPLETELY OVERLOOKED THE OBJECTIVES OF NTP 1999 AND THE DECISION OF GoM – 2003

Unfortunately, while doing so, TRAI completely overlooked that one of the main objectives of NTP 1999 was that spectrum should be utilised efficiently, economically, rationally and optimally and there should be a transparent process of allocation of frequency spectrum as also the fact that in terms of the decision taken by the Council of Ministers in 2003 to approve the recommendations of the Group of Ministers, the DoT and Ministry of Finance were required to discuss and finalise the spectrum pricing formula.

MINISTER C&IT (A. RAJA) AND OFFICERS OF DoT VIRTUALLY GIFTED AWAY THE NATIONAL ASSET AT THROW AWAY PRICES

91. To say the least, the entire approach adopted by TRAI was lopsided and contrary to the decision taken by the Council of Ministers and its recommendations became a handle for the then Minister of C&IT and the officers of the DoT who virtually gifted away the important national asset at throw away prices by willfully ignoring the concerns raised from various quarters including the Prime Minister, Ministry of Finance and also some of its own officers. This becomes clear from the fact that soon after obtaining the licences, some of the beneficiaries off-loaded their stakes to others, in the name of transfer of equity or infusion of fresh capital by foreign companies, and thereby made huge profits. We have no doubt that if the method of auction had been adopted for grant of licence which could be the only rational transparent method for distribution of national wealth, the nation would have been enriched by many thousand crores.

TRAI MAY BE EXPERT BODY, BUT CANNOT IGNORE CONSTITUTIONAL PRINCIPLES

92. While it cannot be denied that TRAI is an expert body assigned with important functions under the 1997 Act, it cannot make recommendations overlooking the basic constitutional postulates and established principles and thereby deny people from participating in the distribution of national wealth and benefit a handful of persons. Therefore, even though the scope of judicial review in such matters is extremely limited, as pointed out in *Delhi Science Forum* v. *Union of India*, (supra) and a large number of other judgments relied upon by the learned counsel of the respondents, keeping in view the facts which have been brought to the notice of the Court that the mechanism evolved by TRAI for allocation of spectrum and the methodology adopted by the then Minister of C&IT and the officers of DoT for grant of UAS Licences may have caused huge loss to the nation, we have no hesitation to record a finding that the recommendations made by TRAI were flawed in many respects and implementation thereof by the DoT resulted in gross violation of the objective of NPT 1999 and the decision taken by the Council of Ministers on 31.10.2003.

RECOMMENDATIONS OF TRAI WERE CONTRARY TO THE DECISION OF COUNCIL OF MINISTERS

93. We may also mention that even though in its recommendations dated 28.8.2007, TRAI had not specifically recommended that entry fee be fixed at 2001 rates, but paragraph 2.73 and other related paragraphs of its recommendations state that it has decided not to recommend the standard option for pricing of spectrum in 2G bands keeping in view the level playing field for the new entrants. It is impossible to approve the decision taken by the DoT to act upon those recommendations. We also consider it necessary to observe that in today's dynamism and unprecedented growth of telecom sector, the entry fee determined in 2001 ought to have been treated by the TRAI as wholly unrealistic for grant of licence along with start up spectrum. In our view, the recommendations made by TRAI in this regard were contrary to the decision of the Council of Ministers that the DoT shall discuss the issue of spectrum pricing with the Ministry of Finance along with the issue of incentive for efficient use of spectrum as well as disincentive for sub-optimal usages. Being an expert body, it was incumbent upon the TRAI to make suitable recommendations even for the 2G bands especially in light of the deficiencies of the present system which it had itself pointed out. We do not find merit in the reasoning of TRAI that the consideration of maintaining a level playing field prevented a realistic reassessment of the entry fee.

FIRST COME FIRST SERVED POLICY IS BASICALLY DANGEROUS – TOTALLY ARBITRARY

Question Nos. 3 and 4:

94. There is a fundamental flaw in the first-come-first-served policy inasmuch as it involves an element of pure chance or accident. In matters involving award of contracts or grant of licence or permission to use public property, the invocation of first-come-first-served policy has inherently dangerous implications. Any person who has access to the power corridor at the highest or the lowest level may be able to obtain information from the Government files or the files of the agency/instrumentality of the State that a particular public property or asset is likely to be disposed of or a contract is likely to be awarded or a licence or permission is likely to be given, he would immediately make an application and would become entitled to stand first in the queue at the cost of all others who may have a better claim.

PROCEDURE ADOPTED FOR DISPOSAL MUST BE FAIR AND TRANSPARENT

95. This Court has repeatedly held that wherever a contract is to be awarded or a licence is to be given, the public authority must adopt a transparent and fair method for making selections so that all eligible persons get a fair opportunity of competition. To put it differently, the State and its agencies/instrumentalities must always adopt a rational method for disposal of public property and no attempt should be made to scuttle the claim of worthy applicants. When it comes to alienation of scarce natural resources like spectrum etc., it is the burden of the State to ensure that a non-discriminatory method is adopted for distribution and alienation, which would necessarily result in protection of national/public interest.

PUBLICISED AUCTION CONDUCTED FAIRLY AND IMPARTIALLY WOULD HAVE YIELDED MAXIMUM FINANCIAL BENEFITS – WOULD HAVE UPHELD CONSTITUTIONAL VALUES

96. In our view, a duly publicised auction conducted fairly and impartially is perhaps the best method for discharging this burden and the methods like first-come-first-served when used for alienation of natural resources/public property are likely to be misused by unscrupulous people who are only interested in garnering maximum financial benefit and have no respect for the constitutional ethos and values. In other words, while transferring or alienating the natural resources, the State is duty bound to adopt the method of auction by giving wide publicity so that all eligible persons can participate in the process.

ACTION TAKEN BETWEEN SEPTEMBER, 2007 TO MARCH, 2008 BY DoT LED BY THE MINISTER C&IT, (A. RAJA), WERE ILLEGAL, ARBITRARY – INTENDED TO FAVOUR FEW INDIVIDUALS AT THE COST OF NATIONAL LOSS

97. The exercise undertaken by the officers of the DoT between September, 2007 and March, 2008, under the leadership of the then Minister of C&IT was wholly arbitrary, capricious and contrary to public interest apart from being violative of the doctrine of equality. The material produced before the Court shows that the Minister of C&IT wanted to favour some companies at the cost of the Public Exchequer and for this purpose, he took the following steps:

(i) Soon after his appointment as Minister of C&IT, he directed that all the applications received for grant of UAS Licence should be kept pending till the receipt of TRAI recommendations.

(ii) The recommendations made by TRAI on 28.8.2007 were not placed before the full Telecom Commission which, among others, would have included the Finance Secretary. The notice of the meeting of the Telecom Commission was not given to any of the non-permanent members despite the fact that the recommendations made by TRAI for allocation of spectrum in 2G bands had serious financial implications. This has been established from the pleadings and the records produced before this Court which show that after issue of licences, 3 applicants transferred their equities for a total sum of Rs. 24,493 crores in favour of foreign companies. Therefore, it was absolutely necessary for the DoT to take the opinion of the Finance Ministry as per the requirement of the Government of India (Transaction of Business) Rules, 1961.

(iii) The officers of the DoT who attended the meeting of the Telecom Commission held on 10.10.2007 hardly had any choice but to approve the recommendations made by TRAI. If they had not done so, they would have incurred the wrath of the Minister of C&IT.

(iv) In view of the approval by the Council of Ministers of the recommendations made by the Group of Ministers in 2003, the DoT had to discuss the issue of spectrum pricing with the Ministry of Finance. Therefore, the DoT was under an obligation to involve the Ministry of Finance before any decision could be taken in the context of paragraphs 2.78 and 2.79 of TRAI's recommendations. However, as the Minister of C&IT was very much conscious of the fact that the Secretary, Finance, had objected to the allocation of 2G spectrum at the rates fixed in 2001, he did not consult the Finance Minister or the officers of the Finance Ministry.

(v) The Minister of C&IT brushed aside the suggestion made by the Minister of Law and Justice for placing the matter before the Empowered Group of Ministers. Not only this, within few hours of the receipt of the suggestion made by the Prime Minister in his letter dated 2.11.2007 that keeping in view the inadequacy of spectrum, transparency and fairness should be maintained in the matter of allocation thereof, the Minister of C&IT rejected the same by saying that it will be unfair, discriminatory, arbitrary and capricious to auction the spectrum to new applicants because it will not give them level playing field.

(vi) The Minister C&IT introduced cut-off date as 25.9.2007 for consideration of the applications received for grant of licence despite the fact that only one day prior to this, press release was issued by the DoT fixing 1.10.2007 as the last date for receipt of the applications. This arbitrary action of the Minister of C&IT though appears to be innocuous, actually benefitted some of the real estate companies who did not have any experience in dealing with telecom services and who had made applications only on 24.9.2007, *i.e.*, one day before the cut-off date fixed by the Minister of C&IT on his own.

(vii) The cut-off date, *i.e.*, 25.9.2007 decided by the Minister of C&IT on 2.11.2007 was not made public till 10.1.2008 and the first-come-first-served policy, which was being followed since 2003 was changed by him on 7.1.2008 and was incorporated in press release dated 10.1.2008. This enabled some of the applicants, who had access either to the Minister or the officers of the DoT to get the demand drafts, bank guarantee, etc., prepared in advance for compliance of conditions of the LoIs, which was the basis for determination of seniority for grant of licences and allocation of spectrum.

(viii) The meeting of the full Telecom Commission, which was scheduled to be held on 9.1.2008 to consider issues relating to grant of licences and pricing of spectrum was deliberately postponed on 7.1.2008 so that the Secretary, Finance and Secretaries of three other important Departments may not be able to raise objections against the procedure devised by the DoT for grant of licence and allocation of spectrum by applying the principle of level playing field.

(ix) The manner in which the exercise for grant of LoIs to the applicants was conducted on 10.1.2008 leaves no room for doubt that every thing was stage managed to favour those who were able to know in advance the change in the implementation of the first-come-first served policy. As a result of this, some of the companies which had submitted applications in 2004 or 2006 were pushed down in the priority and those who had applied between August and September, 2007 succeeded in getting higher seniority entitling them to allocation of spectrum on priority basis.

UAS LICENCES GRANTED BETWEEN 2001 TO 2007 CANNOT BE CANCELLED AS PRAYED ON BEHALF OF UOI

98. The argument of Shri Harish Salve, learned senior counsel, that if the Court finds that the exercise undertaken for grant of UAS Licences has resulted in violation of the institutional integrity, then all the licences granted 2001 onwards should be cancelled does not deserve acceptance because those who have got licence between 2001 and 24.9.2007 are not parties to these petitions and legality of the licences granted to them has not been questioned before this Court.

IF THE POLICY OR DECISION TAKEN HITS THE CONSTITUTIONAL PRINCIPLES, COURT IS DUTY BOUND TO INTERVENE – LICENCES ILLEGALLY GRANTED DESERVE TO BE QUASHED

99. In majority of judgments relied upon by learned Attorney-General and learned counsel for the respondents, it has been held that the power of judicial review should be exercised with great care and circumspection and the Court should not ordinarily interfere with the policy decisions of the Government in financial matters. There cannot be any quarrel with the proposition that the Court cannot substitute its opinion for the one formed by the experts in the particular field and due respect should be given to the wisdom of those who are entrusted with the task of framing the policies. We are also conscious of the fact that the Court should not interfere with the fiscal policies of the State. However, when it is clearly demonstrated that the policy framed by the State or its agency/instrumentality and/or its implementation is contrary to public interest or is violative of the constitutional principles, it is the duty of the Court to exercise its jurisdiction in larger public interest and reject the stock plea of the State that the scope of judicial review should not be exceeded beyond the recognised parameters.

100. When matters like these are brought before the judicial constituent of the State by public spirited citizens, it becomes the duty of the Court to exercise its power in larger public interest and ensure that the institutional integrity is not compromised by those in whom the people have reposed trust and who have taken an oath to discharge duties in accordance with the Constitution and the law without fear or favour, affection or ill will and who, as any other citizen, enjoy fundamental rights and, at the same time, are bound to perform the duties enumerated in article 51A. Reference in this connection can usefully be made to the judgment of the three-Judge Bench headed by Chief Justice Kapadia in *Centre for P.I.L.* v. *Union of India*, (2011) 4 SCC 1.

ENLIGHTENED CITIZENS WORK IN LARGER PUBLIC INTEREST

101. Before concluding, we consider it imperative to observe that but for the vigilance of some enlightened citizens who held important constitutional and other positions and discharged their duties in larger public interest and Non-Governmental Organisations who have been constantly fighting for clean governance and accountability of the constitutional institutions, unsuspecting citizens and the Nation would never have known how the scarce natural resource spared by the Army has been grabbed by those who enjoy money power and who have been able to manipulate the system.

WRIT PETITIONS ACCEPTED – SPECTRUM LICENCES ILLEGALLY GRANTED CANCELLED – BENEFICIARIES AT THE COST OF THE NATION BURDENED WITH COSTS

102. In the result, the writ petitions are allowed in the following terms:

(i) The licences granted to the private respondents on or after 10.1.2008 pursuant to two press releases issued on 10.1.2008 and subsequent allocation of spectrum to the licensees are declared illegal and are quashed.

(ii) The above direction shall become operative after four months.

(iii) Keeping in view the decision taken by the Central Government in 2011, TRAI shall make fresh recommendations for grant of licence and allocation of spectrum in 2G band in 22 Service Areas by auction, as was done for allocation of spectrum in 3G band.

(iv) The Central Government shall consider the recommendations of TRAI and take appropriate decision within next one month and fresh licences be granted by auction.

(v) Respondents Nos. 2, 3 and 9 who have been benefited at the cost of Public Exchequer by a wholly arbitrary and unconstitutional action taken by the DoT for grant of UAS Licences and allocation of spectrum in 2G band and who offloaded their stakes for many thousand crores in the name of fresh infusion of equity or transfer of equity shall pay cost of Rs. 5 crores each. Respondent Nos. 4, 6, 7 and 10 shall pay cost of Rs. 50 lakhs each because they too had been benefited by the wholly arbitrary and unconstitutional exercise undertaken by the DoT for grant of UAS Licences and allocation of spectrum in 2G band. We have not imposed cost on the respondents who had submitted their applications in 2004 and 2006 and whose applications were kept pending till 2007.

(vi) Within four months, 50% of the cost shall be deposited with the Supreme Court Legal Services Committee for being used for providing legal aid to poor and indigent litigants. The remaining 50% cost shall be deposited in the funds created for Resettlement and Welfare Schemes of the Ministry of Defence.

(vii) However, it is made clear that the observations made in this judgment shall not, in any manner, affect the pending investigation by the CBI, Directorate of Enforcement and others agencies or cause prejudice to those who are facing prosecution in the cases registered by the CBI or who may face prosecution on the basis of charge-sheet(s) which may be filed by the CBI in future and the Special Judge, CBI shall decide the matter uninfluenced by this judgment. We also make it clear that this judgment shall not prejudice any person in the action which may be taken by other investigating agencies under Income-tax Act, 1961, Prevention of Money Laundering Act, 2002 and other similar statutes.

……………………………….J.
(G.S. SINGHVI)

……………………………...J.
(ASOK KUMAR GANGULY)

New Delhi:
February 02, 2012.

THE UNION OF INDIA had filed review petition which was later on got dismissed as withdrawn.

Author's Note: Since the case relating to 2G was a matter of great public importance in which one of the Ministers of the Government of India was involved and the National loss was in thousands of crores of Rupees and since proper presentation of the case before the Special Court set up for this purpose, was, required therefore, an Application was filed before the Hon'ble Supreme Court. Hence this judgment

SUPREME COURT WAS CONSIDERING IN THIS CASE THE APPOINTMENT OF SPECIAL PUBLIC PROSECUTOR IN VIEW OF NATIONAL IMPORTANCE OF THE CASE

Center for PIL[1]

v.

Union of India

SUPREME COURT OF INDIA

C.A. No. 10660 of 2010

Decided on 11-4-2011.

BENCH

G.S. Singhvi and Asok Kumar Ganguly, JJ.

ORDER

1. Heard Ms. Indira Jaising, Additional-Solicitor-General, Mr. K.K. Venugopal, learned senior counsel for the Central Bureau of Investigation (CBI), Mr. Harin Raval, Additional-Solicitor-General appearing for the Enforcement Directorate (ED) and also Mr. Pranav Sachdeva, the learned counsel assisting Mr. Prashant Bhushan.

2. The question which this Court is now considering is the appointment of a Special Public Prosecutor, to conduct the prosecution on behalf of the CBI and the ED in the 2G Spectrum case, in which charge-sheet has been filed on April 2, 2011 and this Court has been told that a further charge-sheet is likely to be filed very soon.

PROPER INVESTIGATION BY CBI WAS MONITORED BY SUPREME COURT UNDER ARTICLE 136 IN LARGER PUBLIC INTEREST – SPECIAL COURT WAS SET UP FOR TRIAL OF 2G CASE

3. From the various orders passed in this case on different dates, it is clear that this Court has not only directed CBI investigation in the matter, this Court has been monitoring the said investigation at various stages. This monitoring has been undertaken by this Court in view of the prayers made by the appellant and also in view of the very fair stand taken by the prosecuting agency, as also the Government of India, virtually inviting this Court's intervention in the matter of monitoring of the investigation. Having regard to the larger issues of public

---

1. (2012) 3 SCC 117.

interest involved in proper investigation of the case and the ultimate unearthing of the crime, this Court has accepted such prayers of the parties. Acting on such basis, this Court has given direction for establishing a separate Special Court to try this case and pursuant to such direction, a Special Court has been constituted after following the due procedure. All this will appear from various orders passed by this Court from time to time.

4. It may be noted that while monitoring this investigation, this Court, on the prayer made by the counsel for the parties, has also directed the CBI to take over the investigation in respect of the alleged suicide of one Mr. Sadik Batcha and pursuant to that direction, the CBI has expressed its willingness to take over the said investigation and in fact such investigation has been taken over by the CBI, as would appear from the communication dated April 7, 2011 issued by the Government of India, Ministry of Personnel, PG and Pension, Department of Personnel and Training to Ms. Indira Jaising, ASG. The requisite notification under section 5(1) of DSPE Act, 1946 has been issued.

5. From the aforesaid trend of events, it is clear that in larger public interest, this Court, in exercise of its power under article 136 of the Constitution has been monitoring the investigation in a most comprehensive manner.

SPECIAL PUBLIC PROSECUTOR OF IMPECCABLE INTEGRITY WAS REQUIRED TO CONDUCT THE CASE BEFORE THE SPECIAL COURT

6. In view of those peculiar facts of this case, and various orders passed by it from time to time, this Court is of the opinion that in the matter of appointment of the Special Public Prosecutor, utmost fairness and objectivity should be observed. It is beyond dispute that for a successful prosecution, the appointment of a very competent Special Public Prosecutor is of the essence.

7. This Court is aware of the fact that normally, in matter of appointment of a Special Public Prosecutor, the Central Government or State Government, as the case may be, make such appointments. Since the Court is monitoring the case and it is of the view that a competent prosecution is of utmost importance, having regard to the demands of public interest, this Court requested Mr. K.K. Venugopal, learned senior counsel for CBI and ED, to suggest certain names of learned advocates who can undertake the responsibility of conducting the prosecution as a Special Public Prosecutor in the case.

NAME OF U.U. LALIT SENIOR ADVOCATE OF SUPREME COURT PROPOSED FOR BEING APPOINTED AS SPECIAL PUBLIC PROSECUTOR WHO HAD ALSO AGREED TO IT

8. On such request being made, Mr. K.K. Venugopal took some time and after considering several names suggested the name of Mr. U.U. Lalit, a senior advocate of this Court for being considered for appointment as Special Public Prosecutor.

9. There is unanimity among the learned counsel appearing for the parties, that Mr. Lalit is a lawyer of unimpeachable integrity, possessing unquestionable competence and independence to conduct the prosecution in this case. This Court has also been informed by Mr. K.K. Venugopal, that Mr. Lalit has agreed to accept this responsibility if it is conferred on him. This Court has been informed that Mr. Lalit was on the panel of State of Maharashtra for more than 10 years and also conducted prosecution in some important cases involving public interest. About Mr. Lalit's ability, acumen and independence, nobody has expressed any doubt.

THIS PRAYER WAS OPPOSED BY THE UOI ALLEGING THAT IT WAS THE PREROGATIVE OF THE CENTRAL GOVERNMENT TO APPOINT THE PUBLIC PROSECUTOR

10. But, learned Attorney-General, on 5.4.2011, by referring to provision of section 46(2) of the Prevention of Money Laundering Act, 2002 (hereinafter the said Act) urged that the said provision may be considered by this Court before passing any order suggesting the appointment of Mr. Lalit as Special Public Prosecutor.

11. The matter was thereafter taken up on April 8, 2011. On that date, the learned Additional-Solicitor-General, Ms. Indira Jaising, representing Union of India, on instruction, made the following written submissions:

> "1. The Union of India, after an in-depth consideration of the entire matter, and in discharge of its obligations under the statutory provisions will make the necessary appointment of a SPP in respect of both the CBI matter as well as the money laundering matter within one week from today.
>
> 2. In view of this statement, it is not appropriate or necessary to make any submissions with regard to the scope of section 46(2) of the Money Laundering Act at this stage.
>
> 3. It is therefore requested that the matter may be suitably adjourned to enable the Union of India to report the progress made in this matter to this Hon'ble Court."

COUNCIL APPEARING FOR THE ED RELIED UPON THE EARLIER LAW

12. Mr. Harin Raval, ASG appearing for ED, who is normally led by Mr. K.K. Venugopal, learned senior counsel argued by placing reliance on a decision of this Court in the case of *Rajiv Ranjan Singh 'Lalan' (VIII)* v. *Union of India,* (2006) 6 SCC 613: 2006 AIR SCW 4287, especially paragraphs 50 and 51 of the said decision, those paragraphs are set out below: (SCC p. 643)

> "50. The appointment of lawyers is the prerogative of the Government and the prosecuting agency. The petitioners are trying to find fault with every attempt with every step taken. In cases like this the delay is inevitable.

51. It is also settled law that appointment of advocates, Public Prosecutors, etc., is the prerogative of the Government in power and the court has no role to play."

Relying on the aforesaid paragraphs, Mr. Raval submitted that the appointment of lawyers in connection with the present case is the prerogative of the Government.

SUPREME COURT HELD THIS JUDGMENT NOT APPLICABLE

13. Insofar as the ratio in the case of *Rajiv Ranjan Singh* (supra) is concerned, it was rendered in a totally different fact situation. In the said case, a PIL was filed under article 32 of the Constitution at a time when the prosecution evidence was almost over and the trial had reached its final stage. At that stage, a prayer was made for change of public prosecutor at the instance of the petitioners who were total strangers to the case. On these grounds, the petition was dismissed. In this connection, in the concurring judgment of Justice A.R. Lakshmanan the aforesaid observation about government's prerogative to appoint lawyers for the prosecuting agency was recorded.

WHAT DOES PREROGATIVE MEAN – WHEN DOES IT APPLY

14. We are of the view that the expression "prerogative" cannot be used in the context of a statutory provision. Under our Constitutional and statutory framework, there is nothing known as prerogative. In this connection, we may usefully recall what was said by the eminent jurist N.A. Palkhivala in his treatise "Our Constitution: Defaced and Defiled" (Macmillan: December, 1974). The relevant portion reads as follows:

> "Our Constitution recognises no prerogative whatsoever; it recognises merely rights, duties and discretions. The difference between "prerogative" and "discretion" is clear. A person who has a prerogative can act arbitrarily or irrationally and yet his decision must be treated as legal and valid. On the other hand, if a person has the discretion, and not the prerogative, to make a decision, the discretion can only be exercised fairly and reasonably; otherwise his act is void on the ground that there was no valid exercise of discretion in the eyes of law." (page 103)

We are in respectful agreement with this view. In this case, the Court is not changing any public prosecutor who has already been appointed. The question in the present case was never in issue in *Rajiv Ranjan Singh* (supra). Therefore, the decision in *Rajiv Ranjan Singh* (2006 AIR SCW 4287) (*supra*) is not of much relevance here.

DISCUSSION BY THE SUPREME COURT

15. We have taken note of the submission by Ms. Indira Jaising and Mr. Raval. But in the peculiar facts of the case and having regard to the larger issues of public interest of transparent governance, this Court has been passing various orders for monitoring of the investigation and also by giving direction for setting up separate Special Courts. These steps are taken by this Court in exercise of its jurisdiction under article 136 read with article 142. Consistent with those orders and since this Court is of the opinion that for conducting a proper prosecution, an appointment of a competent Special Public Prosecutor is of the essence, the court requested Mr. K.K. Venugopal to suggest a name of a very able and competent lawyer so that such name can be suggested for appointment as Special Public Prosecutor. The court has already noted about the undoubted ability and acumen of Mr. Lalit to become a Special Public Prosecutor to conduct the prosecution in this case.

16. In the background of these facts, the court now proposes to examine the aforesaid contentions of the learned Attorney-General and also by Ms. Indira Jaising and Mr. Harin Raval, both Additional Solicitors-General.

SECTION 46 OF THE PREVENTION OF MONEY LAUNDERING ACT, 2002 AND SECTION 24 OF THE CODE OF CRIMINAL PROCEDURE DO NOT SAY IF THE PUBLIC PROSECUTOR SHOULD BE AN EMPLOYEE OF THE GOVERNMENT

17. In this connection, section 46 of the said Act is set out below:

"**46.** ***Application of the Code of Criminal Procedure, 1973 to proceedings before Special Court.***—(1) Save as otherwise provided in this Act, the provisions of the Code of Criminal Procedure, 1973 (2 of 1974) (including the provisions as to bails or bonds), shall apply to the proceedings before a Special Court and for the purposes of the said provisions, the Special Court shall be deemed to be a Court of Session and the persons conducting the prosecution before the Special Court, shall be deemed to be a Public Prosecutor:

Provided that the Central Government may also appoint for any case or class or group of cases a Special Public Prosecutor.

(2) A person shall not be qualified to be appointed as a Public Prosecutor or a Special Public Prosecutor under this section unless he has been in practice as an Advocate for not less than seven years, under the Union or a State, requiring special knowledge of law.

(3) Every person appointed as a Public Prosecutor or a Special Public Prosecutor under this section shall be deemed to be a Public Prosecutor within the meaning of clause (u) of section 2 of the Code of Criminal Procedure, 1973 (2 of 1974) and the provisions of that Code shall have effect accordingly."

18. The provision of section 2(u) of the Code of Criminal Procedure is also set out:

"**2(u)** "**Public Prosecutor**" means any person appointed under section 24, and includes any person acting under the directions of a Public Prosecutor;"

19. Section 24 of the Code of Criminal Procedure is also set out:

"**24.** ***Public Prosecutors.***—(1) For every High Court, the Central Government or, the State Government shall, after consultation with the High Court, appoint a Public Prosecutor and may also appoint one or more Additional Public Prosecutors, for conducting in such Court, any prosecution, appeal or other proceeding on behalf of the Central Government or State Government, as the case may be.

(2) The Central Government may appoint one or more Public Prosecutors for the purpose of conducting any case or class of cases in any district or local area.

(3) For every district, the State Government shall appoint a Public Prosecutor and may also appoint one or more Additional Public Prosecutors for the district:

Provided that the Public Prosecutor or Additional Public Prosecutor appointed for one district may be appointed also to be a Public Prosecutor or an Additional Public Prosecutor, as the case may be, for another district.

(4) The District Magistrate shall, in consultation with the Sessions Judge, prepare a panel of names of persons, who are, in his opinion, fit to be appointed as Public Prosecutors or Additional Public Prosecutors for the district.

(5) No person shall be appointed by the State Government as the Public Prosecutor or Additional Public Prosecutor for the district unless his name appears in the panel of names prepared by the District Magistrate under sub-section (4).

(6) Notwithstanding anything contained in sub-section (5), where in a State there exists a regular Cadre of Prosecuting Officers, the State Government shall appoint a Public Prosecutor or an Additional Public Prosecutor only from among the persons constituting such Cadre:

Provided that where, in the opinion of the State Government, no suitable person is available in such Cadre for such appointment that Government may appoint a person as Public Prosecutor or Additional Public Prosecutor, as the case may be, from the panel of names prepared by the District Magistrate under sub-section (4).

[*Explanation.*—For the purpose of this sub-section,—

(a) regular "Cadre of Prosecuting Officers" means a Cadre of Prosecuting Officers which includes therein the post of a Public Prosecutor, by whatever name called, and which provides for promotion of Assistant Public Prosecutors, by whatever name called, to that post;

(b) "Prosecuting Officer" means a person, by whatever name called, appointed to perform the functions of a Public Prosecutor, an Additional Public Prosecutor or an Assistant Public Prosecutor under this Code.]

(7) A person shall be eligible to be appointed as a Public Prosecutor or an Additional Public Prosecutor under sub-section (1) or sub-section (2) or sub-section (3) or sub-section (6), only if he has been in practice as an advocate for not less than seven years.

(8) The Central Government or the State Government may appoint, for the purposes of any case or class of cases, a person who has been in practice as an advocate for not less than ten years as a Special Public Prosecutor:

Provided that the Court may permit the victim to engage an advocate of his choice to assist the prosecution under this sub-section.

(9) For the purposes of sub-section (7) and sub-section (8), the period during which a person has been in practice as a pleader, or has rendered (whether before or after the commencement of this Code) service as a Public Prosecutor or as an Additional Public Prosecutor or Assistant Public Prosecutor or other Prosecuting Officer, by whatever name called, shall be deemed to be the period during which such person has been in practice as an advocate."

20. From a perusal of the section 46(1) of the said Act, it appears that every person conducting prosecution is deemed to be a public prosecutor. At the same time, section 2(u) of the Criminal Procedure Code makes it clear that any person who is appointed under section 24 of Criminal Procedure Code is a public prosecutor. Therefore, on a conjoint and harmonious reading of section 46 along with section 24 of the Criminal Procedure Code it appears that the expression "person conducting the prosecution before the Special Court" in sub-section (1) of section 46 of the said Act, would mean that such a person must either be appointed by the Central or the State Government after following the procedure prescribed in sub-sections (4), (5) along with sub-section (7) of section 24 of Criminal Procedure

Code, or in the alternative after following the procedure in sub-section (6) read with sub-section (7) of section 24 of Criminal Procedure Code. We are of the view that both the provisions, namely, the provisions of section 46 of the said Act and section 24 of Criminal Procedure Code must be read together, since section 46 of the said Act, being a later Act, makes an express reference to the provision of the pre-existing Central law namely the provisions of section 24 of Criminal Procedure Code.

21. The expression "under" occurring in section 46(2) must be reasonably construed in a manner which is consistent with the dignity of the office of Public Prosecutor. A Public Prosecutor cannot be equated with a person who is holding an office under the State. He cannot be treated as a government employee. It may be that he should be a lawyer on the government panel. However, the independence of the Public Prosecutor from any governmental control is the hallmark of this high office.

PUBLIC PROSECUTOR IS REPRESENTATIVE OF THE SOVEREIGNTY SUPPOSED TO BE IMPARTIAL AND TO WORK FOR SAVING PUBLIC INTEREST

22. Reference in this connection may be made to the decision of this Court in the case of *Kumari Shrilekha Vidyarthi* v. *State of Uttar Pradesh,* 1991 (1) SCT 575: AIR 1991 SC 537 (547): 1993 AIR SCW 77, wherein the following observations have been made: (SCC 233 para 14)

> "14. ...The function of the Public Prosecutor relates to a public purpose entrusting him with the responsibility of acting only in the interest of administration of justice. In the case of Public Prosecutors, this additional public element flowing from statutory provisions in Criminal Procedure Code, undoubtedly, invest the Public Prosecutors with the attribute of holder of a public office which cannot be whittled down by the assertion that their engagement is purely professional between a client and his lawyer with no public element attaching to it."

23. The role of a public prosecutor in a criminal justice system has been very aptly put in the following words: *Christmas Humphreys*, 1955 Cr LR 739 (740-741)

> "The Prosecutor has a duty to the State, to the accused and to the court. The Prosecutor is at all times a minister of justice, though seldom so described. It is not the duty of the prosecuting counsel to secure a conviction, nor should any prosecutor even feel pride or satisfaction in the mere fact of success."

24. A public prosecutor is really a Minister of justice and his job is none other than assisting the State in the administration of justice and in fact he is not a representative of any party; See *Babu* v. *State of Kerala,* 1984 Cr LJ 499. The same has also been expressed in *R.* v. *Banks, reported in* (1916) 2 KB 621, wherein it has been said that the Public Prosecutor: (Cr. App Rep p. 76)

> "throughout a case ought not to struggle for the verdict against the prisoner but... ought to bear themselves rather in the character of minister of justice assisting the administration of justice."

25. This Court has also expressed the same opinion in *Sidhartha Vashisht* alias *Manu Sharma* v. *State (NCT of Delhi)*, 2010 (2) RCR (Criminal) 692: 2010 (3) Recent Apex Judgments (RAJ) 1: (2010) 6 SCC 1: AIR 2010 SC 2352: 2010 AIR SCW 4302, where this Court held that public prosecutor must observe a wider set of duties than to merely ensure that the accused is punished. His job is to ensure fair play in all proceedings. (Paras 185-188). In the Constitution Bench decision of this Court in *Sheonandan Paswan* v. *State of Bihar*, (1987) 1 SCC 288: AIR 1987 SC 877, this Court held that a public prosecutor is not a representative of any ordinary party to a controversy but of the sovereignty whose obligation to govern impartially is as compelling as its obligation to govern at all.

26. Therefore, there is a public element in such an appointment.

RELATIONSHIP OF MASTER-SERVANT DOES NOT APPLY TO PUBLIC PROSECUTORS

27. In the appointment of Public Prosecutor, the principle of master-servant does not apply. Such an appointment is not an appointment to a civil post; See *State of Uttar Pradesh* v. *Johri Mal*, 2004 (3) RCR (Criminal) 732: 2004 (3) SCT 409: 2004 (3) Apex Criminal 313: (2004) 4 SCC 714: AIR 2004 SC 3800: 2004 AIR SCW 3888.

U.U. LALIT SENIOR ADVOCATE FULLY SATISFIES ALL THESE CONDITIONS

28. In view of the aforesaid well-settled principles, we cannot hold that the expression 'under' in section 46(2) of the said Act can be construed to mean that the Public Prosecutor will be holding an employment under the State. All that it would mean is that the Special Public Prosecutor should be a lawyer on the panel of either the State or Central Government. Mr. U.U. Lalit satisfies the said requirement quite adequately. Therefore, we are unable to accept the contention of the Union of India and we hold that in the interest of a fair prosecution of the case, appointment of Mr. U.U. Lalit is eminently suitable.

ACCORDINGLY SHRI U. U. LALIT SENIOR ADVOCATE IS APPOINTED AS SPECIAL PUBLIC PROSECUTOR IN EXERCISE OF POWER UNDER ARTICLE 136 AND ARTICLE 142 OF THE CONSTITUTION IN THE SPECIAL COURT TRYING 2G SCAM CASE

29. We, therefore, order that Mr. U.U. Lalit shall be appointed Special Public Prosecutor by the Government to conduct the prosecution in this case, on behalf of CBI and ED. On such appointment, Mr. U.U. Lalit may choose the other advocates who are already on the panel of CBI to assist him. Considering the magnitude of the case, we are of the view that Mr. Lalit may choose two persons from the said panel.

NO OTHER COURT WOULD STAY OR IMPEDE TRIAL – ONLY SUPREME COURT CAN BE MOVED

30. We also make it clear that any objection about appointment of Special Public Prosecutor or his assistant advocates or any prayer for staying or impeding the progress of the Trial can be made only before this Court and no other Court shall entertain the same. The trial must proceed on a day-to-day basis.

31. All these directions are given by this Court in exercise of its power under article 136 read with article 142 of the Constitution and in the interest of holding a fair prosecution of the case.

Order accordingly.

Author's Note: This Presidential Reference was answered by theBench of 5 Hon'ble Judges of the Supreme Court consisting of Hon'ble Chief Justice of India, Hon'ble Mr. Jusitice D.K. Jain, Hon'ble Justice Jagdish Singh Khehar, Hon'ble Justice Dipak Misra and Hon'ble Mr. Justice Ranjan Gogoi. The Main Judgment was written by Hon'ble Mr. Justice D.K. Jain. Hon'ble Mr. Justice Jagdish Singh Khehar wrote a separate but concurring judgment.

REFERENCE MADE BY THE PRESIDENT OF INDIA FOR THE OPINION OF THE SUPREME COURT IF THE NATURAL RESOURCES CAN BE DISPOSED OF ONLY BY AUCTION OR BY OTHER MEANS ALSO, WAS ANSWERED BY THE SUPREME COURT IN THIS CASE

Re: Special Reference No. 1 of 2012[1]

[Under Article 143(1) of the Constitution of India]

SUPREME COURT OF INDIA

BENCH

S.H. Kapadia, CJ, and D.K. Jain, J.S. Khehar, Dipak Mishra and Ranjan Gogoi, JJ.

D.K. Jain, J. [For S.H. Kapadia, CJ, himself, Dipak Misra and Ranjan Gogoi, JJ.]

In exercise of powers conferred under article 143(1) of the Constitution of India, the President of India has on 12th April, 2012, made the present Reference. The full text of the Reference (sans the annexures) is as follows:

"WHEREAS in 1994, the Department of Telecommunication, Government of India ("GOI"), issued 8 Cellular Mobile Telephone Services Licenses ("CMTS Licenses"), 2 in each of the four Metro cities of Delhi, Mumbai, Kolkata and Chennai for a period of 10 years (the "1994 Licenses"). The 1994 licensees were selected based on rankings achieved by them on the technical and financial evaluation based on parameters set out by the Government of India in the tender and were required to pay a fixed licence fee for initial three years and subsequently based on number of subscribers subject to minimum commitment mentioned in the tender document and licence agreement. The 1994 Licenses issued by GoI mentioned that a cumulative maximum of upto 4.5 MHz in the 900 MHz bands would be permitted based on appropriate justification. There was no separate upfront charge for the allocation of Spectrum to the licensees, who only paid annual Spectrum usage charges, which will be subject to revision from time to time and which under the terms of the license bore the nomenclature "licence fee and royalty". A copy of the 1994 Licenses, along with a table setting out the predetermined Licence Fee as prescribed by Department of Telecommunication in the Tender, is annexed hereto as Annexure I (Colly).

WHEREAS in December, 1995, 34 CMTS Licenses were granted based on auction for 18 telecommunication circles for a period of 10 years (the "1995 Licenses"). The 1995 Licenses mentioned that a cumulative maximum of up

1. (2012) 10 SCC 1.

to 4.4 MHz in the 900 MHz bands shall be permitted to the licensees, based on appropriate justification. There was no separate upfront charge for allocation of spectrum to the licensees who were also required to pay annual spectrum usage charges, which under the terms of the license bore the nomenclature "licence fee and royalty" which will be subject to revision from time to time. A copy of the 1995 Licenses, along with a table setting out the fees payable by the highest bidder, is annexed hereto as Annexure II (Colly).

WHEREAS in 1995, bids were also invited for basic telephone service licenses ("BTS Licenses") with the license fee payable for a 15 year period. Under the terms of the BTS Licenses, a licensee could provide fixed line basic telephone services as well as wireless basic telephone services. Six licenses were granted in the year 1997-98 by way of auction through tender for providing basic telecom services (the "1997 BTS Licenses"). The license terms, *inter-alia,* provided that based on the availability of the equipment for Wireless in Local Loop (WLL), in the world market, the spectrum in bands specified therein would be considered for allocation subject to the conditions mentioned therein. There was no separate upfront charge for allocation of spectrum and the licensees offering the basic wireless telephone service were required to pay annual Spectrum usage charges, which under the terms of the license bore the nomenclature "licence fee and royalty". A sample copy of the 1997 BTS Licenses containing the table setting out the license fees paid by the highest bidder is annexed hereto as Annexure III (Colly).

WHEREAS in 1997, the Telecom Regulatory Authority of India Act, 1997 was enacted and the Telecom Regulatory Authority of India (the "TRAI") was established.

WHEREAS on 1st April, 1999, the New Telecom Policy, 1999 ("NTP 1999") was brought into effect on the recommendation of a Group on Telecom ("GoT") which had been constituted by Government of India. A copy of NTP 1999 is annexed hereto as Annexure IV. NTP 1999 provided that Cellular Mobile Service Providers ("CMSP") would be granted a license for a period of 20 years on the payment of a one-time entry fee and licence fee in the form of revenue share. NTP 1999 also provided that BTS (Fixed Service Provider or FSP) Licenses for providing both fixed and wireless (WLL) services would also be issued for a period of 20 years on payment of a one-time entry fee and licence fee in the form of revenue share and prescribed charges for spectrum usage, appropriate level of which was to be recommended by TRAI. The licensees both cellular and basic were also required to pay annual Spectrum usage charges.

WHEREAS based on NTP 1999, a migration package for migration from fixed license fee to one time entry fee and licence fee based on revenue share regime was offered to all the existing licenses on 22nd July, 1999. This came into effect on 1st August, 1999. Under the migration package, the licence period for all the CMTS and FSP licensees was extended to 20 years from the date of issuance of the Licenses.

WHEREAS in 1997 and 2000, CMTS Licenses were also granted in 2 and 21 Circles to Mahanagar Telephone Nigam Limited ("MTNL") and Bharat

Sanchar Nigam Limited ("BSNL") respectively (the "PSU Licenses"). However, no entry fee was charged for the PSU Licenses. The CMTS Licenses issued to BSNL and MTNL mentioned that they would be granted GSM Spectrum of 4.4 + 4.4 MHz in the 900 MHz band. The PSU Licensees were also required to pay annual spectrum usage charges. A copy of the PSU Licenses is annexed hereto as Annexure V (Colly).

WHEREAS in January, 2001, based on TRAI's recommendation, DoT issued guidelines for issuing CMTS Licenses for the 4th Cellular Operator based on tendering process structured as "Multistage Informed Ascending Bidding Process". Based on a tender, 17 new CMTS Licenses were issued for a period of 20 years in the 4 Metro cities and 13 Telecom Circles (the "2001 Cellular Licenses"). The 2001 Licenses required that the licensees pay a one-time non-refundable entry fee as determined through auction as above and also annual license fee and annual spectrum usage charges and there was no separate upfront charge for allocation of spectrum. In accordance with the terms of tender document, the license terms, *inter alia*, provided that a cumulative maximum of upto 4.4 MHz + 4.4 MHz will be permitted and further based on usage, justification and availability, additional spectrum upto 1.8 MHz + 1.8 MHz making a total of 6.2 MHz + 6.2 MHz, may be considered for assignment, on case by case basis, on payment of additional Licence fee. The bandwidth upto maximum as indicated *i.e.*, 4.4 MHz and 6.2 MHz as the case may be, will be allocated based on the technology requirements (*e.g.*, CDMA @ 1.25 MHz, GSM @ 200 KHz etc.). The frequencies assigned may not be contiguous and may not be same in all cases, while efforts would be made to make available larger chunks to the extent feasible. A copy of the 2001 Cellular License, along with a table setting out the fees payable by the highest bidder, is annexed hereto as Annexure VI.

WHEREAS in 2001, BTS Licenses were also issued for providing both fixed line and wireless basic telephone services on a continual basis (2001 Basic Telephone Licenses). Service area-wise one-time Entry Fee and annual license fee as a percentage of Adjusted Gross Revenue (AGR) was prescribed for grant of BTS Licenses. The licence terms, *inter-alia*, provided that for Wireless Access System in local area, not more than 5 + 5 MHz in 824-844 MHz paired with 869-889 MHz band shall be allocated to any basic service operator including existing ones on FCFS basis. A detailed procedure for allocation of spectrum on FCFS basis was given in Annexure-IX of the 2001 BTS license. There was no separate upfront charge for allocation of spectrum and the Licensees were required to pay revenue share of 2% of the AGR earned from wireless in local loop subscribers as spectrum charges in addition to the one time entry fee and annual license fee. A sample copy of the 2001 Basic Telephone License along with a table setting out the entry fees is annexed hereto as Annexure VII.

WHEREAS on 27th October, 2003, TRAI recommended a Unified Access Services Licence ("UASL") Regime. A copy of TRAI's recommendation is annexed hereto as Annexure VIII.

WHEREAS on 11.11.2003, Guidelines were issued, specifying procedure for migration of existing operators to the new UASL regime. As per the Guidelines, all applications for new Access Services License shall be in the category of Unified Access Services Licence. Later, based on TRAI clarification dated 14.11.2003, the entry fee for new Unified Licensee was fixed same as the entry fee of the 4th cellular operator. Based on further recommendations of TRAI dated 19.11.2003, spectrum to the new licensees was to be given as per the existing terms and conditions relating to spectrum in the respective license agreements. A copy of the Guidelines dated 11.11.2003 is annexed hereto as Annexure IX.

WHEREAS consequent to enhancement of FDI limit in telecom sector from 49% to 74%, revised Guidelines for grant of UAS Licenses were issued on 14.12.2005. These Guidelines, *inter alia* stipulate that Licenses shall be issued without any restriction on the number of entrants for provision of Unified Access Services in a Service Area and the applicant will be required to pay one time non-refundable Entry, annual License fee as a percentage of Adjusted Gross Revenue (AGR) and spectrum charges on revenue share basis. No separate upfront charge for allocation of spectrum was prescribed. Initial Spectrum was allotted as per UAS License conditions to the service providers in different frequency bands, subject to availability. Initially allocation of a cumulative maximum up to 4.4 MHz + 4.4 MHz for TDMA based systems or 2.5 MHz + 2.5 MHz for CDMA based systems subject to availability was to be made. Spectrum not more than 5 MHz + 5 MHz in respect of CDMA system or 6.2 MHz + 6.2 MHz in respect of TDMA based system was to be allocated to any new UAS licensee. A copy of the UASL Guidelines dated 14.12.2005 is annexed hereto as Annexure X.

WHEREAS after the introduction of the UASL in 2003 and until March, 2007, 51 new UASL Licenses were issued based on policy of First Come-First Served, on payment of the same entry fee as was paid for the 2001 Cellular Licenses (the "2003-2007 Licenses") and the spectrum was also allocated based on FCFS under a separate wireless operating license on case by case basis and subject to availability. Licensees had to pay annual spectrum usage charges as a percentage of AGR, there being a no upfront charge for allocation of spectrum. A copy of the 2003-2007 License, along with a table setting out the fees payable, is annexed hereto as Annexure XI (Colly).

WHEREAS on 28th August, 2007, TRAI revisited the issue of new licenses, allocation of Spectrum, Spectrum charges, entry fees and issued its recommendations, a copy of which is annexed hereto as Annexure XII. TRAI made further recommendations dated 16.07.2008 which is annexed hereto as Annexure XIII.

WHEREAS in 2007 and 2008, Government of India issued Dual Technology Licences, where under the terms of the existing licenses were amended to allow licensees to hold a license as well as Spectrum for providing services through both GSM and CDMA network. First amendment was issued in December, 2007. All licensees who opted for Dual Technology Licences paid the same entry fee, which was an amount equal to the amount prescribed as entry fee for getting a new UAS licence in the same service area. The amendment to the license *inter-alia* mentioned that initially a cumulative maximum of upto 4.4 MHz + 4.4 MHz was to be allocated in the case of TDMA based systems (@ 200 KHz per carrier or 30 KHz per carrier) and a maximum of 2.5 MHz + 2.5 MHz was to be allocated in the case of CDMA based systems (@ 1.25 MHz per carrier), on case by case basis subject to availability. It was also, *inter alia,* mentioned that additional spectrum beyond the above stipulation may also be considered for allocation after ensuring optimal and efficient utilization of the already allocated spectrum taking into account all types of traffic and guidelines/criteria prescribed from time to time. However, spectrum not more than 5 + 5 MHz in respect of CDMS system and 6.2 + 6.2 MHz in respect of TDMA based system was to be allocated to the licensee. There was no separate upfront charge for allocation of Spectrum. However, Dual Technology licensees were required to pay Spectrum usage charges in addition to the license fee on revenue share basis as a percentage of AGR. Spectrum to these licensees was allocated 10.1.2008 onwards.

WHEREAS subscriber based criteria for CMTS was prescribed in the year 2002 for allocation of additional spectrum of 1.8 + 1.8 MHz beyond 6.2 + 6.2 MHz with a levy of additional spectrum usage charge of 1% of AGR. The allocation criteria was revised from time to time. A copy of the DoT letter dated 1.2.2002 in this regard is annexed hereto as Annexure XIV.

WHEREAS for the spectrum allotted beyond 6.2 MHz, in the frequency allocation letters issued by DoT May, 2008 onwards, it was mentioned *inter alia* that allotment of spectrum is subject to pricing as determined in future by the Government of India for spectrum beyond 6.2 MHz + 6.2 MHz and the outcome of Court orders. However, annual spectrum usage charges were levied on the basis of AGR, as per the quantum of spectrum assigned. A sample copy of the frequency allocation letter is annexed hereto as Annexure XV.

WHEREAS spectrum for the 3G Band (*i.e.,* 2100 MHz band) was auctioned in 2010. The terms of the auction stipulated that, for successful new entrants, a fresh license agreement would be entered into and for existing licensees who were successful in the auction, the license agreement would be amended for use of Spectrum in the 3G band. A copy of the Notice inviting Applications and Clarifications thereto are annexed hereto and marked as Annexure XVI (Colly). The terms of the amendment letter provided, *inter alia,* that the 3G spectrum would stand withdrawn if the license stood terminated for any reason. A copy of the standard form of the amendment letter is annexed hereto and marked as Annexure XVII.

WHEREAS letters of intent were issued for 122 Licenses for providing 2G services on or after 10 January, 2008, against which licenses (the "2008 Licenses") were subsequently issued. However, pursuant to the judgment of this Hon'ble Court dated 2nd February, 2012 in Writ Petition (Civil) No. 423 of 2010 (the "Judgment"), the 2008 Licenses have been quashed. A copy of the judgment is annexed hereto and marked Annexure XVIII.

WHEREAS the Government of India has also filed an Interlocutory Application for clarification of the Judgment, wherein the Government of India has placed on record the manner in which the auction is proposed to be held pursuant to the Judgment and sought appropriate clarificatory orders/ directions from the Hon'ble Court. A copy of the Interlocutory Application is annexed hereto and marked as Annexure XIX.

WHEREAS while the Government of India is implementing the directions set out in the Judgment at paragraph 81 and proceeding with a fresh grant of licences and allocation of spectrum by auction, the Government of India is seeking a limited review of the Judgment to the extent it impacts generally the method for allocation of national resources by the State. A copy of the Review Petition is annexed hereto and marked as Annexure XX.

WHEREAS by the Judgment, this Hon'ble Court directed TRAI to make fresh recommendations for grant of licenses and allocation of Spectrum in the 2G band by holding an auction, as was done for the allocation of Spectrum for the 3G licenses.

WHEREAS, in terms of the directions of this Hon'ble Court, Government of India would now be allocating Spectrum in the relevant 2G bands at prices discovered through auction.

WHEREAS based on the recommendations of TRAI dated 11.5.2010 followed by further clarifications and recommendations, the Government of India has prescribed in February 2012, the limit for spectrum assignment in the Metro Service Areas as 2x10MHz/2x6.25 MHz and in rest of the Service Areas as 2x8MHz/2x5 MHz for GSM (900 MHz, 1800 MHz band)/CDMA (800 MHZ band), respectively subject to the condition that the Licensee can acquire additional spectrum beyond prescribed limit in the open market should there be an auction of spectrum subject to the further condition that total spectrum held by it does not exceed the limits prescribed for merger of licenses *i.e.,* 25% of the total spectrum assigned in that Service Area by way of auction or otherwise. This limit for CDMS spectrum is 10 MHz.

WHEREAS, in view of the fact that Spectrum may need to be allocated to individual entities from time to time in accordance with criteria laid down by the Government of India, such as subscriber base, availability of Spectrum in a particular circle, *inter-se* priority depending on whether the Spectrum comprises the initial allocation or additional allocation, etc., it may not always be possible to conduct an auction for the allocation of Spectrum.

AND WHEREAS in view of the aforesaid, the auctioning of Spectrum in the 2G bands may result in a situation where none of the Licensees, using the 2G bands of 800 MHz, 900 MHz and 1800 MHz would have paid any separate upfront fee for the allocation of Spectrum.

AND WHEREAS the Government of India has received various notices from companies based in other countries, invoking bilateral investment agreements and seeking damages against the Union of India by reason of the cancellation/ threat of cancellation of the licenses.

AND WHEREAS in the circumstance certain questions of law of far reaching national and international implications have arisen, including in relation to the conduct of the auction and the regulation of the telecommunications industry in accordance with the Judgment [*Centre for Public Interest Litigation* v. *Union of India,* (2012) 3 SCC 1] and FDI into this country in the telecom industry and otherwise in other sectors.

Given that the issues which have arisen are of great public importance, and that questions of law have arisen of public importance and with such far reaching consequences for the development of the country that it is expedient to obtain the opinion of the Hon'ble Supreme Court of India thereon.

QUESTIONS ON WHICH THE PRESIDENT OF INDIA SOUGHT THE OPINION OF THE SUPREME COURT

NOW THEREFORE, in exercise of powers conferred upon me by clause (1) of article 143 of the Constitution of India, I, Pratibha Devisingh Patil, President of India, hereby refer the following questions to the Supreme Court of India for consideration and report thereon, namely:

Q.1 Whether the only permissible method for disposal of all natural resources across all sectors and in all circumstances is by the conduct of auctions?

Q.2 Whether a broad proposition of law that only the route of auctions can be resorted to for disposal of natural resources does not run contrary to several judgments of the Supreme Court including those of Larger Benches?

Q.3 Whether the enunciation of a broad principle, even though expressed as a matter of constitutional law, does not really amount to formulation of a policy and has the effect of unsettling policy decisions formulated and approaches taken by various successive governments over the years for valid considerations, including lack of public resources and the need to resort to innovative and different approaches for the development of various sectors of the economy?

Q.4 What is the permissible scope for interference by courts with policy making by the Government including methods for disposal of natural resources?

Q.5 Whether, if the court holds, within the permissible scope of judicial review, that a policy is flawed, is the court not obliged to take into account investments made under the said policy including investments made by foreign investors under multilateral/bilateral agreements?

Q.6 If the answers to the aforesaid questions lead to an affirmation of the judgment dated 2.2.2012 then the following questions may arise, *viz.*

(i) Whether the judgment is required to be given retrospective effect so as to unsettle all licences issued and 2G spectrum (800, 900, and 1800 MHz bands) allocated in and after 1994 and prior to 10.1.2008?

(ii) Whether the allocation of 2G spectrum in all circumstances and in all specific cases for different policy considerations would nevertheless have to be undone? And specifically

(iii) Whether the telecom licences granted in 1994 would be affected?

(iv) Whether the Telecom licences granted by way of basic licences in 2001 and licences granted between the period 2003-2007 would be affected?

(v) Whether it is open to the Government of India to take any action to alter the terms of any licence to ensure a level playing field among all existing licensees?

(vi) Whether dual technology licences granted in 2007 and 2008 would be affected?

(vii) Whether it is necessary or obligatory for the Government of India to withdraw the Spectrum allocated to all existing licensees or to charge for the same with retrospective effect and if so on what basis and from what date?

Q.7 Whether, while taking action for conduct of auction in accordance with the orders of the Supreme Court, it would remain permissible for the Government to:

(i) Make provision for allotment of Spectrum from time to time at the auction discovered price and in accordance with laid down criteria during the period of validity of the auction determined price?

(ii) Impose a ceiling on the acquisition of Spectrum with the aim of avoiding the emergence of dominance in the market by any licensee/applicant duly taking into consideration TRAI recommendations in this regard?

(iii) Make provision for allocation of Spectrum at auction related prices in accordance with laid down criteria in bands where there may be inadequate or no competition (for *e.g.*, there is expected to be a low level of competition for CDMA in 800 MHz band and TRAI has recommended an equivalence ratio of 1.5 or 1.3X1.5 for 800 MHz and 900 MHz bands depending upon the quantum of spectrum held by the licensee that can be applied to auction price in 1800 MHz band in the absence of a specific price for these bands)?

Q.8 What is the effect of the judgment on 3G Spectrum acquired by entities by auction whose licences have been quashed by the said judgment?

NEW DELHI;

DATED: 12 April 2012 **PRESIDENT OF INDIA"**

SUPREME COURT ISSUED NOTICE TO THE PARTIES

2. A bare reading of the Reference shows that it is occasioned by the decision of this Court, rendered by a Bench of two learned Judges on 2nd February, 2012 in *Centre for Public Interest Litigation* v. *Union of India,* (2012) 3 SCC 1 (for brevity "2G Case").

3. On receipt of the Reference, *vide* order dated 9th May, 2012, notice was issued to the Attorney-General for India. Upon hearing the learned Attorney General, it was directed *vide* order dated 11th May, 2012, that notice of the Reference shall be issued to all the States through their Standing Counsel; on Centre for Public Interest Litigation (CPIL) and Dr. Subramanian Swamy (petitioners in the 2G Case); as also on the Federation of Indian Chambers of Commerce and Industry (FICCI) and Confederation of Indian Industry (CII), as representatives of the Indian industry. On the suggestion of the learned Attorney-General, it was also directed (though not recorded in the order), that the reference shall be dealt with in two parts *viz.*, in the first instance, only questions Nos. 1 to 5 would be taken up for consideration and the remaining questions shall be taken up later in the light of our answers to the first five questions.

4. At the commencement of the hearing of the Reference on 10th July, 2012, a strong objection to the maintainability of the Reference was raised by the writ petitioners in the 2G case. Accordingly, it was decided to first hear the learned counsel on the question of validity of the Reference.

OPPOSING PARTIES QUESTIONED THE MAINTAINABILITY OF THE REFERENCE – REFERRED TO THE JUDGMENTS ON EARLIER REFERENCES

Submissions on Maintainability

5. Mr. Soli Sorabjee, learned senior counsel, appearing for CPIL, strenuously urged that in effect and substance, the Reference seeks to question the correctness of the judgment in the 2G Case, which is not permissible once this Court has pronounced its authoritative opinion on the question of law now sought to be raised. The learned counsel argued that reference under article 143(1) of the Constitution does not entail appellate or review jurisdiction, especially in respect of a judgment which has attained finality. According to the learned counsel, it is evident from the format of the Reference that it does not express or suggest any 'doubt' as regards the question of fact or law relating to allocation of all natural resources, a *sine-qua-non* for a valid reference. In support of the proposition, learned counsel placed reliance on observations in earlier references – *In re: The Delhi Laws Act,* 1912, the Ajmer-Merwara (Extension of Laws) Act, 1947 And The Part C States (Laws) Act, 1950, [1951] SCR 747 *In re: The Berubari Union and Exchange of Enclaves Reference Under Article 143(1) of the Constitution of India,* [1960] 3 SCR 250, *In re: The Kerala Education Bill,* 1957, *In Reference Under Article 143(1) of the Constitution of India,* [1959] SCR 995, Special Reference No. 1 of 1964, [1965] 1 SCR 413 (commonly referred to as "Keshav Singh"), *In re: Presidential Poll,* (1974) 2 SCC 33, *In re: The Special Courts Bill,* 1978, (1979) 1 SCC 380, *In the Matter of: Cauvery Water Disputes Tribunal,* 1993 Supp (1) SCC 96 (II) (hereinafter referred to as "Cauvery-II") and Special Reference No. 1 of 1998 *Re.,* (1998) 7 SCC 739

6. Next, it was contended by the learned senior counsel that if for any reason, the Executive feels that the 2G Case does not lay down a correct proposition of law, it is open to it to persuade another Bench, before which the said judgment is relied upon, to refer the issue to a larger Bench for reconsideration. In short, the submission was that an authoritative pronouncement, like the one in the 2G Case, cannot be short circuited by recourse to article 143(1).

7. Learned counsel also contended that the Reference as framed is of an *omnibus* nature, seeking answers on hypothetical and vague questions, and therefore, must not be answered. Commending us to *In re: The Special Courts Bill,* 1978 (supra) and several other decisions, learned counsel urged that a reference under article 143(1) of the Constitution for opinion has to be on a specific question or questions. It was asserted that by reason of the construction of the terms of Reference, the manner in which the questions have been framed and the nature of the answers proposed, this Court would be entitled to return the Reference unanswered by pointing out the aforesaid impediments in answering it. *Lastly,* it was fervently pleaded that if the present Reference is entertained, it would pave the way for the Executive to circumvent or negate the effect of inconvenient judgments, like the decision in the 2G Case, which would not only set a dangerous and unhealthy precedent, but would also be clearly contrary to the ratio of the decision in Cauvery II (*supra*)

8. Mr. Prashant Bhushan, learned senior counsel, while adopting the arguments advanced by Mr. Soli Sorabjee, reiterated that from the format of questions No. 1 to 5, as well as from the review petition filed by the government in the 2G case, (2012) 3 SCC 1 it is clear that the present Reference seeks to overrule the decision in the 2G case (*supra*) by reading down the direction that allowed only 'auction' as the permissible means for allocation of all natural resource, in paragraphs 94 to 96 of the 2G case (*supra*), to the specific case of spectrum. It was argued by the learned counsel that it is apparent from the grounds urged in the review petition filed by the government that it understood the ratio of the 2G case (*supra*), binding them to the form of procedure to be followed while alienating precious natural resources belonging to the people, and yet it is seeking to use the advisory jurisdiction of this Court as an appeal over its earlier decision. It was contended that even if it be assumed that a doubt relating to the disposal of all natural resources has arisen on account of conflict of decisions on the point, such a conflict cannot be resolved by way of a Presidential reference; that would amount to holding that one or the other judgments is incorrectly decided, which, according to the learned counsel, is beyond the scope of article 143(1). Learned counsel alleged that the language in which the Reference is couched, exhibits *mala fides* on the part of the Executive. He thus, urged that we should refrain from giving an opinion.

9. Dr. Subramanian Swamy, again vehemently objecting to the maintainability of the Reference, on similar grounds, added that the present Reference is against the very spirit of article 143(1), which, according to the Constituent Assembly debates, was meant to be invoked sparingly, unlike the case here. It was pleaded that the Reference is yet another attempt to delay the implementation of the directions in the 2G Case. Relying on the decision of this Court in *Dr. M. Ismail Faruqui* v. *Union of India*, 10 (1994) 6 SCC 360 Dr. Swamy submitted that we will be well advised to return the Reference unanswered.

SUBMISSIONS FOR UNION OF INDIA ON MAINTAINABILITY

10. Mr. G.E. Vahanvati, the learned Attorney-General for India, defending the Reference, submitted that the plea regarding non-maintainability of the Reference on the ground that it does not spell out a 'doubt', is fallacious on a plain reading of the questions framed therein. According to him, article 143(1) uses the word 'question' which arises only when there is a 'doubt' and the very fact that the President has sought the opinion of this Court on the questions posed, shows that there is a doubt in the mind of the Executive on those issues. It was stressed that merely because the Reference does not use the word 'doubt' in the recitals, as in other cited cases, does not imply that in substance no doubt is entertained in relation to the mode of alienation of all natural resources, other than spectrum, moreso when the questions posed for opinion have far reaching national and international implications. It was urged that the content of the Reference is to be appreciated in proper perspective, keeping in view the context and not the form.

11. It was urged that maintainability and the discretion to decline to answer a reference are two entirely different things. The question of maintainability arises when *ex facie*, the Presidential reference does not meet the basic requirements of article 143(1), contrastive to the question of discretion, which is the power of the Court to decline to answer a reference, for good reasons, once the reference is maintainable. In support of the proposition, reliance was placed on *In re: The Kerala Education Bill*, 1957 (supra), *Keshav Singh* and *In re: The Special Courts Bill*, 1978 (supra). According to the learned counsel, the question as to whether the reference is to be answered or not, is not an aspect of maintainability, and is to be decided only after hearing the reference on merits.

12. Learned Attorney-General, while contesting the plea that in a reference under Article 143(1), correctness or otherwise of earlier decisions can never be gone into, submitted that in a Presidential reference, there is no constitutional embargo against reference to earlier decisions in order to clarify, restate or even to form a fresh opinion on a principle of law, as long as an *inter partes* decision is left unaffected. In support of the contention that in the past, references have been made on questions in relation to the correctness of judgments, learned counsel placed reliance on the decisions of this Court *In re: The Delhi Laws Act*, 1912 (supra), Special Reference No. 1 of 1998 (supra), *Keshav Singh* (supra) and of the Privy Council *In re: Piracy Jure Gentium*, (1934) AC 586. It was asserted that it has been repeatedly clarified on behalf of the Executive that the decision in the 2G Case has been accepted and is not being challenged. The Reference was necessitated by certain observations made as a statement of law in the said judgment which require to be explicated. Referring to certain observations *In re: The Berubari Union and Exchange of Enclaves* (supra), learned counsel submitted that this Court had accepted that a reference could be answered to avoid protracted litigation.

13. Learned Attorney-General also contended that withdrawal of the review petition by the government is of no consequence; its withdrawal does not imply that the question about the permissible manner of disposal of other natural resources, and the issues regarding the environment for investment in the country, stood settled. Stoutly refuting the allegation that the reference is *mala fide*, learned counsel submitted that in *In re: Presidential Poll* (supra), it is clearly laid down that the Court cannot question the *bona fides* of the President making the reference.

14. Mr. T.R. Andhyarujina, learned senior counsel, voiced concerns arising out of an apparent conflict between provisions of the statutes and the judgment delivered in the *2G* case (*supra*); specifically with reference to sections 10 and 11 of the Mines and Minerals (Regulation and Development) Act, 1957 (for short, "MMRD Act"), which prescribe a policy of preferential treatment and first come first served, unlike the *2G* case (*supra*), which according to the learned counsel only mandates auction for all natural resources. He thus, urged this Court to dispel all uncertainties regarding the true position of law after the judgment in the *2G* case (*supra*), by holding it as *per incuriam* in light of the provisions of the MMRD Act and other statutes.

SUBMISSIONS OF PRIVATE PARTIES/STATE GOVERNMENTS IN FAVOUR OF REFERENCE

15. Mr. Harish Salve, learned senior counsel, appearing on behalf of CII, while supporting the Reference, fervently urged that the contention that the Reference deserves to be returned unanswered due to the absence of the use of the word 'doubt' in the recitals of the Reference, is untenable. According to the learned counsel, under article 143(1), the President can seek an opinion on any question of law or fact that has arisen, or is likely to arise, which is of such a nature and such public importance that it is expedient to seek the opinion of this Court. There is no additional condition that there should be any 'doubt' in the mind of the President. It was submitted by the learned counsel that the need for a Presidential reference may also arise to impart certainty to certain questions of law or fact which are of such a nature and of such moment as to warrant seeking opinion of this Court. It was urged that a pedantic interpretation, by which a Presidential reference would be declined on semantic considerations, such as the failure to use the word 'doubt' in the reference, should be eschewed.

16. Learned counsel contended that at the stage of making a reference, it is the satisfaction of the President in relation to the nature of the question and its importance that is relevant. As a matter of comity of institutions, this Court has always declined to go behind the reasons that prevailed upon the President to make a reference and its *bona fides*. Nevertheless, this Court always has the discretion not to answer any such Reference or the questions raised therein for good reasons. It was stressed that since this Court does not sit in review over the satisfaction of the President, the question of jurisdiction and of maintainability does not arise.

17. Learned counsel also argued that the premise that earlier judgments of this Court are binding in Reference jurisdiction, and thus any Reference, which impinges upon an earlier judgment should be returned unanswered, is equally fallacious. It was argued that the principle of *stare decisis* and the doctrine of precedent are generally accepted and followed as rules of judicial discipline and not jurisdictional fetters and, therefore, this Court is not prevented from re-examining the correctness of an earlier decision. On the contrary, the precedents support the proposition that this Court can, when exercising its jurisdiction under article 143(1), examine the correctness of past precedents. According to the learned counsel, in *Keshav Singh*, this Court did examine the correctness of the judgment in *Pandit M.S.M. Sharma* v. *Shri Sri Krishna Sinha*, [1959] Supp 1 SCR 806 (hereinafter referred to as "Sharma"). Explaining the ratio of the decision in Cauvery-II, learned counsel submitted that it is clear beyond any pale of doubt that the said pronouncement does not lay down, as an abstract proposition of law, that under article 143(1), this Court cannot consider the correctness of any precedent. What it lays down is that once a *lis* between the parties is decided, the operative decree can only be opened by way of a review. According to the learned counsel, overruling a judgment — as a precedent — does not tantamount to reopening the decree.

18. Arguing on similar lines, Mr. C.A. Sundaram, learned senior counsel appearing on behalf of FICCI, contended that if the observations in the 2G case (*supra*) are read as applying to all natural resources and not limited to spectrum, it would tantamount to *de facto* policy formulation by the Court, which is beyond the scope of judicial review. He also took a nuanced stance on this Court's power of reconsideration over its precedents. It was submitted that a precedent can be sliced into two parts *viz.*, the decision or operative part of an order or decree pertaining to the *inter partes* dispute and the ratio with respect to the position of law; the former being beyond this Court's powers of review once an earlier Bench of this Court has pronounced an authoritative opinion on it, but not the latter. He thus, urged that this Court does have the power to reconsider the principles of law laid down in its previous pronouncements even under article 141.

19. Mr. Darius Khambata, learned Advocate-General of Maharashtra, submitted that observations in the *2G* case (*supra*) were made only with regard to spectrum thus, leaving it open to this Court to examine the issue with regard to alienation of other natural resources. It was urged that even if broader observations were made with respect to all natural resources, it would still be open to this Court under article 143(1) to say otherwise. He also pointed to certain State legislations that prescribe methods other than auction and thus, urged this Court to answer the first question in the negative lest all those legislations be deemed unconstitutional.

20. Mr. Sunil Gupta, learned senior counsel, appearing on behalf of the State of Uttar Pradesh, added that when article 143(1) of the Constitution unfolds a high prerogative of a constitutional authority, namely, the President, to consult this Court on question of law or fact, it contains a no less high prerogative of this Court to report to the President its opinion on the question referred, either by making or declining to give an answer to the question. In other words, according to the learned counsel, the issue of a Reference being maintainable at the instance of the President is an issue different from the judicial power of this Court to answer or not to answer the question posed in the Reference.

21. Mr. Ravindra Shrivastava, learned senior counsel appearing on behalf of the State of Chhattisgarh, contended that neither history supports nor reality warrants auction to be a rule of disposal of all natural resources in all situations. He referred to decisions of this Court that unambiguously strike a just balance between considerations of power of the State and duty towards public good, by leaving the choice of method of allocation of natural resources to the State, as long as it conforms to the requirements of article 14. It was pleaded that the State be allowed the choice of methodology of allocation, especially in cases where it intends to incentivize investments and job creation in backward regions that would otherwise have been left untouched by private players if resources were given at market prices.

OBJECTIONS IN BRIEF ON MAINTAINABILITY

22. To sum up, the objections relating to the maintainability of the Reference converge mainly on the following points:

(i) the foundational requirement for reference under article 143(1) *viz.* a genuine 'doubt' about questions of fact or law that the Executive labours under, is absent;

(ii) the filing and withdrawal of a review petition whose recitals pertain to the 2G Case would be an impediment in the exercise of discretion under article 143(1);

(iii) the language in which the Reference is couched exhibits *mala fides* on the part of the Executive;

(iv) in light of enunciation of law on the point in Cauvery II, entertaining a Presidential Reference on a subject-matter, which has been decided upon directly and with finality, is barred;

(v) the present Reference is an attempt to overturn the judgment of this Court in the 2G Case, which is against the spirit of article 143(1) of the Constitution; and

(vi) the Executive is adopting the route of this Reference to wriggle out of the directions in the 2G Case as the same are inconvenient for them to follow.

ARTICLE 143 OF THE CONSTITUTION REFERS TO THE POWER OF THE PRESIDENT TO CONSULT SUPREME COURT

Discussion

23. Before we evaluate the rival stands on the maintainability of the Reference, it would be necessary to examine the scope and breadth of article 143 of the Constitution, which reads thus:

> "**143.** ***Power of President to consult Supreme Court.***—(1) If at any time it appears to the President that a question of law or fact has arisen, or is likely to arise, which is of such a nature and of such public importance that it is expedient to obtain the opinion of the Supreme Court upon it, he may refer the question to that Court for consideration and the Court may, after such hearing as it thinks fit, report to the President its opinion thereon.
>
> (2) The President may, notwithstanding anything in the proviso to article 131, refer a dispute of the kind mentioned in the said proviso to the Supreme Court for opinion and the Supreme Court shall, after such hearing as it thinks fit, report to the President its opinion thereon."

SUPREME COURT MAY GIVE ITS OPINION, DECLINE TO DO SO, OR RETURN IT UNANSWERED

A bare reading at the article would show that it is couched in broad terms. It is plain from the language of article 143(1) that it is not necessary that the question on which the opinion of the Supreme Court is sought must have actually arisen. The President can make a reference under the said article even at an anterior stage, namely, at the stage when the President is satisfied that the question is likely to arise. The satisfaction whether the question meets the pre-requisites of article 143(1) is essentially a matter for the President to decide. Upon receipt of a reference under article 143(1), the function of this Court is to consider the Reference; the question(s) on which the President has made the reference, on the facts as stated in the reference and report to the President its opinion thereon.

24. Nevertheless, the usage of the word "may" in the latter part of article 143(1) implies that this Court is not bound to render advisory opinion in every Reference and may refuse to express its opinion for strong, compelling and good reasons. In *Keshav Singh*, highlighting the difference in the phraseology used in clauses (1) and (2) of article 143, P.B. Gajendragadkar, C.J., speaking for the majority, held as follows (AIR p. 756, para 15):

> "15. ...whereas in the case of reference made under article 143(2) it is the constitutional obligation of this Court to make a report on that Reference embodying its advisory opinion, in a reference made under article 143(1) there is no such obligation. In dealing with this latter class of reference, it is open to this Court to consider whether it should make a report to the President giving its advisory opinion on the questions under reference."

25. Further, even in an earlier judgment in *In re: Allocation of Lands and Buildings Situate in a Chief Commissioner's Province* and in the matter of Reference by the Governor-General under section 213, Government of India Act, 1935, AIR (30) 1943 FC 13 the Federal Court had said that even though the Court is within its authority to refuse to answer a question on a Reference, it must be unwilling to exercise its power of refusal "except for good reasons." A similar phrase was used in *In re: The Kerala Education Bill*, 1957 (supra) when this Court observed that opinion on a Reference under article 143(1), may be declined in a "proper case" and "for good reasons". In *Dr. M. Ismail Faruqui* (supra), it was added that a Reference may not be answered when the Court is not competent to decide the question which is based on expert evidence or is a political one.

DISCUSSION ON THE MAINTAINABILITY FOR NOT USING THE WORD 'DOUBT' IN THE REFERENCE

26. Having noted the relevant contours of article 143(1) of the Constitution, we may now deal with the objections to the maintainability of the Reference.

27. There is no denying the fact that in the entire Reference the word 'doubt' has not been used. It is also true that in all previous References, noted in para 5 (supra), it had been specifically mentioned that doubts had arisen about various issues. Nonetheless, the fact remains that article 143(1) does not use the term 'doubt'. No specific format has been provided in any of the Schedules of the Constitution as to how a reference is to be drawn. The use of the word 'doubt' in a Reference is also not a constitutional command or mandate. Needless to emphasise that the expression, 'doubt', which refers to a state of uncertainty, may be with regard to a fact or a principle.

28. In *P. Ramanatha Aiyar's, The Major Law Lexicon*, 4th Edition, the words 'doubt' and 'question' have been dealt with in the following manner:

> "Doubt, Question. These terms express the act of the mind in staying its decision. *Doubt* lies altogether in the mind; it is a less active feeling than *question;* by the former we merely suspend decision; by the latter we actually demand proofs in order to assist us in deciding. We may *doubt* in silence. We cannot *question* without expressing it directly or indirectly. He who suggests *doubts* does it with caution: he who makes a question throws in difficulties with a degree of confidence. We doubt the truth of a *position;* we question the veracity of an author. (Crabb.)"

As per the *Concise Oxford Dictionary* (Tenth Edition), 'question' means: "a doubt; the raising of a doubt or objection; a problem requiring solution". In *Black's Law Dictionary* 'doubt', as a verb, has been defined as follows:

"To question or hold questionable."

The word 'doubt', as a noun, has been described as under:—

> "Uncertainty of mind; the absence of a settled opinion or conviction; the attitude of mind towards the acceptance of or belief in a proposition, theory, or statement, in which the judgment is not at rest but inclines alternately to either side."

29. The afore-extracted recitals of the instant Reference state that in the current circumstances, certain questions of law with far reaching national and international implications have arisen, including in relation to conduct of the auction and the regulation of the telecommunications industry in accordance with the judgment (2G Case) (*supra)* that may affect the flow of FDI in the telecom industry and otherwise in other sectors into this country. Thereafter, it is also stated that questions of law that have arisen are of great public importance and are of far reaching consequences for the development of the country and hence, it is thought expedient to obtain the opinion of this Court. Question No. 1 of the reference reads as follows:

> "Whether the only permissible method for disposal of all natural resources across all sectors and in all circumstances is by the conduct of auctions?"

PRINCIPLES TO BE FOLLOWED ON DEFECTIVE REFERENCE

30. At this juncture, reference may profitably be made to the decision in I*n re: The Special Courts Bill*, 1978 (supra), an opinion by a Bench of seven learned Judges, wherein it was observed as follows (SCC p. 403, para 27):

> "27. We were, at one stage of the arguments, so much exercised over the undefined breadth of the reference that we were considering seriously whether in the circumstances it was not advisable to return the reference unanswered. But the written briefs filed by the parties and the oral arguments advanced before us have, by their fullness and ability, helped to narrow down the legal controversies surrounding the Bill and to crystallize the issues which arise for our consideration. We propose to limit our opinion to the points specifically raised before us. It will be convenient to indicate at this stage what those points are."

While expressing the hope that, in future, specific questions would be framed for the opinion of this Court, Y.V. Chandrachud (as his Lordship then was), speaking for the majority, said: [*Special Courts Bill* case (*supra*) SCC p. 404, para 30]

> "30. We hope that in future, whenever a reference is made to this Court under article 143 of the Constitution, care will be taken to frame specific questions for the opinion of the Court. Fortunately, it has been possible in the instant reference to consider specific questions as being comprehended within the terms of the reference but the risk that a vague and general reference may be returned unanswered is real and ought to engage the attention of those whose duty it is to frame the reference. Were the Bill not as short as it is, it

would have been difficult to infuse into the reference the comprehension of the two points mentioned by us above and which we propose to decide. A long Bill would have presented to us a rambling task in the absence of reference on specific points, rendering it impossible to formulate succinctly the nature of constitutional challenge to the provisions of the Bill."

31. From the afore-extracted paragraphs, three broad principles emerge:

(i) a reference should not be vague, general and undefined,

(ii) this Court can go through the written briefs and arguments to narrow down the legal controversies, and

(iii) when the question becomes unspecific and incomprehensible, the risk of returning the reference unanswered arises.

32. In *Keshav Singh*, this Court while dealing with the validity of the reference, referred to earlier decisions and opined as follows (AIR p. 756, para 17):

> "17. ...It would thus be seen that the questions so far referred by the President for the Advisory opinion of this Court under article 143(1) do not disclose a uniform pattern and that is quite clearly consistent with the broad and wide words used in article 143(1)."

NO PARTICULAR FORMAT OR PATTERN OF MAKING REFERENCE

33. An analysis of the afore-noted cases, indicates that neither has a particular format been prescribed nor any specific pattern been followed in framing references. The first principle relates to the 'form' and the second pertains to the 'pattern of content'. Holistically understood, on the ground of form or pattern alone, a reference is not to be returned unanswered. It requires appropriate analysis, understanding and appreciation of the content or the issue on which doubt is expressed, keeping in view the concept of constitutional responsibility, juridical propriety and judicial discretion.

OBJECTION OF NON-MAINTAINABILITY OVER-RULED

34. Thus, we find it difficult to accept the stand that use of the word 'doubt' is a necessary condition for a reference to be maintainable under article 143(1). That apart, in our view, question No. 1, quoted above, is neither vague nor general or unspecific, but is in the realm of comprehension which is relatable to a question of law. It expresses a 'doubt' and seeks the opinion of the Court on that question, besides others.

FILING OF REVIEW PETITION AGAINST 2G JUDGMENT AND ITS WITHDRAWAL HAS NO IMPACT ON THIS REFERENCE

35. Insofar as the impact of filing and withdrawal of the review application by the Union of India, against the decision in the 2G Case (*supra*) on the maintainability of the instant Reference is concerned, it is a matter of record that in the review petition, certain aspects of the grounds for review which have been stated in the recitals of the Reference as well as in some questions, were highlighted. However, there is a gulf of difference between the jurisdiction exercised by this Court in a review and the discretion exercised in answering a reference under article 143(1) of the Constitution. A review is basically guided by the well-settled principles for review of a judgment and a decree or order passed *inter se* parties. The Court in exercise of power of review may entertain the review under the acceptable and settled parameters. But, when an opinion of this Court is sought by the Executive taking recourse to a constitutional power, needless to say, the same stands on a different footing altogether. A review is *lis* specific and the rights of the parties to the controversy are dealt with therein, whereas a reference is answered keeping in view the terms of the reference and scrutinizing whether the same satisfies the requirements inherent in the language employed under article 143(1) of the Constitution. In our view, therefore, merely because a review had been filed and withdrawn and in the recital the narration pertains to the said case, the same would not be an embargo or impediment for exercise of discretion to answer the Reference.

MALA FIDE OR *BONA FIDE* CANNOT BE GONE INTO IN PRESIDENTIAL REFERENCE

36. As far as the allegation of *mala fide* is concerned, it is trite that this Court is neither required to go into the truth or otherwise of the facts of the recitals nor can it go into the question of *bona fides* or otherwise of the authority making a reference. [See: *In re: Presidential Poll* (supra)]. To put it differently, the constitutional power to seek opinion of this Court rests with the President. The only discretion this Court has is either to answer the reference or respectfully decline to send a report to the President. Therefore, the challenge on the ground of *mala fide,* as raised, is unsustainable.

IT IS VIRTUALLY AN APPEAL AGAINST 2G JUDGMENT – SUBMISSION OF THE OPPOSITE PARTY

37. The principal objection to the maintainability of the Reference is that it is an indirect endeavour to unsettle and overturn the verdict in the 2G Case, which is absolutely impermissible. The stand of the objectors is that the 2G Case is an authoritative precedent in respect of the principle or proposition of law that all natural resources are to be disposed of by way of public auction and, therefore, the Reference should be held as not maintainable. Emphasis in this behalf was on paragraphs 85 and 94 to 96 of the said judgment. In support of the proposition, heavy reliance was placed on Cauvery II (*supra).*

UOI SUBMITTED 2G JUDGMENT NOT QUESTIONED ON MERITS

38. At the outset, we may note that the learned Attorney-General has more than once stated that the Government of India is not questioning the correctness of the directions in the 2G Case, insofar as the allocation of spectrum is concerned, and in fact the Government is in the process of implementing the same, in letter and spirit. Therefore, in the light of the said statement, we feel that it would be unnecessary to comment on the submission that the Reference is an attempt to get an opinion to unsettle the decision and directions of this Court in the 2G Case. Nevertheless, since in support of the aforesaid submission, the opinion of this Court in Cauvery II has been referred to and relied upon *in extenso,* it would be appropriate to decipher the true ratio of Cauvery II, the linchpin of the opposition to maintainability of the present Reference.

RATIO OF LAW LAID DOWN IN CAUVERY-II IS THE BASIS TO DECIDE THE OBJECTION

39. Cauvery II (*supra*) was preceded by *State of Tamil Nadu* v. *State of Karnataka*, 1991 Supp (1) SCC 240 (hereinafter referred to as "Cauvery I"), which dwelled on the issue whether the Cauvery Water Disputes Tribunal (for short "the Tribunal") had the power to grant interim relief. In that case, applications filed by the State of Tamil Nadu for urgent interim reliefs were rejected by the Tribunal on the ground that they were not maintainable. This order was challenged, resulting in the judgment dated 26th April, 1991 by this Court, where it was held as follows (SCC p. 247, para 15):

> "15. Thus, we hold that this Court is the ultimate interpreter of the provisions of the Interstate Water Disputes Act, 1956 and has an authority to decide the limits, powers and the jurisdiction of the Tribunal constituted under the Act. This Court has not only the power but obligation to decide as to whether the Tribunal has any jurisdiction or not under the Act, to entertain any interim application till it finally decides the dispute referred to it..."

40. The Tribunal had ruled that since it was not like other courts with inherent powers to grant interim relief, only in case the Central Government referred a case for interim relief to it, would it have the jurisdiction to grant the same. *Inter-alia*, the Court in *Cauvery (I)* (supra) observed that the Tribunal was wrong in holding that the Central Government had not made any reference for granting any interim relief, and concluded that the interim reliefs prayed for clearly fell within the purview of the dispute referred by the Central Government. Accordingly, the appeals preferred by the State of Tamil Nadu were allowed and the Tribunal was directed to decide the applications for interim relief. However, the Court did not decide the larger question of whether a Tribunal, constituted under the Interstate Water Disputes Act, 1956 had the power to grant an interim relief, though the answer to the same may be deduced from the final direction.

41. In pursuance of these directions in *Cauvery (I)* (supra), the Tribunal decided the application and *vide* its order dated 25th June, 1991, proceeded to issue certain directions to the State of Karnataka. Thereafter, on 25th July, 1991, the Governor of Karnataka issued an Ordinance named "The Karnataka Cauvery Basin Irrigation Protection Ordinance, 1991". Hot on the heels of the Ordinance, the State of Karnataka also instituted a suit under article 131 of the Constitution against the State of Tamil Nadu for a declaration that the Tribunal's order granting interim relief was without jurisdiction and, therefore, *null* and *void*, etc. The Ordinance was replaced by Act 27 of 1991. In the context of these developments, the President made a reference to this Court under article 143(1) of the Constitution, posing three questions for opinion. The third question of the reference, relevant for the present Reference, was (*Cauvery II* supra, SCC p. 106, para 1):

> "1.(3) Whether a Water Disputes Tribunal constituted under the Act is competent to grant any interim relief to the parties to the dispute."

However, while dealing with the reference in Cauvery II, the Court split the question, *viz.*, whether a Water Disputes Tribunal constituted under the Act is competent to grant any interim relief into two parts: (i) when a reference for grant of interim relief is made to the Tribunal, and (ii) when no such reference is made to it. It was contended by the States of Karnataka and Kerala that if the Tribunal did not have power to grant interim relief, the Central Government would be incompetent to make a reference for the purpose in the first place and the Tribunal in turn would have no jurisdiction to entertain such reference, if made. Dealing with the said submission, after making a reference to the earlier order, this Court observed (at SCC p. 144, para 83) that once

> "the Central Government had made a reference to the Tribunal for consideration of the claim for interim relief, prayed for by the State of Tamil Nadu, the Tribunal had jurisdiction to consider the said request being a part of the reference itself. Implicit in the said decision was the finding that the subject of interim relief was a matter connected with or relevant to the water dispute within the meaning of section 5(1) of the said Act."

It was held that the Central Government could refer the matter for granting interim relief to the Tribunal for adjudication.

42. The consequence of the Court in coming to the conclusion, while replying to the third question was that the Tribunal did not have the jurisdiction to make an interim award or grant interim relief, would have not only resulted in the Court overruling its earlier decision between the two contending parties *i.e.*, the two States, but it would have also then required the Court to declare the order of the Tribunal as being without jurisdiction. The Court therefore, said in [*Cauvery II* case (supra) SCC p. 144, para 83]:

> "83...Although this Court by the said decision has kept open the question, *viz.*, whether the Tribunal has incidental, ancillary, inherent or implied power to grant the interim relief when no reference for grant of such relief is made to it, it has in terms concluded the second part of the question. We cannot, therefore, countenance a situation whereby question 3 and for that matter questions 1 and 2 may be so construed as to invite our opinion on the said decision of this Court. That would obviously be tantamount to our sitting in appeal on the said decision which it is impermissible for us to do even in adjudicatory jurisdiction. Nor is it competent for the President to invest us with an appellate jurisdiction over the said decision through a Reference under article 143 of the Constitution."

These observations would suggest that the Court declined to construe article 143 as a power any different from its adjudicative powers and for that reason, said that what could not be done in the adjudicatory process would equally not be achieved through the process of a reference.

THE CONSTITUENTS OF "SITTING IN APPEAL"

43. The expression, "sitting in appeal" was accurately used. An appellate court vacates the decree (or writ, order or direction) of the lower court when it allows an appeal – which is what this Court was invited to do in Cauvery I. This Court, in that appeal decided earlier, held that the Tribunal had the jurisdiction to pass the interim order sought by the State of Tamil Nadu. To nullify the interim order passed by the Tribunal, pursuant to a direction of the Supreme Court, on the ground that it was without jurisdiction, would necessarily require vacating the direction of the Supreme Court to the Tribunal to exercise its jurisdiction and decide the interim matter. Para 85 of that decision puts the matter beyond any pale of doubt [*Cauvery II* case (supra) SCC p. 145]:

> "85... In the first instance, the language of clause (1) of article 143 far from supporting Shri Nariman's contention is opposed to it. The said clause empowers the President to refer for this Court's opinion a question of law or fact which has arisen or is likely to arise. When this Court in its adjudicatory jurisdiction pronounces its authoritative opinion on a question of law, it cannot be said that there is any doubt about the question of law or the same is *res integra* so as to require the President to know what the true position of law on the question is. The decision of this Court on a question of law is binding on all courts and authorities. Hence, under the said clause the President can refer a question of law only when this Court has not decided it. *Secondly*, a decision given by this Court can be reviewed only under article 137 read with rule 1 of Order XL of the Supreme Court Rules, 1966 and on the conditions mentioned therein. When, further, this Court overrules the view of law expressed by it in an earlier case, it does not do so sitting in appeal and exercising an appellate jurisdiction over the earlier decision. It does so in exercise of its inherent power and only in exceptional circumstances such as when the earlier decision is *per incuriam* or is delivered in the absence of relevant or material facts or if it is manifestly wrong and productive of public mischief; See: *Bengal Immunity Company Ltd.* v. *State of Bihar*, (1955) 2 SCR 603. Under the Constitution such appellate jurisdiction does not vest in this Court, nor can it be vested in it by the President under article 143. To accept Shri Nariman's contention would mean that the advisory jurisdiction under article 143 is also an appellate jurisdiction of this Court over its own decision between the same parties and the executive has a power to ask this Court to revisits decision. If such power is read in article 143 it would be a serious inroad into the independence of judiciary." (Emphasis in original)

44. Eventually, the reference was answered in respect of question No. 3 in the following terms [*Cauvery II* case (supra) SCC pp. 152-53, para 101]:

> "*101. Question No. 3:* (i) A Water Disputes Tribunal constituted under the Act is competent to grant any interim relief to the parties to the dispute when a reference for such relief is made by the Central Government;
>
> (ii) Whether the Tribunal has power to grant interim relief when no reference is made by the Central Government for such relief is a question which does not arise in the facts and circumstances under which the Reference is made. Hence, we do not deem it necessary to answer the same."

DISTINCTION IN CONCEPTS 'VIEW OF LAW' AND 'DECISION'

45. The main emphasis of Mr. Soli Sorabjee was on the second part of paragraph 85, which, according to him, prohibits this Court from overruling a view expressed by it previously under article 143(1). We are not persuaded to agree with the learned senior counsel. The paragraph has to be read carefully. Sawant J. first considers the case of a "decision" of this Court whereas in the subsequent sentence he considers a "view of law" expressed by the Court, and attempts to explain the difference between the approaches to these two situations. These words are sometimes used interchangeably but not hereinabove. We believe that Justice Sawant consciously draws a difference between the two by using the words "When, further, this Court overrules the view of law..." after discussing the case of a "decision".

46. *Black's Law Dictionary* defines a "decision" as "a determination arrived at after consideration of facts, and, in legal context, law"; an "opinion" as

> "the statement by a judge or court of the decision reached in regard to a cause tried or argued before them, expounding the law as applied to the case, and detailing the reasons upon which the judgment is based";

and explains the difference between a "decision" and "opinion" as follows:

> "Decision is not necessarily synonymous with 'opinion'. A decision of the Court is its judgment; the opinion is the reasons given for that judgment, or the expression of the views of the judge."

47. Therefore, references in Para 85 of *Cauvery II* case (supra) to "decision" and "view of law" must be severed from each other. The learned Judge observes that in case of a decision, the appellate structure is exhausted after a pronouncement by the Supreme Court. Therefore, the only option left to the parties is of review or curative jurisdiction [a remedy carved out in the judgment in *Rupa Ashok Hurra* v. *Ashok Hurra*, (2002) 4 SCC 388]. After the exercise of those limited options, the concerned parties have absolutely no relief with regard to the dispute; it is considered settled for eternity in the eyes of the law. However, what is not eternal and still malleable in the eyes of law is the opinion or "view of law" pronounced in the course of reaching the decision. Justice Sawant in *Cauvery II* case (supra) clarifies that unlike this Court's appellate power, its power to overrule a previous precedent is an outcome of its inherent power when he says (SCC p. 145, para 85),

> "...it does not do so sitting in appeal and exercising an appellate jurisdiction over the earlier decision. It does so in exercise of its inherent power and only in exceptional circumstances...."

This Court has pointed out the difference between the two expressions in *Rupa Ashok Hurra* (supra), in the following words (SCC p. 406, para 24):

> "24. There is no gainsaying that the Supreme Court is the court of last resort—the final court on questions both of fact and of law including constitutional law. The law declared by this Court is the law of the land; it is precedent for itself and for all the courts/tribunals and authorities in India. In a judgment there will be declaration of law and its application to the facts of the case to render a decision on the dispute between the parties to the *lis*. It is necessary to bear in mind that the principles in regard to the highest court departing from its binding precedent are different from the grounds on which a final judgment between the parties, can be reconsidered. Here, we are mainly concerned with the latter. However, when reconsideration of a judgment of this Court is sought the finality attached both to the law declared as well as to the decision made in the case, is normally brought under challenge."

CHANGING OF OPINION ON A LEGAL ISSUE OR PRINCIPLE OF LAW IS NOT AN APPEAL AGAINST THE JUDGMENT

48. Therefore, there are two limitations – one jurisdictional and the other self-imposed.

48.1 The first limitation is that a decision of this Court can be reviewed only under article 137 or a Curative Petition and in no other way. It was in this context that in para 85 of Cauvery II, this Court had stated that the President can refer a question of law when this Court has not decided it. Mr. Harish Salve, learned senior counsel, is right when he argues that once a *lis* between parties is decided, the operative decree can only be opened in review. Overruling the judgment – as a precedent – does not reopen the decree.

48.2 The second limitation, a self-imposed rule of judicial discipline, was that overruling the opinion of the Court on a legal issue does not constitute sitting in appeal, but is done only in exceptional circumstances, such as when the earlier decision is *per incuriam* or is delivered in the absence of relevant or material facts or if it is manifestly wrong and capable of causing public mischief. For this proposition, the Court relied upon the judgment in the *Bengal Immunity* case (supra) wherein it was held that when article 141 lays down that the law declared by this Court shall be binding on all courts within the territory of India, it quite obviously refers to courts other than this Court; and that the Court would normally follow past precedents save and except where it was necessary to reconsider the correctness of law laid down in that judgment. In fact, the overruling of a principle of law is not an outcome of appellate jurisdiction but a consequence of its inherent power. This inherent power can be exercised as long as a previous decree *vis-à-vis* lis *inter partes* is not affected. It is the attempt to overturn the decision of a previous case that is problematic which is why the Court observes that [*Cauvery II* case (supra) SCC p. 145, para 85]

> "85. ...under the Constitution such appellate jurisdiction does not vest in this Court, nor can it be vested in it by the President under article 143."

49. Therefore, the controversy in *Cauvery II* (supra) was covered by the decision rendered by this Court in *Cauvery I* (supra) between the parties and the decision operated as *res judicata* and hence, it was opined that discretion under article 143(1) could not be exercised. It has also been observed that this Court had analysed the relevant provisions of the Inter-State Water Disputes Act, 1956 and thereafter had come to the conclusion that the Tribunal had jurisdiction to grant interim relief if the question of granting interim relief formed part of the reference. On this bedrock it was held that the decision operated as *res judicata*. It is, therefore, manifest from *Cauvery-II* that the Court was clearly not opposed to clarifying the ratio of a previous judgment in *Cauvery I*, in the course of an advisory jurisdiction. Afore extracted para 85 of *Cauvery II*, restricts this Court's advisory jurisdiction on the limited point of overturning a decided issue *vis-à-vis* a 'dispute' or *lis inter partes*.

SUPREME COURT HAS POWER TO OVER-RULE A PREVIOUS VIEW OF LAW

50. Finally a seven-Judge Bench of this Court has clearly held that this Court, under article 143(1), does have the power to overrule a previous view delivered by it. Justice Chandrachud, C.J. in *In re: The Special Courts Bill* (supra) held (SCC pp. 437-38, para 101):

> "101...We are inclined to the view that though it is always open to this Court to re-examine the question already decided by it and to overrule, if necessary, the view earlier taken by it, insofar as all other courts in the territory of India are concerned they ought to be bound by the view expressed by this Court even in the exercise of its advisory jurisdiction under article 143(1) of the Constitution."

SUPREME COURT HAS EXPLAINED, CLARIFIED, READ DOWN, THE RATIO OF LAW LAID DOWN IN EARLIER R. JUDGMENTS

51. There is a catena of pronouncements in which this Court has either explained, clarified or read down the ratio of previous judgments. In the very first reference, *In re: Delhi Laws Act*, 1912 (supra), the reference was made by reason of a judgment of the Federal Court in *Jatindra Nath Gupta* v. *The Province of Bihar*, [1949-50] FCR 595. The background of that reference was explained by Mukherjea, J. as under [*Delhi Laws Act, 1912* (supra) AIR p. 393, para 210]:

> "210. The necessity of seeking the advisory opinion of this Court is stated to have arisen from the fact that because of the decision of the Federal Court in *Jatindra Nath Gupta* v. *The Province of Bihar*, which held the proviso to sub-section (3) of section 1 of the Bihar Maintenance of Public Order Act, 1947, *ultra vires* the Bihar Provincial Legislature, by reason of its amounting to a delegation of its legislative powers to an extraneous authority, doubts have arisen regarding the validity of the three legislative provisions mentioned above, the legality of the first and the second being actually called in question in certain judicial proceedings which are pending before some of the High Courts in India."

Justice Das in the same opinion, while noting that reliance was placed by learned counsel for the interveners on the judgment of the Federal Court in *Jatindra Nath Gupta* (supra), recorded that the learned Attorney-General had strenuously challenged the correctness of the decision of the majority of the Federal Court in that case. *Inter alia*, observing that the reference was in a way occasioned by that decision, the learned Judge held as follows (AIR pp. 429, para 334):

> "334. ...I feel bound to say, with the utmost humility and for reasons given already, that the observations of the majority of the Federal Court in that case went too far and, in agreement with the learned Attorney-General, I am unable to accept them as correct exposition of the principles relating to the delegation of legislative power."

52. In this context, it would be beneficial to refer to *Keshav Singh's* case. In the said case, a reference was made by the President which fundamentally pertained to the privileges of the Legislative Assembly and exercise of jurisdiction by a Bench of the High Court. The High Court entertained a writ petition under article 226 of the Constitution, challenging the decision of the Assembly committing one *Keshav Singh*, who was not one of its members, to prison for its contempt. The issue was whether by entertaining the writ petition, the Judges of the High Court were in contempt of the Legislature for infringement of its privileges and immunities. For the same, this Court proceeded to construe the relevant provisions contained in article 194(3) and its harmonization with other articles of the Constitution, especially articles 19(1)(a), 21 and 22. In that context, the decision in "Sharma" AIR 1959 SC 395 came up for consideration. One of the questions that arose in *Sharma's* case (supra) was the impact of articles 19(1)(a) and 21 on the provisions contained in the latter part of article 194(3). The majority view was that the privilege in question was subsisting at the relevant time and must, therefore, deemed to be included under the latter part of article 194(3). It was held that article 19(1)(a) did not apply under the rule of harmonious construction, where article 19(1)(a) was in direct conflict with article 194(3). The particular provision in the latter article would prevail over the general provision contained in the former. It was further held that though article 21 applied, it had not been contravened. The minority view, on the other hand, held that the privilege in question had not been established; even assuming the same was established and it was to be included in the latter part of article 194(3), yet it must be controlled by article 19(1)(a) on the ground that Fundamental Rights guaranteed by Part III of the Constitution were of paramount importance and must prevail over a provision like the one contained in article 194(3) which may be inconsistent with them. The majority decision also commented on the decision in *Gunupati Keshavram Reddy* v. *Nafisul Hasan and the State of Uttar Pradesh*, AIR 1954 SC 636 and observed that the said decision was based entirely on a concession and could not, therefore, be deemed to be a considered decision of this Court.

53. The decision in *Keshavram Reddy* (supra) dealt with the applicability of article 22(2) to a case falling under the latter part of article 194(3). It is worth noting that the minority opinion of *Sharma* (supra) treated *Keshavram Reddy*, as expressing a considered opinion, which was binding on the Court. In *Keshav Singh* (supra) it was opined that in *Sharma's* case, (supra) the majority decision held in terms that Article 21 was applicable to the contents of article 194(3), but on merits, it came to the conclusion that the alleged contravention had not been proved. Commenting on the minority view it was opined that it was unnecessary to consider whether article 21 as such applied because the said view treated all the Fundamental Rights guaranteed by Part III as paramount, and therefore, each one of them could control the provisions of article 194(3).

54. At that juncture, the Bench in *Keshav Singh* case (supra) stated that in the case of *Sharma*, (supra) contentions urged by the petitioner did not raise a general issue as to the relevance and applicability of all the fundamental rights guaranteed by Part III at all. The contravention of only two articles was pleaded and they were articles 19(1)(a) and 21. Strictly speaking, it was, therefore, unnecessary to consider the larger issue as to whether the latter part of article 194(3) was subject to the fundamental rights in general, and indeed, even on the majority view it could not be said that the said view excluded the application of all fundamental rights, for the obvious and simple reason that article 21 was held to be applicable and the merits of the petitioner's arguments about its alleged contravention in his case were examined and rejected. Therefore, it was not right to read the majority decision as laying down a general proposition that whenever there is a conflict between the provisions of the latter part of article 194(3) and any of the provisions of the fundamental rights guaranteed by Part III, the latter must always yield to the former.

55. It was further observed in *Keshav Singh* case (supra) that the majority decision in *Sharma* case (supra) had incidentally commented on the decision in *Keshavram Reddy's* case (supra). Apart from that there was no controversy about the applicability of article 22 in that case, and, therefore, the comment made by the majority judgment on the earlier decision was partly not accurate. Their Lordships adverted to the facts in *Sharma's* case (supra) wherein the majority judgment had observed that it "proceeded entirely on a concession of counsel and cannot be regarded as a considered opinion on the subject." After so stating, the Bench opined thus [*Keshav Singh* case (supra) AIR pp. 766, para 55]:

> "55. ...There is no doubt that the first part of this comment is not accurate. A concession was made by the Attorney-General not on a point of law which was decided by the Court, but on a point of fact; and so, this part of the comment cannot strictly be said to be justified. It is, however, true that there is no discussion about the merits of the contention raised on behalf of Mr. Mistry and to that extent, it may have been permissible to the majority judgment to say that it was not a considered opinion of the Court. But, as we have already pointed out, it was hardly necessary for the majority decision to deal with the point pertaining to the applicability of article 22(2), because that point did not arise in the proceedings before the Court in *Pandit Sharma's* case (supra). That is why we wish to make it clear that the *obiter* observations made in the majority judgment about the validity or correctness of the earlier decision of this Court in *Gunupati Keshavram Reddy's* case should not be taken as having decided the point in question. In other words, the question as to whether article 22(2) would apply to such a case may have to be considered by this Court if and when it becomes necessary to do so."

WHILE EXERCISING JURISDICTION UNDER ARTICLE 143 SUPREME COURT CAN LOOK EARLIER DECISIONS AND THE RATIO OF LAW LAID DOWN

56. From the aforesaid decision in *Keshav Singh* case (supra) it is clear that while exercising jurisdiction under article 143(1) of the Constitution this Court can look into an earlier decision for the purpose of whether the contentions urged in the previous decision did raise a general issue or not; whether it was necessary to consider the larger issue that did not arise; and whether a general proposition had been laid down. It has also been stated that where no controversy arose with regard to applicability of a particular facet of constitutional law, the comments made in a decision could be treated as not accurate; and further it could be opined that in an earlier judgment there are certain *obiter* observations.

57. Thus, in *Keshav Singh* case (supra), a seven-Judge Bench, while entertaining a reference under article 143(1), dealt with a previous decision in respect of its interpretation involving a constitutional principle in respect of certain articles, and proceeded to opine that the view expressed in *Sharma's* case (supra), in relation to a proposition laid down in *Keshavram Reddy's* case (supra), was inaccurate.

58. At this stage, it is worthy to refer to *Supreme Court Advocates-on-Record Association* v. *Union of India,* (1993) 4 SCC 441; commonly known as "Second Judges case" J.S. Verma, J., (as his Lordship then was) speaking for the majority, apart from other conclusions relating to appointment of Judges and the Chief Justices, while dealing with transfer, expressed thus [*Second Judges* case(supra) SCC p. 710, para 486]:

> "486. (8) Consent of the transferred Judge/Chief Justice is not required for either the first or any subsequent transfer from one High Court to another.
>
> (9) Any transfer made on the recommendation of the Chief Justice of India is not to be deemed to be punitive, and such transfer is not justiciable on any ground.
>
> (10) In making all appointments and transfers, the norms indicated must be followed. However, the same do not confer any justiciable right in anyone.
>
> (11) Only limited judicial review on the grounds specified earlier is available in matters of appointments and transfers."

59. As far as the ground of limited judicial review is concerned the majority opined thus [*Second Judges* case (supra) SCC p. 708 para 481-82]:

> "481. These guidelines in the form of norms are not to be construed as conferring any justiciable right in the transferred Judge. Apart from the constitutional requirement of a transfer being made only on the recommendation of the Chief Justice of India, the issue of transfer is not justiciable on any other ground, including the reasons for the transfer or their sufficiency. The opinion of the Chief Justice of India formed in the manner indicated is sufficient safeguard and protection against any arbitrariness or bias, as well as any erosion of the independence of the Judiciary.
>
> 482. ...Except on the ground of want of consultation with the named constitutional functionaries or lack of any condition of eligibility in the case of an appointment, or of a transfer being made without the recommendation of the Chief Justice of India, these matters are not justiciable on any other ground, including that of bias, which in any case is excluded by the element of plurality in the process of decision-making."

60. In *Special Reference No. 1 of 1998* (supra), (commonly referred as the "*Third Judges* case"), question No. 2 reads as follows (SCC p. 747, para 1):

> "1.(2) Whether the transfer of Judges is judicially reviewable in the light of the observation of the Supreme Court in the aforesaid judgment that 'such transfer is not justiciable on any ground' and its further observation that limited judicial review is available in matters of transfer, and the extent and scope of judicial review;"

While answering the same, the Bench opined thus [*Third Judges* case (supra) SCC 771 para 37]:

> "37. It is to our mind imperative, given the gravity involved in transferring High Court Judges, that the Chief Justice of India should obtain the views of the Chief Justice of the High Court from which the proposed transfer is to be effected as also the Chief Justice of the High Court to which the transfer is to

be effected. This is in accord with the majority judgment in the *Second Judges* case which postulates consultation with the Chief Justice of another High Court. The Chief Justice of India should also take into account the views of one or more Supreme Court Judges who are in a position to provide material which would assist in the process of deciding whether or not a proposed transfer should take place. These views should be expressed in writing and should be considered by the Chief Justice of India and the four senior-most puisne Judges of the Supreme Court. These views and those of each of the four senior-most puisne Judges should be conveyed to the Government of India along with the proposal of transfer. Unless the decision to transfer has been taken in the manner aforestated, it is not decisive and does not bind the Government of India."

In the conclusion their Lordships clearly state as follows [*Third Judges* case (supra) SCC p. 772 para 44]:

"1. The expression "consultation with the Chief Justice of India" in articles 217(1) and 222(1) of the Constitution of India requires consultation with a plurality of Judges in the formation of the opinion of the Chief Justice of India. The sole individual opinion of the Chief Justice of India does not constitute "consultation" within the meaning of the said articles.

2. The transfer of puisne Judges is judicially reviewable only to this extent: that the recommendation that has been made by the Chief Justice of India in this behalf has not been made in consultation with the four senior-most puisne Judges of the Supreme Court and/or that the views of the Chief Justice of the High Court from which the transfer is to be effected and of the Chief Justice of the High Court to which the transfer is to be effected have not been obtained."

IN THE REFERENCE UNDER ARTICLE 143(1) SUPREME COURT CAN MAKE CERTAIN MODIFICATIONS AND EXPAND LIMITED JUDICIAL REVIEW

61. From the aforesaid, it is demonstrable that while entertaining the reference under article 143(1), this Court had analysed the principles enunciated in the earlier judgment and also made certain modifications. The said modifications may be stated as one of the mode or method of inclusion by way of modification without changing the *ratio decidendi*. For the purpose of validity of a reference, suffice it to say, dwelling upon an earlier judgment is permissible. That apart, one cannot be oblivious of the fact that the scope of limited judicial review, in the Second Judges case (supra), which otherwise is quite restricted, was slightly expanded in the Court's opinion to the Presidential reference [SIC in the Third Judges case (supra)].

WHEN REFERENCE CAN BE RETURNED UNANSWERED

62. It is of some interest to note that almost every reference, filed under article 143(1), has witnessed challenge as to its maintainability on one ground or the other, but all the same, the references have been answered, except in *Dr. M. Ismail Faruqui* (supra), which was returned unanswered, mainly on the ground that the reference did not serve a constitutional purpose.

63. From the aforesaid analysis, it is quite vivid that this Court would respectfully decline to answer a reference if it is improper, inadvisable and undesirable; or the questions formulated have purely socio-economic or political reasons, which have no relation whatsoever with any of the provisions of the Constitution or otherwise are of no constitutional significance; or are incapable of being answered; or would not subserve any purpose; or there is authoritative pronouncement of this Court which has already decided the question referred.

UNDER THIS REFERENCE WITHOUT TOUCHING MERITS OF 2G JUDGMENT THE CONSTITUTIONAL PRINCIPLES RELATING TO ALLOCATION/ALIENATION/DISPOSAL/DISTRIBUTION OF NATURAL RESOURCES CAN BE DEALT WITH

64. In the case at hand, it is to be scrutinized whether the 2G case is a decision which has dealt with and decided the controversy encapsulated in question No. 1 or meets any of the criteria mentioned above. As we perceive, the question involves interpretation of a constitutional principle inherent under article 14 of the Constitution and it is of great public importance as it deals with allocation/ alienation/disposal/distribution of natural resources. Besides, the question whether the 2G case is on authoritative pronouncement in that regard, has to be looked into and only then an opinion can be expressed. For the said purpose all other impediments do not remotely come into play in the present Reference.

REFERENCE WAS HELD MAINTAINABLE

65. We are, therefore, of the view that as long as the decision with respect to the allocation of spectrum licenses is untouched, this Court is within its jurisdiction to evaluate and clarify the ratio of the judgment in the 2G case. For the purpose of this stage of argumentation, it needs little emphasis, that we have the jurisdiction to clarify the ratio of the judgment in 2G case, irrespective of whether we actually choose to do so or not. Therefore, the fact that this Reference may require us to say something different to what has been enunciated in the 2G case as a proposition of law, cannot strike at the root of the maintainability of the Reference. Consequently, we reject the preliminary objection and hold that this Reference is maintainable, notwithstanding its effect on the ratio of the 2G case, as long as the decision in that case *qua lis inter partes* is left unaffected.

DISCUSSION BY SUPREME COURT ON THE QUESTIONS RAISED IN THIS PRESIDENTIAL REFERENCE

On Merits

66. This leads us to the merits of the controversy disclosed in the questions framed in the Reference for our advisory opinion.

IN 2G JUDGMENT PUBLIC AUCTION WAS HELD AS THE ONLY METHOD OF DISPOSAL OF NATURAL RESOURCES

67. As already pointed out, the judgment in the 2G case triggered doubts about the validity of methods other than 'auction' for disposal of natural resources which, ultimately led to the filing of the present Reference. Therefore, before we proceed to answer question No. 1, it is imperative to understand what has been precisely stated in the 2G case and decipher the law declared in that case.

68. All the counsel agreed that paragraphs 94 to 96 in the said decision are the repository of the ratio *vis-à-vis* disposal of natural resources in the 2G case. On the one hand it was argued that these paragraphs lay down, as a proposition of law, that all natural resources across all sectors, and in all circumstances are to be disposed of by way of public auction, and on the other, it was urged that the observations therein were made only *qua* spectrum. Before examining the strength of the rival stands, we may briefly recapitulate the principles that govern the determination of the 'law declared' by a judgment and its true ratio.

IMPACT OF LAW DECLARED BY SUPREME COURT

69. Article 141 of the Constitution lays down that the 'law declared' by the Supreme Court is binding upon all the courts within the territory of India. The 'law declared' has to be construed as a principle of law that emanates from a judgment, or an interpretation of a law or judgment by the Supreme Court, upon which, the case is decided. See *Fida Hussain* v. *Moradabad Development Authority,* (2011) 12 SCC 615. Hence, it flows from the above that the 'law declared' is the principle culled out on the reading of a judgment as a whole in light of the questions raised, upon which the case is decided; Also see *Ambica Quarry Works* v. *State of Gujarat,* (1987) 1 SCC 213 and *Commissioner of Income-tax* v. *Sun Engineering Works (P) Ltd.,* (1992) 4 SCC 363. In other words, the 'law declared' in a judgment, which is binding upon courts, is the *ratio decidendi* of the judgment. It is the essence of a decision and the principle upon which, the case is decided, which has to be ascertained in relation to the subject-matter of the decision.

EACH CASE HAS ITS OWN FACTS – JUDGMENT TO BE READ AS A WHOLE TO DERIVE ITS *RATIO-DECIDENDI*

70. Each case entails a different set of facts and a decision is a precedent on its own facts; not everything said by a Judge while giving a judgment can be ascribed precedential value. The essence of a decision that binds the parties to the case is the principle upon which the case is decided and for this reason, it is important to analyse a decision and cull out from it, the *ratio decidendi*. In the matter of applying precedents, the erudite Justice Benjamin Cardozo in "The Nature of a Judicial Process", had said that "if the judge is to pronounce it wisely, some principles of selection there must be to guide him along all potential judgments that compete for recognition" and "almost invariably his first step is to examine and compare them;" "it is a process of search, comparison and little more" and ought not to be akin to matching "the colors of the case at hand against the colors of many sample cases" because in that case "the man who had the best card index of the cases would also be the wisest judge". Warning against comparing precedents with matching colours of one case with another, he summarized the process, in case the colours don't match, in the following wise words:

> "It is when the colors do not match, when the references in the index fail, when there is no decisive precedent, that the serious business of the judge begins. He must then fashion law for the litigants before him. In fashioning it for them, he will be fashioning it for others. The classic statement is Bacon's: "For many times, the things deduced to judgment may be *meum* and *tuum*,

when the reason and consequence thereof may trench to point of estate. The sentence of today will make the right and wrong of tomorrow."

71. With reference to the precedential value of decisions, in *State of Orissa* v. *Md. Illiyas*, (2006) 1 SCC 275 this Court observed (SCC p. 282, para 12):

> "12. ...According to the well-settled theory of precedents, every decision contains three basic postulates: (*i*) findings of material facts, direct and inferential. An inferential finding of facts is the inference which the Judge draws from the direct, or perceptible facts; (*ii*) statements of the principles of law applicable to the legal problems disclosed by the facts; and (*iii*) judgment based on the combined effect of the above. A decision is an authority for what it actually decides. What is of the essence in a decision is its ratio and not every observation found therein nor what logically flows from the various observations made in the judgment..."

72. Recently, in *Union of India* v. *Amrit Lal Manchanda*, (2004) 3 SCC 75, this Court has observed as follows (SCC p. 83, para 15):

> "...Observations of courts are neither to be read as Euclid's theorems nor as provisions of the statute and that too taken out of their context. These observations must be read in the context in which they appear to have been stated. Judgments of courts are not to be construed as statutes. To interpret words, phrases and provisions of a statute, it may become necessary for Judges to embark into lengthy discussions but the discussion is meant to explain and not to define. Judges interpret statutes, they do not interpret judgments. They interpret words of statutes; their words are not to be interpreted as statutes."

73. It is also important to read a judgment as a whole keeping in mind that it is not an abstract academic discourse with universal applicability, but heavily grounded in the facts and circumstances of the case. Every part of a judgment is intricately linked to others constituting a larger whole and thus, must be read keeping the logical thread intact. In this regard, in *Islamic Academy of Education* v. *State of Karnataka*, (2003) 6 SCC 697, the Court made the following observations (SCC p. 719 para 2):

> "2. ...The *ratio decidendi* of a judgment has to be found out only on reading the entire judgment. In fact, the ratio of the judgment is what is set out in the judgment itself. The answer to the question would necessarily have to be read in the context of what is set out in the judgment and not in isolation. In case of any doubt as regards any observations, reasons and principles, the other part of the judgment has to be looked into. By reading a line here and there from the judgment, one cannot find out the entire *ratio decidendi* of the judgment."

QUESTIONS FRAMED IN 2G JUDGMENTS

74. The ratio of the 2G case must, therefore, be understood and appreciated in light of the above guiding principles.

75. In the 2G case, the Bench framed five questions.

Questions No. (ii) and (v) pertain to the factual matrix and are not relevant for settling the controversy at hand. The remaining three questions are reproduced below:

"(i) Whether the Government has the right to alienate, transfer or distribute natural resources/national assets otherwise than by following a fair and transparent method consistent with the fundamentals of the equality clause enshrined in the Constitution?

(iii) Whether the exercise undertaken by DoT from September, 2007 to March, 2008 for grant of UAS licences to the private respondents in terms of the recommendations made by TRAI is vitiated due to arbitrariness and *mala fides* and is contrary to public interest?

(iv) Whether the policy of first-come-first-served followed by DoT for grant of licences is *ultra vires* the provisions of article 14 of the Constitution and whether the said policy was arbitrarily changed by the Minister of Communications and Information Technology (hereinafter referred to as "the Minister of Communications and Information Technology"), without consulting TRAI, with a view to favour some of the applicants?"

76. While dealing with question No. (i), the Court observed that the State is empowered to distribute natural resources as they constitute public property/ national assets. Thereafter, the Bench observed as follows [2G judgment (supra) SCC p. 53, para 75]:

"75....while distributing natural resources the State is bound to act in consonance with the principles of equality and public trust and ensure that no action is taken which may be detrimental to public interest. Like any other State action, constitutionalism must be reflected at every stage of the distribution of natural resources. In article 39(b) of the Constitution it has been provided that the ownership and control of the material resources of the community should be so distributed so as to best subserve the common good, but no comprehensive legislation has been enacted to generally define natural resources and a framework for their protection..."

IN ANSWER TO QUESTION NO. 1 PUBLIC TRUST DOCTRINE WAS ADOPTED IN 2G JUDGMENT

77. The learned Judges adverted to the 'public trust doctrine' as enunciated in *The Illinois Central Railroad Co.* v. *The People of the State of Illinois*, 36 L ED 1018: 146 US 387 (1892); *M.C. Mehta* v. *Kamal Nath*, (1997) 1 SCC 388; *Jamshed Hormusji Wadia* v. *Board of Trustees, Port of Mumbai*, (2004) 3 SCC 214; *Intellectuals Forum, Tirupathi* v. *State of Andhra Pradesh*, (2006) 3 SCC 549; *Fomento Resorts and Hotels Limited* v. *Minguel Martins*, (2009) 3 SCC 571; and *Reliance Natural Resources Limited* v. *Reliance Industries Limited*, (2010) 7 SCC 1; And held [2G judgment (supra) SCC p. 56, para 85]:

"85. As natural resources are public goods, the doctrine of equality, which emerges from the concepts of justice and fairness, must guide the State in determining the actual mechanism for distribution of natural resources. In this regard, the doctrine of equality has two aspects: *first*, it regulates the rights and obligations of the State *vis-à-vis* its people and demands that the people be granted equitable access to natural resources and/or its products and that they are adequately compensated for the transfer of the resource to the private domain; and *second*, it regulates the rights and obligations of the State *vis-à-*

vis private parties seeking to acquire/use the resource and demands that the procedure adopted for distribution is just, non-arbitrary and transparent and that it does not discriminate between similarly placed private parties."

Referring to the decisions of this Court in *Akhil Bhartiya Upbhokta Congress* v. *State of Madhya Pradesh*, (2011) 5 SCC 29; and *Sachidanand Pandey* v. *State of West Bengal*, (1987) 2 SCC 295, the Bench ultimately concluded thus [2G Judgment (supra) SCC p. 58, para 89]:

"89. In conclusion, we hold that the State is the legal owner of the natural resources as a trustee of the people and although it is empowered to distribute the same, the process of distribution must be guided by the constitutional principles including the doctrine of equality and larger public good."

78. On a reading of the above paragraphs, it can be noticed that the doctrine of equality; larger public good, adoption of a transparent and fair method, opportunity of competition; and avoidance of any occasion to scuttle the claim of similarly situated applicants were emphasized upon. While dealing with alienation of natural resources like spectrum, it was stated that it is the duty of the State to ensure that a non-discriminatory method is adopted for distribution and alienation which would necessarily result in the protection of national/public interest.

79. Paragraphs 85 and 89, while referring to the concept of 'public trust doctrine', lay emphasis on the doctrine of equality, which has been segregated into two parts – one is the substantive part and the other is the regulatory part. In the regulatory facet, paragraph 85 states that the procedure adopted for distribution should be just and non-arbitrary and must be guided by constitutional principles including the doctrine of equality and larger public good. Similarly, in paragraph 89 stress has been laid on transparency and fair opportunity of competition. It is further reiterated that the burden of the State is to ensure that a non-discriminatory method is adopted for distribution and alienation which would necessarily result in the protection of national and public interest.

ANSWER TO QUESTION NOS. III & IV IN 2G JUDGMENT – IN PARAGRAPHS 94 TO 96 AUCTION WAS LAID DOWN AS THE NORMAL PRINCIPLE OF DISPOSAL

80. Dealing with Questions No. (iii) and (iv) in paragraphs 94 to 96 of the judgment, the Court opined as follows [2G Judgment (supra) SCC p. 59-60]:

"94. There is a fundamental flaw in the first-come-first-served policy inasmuch as it involves an element of pure chance or accident. In matters involving award of contracts or grant of licence or permission to use public property, the invocation of first-come-first-served policy has inherently dangerous implications. Any person who has access to the power corridor at the highest or the lowest level may be able to obtain information from the government files or the files of the agency/instrumentality of the State that a particular public property or asset is likely to be disposed of or a contract is likely to be awarded or a licence or permission is likely to be given, he would immediately make an application and would become entitled to stand first in the queue at the cost of all others who may have a better claim.

95. This Court has repeatedly held that wherever a contract is to be awarded or a licence is to be given, the public authority must adopt a transparent and fair method for making selections so that all eligible persons get a fair opportunity of competition. To put it differently, the State and its agencies/ instrumentalities must always adopt a rational method for disposal of public property and no attempt should be made to scuttle the claim of worthy applicants. When it comes to alienation of scarce natural resources like spectrum, etc., it is the burden of the State to ensure that a non-discriminatory method is adopted for distribution and alienation, which would necessarily result in protection of national/public interest.

96. In our view, a duly publicised auction conducted fairly and impartially is perhaps the best method for discharging this burden and the methods like first-come- first-served when used for alienation of natural resources/public property are likely to be misused by unscrupulous people who are only interested in garnering maximum financial benefit and have no respect for the constitutional ethos and values. In other words, while transferring or alienating the natural resources, the State is duty-bound to adopt the method of auction by giving wide publicity so that all eligible persons can participate in the process."

USE OF THE WORD 'PERHAPS' IN PARA 96 IN 2G JUDGMENT, SCOPE OTHER THAN AUCTION WAS LEFT OPEN FOR DISPOSAL OF NATURAL RESOURCES

81. Our reading of these paragraphs suggests that the Court was not considering the case of auction in general, but specifically evaluating the validity of those methods adopted in the distribution of spectrum from September, 2007 to March, 2008. It is also pertinent to note that reference to auction is made in the subsequent paragraph (96) with the rider '*perhaps*'. It has been observed that "a duly publicized auction conducted fairly and impartially is *perhaps* the best method for discharging this burden." We are conscious that a judgment is not to be read as a statute, but at the same time, we cannot be oblivious to the fact that when it is argued with vehemence that the judgment lays down auction as a constitutional principle, the word "*perhaps*" gains significance. This suggests that the recommendation of auction for alienation of natural resources was never intended to be taken as an absolute or blanket statement applicable across all natural resources, but simply a conclusion made at first blush over the attractiveness of a method like auction in disposal of natural resources. The choice of the word '*perhaps*' suggests that the learned Judges considered situations requiring a method other than auction as conceivable and desirable.

IN FINAL CONCLUSION OF 2G JUDGMENT, AUCTION WAS NOT MENTIONED AS THE ONLY METHOD

82. Further, the final conclusions summarized in paragraph 102 of the judgment (SCC) make no mention about auction being the only permissible and *intra vires* method for disposal of natural resources; the findings are limited to the case of spectrum. In case the Court had actually enunciated, as a proposition of law, that auction is the only permissible method or mode for alienation/allotment of natural resources, the same would have found a mention in the summary at the end of the judgment.

2G JUDGMENT ONLY DIRECTED AUCTION IN SPECTRUM NOT FOR ALL NATURAL RESOURCES

83. Moreover, if the judgment in 2G case (supra) is to be read as holding auction as the only permissible means of disposal of all natural resources, it would lead to the quashing of a large number of laws that prescribe methods other than auction, *e.g.*, the MMRD Act. While dealing with the merits of the Reference, at a later stage, we will discuss whether or not auction can be a constitutional mandate under article 14 of the Constitution, but for the present, it would suffice to say that no court would ever implicitly, indirectly, or by inference, hold a range of laws as *ultra vires* the Constitution, without allowing every law to be tested on its merits. One of the most profound tenets of constitutionalism is the presumption of constitutionality assigned to each legislation enacted. We find that the 2G case does not even consider a plethora of laws and judgments that prescribe methods, other than auction, for dispensation of natural resources; something that it would have done, in case, it intended to make an assertion as wide as applying auction to all natural resources. Therefore, we are convinced that the observations in Paras 94 to 96 could not apply beyond the specific case of spectrum, which according to the law declared in the 2G case, is to be alienated only by auction and no other method.

84. Thus, having come to the conclusion that the 2G case does not deal with modes of allocation for natural resources, other than spectrum, we shall now proceed to answer the first question of the Reference pertaining to other natural resources, as the question subsumes the essence of the entire reference, particularly the set of first five questions.

REFERENCE SEEKS OPINION IF AUCTION WAS ONLY METHOD FOR DISPOSAL OF ALL OTHER NATURAL RESOURCES

85. The President seeks this Court's opinion on the limited point of permissibility of methods other than auction for alienation of natural resources, other than spectrum. The question also harbours several concepts, which were argued before us through the hearing of the Reference, that require to be answered in order to derive a comprehensive answer to the parent question:

(i) Are some methods *ultra vires* and others *intra vires* the Constitution of India, especially article 14?

(ii) Can disposal through the method of auction be elevated to a Constitutional principle?

(iii) Is this Court entitled to direct the executive to adopt a certain method because it is the 'best' method? If not, to what extent can the executive deviate from such 'best' method?

An answer to these issues, in turn, will give an answer to the first question which, as noted above, will answer the Presidential Reference.

86. Before proceeding to answer these questions, we would like to dispose of a couple of minor objections. The first pertained to the classification of resources made in the 2G case. Learned counsel appearing for CPIL argued that all that the judgment in the 2G case has done is to carve out a special category of cases where public auction is the only legally sustainable method of alienation *viz.*, natural resources that are scarce, valuable and are allotted to private entities for commercial exploitation. The learned Attorney-General, however, contested this claim and argued that no such proposition was laid down in the 2G judgment. He pointed out that the words "commercial exploitation" were not even used anywhere in the judgment except in an extract from another judgment in a different context. We agree that the judgment itself does not carve out any special case for scarce natural resources only meant for commercial exploitation. However, we feel, despite that, in this Reference, CPIL is not barred from making a submission drawing a distinction between natural resources meant for commercial exploitation and those meant for other purposes. This Court has the jurisdiction to classify the subject-matter of a reference, if a genuine case for it exists.

ARTICLES 14 AND 39(b) OF THE CONSTITUTION – CONCEPTS OF 'PUBLIC TRUST DOCTRINE' AND 'TRUSTEESHIP' FOR ALL NATURAL RESOURCES – SUBMISSION

87. Mr. Shanti Bhushan, learned Senior Counsel, in support of his stand that the first question of the Reference must be answered in a way so as to allow auction as the only mode for the disposal of natural resources, submitted that a combined reading of article 14, which dictates non-arbitrariness in State action and equal opportunity to those similarly placed; Article 39(b) which is a Directive Principle of State Policy dealing with distribution of natural resources for the common good of the people; and the "trusteeship" principle found in the Preamble which mandates that the State holds all natural resources in the capacity of a trustee, on behalf of the people, would make auction a constitutional mandate under article 14 of the Constitution. It is imperative, therefore, that we evaluate each of these principles before coming to any conclusion on the constitutional verdict on auction.

88. In the 2G case (supra), two concepts namely, "public trust doctrine" and "trusteeship" have been adverted to, which were also relied upon by learned counsel for CPIL, in defence of the argument that the State holds natural resources in a fiduciary relationship with the people. As far as "trusteeship" is concerned, there is no cavil that the State holds all natural resources as a trustee of the public and must deal with them in a manner that is consistent with the nature of such a trust. However, what was asserted on behalf of CPIL was that all natural resources fall within the domain of the "public trust doctrine", and therefore, there is an obligation on the Government to ensure that their transfer or alienation for commercial exploitation is in a fair and transparent manner and only in pursuit of public good. The learned Attorney-General on the other hand, zealously urged that the subject-matter of the doctrine and the nature of restrictions, it imposes, are of limited scope; that the applicability of the doctrine is restricted to certain common properties pertaining to the environment, like rivers, seashores, forest and air, meant for free and unimpeded use of the general public and the restrictions it imposes is in the term of a complete embargo on any alienation of such resources, for private ownership. According to him, the extension of the public trust doctrine to all natural resources has led to a considerable confusion and needs to be clarified.

LAW ON 'PUBLIC TRUST DOCTRINE'

89. The doctrine of public trust enunciated more thoroughly by the United States Supreme Court in *Illinois* (supra) was introduced to Indian environmental jurisprudence by this Court in *M.C. Mehta* (supra). Speaking for the majority, Kuldip Singh, J. observed as follows [*M.C. Mehta* case (supra) SCC pp. 407-08 para 25]:

> "25. The Public Trust Doctrine primarily rests on the principle that certain resources like air, sea, waters and the forests have such a great importance to the people as a whole that it would be wholly unjustified to make them a subject of private ownership. The said resources being a gift of nature, they should be made freely available to everyone irrespective of the status in life. The doctrine enjoins upon the Government to protect the resources for the enjoyment of the general public rather than to permit their use for private ownership or commercial purposes. According to Professor Sax the Public Trust Doctrine imposes the following restrictions on governmental authority:
>
> 'Three types of restrictions on governmental authority are often thought to be imposed by the public trust: *first*, the property subject to the trust must not only be used for a public purpose, but it must be held available for use by the general public; *second*, the property may not be sold, even for a fair cash equivalent; and *third* the property must be maintained for particular types of uses'."

The learned Judge further observed [*M.C. Mehta* case (supra) SCC p. 413 para 34]:

> "34. Our legal system – based on English common law – includes the public trust doctrine as part of its jurisprudence. The State is the trustee of all natural resources which are by nature meant for public use and enjoyment. Public at large is the beneficiary of the seashore, running waters, airs, forests and ecologically fragile lands. The State as a trustee is under a legal duty to protect the natural resources. These resources meant for public use cannot be converted into private ownership."

90. The judgment in *M.C. Mehta* case (supra) was explained in *Intellectuals Forum* (supra). Reiterating that the State is the trustee of all natural resources which are by nature meant for public use and enjoyment, the Court observed thus [*Intellectuals Forum* case (supra) SCC p. 575 para 76]:

> "76. The Supreme Court of California, in *National Audubon Society* v. *Superior Court of Alpine Country* also known as *Mono Lake* case summed up the substance of the doctrine. The Court said:
>
> "Thus, the public trust is more than an affirmation of State power to use public property for public purposes. It is an affirmation of the duty of the State to protect the people's common heritage of streams, lakes, marshlands and tidelands, surrendering the right only in those rare cases when the abandonment of the right is consistent with the purposes of the trust."

This is an articulation of the doctrine from the angle of the affirmative duties of the State with regard to public trust. Formulated from a nugatory angle, the doctrine does not exactly *prohibit* the alienation of the property held as a public trust. However, when the State holds a resource that is freely available for the use of the public, it provides for a high degree of judicial scrutiny on any action of the Government, no matter how consistent with the existing legislations, that attempts to restrict such free use. To properly scrutinise such actions of the Government, the courts must make a distinction between the Government's general obligation to act for the public benefit, and the special, more demanding obligation which it may have as a trustee of certain public resources..." (Emphasis in original)

It was thus, held that when the affirmative duties are set out from a nugatory angle, the doctrine does not exactly prohibit the alienation of property held as a public trust, but mandates a high degree of judicial scrutiny.

91. In *Fomento* (supra), the Court was concerned with the access of the public to a beach in Goa. Holding that it was a public beach which could not be privatized or blocked denying traditional access, this Court reiterated the public trust doctrine as follows (SCC p. 614, para 52):

"52. The matter deserves to be considered from another angle. The public trust doctrine which has been invoked by Ms. Indira Jaising in support of her argument that the beach in question is a public beach and the appellants cannot privatise the same by blocking/obstructing traditional access available through Survey No. 803 (new No. 246/2) is implicitly engrafted by the State Government in Clause 4(*ix*) of the agreement. That doctrine primarily rests on the principle that certain resources like air, sea, waters and the forests have such a great importance to the people as a whole that it would be wholly unjustified to make them a subject of private ownership. These resources are gift of nature, therefore, they should be freely available to everyone irrespective of one's status in life."

92. In *Reliance Natural Resources* (supra), it has been observed that even though the doctrine of public trust has been applied in cases dealing with environmental jurisprudence, "it has broader application". Referring to *M.C. Mehta* (supra), the Court held that: (SCC p. 65 para 116)

"116. ...It is the duty of the Government to provide complete protection to the natural resources as a trustee of the people at large."

93. The public trust doctrine is a specific doctrine with a particular domain and has to be applied carefully. It has been seriously debated before us as to whether the doctrine can be applied beyond the realm of environmental protection. Richard J. Lazarus in his article, "Changing Conceptions of Property and Sovereignty in Natural Resources: Questioning the Public Trust Doctrine", while expressing scepticism over the 'liberation' of the doctrine, makes the following observations:

"The strength of the public trust doctrine necessarily lies in its origins; navigable waters and submerged lands are the focus of the doctrine, and the basic trust interests in navigation, commerce, and fishing are the object of its guarantee of public access. Commentators and judges alike have made efforts to "liberate", "expand", and "modify" the doctrine's scope yet its basic focus remains relatively unchanged. Courts still repeatedly return to the doctrine's historical function to determine its present role. When the doctrine is expanded, more often than not the expansions require tortured constructions of the present rather than repudiations of the doctrine's past."

PUBLIC TRUST MANDATES A HIGH DEGREE OF JUDICIAL SCRUTINY

However, we feel that for the purpose of the present opinion, it is not necessary to delve deep into the issue as in *Intellectuals Forum* (supra), the main departure from the principle explained by Joseph. L. Sax in his Article "The Public Trust Doctrine in Natural Resource Law: Effective Judicial Intervention" is that public trust mandates a high degree of judicial scrutiny, an issue that we will anyway elaborately discuss while enunciating the mandate of article 14 of the Constitution.

94. We would also like to briskly deal with a similar argument made by Mr. Shanti Bhushan. The learned senior counsel submitted that the repository of sovereignty in our framework is the people of this country since the opening words of the Constitution read "We The People of India...do hereby adopt, enact and give to ourselves this Constitution," and therefore the government, as the agent of the Sovereign, the people, while alienating natural resources, must heed to judicial care and due process. *Firstly*, this Court has held in *Raja Ram Pal* v. *Hon'ble Speaker, Lok Sabha*, (2007) 3 SCC 184; Para 21 that the "Constitution is the *suprema lex* in this country" and

> "all organs of the State derive their authority, jurisdiction and powers from the Constitution and owe allegiance to it". (SCC p. 246 para 21)

Further, the notion that the Parliament is an agent of the people was squarely rebutted in *In re: Delhi Laws Act*, 1912 (supra), where it was observed that "the Legislature as a body cannot be seen to be an agency of the electorate as a whole" and "acts on its own authority or power which it derives from the Constitution".

BY RECKLESSNESS IN DISPOSAL OF NATURAL RESOURCES – NOT ONLY EXECUTIVE AND LEGISLATURE WOULD BE ANSWERABLE TO THE CONSTITUTION BUT JUDICIARY WOULD ALSO STEP IN

95. In *Municipal Corporation of Delhi* v. *Birla Cotton Spinning and Weaving Mills, Delhi*, [1968] 3 SCR 251 (AIR p. 1253 para 56) this Court held that "the doctrine that it (the Parliament) is a delegate of the people coloured certain American decision does not arise here" and that in fact the

> "Parliament which by a concentration of all the powers of legislation derived from all the three Legislative Lists becomes the most competent and potent Legislature it is possible to erect under our Constitution."

We however, appreciate the concern of Mr. Shanti Bhushan that the lack of any such power in the hands of the people must not be a sanction for recklessness during disposal of natural resources. The Legislature and the Executive are answerable to the Constitution and it is there where the Judiciary, the guardian of the Constitution, must find the contours to the powers of disposal of natural resources, especially article 14 and article 39(b).

ARTICLE 14 OF THE CONSTITUTION AND THE CASE LAW ON IT

Mandate of Article 14

96. Article 14 runs as follows:

> "**14. *Equality before law.***—The State shall not deny to any person equality before the law or the equal protection of the laws within the territory of India."

The underlying object of article 14 is to secure to all persons, citizens or non-citizens, the equality of status and opportunity referred to in the Preamble to our Constitution. The language of article 14 is couched in negative terms and is in form, an admonition addressed to the State. It does not directly purport to confer any right on any person as some of the other articles, *e.g.*, article 19, do. The right to equality before law is secured from all Legislative and Executive tyranny by way of discrimination since the language of article 14 uses the word "State" which as per article 12, includes the Executive organ; See *Basheshar Nath* v. *The Commissioner of Income-tax, Delhi and Rajasthan*, 1959 Supp (1) SCR 528.

> "13. ...Coming then to the language of the article it must be noted, first and foremost that this article is, in form, an admonition addressed to the State and does not directly purport to confer any right on any person as some of the other articles, *e.g.*, article 19, do. The obligation thus imposed on the State, no doubt, ensures for the benefit of all persons, for, as a necessary result of the operation of this Article, they all enjoy equality before the law. That is, however, the indirect, though necessary and inevitable, result of the mandate. The command of the Article is directed to the State and the reality of the obligation thus imposed on the State is the measure of the fundamental right which every person within the territory of India is to enjoy."

Besides, article 14 is expressed in absolute terms and its effect is not curtailed by restrictions like those imposed on article 19(1) by articles 19(2) to (6). However, notwithstanding the absence of such restrictions, certain tests have been devised through judicial decisions to test if article 14 has been violated or not.

97. For the first couple of decades after the establishment of this Court, the 'classification' test was adopted which allowed for a classification between entities as long as it was based on an intelligible differentia and displayed a rational nexus with the ultimate objective of the policy; *Budhan Choudhry* v. *State of Bihar*, AIR 1955 SC 191 referred to in *Ram Krishna Dalmiya* v. *Shri Justice S.R. Tendolkar*, [1959] 1 SCR 279 explained it in the following terms: (*Budhan Choudhry*, AIR p. 193 para 5)

> "5. ...It is now well-established that while article 14 forbids class legislation, it does not forbid reasonable classification for the purposes of legislation. In order, however, to pass the test of permissible classification two conditions must be fulfiled, namely, (i) that the classification must be founded on an intelligible differentia which distinguishes persons or things that are grouped together from others left out of the group and, (ii) that that differentia must have a rational relation to the object sought to be achieved by the statute in question. The classification may be founded on different bases, namely, geographical, or according to objects or occupations or the like. What is necessary is that there must be a nexus between the basis of classification and

the object of the Act under consideration. It is also well-established by the decisions of this Court that article 14 condemns discrimination not only by a substantive law but also by a law of procedure."

98. However, after the judgment of this Court in *E.P. Royappa* v. *State of Tamil Nadu*, (1974) 4 SCC 3 the 'arbitrariness' doctrine was introduced which dropped a pedantic approach towards equality and held the mere existence of arbitrariness as violative of article 14, however equal in its treatment. Justice Bhagwati (as his Lordship was then) articulated the dynamic nature of quality and borrowing from Shakespeare's Macbeth, said that the concept must not be "cribbed, cabined and confined" within doctrinaire limits: (SCC p. 38 para 85)

> "85. ...Now, what is the content and reach of this great equalising principle? It is a founding faith, to use the words of Bose. J., "a way of life", and it must not be subjected to a narrow pedantic or lexicographic approach. We cannot countenance any attempt to truncate its all-embracing scope and meaning, for to do so would be to violate its activist magnitude. Equality is a dynamic concept with many aspects and dimensions and it cannot be "cribbed, cabined and confined" within traditional and doctrinaire limits."

His Lordship went on to explain the length and breadth of article 14 in the following lucid words: [*Royappa* case (supra) SCC p. 381, para 85]

> "85... From a positivistic point of view, equality is antithetic to arbitrariness. In fact equality and arbitrariness are sworn enemies; one belongs to the rule of law in a republic while the other, to the whim and caprice of an absolute monarch. Where an act is arbitrary, it is implicit in it that it is unequal both according to political logic and constitutional law and is therefore violative of article 14, and if it effects any matter relating to public employment, it is also violative of article 16. Articles 14 and 16 strike at arbitrariness in State action and ensure fairness and equality of treatment. They require that State action must be based on valid relevant principles applicable alike to all similarly situate and it must not be guided by any extraneous or irrelevant considerations because that would be denial of equality. Where the operative reason for State action, as distinguished from motive inducing from the ante chamber of the mind, is not legitimate and relevant but is extraneous and outside the area of permissible considerations, it would amount to *mala fide* exercise of power and that is hit by articles 14 and 16. *Mala fide* exercise of power and arbitrariness are different lethal radiations emanating from the same vice: in fact the latter comprehends the former. Both are inhibited by articles 14 and 16."

99. Building upon his opinion delivered in *Royappa's* case (supra), Bhagwati, J., held in *Maneka Gandhi* v. *Union of India*, (1978) 1 SCC 248: (SCC p. 284, para 7)

> "7. ...The principle of reasonableness, which legally as well as philosophically, is an essential element of equality or non-arbitrariness pervades article 14 like a brooding omnipresence and the procedure contemplated by article 21 must answer the test of reasonableness in order to be in conformity with article 14. It must be "right and just and fair" and not arbitrary, fanciful or oppressive."

100. In *Ajay Hasia* v. *Khalid Mujib Sehravardi,* (1981) 1 SCC 722, this Court said that the 'arbitrariness' test was lying "latent and submerged" in the "simple but pregnant" form of article 14 and explained the switch from the 'classification' doctrine to the 'arbitrariness' doctrine in the following words: (SCC p. 741, para 16)

> "16...The doctrine of classification which is evolved by the courts is not paraphrase of article 14 nor is it the objective and end of that article. It is merely a judicial formula for determining whether the legislative or executive action in question is arbitrary and therefore constituting denial of equality. If the classification is not reasonable and does not satisfy the two conditions referred to above, the impugned legislative or executive action would plainly be arbitrary and the guarantee of equality under article 14 would be breached. Wherever therefore there is arbitrariness in State action whether it be of the legislature or of the executive or of an 'authority' under article 12, article 14 immediately springs into action and strikes down such State action. In fact, the concept of reasonableness and non-arbitrariness pervades the entire constitutional scheme and is a golden thread which runs through the whole of the fabric of the Constitution."

101. *Ramana Dayaram Shetty* v. *International Airports Authority of India,* (1979) 3 SCC 489: AIR 1979 SC 1628 explained the limitations of article 14 on the functioning of the Government as follows: (SCC p. 506, para 12)

> "12...It must, therefore, be taken to be the law that where the Government is dealing with the public, whether by way of giving jobs or entering into contracts or issuing quotas or licences or granting other forms of largesse, the Government cannot act arbitrarily at its sweet will and, like a private individual, deal with any person it pleases, but its action must be in conformity with standard or norms which is not arbitrary, irrational or irrelevant. The power or discretion of the Government in the matter of grant of largesse including award of jobs, contracts, quotas, licences, etc. must be confined and structured by rational, relevant and non-discriminatory standard or norm and if the Government departs from such standard or norm in any particular case or cases, the action of the Government would be liable to be struck down, unless it can be shown by the Government that the departure was not arbitrary, but was based on some valid principle which in itself was not irrational, unreasonable or discriminatory."

EQUALITY AND ARBITRARINESS ARE SWORN ENEMIES

102. Equality and arbitrariness were thus, declared "sworn enemies" and it was held that an arbitrary act would fall foul of the right to equality. Non-arbitrariness was equated with the rule of law about which Jeffrey Jowell in his seminal article "The Rule of Law Today" said:

> "Rule of law principle primarily applies to the power of implementation. It mainly represents a state of *procedural fairness.* When the rule of law is ignored by an official it may on occasion be enforced by courts."

103. As is evident from the above, the expressions 'arbitrariness' and 'unreasonableness' have been used interchangeably and in fact, one has been defined in terms of the other. More recently, in *Sharma Transport* v. *Government of Andhra Pradesh*, (2002) 2 SCC 188, this Court has observed thus: (SCC pp. 203-04 para 25)

> "25...In order to be described as arbitrary, it must be shown that it was not reasonable and manifestly arbitrary. The expression "arbitrarily" means: in an unreasonable manner, as fixed or done capriciously or at pleasure, without adequate determining principle, not founded in the nature of things, non-rational, not done or acting according to reason or judgment, depending on the will alone."

104. Further, even though the 'classification' doctrine was never overruled, it has found less favour with this Court as compared to the 'arbitrariness' doctrine. In *Om Kumar* v. *Union of India*, (2001) 2 SCC 386, this Court held thus: (SCC p. 409, para 59)

> "59. But, in *E.P. Royappa* v. *State of Tamil Nadu*, Bhagwati, J laid down another test for purposes of article 14. It was stated that if the administrative action was "arbitrary", it could be struck down under article 14. This principle is now uniformly followed in all courts more rigorously than the one based on classification. Arbitrary action by the administrator is described as one that is irrational and not based on sound reason. It is also described as one that is unreasonable."

105. However, this Court has also alerted against the arbitrary use of the 'arbitrariness' doctrine. Typically, laws are struck down for violating Part III of the Constitution of India, legislative incompetence or excessive delegation. However, since *Royappa's* case (supra), the doctrine has been loosely applied, this Court in *State of Andhra Pradesh* v. *McDowell and Co.*, (1996) 3 SCC 709, stressed on the need for an objective and scientific analysis of arbitrariness, especially while striking down legislations. Justice Jeevan Reddy observed: (SCC pp. 737-38, para 43)

> "43...The power of Parliament or for that matter, the State Legislatures is restricted in two ways. A law made by Parliament or the legislature can be struck down by courts on two grounds and two grounds alone, *viz.*, (i) lack of legislative competence; and (ii) violation of any of the fundamental rights guaranteed in Part III of the Constitution or of any other constitutional provision. There is no third ground. We do not wish to enter into a discussion of the concepts of procedural unreasonableness and substantive unreasonableness — concepts inspired by the decisions of United States Supreme Court. Even in USA, these concepts and in particular the concept of substantive due process have proved to be of unending controversy, the latest thinking tending towards a severe curtailment of this ground (substantive due process). The main criticism against the ground of substantive due process being that it seeks to set up the courts as arbiters of the wisdom of the Legislature in enacting the particular piece of legislation. It is enough for us to say that by whatever name it is characterised, the ground of invalidation must fall within the four corners of the two grounds mentioned above. In other words, say, if an enactment is challenged as violative of article 14, it can be struck down only if it is found that it is violative of the equality clause/equal

protection clause enshrined therein. Similarly, if an enactment is challenged as violative of any of the fundamental rights guaranteed by clauses (a) to (g) of article 19(1), it can be struck down only if it is found not saved by any of the clauses (s) to (6) of article 19 and so on. No enactment can be struck down by just saying that it is arbitrary* or unreasonable. Some or other constitutional infirmity has to be found before invalidating an Act. An enactment cannot be struck down on the ground that court thinks it unjustified. Parliament and the Legislatures, composed as they are of the representatives of the people, are supposed to know and be aware of the needs of the people and what is good and bad for them. The court cannot sit in judgment over their wisdom. In this connection, it should be remembered that even in the case of administrative action, the scope of judicial review is limited to three grounds, *viz.*, (i) unreasonableness, which can more appropriately be called irrationality, (ii) illegality, and (iii) procedural impropriety (see *Council of Civil Service Unions* v. *Minister for Civil Service*, 1985 AC 374 which decision has been accepted by this Court as well)."

106. Therefore, ever since the *Royappa* era, the conception of 'arbitrariness' has not undergone any significant change. Some decisions have commented on the doctrinal looseness of the arbitrariness test and tried keeping its folds within permissible boundaries. For instance, cases where legislation or rules have been struck down as being arbitrary in the sense of being unreasonable; See *Air India* v. *Nergesh Meerza*, (1981) 4 SCC 335, (SCC at pp. 372-373) only on the basis of "arbitrariness", as explained above, have been doubted in *McDowell's* case (supra). But otherwise, the subject-matter, content and tests for checking violation of article 14 have remained, more or less, unaltered.

STATE ACTION OF DISTRIBUTION OF LARGESSE, GRANT OF CONTRACTS OR ALLOTMENT OF LAND TO BE TESTED ON THE TOUCHSTONE OF ARTICLE 14

107. From a scrutiny of the trend of decisions it is clearly perceivable that the action of the State, whether it relates to distribution of largesse, grant of contracts or allotment of land, is to be tested on the touchstone of article 14 of the Constitution. A law may not be struck down for being arbitrary without the pointing out of a constitutional infirmity as *McDowell's* case (supra) has said. Therefore, a State action has to be tested for constitutional infirmities *qua* article 14 of the Constitution. The action has to be fair, reasonable, non-discriminatory, transparent, non-capricious, unbiased, without favouritism or nepotism, in pursuit of promotion of healthy competition and equitable treatment. It should conform to the norms which are rational, informed with reasons and guided by public interest, etc. All these principles are inherent in the fundamental conception of article 14. This is the mandate of article 14 of the Constitution of India.

---

* An expression used widely and rather indiscriminately — an expression of inherently imprecise import. The extensive use of this expression in India reminds one of what Frankfurter, J said in *Hattie Mae Tiller* v. *Atlantic Coast Line Railroad Co.*, 87 L ED 610: 318 US 54 (1943). "The phrase begins life as a literary expression; its felicity leads to its lazy repetition and repetition soon establishes it as a legal formula, undiscriminatingly used to express different and sometimes contradictory ideas", said the learned Judge."

'AUCTION' DOES NOT HAVE CONSTITUTIONAL MANDATE UNDER ARTICLE 14 OF THE CONSTITUTION

Whether 'Auction' has a Constitutional Mandate:

108. Such being the constitutional intent and effect of article 14, the question arises – can auction as a method of disposal of natural resources be declared a constitutional mandate under article 14 of the Constitution of India? We would unhesitatingly answer it in the negative since any other answer would be completely contrary to the scheme of article 14. *Firstly*, article 14 may imply positive and negative rights for an individual, but with respect to the State, it is only couched in negative terms; like an admonition against the State which prohibits the State from taking up actions that may be arbitrary, unreasonable, capricious or discriminatory. Article 14, therefore, is an injunction to the State against taking certain type of actions rather than commanding it to take particular steps. Reading the mandate of auction into its scheme would thus, be completely contrary to the intent of the article 14 apparent from its plain language.

109. *Secondly*, a constitutional mandate is an absolute principle that has to be applied in all situations; it cannot be applied in some and not tested in others. The absolute principle is then applied on a case by case basis to see which actions fulfil the requirements of the constitutional principle and which do not.

110. Justice K. Subba Rao in his lectures compiled in a book titled *"Some Constitutional Problems"*, critically analyzing the trends of Indian constitutional development, stated as follows:

> "If the Courts, instead of limiting the scope of the articles by construction, exercise their jurisdiction in appropriate cases, I have no doubt that the arbitrariness of the authorities will be minimised. If these authorities entrusted with the discretionary powers, realize that their illegal orders infringing the rights of the people would be quashed by the appropriate authority, they would rarely pass orders in excess of their powers. If they knew that not only the form but the substance of the orders would be scrutinized in open court, they would try to keep within their bounds. The fear of ventilation of grievance in public has always been an effective deterrent. The apprehension that the High Courts would be swamped with writs has no basis."

111. Similar sentiments were expressed by Justice K.K. Mathew in series of lectures incorporated in the form of a book titled *"Democracy, Equality and Freedom"* in which it is stated that "the strength of judicial review lies in case to case adjudication." This is precisely why this Court in His Holiness *Kesavananda Bharati Sripadagalvaru* v. *State of Kerala*, (1973) 4 SCC 225, quoting from an American decision, observed as follows: (SCC p. 873, para 1695)

> "1695...The reason why the expression "due process" has never been defined is that it embodies a concept of fairness which has to be decided with reference to the facts and circumstances of each case and also according to the mores for the time being in force in a society to which the concept has to be applied. As Justice Frankfurter said, "due process" is not a technical conception with a fixed content unrelated to time, place and circumstances (See *Joint Anti-Fascist Refugee Committee* v. *McGrath*, 341 US 123)".

112. Equality, therefore, cannot be limited to mean only auction, without testing it in every scenario. In *The State of West Bengal* v. *Anwar Ali Sarkar*, 1952 SCR 284 at pp. 297, this Court, quoting from *Kotch* v. *Pilot Commrs.*, 330 US 552, had held that; [*Anwar Ali Sarkar* case (supra) AIR p. 80, para 10]

> "10. ...The constitutional command for a State to afford equal protection of the laws sets a goal not attainable by the invention and application of a precise formula. This Court has never attempted that impossible task".

One cannot test the validity of a law with reference to the essential elements of ideal democracy, actually incorporated in the Constitution; See *Indira Nehru Gandhi* v. *Raj Narain*, 1975 (Supp) 1 SCC 198. The Courts are not at liberty to declare a statute void, because in their opinion it is opposed to the spirit of the Constitution. Courts cannot declare a limitation or constitutional requirement under the notion of having discovered some ideal norm. Further, a constitutional principle must not be limited to a precise formula but ought to be an abstract principle applied to precise situations. The repercussion of holding auction as a constitutional mandate would be the voiding of every action that deviates from it, including social endeavours, welfare schemes and promotional policies, even though CPIL itself has argued against the same, and asked for making auction mandatory only in the alienation of scarce natural resources meant for private and commercial business ventures. It would be odd to derive auction as a constitutional principle only for a limited set of situations from the wide and generic declaration of article 14. The strength of constitutional adjudication lies in case to case adjudication and therefore auction cannot be elevated to a constitutional mandate.

ARTICLE 39(b) OF THE CONSTITUTION DOES NOT WARRANT 'AUCTION' AS A CONSTITUTIONAL MANDATE

113. Finally, reading auction as a constitutional mandate would be impermissible because such an approach may distort another constitutional principle embodied in article 39(b). The said article enumerating certain principles of policy, to be followed by the State, reads as follows:

> "*39. Certain principles of policy to be followed by the State.*—The State shall, in particular, direct its policy towards securing—
>
> (a) … … …
>
> (b) that the ownership and control of the material resources of the community are so distributed as best to subserve the common good;
>
> … ……"

The disposal of natural resources is a facet of the use and distribution of such resources. Article 39(b) mandates that the ownership and control of natural resources should be so distributed so as to best subserve the common good. Article 37 provides that the provisions of Part IV shall not be enforceable by any Court, but the principles laid down therein are nevertheless fundamental in the governance of the country and it shall be the duty of the State to apply these principles in making laws.

ARTICLE 39(b) OF THE CONSTITUTION SPEAKS ABOUT THE 'OBJECT' OF DISTRIBUTION NOT ABOUT THE 'MEANS'

Therefore, this Article, in a sense, is a restriction on 'distribution' built into the Constitution. But the restriction is imposed on the object and not the means. The overarching and underlying principle governing 'distribution' is furtherance of common good. But for the achievement of that objective, the Constitution uses the generic word 'distribution'. Distribution has broad contours and cannot be limited to meaning only one method *i.e.*, auction. It envisages all such methods available for distribution/allocation of natural resources which ultimately subserve the "common good".

114. In *State of Tamil Nadu* v. *L. Abu Kavur Bai*, (1984) 1 SCC 515, this Court explained the broad-based concept of 'distribution' as follows: (SCC p. 548, para 89)

> "89. ...The word 'distribution' used in article 39(b) must be broadly construed so that a court may give full and comprehensive effect to the statutory intent contained in article 39(b). A narrow construction of the word 'distribution' might defeat or frustrate the very object which the article 39(b) seeks to subserve..."

After noting definitions of 'distribution' from different dictionaries, this Court held: (SCC p. 548, para 92)

> "92. It is obvious, therefore, that in view of the vast range of transactions contemplated by the word 'distribution' as mentioned in the dictionaries referred to above, it will not be correct to construe the word 'distribution' in a purely literal sense so as to mean only division of a particular kind or to particular persons. The words, apportionment, allotment, allocation, classification, clearly fall within the broad sweep of the word 'distribution'. So construed, the word 'distribution' as used in article 39(b) will include various facets, aspects, methods and terminology of a broad-based concept of distribution..."

MEANING OF THE WORD "DISTRIBUTE" IN ARTICLE 39(b) CANNOT BE CONTROLLED BY ARTICLE 14

115. It can thus, be seen from the afore-quoted paragraphs that the term "distribute" undoubtedly, has wide amplitude and encompasses all manners and methods of distribution, which would include classes, industries, regions, private and public sections, etc. Having regard to the basic nature of article 39(b), a narrower concept of equality under article 14 than that discussed above, may frustrate the broader concept of distribution, as conceived in article 39(b). There cannot, therefore, be a cavil that "common good' and "larger public interests" have to be regarded as constitutional reality deserving actualization.

MAXIMUM REVENUE COLLECTION DOES NOT ALWAYS SUBSERVE PUBLIC GOOD

116. Learned counsel for CPIL argued that revenue maximization during the sale or alienation of a natural resource for commercial exploitation is the only way of achieving public good since the revenue collected can be channelized to welfare policies and controlling the burgeoning deficit. According to the learned counsel, since the best way to maximize revenue is through the route of auction, it becomes a constitutional principle even under article 39(b). However, we are not persuaded to hold so. Auctions may be the best way of maximizing revenue but revenue maximization may not always be the best way to subserve public good. "Common good" is the sole guiding factor under article 39(b) for distribution of natural resources. It is the touchstone of testing whether any policy subserves the "common good" and if it does, irrespective of the means adopted, it is clearly in accordance with the principle enshrined in article 39(b).

117. In *The State of Karnataka* v. *Shri Ranganatha Reddy*, (1977) 4 SCC 471, Justice Krishna Iyer observed that keeping in mind the purpose of an article like 39(b), a broad rather than a narrow meaning should be given to the words of that article. In his inimitable style, his Lordship opined thus: (SCC p. 516, para 83)

> "83. Two conclusions strike us as quintessential. Part IV, especially article 39(b) and (c), is a futuristic mandate to the state with a message of transformation of the economic and social order. *Firstly*, such change calls for collaborative effort from all the legal institutions of the system: the Legislature, the Judiciary and the administrative machinery. *Secondly* and consequentially, loyalty to the high purpose of the Constitution, *viz.*, social and economic justice in the context of material want and utter inequalities on a massive scale, compels the court to ascribe expansive meaning to the pregnant words used with hopeful foresight, not to circumscribe their connotation into contradiction of the objectives inspiring the provision. To be Pharisaic towards the Constitution through ritualistic construction is to weaken the social-spiritual thrust of the founding fathers' dynamic faith."

118. In the case of *Bennett Coleman and Co.* v. *Union of India*, (1972) 2 SCC 788, it has been held by this Court that: (SCC p. 845 para 162)

> "162. ...the only norm which the Constitution furnishes for distribution of material resources of the community is elastic norm of common good."

Thus, "common good" is a norm in article 39(b) whose applicability was considered by this Court on the facts of the case. Even in that case, this Court did not evolve economic criteria of its own to achieve the goal of "common good" in article 39(b), which is part of the Directive Principles.

HOW THE TERM 'COMMON GOOD' USED IN ARTICLE 39(b) TO BE UNDERSTOOD

119. The norm of "common good" has to be understood and appreciated in a holistic manner. It is obvious that the manner in which the common good is best subserved is not a matter that can be measured by any constitutional yardstick – it would depend on the economic and political philosophy of the government. Revenue maximization is not the only way in which the common good can be subserved. Where revenue maximization is the object of a policy, being considered *qua* that resource at that point of time to be the best way to subserve the common good, auction would be one of the preferable methods, though not the only method. Where revenue maximization is not the object of a policy of distribution, the question of auction would not arise. Revenue considerations may assume secondary consideration to developmental considerations.

NEITHER ARTICLE 14 NOR ARTICLE 39(B) OF THE CONSTITUTION MANDATES DISPOSAL BY 'AUCTION'

120. Therefore, in conclusion, the submission that the mandate of article 14 is that any disposal of a natural resource for commercial use must be for revenue maximization, and thus by auction, is based neither on law nor on logic. There is no constitutional imperative in the matter of economic policies – article 14 does not pre-define any economic policy as a constitutional mandate. Even the mandate of 39(b) imposes no restrictions on the means adopted to subserve the public good and uses the broad term 'distribution', suggesting that the methodology of distribution is not fixed. Economic logic establishes that alienation/allocation of natural resources to the highest bidder may not necessarily be the only way to subserve the common good, and at times, may run counter to public good. Hence, it needs little emphasis that disposal of all natural resources through auctions is clearly not a constitutional mandate.

DISPOSAL OTHER THAN BY 'AUCTION' PERMISSIBLE

Legitimate Deviations from Auction

121. As a result, this Court has, on a number of occasions, delivered judgments directing means for disposal of natural resources other than auction for different resources in different circumstances. It would be profitable to refer to a few cases and appreciate the reasons this Court has adopted for deviating from the method of auction.

122. In *Kasturi Lal Lakshmi Reddy* v. *State of Jammu and Kashmir*, (1980) 4 SCC 1, while comparing the efficacy of auction in promoting a domestic industry, P.N. Bhagwati, J. observed: (SCC p. 20 para 22)

> "22. ...If the State were giving tapping contract simpliciter there can be no doubt that the State would have to auction or invite tenders for securing the highest price, subject, of course, to any other relevant overriding considerations of public weal or interest, but in a case like this where the State is allocating resources such as water, power, raw materials etc., for the purpose of encouraging setting up of industries within the State, we do not think the State is bound to advertise and tell the people that it wants a particular industry to be set up within the State and invite those interested to come up with proposals for the purpose. The State may choose to do so, if it thinks fit and in a given situation, it may even turn out to be advantageous for the State to do so, but if any private party comes before the State and offers to set up an industry, the State would not be committing breach of any constitutional or legal obligation if it negotiates with such party and agrees to provide resources and other facilities for the purpose of setting up the industry. The State is not obliged to tell such party: "Please wait I will first advertise, see whether any other offers are forthcoming and then after considering all offers, decide whether I should let you set up the industry"...The State must be free in such a case to negotiate with a private

entrepreneur with a view to inducing him to set up an industry within the State and if the State enters into a contract with such entrepreneur for providing resources and other facilities for setting up an industry, the contract cannot be assailed as invalid so long as the State has acted *bona fide*, reasonably and in public interest. If the terms and conditions of the contract or the surrounding circumstances show that the State has acted *mala fide* or out of improper or corrupt motive or in order to promote the private interests of someone at the cost of the State, the court will undoubtedly interfere and strike down State action as arbitrary, unreasonable or contrary to public interest. But so long as the State action is *bona fide* and reasonable, the court will not interfere merely on the ground that no advertisement was given or publicity made or tenders invited."

123. In *Sachidanand Pandey* (supra) after noticing *Kasturi Lal's* case (supra), it was concluded as under: (*Sachidanand Pandey* case SCC p. 330 para 40)

"40. On a consideration of the relevant cases cited at the Bar the following propositions may be taken as well established: State-owned or public-owned property is not to be dealt with at the absolute discretion of the Executive. Certain precepts and principles have to be observed. Public interest is the paramount consideration. One of the methods of securing the public interest, when it is considered necessary to dispose of a property, is to sell the property by public auction or by inviting tenders. Though that is the ordinary rule, it is not an invariable rule. There may be situations where there are compelling reasons necessitating departure from the rule but then the reasons for the departure must be rational and should not be suggestive of discrimination. Appearance of public justice is as important as doing justice. Nothing should be done which gives an appearance of bias, jobbery or nepotism."

124. In *Haji T.M. Hassan Rawther* v. *Kerala Financial Corporation*, (1988) 1 SCC 166, after an exhaustive review of the law including the decisions in *Kasturi Lal* (supra) and *Sachidanand Pandey* (supra), it was held that public disposal of State owned properties is not the only rule. It was, *inter alia*, observed that: [*Haji T.M. Hassan* case, SCC p. 173 para 14]

"14. The public property owned by the State or by any Instrumentality of the State should be generally sold by public auction or by inviting tenders. This Court has been insisting upon that rule, not only to get the highest price for the property but also to ensure fairness in the activities of the State and public authorities. They should undoubtedly act fairly. Their actions should be legitimate. Their dealings should be aboveboard. Their transactions should be without aversion or affection. Nothing should be suggestive of discrimination. Nothing should be done by them which gives an impression of bias, favouritism or nepotism. Ordinarily these factors would be absent if the matter is brought to public auction or sale by tenders. That is why the court repeatedly stated and reiterated that the State-owned properties are required to be disposed of publicly. But that is not the only rule. As O. Chinnappa Reddy, J. observed "that though that is the ordinary rule, it is not an invariable rule". There may be situations necessitating departure from the rule, but then such instances must be justified by compulsions and not by compromise. It must be justified by compelling reasons and not by just convenience."

Here, the Court added to the previous decisions and said that a blithe deviation from public disposal of resources would not be tolerable; such a deviation must be justified by compelling reasons and not by just convenience.

125. In *M.P. Oil Extraction* v. *State of Madhya Pradesh*, (1997) 7 SCC 592, this Court held as follows: (SCC pp. 612-13, para 45)

> "45. Although to ensure fair play and transparency in State action, distribution of largesse by inviting open tenders or by public auction is desirable, it cannot be held that in no case distribution of such largesse by negotiation is permissible. In the instant case, as a policy decision protective measure by entering into agreements with selected industrial units for assured supply of sal seeds at concessional rate has been taken by the government. The rate of royalty has also been fixed on some accepted principle of pricing formula as will be indicated hereafter. Hence, distribution or allotment of sal seeds at the determined royalty to the respondents and other units covered by the agreements cannot be assailed. It is to be appreciated that in this case, distribution by public auction or by open tender may not achieve the purpose of the policy of protective measure by way of supply of sal seeds at concessional rate of royalty to the industrial units covered by the agreements on being selected on valid and objective considerations."

126. In *Netai Bag* v. *State of West Bengal*, (2000) 8 SCC 262, this Court observed that non-floating of tenders or not holding of public auction would, not in all cases, be deemed to be the result of the exercise of the Executive power in an arbitrary manner. It was stated: (SCC p. 275, para 19)

> "19. ...There cannot be any dispute with the proposition that generally when any State land is intended to be transferred or the State largesse decided to be conferred, resort should be had to public auction or transfer by way of inviting tenders from the people. That would be a sure method of guaranteeing compliance with the mandate of article 14 of the Constitution. Non-floating of tenders or not holding of public auction would not in all cases be deemed to be the result of the exercise of the Executive power in an arbitrary manner. Making an exception to the general rule could be justified by the State Executive, if challenged in appropriate proceedings. The constitutional courts cannot be expected to presume the alleged irregularities, illegalities or unconstitutionality nor the courts can substitute their opinion for the *bona fide* opinion of the State Executive. The courts are not concerned with the ultimate decision but only with the fairness of the decision-making process."

This Court once again pointed out that there can be exceptions from auction; the ultimate test is only that of fairness of the decision making process and compliance with article 14 of the Constitution.

127. In *M & T Consultants, Secunderabad* v. *S.Y. Nawab*, (2003) 8 SCC 100, this Court again reiterated that non-floating of tenders does not always lead to the conclusion that the exercise of the power is arbitrary: (SCC p. 116, para 17)

"17. A careful and dispassionate assessment and consideration of the materials placed on record does not leave any reasonable impression, on the peculiar facts and circumstances of this case, that anything obnoxious which requires either public criticism or condemnation by courts of law had taken place. It is by now well-settled that non-floating of tenders or absence of public auction or invitation alone is no sufficient reason to castigate the move or an action of a public authority as either arbitrary or unreasonable or amounting to *mala fide* or improper exercise or improper abuse of power by the authority concerned. Courts have always leaned in favour of sufficient latitude being left with the authorities to adopt their own techniques of management of projects with concomitant economic expediencies depending upon the exigencies of a situation guided by appropriate financial policy in the best interests of the authority motivated by public interest as well in undertaking such ventures."

128. In *Villianur Iyarkkai Padukappu Maiyam* v. *Union of India*, (2009) 7 SCC 561, a three-Judge Bench of this Court was concerned with the development of the Port of Pondicherry where a contractor had been selected without floating a tender or holding public auction. It was held as under: (SCC pp. 604-05 paras 164 and 171)

"164. The plea raised by the learned counsel for the appellants that the Government of Pondicherry was arbitrary and unreasonable in switching the whole public tender process into a system of personal selection and, therefore, the appeals should be accepted, is devoid of merits. It is well-settled that non-floating of tenders or not holding of public auction would not in all cases be deemed to be the result of the exercise of the Executive power in an arbitrary manner.

* * * * *

171. In a case like this where the State is allocating resources such as water, power, raw materials, etc., for the purpose of encouraging development of the port, this Court does not think that the State is bound to advertise and tell the people that it wants development of the port in a particular manner and invite those interested to come up with proposals for the purpose. The State may choose to do so if it thinks fit and in a given situation it may turn out to be advantageous for the State to do so, but if any private party comes before the State and offers to develop the port, the State would not be committing breach of any constitutional obligation if it negotiates with such a party and agrees to provide resources and other facilities for the purpose of development of the port."

HOWEVER MEANS ADOPTED FOR DISPOSAL MUST NOT BE ARBITRARY OR UNFAIR

129. Hence, it is manifest that there is no constitutional mandate in favour of auction under article 14. The Government has repeatedly deviated from the course of auction and this Court has repeatedly upheld such actions. The judiciary tests such deviations on the limited scope of arbitrariness and fairness under article 14 and its role is limited to that extent. Essentially, whenever, the object of policy is anything but revenue maximization, the Executive is seen to adopt methods other than auction.

MANDATORY AUCTION MAY BE CONTRARY TO ECONOMIC LOGIC ALSO

130. A fortiori, besides legal logic, mandatory auction may be contrary to economic logic as well. Different resources may require different treatment. Very often, exploration and exploitation contracts are bundled together due to the requirement of heavy capital in the discovery of natural resources. A concern would risk undertaking such exploration and incur heavy costs only if it was assured utilization of the resource discovered; a prudent business venture, would not like to incur the high costs involved in exploration activities and then compete for that resource in an open auction. The logic is similar to that applied in patents. Firms are given incentives to invest in research and development with the promise of exclusive access to the market for the sale of that invention. Such an approach is economically and legally sound and sometimes necessary to spur research and development. Similarly, bundling exploration and exploitation contracts may be necessary to spur growth in a specific industry.

131. Similar deviation from auction cannot be ruled out when the object of a State policy is to promote domestic development of an industry, like in *Kasturi Lal's* case, discussed above. However, these examples are purely illustrative in order to demonstrate that auction cannot be the sole criteria for alienation of all natural resources.

DISPOSAL METHOD OTHER THAN 'AUCTION' IS NOT NECESSARILY ABUSED

Potential of Abuse

132. It was also argued that even if the method of auction is not a mandate under Article 14, it must be the only permissible method, due to the susceptibility of other methods to abuse. This argument, in our view, is contrary to an established position of law on the subject cemented through a catena of decisions.

133. In *R.K. Garg* v. *Union of India*, (1981) 4 SCC 675, Justice P.N. Bhagwati, speaking for a Constitution Bench of five learned Judges, held: (SCC p. 691 para 8)

> "8....The Court must always remember that "legislation is directed to practical problems, that the economic mechanism is highly sensitive and complex, that many problems are singular and contingent, that laws are not abstract propositions and do not relate to abstract units and are not to be measured by abstract symmetry"; "that exact wisdom and nice adaption of remedy are not always possible" and that "judgment is largely a prophecy based on meager and uninterpreted experience". Every legislation particularly in economic matters is essentially empiric and it is based on experimentation or what one may call trial and error method and therefore it cannot provide for all possible situations or anticipate all possible abuses. There may be crudities and inequities in complicated experimental economic legislation but on that account alone it cannot be struck down as invalid. The courts cannot, as pointed out by the United States Supreme Court in *Secretary of Agriculture* v. *Central Reig Refining Company*, 94 L Ed 381: 338 US 604 (1950) be converted into tribunals for relief from such crudities and inequities. There may even be

possibilities of abuse, but that too cannot of itself be a ground for invalidating the legislation, because it is not possible for any legislature to anticipate as if by some divine prescience, distortions and abuses of its legislation which may be made by those subject to its provisions and to provide against such distortions and abuses. Indeed, howsoever great may be the care bestowed on its framing, it is difficult to conceive of a legislation which is not capable of being abused by perverted human ingenuity. The Court must therefore adjudge the constitutionality of such legislation by the generality of its provisions and not by its crudities or inequities or by the possibilities of abuse of any of its provisions. If any crudities, inequities or possibilities of abuse come to light, the Legislature can always step in and enact suitable amendatory legislation. That is the essence of pragmatic approach which must guide and inspire the Legislature in dealing with complex economic issues."

134. Then again, in *D.K. Trivedi and Sons* v. *State of Gujarat,* (1986) Supp SCC 20, while upholding the constitutional validity of section 15(1) of the MMRD Act, this Court explained the principle in the following words: (SCC pp. 60-61, para 50)

"50. Where a statute confers discretionary powers upon the executive or an administrative authority, the validity or constitutionality of such power cannot be judged on the assumption that the executive or such authority will act in an arbitrary manner in the exercise of the discretion conferred upon it. If the executive or the administrative authority acts in an arbitrary manner, its action would be bad in law and liable to be struck down by the courts but the possibility of abuse of power or arbitrary exercise of power cannot invalidate the statute conferring the power or the power which has been conferred by it."

135. Therefore, a potential for abuse cannot be the basis for striking down a method as *ultra vires* the Constitution. It is the actual abuse itself that must be brought before the Court for being tested on the anvil of constitutional provisions. In fact, it may be said that even auction has a potential of abuse, like any other method of allocation, but that cannot be the basis of declaring it as an unconstitutional methodology either. These drawbacks include cartelization, "winners curse" (the phenomenon by which a bidder bids a higher, unrealistic and unexecutable price just to surpass the competition; or where a bidder, in case of multiple auctions, bids for all the resources and ends up winning licenses for exploitation of more resources than he can pragmatically execute), etc. However, all the same, auction cannot be called *ultra vires* for the said reasons and continues to be an attractive and preferred means of disposal of natural resources especially when revenue maximization is a priority. Therefore, neither auction, nor any other method of disposal can be held *ultra vires* the Constitution, merely because of a potential abuse.

POLICY DECISIONS ESPECIALLY ECONOMIC POLICY DECISIONS AND PRICING NORMALLY NOT OPEN TO JUDICIAL REVIEW

Judicial Review of Policy Decision

136. The learned Attorney-General also argued that dictating a method of distribution for natural resources violates the age old established principle of non-interference by the Judiciary in policy matters. Even though the contours of the power of judicial review of policy decisions has become a trite subject, as the Courts have repeatedly delivered opinions on it, we wish to reiterate some of the principles in brief, especially with regard to economic policy choices and pricing.

137. One of the earliest pronouncements on the subject came from this Court in *Rustom Cavasjee Cooper* v. *Union of India*, (1970) 1 SCC 248, (commonly known as "Bank Nationalization case") wherein this Court held that it is not the forum where conflicting policy claims may be debated; it is only required to adjudicate the legality of a measure which has little to do with relative merits of different political and economic theories. The Court observed: (SCC p. 294, para 63)

> "63. This Court is not the forum in which these conflicting claims may be debated. Whether there is a genuine need for banking facility in the rural sector, whether certain classes of the community are deprived of the benefit of the resources of the banking industry, whether administration by the Government of the commercial banking sector will not prove beneficial to the community and will lead to rigidity in the administration, whether the Government administration will eschew the profit-motive, and even if it be eschewed, there will accrue substantial benefits to the public, whether an undue accent on banking as a means of social regeneration, especially in the backward areas, is a doctrinaire approach to a rational order of priorities for attaining the national objectives enshrined in our Constitution, and whether the policy followed by the Government in office or the policy propounded by its opponents may reasonably attain the national objectives are matters which have little relevance in determining the legality of the measure. It is again not for this Court to consider the relative merits of the different political theories or economic policies. The Parliament has under Entry 45, List I the power to legislate in respect of banking and other commercial activities of the named banks necessarily incidental thereto: it has the power to legislate for acquiring the undertaking of the named banks under Entry 42, List III. Whether by the exercise of the power vested in the Reserve Bank under the pre-existing laws, results could be achieved which it is the object of the Act to achieve, is, in our judgment, not relevant in considering whether the Act amounts to abuse of legislative power. This Court has the power to strike down a law on the ground of want of authority, but the Court will not sit in appeal over the policy of the Parliament in enacting a law. The Court cannot find fault with the Act merely on the ground that it is inadvisable to take over the undertaking of banks which, it is said by the petitioner, by thrift and efficient management had set up an impressive and efficient business organisation serving large sectors of industry."

138. In *R.K. Garg* (supra), this Court even observed that greater judicial deference must be shown towards a law relating to economic activities due to the complexity of economic problems and their fulfilment through a methodology of trial and error. As noted above, it was also clarified that the fact that an economic legislation may be troubled by crudities, inequities, uncertainties or the possibility of abuse cannot be the basis for striking it down. The following observations which refer to a couple of American Supreme Court decisions are a limpid enunciation on the subject: (SCC pp. 690-91 para 8)

"8. Another rule of equal importance is that laws relating to economic activities should be viewed with greater latitude than laws touching civil rights such as freedom of speech, religion etc. It has been said by no less a person than Holmes, J., that the legislature should be allowed some play in the joints, because it has to deal with complex problems which do not admit of solution through any doctrinaire or strait-jacket formula and this is particularly true in case of legislation dealing with economic matters, where, having regard to the nature of the problems required to be dealt with, greater play in the joints has to be allowed to the legislature. The court should feel more inclined to give judicial deference to legislative judgment in the field of economic regulation than in other areas where fundamental human rights are involved. Nowhere has this admonition been more felicitously expressed than in *Morey* v. *Doud*, 354 US 457 (1957) where Frankfurter, J., said in his inimitable style:

'In the utilities, tax and economic regulation cases, there are good reasons for judicial self-restraint if not judicial deference to legislative judgment. The legislature after all has the affirmative responsibility. The courts have only the power to destroy, not to reconstruct. When these are added to the complexity of economic regulation, the uncertainty, the liability to error, the bewildering conflict of the experts, and the number of times the judges have been overruled by events – self limitation can be seen to be the path to judicial wisdom and institutional prestige and stability'..."

139. In *Premium Granites* v. *State of Tamil Nadu*, (1994) 2 SCC 691 this Court clarified that it is the validity of a law and not its efficacy that can be challenged: (SCC p. 715, para 54)

"54. It is not the domain of the court to embark upon unchartered ocean of public policy in an exercise to consider as to whether a particular public policy is wise or a better public policy can be evolved. Such exercise must be left to the discretion of the executive and legislative authorities as the case may be. The court is called upon to consider the validity of a public policy only when a challenge is made that such policy decision infringes fundamental rights guaranteed by the Constitution of India or any other statutory right..."

140. In *Delhi Science Forum* v. *Union of India*, (1996) 2 SCC 405, a Bench of three learned Judges of this Court, while rejecting a claim against the opening up of the telecom sector reiterated that the forum for debate and discourse over the merits and demerits of a policy is the Parliament. It restated that the services of this Court are not sought till the legality of the policy is disputed, and further, that no direction can be given or be expected from the courts, unless while implementing such policies, there is violation or infringement of any of the constitutional or statutory provisions. It held thus: (SCC p. 413 para 7)

"7. What has been said in respect of legislations is applicable even in respect of policies which have been adopted by Parliament. They cannot be tested in Court of Law. The Courts cannot express their opinion as to whether at a particular juncture or under a particular situation prevailing in the country any such national policy should have been adopted or not. There may be views and views, opinions and opinions which may be shared and believed by citizens of the country including the representatives of the people in Parliament. But that has to be sorted out in Parliament which has to approve such policies..."

141. In *BALCO Employees' Union (Regd.)* v. *Union of India*, (2002) 2 SCC 333, this Court further pointed out that the Court ought to stay away from judicial review of efficacy of policy matters, not only because the same is beyond its jurisdiction, but also because it lacks the necessary expertise required for such a task. Affirming the previous views of this Court, the Court observed that while dealing with economic legislations, the Courts, while not jettisoning its jurisdiction to curb arbitrary action or unconstitutional legislation, should interfere only in those cases where the view reflected in the legislation is not possible to be taken at all. The Court went on to emphasize that unless the economic decision, based on economic expediencies, is demonstrated to be so violative of constitutional or legal limits on power or so abhorrent to reason, that the courts would decline to interfere.

142. In *BALCO* (supra), the Court took notice of the judgment in *Peerless General Finance and Investment Co. Ltd.* v. *Reserve Bank of India*, (1992) 2 SCC 343 and observed that some matters like price fixation are based on such uncertainties and dynamics that even experts face difficulty in making correct projections, making it all the more necessary for this Court to exercise non-interference:

> "31. The function of the Court is to see that lawful authority is not abused but not to appropriate to itself the task entrusted to that authority. It is well-settled that a public body invested with statutory powers must take care not to exceed or abuse its power. It must keep within the limits of the authority committed to it. It must act in good faith and it must act reasonably. Courts are not to interfere with economic policy which is the function of experts. It is not the function of the courts to sit in judgment over matters of economic policy and it must necessarily be left to the expert bodies. In such matters even experts can seriously and doubtlessly differ. Courts cannot be expected to decide them without even the aid of experts."

143. In an earlier case in *Prag Ice & Oil Mills* v. *Union of India*, (1978) 3 SCC 459, this Court had observed as under: (SCC p. 478, Para 24)

> "24. ...We do not think that it is the function of this Court or of any court to sit in judgment over such matters of economic policy as must necessarily be left to the government of the day to decide. Many of them, as a measure of price fixation must necessarily be, are matters of prediction of ultimate results on which even experts can seriously err and doubtlessly by differ. Courts can certainly not be expected to decide them without even the aid of experts."

144. In *State of Madhya Pradesh* v. *Narmada Bachao Andolan*, (2011) 7 SCC 639, this Court said that the judiciary cannot engage in an exercise of comparative analysis over the fairness, logical or scientific basis, or wisdom of a policy. It held that: (SCC pp. 670-71 para 36)

> "36. The Court cannot strike down a policy decision taken by the Government merely because it feels that another decision would have been fairer, or more scientific or logical, or wiser. The wisdom and advisability of

the policies are ordinarily not amenable to judicial review unless the policies are contrary to statutory or constitutional provisions or arbitrary or irrational or an abuse of power."

CHAWLA COMMITTEE REPORT ALSO RECOMMENDED 'AUCTION' OF NATURAL RESOURCES BUT NOT YET ACCEPTED BY THE GOVERNMENT

145. Mr. Subramanian Swamy also brought to our notice a Report on Allocation of Natural Resources, prepared by a Committee, chaired by Mr. Ashok Chawla (hereinafter referred to as the "Chawla Committee Report"), which has produced a copious conceptual framework for the Government of India on the allocation and pricing of scarce natural resources *viz.* coal, minerals, petroleum, natural gas, spectrum, forests, land and water. He averred to observations of the report in favour of auction as a means of disposal. However, since the opinion rendered in the Chawla Committee Report is pending acceptance by the Government, it would be inappropriate for us to place judicial reliance on it. Besides, the Report conducts an economic, and not legal, analysis of the means of disposal of natural resources. The purpose of this Reference would be best served if this Court gave a constitutional answer rather than economic one.

THOUGH AUCTION IS NOT THE CONSTITUTIONAL MANDATE BUT LEGALITY AND CONSTITUTIONALITY OF THE METHOD ADOPTED CAN BE EXAMINED BY THE COURTS

146. To summarize in the context of the present Reference, it needs to be emphasized that this Court cannot conduct a comparative study of the various methods of distribution of natural resources and suggest the most efficacious mode, if there is one universal efficacious method in the first place. It respects the mandate and wisdom of the executive for such matters. The methodology pertaining to disposal of natural resources is clearly an economic policy. It entails intricate economic choices and the Court lacks the necessary expertise to make them. As has been repeatedly said, it cannot, and shall not, be the endeavour of this Court to evaluate the efficacy of auction *vis-à-vis* other methods of disposal of natural resources. The Court cannot mandate one method to be followed in all facts and circumstances. Therefore, auction, an economic choice of disposal of natural resources, is not a constitutional mandate. We may, however, hasten to add that the Court can test the legality and constitutionality of these methods. When questioned, the Courts are entitled to analyse the legal validity of different means of distribution and give a constitutional answer as to which methods are *ultra vires* and *intra vires* the provisions of the Constitution. Nevertheless, it cannot and will not compare which policy is fairer than the other, but, if a policy or law is patently unfair to the extent that it falls foul of the fairness requirement of article 14 of the Constitution, the Court would not hesitate in striking it down.

VALUATION – A SCIENCE BASED ON SEVERAL DYNAMIC VARIABLES

147. Finally, market price, in economics, is an index of the value that a market prescribes to a goods. However, this valuation is a function of several dynamic variables; it is a science and not a law. Auction is just one of the several price discovery mechanisms. Since multiple variables are involved in such valuations, auction or any other form of competitive bidding, cannot constitute even an economic mandate, much less a constitutional mandate.

AUCTION OF NATURAL RESOURCES IS PREFERABLE BUT NOT THE ONLY OPTION

148. In our opinion, auction despite being a more preferable method of alienation/allotment of natural resources, cannot be held to be a constitutional requirement or limitation for alienation of all natural resources and therefore, every method other than auction cannot be struck down as *ultra-vires* the constitutional mandate.

IF THE POLICY DECISION IS NOT BACKED BY SOCIAL PURPOSE – CAN INCUR WRATH OF ARTICLE 14 OF THE CONSTITUTION

149. Regard being had to the aforesaid precepts, we have opined that auction as a mode cannot be conferred the status of a constitutional principle. Alienation of natural resources is a policy-decision, and the means adopted for the same are thus, Executive prerogatives. However, when such a policy decision is not backed by a social or welfare purpose, and precious and scarce natural resources are alienated for commercial pursuits of profit maximizing private entrepreneurs, adoption of means other than those that are competitive and maximize revenue may be arbitrary and face the wrath of article 14 of the Constitution. Hence, rather than prescribing or proscribing a method, we believe, a judicial scrutiny of methods of disposal of natural resources should depend on the facts and circumstances of each case, in consonance with the principles which we have culled out above. Failing which, the Court, in exercise of power of judicial review, shall term the Executive action as arbitrary, unfair, unreasonable and capricious due to its antimony with article 14 of the Constitution.

ANSWER TO FIRST SET OF FIVE QUESTIONS IS THAT AUCTION IS NOT THE ONLY OPTION IN ALL THE CASES

150. In conclusion, our answer to the first set of five questions is that auctions are not the only permissible method for disposal of all natural resources across all sectors and in all circumstances.

OTHER QUESTIONS TOUCH THE MERITS OF 2G JUDGMENT – HENCE DECLINED TO ANSWER

151. As regards the remaining questions, we feel that answer to these questions would have a direct bearing on the mode of alienation of Spectrum and therefore, in light of the statement by the learned Attorney-General that the Government is not questioning the correctness of judgment in the 2G case, we respectfully decline to answer these questions. The Presidential Reference is answered accordingly.

TRANSMIT THIS OPINION

152. This opinion shall be transmitted to the President in accordance with the procedure prescribed in Part V of the Supreme Court Rules, 1966.

....

(S.H. Kapadia, CJI)

....

(D.K. Jain, J.)

....

(Dipak Misra, J.)

....

(Ranjan Gogoi, J.)
NEW DELHI;
SEPTEMBER 27, 2012.

Author's Note: Hon'ble Mr. Justice Jagdish Singh Khehar, Hon'ble member of the Constitutional Bench though concurred with the main opinion but His Lordship recorded separate reasons expressing the view about what care should be taken if disposal of natural resources is not by way of auction.

MAIN OPINION PERUSED – CONCURRED – SEPARATE REASONING
JAGDISH SINGH KHEHAR, J.

153. I have had the privilege of perusing the opinion rendered by my esteemed brother, D.K. Jain, J. Every bit of the opinion (which shall hereinafter be referred to by me, as the "main opinion") is based on settled propositions of law declared by this Court. There can, therefore, be no question of any disagreement therewith. I fully endorse the opinion expressed therein.

TENOR OF THE FIRST QUESTION OF THE PRESIDENTIAL REFERENCE HAS OTHER FACETS ALSO – HENCE THE CAUSE FOR RECORDING SEPARATE REASONS

154. The first question posed in the Presidential reference, is in fact the reason, for my having to record, some other nuances on the subject whereof advice has been sought. The first question in the Presidential reference requires the Supreme Court to tender advice on, "Whether the only permissible method for disposal of all natural resources across all sectors and in all circumstances, is by the conduct of auctions?".

155. It is of utmost importance to understand, the tenor of the first question in the Presidential reference. Take for instance a hypothetical situation where, the legality of 100 instances of disposal of different types of natural resources is taken up for consideration. If the first question is taken in its literal sense, as to whether the method of disposal of all natural resources in all circumstances is by auction alone, then, even if 99 out of the aforesaid 100 different natural resources are such, which can only be disposed of by way of auction, the answer to the first question would still be in the negative. This answer in the negative would give the erroneous impression, that it is not necessary to dispose of natural resources by way of auction. Surely, the Presidential reference has not been made, to seek such an innocuous advice.

CENTRAL GOVERNMENT KNOWS THAT CERTAIN NATURAL RESOURCES CAN BE DISPOSED OF ONLY BY AUCTION – FOR EXAMPLE COAL

The instant reference has been made despite the Central Government being alive to the fact, that there are natural resources which can only be disposed of by way of auction. A mining lease for coal under section 11A of the Mines and Minerals (Development and Regulation) Act, 1957 can be granted, only by way of selection through auction by competitive bidding. Furthermore, the learned Attorney-General for India informed us, about a conscious decision having been taken by the Central Government to henceforth allot spectrum only through competitive bidding by way of auction. Such instances can be multiplied. It is therefore obvious, that Government is alive to the fact, that disposal of some natural resources have to be made only by auction.

THE FIRST QUESTION DOES NOT SEEK LITERAL ANSWER

If that is so, the first question in the reference does not seek a literal response. The first question must be understood to seek this Court's opinion on whether there are circumstances in which natural resources ought to be disposed of only by auction. Tendering an opinion, without a response to this facet of the matter, would not make the seeker of advice, any wiser. It is this aspect alone, which will be the main subject of focus of my instant opinion.

AUCTION ADMITTEDLY LEADS TO MAXIMUM REVENUE

156. Before venturing into the area of consideration expressed in the foregoing paragraph,it is necessary to record, that there was extensive debate during the course of hearing, on whether, maximization of revenue must be the sole permissible consideration, for disposal of all natural resources, across all sectors and in all circumstances. During the course of this debate, the learned Attorney-General for India acknowledged, that auction by way of competitive bidding, was certainly an indisputable means, by which maximization of revenue returns is assured. It is not as if, one would like to bind the learned Attorney-General to the acquiesced proposition. During the course of the days and weeks of erudite debate, learned counsel emphasized, that disposal of assets by processes of tender, tender-cum-auction and auction, could assure maximization of revenue returns. Of course, there are a large variety of tender and auction processes, each one with its own nuances. And we were informed, that a rightful choice, would assure maximization of revenue returns.

THE WORD 'AUCTION' IS USED IN THIS OPINION AS A MEANS TO MAXIMISE REVENUE

The term "auction" expressed in my instant opinion, may therefore be read as a means to maximize revenue returns, irrespective of whether the means adopted should technically and correctly be described as tender, tender-cum-auction, or auction.

PRESENT CONTROVERSY DEPICTS CONFLICT BETWEEN INDIVIDUAL RIGHTS AND SOCIETAL OR PLURAL RIGHTS – REMEDY UNDER ARTICLE 14 IS AVAILABLE

157. The concept of equality before the law and equal protection of the laws, emerges from the fundamental right expressed in article 14 of the Constitution of India. Equality is a definite concept. The variation in its understanding may at best have reference to the maturity and evolution of the nation's thought. To start with, breach of equality was a plea advanced by individuals claiming fair treatment. Challenges were raised also on account of discriminatory treatment. Equality was sought by those more meritorious, when benefits were bestowed on those with lesser caliber. Gradually, judicial intervention came to be sought for equitable treatment, even for a section of the society put together. A jurisdiction, which in due course, came to be described as public interest litigation. It all started with a demand for the basic rights for respectable human existence. Over the years, the concept of determination of societal rights, has traversed into different directions and avenues. So much so, that now rights in equity, sometimes even present situations of conflict between individual rights and societal rights. The present adjudication can be stated to be a dispute of such nature. In a maturing society, individual rights and plural rights have to be balanced, so that the oscillating pendulum of rights, fairly and equally, recognizes their respective parameters. For a country like India, the pendulum must be understood to balance the rights of one citizen on the one side, and 1241491960 (the present estimated population of India) citizens of the country on the other. The true effect of the article 14 of the Constitution of India is to provide equality before the law and equal protection of the laws not only with reference to individual rights, but also by ensuring that its citizens on the other side of the balance are likewise not deprived of their right to equality before the law, and their right to equal protection of the laws.

AN INDIVIDUAL CANNOT BECOME RICH AT THE COST OF THE COUNTRY

An individual citizen cannot be a beneficiary, at the cost of the country (the remaining 1241491960 citizens) *i.e.*, the plurality. Enriching one at the cost of all others would amount to deprivation to the plurality *i.e.*, the nation itself. The gist of the first question in the Presidential reference, raises the issue whether ownership rights over the nation's natural resources, vest in the citizens of the country. An answer to the instant issue in turn would determine, whether or not it is imperative for the executive while formulating a policy for the disposal of natural resources, to ensure that it subserves public good and public interest.

PUBLIC INTEREST LITIGATION IS INVOKED TO SAFEGUARD NATION'S WEALTH AND NATURAL RESOURCES

158. The introduction and acceptance of public interest litigation as a jurisprudential concept is a matter of extensive debate in India, and even more than that, outside India. This concept brings into focus the rights of the plurality (as against individual's right) specially when the plurality is, for one or the other reason, not in a position to seek redressal of its grievances. This inadequacy may not always emerge from financial constrains. It may sometimes arise out of lack of awareness. At other times merely from the overwhelming might of executive authority. The jurisprudential thought in this country, after the emergence of public interest litigation, is seeking to strike a balance between individual rights and the rights of the plurality. After all, all natural resources are the nation's collective wealth. This Court has had the occasion over the last few decades, to determine rights of citizens with reference to natural resources. The right of an individual citizen to those assets, as also, the rights of the remaining citizens of the country, have now emerged on opposite sides in a common litigation. One will endeavour to delineate the legal position expressed in decisions rendered by this Court, on issues relatable to disposal of resources by the State, to determine whether the instant issue stands settled, by law declared by this Court.

DISPOSAL OF NATURAL RESOURCES MUST NOT BE ARBITRARY – IT SHOULD SUBSERVE PUBLIC GOOD AND PUBLIC INTEREST – SHOULD BE TRANSPARENT AND FAIR

159. First of all reference was made to the decision of this Court in *S.G. Jaisinghani* v. *Union of India*, AIR 1967 SC 1427, wherein this Court observed as under: (AIR p. 1434, para 14)

> "*14. In this context it is important to emphasize that the absence of arbitrary power is the first essential of the rule of law upon which our whole constitutional system is based. In a system governed by rule of law, discretion, when conferred upon executive authorities, must be confined within clearly defined limits. The rule of law from this point of view means that decisions should be made by the application of known principles and rules and, in general, such decisions should be predictable and the citizen should know where he is.* If a decision is taken without any principle or without any rule it is unpredictable and such a decision is the antithesis of a decision taken in accordance with the Rule of law; *See* Dicey – *Law of the Constitution* – 10th Edn., Introduction cx. "Law has reached its finest moments," stated Douglas, J. in *United States* v. *Wunderlich*, (1951) 342 US 98, "when it has freed man from the unlimited discretion of some ruler. Where discretion, is absolute, man has always suffered." It is in this sense that the rule of law may be said to be the sworn enemy of caprice. Discretion, as Lord Mansfield slated it in classic terms in the case of *John Wilkes*, (1770) 4 Burr 2528 (2539) "means sound discretion guided by law. It must be governed by Rule, not by humour: it must not be arbitrary, vague, and fanciful."
>
> (emphasis is mine)

In the aforesaid case, it came to be emphasized that Executive action should have clearly defined limits and should be predictable. In other words, the man on the street should know why the decision has been taken in favour of a particular party. What came to be impressed upon was, that lack of transparency in the decision-making process would render it arbitrary.

GOVERNMENT FUNCTIONARIES CANNOT GAIN AT THE COST OF THE NATION OR ITS PEOPLE

160. Also cited for our consideration was the judgment in *Rashbihari Panda* v. *State of Orissa*, (1969) 1 SCC 414. In this case it was canvassed on behalf of the appellants, that the machinery devised by the Government for sale of *Kendu* leaves in which they had acquired a trade monopoly, was violative of the fundamental rights guaranteed under articles 14 and 19(1)(*g*) of the Constitution. It was pointed out, that in the scheme of events the purchasers were merely nominees of the agents. It is also contended, that after the Supreme Court had struck down the policy under which the agents were to carry on business in *Kendu* leaves on their own and to make profit for themselves, the Government to help their party-men set up a body of persons who were to be purchasers to whom the monopoly sales were to be made at concessional rates and that the benefit which would have otherwise been earned by the State would now get diverted to those purchasers. It was held: (SCC pp. 420-22 paras 15-23)

"15. Section 10 of the Act is a counterpart of section 3 and authorises the Government to sell or otherwise dispose of *Kendu* leaves in such manner as the Government may direct. If the monopoly of purchasing *Kendu* leaves by section 3 is valid, insofar as it is intended to be administered only for the benefit of the State, the sale or disposal of *Kendu* leaves by the Government must also be in the public interest and not to serve the private interest of any person or class of persons. *It is true that it is for the Government, having regard to all the circumstances, to act as a prudent businessman would, and to sell or otherwise dispose of Kendu leaves purchased under the monopoly acquired under section 3, but the profit resulting from the sale must be for the public benefit and not for private gain.* Section 11 which provides that out of the net profits derived by the Government from the trade in Kendu leaves an amount not less than one half is to be paid to the Samitis and Gram Panchayats emphasises the concept that the machinery of sale or disposal of Kendu leaves must also be quashed to serve the public interest. *If the scheme of disposal creates a class of middlemen who would purchase from the Government Kendu leaves at concessional rates and would earn large profits disproportionate to the nature of the service rendered or duty performed by them , it cannot claim the protection of article 19(6)(ii).*

16. Section 10 leaves the method of sale or disposal of Kendu leaves to the Government as they think fit. *The action of the Government if conceived and executed in the interest of the general public is not open to judicial scrutiny. But it is not given to the Government thereby to create a monopoly in favour of third parties from their own monopoly.*

17. Validity of the schemes adopted by the Government of Orissa for sale of *Kendu* leaves must be adjudged in the light of article 19(1)(*g*) and Article 14. Instead of inviting tenders the Government offered to certain old contractors the option to purchase *Kendu* leaves for the year 1968 on terms mentioned therein. The reason suggested by the Government that these offers were made because the purchasers had carried out their obligations in the previous year to the satisfaction of the Government is not of any significance. *From the affidavit filed by the State Government it appears that the price fetched at public auctions before and after January 1968, were much higher than the prices at which Kendu leaves were offered to the old contractors.* The Government realised that the scheme of offering to enter into contracts with the old licensees and to renew their terms was open to grave objection, since it sought arbitrarily to exclude many persons interested in the trade. The Government then decided to invite offers for advance purchases of *Kendu* leaves but restricted the invitation to those individuals who had carried out the contracts in the previous year without default and to the satisfaction of the Government. By the new scheme instead of the Government making an offer, the existing contractors were given the exclusive right to make offers to purchase *Kendu* leaves. But insofar as the right to make tenders for the purchase of *Kendu* leaves was restricted to those persons who had obtained contracts in the previous year the scheme was open to the same objection. *The right to make offers being open to a limited class of persons it effectively shut out all other persons carrying on trade in Kendu leaves and also new entrants into that business. It was ex facie discriminatory, and imposed*

unreasonable restrictions upon the right of persons other than existing contractors to carry on business. In our view, both the schemes evolved by the Government were violative of the fundamental right of the petitioners under article 19(1)(g) and article 14 because the schemes gave rise to a monopoly in the trade in Kendu leaves to certain traders, and singled out other traders for discriminatory treatment.

18. The classification based on the circumstance that certain existing contractors had carried out their obligations in the previous year regularly and to the satisfaction of the Government is not based on any real and substantial distinction bearing a just and reasonable relation to the object sought to be achieved *i.e.,* effective execution of the monopoly in the public interest. Exclusion of all persons interested in the trade, who were not in the previous year licensees is *ex facie* arbitrary, it had no direct relation to the object of preventing exploitation of pluckers and growers of *Kendu* leaves, nor had it any just or reasonable relation to the securing of the full benefit from the trade to the State.

19. *Validity of the law by which the State assumed the monopoly to trade in a given commodity has to be judged by the test whether the entire benefit arising therefrom is to enure to the State, and the monopoly is not used as a cloak for conferring private benefit upon a limited class of persons.* The scheme adopted by the Government first of offering to enter into contracts with certain named licensees, and later inviting tenders from licensees who had in the previous year carried out their contracts satisfactorily is liable to be adjudged void on the ground that it unreasonably excludes traders in *Kendu* leaves from carrying on their business. The scheme of selling *Kendu* leaves to selected purchasers or of accepting tenders only from a specified class of purchasers was not "integrally and essentially" connected with the creation of the monopoly and was not on the view taken by this Court in *Akadasi Padhan* case, (1963) Supp 2 SCC 691, protected by article 19(6)(*ii*): it had therefore to satisfy the requirement of reasonableness under the first part of article 19(6). No attempt was made to support the scheme on the ground that it imposed reasonable restrictions on the fundamental rights of the traders to carry on business in *Kendu* leaves. The High Court also did not consider whether the restrictions imposed upon persons excluded from the benefit of trading satisfied the test of reasonableness under the first part of article 19(6). The High Court examined the problem from the angle whether the action of the State Government was vitiated on account of any oblique motive, and whether it was such as a prudent person carrying on business may adopt.

20. *No explanation has been attempted on behalf of the State as to why an offer made by a well-known manufacturer of bidis interested in the trade to purchase the entire crop of Kendu leaves for the year 1968 for rupees three crores was turned down. If the interests of the State alone were to be taken into consideration, the State stood to gain more than rupees one crore by accepting that offer.* We are not suggesting that merely because that offer was made, the Government was bound to accept it. The Government had to consider, as prudent businessman, whether, having regard to the circumstances, it should accept the offer, especially in the light of the financial position of the offeror, the security which he was willing to

give and the effect which the acceptance of the offer may have on the other traders and the general public interest.

21. The learned Judges of the High Court have observed that in their view the exercise of the discretion was not shown to be arbitrary, nor was the action shown to be lacking in *bona fides*. But that conclusion is open to criticism that the Government is not shown to have considered the prevailing prices of *Kendu* leaves about the time when offers were made, the estimated crop of *Kendu* leaves, the conditions in the market and the likelihood of offerers at higher prices carrying out their obligations, and whether it was in the interests of the State to invite tenders in the open market from all persons whether they had or had not taken contracts in the previous year. If the Government was anxious to ensure due performance by those who submitted tenders for purchase of *Kendu* leaves, it was open to the Government to devise adequate safeguards in that behalf. *In our judgment, the plea that the action of the Government was* bona fide *cannot be an effective answer to a claim made by a citizen that his fundamental rights were infringed by the action of the Government,* nor can the claim of the petitioners be defeated on the plea that the Government in adopting the impugned scheme committed an error of judgment.

22. That plea would have assisted the Government if the action was in law valid and the objection was that the Government erred in the exercise of its discretion. It is unnecessary in the circumstances to consider whether the Government acted in the interest of their party-men and to increase party funds in devising the schemes for sale of *Kendu* leaves in 1968.

23. During the pendency of these proceedings the entire year for which the contracts were given has expired. The persons to whom the contracts were given are not before us, and we cannot declare the contracts which had been entered into by the Government for the sale of *Kendu* leaves for the year 1968 unlawful in these proceedings. *Counsel for the appellants agrees that it would be sufficient if it be directed that the tenders for purchase of Kendu leaves be invited by the Government in the next season from all persons interested in the trade. We trust that in accepting tenders, the State Government will act in the interest of the general public and not of any class of traders so that in the next season the State may get the entire benefit of the monopoly in the trade in Kendu leaves and no disproportionate share thereof may be diverted to any private agency.* Subject to these observations we make no further order in the petitions out of which these appeals arise."

(emphasis is mine)

GOVERNMENT MUST ACT AS PRUDENT BUSINESSMAN – PROFITS SHOULD BE FOR, PUBLIC BENEFIT

161. A perusal of the observations made by this Court reveal, that the Government must act as a prudent businessman, and that, the profit earned should be for public benefit and not for private gains. A plea of reasonable restriction raised under article 19(6)of the Constitution of India to save the governmental action was rejected on the ground that the scheme created middlemen who would earn large disproportionate profits. This Court also held the action to be discriminatory because it excluded others like the petitioners from the zone of consideration. Finally, a direction came to be issued by this Court requiring the Government to act in the interest of the general public and to invite tenders so that the State may earn the entire benefit in a manner that no disproportionate profits are diverted to any private agency.

GOVERNMENT POLICY MUST BE BASED ON THE PRINCIPLE OF EQUALITY REASONABLENESS RATIONALITY NON-ARBITRARINESS AND NOT ON EXTRANEOUS CONSIDERATIONS

162. Reliance was also placed on *Ramana Dayaram Shetty* v. *International Airports Authority of India*, (1979) 3 SCC 489, wherein this Court held as under: (SCC pp. 511-12 and 514 paras 21-22)

> "21. This rule also flows directly from the doctrine of equality embodied in article 14. It is now well-settled as a result of the decisions of this Court in *E.P. Royappa* v. *State of Tamil Nadu*, (1974) 4 SCC 3, and *Maneka Gandhi* v. *Union of India*, (1978) 1 SCC 248, *that article 14 strikes at arbitrariness in State action and ensures fairness and equality of treatment. It requires that State action must not be arbitrary but must be based on some rational and relevant principle which is non-discriminatory: it must not be guided by any extraneous or irrelevant considerations, because that would be denial of equality.* The principle of reasonableness and rationality which is legally as well as philosophically an essential element of equality or non-arbitrariness is projected by article 14 and it must characterize every State action, whether it be under authority of law or in exercise of executive power without making of law. *The State cannot, therefore, act arbitrarily in entering into relationship, contractual or otherwise with a third party, but its action must conform to some standard or norm which is rational and non-discriminatory.* This principle was recognised and applied by a Bench of this Court presided over by Ray, C.J., in *Erusian Equipment and Chemicals Ltd.* v. *State of West Bengal* (supra) where the learned Chief Justice pointed out that— (SCC pp. 74-75, paras 12, 14, 17)
>
>> "12. ...*the State can carry on executive function by making a law or without making a law. The exercise of such powers and functions in trade by the State is subject to Part III of the Constitution. Article 14 speaks of equality before the law and equal protection of the laws. Equality of opportunity should apply to matters of public contracts. The State has the right to trade. The State has there the duty to observe equality. An ordinary individual can choose not to deal with any person. The Government cannot choose to exclude persons by discrimination.* The order of blacklisting has the effect of depriving a person of equality of opportunity in the matter of public contract. A person who is on the approved list is unable to enter into advantageous relations with the Government because of the order of blacklisting....
>>
>> 14. A citizen has a right to claim equal treatment to enter into a contract which may be proper, necessary and essential to his lawful calling....
>>
>> 17. It is true that neither the petitioner nor the respondent has any right to enter into a contract but they are entitled to equal treatment with others who offer tender or quotations for the purchase of the goods".

It must, therefore, follow was a necessary corollary from the principle of equality enshrined in article 14 that though the State is entitled to refuse to enter into relationship with any one, yet if it does so, it cannot arbitrarily choose any person it likes for entering into such relationship and discriminate between persons similarly circumstanced, but it must act in conformity with some standard or principle which meets the test of reasonableness and non-discrimination and any departure from such standard or principle would be invalid unless it can be supported or justified on some rational and non-discriminatory ground.

22. It is interesting to find that this rule was recognised and applied by a Constitution Bench of this Court in a case of sale of *kendu* leaves by the Government of Orissa in *Rashbihari Panda* v. *State of Orissa,* (1969) 1 SCC 414..... This decision wholly supports the view we are taking in regard to the applicability of the rule against arbitrariness in State action."

(emphasis is mine)

163. An analysis of the aforesaid determination by this Court *Rashbihari Panda* (supra) would lead to the inference that the State has the right to trade. In executing public contracts in its trading activity the State must be guided by relevant principles, and not by extraneous or irrelevant consideration. The same should be based on reasonableness and rationality as well as non-arbitrariness. It came to be concluded, that the State while entering into a contractual relationship, was bound to maintain the standards referred to above. And any departure from the said standards would be invalid unless the same is supported by good reasons

STATE MUST ACT TO BEST SUBSERVE THE COMMON GOOD AND IN PUBLIC INTEREST

164. Our attention was also invited to the decision rendered in *Kasturi Lal Lakshmi Reddy* v. *State of Jammu and Kashmir,* (1980) 4 SCC 1, wherein the factual background as well as, the legal position came to be expressed in paragraph 19 of the judgment which is being set out below: (SCC pp. 16-18)

"19. It is clear from the backdrop of the facts and circumstances in which the impugned Order came to be made and the terms and conditions set out in the impugned Order that it was not a tapping contract simpliciter which was intended to be given to the second respondents. The second respondents wanted to be assured of regular supply of raw material in the shape of resin before they could decide to set up a factory within the State and it was for the purpose of ensuring supply of such raw material that the impugned Order was made giving tapping contract to the second respondents. It was really by way of allocation of raw material for running the factory that the impugned Order was passed. The terms of the impugned Order show beyond doubt that the second respondents were under an obligation to set up a factory within the State and that 3500 metric tonnes of resin which was permitted to be retained by the second respondents out of the resin extracted by them was required to be utilised in the factory to be set up by them and it was provided that no part of the resin extracted should be allowed to be removed outside the State. The whole object of the impugned Order was to make available 3500 metric tonnes of resin to the second respondents for the purpose of running the factory to be set up by them.

The advantage to the State was that a new factory for manufacture of resin, turpentine oil and other derivatives would come up within its territories offering more job opportunities to the people of the State increasing their prosperity and augmenting the State revenues and in addition the State would be assured of a definite supply of at least 1500 metric tonnes of resin for itself without any financial involvement or risk and with this additional quantity of resin available to it, it would be able to set up another factory creating more employment opportunities and, in fact, as the counter-affidavit of Ghulam Rasul, Under- Secretary to the Government filed on behalf of the State shows the Government lost no time in taking steps to set up a public sector resin distillation plant in a far-flung area of the State, namely, Sundarbani, in Rajouri District.

Moreover, the State would be able to secure extraction of resin from these inaccessible areas on the best possible terms instead of allowing them to remain unexploited or given over at ridiculously low royalty. We cannot accept the contention of the petitioners that under the impugned Order a huge benefit was conferred on the second respondents at the cost of the State. It is clear from the terms of the impugned Order that the second respondents would have to extract at least 5000 metric tonnes of resin from the blazes allotted to them in order to be entitled to retain 3500 metric tonnes. The counter-affidavit of Ghulam Rasul on behalf of the first respondent and Guran Devaya on behalf of the second respondents show that the estimated cost of extraction and collection of resin from these inaccessible areas would be at the least Rs. 175 per quintal, though according to Guran Devaya it would be in the neighbourhood of Rs. 200 per quintal, but even if we take the cost at the minimum figure of Rs. 175 per quintal, the total cost of extraction and collection would come to Rs. 87,50,000 and on this investment of Rs.87,50,000 required to be made by the second respondents the amount of interest at the prevailing bank rate would work out to about Rs. 13,00,000. Now, as against this expenditure of Rs. 87,50,000 plus Rs. 13,00,000 the second respondents would be entitled to claim from the State, in respect of 1500 metric tonnes of resin to be delivered to it only at the rate sanctioned by the Forest Department for the adjoining accessible forests which were being worked on wage-contract basis.

It is stated in the counter-affidavits of Ghulam Rasul and Guran Devaya and this statement is not seriously challenged on behalf of the petitioners, that the cost of extraction and collection as sanctioned by the Forest Department for the adjoining accessible forests given on wage-contract basis in the year 1978-79 was Rs. 114 per quintal and the second respondents would, thus, be entitled to claim from the State no more than Rs. 114 per quintal in respect of 1500 metric tonnes to be delivered to it and apart from bearing the difference between the actual cost of extraction and collection and the amount received from the State at the rate of Rs. 114 per quintal in respect of 1500 metric tonnes, the second respondents would have to pay the price of the remaining 3500 metric tonnes to be retained by them at the rate of Rs. 350 per quintal. On this reckoning, the cost of 3500 metric tonnes to be retained by the second respondents would work out at Rs. 474 per quintal. The result would be that under the impugned Order the State would get 1500 metric tonnes of resin at the rate of Rs. 114 per quintal while the second respondents would have to pay at the rate of Rs. 474 per quintal for the balance of 3500 metric tones retained by them.

Obviously, a large benefit would accrue to the State under the impugned Order. If the State were to get the blazes in these inaccessible areas tapped through wage contract, the minimum cost would be Rs. 175 per quintal, without taking into account the additional expenditure on account of interest, but under the impugned Order the State would get 1500 metric tonnes of resin at a greatly reduced rate of Rs. 114 per quintal without any risk or hazard. The State would also receive for 3500 metric tonnes of resin retained by the second respondents price or royalty at the rate of Rs. 474 per quintal which would be much higher than the rate of Rs. 260 per quintal at which the State was allotting resin to medium scale industrial units and the rate of Rs. 320 per quintal at which it was allotting resin to small scale units within the State.

It is difficult to see how on these facts the impugned Order could be said to be disadvantageous to the State or in any way favouring the second respondents at the cost of the State. The argument of the petitioners was that at the auctions held in December, 1978, January, 1979 and April, 1979, the price of resin realised was as much as Rs. 484, Rs. 520 and Rs. 700 per quintal respectively and when the market price was so high, it was improper and contrary to public interest on the part of the State to sell resin to the second respondents at the rate of Rs. 320 per quintal under the impugned Order. This argument, plausible though it may seem, is fallacious because it does not take into account the policy of the State not to allow export of resin outside its territories but to allot it only for use in factories set up within the State.

It is obvious that, in view of this policy, no resin would be auctioned by the State and there would be no question of sale of resin in the open market and in this situation, it would be totally irrelevant to import the concept of market price with reference to which the adequacy of the price charged by the State to the 2nd respondents could be judged. If the State were simply selling resin, there can be no doubt that the State must endeavour to obtain the highest price subject, of course, to any other overriding considerations of public interest and in that event, its action in giving resin to a private individual at a lesser price would be arbitrary and contrary to public interest. But, where the State has, as a matter of policy, stopped selling resin to outsiders and decided to allot it only to industries set up within the State for the purpose of encouraging industrialisation, there can be no scope for complaint that the State is giving resin at a lesser price than that which could be obtained in the open market. The yardstick of price in the open market would be wholly inept, because in view of the State policy, there would be no question of any resin being sold in the open market. The object of the State in such a case is not to earn revenue from sale of resin, but to promote the setting up of industries within the State.

Moreover, the prices realized at the auctions held in December, 1978, January, 1979 and April, 1979 did not reflect the correct and genuine price of resin, because by the time these auctions came to be held, it had become known that the State had taken a policy decision to ban export of resin from its territories with effect from 1979-80 and the prices realised at the auctions were therefore scarcity prices. In fact, the auction held in April, 1979 was the last auction in the State and since it was known that in future no resin would be available for sale by auction in the open market to outsiders, an unduly high price of Rs. 700 per quintal was offered by the factory owners having their factories outside the State, so that they would get as much resin for the purpose of feeding their industrial units for some time. The counter-affidavits show that, in fact, the average sale price of resin realised during the year 1978-79 was only Rs. 433 per quintal and as compared to this price, the 2nd respondents were required to pay price or royalty at a higher rate of Rs. 474 per quintal for 3500 metric tonnes of resin to be retained by them under the impugned Order. It is in the circumstances impossible to see how it can at all be said that any benefit was conferred on the second respondents at the cost of the State. The first head of challenge against the impugned Order must, therefore, be rejected." *(emphasis is mine)*

165. An examination of the factual position of the controversy dealt with in the judgment extracted above reveals, that the State Government formulated a policy to set up a factory within the State, which would result in creation of more job opportunities for the people of the State. The setting up of the said factory would assure the State of atleast 1500 metric tones of resin without any financial involvement. This in turn would enable the State to set up another factory creating further employment opportunities for the people of the State.

It is, therefore, that this Court concluded that the impugned order passed by the State in favour of the second respondent could not be said to be disadvantageous to the State and favouring the second respondent. In a manner of understanding, this Court found no infirmity in the impugned order passed by the State Government because the State Government had given effect to a policy which would "best subserve the common good" of the inhabitants of the State (as in article 39(b) of the Constitution of India) while assigning a material resource, though no reference was made to article 39(b) of the Constitution of India in the judgment. What is also of importance is, that this Court expressly noticed, that if the State Government was simply selling resin, it was obliged to obtain the highest possible price.

JUDICIAL REVIEW MAINTAINABLE WHERE ILLEGALITY, IRRATIONALITY AND PROCEDURAL IMPROPRIETY ARE INVOLVED

166. Reference was then made to *Dwarkadas Marfatia and Sons* v. *Board of Trustees of the Port of Bombay*, (1989) 3 SCC 293, wherein the case of the respondent was, that in his evidence it had been mentioned by Katara that the plot had been allotted to Dhanji Mavji since it was the policy of the Bombay Port Trust to allot a reconstituted plot to a person occupying a major portion of such plot. It was further asserted, that there was no challenge to this evidence in cross-examination. It was also asserted, that there was no evidence on the alleged policy of the Port Trust of giving plots on joint tenancy to all the occupants. According to learned counsel for the respondent, in the letters addressed by the Port Trust and in the letters by and on behalf of the appellant and/or their alleged associate concerns they had specifically admitted, that there was a policy of the Port Trust to allot plots to the occupants of the major portions thereof and in fact a grievance was made by them, that in accordance with the said policy of the Bombay Port Trust, a plot was not being allotted to the associates of the appellant.

In that view of the matter it was contended, that the issue whether the plot should have been given on joint tenancy or not, could not have been gone into by the court in exercise of its jurisdiction of judicial review. Reliance was placed on the observations of Lord Justice Diplock in *Council of Civil Service Unions* v. *Minister for the Civil Service,* (1984) 3 All ER 935, 950, where the learned Lord Justice classified 3 grounds subject to control of judicial review, namely, illegality, irrationality and procedural impropriety. In the aforesaid factual background this Court concluded as under: [*Dwarkadas* case (supra) SCC pp. 304, 306 & 310 paras 21, 28 & 37]

> "21. We are unable to accept the submissions. *Being a public body even in respect of its dealing with its tenant, it must act in public interest, and an infraction of that duty is amenable to examination either in civil suit or in writ jurisdiction.*
>
> ….. …..
>
> 28. Learned Additional Solicitor-General reiterated on behalf of the respondent that no question of *mala fide* had been alleged or proved in these proceedings. Factually, he is right. *But it has to be borne in mind that governmental policy would be invalid as lacking in public interest, unreasonable or contrary to the professed standards and this is different from the fact that it was not done* bona fide. It is true as learned Additional Solicitor-General contended that there is always a presumption that a governmental action is reasonable and in public interest. It is for the party challenging its validity to show that the action is unreasonable, arbitrary or contrary to the professed norms or not informed by public interest, and the burden is a heavy one.
>
> ….. ……
>
> 37. As we look upon the facts of this case, *there was an implied obligation in respect of dealings with the tenants/occupants of the Port Trust authority to act in public interest/purpose. That requirement is fulfiled if it is demonstrated that the Port Trust authorities have acted in pursuance of a policy which is referable to public purpose.* Once that norm is established whether that policy is the best policy or whether another policy was possible, is not relevant for consideration. It is, therefore, not necessary for our present purposes to dwell on the question whether the obligation of the Port Trust authorities to act in pursuance of a public purpose was a public law purpose or a private law purpose. *Under the constitutional scheme of this country the Port Trust authorities were required by relevant law to act in pursuance of public purpose. We are satisfied that they have proceeded to so act."* (emphasis is mine).

In the instant matter, even though the controversy pertained to a tenancy issue, this Court held, that a public body was bound to act in public interest.

ARTICLE 14 OF THE CONSTITUTION AND PRINCIPLES OF FAIR, JUST AND REASONABLENESS ARE APPLICABLE EVEN IN CONTRACTUAL AGREEMENTS

167. In chronological sequence, learned counsel then cited *Mahabir Auto Stores* v. *Indian Oil Corporation*, (1990) 3 SCC 752. Relevant observations made therein, with reference to the present controversy, are being placed below: (SCC pp. 760-61, 763-64 paras 12, 17-20 & 23)

"12. It is well-settled that every action of the State or an instrumentality of the State in exercise of its executive power, must be informed by reason. In appropriate cases, actions uninformed by reason may be questioned as arbitrary in proceedings under article 226 or article 32 of the Constitution. Reliance in this connection may be placed on the observations of this Court in *Radha Krishna Agarwal* v. *State of Bihar*, (1977) 3 SCC 457. It appears to us, at the outset, that in the facts and circumstances of the case, the respondent company IOC is an organ of the State or an instrumentality of the State as contemplated under article 12 of the Constitution.

The State acts in its Executive power under article 298 of the Constitution in entering or not entering in contracts with individual parties. Article 14 of the Constitution would be applicable to those exercises of power.

Therefore, the action of State organ under article 14 can be checked. See *Radha Krishna Agarwal* v. *State of Bihar* at p. 462, but article 14 of the Constitution cannot and has not been construed as a charter for judicial review of State action after the contract has been entered into, to call upon the State to account for its actions in its manifold activities by stating reasons for such actions. In a situation of this nature certain activities of the respondent company which constituted State under article 12 of the Constitution may be in certain circumstances subject to article 14 of the Constitution in entering or not entering into contracts and must be reasonable and taken only upon lawful and relevant consideration; it depends upon facts and circumstances of a particular transaction whether hearing is necessary and reasons have to be stated. In case any right conferred on the citizens which is sought to be interfered, such action is subject to article 14 of the Constitution, and must be reasonable and can be taken only upon lawful and relevant grounds of public interest.

Where there is arbitrariness in State action of this type of entering or not entering into contracts, article 14 springs up and judicial review strikes such an action down. Every action of the State executive authority must be subject to rule of law and must be informed by reason. So, whatever be the activity of the public authority, in such monopoly or semi-monopoly dealings, it should meet the test of article 14 of the Constitution. If a governmental action even in the matters of entering or not entering into contracts, fails to satisfy the test of reasonableness, the same would be unreasonable.

In this connection reference may be made to *E.P. Royappa* v. *State of Tamil Nadu*, (1974) 4 SCC 3; *Maneka Gandhi* v. *Union of India*, (1978)1 SCC 248; *Ajay Hasia* v. *Khalid Mujib Sehravardi*, (1981) 1 SCC 722; *R.D. Shetty* v. *International Airports Authority of India*, (1979) 3 SCC 489, and also *Dwarkadas Marfatia and Sons* v. *Board of Trustees of the Port of Bombay*, (1989) 3 SCC 293. It appears to us that rule of reason and rule against arbitrariness and discrimination, rules of fair play and natural justice are part of the rule of law applicable in situation or action by State instrumentality in dealing with citizens in a situation like the present one.

Even though the rights of the citizens are in the nature of contractual rights, the manner, the method and motive of a decision of entering or not entering into a contract, are subject to judicial review on the touchstone of relevance and reasonableness, fair play, natural justice, equality and non-discrimination in the type of the transactions and nature of the dealing as in the present case.

….. …..

17. We are of the opinion that in all such cases whether public law or private law rights are involved, depends upon the facts and circumstances of the case. The dichotomy between rights and remedies cannot be obliterated by any strait-jacket formula. It has to be examined in each particular case. Mr. Salve sought to urge that there are certain cases under article 14 of arbitrary exercise of such "power" and not cases of exercise of a "right" arising either under a contract or under a statute. We are of the opinion that that would depend upon the factual matrix.

18. Having considered the facts and circumstances of the case and the nature of the contentions and the dealing between the parties and in view of the present state of law, we are of the opinion that decision of the State/public authority under article 298 of the Constitution, is an administrative decision and can be impeached on the ground that the decision is arbitrary or violative of article 14 of the Constitution of India on any of the grounds available in public law field.

It appears to us that in respect of corporation like IOC when without informing the parties concerned, as in the case of the appellant-firm herein on alleged change of policy and on that basis action to seek to bring to an end to course of transaction over 18 years involving large amounts of money is not fair action, especially in view of the monopolistic nature of the power of the respondent in this field.

Therefore, it is necessary to reiterate that even in the field of public law, the relevant persons concerned or to be affected, should be taken into confidence. Whether and in what circumstances that confidence should be taken into consideration cannot be laid down on any strait-jacket basis. It depends on the nature of the right involved and nature of the power sought to be exercised in a particular situation. It is true that there is discrimination between power and right but whether the State or the instrumentality of a State has the right to function in public field or private field is a matter which, in our opinion, depends upon the facts and circumstances of the situation, but such exercise of power cannot be dealt with by the State or the instrumentality of the State without informing and taking into confidence,the party whose rights and powers are affected or sought to be affected, into confidence. In such situations most often people feel aggrieved by exclusion of knowledge if not taken into confidence.

19. Such transaction should continue as an administrative decision with the organ of the State. *It may be contractual or statutory but in a situation of transaction between the parties for nearly two decades, such procedure should be followed which will be reasonable, fair and just, that is, the process which normally be accepted (sic is expected) to be followed by an organ of the State and that process must be conscious and all those affected should be taken into confidence.*

20. Having regard to the nature of the transaction, we are of the opinion that it would be appropriate to state that in cases where the instrumentality of the State enters the contractual field, it should be governed by the incidence of the

contract. It is true that it may not be necessary to give reasons but, in our opinion, in the field of this nature fairness must be there to the parties concerned, and having regard to the large number or the long period and the nature of the dealings between the parties, the appellant should have been taken into confidence. Equality and fairness at least demands this much from an instrumentality of the State dealing with a right of the State not to treat the contract as subsisting. We must, however, evolve such process which will work.

….. …..

23. *It is not our decision which is important but a decision on the above basis should be arrived at, which should be fair, just and reasonable – and consistent with good government – which will be arrived at fairly and should be taken after taking the persons concerned whose rights/obligations are affected, into confidence. Fairness in such action should be perceptible, if not transparent."* (emphasis is mine)

168. What came to be concluded in the judgment *Mahabir* case (supra) extracted above can be described as an extension of the applicability of article 14 of the Constitution of India on the subject of contractual agreements. Hithertobefore, an act of awarding contracts was adjudged on the touchstone of fairness. For the first time, even a decision of not entering into a contractual arrangement has been brought under the scope of judicial review. The requirement of being fair, just and reasonable, *i.e.*, principles applicable in good governance, have been held to be equally applicable for not entering into a contractual arrangement.

Another facet of the aforesaid decision was, that this Court expressed, that the contracting party had the right to be informed (the right to know) why the contractual arrangement which had continued for long years (from 1965 to 1983) was being terminated.

EVERY STATE ACTION MUST BE TRANSPARENT – WHERE ON THE FACE OF IT, IT APPEARS TO BE ARBITRARY, MAY BE CONTRACTUAL FIELD STATE MUST JUSTIFY ITS FAIRNESS AS EVERY PUBLIC OFFICE HOLDER IS ACCOUNTABLE

169. Much emphasis was placed on the judgment rendered by this Court in *Kumari Shrilekha Vidyarthi* v. *State of Uttar Pradesh*, (1991) 1 SCC 212. Observations which relied upon during the course of hearing are being set out hereinunder: (SCC pp. 236-46 paras 21-29, 33 & 36)

"21. The Preamble of the Constitution of India resolves to secure to all its citizens *Justice*, social, economic and political; and *Equality* of status and opportunity. Every State action must be aimed at achieving this goal. Part IV of the Constitution contains 'Directives Principles of State Policy' which are fundamental in the governance of the country and are aimed at securing social and economic freedoms by appropriate State action which is complementary to individual fundamental rights guaranteed in Part III for protection against excesses of State action, to realise the vision in the Preamble.

This being the philosophy of the Constitution, can it be said that it contemplates exclusion of article 14 — non-arbitrariness which is basic to rule of law — from State actions in contractual field when all actions of the State are meant for public good and expected to be fair and just? We have no doubt that the Constitution does not envisage or permit unfairness or unreasonableness in State actions in any sphere of its activity contrary to the professed ideals in the Preamble. In our opinion, it would be alien to the constitutional scheme to accept the argument of exclusion of article 14 in contractual matters. The scope and permissible grounds of judicial review in such matters and the relief which may be available are different matters but that does not justify the view of its total exclusion. This is moreso when the modern trend is also to examine the unreasonableness of a term in such contracts where the bargaining power is unequal so that these are not negotiated contracts but standard form contracts between unequals.

22. There is an obvious difference in the contracts between private parties and contracts to which the State is a party. Private parties are concerned only with their personal interest whereas the State while exercising its powers and discharging its functions, acts indubitably, as is expected of it, for public good and in public interest. The impact of every State action is also on public interest. This factor alone is sufficient to import at least the minimal requirements of public law obligations and impress with this character the contracts made by the State or its instrumentality.

It is a different matter that the scope of judicial review in respect of disputes falling within the domain of contractual obligations may be more limited and in doubtful cases the parties may be relegated to adjudication of their rights by resort to remedies provided for adjudication of purely contractual disputes.

However, to the extent, challenge is made on the ground of violation of article 14 by alleging that the impugned act is arbitrary, unfair or unreasonable, the fact that the dispute also falls within the domain of contractual obligations would not relieve the State of its obligation to comply with the basic requirements of article 14.

To this extent, the obligation is of a public character invariably in every case irrespective of there being any other right or obligation in addition thereto. An additional contractual obligation cannot divest the claimant of the guarantee under article 14 of non-arbitrariness at the hands of the State in any of its actions.

23. Thus, in a case like the present, if it is shown that the impugned State action is arbitrary and, therefore, violative of article 14 of the Constitution, there can be no impediment in striking down the impugned act irrespective of the question whether an additional right, contractual or statutory, if any, is also available to the aggrieved persons.

24. The State cannot be attributed the split personality of Dr. Jekyll and Mr. Hyde in the contractual field so as to impress on it all the characteristics of the State at the threshold while making a contract requiring it to fulfil the obligation of article 14 of the Constitution and thereafter permitting it to cast off its garb of State to adorn the new robe of a private body during the subsistence of the contract enabling it to act arbitrarily subject only to the contractual obligations and remedies flowing from it.

It is really the nature of its personality as State which is significant and must characterize all its actions, in whatever field, and not the nature of function, contractual or otherwise, which is decisive of the nature of scrutiny permitted for examining the validity of its act. The requirement of article 14 being the duty to act fairly, justly and reasonably, there is nothing which militates against the concept of requiring the State always to so act, even in contractual matters.

There is a basic difference between the acts of the State which must invariably be in pubic interest and those of a private individual, engaged in similar activities, being primarily for personal gain, which may or may not promote public interest.

Viewed in this manner, in which we find no conceptual difficulty or anachronism, we find no reason why the requirement of article 14 should not extend even in the sphere of contractual matters for regulating the conduct of the State activity.

25. In *Wade: Administrative Law*, 6th Edn. after indicating that 'the powers of public authorities are essentially different from those of private persons', it has been succinctly stated at pp. 400-01 as under:

> "... *The whole conception of unfettered discretion is inappropriate to a public authority, which possesses powers solely in order that it may use them for the public good.*"

There is nothing paradoxical in the imposition of such legal limits. It would indeed be paradoxical if they were not imposed. Nor is this principle an oddity of British or American law: it is equally prominent in French law. Nor is it a special restriction which fetters only local authorities: it applies no less to Ministers of the Crown.

Nor is it confined to the sphere of administration: it operates wherever discretion is given for some public purpose, for example where a judge has a discretion to order jury trial. It is only where powers are given for the personal benefit of the person empowered that the discretion is absolute. Plainly this can have no application in public law.

> *For the same reasons there should in principle be no such thing as unreviewable administrative discretion, which should be just as much a contradiction in terms as unfettered discretion*. The question which has to be asked is what is the scope of judicial review, and in a few special cases the scope for the review of discretionary decisions may be minimal. It remains axiomatic that all discretion is capable of abuse, and that legal limits to every power are to be found somewhere." (Emphasis in original)

The view, we are taking, is, therefore, in consonance with the current thought in this field. We have no doubt that the scope of judicial review may vary with reference to the type of matter involved, but the fact that the action is reviewable, irrespective of the sphere in which it is exercised, cannot be doubted.

26. A useful treatment of the subject is to be found in an article *"Judicial Review and Contractual Powers of Public Authorities"*, (1990) 106 LQR 277-92. The conclusion drawn in the article on the basis of recent English decisions is that "public law principles designed to protect the citizens should apply because of the public nature of the body, and they may have some role in protecting the public interest". The trend now is towards judicial review of contractual powers and the other activities of the government. Reference is made also to the recent decision of the Court of Appeal in *Jones* v. *Swansea City Council*, (1990) 1 WLR 54, where the court's clear inclination to the view that contractual powers should generally be

reviewable is indicated, even though the Court of Appeal faltered at the last step and refrained from saying so.

It is significant to note that emphasis now is on reviewability of every State action because it stems not from the nature of function, but from the public nature of the body exercising that function; and all powers possessed by a public authority, howsoever conferred, are possessed 'solely in order that it may use them for the public good'. The only exception limiting the same is to be found in specific cases where such exclusion may be desirable for strong reasons of public policy. This, however, does not justify exclusion of reviewability in the contractual field involving the State since it is no longer a mere private activity to be excluded from public view or scrutiny.

27. Unlike a private party whose acts uninformed by reason and influenced by personal predilections in contractual matters may result in adverse consequences to it alone without affecting the public interest, any such act of the State or a public body even in this field would adversely affect the public interest.

Every holder of a public office by virtue of which he acts on behalf of the State or public body is ultimately accountable to the people in whom the sovereignty vests. As such, all powers so vested in him are meant to be exercised for public good and promoting the public interest. This is equally true of all actions even in the field of contract. Thus, every holder of a public office is a trustee whose highest duty is to the people of the country and, therefore, every act of the holder of a public office, irrespective of the label classifying that act, is in discharge of public duty meant ultimately for public good. *With the diversification of State activity in a Welfare State requiring the State to discharge its wide ranging functions even through its several instrumentalities, which requires entering into contracts also, it would be unreal and not pragmatic, apart from being unjustified to exclude contractual matters from the sphere of State actions required to be non-arbitrary and justified on the touchstone of article 14.*

28. Even assuming that it is necessary to import the concept of presence of some public element in a State action to attract article 14 and permit judicial review, we have no hesitation in saying that the ultimate impact of all actions of the State or a public body being undoubtedly on public interest, the requisite public element for this purpose is present also in contractual matters. *We, therefore, find it difficult and unrealistic to exclude the State actions in contractual matters, after the contract has been made, from the purview of judicial review to test its validity on the anvil of article 14.*

29. *It can no longer be doubted at this point of time that article 14 of the Constitution of India applies also to matters of governmental policy and if the policy or any action of the government, even in contractual matters, fails to satisfy the test of reasonableness, it would be unconstitutional;* See *Ramana Dayaram Shetty* v. *International Airports Authority of India,* (1979) 3 SCC 489, and *Kasturi Lal Lakshmi Reddy* v. *State of Jammu and Kashmir,* (1980) 4 SCC 1. In *Col. A.S. Sangwan* v. *Union of India,* (1980) Supp SCC 559, while the discretion to change the policy in exercise of the executive power, when not trammelled by the statute or rule, was held to be wide, it was emphasised as imperative and implicit in article 14 of the Constitution that a change in policy must be made fairly and should not give the impression that it was so done arbitrarily or by any ulterior criteria. The wide sweep of article 14 and the

requirement of every State action qualifying for its validity on this touchstone, irrespective of the field of activity of the State, has long been settled. Later decisions of this Court have reinforced the foundation of this tenet and it would be sufficient to refer only to two recent decisions of this Court for this purpose.

....

33. No doubt, it is true, as indicated by us earlier, that there is a presumption of validity of the State action and the burden is on the person who alleges violation of article 14 to prove the assertion. *However, where no plausible reason or principle is indicated nor is it discernible and the impugned State action, therefore, appears to be ex facie arbitrary, the initial burden to prove the arbitrariness is discharged shifting onus on the State to justify its action as fair and reasonable. If the State is unable to produce material to justify its action as fair and reasonable, the burden on the person alleging arbitrariness must be held to be discharged.*

The scope of judicial review is limited as indicated in *Dwarkadas Marfatia* case *(supra)* to oversee the State action for the purpose of satisfying that it is not vitiated by the vice of arbitrariness and no more. The wisdom of the policy or the lack of it or the desirability of a better alternative is not within the permissible scope of judicial review in such cases. It is not for the courts to recast the policy or to substitute it with another which is considered to be more appropriate, once the attack on the ground of arbitrariness is successfully repelled by showing that the act which was done, was fair and reasonable in the facts and circumstances of the case. As indicated by Diplock, L.J., in *Council of Civil Service Unions* v. *Minister for the Civil Service*, (1984) 3 All ER 935, the power of judicial review is limited to the grounds of illegality, irrationality and procedural impropriety. In the case of arbitrariness, the defect of irrationality is obvious.

....

36. The meaning and true import of arbitrariness is more easily visualized than precisely stated or defined. The question, whether an impugned act is arbitrary or not, is ultimately to be answered on the facts and in the circumstances of a given case. An obvious test to apply is to see whether there is any discernible principle emerging from the impugned act and if so, does it satisfy the test of reasonableness. Where a mode is prescribed for doing an act and there is no impediment in following that procedure, performance of the act otherwise and in a manner which does not disclose any discernible principle which is reasonable, may itself attract the vice of arbitrariness.

Every State action must be informed by reason and it follows that an act uninformed by reason, is arbitrary. Rule of law contemplates governance by laws and not by humour, whims or caprices of the men to whom the governance is entrusted for the time being. It is trite that 'be you ever so high, the laws are above you'. This is what men in power must remember, always." (emphasis is mine)

170. The legal proposition laid down in the instant judgment may be summarized as follows.

170.1 *Firstly*, State action in the contractual field are meant for public good and in public interest and are expected to be fair and just.

170.2 *Secondly,* it would be alien to the constitutional scheme to accept the argument of exclusion of article 14 of the Constitution of India in contractual matters.

170.3 *Thirdly,* the fact that a dispute falls in the domain of contractual obligation, would make no difference, to a challenge raised under article 14 of the Constitution of India on the ground that the impugned act is arbitrary, unfair and unreasonable.

170.4 *Fourthly,* every State action must be informed of reason and it follows that an act uninformed by reason is arbitrary.

170.5 *Fifthly,* where no plausible reason or principle is indicated (or is discernible), and where the impugned action *ex facie* appears to be arbitrary, the *onus* shifts on the State to justify its action as fair and reasonable.

170.6 *Sixthly,* every holder of public office is accountable to the people in whom the sovereignty vests. All powers vested in a public office, even in the field of contract, are meant to be exercised for public good and for promoting public interest.

170.7 And *Seventhly,* article 14 of the Constitution of India applies also to matters of governmental policy even in contractual matters, and if the policy or any action of the government fails to satisfy the test of reasonableness, the same would be unconstitutional.

FOUNDATIONAL PRINCIPLE OF EXECUTIVE GOVERNANCE IS THAT SOVEREIGNTY VESTS IN THE PEOPLE

171. Thereafter our attention was invited to the decision rendered in *Lucknow Development Authority* v. *M.K. Gupta,* (1994) 1 SCC 243. Seriously, the instant judgment has no direct bearing to the issue in hand. The judgment determines whether compensation can be awarded to an aggrieved consumer under the Consumer Protection Act, 1986. It also settles who should shoulder the responsibility of paying the compensation awarded. But all the same it has some interesting observations which may be noticed in the context of the matter under deliberation. Portions of the observations emphasized upon are being noticed below: (SCC pp. 260-64 paras 8, 10-11)

> "8. ..... *Under our Constitution sovereignty vests in the people. Every limb of the constitutional machinery is obliged to be people oriented. No functionary in exercise of statutory power can claim immunity, except to the extent protected by the statute itself. Public authorities acting in violation of constitutional or statutory provisions oppressively are accountable for their behavior before authorities created under the statute like the commission or the courts entrusted with responsibility of maintaining the rule of law.*
>
> Each hierarchy in the Act is empowered to entertain a complaint by the consumer for value of the goods or services and compensation. The word 'compensation' is again of very wide connotation. It has not been defined in the Act. According to dictionary it means, 'compensating or being compensated; thing given as recompense;'. In legal sense it may constitute actual loss or expected loss and may extend to physical, mental or even emotional suffering, insult or injury or loss. Therefore, when the Commission

has been vested with the jurisdiction to award value of goods or services and compensation it has to be construed widely enabling the Commission to determine compensation for any loss or damage suffered by a consumer which in law is otherwise included in wide meaning of compensation. The provision in our opinion enables a consumer to claim and empowers the Commission to redress any injustice done to him. Any other construction would defeat the very purpose of the Act. The Commission or the Forum in the Act is thus entitled to award not only value of the goods or services but also to compensate a consumer for injustice suffered by him.

....

10. Who should pay the amount determined by the Commission for harassment and agony, the statutory authority or should it be realized from those who were responsible for it? Compensation as explained includes both the just equivalent for loss of goods or services and also for sufferance of injustice. For instance in Civil Appeal No.. ..of 1993 arising out of (Civil) No. 659 of 1991 the Commission directed the Bangalore Development Authority to pay Rs. 2446 to the consumer for the expenses incurred by him in getting the lease-cum-sale agreement registered as it was additional expenditure for alternative site allotted to him. No misfeasance was found. The moment the authority came to know of the mistake committed by it, it took immediate action by allotting alternative site to the respondent. It was compensation for exact loss suffered by the respondent. It arose in due discharge of duties. For such acts or omissions the loss suffered has to be made good by the authority itself. But when the sufferance is due to *mala fide* or oppressive or capricious acts etc., of a public servant, then the nature of liability changes. The Commission under the Act could determine such amount if in its opinion the consumer suffered injury due to what is called misfeasance of the officers by the English Courts. Even in England where award of exemplary or aggravated damages for insult etc., to a person has now been held to be punitive, exception has been carved out if the injury is due to, 'oppressive, arbitrary or unconstitutional action by servants of the Government' (Salmond and Heuston on the *Law of Torts*). Misfeasance in public office is explained by Wade in his book on *Administrative Law* thus:

"Even where there is no Ministerial duty as above, and even where no recognised tort such as trespass, nuisance, or negligence is committed, public authorities or officers may be liable in damages for malicious, deliberate or injurious wrongdoing. There is thus a tort which has been called misfeasance in public office, and which includes malicious abuse of power, deliberate maladministration, and perhaps also other unlawful acts causing injury." (p. 777)

The jurisdiction and power of the courts to indemnify a citizen for injury suffered due to abuse of power by public authorities is founded as observed by Lord Hailsham in *Cassell and Co. Ltd.* v. *Broome,* 1972 AC 1027, on the principle that, 'an award of exemplary damages can serve a useful purpose in vindicating the strength of law'. An ordinary citizen or a common man is hardly equipped to match the might of the State or its instrumentalities. That is provided by the rule of law. It acts as a check on arbitrary and capricious exercise of power. In *Rookes* v. *Barnard,* 1964 AC 1129, it was observed by Lord Devlin, 'the servants of the government are also the servants of the people and the use of their power must always be subordinate to their duty of service'. A public functionary if he acts maliciously or oppressively and the exercise of suits in harassment and agony then it is not an exercise of power but its abuse. No law provides protection against it. He who is responsible for it must suffer it. Compensation or damage as explained earlier may arise even when the officer discharges his duty honestly and *bona fide.*

But when it arises due to arbitrary or capricious behaviour then it loses its individual character and assumes social significance. Harassment of a common man by public authorities is socially abhorring and legally impermissible. It may harm him personally but the injury to society is far more grievous.

Crime and corruption thrive and prosper in the society due to lack of public resistance. Nothing is more damaging than the feeling of helplessness. An ordinary citizen instead of complaining and fighting succumbs to the pressure of undesirable functioning in offices instead of standing against it. Therefore, the award of compensation for harassment by public authorities not only compensates the individual, satisfies him personally but helps in curing social evil. It may result in improving the work culture and help in changing the outlook. Wade in his book *Administrative Law* has observed that it is to the credit of public authorities that there are simply few reported English decisions on this form of malpractice, namely, misfeasance in public offices which includes malicious use of power, deliberate maladministration and perhaps also other unlawful acts causing injury.

One of the reasons for this appears to be development of law which, apart, from other factors succeeded in keeping a salutary check on the functioning in the government or semi-government offices by holding the officers personally responsible for their capricious or even ultra vires *action resulting in injury or loss to a citizen by awarding damages against them.*

Various decisions rendered from time to time have been referred to by Wade on *Misfeasance by Public Authorities.* We shall refer to some of them to demonstrate how necessary it is for our society. In *Ashby* v. *White,* (1703) 2 LD Raym 938, the House of Lords invoked the principle of *ubi jus ibi remedium* in favour of an elector who was wrongfully prevented from voting and decreed the claim of damages. The ratio of this decision has been applied and extended by English Courts in various situations...

11. Today the issue thus is not only of award of compensation but who should bear the brunt. *The concept of authority and power exercised by public functionaries has many dimensions. It has undergone tremendous change with passage of time and change in socio-economic outlook. The authority empowered to function under a statute while exercising power discharges public duty. It has to act to subserve general welfare and common good. In discharging this duty honestly and* bona fide, *loss may accrue to any person. And he may claim compensation which may in circumstances be payable. But where the duty is performed capriciously or the exercise*

of power results in harassment and agony then the responsibility to pay the loss determined should be whose? In a modern society no authority can arrogate to itself the power to act in a manner which is arbitrary. It is unfortunate that matters which require immediate attention linger on and the man in the street is made to run from one end to other with no result. The culture of window clearance appears to be totally dead. Even in ordinary matters a common man who has neither the political backing nor the financial strength to match the inaction in public oriented departments gets frustrated and it erodes the credibility in the system. Public administration, no doubt involves a vast amount of administrative discretion which shields the action of administrative authority. But where it is found that exercise of discretion was mala fide *and the complainant is entitled to compensation for mental and physical harassment then the officer can no more claim to be under protective cover.*

When a citizen seeks to recover compensation from a public authority in respect of injuries suffered by him for capricious exercise of power and the National Commission finds it duly proved then it has a statutory obligation to award the same. It was never more necessary than today when even social obligations are regulated by grant of statutory powers.

The test of permissive form of grant is over. It is now imperative and implicit in the exercise of power that it should be for the sake of society. When the court directs payment of damages or compensation against the State the ultimate sufferer is the common man. It is the tax payers' money which is paid for inaction of those who are entrusted under the Act to discharge their duties in accordance with law. It is, therefore, necessary that the Commission when it is satisfied that a complainant is entitled to compensation for harassment or mental agony or oppression, which finding of course should be recorded carefully on material and convincing circumstances and not lightly, then it should further direct the department concerned to pay the amount to the complainant from the public fund immediately but to recover the same from those who are found responsible for such unpardonable behaviour by dividing it proportionately where there are more than one functionaries." (emphasis is mine).

172. The judgment brings out the foundational principle of executive governance. The said foundational principle is based on the realization that sovereignty vests in the people. The judgment therefore records that every limb of the constitutional machinery is obliged to be people oriented. The fundamental principle brought out by the judgment is, that a public authority exercising public power discharges a public duty, and therefore, has to subserve general welfare and common good. All power should be exercised for the sake of society. The issue which was the subject matter of consideration, and has been noticed along with the citation, was decided by concluding that compensation shall be payable by the State (or its instrumentality) where inappropriate deprivation on account of improper exercise of discretion has resulted in a loss, compensation is payable by the State (or its instrumentality). But where the public functionary exercises his discretion capriciously, or for considerations which are *mala fide,* the public functionary himself must shoulder the burden of compensation held as payable. The reason for shifting the *onus* to the public functionary deserves notice. This Court felt, that when a court directs payment of damages or compensation against the State, the ultimate sufferer is the common man, because it is tax payers money out of which damages and costs are paid.

OBJECT IN DISCRETION IN STATE LARGESSE SHOULD BE TO "BEST SUBSERVE THE COMMON GOOD"

173. Next cited for our consideration was the judgment in *Common Cause, A Registered Society* v. *Union of India*, (1996) 6 SCC 530. The instant case dealt with a challenge to the allotment of retail outlets for petroleum products (petrol pumps). Allotment was made in favour of 15 persons on the ground of poverty or unemployment. Rest of the relevant facts emerge from the extracts from the judgment reproduced below: (SCC pp. 554-55 paras 24 & 26)

> "24. The orders of the Minister reproduced above read: "the applicant has no regular income to support herself and her family", "the applicant is an educated lady and belongs to Scheduled Tribe community", "the applicant is unemployed and has no regular source of income", "the applicant is an uneducated, unemployed Scheduled Tribe youth without regular source of livelihood", "the applicant is a housewife whose family is facing difficult financial circumstances" etc. etc. There would be literally millions of people in the country having these circumstances or worse. There is no justification whatsoever to pick up these persons except that they happen to have won the favour of the Minister on *mala fide* considerations. None of these cases fall within the categories placed before this Court in *Centre for Public Interest Litigation* v. *Union of India*, 1995 Supp (3) SCC 382, but even if we assume for argument sake that these cases fall in some of those or similar guidelines the exercise of discretion was wholly arbitrary.
>
> *Such a discretionary power which is capable of being exercised arbitrarily is not permitted by article 14 of the Constitution of India. While article 14 permits a reasonable classification having a rational nexus to the objective sought to be achieved, it does not permit the power to pick and choose arbitrarily out of several persons falling in the same category. A transparent and objective criteria/procedure has to be evolved so that the choice among the members belonging to the same class or category is based on reason, fair play and non-arbitrariness. It is essential to lay down as a matter of policy as to how preferences would be assigned between two persons falling in the same category. If there are two eminent sportsmen in distress and only one petrol pump is available, there should be clear, transparent and objective criteria/procedure to indicate who out of the two is to be preferred. Lack of transparency in the system promotes nepotism and arbitrariness.* It is absolutely essential that the entire system should be transparent right from the stage of calling for the applications upto the stage of passing the orders of allotment. *The names of the allottees, the orders and the reasons for allotment should be available for public knowledge and scrutiny.* Mr. Shanti Bhushan has suggested that the petrol pumps, agencies etc., may be allotted by public auction – category-wise amongst the eligible and objectively selected applicants. *We do not wish to impose any procedure on the Government. It is a matter of policy for the Government to lay down. We, however, direct that any procedure laid down by the Government must be transparent, just, fair and non-arbitrary.*
>
> ….. …..

26. ...*With the change in socio-economic outlook, the public servants are being entrusted with more and more discretionary powers even in the field of distribution of government wealth in various forms.* We take it to be perfectly clear, that if a public servant abuses his office either by an act of omission or commission, and the consequence of that is injury to an individual or loss of public property, an action may be maintained against such public servant. No public servant can say "you may set aside an order on the ground of *mala fide* but you cannot hold me personally liable". *No public servant can arrogate to himself the power to act in a manner which is arbitrary."* (emphasis is mine).

174. This judgment has a direct bearing on the controversy in hand. It clearly delineates the manner in which discretion must be exercised, specially when the object of discretion is State largesse. A perusal of the observations reproduced above reveal, that the State largesse under reference (petrol pumps) were to be allotted on the ground of poverty and unemployment. Such an allotment was obviously based on a policy to "best subserve the common good" enshrined in article 39(b) of the Constitution of India.

This Court found no fault in the policy itself. The fault was with the manner of giving effect to the policy. It was held, that a transparent and objective criteria/ procedure has to be evolved, so that the choice out of those who are eligible can be made fairly and without any arbitrariness. The exercise of discretion which enables the competent authority to arbitrarily pick and choose out of several persons falling in the same category, according to the above decision would be arbitrary, and as such violative of article 14 of the Constitution of India.

PUBLIC AUTHORITIES SHOULD NOT HAVE HIDDEN AGENDA – MUST GET FULL VALUE OF THE NATURAL RESOURCES

175. Out of the more recent judgments our attention was invited to *Meerut Development Authority* v. *Association of Management Studies*, (2009) 6 SCC 171. The controversy adjudicated upon in this case emerges from the decision of the appellant to allotment of 2 plots of land. For the said purpose the appellant invited tenders from interested persons. In response the respondent submitted its tender. After the allotment of one of the plots to the respondent, the respondent raised an objection that the appellant had fixed the reserved price of the second plot at a rate much higher than its adjoining plots. The respondent assail the action of the appellant in issuing a fresh advertisement for the allotment of the second plot. In the course of determination of the aforesaid controversy this Court held: (SCC pp. 181-82, 185 & 187-88 para 26-29, 39-41 & 50)

"26. A tender is an offer. It is something which invites and is communicated to notify acceptance. Broadly stated it must be unconditional; must be in the proper form, the person by whom tender is made must be able to and willing to perform his obligations. The terms of the invitation to tender cannot be open to judicial scrutiny because the invitation to tender is in the realm of contract. However, a limited judicial review may be available in cases where it is established that the terms of the invitation to tender were so tailor-made to suit the convenience of any particular person with a view to eliminate all others from participating in the bidding process.

27. *The bidders participating in the tender process have no other right except the right to equality and fair treatment in the matter of evaluation of competitive bids offered by interested persons in response to notice inviting tenders in a transparent manner and free from hidden agenda.* One cannot challenge the terms and conditions of the tender except on the abovestated ground, the reason being the terms of the invitation to tender are in the realm of the contract. No bidder is entitled as a matter of right to insist the authority inviting tenders to enter into further negotiations unless the terms and conditions of notice so provided for such negotiations.

28. *It is so well-settled in law and needs no restatement at our hands that disposal of the public property by the State or its instrumentalities partakes the character of a trust. The methods to be adopted for disposal of public property must be fair and transparent providing an opportunity to all the interested persons to participate in the process.*

29. The Authority has the right not to accept the highest bid and even to prefer a tender other than the highest bidder, if there exist good and sufficient reasons, such as, the highest bid not representing the market price but there cannot be any doubt that the Authority's action in accepting or refusing the bid must be free from arbitrariness or favouritism.

....

39. The law has been succinctly stated by Wade in his treatise, *Administrative Law*:

"The powers of public authorities are therefore essentially different from those of private persons. A man making his will may, subject to any rights of his dependants, dispose of his property just as he may wish. He may act out of malice or a spirit of revenge, but in law this does not affect his exercise of his power. In the same way a private person has an absolute power to allow whom he likes to use his land, to release a debtor, or, where the law permits, to evict a tenant, regardless of his motives. This is unfettered discretion. But a public authority may do none of these things unless it acts reasonably and in good faith and upon lawful and relevant grounds of public interest. So a city council acted unlawfully when it refused unreasonably to let a local rugby football club use the city's sports ground, though a private owner could of course have refused with impunity. *Nor may a local authority arbitrarily release debtors, and if it evicts tenants, even though in accordance with a contract, it must act reasonably and 'within the limits of fair dealing'. The whole conception of unfettered discretion is inappropriate to a public authority, which possesses powers solely in order that it may use them for the public good." Administrative Law,* 9th Edn. H.W.R. Wade and C.F. Forsyth.

40. There is no difficulty to hold that the authorities owe a duty to act fairly but it is equally well-settled in judicial review, the court is not concerned with the merits or correctness of the decision, but with the manner in which the decision is taken or the order is made. The court cannot substitute its own opinion for the opinion of the authority deciding the matter.

41. The distinction between appellate power and a judicial review is well-known but needs reiteration. By way of judicial review, the court cannot examine the details of the terms of the contract which have been entered into by the public

bodies or the State. The courts have inherent limitations on the scope of any such enquiry. *If the contract has been entered into without ignoring the procedure which can be said to be basic in nature and after an objective consideration of different options available taking into account the interest of the State and the public, then the court cannot act as an appellate court by substituting its opinion in respect of selection made for entering into such contract. But at the same time the courts can certainly examine whether the "decision-making process" was reasonable, rational, not arbitrary and violative of article 14.* See *Sterling Computers Ltd.* v. *M&N Publications Ltd.*, (1993) 1 SCC 445.

....

50. We are, however, of the opinion that the effort, if any, made by MDA to augment its financial resources and revenue itself cannot be said to be an unreasonable decision. *It is well said that the struggle to get for the State the full value of its resources is particularly pronounced in the sale of State-owned natural assets to the private sector. Whenever the Government or the authorities get less than the full value of the asset, the country is being cheated; there is a simple transfer of wealth from the citizens as a whole to whoever gets the assets "at a discount"*. Most of the times the wealth of the State goes to the individuals within the country rather than to multinational corporations; still, wealth slips away that ought to belong to the nation as a whole.

(emphasis is mine)

176. In the judgment in *Meerut Development Authority* case (supra) this Court laid down, that in a tender process, a tenderer has the right to fair treatment and the right to be treated equally. The evaluation of tenders, it has been held, must be transparent and free from any hidden agenda. The view expressed in Wades Tretise on Administrative Law, that public authorities cannot act in a manner which is open to private persons, was accepted. Public authorities, it was held, can neither act out of malice nor a spirit of revenge. A public authority is ordained to act, reasonably and in good faith and upon lawful and relevant grounds of public interest. Most importantly it was concluded, that the State "must" get the "full value" of the resources, specially when State owned assets are passed over to private individuals/entities. Not stopping there the Court added further, that whoever pays less than the full value, get the assets belonging to the citizens "at a discount", and as such the wealth that belongs to the nation slips away.

IN ONE CASE CENTRAL GOVERNMENT ITSELF HAD TAKEN A STAND THAT NATURAL RESOURCES WERE A TRUST IN ITS HANDS ON BEHALF OF THE PEOPLE OF INDIA – NATURAL RESOURCES WOULD BE USED IN THE BEST INTEREST OF THE COUNTRY AND NOT FOR PRIVATE INTEREST

177. Also cited for our consideration was the judgment in *Reliance Natural Resources Ltd.* v. *Reliance Industries Ltd.*, (2010) 7 SCC 1. The Court's attention was invited to the following: (SCC pp. 36, 67-68, 103 & 105 paras 33, 122, 128, 243 & 250)

"33. Mr R.F. Nariman, learned Senior Counsel appearing for RIL concentrated his argument with reference to sections 391 to 394 of the Companies Act. According to him, section 392 of the Act had no predecessors either in English law or in the Companies Act of 1913. The reason why the

Legislature appears to have felt the necessity of enacting section 392 is to bring section 391 on a par with section 394. Section 394 applies only to companies which are reconstructing and or amalgamating, involving the transfer of assets and liabilities to another company. It is thus, applicable to a species of the genus of company referred to under section 391. Section 394, sub-section 1 specifically gives the Company Court the power not merely to sanction the compromise or arrangement but also gives the Company Court the power, by a subsequent order, to make provisions for "such incidental, consequential and supplemental matters as are necessary to secure that the reconstruction or amalgamation shall be fully and effectively carried out" [Section 394(1)(*vi*)]. This power is absent in section 391, so that companies falling within section 391, but not within section 394, would not be amenable to the Company Court's jurisdiction to enforce a compromise or arrangement made under section 391 and to see that they are fully carried out. Hence, the power under section 392 has to be understood in the above context, and is of the same quality as the power expressly given to the Company Court post-sanction under section 394.

....

122. From the above analysis, the following are the broad sustainable conclusions which can be derived from the position of the Union:

(1) *The natural resources are vested with the Government as a matter of trust in the name of the people of India. Thus, it is the solemn duty of the State to protect the national interest.*

(2) Even though exploration, extraction and exploitation of natural resources are within the domain of governmental function, the Government has decided to privatise some of its functions. For this reason, the constitutional restrictions on the Government would equally apply to the private players in this process. *Natural resources must always be used in the interests of the country, and not private interests.*

(3) The broader constitutional principles, the statutory scheme as well as the proper interpretation of the PSC mandates the Government to determine the price of the gas before it is supplied by the contractor.

(4) The policy of the Government, including the gas utilisation policy and the decision of EGOM would be applicable to the pricing in the present case.

(5) *The Government cannot be divested of its supervisory powers to regulate the supply and distribution of gas.*

....

128. *In a constitutional democracy like ours, the national assets belong to the people. The Government holds such natural resources in trust. Legally, therefore, the Government owns such assets for the purposes of developing them in the interests of the people.* In the present case, the Government owns the gas till it reaches its ultimate consumer. A mechanism is provided under the PSC between the Government and the contractor (RIL, in the present case). The PSC shall override any other contractual obligation between the contractor and any other party.

....

243. The structure of our Constitution is not such that it permits the reading of each of the Directive Principles of State Policy, that have been framed for the achievement of conditions of social, economic and political justice in isolation. The structural lines of logic, of ethical imperatives of the State and the lessons of history flow from one to the other. *In the quest for national development and unity of the nation, it was felt that the "ownership and control of the material resources of the community" if distributed in a manner that does not result in common good, it would lead to derogation from the quest for national Development and the unity of the nation*. Consequently, article 39(b) of the Constitution should be construed in light of article 38 of the Constitution and be understood as placing an affirmative obligation upon the State to ensure that distribution of material resources of the community does not result in heightening of inequalities amongst people and amongst regions. In line with the logic of the constitutional matrix just enunciated, and in the sweep of the quest for national development and unity, is another provision. Inasmuch as inequalities between people and regions of the nation are inimical to those goals, article 39(c) posits that the "operation of the economic system" when left unattended and unregulated, leads to "concentration of wealth and means of production to the common detriment" and commands the State to ensure that the same does not occur.

....

250. We hold that with respect to the natural resources extracted and exploited from the geographic zones specified in article 297 the Union may not:

(1) transfer title of those resources after their extraction unless the Union receives just and proper compensation for the same;

(2) allow a situation to develop wherein the various users in different sectors could potentially be deprived of access to such resources;

(3) allow the extraction of such resources without a clear policy statement of conservation, which takes into account total domestic availability, the requisite balancing of current needs with those of future generations, and also India's security requirements;

(4) allow the extraction and distribution without periodic evaluation of the current distribution and making an assessment of how greater equity can be achieved, as between sectors and also between regions;

(5) allow a contractor or any other agency to extract and distribute the resources without the explicit permission of the Union of India, which permission can be granted only pursuant to a rationally framed utilisation policy; and

(6) no end user may be given any guarantee for continued access and of use beyond a period to be specified by the Government.

Any contract including a PSC which does not take into its ambit stated principles may itself become vulnerable and fall foul of article 14 of the Constitution.

(emphasis is mine).

178. Interestingly, in this case the position adopted by the Union needs to be highlighted. This Court was informed, that natural resources are vested in the Government, as a matter of trust, in the name of the people of India. And that, it was the solemn duty of the State to protect the national interest. The most significant assertion expressed on behalf of the Union was, that natural resources must always be used in the interest of the country and not in private interest. It is in the background of the stance adopted by the Union, that this Court issued the necessary directions extracted above.

STATE LARGESSE CANNOT BE DISPOSED OF ON THE WHIMS AND SWEET WILL OF POLITICAL BOSSES OR OFFICERS OF THE STATE

179. Last of all reference was made to the decision of this Court in *Akhil Bhartiya Upbhokta Congress* v. *State of Madhya Pradesh*, (2011) 5 SCC 29: (SCC p. 60 paras 65-67)

> *65. What needs to be emphasised is that the State and/or its agencies/ instrumentalities cannot give largesse to any person according to the sweet will and whims of the political entities and/or officers of the State. Every action/decision of the State and/or its agencies/instrumentalities to give largesse or confer benefit must be founded on a sound, transparent, discernible and well-defined policy, which shall be made known to the public by publication in the Official Gazette and other recognised modes of publicity and such policy must be implemented/executed by adopting a non-discriminatory and non-arbitrary method irrespective of the class or category of persons proposed to be benefited by the policy. The distribution of largesse like allotment of land, grant of quota, permit licence, etc., by the State and its agencies/ instrumentalities should always be done in a fair and equitable manner and the element of favouritism or nepotism shall not influence the exercise of discretion, if any, conferred upon the particular functionary or officer of the State.*
>
> *66. We may add that there cannot be any policy, much less, a rational policy of allotting land on the basis of applications made by individuals, bodies, organisations or institutions dehors an invitation or advertisement by the State or its agency/ instrumentality. By entertaining applications made by individuals, organizations or institutions for allotment of land or for grant of any other type of largesse the State cannot exclude other eligible persons from lodging competing claim. Any allotment of land or grant of other form of largesse by the State or its agencies/instrumentalities by treating the exercise as a private venture is liable to be treated as arbitrary, discriminatory and an act of favouritism and/or nepotism violating the soul of the equality clause embodied in article 14 of the Constitution.*
>
> *67. This, however, does not mean that the State can never allot land to the institutions/organisations engaged in educational, cultural, social or philanthropic activities or are rendering service to the society except by way of auction. Nevertheless, it is necessary to observe that once a piece of land is earmarked or identified for allotment to institutions/organisations engaged in any such activity, the actual exercise of allotment must be done in a manner consistent with the doctrine of equality. The competent authority should, as a matter of course, issue an advertisement incorporating therein the conditions of eligibility so as to enable all similarly situated eligible persons, institutions/organisations to participate in the process of allotment, whether by way of auction or otherwise. In a given case the Government may allot land at a fixed price but in that case also allotment must be preceded by a wholesome exercise consistent with article 14 of the Constitution."* (emphasis is mine).

The observations of this Court in the judgment extracted above neither need any summarization, nor any further elaboration.

PRINCIPLE OF 'FIRST-COME-FIRST-SERVED' FOR ALLOCATING SPECTRUM LICENCE WAS ARBITRARY HAVING DANGEROUS IMPLICATIONS – HENCE 2G JUDGMENT AND DIRECTIONS – HENCE PRESIDENTIAL REFERENCE

180. Surely, there cannot be any escape from a reference to the judgment rendered by this Court in *Centre for Public Interest Litigation* v. *Union of India*, (2012) 3 SCC 1, which according to the Preamble of the Presidential reference, seems to be the reason why the reference came to be made. During the course of hearing extensive debate, between rival parties, ensued on the effect of the observations recorded by this Court in paragraphs 95 and 96 of the judgment. The aforesaid paragraphs are being extracted hereinbelow: (SCC pp. 59-60)

> "95. This Court has repeatedly held that wherever a contract is to be awarded or a licence is to be given, the public authority must adopt a transparent and fair method for making selections so that all eligible persons get a fair opportunity of competition. To put it differently, the State and its agencies/instrumentalities must always adopt a rational method for disposal of public property and no attempt should be made to scuttle the claim of worthy applicants. When it comes to alienation of scarce natural resources like spectrum etc., it is the burden of the State to ensure that a non-discriminatory method is adopted for distribution and alienation, which would necessarily result in protection of national/public interest.
>
> 96. In our view, a duly publicized auction conducted fairly and impartially is perhaps the best method for discharging this burden and the methods like first-come-first-served when used for alienation of natural resources/public property are likely to be misused by unscrupulous people who are only interested in garnering maximum financial benefit and have no respect for the constitutional ethos and values. In other words, while transferring or alienating the natural resources, the State is duty bound to adopt the method of auction by giving wide publicity so that all eligible persons can participate in the process."

181. Insofar as the controversy in the aforesaid case is concerned, it would be relevant to mention that the petitioner approached this Court by invoking the extraordinary writ jurisdiction of this Hon'ble Court under article 32 of the Constitution of India. The petition came to be filed as a cause in public interest. The reason which promoted the petitioner to approach this Court was that the Union had adopted the policy of "first-come-first-serve" for allocation of licences of spectrum. It was alleged that the aforesaid policy involved the element of pure chance or accident. It was asserted on behalf of the petitioners that invocation of the principles of "first-come-first-serve" for permission to use natural resources had inherently dangerous implications.

The implications expressed by the petitioners were duly taken into consideration and the plea raised on behalf of the petitioners was accepted.

Thereupon, the following directions came to be issued in paragraph 102 of the judgment: (2G case SCC p. 63)

"102. In the result, the writ petitions are allowed in the following terms:

(i) The licences granted to the private Respondents on or after 10.1.2008 pursuant to two press releases issued on 10.1.2008 and subsequent allocation of spectrum to the licensees are declared illegal and are quashed.

(ii) The above direction shall become operative after four months.

(iii) Keeping in view the decision taken by the Central Government in 2011, TRAI shall make fresh recommendations for grant of licence and allocation of spectrum in 2G band in 22 Service Areas by auction, as was done for allocation of spectrum in 3G band.

(iv) The Central Government shall consider the recommendations of TRAI and take appropriate decision within next one month and fresh licences be granted by auction.

(v) Respondent Nos. 2, 3 and 9 who have been benefited at the cost of Public Exchequer by a wholly arbitrary and unconstitutional action taken by the DoT for grant of UAS Licences and allocation of spectrum in 2G band and who off-loaded their stakes for many thousand crores in the name of fresh infusion of equity or transfer of equity shall pay cost of Rs. 5 crores each. Respondent Nos. 4, 6, 7 and 10 shall pay cost of Rs. 50 lakhs each because they too had been benefited by the wholly arbitrary and unconstitutional exercise undertaken by the DoT for grant of UAS Licences and allocation of spectrum in 2G band. We have not imposed cost on the Respondents who had submitted their applications in 2004 and 2006 and whose applications were kept pending till 2007.

(vi) Within four months, 50% of the cost shall be deposited with the Supreme Court Legal Services Committee for being used for providing legal aid to poor and indigent litigants. The remaining 50% cost shall be deposited in the funds created for Resettlement and Welfare Schemes of the Ministry of Defence.

(vii) However, it is made clear that the observations made in this judgment shall not, in any manner, affect the pending investigation by the CBI, Directorate of Enforcement and others agencies or cause prejudice to those who are facing prosecution in the cases registered by the CBI or who may face prosecution on the basis of chargesheet(s) which may be filed by the CBI in future and the Special Judge, CBI shall decide the matter uninfluenced by this judgment. We also make it clear that this judgment shall not prejudice any person in the action which may be taken by other investigating agencies under Income-tax Act, 1961, Prevention of Money-Laundering Act, 2002 and other similar statutes."

REVIEW PETITION FILED BUT WITHDRAWN – THE GOVERNMENT DECIDED TO IMPLEMENT THE 2G JUDGMENT

182. It needs to be noticed that a review petition came to be filed by the Union against the instant judgment in 2G case (supra). The same, however, came to be withdrawn without any reservations. During the course of hearing of the instant petition, the Learned Attorney-General for India informed this Court that the Union had decided to give effect to the judgment, insofar as the allocation of spectrum is concerned. In the above view of the matter, one only needs to notice the observations recorded by this Court in paragraphs 95 and 96 extracted hereinabove (in para 180 above).

IN 2G JUDGMENT THE PRINCIPLE OF TRANSPARENT AND FAIR METHOD OF DISPOSAL, LAID DOWN EARLIER, WAS APPROVED AND RE-ITERATED

A perusal of the aforesaid paragraphs reveals, that in line with the judgments rendered by this Court interpreting article 14 of the Constitution of India, this Court yet again held, that while awarding a contact or a licence, the Executive must adopt a transparent and fair method.

The executive must ensure, that all eligible persons get a fair opportunity to compete. For awarding contracts or licences, the Executive should adopt a rational method, so as to ensure that claims of worthy applicants are not scuttled. On the subject of natural resources like spectrum, etc., this Court held that it was the bounden duty of the State to ensure the adoption of a non-discriminatory method which would result in protection of national/public interest.

This Court also expressed the view that "perhaps" the best method for doing so would be through a duly publicized auction conducted fairly and impartially. Thus viewed, it was affirmed, that the State was duty bound to adopt the method of auction by giving wide publication while alienating natural resources, so as to ensure that all eligible persons can participate in the process.

PARAMETERS OF ARTICLE 14 OF THE CONSTITUTION BOUND THE STATE TO BE FAIR, JUST AND TRANSPARENT EVEN IN CONTRACTUAL TRANSACTIONS – NOT TO ADOPT THE POLICY OF PICK AND CHOOSE

183. The parameters laid by this Court on the scope of applicability of article 14 of the Constitution of India, in matters where the State, its instrumentalities, and their functionaries, are engaged in contractual obligations (as they emerge from the judgments extracted in paragraph 6 above) are being briefly paraphrased. For an action to be able to withstand the test of article 14 of the Constitution of India, it has already been expressed in the "main opinion" that it has to be fair, reasonable, non-discriminatory, transparent, non-capricious, unbiased, without favouritism or nepotism, in pursuit of promotion of healthy competition and equitable treatment. The judgments referred to, endorse all those requirements where the State, its instrumentalities, and their functionaries, are engaged in contractual transactions.

Therefore, all "governmental policy" drawn with reference to contractual matters, it has been held, must conform to the aforesaid parameters. While article 14 of the Constitution of India permits a reasonable classification having a rational nexus to the object sought to be achieved, it does not permit the power of pick and choose arbitrarily out of several persons falling in the same category. Therefore, a criteria or procedure has to be adopted so that the choice among those falling in the same category is based on reason, fair play and non-arbitrariness. Even if there are only two contenders falling in the zone of consideration, there should be a clear, transparent and objective criteria or procedure to indicate which out of the two is to be preferred. It is this, which would ensure transparency.

SETTLED LAW IS THAT THE STATE MUST KEEP IN MIND PUBLIC INTEREST AND PUBLIC GOOD AS IT IS ACCOUNTABLE TO THE PEOPLE OF INDIA

184. Another aspect which emerges from the judgments (extracted in paragraphs 159 to 182 above) is that, the State, its instrumentalities and their functionaries, while exercising their Executive power in matters of trade or business etc., including making of contracts, should be mindful of public interest, public purpose and public good. This is so, because every holder of public office by virtue of which he acts on behalf of the State, or its instrumentalities, is ultimately accountable to the people in whom sovereignty vests. As such, all powers vested in the State are meant to be exercised for public good and in public interest.

STATE DOES NOT HAVE UNFETTERED DISCRETION

Therefore, the question of unfettered discretion in an Executive authority, just does not arise. The fetters on discretion are – a clear, transparent and objective criteria or procedure which promotes public interest, public purpose and public good. A public authority is ordained, therefore to act, reasonably and in good faith and upon lawful and relevant grounds of public interest.

185. Observations recorded by this Court on the subject of revenue returns, during the course of the States engagements in commercial ventures (emerging from the judgments extracted in paragraphs 159 to 182 above), are being summarized hereunder. It has been held, where the State is simply selling a product, there can be no doubt that the State must endeavour to obtain the highest price, subject of course to any other overriding public consideration.

A TRADING AGREEMENT OF NATURAL RESOURCES IS TO BE TESTED WHETHER THE STATE IS THE GAINER OR PRIVATE INDIVIDUAL

The validity of a trading agreement executed by the Government has to be judged by the test, that the entire benefit arising therefrom enures to the State, and is not used as a cloak for conferring private benefits on a limited class of persons. If a contract has been entered into, taking in account the interest of the State and the public, the same would not be interfered with by a Court, by assuming the position of an appellate authority. The endeavour to get the State the "full value" of its resources, it has been held, is particularly pronounced in the sale of State owned natural resources, to the private sector. Whenever the State gets less than the full value of the assets, it has been inferred, that the country has been cheated, in as much as, it amounts to a simple transfer of wealth, from the citizens as a whole, to whoever gets the assets at a discount. And in that sense, it has been concluded, the wealth that belongs to the nation is lost.

NATURAL RESOURCES ARE A TRUST IN THE HANDS OF THE STATE ON BEHALF OF THE PEOPLE OF INDIA

In *Reliance Natural Resources Ltd.'s* case (*supra*), the Union of India adopted the position, that natural resources are vested in the State as a matter of trust, for and on behalf of the citizens of the country. It was also acknowledged, that it was the solemn duty of the State, to protect those natural resources. More importantly, it was accepted, that natural resources must always be used in the common interest of the citizens of the country, and not for private interest.

'MAIN OPINION' IN PARA 149 THAT IF THE POLICY DECISION IS NOT BACKED BY SOCIAL GOOD-OPEN TO THE WRATH OF ARTICLE 14 OF THE CONSTITUTION – CONCURRED

186. Based on the legal/constitutional parameters/requirements culled out in the preceding three paragraphs (*i.e.* paras 183 to 185), I shall venture an opinion on whether there are circumstances in which natural resources ought to be disposed of only by ensuring maximum returns. For this, I shall place reliance on a conclusion drawn in the "main opinion", namely, "Distribution of natural resources is a policy-decision, and the means adopted for the same are thus, Executive prerogatives. However, when such a policy decision is not backed by a social or welfare purpose, and precious and scarce natural resources are alienated for commercial pursuits of profit maximizing private entrepreneurs, adoption of means other than those that are competitive and maximize revenue, may be arbitrary and face the wrath of article 14 of the Constitution." (Refer to paragraph 149 of the "main opinion"). I am in respectful agreement with the aforesaid conclusion, and would accordingly opine, that when natural resources are made available by the State to private persons for commercial exploitation exclusively for their individual gains, the State's endeavour must be towards maximization of revenue returns. This alone would ensure, that the fundamental right enshrined in article 14 of the Constitution of India (assuring equality before the law and equal protection of the laws), and the directive principle contained in article 39(b) of the Constitution of India (that material resources of the community are so distributed as best to subserve the common good), have been extended to the citizens of the country.

REASONABLE CLASSIFICATION ACCEPTED BY ARTICLE 14 – NOT ARBITRARY EXERCISE OF DISCRETION OR PICK AND CHOOSE POLICY

187. A similar conclusion would also emerge in a slightly different situation. This Court in a case dealing with a challenge to the allotment of retail outlets for petroleum products; *Common Cause, A Registered Society* v. *Union of India*, (1996) 6 SCC 530 has held, that article 14 of the Constitution of India, does not countenance discretionary power which is capable of being exercised arbitrarily. While accepting that article 14 of the Constitution of India permits a reasonable classification having a rational nexus to the object sought to be achieved, it was held that article 14 of the Constitution of India does not permit the State to pick and choose arbitrarily out of several persons falling in the same category. A transparent and objective criteria/procedure has to be evolved so that the choice amongst those belonging to the same class or category is based on reason, fair play, and non-arbitrariness. Envisage a situation as the one expressed above, where by reasonable classification based on some public purpose, the choice is limited to a set of private persons, amongst whom alone, the State has decided to dispose of natural resources. Herein again, in my opinion, if the participation of private persons is for commercial exploitation exclusively for their individual gains, then the State's endeavour to maximize revenue alone, would satisfy the constitutional mandate contained in articles 14 and 39(b) of the Constitution of India.

'MAIN OPINION' IN PARA 107 THAT 'AUCTION' IS NOT THE CONSTITUTIONAL MANDATE – CONCURRED

188. In the "main opinion", it has been concluded, that auction is not a constitutional mandate, in the nature of an absolute principle which has to be applied in all situations. And as such, auction cannot be read into article 14 of the Constitution of India, so as to be applied in all situations (refer to paragraphs 107 and 108 also of the "main opinion"). Auction is certainly not a constitutional mandate in the manner expressed, but it can surely be applied in some situations to maximize revenue returns, to satisfy legal and constitutional requirements.

'AUCTION' ESSENTIAL FOR 'MAXIMISATION OF REVENUE' – HENCE SEPARATE EXPRESSION OF VIEW

It is, therefore, that I have chosen to express the manner of disposal of natural resources by using the words "maximization of revenue" in place of the term "auction", in the foregoing two paragraphs. But it may be pointed out, the Attorney-General for India had acknowledged during the course of hearing, that auction by way of competitive bidding was certainly an indisputable means, by which maximization of revenue returns is assured (in this behalf other observations recorded by me in paragraph 3 above may also be kept in mind). In the aforesaid view of the matter, all that needs to be stated is, that if the State arrives at the conclusion, in a given situation, that maximum revenue would be earned by auction of the natural resource in question, then that alone would be the process which it would have to adopt, in the situations contemplated in the foregoing two paragraphs.

JUDICIAL NOTICE OF WASHOUT OF TWO PARLIAMENT SESSIONS BASED ON CAG REPORT ABOUT EXTENSIVE LOSS TO THE NATION ON INAPPROPRIATE ALLOCATION OF NATURAL RESOURCES CAN BE TAKEN

189. One is compelled to take judicial notice of the fact, that allotment of natural resources is an issue of extensive debate in the country, so much so, that the issue of allocation of such resources had recently resulted in a washout of two sessions of Parliament. The current debate on allotment of material resources has been prompted by a report submitted by the Comptroller and Auditor-General, asserting extensive loss in revenue based on inappropriate allocations. The report it is alleged, points out that private and public sector companies had made windfall gains because the process of competitive bidding had not been adopted. The country witnessed a similar political spat a little while earlier, based on the allocation of the 2G spectrum.

EXTENSIVE LOSS TO THE NATION IN WRONGFUL ALLOCATION OF SPECTRUM LICENCE WAS NOTICED IN 2G JUDGMENT

On that occasion the controversy was brought to this Court by way of a public interest litigation, the judgment whereof is reported as *Centre for Public Interest*

Litigation v. *Union of India,* (2012) 3 SCC 1. Extensive revenue loss, in the course of allocation of the 2G spectrum was duly noticed. On each occasion when the issue of allocation of natural resources, results in an alleged loss of revenue, it is portrayed as a loss to the nation. The issue then becomes a subject-matter of considerable debate at all levels of the Indian polity. Loss of one, essentially entails a gain to the other. On each such occasion loss to the nation, translates into the identification of private players as the beneficiaries.

AS PER MEDIA REPORTS, PRIVATE PARTIES MADE LAKHS OF CRORES OF RUPEES AT THE COST OF NATIONAL LOSS

If one were to accept the allegations appearing in the media, on account of defects in the disposal mechanism, private parties have been beneficiaries to the tune of lakhs of crores of Indian Rupees, just for that reason. In the current debate, rival political parties have made allegations against those responsible, which have been repudiated with counter allegations. This Court is not, and should never be seen to be, a part of that debate. But it does seem, that the Presidential reference is aimed at invoking this Court's advisory jurisdiction to iron out the creases, so that legal and constitutional parameters are correctly understood. This would avoid such controversies in future.

CONCURRED WITH THE 'MAIN OPINION' IN PARA 146 THAT THE COURT CAN TEST THE LEGALITY AND CONSTITUTIONALITY OF THE METHOD OF DISPOSAL

It is, therefore, that an opinion is also being rendered by me, on the fourth question, namely, "What is the permissible scope for interference by courts with policy making by the Government including methods for disposal of natural resources?" On this the advice tendered in the "main opinion" *inter alia* expresses, "We may, however, hasten to add that the Court can test the legality and constitutionality of these methods. When questioned, the Courts are entitled to analyse the legal validity of different means of distribution and give a constitutional answer as to which methods are *ultra vires* and *intra vires* the provisions of the Constitution. Nevertheless, it cannot and will not compare which policy is fairer than the other, but, if a policy or law is patently unfair to the extent that it falls fouls of the fairness requirement of article 14 of the Constitution, the Court would not hesitate in striking it down.", (refer to paragraph 146 of the "main opinion"). While fully endorsing the above conclusion, I wish to further elucidate the proposition.

ARTICLE 39(B) OF THE CONSTITUTION COMMANDING, 'BEST TO SUBSERVE THE COMMON GOOD' SHOULD BE THE GUIDING PRINCIPLE IN THE DISPOSAL OF NATURAL RESOURCES

190. Before adverting to anything else, it is essential to refer to article 39(b)of the Constitution of India.

> "39. *Certain principles of policy to be followed by the State.*—The State shall in particular, direct its policy towards securing—
>
> (a) ....
>
> (b) that the ownership and control of the material resources of the community are so distributed as best to subserve the common good;
>
> (emphasis is mine).

The mandate contained in the Article extracted above envisages, that all material resources ought to be distributed in a manner which would "best subserve the common good". It is therefore apparent, that governmental policy for distribution of such resources should be devised by keeping in mind the "common good" of the community *i.e.*, the citizens of this country. It has been expressed in the "main opinion", that matters of policy fall within the realm of the Legislature or the Executive, and cannot be interfered with, unless the policy is in violation of statutory law, or is *ultra vires* the provision(s) of the Constitution of India. It is not within the scope of judicial review for a Court to suggest an alternative policy, which in the wisdom of the Court could be better suited in the circumstances of a case. Thus, far the position is clearly unambiguous.

WHEN LEGITIMATE POLICY IS EXECUTED UNLAWFULLY

191. The legality and constitutionality of policy is one matter, and the manner of its implementation quite another. Even at the implementation stage a forthright and legitimate policy, may take the shape of an illegitimate stratagem (which has been illustrated at a later juncture hereinafter).

PRESIDENTIAL REFERENCE IS NOT BASED ON CONCRETE FACT SITUATION – HENCE HYPOTHETICAL SITUATION CREATED AS GUIDE FOR THE DECISION-MAKING AUTHORITIES

Since the Presidential reference is not based on any concrete fact situation, it would be appropriate to hypothetically create one. This would enable those responsible for decision-making, to be able to appreciate the options available to them, without the fear of trespassing beyond the limitations of legality and constitutionality. This would also ensure that a truly meaningful opinion has been rendered. The illustration, that has been chosen is imaginary, and therefore, should not be taken as a reference to any similar real life situation(s)/ circumstance(s). The focus in the instant consideration is limited to allocation of natural resources for private commercial exploitation, *i.e.,* where a private player will be the beneficiary of such allocation, and will exploit the natural resource to make personal profits therefrom. The illustration chosen will be used to express an opinion on matters which are governed by statutory provisions, as also, those which are based on governmental policy. This is so because insofar as the present controversy is concerned, the parameters for distribution of natural resources must be examined under these two heads separately.

SECTION 11A OF THE MINES AND MINERALS (REGULATION AND DEVELOPMENT) ACT, 1957 INTRODUCED ON 13.2.2012 – COAL IS A NATURAL RESOURCE

192. Coal is a natural resource. It shall constitute the illustrative natural resource for the present consideration. Let us assume a governmental decision to allocate coal lots for private commercial exploitation. *First,* the legislative policy angle. Reference may be made to the Mines and Minerals (Development and Regulation) Act, 1957 (hereinafter referred to as, the MMDR Act). The enactment deals exclusively with natural resources. Section 11A of the MMDR Act has been chosen as the illustrative provision, to demonstrate how a forthright legitimate legislative policy, may take the shape of an illegitimate stratagem. The choice of section 11A aforesaid is on account of the fact that it was added to the MMDR Act only on 13.2.2012, and as such, there may not have been, as of now, any actual allocation of coal lots based thereon.

193. Section 11A of the MMDR Act, is being placed hereunder:

"*11A. Procedure in respect of coal or lignite.*—The Central Government may, for the purpose of granting reconnaissance permit, prospecting licence or mining lease in respect of an area containing coal or lignite, select, through auction by competitive bidding on such terms and conditions as may be prescribed, a company engaged in,—

(i) production of iron and steel;

(ii) generation of power;

(iii) washing of coal obtained from a mine; or

(iv) such other end use as the Central Government may, by notification in the Official Gazette, specify, and the State Government shall grant such reconnaissance permit, prospecting licence or mining lease in respect of coal or lignite to such company as selected through auction by competitive bidding under this section:

Provided that the auction by competitive bidding shall not be applicable to an area containing coal or lignite,—

(a) where such area is considered for allocation to a Government company or corporation for mining or such other specified end use;

(b) where such area is considered for allocation to a company or corporation that has been awarded a power project *on the basis of competitive bids* for tariff (including Ultra Mega Power Projects)."

Explanation.—For the purposes of this section "company" means a company as defined in section 3 of the Companies Act, 1956 and includes a foreign company within the meaning of section 591 of that Act. (emphasis is mine).

For the grant of a mining lease in respect of an area containing coal, the provision leaves no room for any doubt, that selection would be made through auction by competitive bidding. No process other than auction, can therefore be adopted for the grant of a coal mining lease.

SECTION 11A OF MMDR ACT ALSO SPECIFIED ELIGIBILITY ZONE FOR COAL BLOCKS

194. Section 11A of the MMDR Act also defines the zone of eligibility, for participation in such competitive bidding. To be eligible, the contender must be engaged in the production of iron and steel, or generation of power, or washing of coal obtained from a mine, or an activity notified by the Central Government. Only those satisfying the legislatively prescribed zone of eligibility, are permitted to compete for a coal mining lease. For the sake of fairness, and to avoid arbitrariness, the provision contemplates, that the highest bidder amongst those who participate in the process of competitive bidding, would succeed in obtaining the concerned coal mining lease. The legislative policy limiting the zone of consideration could be subject-matter of judicial review. It could be assailed, in case of violation of a legal or constitutional provision.

FACTS OF EACH CASE WOULD BE THE DECIDING FACTOR

As expressed in the "main opinion" the facts of each individual case, will be the deciding factor for such determination. In the absence of any such challenge, the legislative policy would be binding and enforceable. In such an eventuality, those who do not fall within the zone of consideration, would be precluded from the process of competitive bidding for a mining lease over an area having coal deposits.

In the process of auction through competitive bidding, if the objective is to best subserve the common good (as in Article 39(b) of the Constitution of India) the legislative policy would be fully legitimate. If, however, the expressed legislative policy has no nexus to any legitimate objective, or it transgresses the mandate of distribution of material resources to "best subserve the common good", it may well be unfair, unreasonable or discriminatory.

SECTION 11A OF MMDR ACT THOUGH IS AN EXCEPTION TO THE LEGISLATIVE POLICY ALSO ALLOWS MINING LEASE WITHOUT THE AUCTION ROUTE

195. For an effective analysis, section 11A of the MMDR Act needs a further closer examination.

Section 11A aforesaid, as an exception to the legislative policy referred to in the foregoing paragraph,also provides for the grant of a mining lease for coal to a private player, without following the auction route. The provision contemplates the grant of a mining lease for coal, without any reciprocal monetary or other consideration from the lessee. The proviso in section 11A of the MMDR Act, excludes the auction route where the beneficiary is engaged in power generation. Such exclusion, is contemplated only when the power generating concern, was awarded the power project, on the basis of "competitive bids for tariff".

It is important to highlight, that there is no express assurance in section 11A aforesaid, that every entrepreneur who sets up a power project, having succeeded on the basis of competitive bidding, would be allotted a coal mining lease. But if such an allotment is actually made, it is apparent, that such entrepreneur would get the coal lot, without having to participate in an auction, free of cost. The legislative policy incorporated in section 11A of the MMDR Act, if intended to best subserve the common good, may well be valid, even in a situation where the material resource is being granted free of cost.

What appears to be free of cost in the proviso in section 11A of the MMDR Act, is in actuality consideration enmeshed in providing electricity at a low tariff. The aforesaid proviso may be accepted as fair, and may not violate the mandate contained in article 14 of the Constitution of India, or even the directive principles contained in article 39(b) of the Constitution of India.

EXCEPTION OF COAL MINING LEASE WHEN IMPLEMENTED MAY BE OR MAY NOT BE FAIR, REASONABLE OR EQUITABLE

196. Hypothetically, assume a competitive bidding process for tariff, amongst private players interested in a power generation project. The private party which agrees to supply electricity at the lowest tariff would succeed in such an auction.

The important question is, if the private party who succeeds in the award of the project, is granted a mining lease in respect of an area containing coal, free of cost, would such a grant satisfy the test of being fair, reasonable, equitable and impartial. The answer to the instant query would depend on the facts of each individual case. Therefore, the answer could be in the affirmative, as well as, in the negative. Both aspects of the matter are being explained in the succeeding paragraph.

EXAMPLES WHEN THE ALLOCATIONS WOULD BE VALID AND WHEN NOT

197. Going back to the hypothetical illustration based on section 11A of the MMDR Act. One would add some further facts so as to be able to effectively project the legal point of view. If the bidding process to determine the lowest tariff has been held, and the said bidding process has taken place without the knowledge, that a coal mining lease would be allotted to the successful bidder, yet the successful bidder is awarded a coal mining lease. Would such a grant be valid? In the aforesaid fact situation, the answer to the question posed, may well be in the negative. This is so because, the competitive bidding for tariff was not based on the knowledge of gains, that would come to the vying contenders, on account of grant of a coal mining lease. Such a grant of a coal mining lease would therefore have no nexus to the "competitive bid for tariff".

Grant of a mining lease for coal in this situation would therefore be a windfall, without any nexus to the object sought to be achieved. In the bidding process, the parties concerned had no occasion to bring down the electricity tariff, on the basis of gains likely to accrue to them, from the coal mining lease. In this case, a material resource would be deemed to have been granted without a reciprocal consideration *i.e.,* free of cost. Such an allotment may not be fair and may certainly be described as arbitrary,and violative of the Article 14 of the Constitution of India.

Such an allotment having no nexus to the objective of subserving the common good, would fall foul even of the directive principle contained in article 39(b) of the Constitution of India. Therefore, a forthright and legitimate policy, on account of defective implementation, may become unacceptable in law.

198. In a slightly changed factual scenario, the conclusion may well be different. If before the holding the process of auction, for the award of a power project (based on competitive bids for tariff), it is made known to the contenders, that the successful bidder would be entitled to a mining lease over an area containing coal, those competing for the power project would necessarily incorporate the profit they were likely to make from such mining lease. While projecting the tariff at which they would supply electricity, they would be in a position to offset such profits from their costs. This would result in an opportunity to the contenders to lower the tariff to a level lower than would have been possible without the said lease.

In such a situation the gains from the coal mining lease, would be enmeshed in the competitive bidding for tariff. Therefore, it would not be just to assume in the instant sequence of facts, that the coal lot has been granted free of cost. One must read into the said grant, a reciprocal consideration to provide electricity at a lower tariff. In the instant factual scenario, the allotment of the mining lease would be deemed to be aimed at "subserving the common good" in terms of article 39(b) of the Constitution of India.

Therefore even the allotment of such a mining lease, which appears to result in the allocation of a natural resource free of cost, may well satisfy the test of fairness and reasonableness contemplated in article 14 of the Constitution of India. Moreso, because a fair playing field having been made available to all those competing for the power project, by making them aware of the grant of a coal mining lease, well before the bidding process. The question of favouritism therefore would not arise. Would such a grant of a natural resource, free of cost, be valid? The answer to the query, in the instant fact situation, may well be in the affirmative.

THE 'MAIN OPINION' THAT 'AUCTION' IS ONE OF THE SEVERAL METHODS OF DISPOSAL OF NATURAL RESOURCES IS CONCURRED

199. The policy of allocation of natural resources for public good can be defined by the Legislature, as has been discussed in the foregoing paragraphs. Likewise, policy for allocation of natural resources may also be determined by the Executive. The parameters for determining the legality and constitutionality of the two are exactly the same. In the aforesaid view of the matter, there can be no doubt about the conclusion recorded in the "main opinion" that auction which is just one of the several price recovery mechanisms, cannot be held to be the only constitutionally recognised method for alienation of natural resources. That should not be understood to mean, that it can never be a valid method for disposal of natural resources (refer to paragraphs 186 to 188 of my instant opinion).

NATURAL RESOURCES SHOULD NOT BE GIVEN AS CHARITY OR LARGESSE OR DONATION OR ENDOWMENT BY THE PEOPLE IN POWER AT THE COST OF THE NATION OR ITS PEOPLE

200. I would, therefore, conclude by stating that no part of the natural resource can be dissipated as a matter of largess, charity, donation or endowment, for private exploitation. Each bit of natural resource expended must bring back a reciprocal consideration. The consideration may be in the nature of earning revenue or may be to "best subserve the common good". It may well be the amalgam of the two. There cannot be a dissipation of material resources free of cost or at a consideration lower than their actual worth. One set of citizens cannot prosper at the cost of another set of citizens, for that would not be fair or reasonable.

..........................J.

(Jagdish Singh Khehar)

New Delhi;

September 27, 2012.

Author' Note: Since the 2G spectrum scam involved Loss to the Nation to the tune of Rs. 1.75 lakh crores as per the Report of Comptroller and Auditor General of India which is the Constitutional Organ of the Country, the Supreme Court had directed day-to-day basis trial *vide* order dated 11-4-2011 in its Constitutional Jurisdiction and further that no Court shall pass orders to impede the trial. Still some parties had filed Legal Proceedings including Writ Petitions in the Delhi High Court. On the application of the CBI, the Supreme Court *vide* orders dated 9-11-2012 had stayed the proceedings before the Delhi High Court. Consequently a number of writ petitions and interim applications were filed in the Supreme Court for withdrawal of those orders. Hence this judgment.

SUPREME COURT CONSIDERED THE QUESTION IF THE ORDERS DATED 11-4-2011 AND 9-11-2012 PASSED BY IT CAN BE RECALLED

Shahid Balwa
v.
Union of India

SUPREME COURT OF INDIA

CIVIL ORIGINAL JURISDICTION

Writ Petition (C) No. 548 of 2012

with

Writ Petition (c) No. 550, 551, 552 of 2012, 17 of 2013,

and

I.A. Nos. 59, 61, 63 and 68 in

Civil Appeal No. 10660 of 2010

JUDGMENT

K.S. Radhakrishnan, J.

1. We are, in these cases, called upon to examine the question whether two orders passed by this Court on 11-4-2011 and 9-11-2012 in Civil Appeal No. 10660 of 2010, in exercise of powers conferred on this Court under articles 136 and 142 of the Constitution of India, while monitoring the investigation of 2G related cases, are liable to be recalled, *de hors* the rights guaranteed to the Petitioners to invoke the jurisdiction of this Court under articles 32 and 136 of the Constitution of India, if aggrieved by the orders passed by the Special Court dealing with 2G Spectrum case.

THESE ORDERS WERE PASSED IN CIVIL APPEAL NO. 10660 RELATING TO 2G SPECTRUM SCAM CASE

2. Civil Appeal No. 10660 of 2010, in which the abovementioned orders have been passed, was filed under article 136 of the Constitution of India by special leave, praying for a Court monitored investigation by the Central Bureau of Investigation (CBI) or by a Special Investigating Team into what was described as the 2G Spectrum Scam and also for a direction to investigate the role played by A. Raja, the then Union Minister for Department of Telecommunications (DoT), senior officers of DoT, middlemen, businessmen and others.

F.I.R. FOR LOSS TO THE NATION FOR MORE THAN RS. 22,000 CRORES IN 2G SCAM-WAS REGISTERED

Before this Court, it was pointed out that the CBI had lodged a First Information Report on 21-10-2009 alleging that during the years 2000-2008 certain officials of the DoT entered into a criminal conspiracy with certain private companies and misused their official position in the grant of Unified Access Licenses causing wrongful loss to the nation, which was estimated to be more than Rs. 22,000 crores. CBI, following that, registered a case No. RC-DAI-2009-A-0045 (2G Spectrum Case) on 21-10-2009 under section 120B IPC, 13(1)(d) of the PC Act against a former Cabinet Minister and others.

REPORT OF CAG SUBMITTED TO THE PRESIDENT OF INDIA UNDER ARTICLE 151 OF THE CONSTITUTION

3. Before this Court parties produced large number of documents, including the Performance Audit Report (Draft and Final) prepared by the Comptroller and Auditor General of India (CAG) on the issue of licence and allocation of 2G Spectrum by DoT, Ministry of Communications and Information and Technology for the period from 2003-2004 to 2009-2010. Report of the CAG, was submitted to the President of India, as per article 151 of the Constitution of India. The Central Vigilance Commission (CVC) also conducted an inquiry under section 8(d) of the Central Vigilance Commission Act, 2003 and noticed grave irregularities in the grant of licences. The CVC on 12-10-2009 had forwarded the enquiry report to the Director, CBI to investigate into the matter to establish the criminal conspiracy in the allocation of 2G Spectrum under UASL policy of DoT and to bring to book all wrongdoers.

COURT-MONITORED INVESTIGATION IN 2G SCAM WAS ORDERED BY THE SUPREME COURT

4. After taking into consideration of all those factors, including the report of the CVC as well as the findings recorded by the CAG, this Court agreed for a Court monitored investigation and held as follows:

> "We are, *prima facie*, satisfied that the allegations contained in the writ petition and the affidavits filed before this Court, which are supported not only by the documents produced by them, but also the report of the Central Vigilance Commission, which was forwarded to the Director, CBI on 12-10-2009 and the findings recorded by the CAG in the Performance Audit Report, need a thorough and impartial investigation. However, at this stage, we do not consider it necessary to appoint a Special Team to investigate what the appellants have described as 2G Spectrum Scam because the Government of India has, keeping in view the law laid down in *Vineet Narain's* case and others passed in other cases, agreed for a Court Monitored Investigation."

DIRECTIONS BY SUPREME COURT *VIDE* ORDER DATED 16.12.2010

5. This Court, with a view to ensure a comprehensive and coordinated investigation by the CBI and the Enforcement Directorate, gave the following directions *vide* its order dated 16-12-2010:

(i) The CBI shall conduct thorough investigation into various issues highlighted in the report of the Central Vigilance Commission, which was forwarded to the director, CBI *vide* letter dated 12-10-2009 and the report of the CAG, who have *prima facie* found serious irregularities in the grant of licences to 122 applicants, majority of whom are said to be ineligible, the blatant violation of the terms and conditions of licences and huge loss to the public exchequer running into several thousand crores. The CBI should also probe how licences were granted to large number of ineligible applicants and who was responsible for the same and why the TRAI and the DoT did not take action against those licensees who sold their stake/equities for many thousand crores and also against those who failed to fulfil rollout obligations and comply with other conditions of licence.

(ii) The CBI shall conduct the investigation without being influenced by any functionary, agency or instrumentality of the State and irrespective of the position, rank or status of the person to be investigated/probed.

(iii) The CBI shall, if it has already not registered first information report in the context of the alleged irregularities committed in the grant of licences from 2001 to 2006-2007, now register a case and conduct thorough investigation with particular emphasis on the loss caused to the public exchequer and corresponding gain to the licensees/service providers and also on the issue of allowing use of dual/alternate technology by some service providers even before the decision was made public *vide* press release dated 19-10-2007.

(iv) The CBI shall also make investigation into the allegation of grant of huge loans by the public sector and other banks to some of the companies which have succeeded in obtaining licences in 2008 and find out whether the officers of the DoT were signatories to the loan agreement executed by the private companies and if so, why and with whose permission they did so.

(v) The Directorate of Enforcement/concerned agencies of the Income Tax Department shall continue their investigation without any hindrance or interference by any one.

(vi) Both the agencies, *i.e.* the CBI and the Directorate of Enforcement shall share information with each other and ensure that the investigation is not hampered in any manner whatsoever.

(vii) The Director General, Income Tax (Investigation) shall, after completion of analysis of the transcripts of the recording made pursuant to the approval accorded by the Home Secretary, Government of India, hand over the same to CBI to facilitate further investigation into the FIR already registered or which may be registered hereinafter."

NO COURT SHALL STAY INVESTIGATION IN 2G SCAM CASE – ORDER OF SUPREME COURT DATED 10-2-2011

6. CBI and the Enforcement Directorate then used to apprise this Court of the various stages of investigation and this Court, on 10-2-2011, passed an order stating that since this Court is monitoring the investigation of 2G Spectrum Scam no court shall pass any order which may, in any manner, impede the investigation being carried out by the CBI and the Directorate of Enforcement.

SEPARATE SPECIAL COURT SET-UP FOR TRIAL OF 2G SCAM CASE

7. Learned Attorney-General of India, it was pointed out, had written to the Law Minister on the issue of creation of separate Special Court for dealing with the cases relating to 2G Scam and, for the said purpose, the Law Minister, in turn, had written to the Chief Justice of the Delhi High Court seeking nomination of a Special Court for the said purpose. Learned Attorney-General submitted before this Court on 16-3-2011 that the Registrar-General of the High Court of Delhi had conveyed its decision to nominate Shri O.P. Saini, an officer of the Delhi Higher Judicial Service, as the Special Judge to take up the trial of cases relating to what has been described as 2G Scam. The Court was also informed that two separate notifications would be issued by the Central Government in terms of section 3(1) the PC Act, 1988 and section 43(1) of the Prevention of Money Laundering Act, 2002 for establishment of the Special Court to exclusively try the offences relating to 2G Scam and other related offences. Following that, two notifications dated 28-3-2011 were published in the Gazette of India Extraordinary on Monday, the 28th March, 2011.

THE DEATH CASE OF SADIQ BATCHA ENTRUSTED TO CBI

8. The CBI submitted before this Court on 1-4-2011 that a notification had been issued under section 6 of the Delhi Police Establishment Act by the State Government for entrusting the case relating to death of Sadiq Batcha to the CBI and the CBI had indicated that it had no objection to take up the investigation. The CBI also submitted before this Court that a Special Public Prosecutor had to be appointed to lead and supervise the prosecution of the case relating to the 2G Scam for which the CBI had suggested the name of Shri U.U. Lalit, senior advocate of this Court.

DETAILS OF THE OFFENCES MADE OUT AGAINST THE PERSONS INVOLVED IN 2G SCAM CASE

9. The CBI, after completion of the investigation in the main case, noticed the commission of various other offences during 2007-09 punishable under sections 120B, 420, 468, 471 of IPC against the accused persons, namely, Shri A. Raja and others and the following substantive offences were stated to have been made out against the following accused persons:

"(a) Sh. A. Raja, then MOC&IT – the offence punishable under sections 420, 468, 471 IPC & 13(2) read with 13(1)(d) PC Act, 1988.

(b) Sh. Siddartha Behura, then Secretary, Department of Telecom—the offence punishable under section 420 IPC & 13(2) read with 13(1)(d) PC Act, 1988.

(c) Sh. R.K. Chandolia, then PS to MOC & IT—the offence punishable under section 420 IPC & 13(2) read with 13(1)(d) PC Act.

(d) Sh. Shahid Usman Balwa, Director, M/s Swan Telecom Pvt. Ltd.; Sh. Vinod Goenka, Director, M/s Swan Telecom Pvt. Ltd. and M/s Swan Telecom Pvt. Ltd. (now M/s Etisalat DB Telecom Pvt. Ltd.) through its Director – offences punishable under sections 420/468/471 IPC.

(e) Sh. Sanjay Chandra, Managing Director, M/s Unitech Ltd. and M/s Unitech Wireless (Tamil Nadu) Pvt. Ltd. through its Director-offences punishable under section 420 IPC.

(f) Sh. Gautam Doshi, Group Managing Director, Reliance ADA Group, Sh. Hari Nair, Senior Vice-President of Reliance ADA Group & Sh. Surendra Pipara, Senior Vice-President of Reliance ADA Group & M/s Reliance Telecom Ltd. through its Director – offences punishable under section 109 read with 420 IPC."

CBI SUBMITTED CHARGE-SHEET IN ONE CASE ON 2-4-2011

10. The CBI, on the basis of the investigation conducted, submitted a charge-sheet against the abovementioned persons/companies before a Special Judge on 2-4-2011 and Special Judge took cognizance of the aforesaid offences on the same day.

SUPREME COURT MONITORED INVESTIGATION DUE TO LARGER PUBLIC INTEREST

11. This Court undertook the monitoring of the investigation in view of the prayers made by the appellants and the request made by the prosecution agency and the Government of India, having regard to the larger public interest involved, and the necessity of a proper investigation and also with the ultimate object of unearthing the crime.

U.U. LALIT SENIOR ADVOCATE APPOINTED SPECIAL PUBLIC PROSECUTOR – TRIAL ON DAY-TO-DAY BASIS – NO COURT SHALL STAY TRIAL *VIDE* ORDER 11-4-2011

12. Counsel appearing for the CBI suggested to this Court, on 11-4-2011, the name of Shri U.U. Lalit, senior advocate, for the conduct of the criminal prosecution in the case on behalf of the CBI as well as the Directorate of Enforcement and the Court on that date *inter alia* ordered as follows:

> "We also make it clear that any objection about appointment of Special Public Prosecutor or his assistant advocates or any prayer for staying or impeding the progress of the Trial can be made only before this Court and no other Court shall entertain the same. The trial must proceed on a day-to-day basis.
>
> All these directions are given by this Court in exercise of its power under article 136 read with article 142 of the Constitution and in the interest of holding a fair prosecution of the case."

LARGE NUMBER OF LEGAL PROCEEDINGS FILED IN DELHI HIGH COURT FOR STAY OF TRIAL

13. We found, in spite of the order passed by this Court on 11-4-2011 that no Court should entertain any prayer for staying or impeding the progress of the trial, large number of writ petitions were seen filed before the Delhi High Court praying for stay of the trial proceedings on one or the other ground. The CBI noticing that entertaining of those cases would violate the order passed by this Court on 11-4-2011, filed an application before this Court for summoning the records of Writ Petition (Criminal) No. 1587 of 2012, Writ Petition (Criminal) No. 1588 of 2012, Writ Petition (Criminal) No. 913 of 2012, Writ Petition (Criminal) No. 111 of 2012, Writ Petition (Criminal) No. 207 of 2012, Writ Petition (Criminal) No. 1478 of 2012, Writ Petition (Criminal) No. 1751 of 2012, Writ Petition (Criminal) No. 1752 of 2012, Writ Petition (Criminal) No. 1754 of 2012, Writ Petition (Criminal) No. 206 of 2012, Writ Petition (Criminal) No. 159 of 2012, Writ Petition (Criminal) No. 208 of 2012, Criminal M.C. No. 4197 of 2011, Criminal M.C. No. 67 of 2012, Writ Petition (Criminal) No. 129 of 2012, Writ Petition (Criminal) No. 656 of 2012, Criminal M.C. No. 4199 of 2011, Writ Petition (Criminal) No. 467 of 2012 and Criminal M.C. No. 1060 of 2012 pending before the Delhi High Court and also prayed for stay of all the proceedings of these cases.

SUPREME COURT STAYED THOSE CASES PENDING IN DELHI HIGH COURT *VIDE* ORDER DATED 9-11-2012

14. This Court felt entertaining those cases by the Delhi High Court, at this stage, would violate the order passed by this Court on 11-4-2011, passed an order on 9-11-2012 staying those proceedings pending before the Delhi High Court.

SUBMISSIONS OF THE PETITIONERS AND LAW RELIED ON

15. Shri Ram Jethmalani, learned senior counsel, appearing for the petitioner in Writ Petition (C) No. 548 of 2012, prayed for recalling orders dated 11-4-2011 and 9-11-2012 on the ground that those orders would violate the rights guaranteed to the petitioners under section 482 of the Cr.P.C. and articles 226 and 227 of the Constitution of India for moving the High Court. Learned senior counsel also submitted that remedy, if at all, available under article 32 is limited to safeguarding the rights guaranteed under Part III of the Constitution while the remedies available under articles 226 and 227 of the Constitution have a wider scope, which cannot be taken away by the impugned orders passed by this Court while monitoring the 2G Scam.

16. Learned senior counsel also submitted that the impugned orders have the effect of taking away the power of the Court in granting reasonable adjournments under section 309 of the Cr.P.C. and submitted neither sub-section (4) of section 4 nor section 19(3) of the PC Act can take away that right of the petitioners, but has been effectively curtailed by the impugned orders passed by this Court. Learned senior counsel also submitted that this Court exercising powers under articles 136 and 142 of the Constitution, has the power to only monitor the investigation and once the investigation is over and charge-sheet has been filed, this Court should leave the matter to the trial court safeguarding the rights of parties in questioning the correctness or otherwise of the orders passed by the trial Court in appropriate Forums. Reference was made to the decision of this Court in *Rajiv Ranjan Singh 'Lalan' (VIII)* v. *Union of India,* (2006) 6 SCC 613 and *Vineet Narain* v. *Union of India,* (1996) 2 SCC 199.

17. Shri Mukul Rohtagi, learned senior counsel, submitted that right to fair trial is a right guaranteed to the parties under articles 14 and 21 of the Constitution of India and the impugned order has the effect of negating those rights by shutting out all remedies available to the parties under articles 226 and 227 of the

Constitution of India to move the High Court. Learned senior counsel placed reliance on the Judgment of this Court in *A.R. Antulay* v. *R.S. Nayak*, (1988) 2 SCC 602 and submitted that in appropriate cases this Court has got the power to recall its earlier order in the interest of justice, if it is satisfied that its directions will result in the deprivation of fundamental rights guaranteed to the citizens or any other legal rights. Placing reliance on the Judgment of this Court in *L. Chandra Kumar* v. *Union of India*, (1997) 3 SCC 261 and *Shalini Shyam Shetty* v. *Rajendra Shankar Patil*, (2010) 8 SCC 600, learned senior counsel submitted that the rights conferred under articles 226 and 227 of the Constitution of India are the basic structure of the Constitution and the same cannot be taken away by exercising powers under articles 136 and 142 of the Constitution of India.

18. Shri Harish Salve, learned senior counsel, submitted that the power of the Court to monitor the criminal investigation should stop once the charge-sheet has been filed, leaving the trial court to proceed with trial in accordance with the law. In support of his contention reliance was placed on the Judgment of this Court in *Jakia Nasim Ahesan* v. *State of Gujarat*, (2011) 12 SCC 302 and the Judgment in *Ankul Chandra Pradhan* v. *Union of India*, (1996) 6 SCC 354.

SUBMISSIONS ON BEHALF OF CBI

19. Shri K.K. Venugopal, learned senior counsel appearing for the CBI, submitted that there are no justifiable reasons for recalling the impugned orders since those orders had been passed in the larger public interest and that too based on the request made by the Government of India virtually inviting this Court's intervention for monitoring the investigation relating to 2G Scam.

REPORT OF CAG REVEALS MAGNITUDE OF NATIONAL LOSS SUBMISSION

Learned senior counsel referred to the CAG report as well as the report sent by the CVC to the CBI and submitted that those reports would highlight the magnitude of loss suffered by the public exchequer, which has been revealed by the investigation conducted by the CBI. Learned senior counsel also submitted that this Court has undertaken monitoring of the investigation due to the involvement of highly placed officers of DoT and the then Union Minister for Telecommunications, Members of Parliament, bureaucrats and businessmen.

ORDERS DATED 11-4-2011 AND 9-11-2012 ONLY MEANT NOT TO IMPEDE TRIAL SUBMISSION

20. Learned senior counsel also submitted that this Court, while issuing the orders dated 11-4-2011 or 9-11-2012, has neither interfered with the proceedings pending before the Special Court, nor attempted to supervise or investigate the trial proceedings. On the other hand, this Court only ensured that the progress of the trial be not impeded and the trial should go on day-to-day basis. Learned senior counsel also submitted that this Court has reserved its powers to entertain any challenge against the orders passed by the Special Judge under articles 136, 32 as well as article 142 of the Constitution and hence, no prejudice is caused to the petitioners.

DISCUSSION INVESTIGATION BY CBI WAS STILL IN PROGRESS

21. We may, at the very outset, point out that CBI as well as the Enforcement Directorate is yet to complete the investigation of the cases relating to 2G Scam and the case which is being tried by the Special Judge is only one among them, wherein the charge-sheet has been filed and the trial is in progress.

AGGRIEVED PARTY COULD APPROACH SUPREME COURT

This Court, taking into consideration the width and ambit of the investigation which even spreads overseas and the larger public interest involved, passed the orders impugned, reserving the right of all, including the accused persons, to move this Court if their prayer would amount to staying or impeding the progress of the trial. In case they have any grievance against the orders passed by the Special Judge during trial, they are free to approach this Court so that the progress of the trial would not be hampered by indulging in cumbersome and time consuming proceedings in the other Forums, thereby stultifying the preemptory direction given by this Court for day-to-day trial.

SUPREME COURT PASSED THESE ORDERS IN EXERCISE OF CONSTITUTIONAL JURISDICTION – ARTICLES 226 AND 227 AND SECTION 482 Cr. P.C. NOT AVAILABLE

22. Article 136 read with article 142 of the Constitution of India enables this Court to pass such orders, which are necessary for doing complete justice in any cause or matter pending before it and, any order so made, shall be enforceable throughout the territory of India. Parties, in such a case, cannot invoke the jurisdiction under articles 226 or 227 of the Constitution of India or under section 482 Cr.P.C. so as to interfere with those orders passed by this Court, in exercise of its constitutional powers conferred under article 136 read with article 142 of the Constitution of India. Or, else, the parties will move Courts inferior to this Court under article 226 or article 227 of the Constitution of India or section 482 Cr.P.C., so as to defeat the very purpose and object of the various orders passed by this Court in exercise of its powers conferred under article 136 read with article 142 of the Constitution of India.

LARGER PUBLIC INTEREST COMPELLED SUPREME COURT TO PASS THESE ORDERS IN PUBLIC INTEREST

Public Interest

23. Public Interest compelled this Court to take up the investigation in 2G related cases in exercise of its powers under article 136 read with article 142, that too, on a request made by the Central Government.

CAG GUARDIAN OF PUBLIC PURSE

CAG is stated to be the most important Officer under the Constitution of India and his duty, being the guardian of the public Purse, is to see that not a farthing of it is spent without the authority of the Parliament. Article 149 of the Constitution of India empowers the CAG to perform such duties and exercise such powers in relation to the accounts of the Union and the State and Audit plays an important role in the scheme of Parliamentary Financial Control and it is also directed towards discovering waste, extravagance and disallow any expenditure violating the Constitution, or any Law.

CAG REPORTED THE NATIONAL LOSS AT RS. 1.76 LAC CRORE IN 2G SCAM

CAG, in its report submitted to the President of India under article 151 of the Constitution of India, has commented upon the manner in which the Unified

Access Licences were granted and projected that it caused wrongful loss to the Government to the tune of Rs. 1.76 lac crore. Of course, some acrimony had erupted between the Central Government and the CAG's estimate of loss, but it is reported to be substantial. CVC also conducted an enquiry under section 8(d) of the Central Vigilance Act, 2003 and noticed grave irregularities in the grant of licences. CVC, on 12-10-2009, had forwarded the enquiry report to that effect to the Directorate of CBI.

SUPREME COURT IS THE GUARDIAN OF THE CONSTITUTION OF INDIA

24. The nation and the people of this country are seriously concerned with the outcome of cases involving larger public interest, like one concerning 2G and this Court, as the guardian of the Constitution, has got the duty and obligation to see that the larger public interest and the interest of the nation is preserved and protected. When larger public interest is involved, it is the responsibility of the Constitutional Court to assure judicial legitimacy and accountability. Public interest demands timely resolution of cases relating to 2G Scam. Prolonged litigation undermines the public confidence and weakens the democracy and rule of law.

PARLIAMENT ALSO FOR EARLY DISPOSAL OF CORRUPTION CASES – NO STAY BY ANY COURT IN THE TRIAL

25. The Parliament, in its wisdom, has also noticed the necessity of early disposal of cases relating to bribery and corruption. Section 4(4) of the Prevention of Corruption Act, 1988 reflects the will of the Parliament that a Special Judge shall hold the trial of an offence on day-to-day basis, notwithstanding anything contained in the Code of Criminal Procedure. Section 19(3)(c) also states that, notwithstanding anything contained in the Code of Criminal Procedure, no Court shall stay the proceedings under the Prevention of Corruption Act on any other ground and no Court shall exercise the powers of the revision in relation to any read with interlocutory order passed in any inquiry, trial, appeal or other proceedings. Statutory provisions highlight the imperative need to eradicate the evils of bribery and corruption.

LARGER PUBLIC INTEREST HAS PRECEDENCE OVER INDIVIDUAL RIGHTS

Larger public interest should have precedence over the prayers of the petitioners, especially when this Court has safeguarded their rights and given freedom to them to move this Court, either under article 136 or article 32 of the Constitution of India. Article 139A also reflects the larger public interest, which enables this Court to transfer certain cases which involve substantial questions of law, from one High Court to another or to this Court, in such an event, it cannot be contended that the parties are deprived of their rights to adjudicate their grievances under articles 226, 227 or section 482 Cr.P.C., before the High Court.

ACCUSED ENJOYED POLITICAL POWER – NATIONAL LOSS WORTH LAKHS OF CRORES OF RUPEES – COURT MONITORING INVESTIGATION IN NATIONAL INTEREST – PUBLIC EXPECT JUSTICE

Court Monitored Investigation

26. Monitoring of criminal investigation is the function of investigating agency and not that of the Court – either of the superior Court or of the trial Court. But unsolved crimes, unsuccessful prosecution, unpunished offenders and wrongful convictions bring our criminal justice system in disrepute. Crores and crores of tax payers' money is being spent for investigating crimes in our country since every such incident is a crime against the society. When the persons involved in the crime wield political power and influence, the possibility of putting pressure on the investigating agency, which is no more independent in our country, is much more. Common people will be left with the feeling that they can get away with any crime which tarnish the image not only of the investigating agency but judicial system as well. Once investigation fails, Court will face with a *fait accompli*. Proper and uninfluenced investigation is necessary to bring about the truth. Truth will be a casualty if investigation is derailed due to external pressure and guilty gets away from the clutches of law.

PUBLIC DEMAND FOR COURT MONITORING OF MORE AND MORE SUCH LIKE CASES

27. More and more demands are now coming before the Courts for its monitoring of investigation relating to crimes committed by influential persons and persons who have political influence, with the apprehension that they could derail the investigation. Courts in public interest sometime have to take such a course in the larger public interest. That burden this Court has discharged in various cases like *Vineet Narayan's* case and *Gujarat Communal Riot's* case, etc. This Court has taken the consistent view that once charge-sheet is submitted in the proper Court, the process of Court monitoring investigation comes to an end and it is for that Court to take cognizance of the offence and deal with the matter. But, so far as the present case is concerned, we have already indicated that charge-sheet has been filed only in one among the various 2G related cases. This Court, while passing the impugned order, only directed speedy trial and, that too, on a day-to-day basis which cannot be termed as interference with the trial proceedings.

ORDERS FOR TRIAL ON DAY TO DAY BASIS AND NO STAY OF TRIAL BY ANY COURT – IS NOT MONITORING OF TRIAL

28. We also, therefore, find no basis in the contention of the petitioners that the orders dated 11-4-2011 and 9-11-2012 have the effect of monitoring the trial proceedings. No Court, other than the Court seized with the trial, has the power to monitor the proceedings pending before it. Order dated 11-4-2011 only facilitates the progress of the trial by ordering that the trial must proceed on a day-to-day basis. Large backlog of cases in the Courts is often an incentive to the litigants to misuse of Court's system by indulging in unnecessary and fraudulent litigation, thereby delaying the entire trial process. Criminal justice system's procedure guarantees and elaborateness sometimes give, create openings for abusive, dilatory tactics and confer unfair advantage on better heeled litigants to cause delay to their advantage.

DELAYED TRIAL BENEFITS THE ACCUSED – LARGER PUBLIC INTEREST DEMANDED QUICK TRIAL IN 2G SCAM CASE

Longer the trial, witnesses will be unavailable, memories will fade and evidence will be stale. Taking into consideration all those aspects, this Court felt that it is in the larger public interest that the trial of 2G Scam be not hampered. Further, when larger public interest is involved, it is the bounden duty of all, including the accused persons, who are presumed to be innocent, until proven guilty, to co-operate with the progress of the trial. Early disposal of the trial is also to their advantage, so that their innocence could be proved, rather than remain enmeshed in criminal trial for years and unable to get on with their lives and business.

A.R. ANTULAY'S CASE NOT APPLICABLE TO THE FACTS OF THIS CASE

29. We fail to see how the principle laid down by this Court in *A.R. Antulay's* case (supra) would apply to the facts of these cases. We have found no error in the orders passed by this Court on 11-4-2011 or on 9-4-2012. Therefore, the question of rectifying any error does not arise. On the other hand, as we have already indicated, the purpose and object of passing those orders was for a larger public interest and for speedy trial, that too on day-to-day basis which has been reflected not only in the various provisions of the PC Act, 1988 but also falls within the realm of judicial accountability.

ORDER FOR TRIAL ON DAY-TO-DAY BASIS OR CONCLUSION BY SPECIFIC DATE – IS NOT INTERFERENCE IN TRIAL

30. We also find no reason to lay down any guidelines as prayed for by the petitioners in a Court monitored investigation. In a Court monitored investigation, as already pointed out the Court is not expected to interfere with the trial proceedings. The conduct of the trial is the business of the trial judge and not the court monitoring the investigation. A superior court exercising the appellate power or constitutional power, if gives a direction to conduct the trial on day-to-day basis or complete the trial in a specific time by giving direction is not interfering with the trial proceedings but only facilitating the speedy trial, which is a facet of article 21 of the Constitution of India. That being the factual situation in these cases, the principle laid down by this Court in *Rajiv Ranjan Singh "Lalan"* v. *Union of India,* (2006) 1 SCC 356; *Brij Narain Singh* v. *Adya Prasad,* (2008) 11 SCC 558 and *Ankul Chandra Pradhan* (supra), are not applicable.

NO GROUND TO RECALL ORDERS DATED 11-4-2011 AND 9-4-2012 – WRIT PETITIONS DISMISSED

31. We, therefore, find no good reason either to frame guidelines to be followed by a constitutional court in relation to monitoring of criminal investigation or any legal infirmity in the orders passed by this Court on 11-4-2011 or 9-4-2012. Writ Petitions lack merits and they are accordingly dismissed, so also IA Nos. 59, 61, 63 and 68 in Civil Appeal No. 10660 of 2010.

..............................J.
(G.S. Singhvi)

..............................J.
(K.S. Radhakrishnan)

New Delhi,
September 3, 2013

WHETHER THE PARLIAMENTARIANS AND LEGISLATORS SHOULD CEASE TO BE SO WHEN CONVICTED AND SENTENCED

FOR THAT PURPOSE THE CONSTITUTIONALITY OF SUB-SECTION (4) OF SECTION 8 OF THE REPRESENTATION OF THE PEOPLE ACT, 1951 WAS CONSIDERED IN THIS CASE

Lily Thomas[1]

v.

Union of India

SUPREME COURT OF INDIA

CIVIL ORIGINAL JURISDICTION

Writ Petition (Civil) No. 490 of 2005

WITH

Lok Prahari, through its General Secretary, S.N. Shukla

v.

Union of India

Writ Petition (Civil) No. 231 of 2005

Decided on 10-7-2013

BENCH

A.K. Patnaik and S.J. Mukhopadhaya

JUDGMENT

A.K. Patnaik, J.

These two writ petitions have been filed as Public Interest Litigations for mainly declaring sub-section (4) of section 8 of the Representation of the People Act, 1951 as *ultra vires* the Constitution. The background facts:

The Background Facts

2. The background facts relevant for appreciating the challenge to sub-section (4) of section 8 of the Act are that the Constituent Assembly while drafting the Constitution intended to lay down some disqualifications for persons being chosen as, and for being, a Member of either House of Parliament as well as a Member of the Legislative Assembly or Legislative Council of the State. Accordingly, in the Constitution which was finally adopted by the Constituent Assembly, article 102(1) laid down the disqualifications for membership of either House of Parliament and article 191(1) laid down the disqualifications for membership of the Legislative Assembly or Legislative Council of the State. These two articles are extracted herein below:

---

1. (2013) 7 SCC 653.

ARTICLE 102 AND ARTICLE 191 OF THE CONSTITUTION OF INDIA

"***102. Disqualifications for membership.***—(1) A person shall be disqualified for being chosen as, and for being, a member of either House of Parliament—

(a) if he holds any office of profit under the Government of India or the Government of any State, other than an office declared by Parliament by law not to disqualify its holder;

(b) if he is of unsound mind and stands so declared by a competent court;

(c) if he is an undischarged insolvent;

(d) if he is not a citizen of India, or has voluntarily acquired the citizenship of a foreign State, or is under any acknowledgment of allegiance or adherence to a foreign State;

(e) if he is so disqualified by or under any law made by Parliament.

191. Disqualifications for membership.—(1) A person shall be disqualified for being chosen as, and for being, a member of the Legislative Assembly or Legislative Council of a State—

(a) if he holds any office of profit under the Government of India or the Government of any State specified in the First Schedule, other than an office declared by the Legislature of the State by law not to disqualify its holder;

(b) if he is of unsound mind and stands so declared by a competent court;

(c) if he is an undischarged insolvent;

(d) if he is not a citizen of India, or has voluntarily acquired the citizenship of a foreign State, or is under any acknowledgment of allegiance or adherence to a foreign State;

(e) if he is so disqualified by or under any law made by Parliament.

Explanation.—For the purposes of this clause, a person shall not be deemed to hold an office of profit under the Government of India or the Government of any State specified in the First Schedule by reason only that he is a Minister either for the Union or for such State."

3. A reading of the aforesaid constitutional provisions will show that besides the disqualifications laid down in clauses (a), (b), (c) and (d), Parliament could lay down by law other disqualifications for membership of either House of Parliament or of Legislative Assembly or Legislative Council of the State. In exercise of this power conferred under article 102(1)(e) and under article 191(1)(e) of the Constitution, Parliament provided in Chapter III of the Representation of the People Act, 1951 (for short 'the Act'), the disqualifications for membership of Parliament and State Legislatures. Sections 7 and 8 in Chapter III of the Act, with which we are concerned in these writ petitions, are extracted hereinbelow:

SECTIONS 7 AND 8 OF THE REPRESENTATION OF THE PEOPLE ACT, 1951

"***7. Definitions.***—In this Chapter,—

(a) "appropriate Government" means in relation to any disqualification for being chosen as or for being a member of either House of Parliament, the Central Government, and in relation to any disqualification for being chosen as or for being a member of the Legislative Assembly or Legislative Council of a State, the State Government;

(b) "disqualified" means disqualified for being chosen as, and for being, a member of either House of Parliament or of the Legislative Assembly or Legislative Council of a State.

8. Disqualification on conviction for certain offences.—(1) A person convicted of an offence punishable under—

(a) section 153A (offence of promoting enmity between different groups on ground of religion, race, place of birth, residence, language, etc., and doing acts prejudicial to maintenance of harmony) or section 171E (offence of bribery) or section 171F (offence of undue influence or personation at an election) or sub-section (1) or sub-section (2) of section 376 or section 376A or section 376B or section 376C or section 376D (offences relating to rape) or section 498A (offence of cruelty towards a woman by husband or relative of a husband) or sub-section (2) or sub-section (3) of section 505 (offence of making statement creating or promoting enmity, hatred or ill-will between classes or offence relating to such statement in any place of worship or in any assembly engaged in the performance of religious worship or religious ceremonies) of the Indian Penal Code (45 of 1860); or

(b) the Protection of Civil Rights Act, 1955 (22 of 1955) which provides for punishment for the preaching and practice of "untouchability", and for the enforcement of any disability arising therefrom; or

(c) section 11 (offence of importing or exporting prohibited goods) of the Customs Act, 1962 (52 of 1962); or

(d) sections 10 to 12 (offence of being a member of an association declared unlawful, offence relating to dealing with funds of an unlawful association or offence relating to contravention of an order made in respect of a notified place) of the Unlawful Activities (Prevention) Act, 1967 (37 of 1967); or

(e) the Foreign Exchange (Regulation) Act, 1973 (46 of 1973); or

(f) the Narcotic Drugs and Psychotropic Substances Act, 1985 (61 of 1985); or

(g) section 3 (offence of committing terrorist acts) or section 4 (offence of committing disruptive activities) of the Terrorist and Disruptive Activities (Prevention) Act, 1987 (28 of 1987); or

(h) section 7 (offence of contravention of the provisions of sections 3 to 6) of the Religious Institutions (Prevention of Misuse) Act, 1988 (41 of 1988); or

(i) section 125 (offence of promoting enmity between classes in connection with the election) or section 135 (offence of removal of ballot papers from polling stations) or section 135A (offence of booth capturing) of clause (a) of sub-section (2) of section 136 (offence of fraudulently defacing or fraudulently destroying any nomination paper) of this Act; or

(j) section 6 (offence of conversion of a place of worship) of the Places of Worship (Special Provisions) Act, 1991, or

(k) section 2 (offence of insulting the Indian National Flag or the Constitution of India) or section 3 (offence of preventing singing of National Anthem) of the Prevention of Insults to National Honour Act, 1971 (69 of 1971), or

(l) the Commission of Sati (Prevention) Act, 1987 (3 of 1988); or

(m) the Prevention of Corruption Act, 1988 (49 of 1988); or

(n) the Prevention of Terrorism Act, 2002 (15 of 2002),

shall be disqualified, where the convicted person is sentenced to—

(i) only fine, for a period of six years from the date of such conviction;

(ii) imprisonment, from the date of such conviction and shall continue to be disqualified for a further period of six years since his release.

(2) A person convicted for the contravention of—

(a) any law providing for the prevention of hoarding or profiteering; or

(b) any law relating to the adulteration of food or drugs; or

(c) any provisions of the Dowry Prohibition Act, 1961 (28 of 1961); and sentenced to imprisonment for not less than six months, shall be disqualified from the date of such conviction and shall continue to be disqualified for a further period of six years since his release.

A MEMBER OF PARLIAMENT OR ASSEMBLY IF CONVICTED AND SENTENCED FOR MORE THAN 2 YEARS SHALL BE DISQUALIFIED

(3) A person convicted of any offence and sentenced to imprisonment for not less than two years other than any offence referred to in sub-section (1) or sub-section (2) shall be disqualified from the date of such conviction and shall continue to be disqualified for a further period of six years since his release.

(4) Notwithstanding anything in sub-section (1), sub-section (2) or sub-section (3) a disqualification under either sub-section shall not, in the case of a person who on the date of the conviction is a Member of Parliament or the Legislature of a State, take effect until three months have elapsed from that date or, if within that period an appeal or application for revision is brought in respect of the conviction or the sentence, until that appeal or application is disposed of by the court.

Explanation.—In this section,—

(a) "law providing for the prevention of hoarding or profiteering" means any law, or any order, rule or notification having the force of law, providing for—

(I) the regulation of production or manufacture of any essential commodity;

(II) the control of price at which any essential commodity may be bought or sold;

(III) the regulation of acquisition, possession, storage, transport, distribution, disposal, use or consumption of any essential commodity;

(IV) the prohibition of the withholding from sale of any essential commodity ordinarily kept for sale;

(b) "drug" has the meaning assigned to it in the Drugs and Cosmetics Act, 1940 (23 of 1940);

(c) "essential commodity" has the meaning assigned to it in the Essential Commodity Act, 1955 (10 of 1955);

(d) "food" has the meaning assigned to it in the Prevention of Food Adulteration Act, 1954 (37 of 1954)."

4. Clause (b) of section 7 of the Act quoted above defines the word "disqualified" to mean disqualified for being chosen as, and for being, a Member of either House of Parliament or of the Legislative Assembly or of Legislative Council of State. Sub-sections (1), (2) and (3) of section 8 of the Act provide that a person convicted of an offence mentioned in any of these sub-sections shall stand disqualified from the date of conviction and the disqualification was to continue for the specific period mentioned in the sub-section.

SECTION 8(4) OF THE REPRESENTATION OF THE PEOPLE ACT, 1951 PROVIDES AN EXCEPTION

However, sub-section (4) of section 8 of the Act provides that notwithstanding anything in sub-section (1), sub-section (2) or sub-section (3) in section 8 of the Act, a disqualification under either sub-section shall not, in the case of a person who on the date of the conviction is a member of Parliament or the Legislature of a State, take effect until three months have elapsed from that date or, if within that period an appeal or application for revision is brought in respect of the conviction or the sentence, until that appeal or application is disposed of by the court. It is this saving or protection provided in sub-section (4) of section 8 of the Act for a Member of Parliament or the Legislature of a State which is challenged in these writ petitions as *ultra vires* the Constitution.

SUB-SECTION (4) OF SECTION 8 OF THE REPRESENTATION OF THE PEOPLE ACT, 1951 IS ILLEGAL-SUBMISSIONS OF THE PETITIONERS

5. Mr. Fali S. Nariman, learned Senior Counsel appearing for the petitioner in Writ Petition No. 490 of 2005 and Mr. S.N. Shukla, the General Secretary of the Petitioner in Writ Petition No. 231 of 2005, submitted that the opening words of clause (1) of articles 102 and 191 of the Constitution make it clear that the same disqualifications are provided for a person being chosen as a member of either House of Parliament, or the State Assembly or Legislative Council of the State and for a person being a member of either House of Parliament or of the Legislative Assembly or Legislative Council of a State and therefore the disqualifications for a person to be elected as a member of either House of the Parliament or of the Legislative Assembly or Legislative Council of the State and for a person to continue as a member of either House of Parliament or of the Legislative Assembly or Legislative Council of the State cannot be different. In support of this submission, Mr. Nariman cited a Constitution Bench judgment of this Court in *Election Commission, India* v. *Saka Venkata Rao*, AIR 1953 SC 210, in which it has been held that article 191 lays down the same set of disqualifications for election as well as for continuing as a member.

6. Mr. Nariman and Mr. Shukla submitted that sub-section (4) of section 8 of the Act, insofar as it provides that the disqualification under sub-sections (1), (2) and (3) of section 8 for being elected as a member of either House of Parliament or the Legislative Assembly or Legislative Council of State shall not take effect in the case of a person who is already a member of Parliament or Legislature of a State on the date of the conviction if he files an appeal or a revision in respect of the conviction or the sentence within three months till the appeal or revision is disposed of by the Court, is in contravention of the provisions of clause (1) of articles 102 and 191 of the Constitution.

7. Mr. Shukla referred to the debates of the Constituent Assembly on article 83 of the Draft Constitution, which corresponds to article 102 of the Constitution. In these debates, Mr. Shibban Lal Saksena, a member of the Constituent Assembly moved an Amendment No. 1590 on 19.05.1949 to provide that when a person who, by virtue of conviction becomes disqualified and is on the date of disqualification a member of Parliament, his seat shall, notwithstanding anything in this article, not become vacant by reason of the disqualification until three months have elapsed from the date thereof or, if within those three months an appeal or petition for revision is brought in respect of the conviction or the sentence, until that appeal or petition is disposed of, but during any period during which his membership is preserved by this provision, he shall not sit or vote. Mr. Shukla submitted that this amendment to article 83 of the Draft Constitution was not adopted in the Constituent Assembly. Instead, in sub-clause (e) of clause (1) of articles 102 and 191 of the Constitution, it was provided that Parliament may make a law providing disqualifications besides those mentioned in sub-clauses (a), (b), (c) and (d) for a person being chosen as, and for being, a member of either House of Parliament and of the Legislative Assembly or Legislative Council of a State. Mr. Shukla submitted that despite the fact that a provision similar to sub-section (4) of section 8 of the Act was not incorporated in the Constitution by the Constituent Assembly, Parliament has enacted sub-section (4) of section 8 of the Act.

NO SUCH POWER HAS BEEN GIVEN TO THE PARLIAMENT IN ARTICLE 102 OR ARTICLE 191 OF THE CONSTITUTION TO ENACT A PROVISION LIKE SUB-SECTION (4) OF SECTION 8 IN THE R.P. ACT, 1951

8. According to Mr. Nariman and Mr. Shukla, in the absence of a provision in articles 102 and 191 of the Constitution conferring power on Parliament to make a provision protecting sitting members of either House of Parliament or the Legislative Assembly or the Legislative Council of a State, from the disqualifications it lays down for a person being chosen as a Member of Parliament or a State Legislature, Parliament lacks legislative powers to enact sub-section (4) of section 8 of the Act and sub-section (4) of section 8 of the Act is therefore *ultra vires* the Constitution.

9. Mr. Nariman next submitted that the legal basis of sub-section (4) of section 8 of the Act is based on an earlier judicial view in the judgment of a Division Bench of this Court in *Shri Manni Lal* v. *Shri Parmal Lal*, (1970) 2 SCC 462 that when a conviction is set aside by an appellate order of acquittal, the acquittal takes effect retrospectively and the conviction and the sentence are deemed to be set aside from the date they are recorded. He submitted that in *B.R. Kapur* v. *State of Tamil Nadu*, (2001) 7 SCC 231 a Constitution Bench of this Court reversed the aforesaid judicial view and held: (SCC p. 297 para 40)

"40. ...that conviction, and the sentence it carries, operate against the accused in all their rigour until set aside in appeal, and a disqualification that attaches to the conviction and sentence applies as well."

He submitted that this later view has been reiterated by a Constitution Bench of this Court in *K. Prabhakaran* v. *P. Jayarajan*, (2005) 1 SCC 754.

10. Mr. Nariman argued that thus as soon as a person is convicted of any of the offences mentioned in sub-sections (1), (2) and (3) of section 8 of the Act, he becomes disqualified from continuing as a Member of Parliament or of a State Legislature notwithstanding the fact that he has filed an appeal or a revision against the conviction and there is no legal basis for providing in sub-section (4) of section 8 of the Act that his disqualification will not take effect if he files an appeal or revision within three months against the order of conviction. He submitted that in case a sitting Member of Parliament or State Legislature feels aggrieved by the conviction and wants to continue as a member notwithstanding the conviction, his remedy is to move the Appellate Court for stay of the order of conviction.

11. He cited the decision in *Navjot Singh Sidhu* v. *State of Punjab*, (2007) 2 SCC 574, in which this Court has clarified that under sub-section (1) of section 389 of the Code of Criminal Procedure, 1973 power has been conferred on the Appellate Court not only to suspend the execution of the sentence and to grant bail, but also to suspend the operation of the order appealed against, which means the order of conviction. He submitted that in appropriate cases, the Appellate Court may stay the order of conviction of a sitting Member of Parliament or State Legislature and allow him to continue as a member notwithstanding the conviction by the trial court, but a blanket provision like sub-section (4) of section 8 of the Act cannot be made to keep the disqualification pursuant to conviction in abeyance till the appeal or revision is decided by the Appellate or Revisional Court.

12. Mr. Nariman and Mr. Shukla submitted that in *K. Prabhakaran* v. *P. Jayarajan* (supra) the validity of sub-section (4) of section 8 of the Act was not under challenge and only a reference was made to the Constitution Bench of this Court on certain questions which arose in civil appeals against judgments delivered by the High Court in election cases under the Act. They submitted that the Constitution Bench of this Court framed three questions with regard to disqualification of a candidate under section 8 of the Act and while answering question No. 3, the Constitution Bench indicated reasons which seem to have persuaded Parliament to classify sitting members of the House into a separate category and to provide in sub-section (4) of section 8 of the Act that if such sitting members file appeal or revision against the conviction within three months, then the disqualification on account of their conviction will not take effect until the appeal or revision is decided by the appropriate court. They submitted that the opinion expressed by the Constitution Bench of this Court in *K. Prabhakaran* v. *P. Jayarajan*, (supra) regarding the purpose for which Parliament classified sitting members of Parliament and State Legislatures into a separate category and protected them from the disqualifications by the saving provision in sub-section (4) of section 8 of the Act are *obiter dicta* and are not binding *ratio* on the issue of the validity of sub-section (4) of section 8 of the Act.

13. Mr. Nariman and Mr. Shukla submitted that sub-section (4) of section 8 of the Act, insofar as it does not provide a rationale for making an exception in the case of Members of Parliament or a Legislature of a State is arbitrary and discriminatory and is violative of article 14 of the Constitution. They submitted that persons to be elected as Members of Parliament or a State Legislature stand on the same footing as sitting Members of Parliament and State Legislatures so far as disqualifications are concerned and sitting Members of Parliament and State Legislatures cannot enjoy the special privilege of continuing as members even though they are convicted of the offences mentioned in sub-sections (1), (2) and (3) of section 8 of the Act.

SUBMISSIONS ON BEHALF OF THE UNION OF INDIA WAS THAT SUB-SECTION (4) OF SECTION 8 OF THE R.P. ACT, 1951 HAS BEEN HELD TO BE VALID

Contentions on behalf of the Respondents

14. Mr. Siddharth Luthra, learned ASG appearing for the Union of India in Writ Petition (C) 231 of 2005, submitted that the validity of sub-section (4) of section 8 of the Act has been upheld by the Constitution Bench of this Court in *K. Prabhakaran* v. *P. Jayarajan* (supra). He submitted that while answering question No. 3, the Constitution Bench has held in *Prabhakaran's* case (supra) that the purpose of carving out a saving in sub-section (4) of section 8 of the Act is not to confer an advantage on sitting Members of Parliament or of a State Legislature but to protect the House. He submitted that in para 58 of the judgment the Constitution Bench has explained that if a member of the House was debarred from sitting in the House and participating in the proceedings, no sooner the conviction was pronounced followed by sentence of imprisonment, entailing forfeiture of his membership, then two consequences would follow: *first*, the strength of membership of the House shall stand reduced, so also the strength of the political party to which such convicted member may belong and the Government in power may be surviving on a razor-edge thin majority where each member counts significantly and disqualification of even one member may have a deleterious effect on the functioning of the Government; *second*, a bye-election shall have to be held which exercise may prove to be futile, also resulting in complications in the event of the convicted member being acquitted by a superior criminal court.

15. Mr. Luthra submitted that for the aforesaid two reasons, Parliament has classified the sitting members of Parliament or a State Legislature in a separate category and provided in sub-section (4) of section 8 of the Act that if on the date of incurring disqualification, a person is a Member of Parliament or of a State Legislature, such disqualification shall not take effect for a period of three months from the date of such disqualification to enable the sitting member to file appeal or revision challenging his conviction, and sentence and if such an appeal or revision is filed, then applicability of the disqualification shall stand deferred until such appeal or revision is disposed of by the appropriate Court.

16. Mr. Luthra next submitted that the reality of the Indian judicial system is that acquittals in the levels of the Appellate Court such as the High Court are very high and it is for this reason that Parliament has provided in sub-section (4) of section 8 of the Act that disqualification pursuant to conviction or sentence in the case of sitting members should stand deferred till the appeal or revision is decided by the Appellate or the Revisional Court. He submitted that the power to legislate on disqualification of Members of Parliament and the State Legislature conferred on Parliament carries with it the incidental power to say when the disqualification will take effect. He submitted that the source of legislative power for enacting sub-section (4) of section 8 of the Act is, therefore, very much there in articles 101(1)(e) and 191(1)(e) of the Constitution and if not in these articles of the Constitution, in article 246(1) read with Entry 97 of List I of the Seventh Schedule of the Constitution and article 248 of the Constitution, which confer powers on Parliament to legislate on any matter not enumerated in List II and List III of the Seventh Schedule of the Constitution.

17. Mr. Paras Kuhad, learned ASG, appearing for the Union of India in Writ Petition (C) No. 490 of 2005 also relied on the judgment of the Constitution Bench of this Court in *K. Prabhakaran* v. *P. Jayarajan* (supra) on the validity of sub-section (4) of section 8 of the Act and the reasoning given in the answer to question No. 3 in the aforesaid judgment of this Court. He further submitted that sub-section (4) of section 8 of the Act does not lay down disqualifications for Members of Parliament and the State Legislatures different from the disqualifications laid down for persons to be chosen as Members of Parliament and the State Legislatures in sub-sections (1), (2) and (3) of section 8 of the Act. He submitted that sub-section (4) of section 8 of the Act merely provides that the very same disqualifications laid down in sub-sections (1), (2) and (3) of section 8 of the Act shall in the case of sitting Members of Parliament and State Legislatures take effect only after the appeal or revision is disposed of by the Appellate or Revisional Court as the case may be if an appeal or revision is filed against the conviction.

18. Mr. Paras Kuhad submitted that Parliament has power under article 102(1)(e) of the Constitution and article 191(1)(e) of the Constitution to prescribe when exactly the disqualification will become effective in the case of sitting Members of Parliament or the State Legislature with a view to protect the House. He also referred to the provisions of articles 101(3)(a) and 190(3)(a) of the Constitution to argue that a Member of Parliament or a State Legislature will vacate a seat only when he becomes subject to any disqualification mentioned in clause (1) of article 102 or clause (1) of article 191, as the case may be, and this will happen only after a decision is taken by the President or the Governor that the Member has become disqualified in accordance with the mechanism provided in article 103 or article 192 of the Constitution.

19. Mr. Kuhad further submitted that Mr. Nariman is not right in his submission that the remedy of a sitting member who is convicted or sentenced and gets disqualified under sub-sections (1), (2) or (3) of section 8 of the Act is to move the Appellate Court under section 389 of the Code of Criminal Procedure for stay of his conviction. He submitted that the Appellate Court does not have any power under section 389, Cr.P.C. to stay the disqualification which would take effect from the date of conviction and therefore a safeguard had to be provided in sub-section (4) of section 8 of the Act that the disqualification, despite the conviction or sentence, will not have effect until the appeal or revision is decided by the Appellate or the Revisional Court. He submitted that there is, therefore, a rationale for enacting sub-section (4) of section 8 of the Act.

POWER OF PARLIAMENT DISCUSSED

Findings of the Court

20. We will first decide the issue raised before us in these writ petitions that Parliament lacked the legislative power to enact sub-section (4) of section 8 of the Act as this issue was not at all considered by the Constitution Bench of this Court in the aforesaid case of *K. Prabhakaran* (supra).

21. In *The Empress* v. *Burah,* (1878) 5 IA 178 the Privy Council speaking through Selborne J. laid down the following fundamental principles for interpretation of a written Constitution laying down the powers of the Indian Legislature: (IA pp. 193-94)

> "...The Indian Legislature has powers expressly limited by the Act of the Imperial Parliament which created it; and it can, of course, do nothing beyond the limits which circumscribes these powers. But, when acting within these limits, it is not in any sense an agent or delegate of the Imperial Parliament, but has, and was intended to have, plenary powers of legislation, as large, and of the same nature, as those of Parliament itself. The established Courts of Justice, when a question arises whether the prescribed limits have been exceeded, must of necessity determine that question; and the only way in which they can properly do so, is by looking to the terms of the instrument by which, affirmatively, the legislative powers were created, and by which, negatively, they are restricted. If what has been done is legislation within the general scope of the affirmative words which give the power, and if it violates no express condition or restriction by which that power is limited (in which category would, of course, be included any Act of the Imperial Parliament at variance with it), it is not for any Court of Justice to inquire further, or to enlarge constructively those conditions and restrictions."

22. The correctness of the aforesaid principles with regard to interpretation of a written Constitution has been reaffirmed by the majority of Judges in *Kesavananda Bharti* v. *State of Kerala,* AIR 1973 SC 1465; (See the *Constitutional Law of India,* H.M. Seervai, 4th Edn., Vol. I, para 2.4 at page 174). Hence, when a question is raised whether Parliament has exceeded the limits of its powers, courts have to decide the question by looking to the terms of the instrument by which affirmatively, the legislative powers were created, and by which negatively, they are restricted.

23. We must first consider the argument of Mr. Luthra, learned Additional-Solicitor General, that the legislative power to enact sub-section (4) of section 8 of the Act is located in article 246(1) read with Entry 97 of List I of the Seventh Schedule and article 248 of the Constitution, if not in articles 102(1)(e) and 191(1)(e) of the Constitution.

24. Articles 246 and 248 of the Constitution are placed in Chapter I of Part XI of the Constitution of India. Part XI is titled "Relations between the Union and the States" and Chapter I of Part XI is titled "Legislative Relations". In Chapter I of Part XI, under the heading "Distribution of Legislative Powers" articles 245 to 255 have been placed. A reading of articles 245 to 255 would show that these relate to distribution of legislative powers between the Union and the Legislatures of the States. Article 246(1) provides that Parliament has exclusive power to make laws with respect to any of the matters enumerated in List I in the Seventh Schedule of the Constitution and under Entry 97 of List I of the Seventh Schedule of the Constitution, Parliament has exclusive power to make law with respect to any other matter not enumerated in List II or List III. Article 248 similarly provides that Parliament has exclusive power to make any law with respect to any matter not enumerated in the Concurrent List (List III) or State List (List II) of the Seventh Schedule of the Constitution. Therefore, article 246(1) read with Entry 97 and article 248 only provide that in residuary matters (other than matters enumerated in List II and List III) Parliament will have power to make law.

25. To quote from *Commentary on the Constitution of India by Durga Das Basu* (8th Edn.) Vol. 8 at page 8988:

> "In short, the principle underlying article 248, read with Entry 97 of List I, is that a written Constitution, which divides legislative power as between two Legislatures in a federation, cannot intend that neither of such Legislatures shall go without power to legislate with respect of any subject simply because that subject has not been specifically mentioned nor can be reasonably comprehended by judicial interpretation to be included in any of the Entries in the Legislative Lists. To meet such a situation, a residuary power is provided, and in the Indian Constitution, this residuary power is vested in the Union Legislature. Once, therefore, it is found that a particular subject-matter has not been assigned to the competence of the State Legislature, 'it leads to the irresistible inference that (the Union) Parliament would have legislative competence to deal with the subject-matter in question.'

POWER TO LAY DOWN DISQUALIFICATIONS OF MPs AND MLAs VESTED IN PARLIAMENT ONLY UNDER ARTICLE 102 AND ARTICLE 191 OF THE CONSTITUTION OF INDIA

26. Articles 102(1)(e) and 191(1)(e) of the Constitution, on the other hand, have conferred specific powers on Parliament to make law providing disqualifications for membership of either House of Parliament or Legislative Assembly or Legislative Council of the State other than those specified in sub-clauses (a), (b), (c) and (d) of clause (1) of articles 102 and 191 of the Constitution. We may note that no power is vested in the State Legislature to make law laying down disqualifications of membership of the Legislative Assembly or Legislative Council of the State and power is vested in Parliament to make law laying down disqualifications also in respect of members of the Legislative Assembly or Legislative Council of the State. For these reasons, we are of the considered opinion that the legislative power of Parliament to enact any law relating to disqualification for membership of either House of Parliament or Legislative Assembly or Legislative Council of the State can be located only in articles 102(1)(e) and 191(1)(e) of the Constitution and not in articles 246(1) read with Entry 97 of List I of the Seventh Schedule and article 248 of the Constitution. We do not, therefore, accept the contention of Mr. Luthra that the power to enact sub-section (4) of section 8 of the Act is vested in Parliament under articles 246(1) read with Entry 97 of List I of the Seventh Schedule and 248 of the Constitution, if not in articles 102(1)(e) and 191(1)(e) of the Constitution.

27. Articles 102(1)(e) and 191(1)(e) of the Constitution, which contain the only source of legislative power to lay down disqualifications for membership of either House of Parliament and Legislative Assembly or Legislative Council of a State, provide as follows:

> "**102.** ***Disqualification for membership.***—A person shall be disqualified for being chosen as, and for being, a member of either House of Parliament—
>
> (e) if he is so disqualified by or under any law made by Parliament.
>
> ***191. Disqualification for membership.***—A person shall be disqualified for being chosen as, and for being, a member of the Legislative Assembly or Legislative Council of a State—
>
> * * * * *
>
> (e) if he is so disqualified by or under any law made by Parliament."

28. A reading of the aforesaid two provisions in articles 102(1)(e) and 191(1)(e) of the Constitution would make it abundantly clear that Parliament is to make one law for a person to be disqualified for being chosen as, and for being, a Member of either House of Parliament or Legislative Assembly or Legislative Council of the State. In the language of the Constitution Bench of this Court in *Election Commission, India* v. *Saka Venkata Rao* (supra), article 191(1) [which is identically worded as article 102(1)] lays down "the same set of disqualifications for election as well as for continuing as a member".

PARLIAMENT DOES NOT HAVE THE POWER TO CREATE DISTINCTION IN DISQUALIFICATION BETWEEN A PERSON TO BE CHOSEN AS MP OR MLA AND THE PERSON CONTINUING AS MP OR MLA

Parliament thus does not have the power under articles 102(1)(e) and 191(1)(e) of the Constitution to make different laws for a person to be disqualified for being chosen as a member and for a person to be disqualified for continuing as a Member of Parliament or the State Legislature. To put it differently, if because of a disqualification a person cannot be chosen as a Member of Parliament or State Legislature, for the same disqualification, he cannot continue as a Member of Parliament or the State Legislature. This is so because the language of articles 102(1)(c) and 191(1)(e) of the Constitution is such that the disqualification for both a person to be chosen as a member of a House of Parliament or the State Legislature or for a person to continue as a Member of Parliament or the State Legislature has to be the same.

SUB-SECTION (4) OF SECTION 8 OF THE REPRESENTATION OF THE PEOPLE ACT, 1951 DOES CREATE SUCH DISTINCTION BETWEEN THESE TWO CLASSES

29. Mr. Luthra and Mr. Kuhad, however, contended that the disqualifications laid down in sub-sections (1),(2) and (3) of section 8 of the Act are the same for persons who are to continue as members of Parliament or a State Legislature and sub-section (4) of section 8 of the Act does not lay down a different set of disqualifications for sitting members but merely states that the same disqualifications will have effect only after the appeal or revision, as the case may be, against the conviction is decided by the Appellate or the Revisional Court if such appeal or revision is filed within 3 months from the date of conviction. We cannot accept this contention also because of the provisions of articles 101(3)(a) and 190(3)(a) of the Constitution which are quoted hereinbelow:

"101. Vacation of seats.—

(1) ....

(2) ....

(3) If a member of either House of Parliament—

(a) becomes subject to any of the disqualifications mentioned in clause (1) or clause (2) of article 102.

....

his seat shall thereupon become vacant:

* * * * *

190. Vacation of seats.—

(1) ....

(2) ....

(3) If a member of a House of the Legislature of a State – (a) becomes subject to any of the disqualifications mentioned in clause (1) or clause (2) of article 191,

his seat shall thereupon become vacant."

30. Thus, article 101(3)(a) provides that if a Member of either House of Parliament becomes subject to any of the disqualifications mentioned in clause (1), his seat shall thereupon become vacant and similarly article 190(3)(a) provides that if a Member of a House of the Legislature of a State becomes subject to any of the disqualifications mentioned in clause (1), his seat shall thereupon become vacant. This is the effect of a disqualification under articles 102(1) and 190(1) incurred by a Member of either House of Parliament or a House of the State Legislature. Accordingly, once a person who was a Member of either House of Parliament or House of the State Legislature becomes disqualified by or under any law made by Parliament under articles 102(1)(e) and 191(1)(e) of the Constitution, his seat automatically falls vacant by virtue of articles 101(3)(a) and 190(3)(a) of the Constitution and Parliament cannot make a provision as in sub-section (4) of section 8 of the Act to defer the date on which the disqualification of a sitting member will have effect and prevent his seat becoming vacant on account of the disqualification under article 102(1)(e) or article 191(1)(e) of the Constitution.

PRESIDENT OR THE GOVERNOR DO NOT HAVE THE POWER TO DECIDE THE DATE WHEN THE MP OR MLA HAS SUFFERED DISQUALIFICATION

31. We cannot also accept the submission of Mr. Kuhad that until the decision is taken by the President or Governor on whether a Member of Parliament or State Legislature has become subject to any of the disqualifications mentioned in clause (1) of article 102 and article 191 of the Constitution, the seat of the member alleged to have been disqualified will not become vacant under articles 101(3)(a) and 190(3)(a) of the Constitution. Articles 101(3)(a) and 190(3)(a) of the Constitution provide that if a member of the House becomes subject to any of the disqualifications mentioned in clause (1), "his seat shall thereupon become vacant".

FILLING OF THAT VACANCY MAY WAIT FOR THE ORDERS OF THE PRESIDENT OR THE GOVERNOR

Hence, the seat of a member who becomes subject to any of the disqualifications mentioned in clause (1) will fall vacant on the date on which the member incurs the disqualification and cannot await the decision of the President or the Governor, as the case may be, under articles 103 and 192 respectively of the Constitution. The filling of the seat which falls vacant, however, may await the decision of the President or the Governor under articles 103 and 192 respectively of the Constitution and if the President or the Governor takes a view that the member has not become subject to any of the disqualifications mentioned in clause (1) of articles 102 and 191 respectively of the Constitution, it has to be held that the seat of the member so held not to be disqualified did not become vacant on the date on which the member was alleged to have been subject to the disqualification.

PARLIAMENT DO NOT HAVE THE POWER UNDER ARTICLE 102(1)(E) OR ARTICLE 191(1)(E) TO DEFER THE DATE OF DISQUALIFICATION

32. The result of our aforesaid discussion is that the affirmative words used in articles 102(1)(e) and 191(1)(e) confer power on Parliament to make one law laying down the same disqualifications for a person who is to be chosen as Member of either House of Parliament or as a Member of the Legislative Assembly or Legislative Council of a State and for a person who is a sitting member of a House of Parliament or a House of the State Legislature and the words in articles 101(3)(a) and 190(3)(a) of the Constitution put express limitations on such powers of the Parliament to defer the date on which the disqualifications would have effect. Accordingly, sub-section (4) of section 8 of the Act which carves out a saving in the case of sitting members of Parliament or State Legislature from the disqualifications under sub-sections (1), (2) and (3) of section 8 of the Act or which defers the date on which the disqualification will take effect in the case of a sitting Member of Parliament or a State Legislature is beyond the powers conferred on Parliament by the Constitution.

PARLIAMENT HAD NO RIGHT TO ENACT SUB-SECTION (4) OF SECTION 8 OF THE REPRESENTATION OF THE PEOPLE ACT, 1951

33. Looking at the affirmative terms of articles 102(1)(e) and 191(1)(e) of the Constitution, we hold that Parliament has been vested with the powers to make law laying down the same disqualifications for person to be chosen as a Member of Parliament or a State Legislature and for a sitting Member of a House of Parliament or a House of a State Legislature. We also hold that the provisions of article 101(3)(a) and 190(3)(a) of the Constitution expressly prohibit Parliament to defer the date from which the disqualification will come into effect in case of a sitting member of Parliament or a State Legislature. Parliament, therefore, has exceeded its powers conferred by the Constitution in enacting sub-section (4) of section 8 of the Act and accordingly sub-section (4) of section 8 of the Act is *ultra vires* the Constitution.

IN FRIVOLOUS CASES CONVICTION CAN BE STAYED BY A COMPETENT COURT OF LAW

34. We do not also find merit in the submission of Mr. Luthra and Mr. Kuhad that if a sitting member of Parliament or the State Legislature suffers from a frivolous conviction by the trial court for an offence given under sub-section (1), (2) or (3) of section 8 of the Act, he will be remediless and he will suffer immense hardship as he would stand disqualified on account of such conviction in the absence of sub-section (4) of section 8 of the Act. A three-Judge Bench of this Court in *Rama Narang* v. *Ramesh Narang*, (1995) 2 SCC 513, has held that when an appeal is preferred under section 374 of the Code of Criminal Procedure [for short 'the Code'] the appeal is against both the conviction and sentence and, therefore, the Appellate Court in exercise of its power under section 389(1) of the Code can also stay the order of conviction and the High Court in exercise of its inherent jurisdiction under section 482 of the Code can also stay the conviction if the power was not to be found in section 389(1) of the Code.

35. In *Ravikant S. Patil* v. *Sarvabhouma S. Bagali*, (2007) 1 SCC 673, a three-Judge Bench of this Court, however, observed: (SCC p. 679, para 15)

> "15. It deserves to be clarified that an order granting stay of conviction is not the rule but is an exception to be resorted to in rare cases depending upon the facts of a case. Where the execution of the sentence is stayed, the conviction continues to operate. But where the conviction itself is stayed, the effect is that the conviction will not be operative from the date of stay. An order of stay, of course, does not render the conviction non-existent, but only non-operative. Be that as it may. Insofar as the present case is concerned, an application was filed specifically seeking stay of the order of conviction specifying the consequences if conviction was not stayed, that is, the appellant would incur disqualification to contest the election. The High Court after considering the special reason, granted the order staying the conviction. As the conviction itself is stayed in contrast to a stay of execution of the sentence, it is not possible to accept the contention of the respondent that the disqualification arising out of conviction continues to operate even after stay of conviction."

In the aforesaid case, a contention was raised by the respondents that the appellant was disqualified from contesting the election to the Legislative Assembly under sub-section (3) of section 8 of the Act as he had been convicted for an offence punishable under sections 366 and 376 of the Indian Penal Code and it was held by the three-Judge Bench that as the High Court for special reasons had passed an order staying the conviction, the disqualification arising out of the conviction ceased to operate after the stay of conviction. Therefore, the disqualification under sub-section (1), (2) or (3) of section 8 of the Act will not operate from the date of order of stay of conviction passed by the Appellate Court under section 389 of the Code or the High Court under section 482 of the Code.

SUB-SECTION (4) OF SECTION 8 OF THE REPRESENTATION OF THE PEOPLE ACT, 1951 IS *ULTRA VIRES* THE CONSTITUTION

36. As we have held that Parliament had no power to enact sub-section (4) of section 8 of the Act and accordingly sub-section (4) of section 8 of the Act is *ultra vires* the Constitution, it is not necessary for us to go into the other issue raised in these writ petitions that sub-section (4) of section 8 of the Act is violative of article 14 of the Constitution. It would have been necessary for us to go into this question only if sub-section (4) of section 8 of the Act was held to be within the powers of the Parliament. In other words, as we can declare sub-section (4) of section 8 of the Act as *ultra vires* the Constitution without going into the question as to whether sub-section (4) of section 8 of the Act is violative of article 14 of the Constitution, we do not think it is necessary to decide the question as to whether sub-section (4) of section 8 of the Act is violative of article 14 of the Constitution.

NOT APPLICABLE TO MPs OR MLAs WHO HAVE ALREADY FILED APPEALS OR REVISION AFTER SUFFERING DISQUALIFICATION

37. The only question that remains to be decided is whether our declaration in this judgment that sub-section (4) of section 8 of the Act is *ultra vires* the Constitution should affect disqualifications already incurred under sub-sections (1), (2) and (3) of section 8 of the Act by sitting members of Parliament and State Legislatures who have filed appeals or revisions against their conviction within a period of three months and their appeals and revisions are still pending before the concerned court.

38. Under sub-sections (1), (2) and (3) of section 8 of the Act, the disqualification takes effect from the date of conviction for any of the offences mentioned in the sub-sections and remains in force for the periods mentioned in the sub-sections. Thus, there may be several sitting members of Parliament and State Legislatures who have already incurred disqualification by virtue of a conviction covered under sub-section (1), or sub-section (2) or sub-section (3) of section 8 of the Act.

In *Golak Nath* v. *State of Punjab,* AIR 1967 SC 1643, Subba Rao, C.J. speaking on behalf of himself, Shah, Sikri, Shelat and Vaidialingam, JJ. has held that articles 32, 141, 142 of the Constitution are couched in such a wide and elastic terms as to enable this Court to formulate legal doctrines to meet the ends of justice and has further held that this Court has the power not only to declare the law but also to restrict the operation of the law as declared to future and save the transactions, whether statutory or otherwise, that were effected on the basis of the earlier law. Sitting Members of Parliament and State Legislature who have already been convicted for any of the offences mentioned in sub-sections (1), (2) and (3) of section 8 of the Act and who have filed appeals or revisions which are pending and are accordingly saved from the disqualifications by virtue of sub-section (4) of section 8 of the Act should not, in our considered opinion, be affected by the declaration now made by us in this judgment.

This is because the knowledge that sitting members of Parliament or State Legislatures will no longer be protected by sub-section (4) of section 8 of the Act will be acquired by all concerned only on the date this judgment is pronounced by this Court. As has been observed by this Court in *Harla* v. *State of Rajasthan,* AIR 1951 SC 467: (AIR p. 458 para 8)

> "8. ....it would be against the principles of natural justice to permit the subjects of a State to be punished or penalized by laws of which they had no knowledge and of which they could not even with exercise of due diligence have acquired any knowledge."

THIS LAW WOULD BE APPLICABLE TO MPS OR MLAS WHO SUFFER DISQUALIFICATION NOW ONWARDS – WRITS ALLOWED

However, if any sitting Member of Parliament or a State Legislature is convicted of any of the offences mentioned in sub-sections (1), (2) and (3) of section 8 of the Act and by virtue of such conviction and/or sentence suffers the disqualifications mentioned in sub-sections (1), (2) and (3) of section 8 of the Act after the pronouncement of this judgment, his Membership of Parliament or the State Legislature, as the case may be, will not be saved by sub-section (4) of section 8 of the Act which we have by this judgment declared as *ultra vires* the Constitution notwithstanding that he files the appeal or revision against the conviction and/or sentence.

39. With the aforesaid declaration, the writ petitions are allowed. No costs.

....J.
K. Patnaik)

....J.
(Sudhansu Jyoti Mukhopadhaya)

New Delhi,
July 10, 2013.

Author's Note: In paragraphs 40 and 41, WP(C) No. 694 of 2004 was disposed of in terms of the judgment delivered in WP(C) No. 490 of 2005 and WP(C) No. 231 of 2005 reproduced above.

Author's Note: The Union of India had filed Review Petition against the Judgment dated 10.7.2013 in which it was held that Members of Parliament if upon conviction are awarded the Punishment of more than 2 years, they will cease to be the Members of Parliament or of Legislative Assemblies as the case may be that Review petition was dismissed by the Hon'ble Supreme Court on 4.9.2013 by the judgment reproduced below.

Union of India

v.

Lily Thomas

SUPREME COURT OF INDIA

CIVIL ORIGINAL JURISDICTION

Review Petition (c) No(s). 1830-1831 of 2013

in

Writ Petition (c) No. 490 of 2005

[for preliminary hearing]

(With application for condonation of delay in filing review petition)

Decided on 4-9-2013 These Petitions were circulated today.

ORDER

DELAY CONDONED – REVIEW PETITION DISMISSED

1. Delay condoned.

2. We have heard the learned Additional-Solicitor-General appearing for the petitioners and we do not find any error apparent on the face of the record in our judgment dated 10th July, 2013 in Writ Petition (C) No. 490 of 2005 and Writ Petition (C) No. 231 of 2005 and hence, we dismiss these review.

....J.
K. Patnaik)

....J.
(Sudhansu Jyoti Mukhopadhaya)

Author's Note: A Bill titled the Representation of the People (2nd Amendment and Validation) Bill, 2013 was introduced in the Rajya Sabha but it was referred to the Standing Committee. Pending this Bill, the Union of India had passed an Ordinance in the same terms and it was sent to the President of India for his signatures. It was strongly opposed by the Public. Then the Central Government decided on 2.10.2013 to withdraw, both the Bill and the Ordinance.

WHETHER A PERSON IN JAIL OR IN POLICE CUSTODY CAN CONTEST ELECTIONS OR NOT WAS DECIDED IN THIS CASE

The Chief Election Commissioner[1]

v.

Jan Chaukidar (Peoples Watch)

SUPREME COURT OF INDIA

CIVIL APPELLATE JURISDICTION

Civil Appeal Nos. 3040-3041 of 2004

Decided on 10-7-2013

BENCH

A.K. Patnaik and Sudhanshu Jyoti Mokhopadhaya.

ORDER

1. These are appeals by way of Special Leave under article 136 of the Constitution against the common order dated 30.4.2004 of the Patna High Court in C.W.J.C. No. 4880 of 2004 and C.W.J.C. No.4988 of 2004: (2004) 2 BLJR 988.

THE REPRESENTATION OF THE PEOPLE ACT, 1951 ENACTED UNDER ARTICLE 326 OF THE CONSTITUTION OF INDIA

2. The facts very briefly are that article 326 of the Constitution provides that the elections to the House of the People and to the Legislative Assembly of every State shall be on the basis of adult suffrage and every person who is a citizen of India and who is not less than eighteen years of age on such date as may be fixed in that behalf by or under any law made by the appropriate Legislature and is not otherwise disqualified under the Constitution any law made by the appropriate Legislature on the grounds of non-residence, unsoundness of mind, crime or corrupt or illegal practice, shall be entitled to be registered as a voter for any such election. In accordance with article 326 of the Constitution, Parliament has enacted the Representation of the People Act, 1950 (for short 'the 1950 Act') for registration of voters at such elections to the House of the People and to the Legislative Assembly of every State and has also enacted the Representation of the People Act, 1951 (for short 'the 1951 Act') for the conduct of elections to the Houses of Parliament and to the Houses of Legislature of each State.

WORD 'ELECTOR' DEFINED IN THE REPRESENTATION OF THE PEOPLE ACT, 1951

3. The word "elector" is defined in the 1951 Act in relation to the constituency to mean a person whose name is entered in electoral rolls of the constituency for the time being in force and who is not subject to any of the disqualifications mentioned in section 16 of the 1950 Act. Section 16(1)(c) of the 1950 Act provides that:

---

1. (2013) 7 SCC 507.

> ***"Section 16. Disqualification for registration in an electoral role.***—(1) A person shall be disqualified for registration in an electoral roll if he is for the time being disqualified from voting under the provisions of any law relating to corrupt practices and other offences in connection with elections."

SECTIONS 4 AND 5 OF THE REPRESENTATION OF THE PEOPLE ACT, 1951

4. Section 4 of the 1951 Act lays down the qualifications for membership of the House of the People and one of the qualifications laid down is that he must be an "elector" for any Parliamentary constituency. Similarly, section 5 of the 1951 Act lays down the qualifications for membership of a Legislative Assembly of a State and one of the qualifications laid down is that he must be an "elector" for any Assembly constituency in that State.

5. Section 62 of the 1951 Act is titled "Right to vote" and it provides in sub-section (5) that:

> "62.(5) No person shall vote at any election if he is confined in a prison, whether under a sentence of imprisonment or transportation or otherwise, or is in the lawful custody of the police;"

The proviso to sub-section (5) of section 62 of the 1951 Act, however, states that the sub-section will not apply to a person subjected to preventive detention under any law for the time being in force.

UNDER SECTION 62(5) OF THE REPRESENTATION OF THE PEOPLE ACT, 1951, A PERSON IN JAIL OR POLICE CUSTODY IS NOT AN ELECTOR

6. Writ petitions C.W.J.C. No. 4880 of 2004 and C.W.J.C. No.4988 of 2004 were filed in the Patna High Court contending that a person, who is confined in prison, whether under a sentence of imprisonment or transportation or otherwise, or is in the lawful custody of the police is not entitled to vote by virtue of sub-section (5) of section 62 of the 1951 Act and accordingly is not an "elector" and is, therefore, not qualified to contest elections to the House of People or the Legislative Assembly of a State because of the provisions in sections 4 and 5 of the 1951 Act. By the impugned common order, the High Court accepted this contention in the writ petitions and held: (*Jan Chaukidar* case BJLR pp. 996-97 para 33)

> "33. A right to vote is a statutory right, the Law gives it, the Law takes it away. Persons convicted of crime are kept away from elections to the Legislature, whether to State Legislature or Parliament, and all other public elections. The Court has no hesitation in interpreting the Constitution and the Laws framed under it, read together, that persons in the lawful custody of the Police also will not be voters, in which case, they will neither be electors. The Law temporarily takes away the power of such persons to go anywhere near the election scene. To vote is a statutory right. It is privilege to vote, which privilege may be taken away. In that case, the elector would not be qualified, even if his name is on the electoral rolls. The name is not struck off, but the qualification to be an elector and the privilege to vote when in the lawful custody of the police is taken away."

FINDINGS OF PATNA HIGH COURT UPHELD – APPEALS DISMISSED

7. Aggrieved, by the findings of the High Court, the appellants have filed these appeals. We have heard learned counsel for the parties and we do not find any infirmity in the findings of the High Court in the impugned common order that a person who has no right to vote by virtue of the provisions of sub-section (5) of section 62 of the 1951 Act is not an elector and is therefore not qualified to contest the election to the House of the People or the Legislative Assembly of a State.

8. These civil appeals are accordingly dismissed. No costs.

....J.
(A.K. Patnaik)

....J.
(Sudhansu Jyoti Mukhopadhaya)

New Delhi,
July 10, 2013.

Review application was filed by the Union of India on which the Hon'ble Supreme Court has issued the notice. Hence this judgment.

Ramesh Dalal

v.

Union of India

SUPREME COURT OF INDIA

Record of Proceedings

Review Petition (C) No(s). 1784-1785 of 2013

in

Civil Appeal Nos. 3040-3041 of 2004

(With application for exemption from filing certified copy of the impugned Judgment, directions, interim Relief, oral hearing, permission to file additional documents and office report)

Decided on 4-9-2013 These Petitions were circulated today.

Hon'ble Mr. Justice A.K. Patnaik

Hon'ble Mr. Justice Sudhanshu Jyoti Mukhopadhaya

ORDER

These review petitions be listed alongwith Review Petition) Nos. 1854-1855 of 2013 on 23rd October, 2013.

Author's note: The Central Government introduced "The Representation of the People (Amendment) Bill, 2013", in the Lok Sabha to negate the above mentioned judgment dated 10.7.2013 passed by the Hon'ble Supreme Court. This Bill has been passed in the Lok Sabha. Then the Bill was sent to the Rajya Sabha where also it was passed on 28.8.2013. It has received the assent of the President of India. The amended provision of the Representation of the People Act, 1951 has become the law of the land.

Author's note: It was reported in almost all the newspapers dated 20-11-2013 (Wednesday) that the review petition was dismissed by the Supreme Court as infructuous in the light of the amendment brought about in Parliament in the Representation of the People Act, 1951 after the passing of the judgment by the Supreme Court on 10-7-2013. It was also ordered that liberty was granted to challenge the amendment by separate legal proceedings.

Author's note: It was noticed that many of the candidates filing nomination papers for being elected as a Member of the Legislative Assembly or for the Lok Sabha either keep the columns of the affidavit accompanying the nomination papers blank or they fill wrong information. The direction was given to the candidates by way of Judgments of the Hon'ble Supreme Court and followed by an amendment in the Representation of the People Act to complete all the columns of the affidavit and to furnish correct information in the affidavits accompanying the nomination papers but these directions were complied with more in breach than the actual and real compliance. Hence this Judgment.

IMPLEMENTATION OF THE DIRECTIONS GIVEN IN THE EARLIER JUDGMENTS TO THE ELECTION COMMISSION OF INDIA RELATING TO THE FILLING OF ALL THE COLUMNS IN THE AFFIDAVIT ACCOMPANYING THE NOMINATION PAPERS WAS CONSIDERED IN THIS CASE

Resurgence India[1]

v.

Election Commission of India

SUPREME COURT OF INDIA

CIVIL ORIGINAL JURISDICTION

[Writ Petition (Civil) No. 121 of 2008]

JUDGMENT

P. Sathasivam, CJI.

1. This writ petition, under article 32 of the Constitution of India, has been filed to issue specific directions to effectuate meaningful implementation of the judgments rendered by this Court in *Union of India* v. *Association for Democratic Reforms*, (2002) 5 SCC 294 and *People's Union for Civil Liberties (PUCL)* v. *Union of India*, (2003) 4 SCC 399 and also to direct the respondents herein to make it compulsory for the Returning Officers to ensure that the affidavits filed by the contestants are complete in all respects and to reject the affidavits having blank particulars. Background:

DIRECTIONS WERE MEANT TO MAINTAIN PURITY IN ELECTIONS

2. In order to maintain purity of elections and to bring transparency in the process of election, this Court, in *Association for Democratic Reforms* (supra), directed the Election Commission of India-Respondent No. 1 hereinto issue necessary orders, in exercise of its power under article 324 of the Constitution, to call for information on affidavit from each candidate seeking election to the Parliament or a State Legislature as a necessary part of his nomination paper furnishing therein information relating to his conviction/acquittal/discharge in any criminal offence in the past, any case pending against him of any offence punishable with imprisonment for 2 years or more, information regarding assets (movable, immovable, bank balance etc.) of the candidate as well as of his/her spouse and that of dependants, liability, if any, and the educational qualification of the candidate.

---

1. JT 2013 (12) SCC 462.

IN PURSUANCE OF THE JUDGMENTS OF THE SUPREME COURT, NECESSARY INSTRUCTIONS WERE ISSUED BY THE ELECTION COMMISSION

3. Pursuant to the above order, the Election Commission, *vide* order dated 28.6.2002, issued certain directions to the candidates to furnish full and complete information in the form of an affidavit, duly sworn before a Magistrate of the First Class, with regard to the matters specified in Association for Democratic Reforms (supra). It was also directed that non-furnishing of the affidavit by any candidate or furnishing of any wrong or incomplete information or suppression of any material information will result in the rejection of the nomination paper, apart from inviting penal consequences under the Indian Penal Code, 1860. It was further clarified that only such information shall be considered to be wrong or incomplete or suppression of material information which is found to be a defect of substantial character by the Returning Officer in the summary inquiry conducted by him at the time of scrutiny of nomination papers.

IN ANOTHER JUDGMENT DIRECTIONS WERE GIVEN NOT TO REJECT THE NOMINATION PAPERS FOR FURNISHING WRONG INFORMATION OR CONCEALING MATERIAL INFORMATION IN SUMMARY ENQUIRY

4. In *People's Union for Civil Liberties (PUCL)* (supra), though this Court reaffirmed the aforementioned decision but also held that the direction to reject the nomination papers for furnishing wrong information or concealing material information and verification of assets and liabilities by means of a summary inquiry at the time of scrutiny of the nominations cannot be justified.

ELECTION COMMISSION ALSO REVISED THE INSTRUCTIONS

5. Pursuant to the above, the Election Commission, *vide* order dated 27.3.2003, held its earlier order dated 28.6.2002 non-enforceable with regard to verification of assets and liabilities by means of summary inquiry and rejection of nomination papers on the ground of furnishing wrong information or suppression of material information.

ELECTION COMMISSION THEN ISSUED INSTRUCTIONS THAT ON THE RECEIPT OF THE COMPLAINT WITH DOCUMENTARY EVIDENCE THAT INFORMATION FURNISHED WAS WRONG, START PROSECUTION OF THE CANDIDATE

6. Again, the Election Commission of India, *vide* letter dated 2.6.2004 directed the Chief Electoral Officers of all the States and Union Territories that where any complaint regarding furnishing of false information by any candidate is submitted by anyone, supported by some documentary evidence, the Returning Officer concerned should initiate action to prosecute the candidate concerned by filing formal complaint before the appropriate authority.

LARGE SCALE IRREGULARITIES WERE FOUND IN THE AFFIDAVITS ACCOMPANYING NOMINATION PAPERS

Brief Facts:

7. In the above backdrop, the brief facts of the case in hand are as under:— Resurgence India-the petitioner herein is a non-governmental organisation (NGO) registered under the Societies Registration Act, 1860 and is working for social awakening, social empowerment, human rights and dignity. During Punjab Legislative Assembly Elections, 2007, the petitioner-organisation undertook a massive exercise under the banner Punjab Election Watch' and affidavits pertaining to the candidates of six major political parties in the State were analyzed in order to verify their completeness. During such campaign, large scale irregularities were found in most of the affidavits filed by the candidates.

8. On 9.2.2007, the petitioner-organization made a representation to the Election Commission of India regarding large number of non-disclosures in the affidavits filed by the contestants in the State of Punjab and poor level of scrutiny by the Returning Officers. *Vide* letter dated 20.2.2007, the Election Commission of India expressed its inability in rejecting the nomination papers of the candidates solely due to furnishing of false/incomplete information in the affidavits in view of the judgment in *People's Union for Civil Liberties (PUCL)* (supra).

HENCE THIS WRIT PETITION

9. Being aggrieved of the same, the petitioner-organisation has preferred this petition for the issuance of a writ of *mandamus* to make it compulsory for the Returning Officers to ensure that the affidavits filed by the contestants should be complete in all respects and to reject those nomination papers which are accompanied by incomplete/blank affidavits. The petitioner-organisation also prayed for deterrent action against the Returning Officers in case of acceptance of such incomplete affidavits in order to remove deficiencies in the format of the prescribed affidavit.

10. Heard Mr. Prashant Bhushan, learned counsel for the petitioner-organisation, Ms. Meenakshi Arora, learned counsel for the Election Commission of India-Respondent No. 1 herein and Mr. A. Mariarputham, learned senior counsel for the Union of India. Prayer/Relief Sought for: Stand of the Petitioner-Organisation:

PRAYER OF THE PETITIONERS THAT THE NOMINATION PAPERS BE REJECTED FOR FILING BLANK AFFIDAVITS

Prayer/Relief Sought for Stand of the Petitioner Organisation

11. The Petitioner-organization pleaded for issuance of appropriate writ/ direction including the writ of *mandamus* directing the respondents herein to make it compulsory for the Returning Officers to ensure that the affidavits filed by the candidates are complete in all respects and to reject those nomination papers, which are accompanied by blank affidavits.

Stand of the Election Commission of India

11.1 It is the stand of the Election Commission of India that the judgment in *People's Union for Civil Liberties (PUCL)* (supra) does not empower the Returning Officers to reject the nomination papers solely due to furnishing of false/ incomplete/blank information in the affidavits signed by the candidates. In succinct, they put forth the argument that they do not have any latitude for rejecting the nomination papers in view of the abovementioned judgment.

ELECTION COMMISSION ALSO AGREED WITH IT

However, learned counsel for the Election Commission of India made an assertion that the Election Commission too is of the opinion that incomplete nomination papers must be rejected. Hence, the Election Commission of India sought for clarification in that regard.

UNION OF INDIA SUBMITTED THAT IT WOULD BE AN ANOMALY TO ACCEPT THE AFFIDAVITS WITH WRONG INFORMATION AND REJECT THE BLANK AFFIDAVITS

11.2 Stand of the Union of India

The Union of India also put forth the similar contention as raised by the Election Commission. Interestingly, the Union of India also raised a query as to how this Court will be justified in accepting the nomination paper with false information but rejecting the nomination paper for filing affidavit with particulars left blank and hence prayed that both the above said situations must be treated at par.

Discussion

12. Both the petitioner-organisation and the respondent/UOI sought divergent remedies against the same situation *viz.*, wherein the affidavit filed by the candidate stating the information given as correct but the particulars of the same are left blank. The petitioner-organisation is seeking for rejection of nomination paper in such a situation whereas the Union of India is pleading for treating it at par with filing false affidavit and to prosecute the candidate under section 125A of the Representation of the People Act, 1951 (in short 'the R.P. Act').

SECTIONS 33A, 36 AND 125 OF THE REPRESENTATION OF THE PEOPLE ACT, 1951

13. In order to appreciate the issue involved, it is desirable to refer the relevant provisions of the R.P. Act. Sections 33A, 36 and 125A of the RP Act read as under:

> "*33A. **Right to information.***—(1) A candidate shall, apart from any information which he is required to furnish, under this Act or the Rules made thereunder, in his nomination paper delivered under sub-section (1) of section 33, also furnish the information as to whether—
>
> (i) he is accused of any offence punishable with imprisonment for two years or more in a pending case in which a charge has been framed by the court of competent jurisdiction;
>
> (ii) he has been convicted of an offence [other than any offence referred to in sub-section (1) or sub-section (2), or covered in sub-section (3), of section 8] and sentenced to imprisonment for one year or more.
>
> (2) The candidate or his proposer, as the case may be, shall, at the time of delivering to the returning officer the nomination paper under sub-section (1) of section 33, also deliver to him an affidavit sworn by the candidate in a prescribed form verifying the information specified in sub-section (1).
>
> (3) The returning officer shall, as soon as may be after the furnishing of information to him under sub-section (1), display the aforesaid information by affixing a copy of the affidavit, delivered under sub-section (2), at a

conspicuous place at his office for the information of the electors relating to a constituency for which the nomination paper is delivered.

36. Scrutiny of nomination.—(1) On the date fixed for the scrutiny of nominations under section 30, the candidates, their election agents, one proposer of each candidate, and one other person duly authorised in writing by each candidate, but no other person, may attend at such time and place as the returning officer may appoint; and the returning officer shall give them all reasonable facilities for examining the nomination papers of all candidates which have been delivered within the time and in the manner laid down in section 33.

(2) The returning officer shall then examine the nomination papers and shall decide all objections which may be made to any nomination and may, either on such objection or on his own motion, after such summary inquiry, if any, as he thinks necessary, reject any nomination on any of the following grounds:—

(a) that on the date fixed for the scrutiny of nominations the candidate either is not qualified or is disqualified for being chosen to fill the seat under any of the following provisions that may be applicable, namely: articles 84, 102, 173 and 191,

Part II of this Act, and sections 4 and 14 of the Government of Union Territories Act, 1963 (20 of 1963); or

(b) that there has been a failure to comply with any of the provisions of section 33 or section 34 ; or

(c) that the signature of the candidate or the proposer on the nomination paper is not genuine.

(3) Nothing contained in clause (b) or clause (c) of sub-section (2) shall be deemed to authorise the rejection of the nomination of any candidate on the ground of any irregularity in respect of a nomination paper, if the candidate has been duly nominated by means of another nomination paper in respect of which no irregularity has been committed.

(4) The returning officer shall not reject any nomination paper on the ground of any defect which is not of a substantial character.

(5) The returning officer shall hold the scrutiny on the date appointed in this behalf under clause (b) of section 30 and shall not allow any adjournment of the proceedings except when such proceedings are interrupted or obstructed by riot or open violence or by causes beyond his control:

Provided that in case an objection is raised by the returning officer or is made by any other person the candidate concerned may be allowed time to rebut it not later than the next day but one following the date fixed for scrutiny, and the returning officer shall record his decision on the date to which the proceedings have been adjourned.

(6) The returning officer shall endorse on each nomination paper his decision accepting or rejecting the same and, if the nomination paper is rejected, shall record in writing a brief statement, of his reasons for such rejection.

(7) For the purposes of this section, a certified copy of an entry in the electoral roll for the time being in force of a constituency shall be conclusive evidence of the fact that the person referred to in that entry is an elector for that constituency, unless it is proved that he is subject to a disqualification mentioned in section 16 of the Representation of the People Act, 1950 (43 of 1950).

(8) Immediately after all the nomination papers have been scrutinized and decisions accepting or rejecting the same have been recorded, the returning officer shall prepare a list of validly nominated candidates, that is to say, candidates whose nominations have been found valid, and affix it to his notice board.

125A. Penalty for filing false affidavit, etc.—A candidate who himself or through his proposer, with intent to be elected in an election,—

(i) fails to furnish information relating to sub-section (1) of section 33A; or

(ii) gives false information which he knows or has reason to believe to be false; or

(iii) conceals any information, in his nomination paper delivered under sub-section (1) of section 33 or in his affidavit which is required to be delivered under sub-section (2) of section 33A, as the case may be, shall, notwithstanding anything contained in any other law for the time being in force, be punishable with imprisonment for a term which may extend to six months, or with fine, or with both."

LAW LAID DOWN BY THE SUPREME COURT IN EARLIER JUDGMENTS

14. In view of the above, the power to reject the nomination paper by the Returning Officer on the instance of candidate filing the affidavit with particulars left blank can be derived from the reasoning of a three-Judge Bench of this Court in *Shaligram Shrivastava* v. *Naresh Singh Patel,* (2003) 2 SCC 176. In the aforesaid case, the nomination paper of a candidate got rejected at the time of scrutiny under section 36(2) of the R.P. Act on the ground that he had not filled up the proforma prescribed by the Election Commission wherein the candidate was required to state whether he had been convicted or not for any offence mentioned in section 8 of the R.P. Act.

In actual, the candidate therein had filed an affidavit stating that the information given in the proforma was correct but the proforma itself was left blank. The candidate therein coincidentally raised somewhat similar contention as pleaded by the Union of India in the present case. The candidate pleaded that his nomination paper could not be rejected on the ground that he had not filled up the proforma prescribed since no such proforma was statutorily provided under the provisions of the Act or under the rules framed thereunder. It was contended that the Commission could not legislate to prescribe a proforma; at best it can only be an Executive instruction of the Election Commission whereas the petitioner had filled the proforma prescribed under the Rules, which did not suffer from any defect.

15. Although, the grounds of contention may not be exactly similar to the case on hand but the reasoning rendered in that verdict will come in aid for arriving at a decision in the given case. In order to arrive at a conclusion in that case, this Court traversed through the objective behind filing the proforma. The proforma mandated in that case was required to be filed as to the necessary and relevant information with regard to the candidate in the light of section 8 of the R.P. Act.

This Court further held that at the time of scrutiny, the Returning Officer is entitled to satisfy himself whether the candidate is qualified and not disqualified, hence, the Returning Officer was authorised to seek such information to be furnished at the time or before scrutiny. It was further held that if the candidate fails to furnish such information and also absents himself at the time of the scrutiny of the nomination papers, then he is obviously avoiding a statutory inquiry being conducted by the Returning Officer under section 36(2) of the R.P. Act relating to his being not qualified or disqualified in the light of section 8 of the R.P. Act. It is bound to result in defect of a substantial character in the nomination. This Court further held as under:—

> "17. In the case in hand the candidate had failed to furnish such information as sought on the proforma given to him and had also failed to be present personally or through his representative at the time of scrutiny. The statutory duty/power of Returning Officer for holding proper scrutiny of nomination paper was rendered nugatory. No scrutiny of the nomination paper could be made under section 36(2) of the Act in the light of section 8 of the Act. It certainly rendered the nomination paper suffering from defect of substantial character and the Returning Officer was within his rights in rejecting the same."

16. It is clear that the Returning Officers derive the power to reject the nomination papers on the ground that the contents to be filled in the affidavits are essential to effectuate the intent of the provisions of the R.P. Act and as a consequence, leaving the affidavit blank will in fact make it impossible for the Returning Officer to verify whether the candidate is qualified or disqualified which indeed will frustrate the object behind filing the same. In concise, this Court in *Shaligram* (supra) evaluated the purpose behind filing the proforma for advancing latitude to the Returning Officers to reject the nomination papers.

17. In the light of the above reasoning, now let us assess the facts of the given case. In *Association for Democratic Reforms* (supra), this Court arrived at a decision that the members of a democratic society should be sufficiently informed so that they may influence intelligently the decisions which may affect themselves and it would include their decision of casting votes in favour of a particular candidate. This Court further held that if there was a disclosure by a candidate with regard to his criminal antecedents, assets and liabilities and educational qualification, then it would strengthen the voters in taking appropriate decision of casting their votes. This Court further stated as under:—

> "38. If right to telecast and right to view to sport games and right to impart such information is considered to be part and parcel of article 19(1)(a), we fail

to understand why the right of a citizen/voter – a little man – to know about the antecedents of his candidate cannot be held to be a fundamental right under article 19(1)(a). In our view, democracy cannot survive without free and fair election, without free and fairly informed voters. Votes cast by uninformed voters in favour of X or Y candidate would be meaningless. As stated in the aforesaid passage, one-sided information, disinformation, misinformation and non-information, all equally create an uninformed citizenry, which makes democracy a farce.

Therefore, casting of vote by a misinformed and non-informed voter or a voter having one-sided information only is bound to affect the democracy seriously. Freedom of speech and expression includes right to impart and receive information, which includes freedom to hold opinions. Entertainment is implied in freedom of 'speech and expression' and there is no reason to hold that freedom of speech and expression would not cover right to get material information with regard to a candidate who is contesting election for a post which is of utmost importance in the democracy.

46...4. To maintain the purity of elections and in particular to bring transparency in the process of election, the Commission can ask the candidates about the expenditure incurred by the political parties and this transparency in the process of election would include transparency of a candidate who seeks election or re- election. In a democracy, the electoral process has a strategic role. The little man of this country would have basic elementary right to know full particulars of a candidate who is to represent him in Parliament where laws to bind his liberty and property may be enacted.

........7. Under our Constitution, article 19(1)(a) provides for freedom of speech and expression. Voters's speech or expression in case of election would include casting of votes, that is to say, voter speaks out or expresses by casting vote. For this purpose, information about the candidate to be selected is a must. Voter's (little man-citizen's) right to know antecedents including criminal past of his candidate contesting election for MP or MLA is much more fundamental and basic for survival of democracy. The little man may think over before making his choice of electing law-breakers as law-makers."

CONCLUSIONS OF EARLIER JUDGMENTS

18. Thus, this Court held that a voter has the elementary right to know full particulars of a candidate who is to represent him in the Parliament and such right to get information is universally recognised natural right flowing from the concept of democracy and is an integral part of article 19(1)(a) of the Constitution. It was further held that the voter's speech or expression in case of election would include casting of votes, that is to say, voter speaks out or expresses by casting vote. For this purpose, information about the candidate to be selected is a must. Thus, in unequivocal terms, it is recognised that the citizen's right to know of the candidate who represents him in the Parliament will constitute an integral part of article 19(1)(a) of the Constitution of India and any act, which is derogative of the fundamental rights is at the very outset *ultra vires*.

SECTION 33A WAS ENACTED IN 2002 IN VIEW OF THAT JUDGMENT

19. With this background, section 33A of the R.P. Act was enacted by Act 72 of 2002 with effect from 24.8.2002. Thus, the purpose of the Act 72 of 2002 was to effectuate the right contemplated in *Association for Democratic Reforms* (supra). However, the legislators did not incorporate all the suggestions as directed by this Court in the above case but for mandating all the candidates to disclose the criminal antecedents under section 33A by filing an affidavit as prescribed along with the nomination paper filed under section 33(1) of the R.P. Act so that the citizens must be aware of the criminal antecedents of the candidate before they can exercise their freedom of choice by casting of votes as guaranteed under the Constitution of India. As a result, at present, every candidate is obligated to file an affidavit with relevant information with regard to their criminal antecedents, assets and liabilities and educational qualifications.

DISCUSSION BY THE SUPREME COURT

20. Let us now test whether the filing of affidavit stating that the information given in the affidavit is correct but leaving the contents blank would fulfil the objective behind filing the same. The reply to this question is a clear denial. The ultimate purpose of filing of affidavit along with the nomination paper is to effectuate the fundamental right of the citizen under article 19(1)(a) of the Constitution of India. The citizens are required to have the necessary information at the time of filing of the nomination paper in order to make a choice of their voting. When a candidate files an affidavit with blank particulars, it renders the affidavit itself nugatory.

CORRECTNESS OF THE INFORMATION FURNISHED SHOULD BE ENSURED AT THE TIME OF SCRUTINY

21. For that purpose, the Returning Officer can very well compel a candidate to furnish information relevant on the date of scrutiny. We were appraised that the Election Commission already has a standard draft format for reminding the candidates to file an affidavit as stipulated. We are of the opinion that along with the above, another clause may be inserted for reminding the candidates to fill the blanks with the relevant information thereby conveying the message that no affidavit with blank particulars will be entertained.

IF THE CANDIDATE FAILS, REJECT HIS NOMINATION PAPERS

We reiterate that it is the duty of the Returning Officer to check whatever the information required is fully furnished at the time of filing of affidavit with the nomination paper since such information is very vital for giving effect to the 'right to know' of the citizens. If a candidate fails to fill the blanks even after the reminder by the Returning Officer, the nomination paper is fit to be rejected.

POWER TO REJECT THE NOMINATION PAPERS BE USED SPARINGLY

We do comprehend that the power of Returning Officer to reject the nomination paper must be exercised very sparingly but the bar should not be laid so high that the justice itself is prejudiced.

HOWEVER POWER OF REJECTION NOT BARRED

22. We also clarify to the extent that in our coherent opinion the above power of rejection by the Returning Officer is not barred by Para 73 of *People's Union for Civil Liberties (PUCL)* (supra) which reads as under:—

> "73. While no exception can be taken to the insistence of affidavit with regard to the matters specified in the judgment in *Association for Democratic Reforms* case, the direction to reject the nomination paper for furnishing wrong information or concealing material information and providing for a summary enquiry at the time of scrutiny of the nominations, cannot be justified. In the case of assets and liabilities, it would be very difficult for the Returning Officer to consider the truth or otherwise of the details furnished with reference to the 'documentary proof'.
>
> Very often, in such matters the documentary proof may not be clinching and the candidate concerned may be handicapped to rebut the allegation then and there. If sufficient time is provided, he may be able to produce proof to contradict the objector's version. It is true that the aforesaid directions issued by the Election Commission are not under challenge but at the same time *prima facie* it appears that the Election Commission is required to revise its instructions in the light of directions issued in *Association for Democratic Reforms* case and as provided under the Representation of the People Act and its third Amendment."

CANDIDATE BE GIVEN AN OPPORTUNITY TO MEET THE OBJECTIONS

23. The aforesaid paragraph, no doubt, stresses on the importance of filing of affidavit, however, opines that the direction to reject the nomination paper for furnishing wrong information or concealing material information and providing for a summary inquiry at the time of scrutiny of the nominations cannot be justified since in such matters the documentary proof may not be clinching and the candidate concerned may be handicapped to rebut the allegation then and there. This Court was of the opinion that if sufficient time is provided, the candidate may be in a position to produce proof to contradict the objector's version.

COLUMNS LEFT BLANK – GOOD GROUND FOR REJECTION

The object behind penning down the aforesaid reasoning is to accommodate genuine situation where the candidate is trapped by false allegations and is unable to rebut the allegation within a short time. Para 73 of the aforesaid judgment nowhere contemplates a situation where it bars the Returning Officer to reject the nomination paper on account of filing affidavit with particulars left blank. Therefore, we hereby clarify that the above said paragraph will not come in the way of the Returning Officer to reject the nomination paper if the said affidavit is filed with blank columns. The candidate must take the minimum effort to explicitly remark as 'NIL' or 'Not Applicable' or 'Not known' in the columns and not to leave the particulars blank, if he desires that his nomination paper be accepted by the Returning Officer.

CANDIDATE WHO LEFT COLUMNS BLANK BE NOT PROSECUTED

24. At this juncture, it is vital to refer to section 125A of the R.P. Act. As an outcome, the act of failure on the part of the candidate to furnish relevant information, as mandated by section 33A of the R.P. Act, will result in prosecution of the candidate. Hence, filing of affidavit with blank space will be directly hit by section 125A(i) of the R.P. Act. However, as the nomination paper itself is rejected by the Returning officer, we find no reason why the candidate must again be penalized for the same act by prosecuting him/her.

GIVING OF FALSE INFORMATION – CANNOT BE AT PAR WITH BLANK COLUMNS IN THE AFFIDAVIT

25. If we accept the contention raised by Union of India, *viz.*, the candidate who has filed an affidavit with false information as well as the candidate who has filed an affidavit with particulars left blank should be treated at par, it will result in breach of fundamental right guaranteed under article 19(1)(a) of the Constitution, *viz.*, 'right to know', which is inclusive of freedom of speech and expression as interpreted in Association for Democratic Reforms (supra).

COLUMNS OF AFFIDAVIT BLANK – STILL ACCEPTANCE – AMOUNTS TO FUNDAMENTAL BREACH OF DUTY BY RETURNING OFFICER

26. In succinct, if the Election Commission accepts the nomination papers in spite of blank particulars in the affidavits, it will directly violate the fundamental right of the citizen to know the criminal antecedents, assets and liabilities and educational qualification of the candidate. Therefore, accepting affidavit with blank particulars from the candidate will rescind the verdict in *Association for Democratic Reforms* (supra). Further, the subsequent act of prosecuting the candidate under section 125A(i) will bear no significance as far as the breach of fundamental right of the citizen is concerned. For the aforesaid reasons, we are unable to accept the contention of the Union of India.

RIGHT OF THE VOTER TO KNOW ABOUT THE CANDIDATE IS HIS FUNDAMENTAL RIGHT – DIRECTIONS ISSUED – WRIT DISPOSED OF

27. What emerges from the above discussion can be summarized in the form of following directions:

(i) The voter has the elementary right to know full particulars of a candidate who is to represent him in the Parliament/Assemblies and such right to get information is universally recognised. Thus, it is held that right to know about the candidate is a natural right flowing from the concept of democracy and is an integral part of article 19(1)(a) of the Constitution.

(ii) The ultimate purpose of filing of affidavit along with the nomination paper is to effectuate the fundamental right of the citizens under article19(1)(a) of the Constitution of India. The citizens are supposed to have the necessary information at the time of filing of nomination paper and for that purpose, the Returning Officer can very well compel a candidate to furnish the relevant information.

(iii) Filing of affidavit with blank particulars will render the affidavit nugatory.

(iv) It is the duty of the Returning Officer to check whether the information required is fully furnished at the time of filing of affidavit with the nomination paper since such information is very vital for giving effect to the 'right to know' of the citizens. If a candidate fails to fill the blanks even after the reminder by the Returning Officer, the nomination paper is fit to be rejected. We do comprehend that the power of Returning Officer to reject the nomination paper must be exercised very sparingly but the bar should not be laid so high that the justice itself is prejudiced.

(v) We clarify to the extent that Para 73 of *People's Union for Civil Liberties* case (supra) will not come in the way of the Returning Officer to reject the nomination paper when affidavit is filed with blank particulars.

(vi) The candidate must take the minimum effort to explicitly remark as 'NIL' or 'Not Applicable' or 'Not known' in the columns and not to leave the particulars blank.

(vii) Filing of affidavit with blanks will be directly hit by section 125A(i) of the R.P. Act. However, as the nomination paper itself is rejected by the Returning Officer, we find no reason why the candidate must be again penalized for the same act by prosecuting him/her.

28. The Writ Petition is disposed of with the above directions.

......................CJI. (P. Sathasivam)
.........................J. (Ranjana Prakash Desai)
.........................J. (Ranjan Gogoi)

New Delhi;
September 13, 2013

Author's note: This judgment is historical in the context of the present scenario when even the persons facing criminal cases or trials or having criminal record are contesting elections for Lok Sabha or State Assemblies. The voters had no choice but to cast vote in favour of one or the other even when all the candidates were no better than the other and had same or similar past history. A Public Interest Litigation was filed to get a right for the voters to reject all the candidates. Hence this judgment.

CONSTITUTIONAL VALIDITY OF RULES 41(2)(3) AND 49-O OF THE CONDUCT OF ELECTION RULES WAS CONSIDERED BY THE SUPREME COURT

***People's Union for Civil Liberties*[1]**

v.

Union of India

SUPREME COURT OF INDIA

CIVIL ORIGINAL JURISDICTION

Writ Petition (c) No. 161 of 2004

BENCH

P. Sathasivam, CJI., Ranjana Parkash Desai and Ranjan Gogoi, JJ.

JUDGMENT

P. Sathasivam, CJI.

1. The present writ petition, under article 32 of the Constitution of India, has been filed by the petitioners herein challenging the constitutional validity of rules 41(2) and (3) and 49-O of the Conduct of Election Rules, 1961 (in short 'the Rules') to the extent that these provisions violate the secrecy of voting which is fundamental to the free and fair elections and is required to be maintained as per section 128 of the Representation of the People Act, 1951 (in short 'the R.P. Act') and rules 39 and 49M of the Rules.

2. The petitioners herein have preferred this petition for the issuance of a writ or direction(s) of like nature on the ground that though the above said Rules, *viz.*, rules 41(2) and (3) and 49-O, recognise the right of a voter not to vote but still the secrecy of his having not voted is not maintained in its implementation and thus the impugned rules, to the extent of such violation of the right to secrecy, are not only *ultra vires* to the said Rules but also violative of articles 19(1)(a) and 21 of the Constitution of India besides International Covenants.

3. In the above backdrop, the petitioners herein prayed for declaring rules 41(2) and (3) and 49-O of the Rules *ultra vires* and unconstitutional and also prayed for a direction to the Election Commission of India – Respondent No. 2 herein, to provide necessary provision in the ballot papers as well as in the electronic voting machines for the protection of the right of not to vote in order to keep the exercise

1. JT 2013 (13) SCC 133.

of such right a secret under the existing RP Act/the Rules or under article 324 of the Constitution.

QUESTION RAISED ABOUT THE MAINTAINABILITY OF THE WRIT PETITION BEFORE THE DIVISION BENCH

4. On 23.2.2009, a Division Bench of this Court, on an objection with regard to maintainability of the writ petition on the ground that right to vote is not a fundamental right but is a statutory right, after considering *Union of India* v. *Association for Democratic Reforms,* (2002) 5 SCC 294 and *People's Union for Civil Liberties* v. *Union of India,* (2003) 4 SCC 399 held that even though the judgment in *Kuldip Nayar* v. *Union of India,* (2006) 7 SCC 1 did not overrule or discard the ratio laid down in the judgments mentioned above, however, it creates a doubt in this regard, referred the matter to a larger Bench to arrive at a decision.

APPLICATIONS FILED FOR IMPLEADMENT – ALLOWED

5. One Centre for Consumer Education and Association for Democratic Reforms have filed applications for impleadment in this Writ Petition. Impleadment applications are allowed.

NAMES OF THE COUNSEL WHO REPRESENTED THE PARTIES

6. Heard Mr. Rajinder Sachhar, learned senior counsel for the petitioners, Mr. P.P. Malhotra, learned Additional Solicitor General for the Union of India-Respondent No. 1 herein, Ms. Meenakshi Arora, learned counsel for the Election Commission of India-Respondent No. 2 herein, Ms. Kamini Jaiswal and Mr. Raghenth Basant, learned counsel for the impleading parties.

CONTENTIONS

Submissions of the Petitioners

7. Mr. Rajinder Sachhar, learned senior counsel for the petitioners, by taking us through various provisions, particularly, section 128 of the R.P. Act as well as rules 39, 41, 49M and 49-O of the Rules submitted that in terms of rule 41(2) of the Rules, an elector has a right not to vote but still the secrecy of his having not voted is not maintained under rules 41(2) and (3) thereof. He further pointed out that similarly according to rule 49-O of the Rules, the right of a voter who decides not to vote has been accepted but the secrecy is not maintained. According to him, in case an elector decides not to record his vote, a remark to this effect shall be made against the said entry in Form 17A by the Presiding Officer and the signature or thumb impression of the elector shall be obtained against such remark.

IFA VOTER DECIDES NOTTO VOTE – SECRECY IS NOT MAINTAINED

Hence, if a voter decides not to vote, his record will be maintained by the Presiding Officer which will thereby disclose that he has decided not to vote. The main substance of the arguments of learned senior counsel for the petitioners is that though right to not to vote is recognised by rules 41 and 49-O of the Rules and is also a part of the freedom of expression of a voter, if a voter chooses to exercise the said right, it has to be kept secret. Learned senior counsel further submitted that both the above provisions, to the extent of such violation of the secrecy clause are not only *ultra vires* but also contrary to section 128 of the R.P.

Act, rules 39 and 49M of the Rules as well as articles 19(1)(a) and 21 of the Constitution.

SUBMISSIONS ON BEHALF OF THE UNION OF INDIA – RIGHT TO VOTE IS NOT CONSTITUTIONAL

8. On the other hand, Mr. P.P. Malhotra, learned Additional Solicitor General appearing for the Union of India submitted that the right to vote is neither a fundamental right nor a constitutional right nor a common law right but is a pure and simple statutory right. He asserted that neither the RP Act nor the Constitution of India declares the right to vote as anything more than a statutory right and hence the present writ petition is not maintainable. He further pointed out that in view of the decision of the Constitution Bench in *Kuldip Nayar* (supra), the reference for deciding the same by a larger Bench was unnecessary. He further pointed out that in view of the above decision, the earlier two decisions of this Court, *viz., Association for Democratic Reforms* (supra) and *People's Union for Civil Liberties* (supra), stood impliedly overruled, hence, on this ground also reference to a larger Bench was not required. He further pointed out that though the power of Election Commission under article 324 of the Constitution is wide enough, but still the same can, in no manner, be construed as to cover those areas, which are already covered by the statutory provisions. He further pointed out that even from the existing provisions, it is clear that secrecy of ballot is a principle which has been formulated to ensure that in no case it shall be known to the candidates or their representatives that in whose favour a particular voter has voted so that he can exercise his right to vote freely and fearlessly.

RIGHT OF SECRECY IS ONLY FOR THOSE WHO VOTE – SUBMITTED UOI

He also pointed out that the right of secrecy has been extended to only those voters who have exercised their right to vote and the same, in no manner, can be extended to those who have not voted at all.

Finally, he submitted that since section 2(d) of the R.P. Act specifically defines "election" to mean an election to fill a seat, it cannot be construed as an election not to fill a seat.

SUBMISSIONS ON BEHALF OF THE ELECTION COMMISSION OF INDIA – SECRECY ESSENTIAL FOR ALL

9. Ms. Meenakshi Arora, learned counsel appearing for the Election Commission of India – Respondent No. 2 herein, by pointing out various provisions both from the R.P. Act and the Rules submitted that inasmuch as secrecy is an essential feature of "free and fair elections", rules 41(2) and (3) and 49-O of the Rules violate the requirement of secrecy.

SUBMISSIONS BY THE IMPLEADED PARTIES – NOTA BUTTON BE PROVIDED

10. Ms. Kamini Jaiswal and Mr. Raghenth Basant, learned counsel appearing for the impleading parties, while agreeing with the stand of the petitioners as well as the Election Commission of India, prayed that necessary directions may be issued for providing another button *viz.*, "None of the Above" (NOTA) in the Electronic Voting Machines (EVMs) so that the voters who come to the polling booth and decide not to vote for any of the candidates, are able to exercise their right not to vote while maintaining their right of secrecy.

11. We have carefully considered the rival submissions and perused the relevant provisions of the R.P. Act and the Rules.

DISCUSSION

Sections 79(d) and 128 of the Representation of the People Act, 1951

12. In order to answer the above contentions, it is vital to refer to the relevant provisions of the RP Act and the Rules. Sections 79(d) and 128 of the R.P. Act read as under:

> "79(d)—"electoral right" means the right of a person to stand or not to stand as, or to withdraw or not to withdraw from being, a candidate, or to vote or refrain from voting at an election.
>
> 128. *Maintenance of secrecy of voting.*—(1) Every officer, clerk, agent or other person who performs any duty in connection with the recording or counting of votes at an election shall maintain, and aid in maintaining, the secrecy of the voting and shall not (except for some purpose authorised by or under any law) communicate to any person any information calculated to violate such secrecy:
>
> Provided that the provisions of this sub-section shall not apply to such officer, clerk, agent or other person who performs any such duty at an election to fill a seat or seats in the Council of States.
>
> (2) Any person who contravenes the provisions of sub-section (1) shall be punishable with imprisonment for a term which may extend to three months or with fine or with both."

RULES 39(1), 41, 49M AND 49-O OF THE CONDUCT OF ELECTION RULES, 1961

Rules 39(1), 41, 49M and 49-O of the Rules read as under:

> "***39. Maintenance of secrecy of voting by electors within polling station and voting procedure.***—(1) Every elector to whom a ballot paper has been issued under rule 38 or under any other provision of these rules, shall maintain secrecy of voting within the polling station and for that purpose observe the voting procedure hereinafter laid down.
>
> ***41. Spoilt and returned ballot papers.***—(1) An elector who has inadvertently dealt with his ballot paper in such manner that it cannot be conveniently used as a ballot paper may, on returning it to the presiding officer and on satisfying him of the inadvertence, be given another ballot paper, and the ballot paper so returned and the counterfoil of such ballot paper shall be marked "Spoilt: cancelled" by the presiding officer.
>
> (2) If an elector after obtaining a ballot paper decides not to use it, he shall return it to the presiding officer, and the ballot paper so returned and the counterfoil of such ballot paper shall be marked as "Returned: cancelled" by the presiding officer.
>
> (3) All ballot papers cancelled under sub-rule (1) or sub-rule (2) shall be kept in a separate packet.

49M. Maintenance of secrecy of voting by electors within the polling station and voting procedures.—(1) Every elector who has been permitted to vote under rule 49L shall maintain secrecy of voting within the polling station and for that purpose observe the voting procedure hereinafter laid down.

(2) Immediately on being permitted to vote the elector shall proceed to the presiding officer or the polling officer in-charge of the control unit of the voting machine who shall, by pressing the appropriate button on the control unit, activate the balloting unit; for recording of elector's vote.

(3) The elector shall thereafter forthwith—

(a) proceed to the voting compartment;

(b) record his vote by pressing the button on the balloting unit against the name and symbol of the candidate for whom he intends to vote; and

(c) come out of the voting compartment and leave the polling station.

(4) Every elector shall vote without undue delay.

(5) No elector shall be allowed to enter the voting compartment when another elector is inside it.

(6) If an elector who has been permitted to vote under rule 49L or rule 49P refuses after warning given by the presiding officer to observe the procedure laid down in sub-rule (3) of the said rules, the presiding officer or a polling officer under the direction of the presiding officer shall not allow such elector to vote.

(7) Where an elector is not allowed to vote under sub-rule (6), a remark to the effect that voting procedure has been violated shall be made against the elector's name in the register of voters in Form 17 by the presiding officer under his signature.

49-O. Elector deciding not to vote.—If an elector, after his electoral roll number has been duly entered in the register of voters in Form 17A and has put his signature or thumb impression thereon as required under sub-rule (1) of rule 49L, decide not to record his vote, a remark to this effect shall be made against the said entry in Form 17A by the presiding officer and the signature or thumb impression of the elector shall be obtained against such remark."

ARTICLE 21(3), UNIVERSAL DECLARATION OF HUMAN RIGHTS AND ARTICLE 25(B), INTERNATIONAL COVENANT ON CIVIL AND POLITICAL RIGHTS

13. Apart from the above provisions, it is also relevant to refer article 21(3) of the Universal Declaration of Human Rights and article 25(b) of the International Covenant on Civil and Political Rights, which read as under:

"21(3). The will of the people shall be the basis of the authority of government; this will shall be expressed in periodic and genuine elections which shall be by universal and equal suffrage and shall be held by secret vote or by equivalent free voting procedures."

"25. Every citizen shall have the right and the opportunity, without any of the distinctions mentioned in article 2 and without unreasonable restrictions:

(a) *** *** ***;

(b) To vote and to be elected at genuine periodic elections which shall be by universal and equal suffrage and shall be held by secret ballot, guaranteeing the free expression of the will of the electors;"

ARTICLE 19(1) AND ARTICLE 21 OF THE CONSTITUTION OF INDIA

14. Articles 19(1)(a) and 21 of the Constitution, which are also pertinent for this matter, are as under:

"19 — Protection of certain rights regarding freedom of speech, etc.—

(1) All citizens shall have the right—

(a) to freedom of speech and expression;

XXXXX

21. Protection of life and personal liberty.—No person shall be deprived of his life or personal liberty except according to procedure established by law."

FORM 17A UNDER RULE 49L OF THE CONDUCT OF ELECTION RULES, 1961

15. From the above provisions, it is clear that in case an elector decides not to record his vote, a remark to this effect shall be made in Form 17A by the Presiding Officer and the signature or thumb impression of the elector shall be obtained against such remark. Form 17A reads as under:

"FORM 17A

(*See* rule 49L)

REGISTER OF VOTERS

Election to the House of the People/Legislative Assembly of the State/Union territory ....from..................Constituency No. and Name of Polling Station...............Part No. of Electoral Roll............

Sl. No.	Sl. No. of elector in the electoral roll	Details of the document produced by the elector in proof of his/her identification	Signature/Thumb impression of elector	Remark
(1)	(2)	(3)	(4)	(5)
1.				
2.				
3.				
4.				
etc.				

Signature of the Presiding Officer"

DISCUSSION ON THE OBJECTION OF THE UNION OF INDIA ON MAINTAINABILITY OF THE WRIT PETITION

16. Before elaborating the contentions relating to the above provisions with reference to the secrecy of voting, let us first consider the issue of maintainability of the Writ Petition as raised by the Union of India. In the present Writ Petition, which is of the year 2004, the petitioners have prayed for the following reliefs:

"(i) declaring that rules 41(2) and (3) and 49-O of the Conduct of Election Rules, 1961 are *ultra vires* and unconstitutional to the extent they violate secrecy of vote;

(ii) direct the Election Commission under the existing Representation of People Act, 1951 and the Conduct of Election Rules, 1961 and/or under article 324 to provide necessary provision in the ballot papers and the voting machines for protection of right not to vote and to keep the exercise of such right secret;"

TWO JUDGE-BENCH REFERRED THE MATTER TO A LARGER BENCH

17. It is relevant to point out that initially the present Writ Petition came up for hearing before a Bench of two-Judges. During the course of hearing, an objection was raised with regard to the maintainability of the Writ Petition under article 32 on the ground that the right claimed by the petitioners is not a fundamental right as enshrined in Part III of the Constitution. It is the categorical objection of the Union of India that inasmuch as the writ petition under article 32 would lie to this Court only for the violation of fundamental rights and since the right to vote is not a fundamental right, the present Writ Petition under article 32 is not maintainable. It is the specific stand of the Union of India that right to vote is not a fundamental right but merely a statutory right. It is further pointed out that this Court, in para 20 of the referral order dated 23.2.2009, reported in (2009) 3 SCC 200, observed that since in *Kuldip Nayar* (supra), the judgments of this Court in *Association for Democratic Reforms* (supra) and *People's Union for Civil Liberties* (supra) have not been specifically overruled which tend to create a doubt whether the right to vote is a fundamental right or not and referred the same to a larger Bench stating that the issue requires clarity. In view of the reference, we have to decide:

(i) Whether there is any doubt or confusion with regard to the right of a voter in *Kuldip Nayar* (supra);

(ii) Whether earlier two judgments *viz.*, *Association for Democratic Reforms* (supra) and *People's Union for Civil Liberties* (supra) referred to by the Constitution Bench in *Kuldip Nayar* (supra) stand impliedly overruled.

PRIOR LAW RELIED UPON BY THE UNION OF INDIA

18. Though, Mr. Malhotra relied on a large number of decisions, we are of the view that there is no need to refer to those decisions except a reference to the decision of this Court in *Kuldip Nayar* (supra), *Association for Democratic Reforms* (supra) and *People's Union for Civil Liberties* (supra).

19. A three-Judge Bench of this Court comprising M.B Shah, P. Venkatarama Reddi and D.M. Dharmadhikari, JJ. expressed separate but concurring opinions in the *People's Union for Civil Liberties* (supra). In para 97, Reddi, J. made an observation as to the right to vote being a Constitutional right if not a fundamental right which reads as under:

"97. In *Jyoti Basu* v. *Debi Ghosal*, (1982) 3 SCR 318 this Court again pointed out in no uncertain terms that:

8 "a right to elect, fundamental though it is to democracy, is, anomalously enough, neither a fundamental right nor a common law right. It is pure and simple a statutory right."

With great reverence to the eminent Judges, I would like to clarify that the right to vote, if not a fundamental right, is certainly a constitutional right. The right originates from the Constitution and in accordance with the constitutional mandate contained in article 326, the right has been shaped by the statute, namely, R.P. Act. That, in my understanding, is the correct legal position as regards the nature of the right to vote in elections to the House of the People and Legislative Assemblies. It is not very accurate to describe it as a statutory right, pure and simple. Even with this clarification, the argument of the learned Solicitor-General that the right to vote not being a fundamental right, the information which at best facilitates meaningful exercise of that right cannot be read as an integral part of any fundamental right, remains to be squarely met...."

19.1 Similarly, in para 123, point No. 2 Reddi, J., held as under:—

"(2) The right to vote at the elections to the House of the People or Legislative Assembly is a constitutional right but not merely a statutory right; freedom of voting as distinct from right to vote is a facet of the fundamental right enshrined in article 19(1)(a). The casting of vote in favour of one or the other candidate marks the accomplishment of freedom of expression of the voter."

19.2 Except the above two paragraphs, this aspect has nowhere been discussed or elaborated wherein all the three Judges, in their separate but concurring judgments, have taken the pains to specifically distinguish between right to vote and freedom of voting as a species of freedom of expression. In succinct, the ratio of the judgment was that though the right to vote is a statutory right but the decision taken by a voter after verifying the credentials of the candidate either to vote or not is his right of expression under article 19(1)(a) of the Constitution.

JUDGMENTS RELIED UPON BY THE UNION OF INDIA HAD NOT DEALT WITH THE QUESTION INVOLVED IN THIS WRIT PETITION

20. As a result, the judgments in *Association for Democratic Reforms* (supra) and *People's Union for Civil Liberties* (supra) have not disturbed the position that right to vote is a statutory right. Both the judgments have only added that the right to know the background of a candidate is a fundamental right of a voter so that he can take a rational decision of expressing himself while exercising the statutory right to vote. In *People's Union for Civil Liberties* (supra), Shah J., in para 78D, held as under:

"...However, voters' fundamental right to know the antecedents of a candidate is independent of statutory rights under the election law. A voter is first citizen of this country and apart from statutory rights, he is having fundamental rights conferred by the Constitution..."

20.1 P. Venkatrama Reddi, J., in para 97, held as under:

"...Though the initial right cannot be placed on the pedestal of a fundamental right, but, at the stage when the voter goes to the polling booth and casts his vote, his freedom to express arises. The casting of vote in favour of one or the other candidate tantamounts to expression of his opinion and preference and that final stage in the exercise of voting right marks the accomplishment of freedom of expression of the voter. That is where article 19(1)(a) is attracted. Freedom of voting as distinct from right to vote is thus a species of freedom of expression and therefore carries with it the auxiliary and complementary rights such as right to secure information about the candidate which are conducive to the freedom..."

20.2 Dharmadhikari, J., in para 127, held as under:

"...This freedom of a citizen to participate and choose a candidate at an election is distinct from exercise of his right as a voter which is to be regulated by statutory law on the election like the RP Act..."

20.3 In view of the above, para 362 in *Kuldip Nayar* (supra) does not hold to the contrary, which reads as under:

"We do not agree with the above submission. It is clear that a fine distinction was drawn between the right to vote and the freedom of voting as a species of freedom of expression, while reiterating the view in *Jyoti Basu* v. *Debi Ghosal* that a right to elect, fundamental though it is to democracy, is neither a fundamental right nor a common law right, but pure and simple, a statutory right".

JUDGMENT IN KULDIP NAYAR REAFFIRMS THAT RIGHT TO VOTE IS STATUTORY NOT FUNDAMENTAL

21. After a careful perusal of the verdicts of this Court in *Kuldip Nayar* (supra), *Association for Democratic Reforms* (supra) and *People's Union for Civil Liberties* (supra), we are of the considered view that *Kuldip Nayar* (supra) does not overrule the other two decisions rather it only reaffirms what has already been said by the two aforesaid decisions. The said paragraphs recognize that right to vote is a statutory right and also in *People's Union for Civil Liberties* (supra) it was held that "a fine distinction was drawn between the right to vote and the freedom of voting as a species of freedom of expression". Therefore, it cannot be said that *Kuldip Nayar* (supra) has observed anything to the contrary. In view of the whole debate of whether these two decisions were overruled or discarded because of the opening line in Para 362 of *Kuldip Nayar* (supra) *i.e.*, "we do not agree with the above submissions..." we are of the opinion that this line must be read as a whole and not in isolation. The contention of the petitioners in *Kuldip Nayar* (supra) was that majority view in *People's Union for Civil Liberties* (supra) held that right to vote is a Constitutional right besides that it is also a facet of fundamental right under article 19(1)(a) of the Constitution. It is this contention on which the Constitution Bench did not agree too in the opening line in para 362 and thereafter went on to clarify that in fact in *People's Union for Civil Liberties (supra)*, a fine distinction was drawn between the right to vote and the freedom of voting as a species of freedom of expression.

Thus, there is no contradiction as to the fact that right to vote is neither a fundamental right nor a Constitutional right but a pure and simple statutory right. The same has been settled in a catena of cases and it is clearly not an issue in dispute in the present case. With the above observation, we hold that there is no doubt or confusion persisting in the Constitution Bench judgment of this Court in *Kuldip Nayar* (supra) and the decisions in *Association for Democratic Reforms* (supra) and *People's Union for Civil Liberties (PUCL) (supra)* do not stand impliedly overruled.

SUBMISSION ON BEHALF OF UNION OF INDIA – WRIT NOT MAINTAINABLE – REJECTED – HELD WRIT MAINTAINABLE

Whether the present writ petition under article 32 is maintainable:

22. In the earlier part of our judgment, we have quoted the reliefs prayed for by the petitioners in the writ petition. Mr. Malhotra, learned Additional Solicitor General, by citing various decisions submitted that since right to vote is not a fundamental right but is merely a statutory right, hence, the present writ petition under article 32 is not maintainable and is liable to be dismissed. He referred to the following decisions of this Court in *N.P. Ponnuswami* v. *Returning Officer*, 1952 SCR 218; *Jamuna Prasad Mukhariya* v. *Lachhi Ram*, (1955) 1 SCR 608; *University of Delhi* v. *Anand Vardhan Chandal*, (2000) 10 SCC 648; *Kuldip Nayar* (supra) and *K. Krishna Murthy (Dr.)* v. *Union of India*, (2010) 7 SCC 202, wherein it has been held that the right to vote is not a fundamental right but is merely a statutory right.

23. In *Kochunni* v. *State of Madras*, 1959 (2) Supp SCR 316, this Court held that the right to move before this Court under article 32, when a fundamental right has been breached, is a substantive fundamental right by itself. In a series of cases, this Court has held that it is the duty of this Court to enforce the guaranteed fundamental rights. Vide *Daryo* v. *State of Uttar Pradesh*, (1962) 1 SCR 574.

24. The decision taken by a voter after verifying the credentials of the candidate either to vote or not is a form of expression under article 19(1)(a) of the Constitution. The fundamental right under article 19(1)(a) read with statutory right under section 79(d) of the R.P. Act is violated unreasonably if right not to vote effectively is denied and secrecy is breached. This is how articles 14 and 19(1)(a) are required to be read for deciding the issue raised in this writ petition. The casting of the vote is a facet of the right of expression of an individual and the said right is provided under article 19(1)(a) of the Constitution of India (Vide: *Association for Democratic Reforms* (supra) and *People's Union for Civil Liberties* (supra). Therefore, any violation of the said rights gives the aggrieved person the right to approach this Court under article 32 of the Constitution of India. In view of the above said decisions as well as the observations of the Constitution Bench in *Kuldip Nayar* (supra), a *prima facie* case exists for the exercise of jurisdiction of this Court under article 32.

25. Apart from the above, we would not be justified in asking the petitioners to approach the High Court to vindicate their grievance by way of a writ petition under article 226 of the Constitution of India at this juncture. Considering the reliefs prayed for which relate to the right of a voter and applicable to all eligible voters, it may not be appropriate to direct the petitioners to go to each and every High Court and seek appropriate relief. Accordingly, apart from our conclusion on legal issue, in view of the fact that the writ petition is pending before this Court for the last more than nine years, it may not be proper to reject the same on the ground, as pleaded by learned ASG. For the reasons mentioned above, we reject the said contention and hold that this Court is competent to hear the issues raised in this writ petition filed under article 32 of the Constitution.

SECRECY IN VOTING ESSENTIAL FOR STRENGTHENING DEMOCRACY

Discussion about the relief prayed for in the writ petition

26. We have already quoted the relevant provisions, particularly, section 128 of the R.P. Act, rules 39, 41, 49M and 49-O of the Rules. It is clear from the above provisions that secrecy of casting vote is duly recognised and is necessary for strengthening democracy. We are of the opinion that paragraph Nos. 441, 442 and 452 to 454 of the decision of the Constitution Bench in *Kuldip Nayar* (supra), are relevant for this purpose which are extracted hereinbelow:

> "441. Voting at elections to the Council of States cannot be compared with a general election. In a general election, the electors have to vote in a secret manner without fear that their votes would be disclosed to anyone or would result in victimisation. There is no party affiliation and hence the choice is entirely with the voter. This is not the case when elections are held to the Council of States as the electors are elected Members of the Legislative Assemblies who in turn have party affiliations.
>
> 442. The electoral systems world over contemplate variations. No one yardstick can be applied to an electoral system. The question whether election is direct or indirect and for which House members are to be chosen is a relevant aspect. All over the world in democracies members of the House of Representatives are chosen directly by popular vote. Secrecy there is a must and insisted upon; in representative democracy, particularly to the upper chamber, indirect means of election adopted on party lines is well-accepted practice.
>
> 452. Parliamentary democracy and multi-party system are an inherent art of the basic structure of the Indian Constitution. It is the political parties that set up candidates at an election who are predominantly elected as Members of the State Legislatures. The context in which general elections are held, secrecy of the vote is necessary in order to maintain the purity of the electoral system. Every voter has a right to vote in a free and fair manner and not disclose to any person how he has voted. But here we are concerned with a voter who is elected on the ticket of a political party. In this view, the context entirely changes.
>
> 453. That the concept of "constituency-based representation" is different from "proportional representation" has been eloquently brought out in *United Democratic Movement* v. *President of the Republic of South Africa* where the question before the Supreme Court was: whether "floor crossing" was fundamental to the Constitution of South Africa. In this judgment the concept of proportional representation *vis-à-vis* constituency-based representation is highlighted…
>
> 454. The distinguishing feature between "constituency-based representation" and "proportional representation" in a representative democracy is that in the case of the list system of proportional representation, members are elected on party lines. They are subject to party discipline. They

are liable to be expelled for breach of discipline. Therefore, to give effect to the concept of proportional representation, Parliament can suggest "open ballot". In such a case, it cannot be said that "free and fair elections" would stand defeated by "open ballot". As stated above, in a constituency-based election it is the people who vote whereas in proportional representation it is the elector who votes. This distinction is indicated also in the Australian judgment in *R.* v. *Jones*. In constituency-based representation, "secrecy" is the basis whereas in the case of proportional representation in a representative democracy the basis can be "open ballot" and it would not violate the concept of "free and fair elections", which concept is one of the pillars of democracy."

MAINTENANCE OF SECRECY OF VOTERS IN DIRECT ELECTIONS FOR LOK SABHA AND STATE ASSEMBLIES IS A MUST

27. The above discussion in the cited paragraphs makes it clear that in direct elections to Lok Sabha or State Legislatures, maintenance of secrecy is a must and is insisted upon all over the world in democracies where direct elections are involved to ensure that a voter casts his vote without any fear of being victimized if his vote is disclosed.

28. After referring to section 128 of the RP Act and rule 39 of the Rules, this Court in *S. Raghbir Singh Gill* v. *S. Gurcharan Singh Tohra*, 1980 (Supp) SCC 53 held as under:

> "14...Secrecy of ballot can be appropriately styled as a postulate of constitutional democracy. It enshrines a vital principle of Parliamentary institutions set up under the Constitution. It subserves a very vital public interest in that an elector or a voter should be absolutely free in exercise of his franchise untrammelled by any constraint, which includes constraint as to the disclosure. A remote or distinct possibility that at some point a voter may under a compulsion of law be forced to disclose for whom he has voted would act as a positive constraint and check on his freedom to exercise his franchise in the manner he freely chooses to exercise. Therefore, it can be said with confidence that this postulate of constitutional democracy rests on public policy."

29. In the earlier part of this judgment, we have referred to article 21(3) of the Universal Declaration of Human Rights and article 25(b) of the International Covenant on Civil and Political Rights, which also recognise the right of secrecy.

SUBMISSION OF UNION OF INDIA THAT RULE OF SECRECY APPLIES TO THOSE WHO VOTE – NOT TO THOSE WHO DO NOT VOTE – REJECTED

30. With regard to the first prayer of the petitioners, *viz.*, extension of principle of secrecy of ballot to those voters who decide not to vote, Mr. Malhotra, learned ASG submitted that principle of secrecy of ballot is extended only to those voters who have cast their votes in favour of one or the other candidates, but the same, in no manner, can be read as extended to even those voters who have not voted in the election. He further pointed out that the principle of secrecy of ballot pre-supposes validly cast vote and the object of secrecy is to assure a voter to allow him to cast his vote without any fear and in no manner it will be disclosed that in whose favour he has voted or he will not be compelled to disclose in whose favour he voted. The pith and substance of his argument is that secrecy of ballot is a principle which has been formulated to ensure a voter (who has exercised his right to vote) that in no case it shall be known to the candidates or their representatives that in whose favour a particular voter has voted so that he can exercise his right to vote freely and fearlessly.

The stand of the Union of India as projected by learned ASG is that the principle of secrecy of ballot is extended only to those voters who have cast their vote and the same in no manner can be extended to those who have not voted at all.

31. Right to vote as well as right not to vote have been statutorily recognised under section 79(d) of the R.P. Act and rules 41(2) and (3) and 49-O of the rules respectively. Whether a voter decides to cast his vote or decides not to cast his vote, in both cases, secrecy has to be maintained. It cannot be said that if a voter decides to cast his vote, secrecy will be maintained under section 128 of the R.P. Act read with rules 39 and 49M of the Rules and if in case a voter decides not to cast his vote, secrecy will not be maintained. Therefore, a part of rule 49-O read with Form 17A, which treats a voter who decides not to cast his vote differently and allows the secrecy to be violated, is arbitrary, unreasonable and violative of article 19 and is also *ultra vires* sections 79(d) and 128 of the R.P. Act.

PRINCIPLE OF SECRECY IN 'CONSTITUENCY BASED' ELECTIONS IS A MUST FOR 'FREE AND FAIR ELECTIONS'

32. As regards the question as to whether the right of expression under article 19 stands infringed when secrecy of the poll is not maintained, it is useful to refer *S. Raghbir Singh* (supra) wherein this Court deliberated on the interpretation of section 94 of the R.P. Act which mandates that no elector can be compelled as a witness to disclose his vote. In that case, this Court found that the "secrecy of ballots constitutes a postulate of constitutional democracy...A remote or distinct possibility that the voter at some point of time may under a compulsion of law be forced to disclose for whom he has voted would act as a positive constraint and check on his freedom to exercise his franchise in the manner he freely chooses to exercise". Secrecy of ballot, thus, was held to be a privilege granted in public interest to an individual. It is pertinent to note that in the said case, the issue of the disclosure by an elector of his vote arose in the first place because there was an allegation that the postal ballot of an MLA was tampered with to secure the victory of one of the candidates to the Rajya Sabha. Therefore, seemingly there was a conflict between the "fair vote" and "secret ballot".

33. In *Kuldip Nayar* (supra), this Court held that though secrecy of ballots is a vital principle for ensuring free and fair elections, the higher principle is free and fair elections. However, in the same case, this Court made a copious distinction between "constituency based representation" and "proportional representation". It was held that while in the former, secrecy is the basis, in the latter the system of open ballot and it would not be violative of "free and fair elections". In the said case, *R* v. *Jones*, (1972) 128 CLR 221 and *United Democratic Movement* v. *President of the Republic of South Africa*, (2003) 1 SA 495 were also cited with approval.

34. Therefore, in view of the decisions of this Court in *S. Raghubir Singh Gill* (supra) and *Kuldip Nayar* (supra), the policy is clear that secrecy principle is integral to free and fair elections which can be removed only when it can be shown that there is any conflict between secrecy and the "higher principle" of free elections. The instant case concerns elections to Central and State Legislatures that are undoubtedly "constituency based". No discernible public interest shall be served by disclosing the elector's vote or his identity. Therefore, secrecy is an essential feature of the "free and fair elections" and rule 49-O undoubtedly violates that requirement.

VOTING IS A FORMAL EXPRESSION OF OPINION – PRACTICE AND PROCEDURE APPLICABLE IN PARLIAMENT REFERRED

35. In *Lily Thomas* v. *Speaker, Lok Sabha,* (1993) 4 SCC 234, this Court held that "voting is a formal expression of will or opinion by the person entitled to exercise the right on the subject or issue in question" and that "right to vote means right to exercise the right in favour of or against the motion or resolution. Such a right implies right to remain neutral as well".

36. In view of the same, this Court also referred to the Practice and Procedure of the Parliament for voting which provides for three buttons: *viz.*, AYES, NOES and ABSTAIN whereby a member can abstain or refuse from expressing his opinion by casting vote in favour or against the motion.

The constitutional interpretation given by this Court was based on inherent philosophy of Parliamentary sovereignty.

A VOTER HAS THE RIGHT NOT TO VOTE CONSIDERING THE CANDIDATES UNWORTHY OF HIS VOTE

37. A perusal of section 79(d) of the R.P. Act, rules 41(2) and (3) and rule 49-O of the Rules make it clear that a right not to vote has been recognised both under the RP Act and the Rules. A positive 'right not to vote' is a part of expression of a voter in a Parliamentary democracy and it has to be recognised and given effect to in the same manner as 'right to vote'. A voter may refrain from voting at an election for several reasons including the reason that he does not consider any of the candidates in the field worthy of his vote. One of the ways of such expression may be to abstain from voting, which is not an ideal option for a conscientious and responsible citizen. Thus, the only way by which it can be made effectual is by providing a button in the EVMs to express that right. This is the basic requirement if the lasting values in a healthy democracy have to be sustained, which the Election Commission has not only recognised but has also asserted.

EVEN THE LAW COMMISSION OF INDIA RECOMMENDED THE RIGHT OF NEGATIVE VOTE

38. The Law Commission of India, in its 170th Report relating to Reform of the Electoral Laws recommended for implementation of the concept of negative vote and also pointed out its advantages.

RIGHT OF NEGATIVE VOTING WAS EXERCISABLE IN BALLOT PAPERS-NOT AVAILABLE IN E.V.M. SYSTEM INTRODUCED FOR THE FIRST TIME IN 1998

39. In India, elections traditionally have been held with ballot papers. As explained by the Election Commission, from 1998 onwards, the Electronic Voting

Machines (EVMs) were introduced on a large scale. Formerly, under the ballot paper system, it was possible to secretly cast a neutral/negative vote by going to the polling booth, marking presence and dropping one's ballot in the ballot box without making any mark on the same. However, under the system of EVMs, such secret neutral voting is not possible, in view of the provision of rule 49B of the Rules and the design of the EVM and other related voting procedures. Rule 49B of the Rules mandates that the names of the candidates shall be arranged on the balloting unit in the same order in which they appear in the list of contesting candidates and there is no provision for a neutral button.

40. It was further clarified by the Election Commission that EVM comprises of two units, *i.e.*, control and balloting units, which are interconnected by a cable. While the balloting unit is placed in a screened enclosure where an elector may cast his vote in secrecy, the control unit remains under the charge of the Presiding Officer and so placed that all polling agents and others present have an unhindered view of all the operations. The balloting unit, placed inside the screened compartment at the polling station gets activated for recording votes only when the button marked "Ballot" on the control unit is pressed by the presiding officer/polling officer in charge. Once the ballot button is pressed, the Control unit emanates red light while the ballot unit which has been activated to receive the vote emanates green light. Once an elector casts his vote by pressing balloting button against the candidate of his choice, he can see a red light glow against the name and symbol of that candidate and a high-pitched beep sound emanates from the machine.

Upon such casting of vote, the balloting unit is blocked, green light emanates on the control unit, which is in public gaze, and the high pitched beep sound is heard by one and all. Thereafter, the EVM has to re-activate for the next elector by pressing "ballot button". However, should an elector choose not to cast his vote in favour of any of the candidates labelled on the EVM, and consequently, not press any of the labeled button neither will the light on the control unit change from red to green nor will the beep sound emanate. Hence, all present in the poll booth at the relevant time will come to know that a vote has not been cast by the elector.

IN EVM SYSTEM SECRECY IS NOT MAINTAINED IN NEGATIVE VOTE

41. Rule 49-O of the Rules provides that if an elector, after his electoral roll number has been entered in the register of electors in Form 17A, decides not to record his vote on the EVM, a remark to this effect shall be made against the said entry in Form 17A by the Presiding Officer and signature/thumb impression of the elector shall be obtained against such remark. As is apparent, mechanism of casting vote through EVM and rule 49-O compromise on the secrecy of the vote as the elector is not provided any privacy when the fact of the neutral/negative voting goes into record.

IN BALLOT PAPER SECRECY OF NEGATIVE VOTE WAS MAINTAINED – ALTHOUGH THE VOTE WAS CONSIDERED AS INVALID

42. Rules 49A to 49X of the Rules come under Chapter II of Part IV of the Rules. Chapter II deals with voting by Electronic Voting Machines only. Therefore, rule 49-O, which talks about Form 17A, is applicable only in cases of voting by EVMs. The said Chapter was introduced in the Rules by way of an amendment dated 24.3.1992. Voting by ballot papers is governed by Chapter I of Part IV of the Rules. Rule 39 talks about secrecy while voting by ballot and rule 41 talks about ballot papers. However, as said earlier, in the case of voting by ballot paper, the candidate always had the option of not putting the cross mark against the names of any of the candidates and thereby record his disapproval for all the candidates in the fray. Even though such a ballot paper would be considered as an invalid vote, the voter still had the right not to vote for anybody without compromising on his/her right of secrecy.

EVMs DO NOT HAVE THE BUTTON 'NONE OF THE ABOVE' (NOTA)

However, with the introduction of EVMs, the said option of not voting for anybody without compromising the right of secrecy is not available to the voter since the voting machines did not have 'None of the Above' (NOTA) button.

ELECTION COMMISSION HAD ALSO WRITTEN TO THE MINISTRY OF LAW AND JUSTICE TO PROVIDE SUCH A BUTTON IN THE EVMs

43. It is also pointed out that in order to rectify this serious defect, on 10.12.2001, the Election Commission addressed a letter to the Secretary, Ministry of Law and Justice stating, *inter alia*, that the "electoral right" under section 79(d) includes a right not to cast vote and sought to provide a panel in the EVMs so that an elector may indicate that he does not wish to vote for any of the aforementioned candidates. The letter also stated that such number of votes expressing dissatisfaction with all the candidates may be recorded in a result sheet. It is also brought to our notice that no action was taken on the said letter dated 10.12.2001.

44. The Election Commission further pointed out that in the larger interest of promoting democracy, a provision for "None of the Above" or "NOTA" button should be made in the EVMs/ballot papers. It is also highlighted that such an action, apart from promoting free and fair elections in a democracy, will provide an opportunity to the elector to express his dissent/disapproval against the contesting candidates and will have the benefit of reducing bogus voting.

DEMOCRACY, FREE AND FAIR ELECTIONS ARE A PART OF THE BASIC STRUCTURE OF THE CONSTITUTION OF INDIA

45. Democracy and free elections are part of the basic structure of the Constitution. In *Indira Nehru Gandhi* v. *Raj Narain*, 1975 Supp 1 SCC 198, Khanna, J., held that democracy postulates that there should be periodic elections where the people should be in a position to re-elect their old representatives or change the representatives or elect in their place new representatives. It was also held that democracy can function only when elections are free and fair and the people are free to vote for the candidates of their choice. In the said case, article 19 was not in issue and the observations were in the context of basic structure of the Constitution. Thereafter, this Court reiterated that democracy is the basic structure of the Constitution in *Mohinder Singh Gill* v. *Chief Election Commissioner, New Delhi*, (1978) 1 SCC 405 and *Kihoto Hollohon* v. *Zachillhu*, 1992 (Supp) 2 SCC 651.

SUPREME COURT HAS THE RIGHT TO DIRECT THE ELECTION COMMISSION TO PROVIDE 'NOTA' BUTTON IN THE EVMs TO PROTECT THE SECRECY OF NEGATIVE VOTE

46. In order to protect the right in terms of section 79(d) and rule 49-O, *viz.*, "right not to vote", we are of the view that this Court is competent/well within its power to issue directions that secrecy of a voter who decides not to cast his vote has to be protected in the same manner as the Statute has protected the right of a voter who decides to cast his vote in favour of a candidate. This Court is also justified in giving such directions in order to give effect to the right of expression under article 19(1)(a) and to avoid any discrimination by directing the Election Commission to provide NOTA button in the EVMs.

SUBMISSION OF THE UNION OF INDIA – NO RIGHT OF NEGATIVE VOTE – REJECTED

47. With regard to the above, Mr. Malhotra, learned ASG, by drawing our attention to section 62 of the RP Act, contended that this Section enables a person to cast a vote and it has no scope for negative voting. Section 62(1) of the R.P. Act reads as under:

> "62. *Right to vote.*—(1) No person who is not, and except as expressly provided by this Act, every person who is, for the time being entered in the electoral roll of any constituency shall be entitled to vote in that constituency."

48. Mr. Malhotra, learned ASG has also pointed out that elections are conducted to fill a seat by electing a person by a positive voting in his favour and there is no concept of negative voting under the R.P. Act. According to him, the Act does not envisage that a voter has any right to cast a negative vote if he does not like any of the candidates. Referring to section 2(d) of the R.P. Act, he asserted that election is only a means of choice or election between various candidates to fill a seat. Finally, he concluded that negative voting (NOTA) has no legal consequence and there shall be no motivation for the voters to travel to the polling booth and reject all the candidates, which would have the same effect of not going to the polling station at all.

49. However, correspondingly, we should also appreciate that the election is a mechanism, which ultimately represents the will of the people. The essence of the electoral system should be to ensure freedom of voters to exercise their free choice. Article 19 guarantees all individuals the right to speak, criticize, and disagree on a particular issue. It stands on the spirit of tolerance and allows people to have diverse views, ideas and ideologies. Not allowing a person to cast vote negatively defeats the very freedom of expression and the right ensured in article 21 *i.e.*, the right to liberty.

LESSER VOTER PARTICIPATION AFFECTS THE INSTITUTION OF DEMOCRACY – 'NOTA' BUTTON IN THE EVMs CAN INCREASE IT

50. Eventually, voters' participation explains the strength of the democracy. Lesser voter participation is the rejection of commitment to democracy slowly but definitely whereas larger participation is better for the democracy. But, there is no yardstick to determine what the correct and right voter participation is. If introducing a NOTA button can increase the participation of democracy then, in our cogent view, nothing should stop the same. The voters' participation in the election is indeed the participation in the democracy itself. Non-participation causes frustration and disinterest, which is not a healthy sign of a growing democracy like India.

CONCLUSION

Best Persons having High Moral and Ethical Values need be Elected for Proper Governance of the Country

51. Democracy being the basic feature of our constitutional set up, there can be no two opinions that free and fair elections would alone guarantee the growth of a healthy democracy in the country. The 'Fair' denotes equal opportunity to all people. Universal adult suffrage conferred on the citizens of India by the Constitution has made it possible for these millions of individual voters to go to the polls and thus participate in the governance of our country. For democracy to survive, it is essential that the best available men should be chosen as people's representatives for proper governance of the country. This can be best achieved through men of high moral and ethical values, who win the elections on a positive vote.

Thus in a vibrant democracy, the voter must be given an opportunity to choose none of the above (NOTA) button, which will indeed compel the political parties to nominate a sound candidate. This situation palpably tells us the dire need of negative voting.

RIGHT TO VOTE – ESSENCE OF DEMOCRACY

52. No doubt, the right to vote is a statutory right but it is equally vital to recollect that this statutory right is the essence of democracy. Without this, democracy will fail to thrive. Therefore, even if the right to vote is statutory, the significance attached with the right is massive. Thus, it is necessary to keep in mind these facets while deciding the issue at hand.

'NOTA' BUTTON IN EVMs WILL FOSTER PURITY IN ELECTORAL PROCESS WHICH IS NEEDED FOR STRONG DEMOCRACY

53. Democracy is all about choice. This choice can be better expressed by giving the voters an opportunity to verbalize themselves unreservedly and by imposing least restrictions on their ability to make such a choice. By providing NOTA button in the EVMs, it will accelerate the effective political participation in the present state of democratic system and the voters in fact will be empowered. We are of the considered view that in bringing out this right to cast negative vote at a time when electioneering is in full swing, it will foster the purity of the electoral process and also fulfil one of its objective, namely, wide participation of people.

AFFORDING SECRECY IS INTEGRAL TO FREE AND FAIR ELECTIONS

54. Free and fair election is a basic structure of the Constitution and necessarily includes within its ambit the right of an elector to cast his vote without fear of reprisal, duress or coercion. Protection of elector's identity and affording secrecy is therefore integral to free and fair elections and an arbitrary distinction between the voter who casts his vote and the voter who does not cast his vote is violative of article 14. Thus, secrecy is required to be maintained for both categories of persons.

DISAPPROVAL OF CANDIDATES – BY VOTERS WILL COMPEL POLITICAL PARTIES TO FIELD GOOD CANDIDATES

55. Giving right to a voter not to vote for any candidate while protecting his right of secrecy is extremely important in a democracy. Such an option gives the voter the right to express his disapproval with the kind of candidates that are being put up by the political parties. When the political parties will realize that a large number of people are expressing their disapproval with the candidates being put up by them, gradually there will be a systemic change and the political parties will be forced to accept the will of the people and field candidates who are known for their integrity.

WITHOUT 'NOTA' BUTTON UNSCRUPULOUS PERSONS ARE THE GAINERS

56. The direction can also be supported by the fact that in the existing system a dissatisfied voter ordinarily does not turn up for voting which in turn provides a chance to unscrupulous elements to impersonate the dissatisfied voter and cast a vote, be it a negative one. Furthermore, a provision of negative voting would be in the interest of promoting democracy as it would send clear signals to political parties and their candidates as to what the electorate think about them.

'NOTA' BUTTON IS LIKE 'ABSTAIN' BUTTON IN PARLIAMENT

57. As mentioned above, the voting machines in the Parliament have three buttons, namely, AYES, NOES, and ABSTAIN. Therefore, it can be seen that an option has been given to the members to press the ABSTAIN button. Similarly, the NOTA button being sought for by the petitioners is exactly similar to the ABSTAIN button since by pressing the NOTA button the voter is in effect saying that he is abstaining from voting since he does not find any of the candidates to be worthy of his vote.

NEGATIVE VOTE FUNDAMENTAL TO VIBRANT DEMOCRACY – MANY COUNTRIES HAVE IT

58. The mechanism of negative voting, thus, serves a very fundamental and essential part of a vibrant democracy. The following countries have provided for neutral/protest/negative voting in their electoral systems:

S. No.	Name of the Country	Method of Voting	Form of Negative Vote
1.	France	Electronic	NOTA
2.	Belgium	Electronic	NOTA
3.	Brazil	Ballot Paper	NOTA
4.	Greece	Ballot Paper	NOTA
5.	Ukraine	Ballot Paper	NOTA
6.	Chile	Ballot Paper	NOTA
7.	Bangladesh	Ballot Paper	NOTA
8.	State of Nevada, USA	Ballot Paper	NOTA

S. No.	Name of the Country	Method of Voting	Form of Negative Vote
9.	Finland	Ballot Paper	Blank Vote and/or 'write in*'
10.	Sweden	Ballot Paper	Blank Vote and/or 'write in*'
11.	United States of America	Electronic/Ballot State	Blank Vote and/or 'write in*'
12.	Colombia	Ballot Paper	Blank Vote
13.	Spain	Ballot Paper	Blank Vote

* Write-in' – The 'write-in' form of negative voting allows a voter to cast a vote in favour of any fictional name/candidate.

EVMs HAS 64 BUTTONS – CAN STILL BE INCREASED-'NOTA' BUTTON CAN BE PROVIDED

59. The Election Commission also brought to the notice of this Court that the present electronic voting machines can be used in a constituency where the number of contesting candidates is up to 64. However, in the event of there being more than 64 candidates in the poll fray, the conventional system of ballot paper is resorted to. Learned counsel appearing for the Election Commission also asserted through supplementary written submission that the Election Commission of India is presently exploring the possibility of developing balloting unit with 200 panels. Therefore, it was submitted that if in case this Court decides to uphold the prayers of the petitioners herein, the additional panel on the balloting unit after the last panel containing the name and election symbol of the last contesting candidate can be utilised as the NOTA button.

Further, it was explicitly asserted in the written submission that the provision for the above facility for a negative or neutral vote can be provided in the existing electronic voting machines without any additional cost or administrative effort or change in design or technology of the existing machines. For illustration, if there are 12 candidates contesting an election, the 13th panel on the balloting unit will contain the words like "None of the above" and the ballot button against this panel will be kept open and the elector who does not wish to vote for any of the abovementioned 12 contesting candidates, can press the button against the 13th panel and his vote will be accordingly recorded by the control unit. At the time of the counting, the votes recorded against serial number 13 will indicate as to how many electors have decided not to vote for any candidate.

'NOTA' BUTTON CAN BE THE LAST BUTTON IN THE EVM PANEL

60. Taking note of the submissions of Election Commission, we are of the view that the implementation of the NOTA button will not require much effort except for allotting the last panel in the EVM for the same.

RULES 41(2) AND (3) AND 49-O OF THE CONDUCT OF ELECTION RULES, 1961 VIOLATE SECRECY OF VOTING – THEREFORE *ULTRA VIRES*

61. In the light of the above discussion, we hold that rules 41(2) and (3) and 49-O of the Rules are *ultra vires* section 128 of the R.P. Act and article 19(1)(a) of the Constitution to the extent they violate secrecy of voting.

DIRECTION GIVEN TO THE ELECTION COMMISSION TO PROVIDE 'NOTA' BUTTON IN THE EVMs – GOVERNMENT OF INDIA TO PROVIDE ALL ASSISTANCE REQUIRED – WRIT PETITION DISPOSED OF

In view of our conclusion, we direct the Election Commission to provide necessary provision in the ballot papers/EVMs and another button called "None of the Above" (NOTA) may be provided in EVMs so that the voters, who come to the polling booth and decide not to vote for any of the candidates in the fray, are able to exercise their right not to vote while maintaining their right of secrecy. Inasmuch as the Election Commission itself is in favour of the provision for NOTA in EVMs, we direct the Election Commission to implement the same either in a phased manner or at a time with the assistance of the Government of India. We also direct the Government of India to provide necessary help for implementation of the above direction.

Besides, we also direct the Election Commission to undertake awareness programmes to educate the masses.

62. The writ petition is disposed of with the aforesaid directions.

........................CJI. (P. Sathasivam)
..........................J. (Ranjana Prakash Desai)
..........................J. (Ranjan Gogoi)

New Delhi;
September 27, 2013

Author's Note: This judgment has not made it clear that if a candidate gets even one thousand votes while all other voters have exercised the negative vote, then what would be the result. Will it mean that if the Negative vote is in majority then all the votes polled in favour of any of the candidates would stand cancelled? If not, the vote would be like a cancelled vote with virtually no effect.

For this reason, it was published in the Newspaper that an application for clarification would be filed in the Supreme Court.

Author's Note: Dr. Subramanian Swami had filed a Writ Petition in Delhi High Court requiring the Election Commission of India to introduce 'Paper Trail' in the Voting EVMs to ensure the voter that his vote has actually gone to the candidate to whom he had voted, as it will also ensure that the EVMs are tamper proof. His Writ Petition was dismissed by the Delhi High Court on which he had filed an appeal in the Hon'ble Supreme Court. Hence this judgment.

QUESTIONS OF LAW AND FACTS CONSIDERED IN THIS CASE WERE IF PAPER TRAIL CAN BE INTRODUCED IN THE EVMs OR NOT

Dr. Subramanian Swamy[1]
v.
Election Commission of India

SUPREME COURT OF INDIA

[Civil Appeal No. 9093 of 2013
arising out of SLP (Civil) No. 13735 of 2012]

AND

[Writ Petition (C) No. 406 of 2012]

P. Sathasivam, CJI. and Ranjan Gogai, J.

P. Sathasivam, CJI.

1. Leave granted. Civil Appeal @ SLP (C) No. 13735 of 2012

2. This appeal is directed against the judgment and order dated 17.1.2012 passed by the Division Bench of the High Court of Delhi at New Delhi in W.P.(C) No. 11879 of 2009 whereby the High Court disposed of the petition by disallowing the prayer made by the appellant herein for issuance of a writ of *mandamus* directing the Election Commission of India (ECI)-Respondent herein to incorporate a system of "paper trail/paper receipt" in the Electronic Voting Machines (EVMs) as a convincing proof that the EVM has rightly registered the vote cast by a voter in favour of a particular candidate.

3. Being aggrieved of the above, the present appeal has been filed by way of special leave. Writ Petition (Civil) No. 406 of 2012

ONE WRIT PETITION ALSO FILED – HEARD WITH THIS APPEAL

4. One Rajendra Satyanarayan Gilda has filed this Writ Petition, under article 32 of the Constitution of India, praying for issuance of a writ of *mandamus*/ direction(s) directing the Union of India, the Chief Election Commissioner and the Technical Experts Committee-Respondent Nos. 1-3 herein respectively to effect the necessary modifications in the EVMs so as to allow the voters to verify their respective votes and to attach the printers to the EVMs with a facility to print the running record of the votes for the purpose of verification by the voters in the process of voting. He also prayed for a direction to frame guidelines and to effect necessary amendments in the Conduct of Election Rules, 1961.

---

1. JT 2013 (13) SC 312.

5. In view of the pendency of the appeal filed by Dr. Subramanian Swamy, this Court issued notice in the writ petition and tagged with the said appeal.

PARTIES WERE HEARD BY THE SUPREME COURT

6. Heard Dr. Subramanian Swamy, appellant-in-person in the appeal, Dr. R.R. Deshpande, learned counsel for the writ petitioner, Mr. Ashok Desai and Ms. Meenakshi Arora, learned senior counsel for the ECI. Contentions:

SUBMISSIONS OF THE APPELLANT – VOTER SHOULD GET RECEIPT

Contentions

7. Dr. Subramanian Swamy, the appellant herein contended before this Court that the present system of EVMs, as utilized in the last few general elections in India, does not meet all the requirements of the international standards and though the ECI maintains that the EVMs cannot be tampered with, but the fact is that EVMs, like all electronic equipments, are open to hacking.

8. The appellant has further highlighted that the instant matter arises out of the refusal of the ECI to incorporate a certain obvious safeguard in the EVMs called "paper backup", "paper receipt" or "paper trail", presently in use and mandated in some countries like USA, which would easily and cheaply meet the requirement of proof that the EVM has rightly registered the vote cast by a voter. The appellant has further highlighted that the "paper trail" system is to supplement the procedure of voting as in this procedure, after recording a vote in the EVM, a print-out will come out which will appraise the voter that his vote has been rightly registered and the same will be deposited in a box which can only be used by the ECI in case of election dispute.

9. It is the categorical stand of the appellant that the above said system will bring more accuracy in the present system and if a particular election is challenged on the ground that some particular identified voter's vote or the votes of a group of voters have been suppressed/have not been correctly assigned by the EVMs, the accepted current procedure is for a re-run of the same EVMs for a re-count, however, under the new procedure, a re-count will be of the receipts in the ballot box containing the printouts the EVMs had issued to the voter thereby ensuring more transparency in the process.

SUBMISSIONS ON BEHALF OF THE PETITIONER

10. The writ petitioner has also raised similar contentions as those of Dr. Swamy. According to the petitioner, in the present system of voting through EVMs, there is no such facility by which a voter can verify and confirm his own voting. At present, a voter presses a button only but cannot ascertain the actual voting. He is not sure whether his vote is recorded or not, if recorded, whether it is recorded in favour of the person to whom it was intended or not. Whether it is valid or invalid and whether it is counted or not. It is submitted by the petitioner that unless and until answers to these questions are personally seen by the voter, it cannot be said that voting is made by him because "pressing a button of choice and getting flashed the red-light" is not actual voting in real sense unless the voter knows well that what has happened in consequence of pressing a button of his choice from the EVMs. Stand of the Election Commission of India:

SUBMISSIONS ON BEHALF OF THE ELECTION COMMISSION OF INDIA – EVMs ARE TAMPER PROOF – 'VOTER VERIFIABLE PAPER AUDIT TRAIL' (VVPAT) NOT SUCCESSFUL

Stand of the Election Commission of India

11. Mr. Ashok Desai, learned senior counsel for the ECI submitted that the apprehension that EVMs could be tampered with is baseless. It was also informed to this Court that the ECI has been exploring the possibility of incorporating a viable Voter Verifiable Paper Audit Trail (VVPAT) system as a part of the presently used EVMs to make the election system more transparent. Further, it was brought to our notice that the ECI conducted field trials for VVPAT system earlier also but the same had not been successful and were discontinued. The ECI also filed a counter-affidavit stating that the EVMs provided by the Commission are of such a high end technology that it cannot be hacked.

12. Referring to section 61A of the Representation of the People Act, 1951, it is submitted that the Statute itself provides for recording of votes by EVMs and the ECI has been given the discretion to prescribe recording of votes by such EVMs as it may deem fit. This discretion has to be exercised in a manner to preserve the sanctity of the election process and ensure that the election is conducted in a free and fair manner. The ECI has exercised due diligence to ensure that EVMs so used are "tamper proof" and it is also in the process of exploring to incorporate VVPAT system which is compatible with the present EVMs used by it. It is asserted that there is no instance of tampering with EVMs so far by anyone.

CONTROL UNIT OF EVMs CAN PRINT-OUT THE VOTING DATA

13. It is further submitted that the EVMs used in India are unique and unlike the ones used in the elections in USA and other countries, which are personal computer based. EVMs deployed by the ECI have been lauded not only in India but also abroad. EVM's Control Unit retains in the memory each vote recorded elector-wise. The information stored in the memory of the Control Unit can be retrieved by using a device called the "decoder" which, when attached to the Control Unit of EVM, can print out the statement of voting data showing the order in which each voter has voted and to whom he has voted.

LIGHT GLOWS WHEN THE BUTTON IS PRESSED IN THE EVMs

14. Insofar as the transparency of the election process as well as the right of a voter to know whether his vote has actually been recorded for the candidate for whom it was cast is concerned, it is submitted that as soon as a vote is recorded by a voter by pressing the "candidate's" button on the Ballot Unit, a light glows against the name and symbol of the candidate, which the voter can see for himself/herself. This is a visual (electronic) assurance to the voter that the candidate for whom he has cast his vote has actually got that vote. Thereafter, the light goes off to protect the secrecy of voting.

VVPAT TRIALS WERE CONDUCTED BY EXPERT COMMITTEES

15. It is further submitted that the feasibility of VVPAT system was sought to be explored to by various political parties and they were explained the technical and administrative safeguards. The ECI also constituted a Technical Experts

Committee to examine the viability of the VVPAT system. On 27.5.2011, the Technical Experts Committee, after discussion with political parties and civil society members and also after seeing the demonstration of the prototype VVPAT system developed by M/s. Bharat Electronics Ltd. (BEL) and M/s. Electronics Corporation of India Ltd. (ECIL), recommended that a field test of the prototype VVPAT system should be carried out in a simulated election under different environmental conditions in Jaisalmer, Thiruvananthapuram, Delhi, Leh and Cherapunji. The ECI also held further meetings with the manufacturers of EVMs on various dates to fine tune the system and expedite the follow up action required. Several meetings were also held with the Expert Committee on VVPAT system.

POLITICAL PARTIES/INDIVIDUALS REQUESTED TO WITNESS IT

16. In wider fulfilment of the objectives of the field trial, the ECI has requested the National and State parties to extend necessary cooperation by getting involved in the trial process actively and also witness the trial in order to have a first hand experience of the system. The ECI has also requested the individuals including the appellant – Dr. Subramanian Swamy and the groups, who have been engaged with the ECI on the issue of EVM-VVPAT, to witness the trial.

VARIOUS ORDERS BY SUPREME COURT AND MONITORING

17. We have carefully perused the relevant materials and considered the rival contentions.

Discussion:

18. When the matter was listed before this Court for hearing on 27.9.2012, Mr. Ashok Desai had brought to our notice that the ECI is contemplating foolproof method in EVMs for which they are taking various steps in consultation with the Technical Experts Committee and the views of all recognised political parties. Mr. Desai also promised to appraise this Court about the deliberations and the ultimate decision to be taken by them in this regard. Accordingly, this Court granted sufficient time to the ECI to file Status Report regarding introduction of VVPAT system in EVMs to be used in the elections.

19. Pursuant to the directions of this Court, the ECI filed a Status Report on the developments of VVPAT system. In the said report, the ECI, citing various technicalities, prayed for further time to make the system more robust for the field conditions.

20. On 15.12.2012, M/s. BEL, Bangalore filed a report showing the status of development of VVPAT system which contains changes that have been carried out in VVPAT from September to December, 2012 and also furnished chronological changes made in VVPAT system after the field trial of the VVPAT system held in July and August, 2012.

AFFIDAVIT FILED BY THE ELECTION COMMISSION OF INDIA

21. Pursuant to the directions of this Court, the Secretary, ECI, filed an affidavit highlighting the following steps/information:

(i) "That *vide* its Affidavit dated 14.1.2013, the Commission had filed the status report regarding introduction of the VVPAT system in the Electronic Voting Machines (EVMs).

(ii) That subsequently, in the Technical Expert Committee meeting held on 4.2.2013, the Committee approved the design of the VVPAT and decided that software fine tuning will be done and completed by the end of February, 2013, and modified design specifications will be submitted to the Technical Expert Committee for approval. The Committee also recommended that the Commission may for using the VVPAT and that the VVPAT should be tried in a bye-election.

(iii) That in the Technical Expert Committee meeting held on 19.2.2013, the Committee finalized the VVPAT design. The manufacturers, namely, M/s. Bharat Electronics Limited and M/s. Electronics Corporation of India Limited have quoted Rs. 16,200 (excluding duties, taxes and transport charges) per VVPAT system. The Commission has decided to purchase sufficient units of VVPAT for trials in a Bye-election, at an approximate cost of Rs. 72,90,000 (Rupees seventy-two lakh ninety thousand) approximately.

(iv) It is submitted that the Commission will require approximately 13 lakh VVPAT units to be manufactures for 13 lakh EVMs presently available and roughly about Rs. 1690 crores (One Thousand Six Hundred Ninety Crores) (*i.e.*, 13 lakh units x Rs. 13,000 per unit) are required for the purpose of implementation of the VVPAT system taking into account the possible reduction in the cost per unit when produced in bulk.

(v) It is further submitted that in order to implement the new system the Conduct of Election Rules, 1961 will require certain amendments. In this connection, *vide* letter No. 3/1/2013/Vol. II/SDR/86 dated 28.3.2013, the Commission has informed the Legislative Department of the Ministry of Law and Justice *inter alia* the various amendments required to the relevant parts of Rules 49A to 49X, 66A, 55C, 56C, 57C and Form 17C of the Conduct of Elections Rules, 1961, as well as introduction of Rules 49MA and 56D in the said Rules.

(vi) That the Commission has called for a meeting of all the recognized National and State Parties on 10th May, 2013 for the purpose of demonstration of VVPAT unit to them and for discussion with them for eliciting their views regarding use of VVPAT system in the elections. The petitioner herein and others interested in the matter would also be invited at the meeting."

TECHNICAL EXPERT COMMITTEE APPROVED THE FINAL DESIGN OF VVPAT – LAW MINISTERY TO AMEND RULES FOR PROVIDING VVPAT

22. It is seen from the records that after various deliberations with the experts and persons concerned with the technology, the Technical Experts Committee approved the final design of VVPAT units in its meeting held on 19.1.2013. In order to meet the directions of this Court and for proper execution of VVPAT system, as noticed above, the ECI in its letter dated 28.3.2013, addressed to the Secretary to the Government of India, Ministry of Law and Justice stated that necessary ground work for amendment to the Conduct of Election Rules, 1961 (in relevant parts in Rules 49A to 49X, 66A, 55C, 56C, 57C and Form 17C) may be made so that the amendment to the Rules can be notified immediately which will enable the ECI to use the VVPAT system in bye-elections in consultation with the political parties. By placing all those materials, the ECI requested the Ministry of Law and Justice for drafting and notifying amendment Rules expeditiously.

23. From the materials placed by the ECI, it is noted that the purchase order has been placed with M/s. BEL and M/s. ECIL for supplying 150 and 300 VVPAT units respectively at Rs. 16,200 per unit excluding excise duty, sales tax and transportation etc. costing Rs. 72,90,000 (approx.). The ECI has also highlighted that if the VVPAT systems are ultimately to be used with all the 13 lakh EVMs available, the total cost in the purchase of VVPAT units may come to about Rs. 1,690 crores, taking into account the possible reduction in the cost per unit due to bulk production the cost may come to Rs. 13,000 per unit approximately.

AMENDMENT IN THE CONDUCT OF ELECTION RULES NOTIFIED

24. The affidavit dated 21.8.2013, filed on behalf of the ECI, shows that the Ministry of Law and Justice, on 24.7.2013, referred the draft notification to amend the Conduct of Election Rules, 1961 to provide for use of VVPAT system of elections to the ECI for its views and comments. The ECI suggested certain minor modifications in the draft notification and sent the same back to the Ministry of Law and Justice on 2.8.2013 with a request to notify the amendment Rules at the earliest. Accordingly, the Ministry of Law and Justice notified the amendments to the Conduct of Election Rules, 1961 in the Gazette of India *vide* notification No. S.O. 2470(E) dated 14.8.2013 to enable use of VVPAT with EVMs.

25. The aforesaid affidavit of the ECI also shows that the ECI had also convened a meeting of all the recognised National and State political parties on 10.5.2013 and demonstrated before their representatives the working of VVPAT system. Separately, on the same day, the ECI also held a meeting with individuals including the appellant herein who had been engaged with the ECI over the past several years regarding the functioning of EVMs. VVPAT system was demonstrated before them as well. Representatives of political parties and other individuals expressed their satisfaction over the VVPAT system. Thereafter, the ECI had decided to use the VVPAT system in the bye-election from 51-Noksen (ST) Assembly Constituency in the State of Nagaland. Instructions were issued to hold special meetings with the contesting candidates in that constituency to brief them about the use of VVPAT system. The ECI also organised special training sessions for poll officers for the use of VVPAT and steps were taken to educate the electors for the same.

VVPAT PROVED SUCCESSFUL IN NAGALAND ASSEMBLY ELECTIONS

26. After various hearings, when the matter was heard on 4.10.2013, an affidavit dated 1.10.2013 filed on behalf of the ECI was placed before this Court. The said affidavit was filed to place on record the performance/result of the introduction of the VVPAT system in the bye-election from 51-Noksen (ST) Assembly Constituency of Nagaland for which the poll was conducted on 4.9.2013 indicating the future course of action to be decided by the ECI on the basis of said performance. By this affidavit, it was brought to our notice that since VVPAT system was being used for the first time, the ECI has decided that intensive training shall be given to the polling officers.

Members of the Technical Experts Committee of the ECI also went to supervise training and the actual use of VVPAT in the bye-election. It is further stated that the ECI also wrote letters to all the recognised political parties and other persons, including the appellant herein, engaged with the ECI on this subject inviting them to witness the use of VVPAT. It is also brought to our notice that VVPAT was successfully used in all the 21 polling stations of 51-Noksen (ST) Assembly Constituency of Nagaland. It was also stated that as per the Rules, the paper slips of VVPAT shall not be counted normally except in case the Returning Officer decides to count them on an application submitted by any of the candidates. However, since VVPAT system was being used for the first time in any election, the ECI decided on its own to count paper slips of VVPAT in respect of all polling stations. According to the ECI, no discrepancy was found between the electronic and paper count.

27. In the said affidavit, it is finally stated that the ECI has decided to increase the use of VVPAT units in a phased manner and for this purpose the ECI has already written to the Government of India, Ministry of Law and Justice to issue administrative and financial sanction for procurement of 20,000 units of VVPAT (10,000 each from M/s BEL and M/s ECIL) costing about Rs. 38.01 crore.

28. Though initially the ECI was little reluctant in introducing "paper trail" by use of VVPAT, taking note of the advantage in the system as demonstrated by Dr. Subramanian Swamy, we issued several directions to the ECI . Pursuant to the same, the ECI contacted several expert bodies, technical advisers, etc. They also had various meetings with National and State level political parties, demonstrations were conducted at various places and finally after a thorough examination and full discussion, VVPAT was used successfully in all the 21 polling stations of 51-Noksen (ST) Assembly Constituency of Nagaland. The information furnished by the ECI, through the affidavit dated 1.10.2013, clearly shows that VVPAT system is a successful one. We have already highlighted that VVPAT is a system of printing paper trail when the voter casts his vote, in addition to the electronic record of the ballot, for the purpose of verification of his choice of candidate and also for manual counting of votes in case of dispute.

'PAPER TRAIL' INDISPENSABLE FOR TRANSPARENT ELECTION

29. From the materials placed by both the sides, we are satisfied that the "paper trail" is an indispensable requirement of free and fair elections. The confidence of the voters in the EVMs can be achieved only with the introduction of the "paper trail". EVMs with VVPAT system ensure the accuracy of the voting system. With an intent to have fullest transparency in the system and to restore the confidence of the voters, it is necessary to set up EVMs with VVPAT system because vote is nothing but an act of expression which has immense importance in democratic system.

ELECTION COMMISSION DIRECTED TO IMPLEMENT VVPAT IN GENERAL ELECTIONS-2014 IN PHASED MANNER

30. In the light of the above discussion and taking notice of the pragmatic and reasonable approach of the ECI and considering the fact that in general elections all over India, the ECI has to handle one million (ten lakhs) polling booths, we permit the ECI to introduce the same in gradual stages or geographical-wise in the ensuing general elections. The area, State or actual booth(s) are to be decided by the ECI and the ECI is free to implement the same in a phased manner. We appreciate the efforts and good gesture made by the ECI in introducing the same.

GOVERNMENT OF INDIA DIRECTED TO PROVIDE FUNDS

31. For implementation of such a system (VVPAT) in a phased manner, the Government of India is directed to provide required financial assistance for procurement of units of VVPAT.

APPEAL/WRIT PETITION DISPOSED OF – APPRECIATION RECORDED

32. Before parting with the case, we record our appreciation for the efforts made by Dr. Subramanian Swamy as well as the ECI, in particular Mr. Ashok Desai and Ms. Meenakshi Arora, learned senior counsel for the ECI.

33. With the above directions, the appeal and the writ petition are disposed of. No separate order is required in the applications for intervention. Both sides are permitted to approach this Court for further direction(s), if need arises.

....

CJI. (P. SATHASIVAM)

....

....

J. (RANJAN GOGOI)

....

NEW DELHI;

OCTOBER 8, 2013.

Author's Note: The Parliament had passed the Act titled, 'The Persons with Disabilities (Equal Opportunities, Protection of Rights and Full Participation) Act, 1995 providing 3% reservation for disabled persons in Government jobs in the Centre, States and all the Instrumentalities of the State. However, the Union of India issued Office Memorandum in 2005 issuing directions which were inconsistent with the provisions of the Act. The legality of said Office Memorandum was challenged by the National Federation of the Blind by filing writ petition in Delhi High Court which was accepted on 19.12.2008. The Union of India and others filed an appeal in the Hon'ble Supreme Court by impleading the National Federation of the Blind as Respondent No. 1. Hence this judgment.

IMPLEMENTATION OF SECTION 33 OF 'THE PERSONS WITH DISABILITIES (EQUAL OPPORTUNITIES, PROTECTION OF RIGHTS AND FULL PARTICIPATION) ACT, 1995, WAS INVOLVED IN THIS CASE

Union of India
v.
National Federation of the Blind

SUPREME COURT OF INDIA

Civil Appellate Jurisdiction

Civil Appeal No. 9096 of 2013

(Arising out of SLP (Civil) No. 7541 of 2009)

P. Sathasivam, CJI., Ranjana Parkash Desai and Ranjan Gogoi, JJ.

JUDGMENT

P. Sathasivam, CJI.

1. Leave granted.

2. This appeal is directed against the final judgment and order dated 19.12.2008 passed by the High Court of Delhi at New Delhi in Writ Petition (C) No. 15828 of 2006 wherein the High Court interpreted section 33 of the Persons with Disabilities (Equal Opportunities, Protection of Rights and Full Participation) Act, 1995 (in short 'the Act') and issued various directions to be complied with by the appellants herein.

FACTUAL BACKGROUND

3. Brief facts:

(a) National Federation of the Blind-Respondent No. 1 herein is an apex organization and a society registered under the Societies Registration Act, 1860, having its Head Office at New Delhi and is working for the protection of the rights of the visually challenged.

(b) In the year 2006, Respondent No. 1 herein filed a writ petition before the High Court in public interest seeking implementation of section 33 of the Act alleging that the appellants herein have failed to provide reservation to the blind and low vision persons and they are virtually excluded from the process of recruitment to the Government posts as stipulated under the said Act.

(c) In the above backdrop, it is relevant to mention that way back in 1977, the erstwhile Ministry of Social Welfare, Government of India, made reservation in favour of the following three categories of disabled persons in Group C and D posts to the extent of 1 per cent. each for the (i) Blind; (ii) Hearing and Speech Impairment; and (iii) persons suffering from locomotor disability. In the year 1986, the Department of Personnel and Training (DoPT), directed all the departments to take into account both identified and unidentified posts for working out the total number of vacancies to be reserved for each of the disabled categories. In spite of the above said executive order, various government departments and public sector undertakings did not give effect to the scheme of reservation which compelled Respondent No. 1 herein to organise a nation wide agitation, as a result of which, an agreement was arrived at between the parties on 27.8.1987 to undertake a Special Recruitment Drive for clearing up the backlog of vacancies.

(d) On 7.2.1996, the Persons with Disabilities (Equal Opportunities, Protection of Rights and Full Participation) Act, 1995 was brought into force making reservation of at least 3 per cent. posts in all government establishments to the extent of 1 per cent each for the persons suffering from (i) blindness or low vision; (ii) hearing impairment; and (iii) locomotor disability or cerebral palsy. After enactment of the said Act, Union of India issued various orders for ensuring proper implementation of the provisions of the Act for the persons with disabilities.

RESPONDENT NO. 1 FILED WRIT PETITION IN DELHI HIGH COURT

(e) Respondent No. 1 herein, by filing the above said petition before the High Court asserted that despite statutory provisions and various executive orders, discrimination against the persons with disabilities continued in filling up the vacancies in various government departments whereas it was contended by the other side that the Office Memorandum (OM) dated 29.12.2005, issued *by the Department of Personnel and Training,* inter alia *provides a* system for ensuring proper implementation of the provisions of the Act for the persons with disabilities.

WRIT PETITION WAS ACCEPTED

(f) *Vide* order dated 19.12.2008, the High Court disposed of the petition directing the Union of India to modify the OM dated 9.12.2005 being inconsistent with the provisions of section 33 of the Act and issued several other directions.

UNION OF INDIA FILED AN APPEAL IN THE SUPREME COURT

(g) Being aggrieved of the above, the appellants have preferred this appeal by way of special leave before this Court.

APPLICATION FOR IMPLEADMENT FILED – ALLOWED TO ACT INTERVENORS

(h) Tamil Nadu Handicapped Federation Charitable Trust, Smt. S. Rajeswari and Association for Physically Challenged People Ordnance Clothing Factory filed applications for impleadment. *Vide* order dated 22.7.2011, this Court did not allow them to implead but to act as intervenors in the proceedings.

PARTIES WERE HEARD

4. Heard Ms. Indra Jaisingh, learned Additional Solicitor-General for the Union of India, Mr. S.K. Rungta, learned senior counsel (R-1) appearing in person and Mr. R. Prabhakaran, learned counsel for Intervenors.

SUBMISSIONS OF THE UNION OF INDIA

Submissions:

5. Ms. Indra Jaisingh, learned Additional Solicitor-General for the Union of India, after taking us through various provisions of the Act and OM(s) issued by the Government of India submitted that the impugned judgment of the High Court is against the provisions of the Act. She further pointed out that the finding of the High Court that in terms of section 33 of the Act, 3% reservation for the disabled persons has to be computed on the basis of total strength of the cadre, *i.e.*, both identified as well as unidentified posts is erroneous. In any event, according to her, the direction of the High Court to work out backlog vacancies for the disabled persons on the total cadre strength in different establishments within one month from the date of the order is impractical and not executable. It is further highlighted that according to section 33 of the Act, reservation to the persons with disabilities in an establishment shall be 3% of the vacancies arising in the posts which are identified for the persons with disabilities. The High Court, by the impugned judgment, disturbed the very basic system of the reservation of posts for the persons with disabilities. She further highlighted that the reservation for Group C and D posts is being calculated on the basis of the vacancies in identified as well as unidentified posts prior to the Act came into existence and in view of the provisions of section 72 of the Act, continued in the same way, however, reservation for Groups A and B posts is being calculated on the basis of the vacancies for identified posts as per the provisions of the Act.

SUBMISSIONS ON BEHALF OF RESPONDENT NO. 1

6. On the other hand, Mr. S.K. Rungta, learned senior counsel (R-1) appearing in person submitted that in terms of the provisions of the Act, more particularly, sections 32 and 33 of the Act, it is obligatory on the part of the Government establishments to provide at least 3% reservation of posts in the total cadre strength and not in the identified vacancies. He further pointed out that though the Act was passed in 1995 since then the provisions have not been strictly implemented. He prayed for further time bound direction for implementation of the same.

7. Mr. R. Prabhakaran, learned counsel for intervenors reiterated the submissions made by Mr. S.K. Rungta.

8. We have perused all the relevant materials and considered the rival submissions.

PROVISIONS OF THE PERSONS WITH DISABILITIES (EQUAL OPPORTUNITIES, PROTECTION OF RIGHTS AND FULL PARTICIPATION) ACT, 1995

Relevant Provisions:

9. In order to answer the rival contentions, it is desirable to quote the relevant provision of the Act. Sections 2(a), 2(i), 2(j) and 2(k) of the Act read as under:

"2(a) "appropriate Government" means,—

(i) in relation to the Central Government or any establishment wholly or substantially financed by that Government, or a Cantonment Board constituted under the Cantonment Act, 1924 (2 of 1924), the Central Government;

(ii) in relation to a State Government or any establishment wholly or substantially financed by that Government or any local authority, other than a Cantonment Board, the State Government;

(iii) in respect of the Central Co-ordination Committee and the Central Executive Committee, the Central Government;

(iv) in respect of the State Co-ordination Committee and the State Executive Committee, the State Government;

2(i) "Disability" means—

(i) blindness;

(ii) low vision;

(iii) leprosy-cured;

(iv) hearing impairment;

(v) locomotor disability;

(vi) mental retardation;

(vii) mental illness;

2(j) "employer" means,—

(i) in relation to a Government, the authority notified by the Head of the Department in this behalf or where no such authority is notified, the Head of the Department; and

(ii) in relation to an establishment, the Chief Executive Officer of that establishment;

2(k) "establishment" means a corporation established by or under a Central, Provincial or State Act, or an authority or a body owned or controlled or aided by the Government or a local authority or a Government company as defined in section 617 of the Companies Act, 1956 (1 of 1956) and includes Departments of a Government;"

SECTION 2(K) OF THE ACT IS VERY EXHAUSTIVE

10. Among the above definitions, we are more concerned with the definition of "establishment" under section 2(k) of the Act, which is an exhaustive definition and covers (i) a corporation established by or under a Central, Provincial or State Act, or (ii) an authority or a body owned or controlled or aided by the Government or a local authority, or (iii) a Government company as defined in section 617 of the Companies Act, 1956 and (iv) Departments of a Government.

CHAPTER VI OF THE ACT DEALS WITH EMPLOYMENT OF DISABLED PERSONS – SECTIONS 32, 33, 36 REPRODUCED

11. Chapter VI of the Act deals with the employment of persons with disabilities. The relevant sections of the said Chapter are as under:—

"32. *Identification of posts which can be reserved for persons with disabilities.*— Appropriate Governments shall—

(a) identify posts, in the establishments, which can be reserved for the persons with disability;

(b) at periodical intervals not exceeding three years, review the list of posts identified and update the list taking into consideration the developments in technology.

33. *Reservation of Posts.*—Every appropriate Government shall appoint in every establishment such percentage of vacancies not less than three per cent. for persons or class of persons with disability of which one per cent. each shall be reserved for persons suffering from—

(i) blindness or low vision;

(ii) hearing impairment;

(iii) locomotor disability or cerebral palsy, in the posts identified for each disability:

Provided that the appropriate Government may, having regard to the type of work carried on in any department or establishment, by notification subject to such conditions, if any, as may be specified in such notification, exempt any establishment from the provisions of this section.

36. *Vacancies not filled up to be carried forward.*—Where in any recruitment year any vacancy under section 33, cannot be filled up due to non-availability of a suitable person with disability or, for any other sufficient reason, such vacancy shall be carried forward in the succeeding recruitment year and if in the succeeding recruitment year also suitable person with disability is not available, it may first be filled by interchange among the three categories and only when there is no person with disability available for the post in that year, the employer shall fill up the vacancy by appointment of a person, other than a person with disability:

Provided that if the nature of vacancies in an establishment is such that a given category of person cannot be employed, the vacancies may be interchanged among the three categories with the prior approval of the appropriate Government."

CENTRAL GOVERNMENT FRAMED RULES

12. In exercise of the powers conferred by sub-sections (1) and (2) of section 73 of the Act, the Central Government enacted the Persons with Disabilities (Equal Opportunities, Protection of Rights and Full Participation) Rules, 1996.

OFFICE MEMORANDUM DATED 29.12.2005 ISSUED BY THE GOVERNMENT OF INDIA AND ITS CONTENTS

13. After enactment of the above Act, in order to consolidate the existing instructions in line with the provisions of the Act, on 29.12.2005, Government of India, Department of Personnel and Training, issued certain instructions by way of an Office Memorandum (OM), with regard to the reservation for the persons with disabilities (physically handicapped persons) in posts and services. The said

Office Memorandum specifically states that it shall supersede all previous instructions issued on the subject so far. Respondent No. 1 herein has commended various clauses of the OM dated 29.12.2005. The relevant clauses of the same are extracted hereinbelow:

"**2. QUANTUM OF RESERVATION.**—(i) Three percent. of the vacancies, in case of direct recruitment to Group A, B, C and D posts shall be reserved for persons with disabilities of which one per cent. each shall be reserved for persons suffering from

(i) blindness or low vision; (ii) hearing impairment and (iii) locomotor disability or cerebral palsy in the posts identified for each disability;

(ii) Three per cent. of the vacancies in case of promotion to Group D, and Group C posts in which the element of direct recruitment, if any, does not exceed 75%, shall be reserved for persons with disabilities of which one per cent. each shall be reserved for persons suffering from (i) blindness or low vision, (ii) hearing impairment and (iii) locomotor disability or cerebral palsy in the posts identified for each disability.

3. EXEMPTION FROM RESERVATION.—If any Department/Ministry considers it necessary to exempt any establishment partly or fully from the provisions of reservation for persons with disabilities of which one per cent. each shall be reserved for persons suffering from (i) blindness or low vision, (ii) hearing impairment and (iii) locomotor disability or cerebral palsy in the posts identified for each disability, it may make a reference to the Ministry of Social Justice and Employment giving full justification for the proposal. The grant of exemption shall be considered by an Inter-Departmental Committee set up by the Ministry of Social Justice and Empowerment.

4. IDENTIFICATION OF JOBS/POSTS.—The Ministry of Social Justice and Empowerment have identified the jobs/posts suitable to be held by persons with disabilities and the physical requirement for all such jobs/posts *vide* their notification No. 16-25/99. NII dated 31.5.2001. The jobs/posts given in Annexure II of the said notification as amended from time to time shall be used to give effect to 3 per cent. reservation to the persons with disabilities. It may, however, be noted that:

(a) The nomenclature used for any job/post shall mean and include nomenclature used for other comparable jobs/posts having identical functions.

(b) The list of jobs/posts notified by the Ministry of Social Justice and Empowerment is not exhaustive. The concerned Ministries/ Departments shall have the discretion to identify jobs/posts in addition to the jobs/posts already identified by the Ministry of Social Justice and Empowerment. However, no Ministry/Department/ Establishment shall exclude any identified job/post from the purview of reservation at its own discretion.

(c) If a job/post identified for persons with disabilities is shifted from one group or grade to another group or grade due to change in the pay-scale or otherwise, the job/post shall remain identified.

13. COMPUTATION OF RESERVATION.—Reservation for persons with disabilities in case of Group C and Group D posts shall be computed on the basis of total number of vacancies occurring in all Group C or Group D posts, as the case may be, in the establishment, although the recruitment of the persons with disabilities would only be in the posts identified suitable for them. The number of vacancies to be reserved for the persons with disabilities in case of direct recruitment to Group C posts in an establishment shall be computed by taking into account the total number of vacancies arising in Group C posts for being filled by direct recruitment in a recruitment year both in the identified and non-identified posts under the establishment. The same procedure shall apply for Group D posts. Similarly, all vacancies in promotion quota shall be taken into account while computing reservation in promotion in Group C and Group D posts. Since reservation is limited to identified posts only and number of vacancies reserved is computed on the basis of total vacancies (in identified posts as well as unidentified posts), it is possible that number of persons appointed by reservation in an identified posts may exceed 3 per cent.

14. Reservation for persons with disabilities in Group A posts shall be computed on the basis of vacancies occurring in direct recruitment quota in all the identified Group A posts in the establishment. The same method of computation applies for Group B posts.

15. EFFECTING RESERVATION – MAINTENANCE OF ROSTERS.—(a) all establishments shall maintain separate 100 point reservation roster registers in the format given in Annexure II for determining/effecting reservation for the disabled – one each for Group A posts filled by direct recruitment, Group B posts filled by direct recruitment, Group C posts filled by direct recruitment, Group C posts filled by promotion, Group D posts filled by direct recruitment and Group D posts filled by promotion.

(b) Each register shall have cycles of 100 points and each cycle of 100 points shall be divided into three blocks, comprising the following points:

1st Block – point No. 1 to point No. 33

2nd Block – point No. 34 to point No. 66

3rd Block – point No. 67 to point No. 100

(c) Points 1, 34, and 67 of the roster shall be earmarked reserved for persons with disabilities – one point for each of the three categories of disabilities. The head of the establishment shall decide the categories of disabilities for which the points 1, 34 and 67 will be reserved keeping in view all relevant facts.

(d) All the vacancies in Group C posts falling in direct recruitment quota arising in the establishment shall be entered in the relevant roster register. If the post falling at point No. 1 is not identified for the disabled or the head of the establishment considers it desirable not to fill up by a disabled person or it is not possible to fill up that post by the disabled for any other person, one of the vacancies falling at any of the points from 2 to 33 shall be treated as reserved for the disabled and filled as such. Likewise a vacancy falling at any of the points from 34 to 66 or from 67 to 100 shall be filled by the disabled.

The purpose of keeping points 1, 34 and 67 as reserved is to fill up the first available suitable vacancy from 1 to 33, first available suitable vacancy from 34 to 66 and first available suitable vacancy from 67 to 100 persons with disabilities.

(e) There is a possibility that none of the vacancies from 1 to 33 is suitable for any category of the disabled. In that case two vacancies from 34 to 66 shall be filled as reserved for persons with disabilities. If the vacancies from 34 to 66 are also not suitable for any category, three vacancies shall be filled as reserved from the third block containing points from 67 to 100. This means that if no vacancy can be reserved in a particular block, it shall be carried into the next block.

(f) After all the 100 points of the roster are covered, a fresh cycle of 100 points shall start.

(g) If the number of vacancies in a year is such as to cover only one block or two, discretion as to which category of the disabled should be accommodated first shall vest in the head of the establishment, who shall decide on the basis of the nature of the post, the level of representation of the specific disabled category in the concerned grade/post etc.

(h) A separate roster shall be maintained for Group C posts filled by promotion and procedure as explained above shall be followed for giving reservation to persons with disabilities. Likewise two separate rosters shall be maintained for Group D posts, one for the posts filled by direct recruitment and another for posts filled by promotion.

(i) Reservation in Group A and Group B posts is determined on the basis of vacancies in the identified posts only. Separate rosters for Group A posts and Group B posts in the establishment shall be maintained. In the rosters maintained for Group A and Group B posts, all vacancies of direct recruitment arising in identified posts shall be entered and reservation shall be effected the same way as explained above.

16. *INTER SE* EXCHANGE AND CARRY FORWARD OF RESERVATION IN CASE OF DIRECT RECRUITMENT.—(a) Reservation for each of the three categories of persons with disabilities shall be made separately. But if the nature of vacancies in an establishment is such that a person of a specific category of disability cannot be employed, the vacancies may be interchanged among the three categories with the approval of the Ministry of Social Justice and Empowerment and reservation may be determined and vacancies filled accordingly.

(b) If any vacancy reserved for any category of disability cannot be filled due to non-availability of a suitable person with that disability or, for any other sufficient reason, such vacancy shall not be filled and shall be carried forward as a 'backlog reserved vacancy' to the subsequent recruitment year.

(c) In the subsequent recruitment year the backlog reserved vacancy shall be treated as reserved for the category of disability for which it was kept reserved in the initial year of recruitment. However, if a suitable person with that disability is not available, it may be filled by interchange among the three categories of disabilities. In case no suitable person with disability is available for filling up the post in the subsequent year also, the employer may fill up the vacancy by appointment of a person other than a person with disability. If the vacancy is filled by a person with disability of the category for which it was reserved or by a person of other category of disability by *inter se* exchange in the subsequent recruitment year, it will be treated to have been filled by reservation. But if the vacancy is filled by a person other than a person with disability in the subsequent recruitment year, reservation shall be carried forward for a further period upto two recruitment years whereafter the reservation shall lapse. In these two subsequent years, if situation so arises, the procedure for filling up the reserved vacancy shall be the same as followed in the first subsequent recruitment year.

19. **HORIZONTALITY OF RESERVATION FOR PERSONS WITH DISABILITIES.**—Reservation for backward classes of citizens (SCs, STs and OBCs) is called vertical reservation and the reservation for categories such as persons with disabilities and ex-servicemen is called horizontal reservation. Horizontal reservation cuts across vertical reservation (in what is called interlocking reservation) and person selected against the quota for persons with disabilities have to be placed in the appropriate category *viz.* SC/ST/OBC/General candidates depending upon the category to which they belong in the roster meant for reservation of SCs/STs/OBCs. To illustrate, if in a given year there are two vacancies reserved for the persons with disabilities and out of two persons with disabilities appointed, one belongs to a Scheduled Caste and the other to general category then the disabled SC candidate shall be adjusted against the SC point in the reservation roster and the general candidate against unreserved point in the relevant reservation roster. In case none of the vacancies falls on point reserved for the SCs, the disabled candidate belonging to SC shall be adjusted in future against the next available vacancy reserved for SCs.

20. Since the persons with disabilities have to be placed in the appropriate category *viz.* SC/ST/OBC/General in the roster meant for reservation of SCs/STs/OBCs, the application form for the post should require the candidates applying under the quota reserved for persons with disabilities to indicate whether they belong to SC/ST/OBC or General category."

GOVERNMENT WAS AUTHORISED IN THE OFFICE MEMORANDUM TO RELAX CONDITIONS

14. Clauses 21 and 22 of the said OM enable the Government for relaxation in age limit as well as standard of suitability.

ON RECEIVING REPRESENTATION, GOVERNMENT ISSUED ANOTHER OFFICE MEMORANDUM ON 26.4.2006

15. After the OM dated 29.12.2005, based on the representations made by Respondent No. 1 herein, another OM dated 26.4.2006 came to be issued. The details and the directions contained in the said OM are as follows:

"Dated the 26th April, 2006

OFFICE MEMORANDUM

Sub: Reservation for the Persons with Disabilities

The undersigned is directed to say that the Persons with Disabilities (Equal Opportunities, Protection of Rights and Full Participation) Act, 1995 which came into existence on 1.1.1996 provides for reservation for persons with disability in the posts identified for three categories of disabilities namely (i) blindness or low vision, (ii) hearing impairment, and (iii) locomotor disability or cerebral palsy. Instructions have also been issued by this Department for providing reservation for such persons. In spite of the Act and the instructions of this Department, vacancies were not earmarked reserved or were not filled by reservation in some establishments.

2. The matter has been considered carefully and it has been decided that reservation for persons with disabilities should be implemented in right earnest and there should be no deviation from the scheme of reservation, particularly after the Act came into effect. In order to achieve this objective, all the establishments should prepare the reservation roster registers as provided in this Department's O.M. No. 36035/3/2004-Estt. (Res.) dated 29.12.2005 starting from the year 1996 and reservation for persons with disabilities be earmarked as per instructions contained in that OM. If some or all the vacancies so earmarked had not been filled by reservation and were filled by able bodied persons either for the reason that points of reservation had not been earmarked properly at the appropriate time or persons with disabilities did not become available, such unutilized reservation may be treated as having been carried forward to the first recruitment year occurring after issue of this OM and be filled as such. If it is not possible to fill up such reserved vacancies during the said recruitment year, reservation would be carried forward for further two years, whereafter it may be treated as lapsed.

3. It has been observed that some recruiting agencies declare in their advertisements that blind/partially blind candidates need not apply and that separate examinations would be conducted for visually handicapped candidates. Attention is invited to para 7 of this Department's O.M. No. 36035/3/2004-Estt. (Res.) dated 29.12.2005 which provides that persons with disabilities selected on their own merit will not be adjusted against the reserved share of vacancies. It means that persons with disabilities who are selected on their own merit have to be adjusted against the unreserved vacancies and reservation has to be given in addition. If visually handicapped candidates or any other category of handicapped candidates are debarred from applying on the ground that a separate examination would be conducted for them, chances of handicapped candidates being selected on their own merit would be eliminated. Thus, debarring of any category of handicapped candidates in the above manner is against the provisions contained in the aforesaid O.M. It is, therefore, requested that persons with disabilities should not be debarred from applying for the posts identified suitable for them and should be provided opportunity to compete for the unreserved vacancies as well by holding a common examination.

4. Contents of this O.M. may be brought to the notice of all concerned.

Sd/-

(K.G. Verma)

Deputy Secretary to the Govt. of India"

OFFICE MEMORANDUM 10.12.2008 ISSUED TO START A SPECIAL RECRUITMENT DRIVE TO FILL IN THE BACKLOG

16. Another O.M. dated 10.12.2008, issued by the Department of Personnel and Training, was also brought to our notice whereunder a Special Recruitment Drive to fill up the backlog reserved vacancies for the persons with disabilities was initiated. The said O.M. mainly speaks about filling up of "backlog reserved vacancies". Relevant portion of the said O.M. is extracted hereinbelow:

> "Dated the 10th December, 2008
>
> OFFICE MEMORANDUM
>
> Sub: Special Recruitment Drive to fill up the backlog reserved vacancies for Persons with Disabilities
>
> The undersigned is directed to say that this Department's O.M. No. 36035/3/2004-Estt. (Res.) dated 29.12.2005 provides that if any vacancy reserved for any category of disability cannot be filled due to non-availability of a suitable person with that disability or for any other sufficient reason, such vacancy is not filled and is carried forward as a 'backlog reserved vacancy' to the subsequent recruitment year. In the subsequent recruitment year, the 'backlog reserved vacancy' is treated as reserved for the category of disability for which it was kept reserved in the initial year of recruitment and filled as such. However, if a suitable person with that disability is not available in the subsequent recruitment also, it may be filled by interchange among the three categories of disabilities, failing which by appointment of a person other than a person with disability. It may, thus, be seen that if a vacancy is earmarked reserved for any category of disability and a suitable person with that disability is not available to fill it up in the initial year of recruitment, it becomes a 'backlog reserved vacancy' for first subsequent recruitment year.
>
> 2. As per instructions existing prior to issue of O.M. dated 29.12.2005, if in any year, suitable physically handicapped candidates were not available to fill up a reserved vacancy, the vacancy was filled by an other category candidate and reservation was carried forward for a period of upto three recruitment years. In the event of non-availability of suitable persons with disabilities, the reserved vacancies were not kept unfilled. Thus, there was no provision of backlog reserved vacancies of persons with disabilities prior to 29.12.2005.
>
> Nevertheless, it is possible that some Ministries/Departments/establishments might have kept some vacancies earmarked reserved for the persons with disability unfilled due to non-availability of persons with disability. If there exist such vacancies, these will be treated as backlog reserved vacancies for the current recruitment year."

17. By issuing such directions, the Department of Personnel and Training directed all the Ministries/Departments to launch a Special Recruitment Drive and fixed target dates for fulfilling various stages.

DISCUSSION ABOUT THE VALIDITY OF OFFICE MEMORANDUM 29.12.2005

Discussion:

18. In the light of the above statutory provisions as well as various clauses of the OM dated 29.12.2005, let us analyze whether the High Court was justified in passing the impugned judgment.

19. Before adverting to the rival contentions submitted by the appellants and the respondents, it is relevant to comprehend the background and the objective of the Persons with Disabilities (Equal Opportunities, Protection of Rights and Full Participation) Act, 1995.

20. India as a welfare State is committed to promote overall development of its citizens including those who are differently abled in order to enable them to lead a life of dignity, equality, freedom and justice as mandated by the Constitution of India. The roots of statutory provisions for ensuring equality and equalization of opportunities to the differently abled citizens in our country could be traced in Part III and Part IV of the Constitution. For the persons with disabilities, the changing world offers more new opportunities owing to technological advancement, however, the actual limitation surfaces only when they are not provided with equal opportunities. Therefore, bringing them in the society based on their capabilities is the need of the hour.

21. Although, the Disability Rights Movement in India commenced way back in 1977, of which Respondent No. 1 herein was an active participant, it acquired the requisite sanction only at the launch of the Asian and Pacific Decade of Disabled Persons in 1993-2002, which gave a definite boost to the movement. The main need that emerged from the meet was for a comprehensive legislation to protect the rights of persons with disabilities. In this light, the crucial legislation was enacted in 1995 *viz.*, the Persons with Disabilities (Equal Opportunities, Protection of Rights and Full Participation) Act, 1995 which empowers persons with disabilities and ensures protection of their rights. The Act, in addition to its other prospects, also seeks for better employment opportunities to persons with disabilities by way of reservation of posts and establishment of a Special Employment Exchange for them.

22. For the same, section 32 of the Act stipulates for identification of posts which can be reserved for persons with disabilities. Section 33 provides for reservation of posts and section 36 thereof provides that in case a vacancy is not filled up due to non-availability of a suitable person with disability, in any recruitment year such vacancy is to be carried forward in the succeeding recruitment year. The difference of opinion between the appellants and the respondents arises on the point of interpretation of these sections.

SUBMISSIONS OF THE PARTIES

23. It is the stand of the Union of India that the Act provides for only 3% reservation in the vacancies in the posts identified for the disabled persons and not on the total cadre strength of the establishment whereas Mr. S.K. Rungta, learned senior counsel (R-1) appearing in person submitted that accepting the interpretation proposed by the Union of India will flout the policy of reservation encompassed under section 33 of the Act. He further submitted that the High Court has rightly held that the reservation of 3% for differently abled persons in conformity with the Act should have to be computed on the basis of the total strength of a cadre and not just on the basis of the vacancies available in the posts that are identified for differently abled persons, thereby declaring certain clauses of the OM dated 29.12.2005 as unacceptable and contrary to the mandate of section 33 of the Act.

SUBMISSIONS RAISED BY UNION OF INDIA AGAINST DELHI HIGH COURT JUDGMENT

24. Two aspects of the impugned judgment have been challenged before this Court:—

(a) The manner of computing 3% reservation for the persons with the disabilities as per section 33 of the Act.

(b) Whether post based reservation must be adhered to or vacancy based reservation.

DESCUSSION BY THE SUPREME COURT

Finding of Delhi High Court that Reservation will apply to Total Cadre Strength – Not Correct

25. Now let us consider the reasoning of the High Court and the submissions made by the parties.

26. Primarily, we would like to clarify that there is a sea of difference in computing reservation on the basis of total cadre strength and on the basis of total vacancies (both inclusive of identified and unidentified) in the cadre strength. At the outset, a reference to the impugned O.M. dated 29.12.2005 would, in unequivocal terms, establish that the matter in dispute in the given case is whether the latter method of computation of reservation will uniformly apply to the posts in Groups A, B, C and D or will it be applicable only to Groups C and D. The question pertaining to computation of reservation on the basis of total cadre strength does not even arise in the given circumstance of the case. However, the High Court, in the impugned judgment, went on to uphold the view that the computation of reservation must be on the basis of total cadre strength which is clearly erroneous on the face of it. Inadvertently, the respondents herein have also adopted the same line of argument in their oral and written submissions. As a result, the point for consideration before this Court is whether the modus of computation of reservation on the basis of total number of vacancies (both inclusive of identified and unidentified) in the cadre strength will uniformly apply to Groups A, B, C and D or will it be applicable only to Groups C and D.

Stand of UOI – Reservation only in Vacancies in the Identified Post – Not Correct

27. It is the stand of the Union of India that for vivid understanding of the reservation policy laid down under section 33 of the Act, it is essential to read together sections 32 and 33 of the Act. It was also submitted that a conjoint reading of the above referred sections, mandates only reservation of vacancies in the identified posts and not in all the posts or against the total number of vacancies in the cadre strength. However, it was also admitted that the computation of reservation is being done in respect of Groups C and D posts on the basis of total number of vacancies (both inclusive of identified and unidentified) in the cadre strength since 1977. In fact, the abovesaid contention has been raised in *Government of India through Secretary* v. *Ravi Prakash Gupta*, (2010) 7 SCC 626 and, therefore, it is no longer *res integra*. (Supra)

RAVI PRAKASH GUPTA'S JUDGMENT (*SUPRA*) RELIED BY UOI DOES NOT SUPPORT IT

28. The question for determination raised in this case is whether the reservation provided for the disabled persons under section 33 of the Act is dependent upon the identification of posts as stipulated by section 32. In the aforementioned case, the Government of India sought to contend that since they have conducted the exercise of identification of posts in civil services in terms of section 32 only in the year 2005, the reservation has to be computed and applied only with reference to the vacancies filled up from 2005 onwards and not from 1996 when the Act came into force. This Court, after examining the inter-dependence of sections 32 and 33 *viz.*, identification of posts and the scheme of reservation, rejected this contention and held as follows:-

> "25. .....The submission made on behalf of the Union of India regarding the implementation of the provisions of section 33 of the Disabilities Act, 1995, only after identification of posts suitable for such appointment, under section 32 thereof, runs counter to the legislative intent with which the Act was enacted. To accept such a submission would amount to accepting a situation where the provisions of section 33 of the aforesaid Act could be kept deferred indefinitely by bureaucratic inaction. Such a stand taken by the petitioners before the High Court was rightly rejected. Accordingly, the submission made on behalf of the Union of India that identification of Grade `A' and `B' posts in the I.A.S. was undertaken after the year 2005 is not of much substance.
>
> 26. As has been pointed out by the High Court, neither section 32 nor section 33 of the aforesaid Act makes any distinction with regard to Groups A, B, C and D posts. They only speak of identification and reservation of posts for people with disabilities, though the proviso to section 33 does empower the appropriate Government to exempt any establishment from the provisions of the said section, having regard to the type of work carried on in any department or establishment. No such exemption has been pleaded or brought to our notice on behalf of the petitioners.
>
> 27. It is only logical that, as provided in section 32 of the aforesaid Act, posts have to be identified for reservation for the purposes of section 33, but such identification was meant to be simultaneously undertaken with the coming into operation of the Act, to give effect to the provisions of section 33. The Legislature never intended the provisions of section 32 of the Act to be used as a tool to deny the benefits of section 33 to these categories of disabled persons indicated therein. Such a submission strikes at the foundation of the provisions relating to the duty cast upon the appropriate Government to make appointments in every establishment.

29. While it cannot be denied that unless posts are identified for the purposes of section 33 of the aforesaid Act, no appointments from the reserved categories contained therein can be made, and that to such extent the provisions of section 33 are dependent on section 32 of the Act, as submitted by the learned ASG, but the extent of such dependence would be for the purpose of making appointments and not for the purpose of making reservation. In other words, reservation under section 33 of the Act is not dependent on identification, as urged on behalf of the Union of India, though a duty has been cast upon the appropriate Government to make appointments in the number of posts reserved for the three categories mentioned in section 33 of the Act in respect of persons suffering from the disabilities spelt out therein. In fact, a situation has also been noticed where on account of non-availability of candidates some of the reserved posts could remain vacant in a given year. For meeting such eventualities, provision was made to carry forward such vacancies for two years after which they would lapse. Since in the instant case such a situation did not arise and posts were not reserved under section 33 of the Disabilities Act, 1995, the question of carrying forward of vacancies or lapse thereof, does not arise.

31. We, therefore, see no reason to interfere with the judgment of the High Court impugned in the Special Leave Petition which is, accordingly, dismissed with costs. All interim orders are vacated. The petitioners are given eight weeks' time from today to give effect to the directions of the High Court."

SCOPE OF IDENTIFICATION COMES INTO PLAY ONLY AFTER APPOINTMENT

29. In the light of the above pronouncement, it is clear that the scope of identification comes into picture only at the time of appointment of a person in the post identified for disabled persons and is not necessarily relevant at the time of computing 3% reservation under section 33 of the Act. In succinct, it was held in *Government of India through Secretary* v. *Ravi Prakash Gupta* (supra) *that section 32 of the Act is not a* precondition for computation of reservation of 3% under Section 33 of the Act rather section 32 is the following effect of Section 33.

SECTION 33 OF THE ACT PROVIDES RESERVATION ON THE BASIS OF TOTAL VACANCIES IN THE CADRE – NOT ON THE VACANCIES AVAILABLE ON THE IDENTIFIED POSTS – SUBMISSION OF UOI REJECTED

30. Apart from the reasoning of this Court in *Ravi Prakash Gupta* (supra), even a reading of section 33, at the outset, establishes vividly the intention of the legislature *viz.*, reservation of 3% for differently abled persons should have to be computed on the basis of total vacancies in the strength of a cadre and not just on the basis of the vacancies available in the identified posts. There is no ambiguity in the language of section 33 and from the construction of the said statutory provision only one meaning is possible.

31. A perusal of section 33 of the Act reveals that this section has been divided into three parts. The first part is "every appropriate Government shall appoint in every establishment such percentage of vacancies not less than 3% for persons or class of persons with disability." It is evident from this part that it mandates every appropriate Government shall appoint a minimum of 3% vacancies in its establishments for persons with disabilities. In this light, the contention of the Union of India that reservation in terms of section 33 has to be computed against identified posts only is not tenable by any method of interpretation of this part of the section.

32. The second part of this section starts as follows:

"...of which one per cent. each shall be reserved for persons suffering from blindness or low vision, hearing impairment and locomotor disability or cerebral palsy in the posts identified for each disability." From the above, it is clear that it deals with distribution of 3% posts in every establishment among 3 categories of disabilities. It starts from the word "of which". The word "of which" has to relate to appointing not less than 3% vacancies in an establishment and, in any way, it does not refer to the identified posts. In fact, the contention of the Union of India is sought to be justified by bringing the last portion of the second part of the section *viz.* "....identified posts" in this very first part which deals with the statutory obligation imposed upon the appropriate Government to "appoint not less than 3% vacancies for the persons or class of persons with disabilities."

MINIMUM LEVEL OF REPRESENTATION AND DISTRIBUTION OF 3% PROVIDED

In our considered view, it is not plausible in the light of established rules of interpretation. The minimum level of representation of persons with disabilities has been provided in this very first part and the second part deals with the distribution of this 3% among the three categories of disabilities. Further, in the last portion of the second part the words used are "in the identified posts for each disability" and not "of identified posts". This can only mean that out of minimum 3% of vacancies of posts in the establishments 1% each has to be given to each of the 3 categories of disability *viz.*, blind and low vision, hearing impaired and locomotor disabled or cerebral palsy separately and the number of appointments equivalent to the 1% for each disability out of total 3% has to be made against the vacancies in the identified posts. The attempt to read identified posts in the first part itself and also to read the same to have any relation with the computation of reservation is completely misconceived.

33. The third part of the section is the proviso which reads thus:

"Provided that the appropriate Government may, having regard to the type of work carried on in any department or establishment, by notification subject to such conditions, if any, as may be specified in such notification, exempt any establishment from the provisions of this section." The proviso also justifies the above said interpretation that the computation of reservation has to be against the total number vacancies in the cadre strength and not against the identified posts. Had the Legislature intended to mandate for computation of reservation against the identified posts only, there was no need for inserting the proviso to Section which empowers the appropriate Government to exempt any establishment either partly or fully from the purview of the section subject to such conditions contained in the notification to be issued in the Official Gazette in this behalf. Certainly, the Legislature did not intend to give such arbitrary power for exemption from reservation for persons with disabilities to be exercised by the appropriate Government when the computation is intended to be made against the identified posts.

SECTION 41 OF THE ACT PROVIDES 5% REPRESENTATION IN PUBLIC AND PRIVATE SECTORS

34. In this regard, another provision of the said Act also supports this interpretation. Section 41 of the said Act mandates the appropriate Government to frame incentive schemes for employers with a view to ensure that 5% of their work force is composed of persons with disabilities. The said section is reproduced hereinbelow:

"41. *Incentives to employers to ensure five per cent. of the work force is composed of persons with disabilities.*—The appropriate Government and the local authorities shall, within limits to their economic capacity and development, provide incentives to employers both in public and private sectors to ensure that at least five per cent of their work force is composed of persons with disabilities."

Thus, on a conjoint reading of sections 33 and 41, it is clear that while Section 33 provides for a minimum level of representation of 3% in the establishments of appropriate Government, the Legislature intended to ensure 5% of representation in the entire work force both in public as well as private sector.

DRAFT 'RIGHT OF PERSONS WITH DISABILITIES' BILL, 2012 REVEALS THE INTENTION OF THE LEGISLATURE – SECTIONS 32 AND 33 OF THE 1995 ACT ARE ALIKE SECTIONS 38 AND 39 IN THE BILL, 2012

35. Moreover, the intention of the Legislature while framing the Act can also be inferred from the Draft Rights of Persons with Disabilities Bill, 2012, which is pending in the Parliament for approval. In Chapter 6 of the Bill, *viz.*, Special Provisions for Persons with Benchmark Disabilities, similar sections like sections 32 and 33 in the Act have been incorporated under sections 38 and 39 which are as under:—

"Section 38. Identification of Posts which can be Reserved for Persons with Benchmark Disabilities:

Appropriate Governments shall – (a) identify posts in establishments under them which can be reserved for persons with benchmark disability as mentioned in section 39;

(b) at periodical intervals not exceeding three years, review and revise the list of identified posts, taking into consideration developments in technology.

Section 39. Reservation of Posts for Persons with Benchmark Disabilities:—

(1) Every appropriate Government shall reserve, in every establishment under them, not less than 5% of the vacancies meant to be filled by direct recruitment, for persons or class of persons with benchmark disability, of which 1% each shall be of all posts reserved for persons with following disabilities:—

(i) blindness and low vision (with reservation of 0.5% of the vacancies for each of the two disabilities).

(ii) hearing impairment and speech impairment.

(iii) locomotor disability including cerebral palsy, leprosy cured and muscular dystrophy.

(iv) autism, intellectual disability and mental illness

(v) multiple disabilities from among (i) to (iv) above including deaf blindness:

Provided that the appropriate Government may, having regard to the type of work carried on in any department or establishment, by notification subject to such conditions, if any, as may be specified in such notification, exempt any establishment from the provisions of this section.

(2) If sufficient number of qualified persons with benchmark disabilities are not available in a particular year, then the reservation may be carried forward for upto the next three recruitment years, and if in such succeeding recruitment years also a suitable person with benchmark disability is not available, then the post in the fourth year may be first filled by interchange among the categories of disabilities; and only when there is no person with any benchmark disability available for the post in that year, the vacancy may be filled by appointment of a person, other than a person with benchmark disability."

35.1 A perusal of sections 38 and 39 of the Bill clarifies all the ambiguities raised in this appeal. The intention of the Legislature is clearly to reserve in every establishment under the appropriate Government, not less than 3% of the vacancies for the persons or class of persons with disability, of which 1% each shall be reserved for persons suffering from blindness or low vision, hearing impairment and locomotor disability or cerebral palsy in the posts identified for each disability.

1995 ACT IS A SOCIAL WELFARE LEGISLATION

36. Admittedly, the Act is a social legislation enacted for the benefit of persons with disabilities and its provisions must be interpreted in order to fulfil its objective. Besides, it is a settled rule of interpretation that if the language of a statutory provision is unambiguous, it has to be interpreted according to the plain meaning of the said statutory provision. In the present case, the plain and unambiguous meaning of section 33 is that every appropriate Government has to appoint a minimum of 3% vacancies in an establishment out of which 1% each shall be reserved for persons suffering from blindness and low vision, persons suffering from hearing impairment and persons suffering from locomotor or cerebral palsy.

ILLUSTRATION

37. To illustrate, if there are 100 vacancies of 100 posts in an establishment, the concerned establishment will have to reserve a minimum of 3% for persons with disabilities out of which at least 1% has to be reserved separately for each of the following disabilities: persons suffering from blindness or low vision, persons suffering from hearing impairment and the persons suffering from locomotor disability or cerebral palsy. Appointment of 1 blind person against 1 vacancy reserved for him/her will be made against a vacancy in an identified post for instance, the post of peon, which is identified for him in group D. Similarly, one hearing impaired will be appointed against one reserved vacancy for that category in the post of store attendant in group D post. Likewise, one person suffering from locomotor disability or cerebral palsy will be appointed against the post of "Farash" group D post identified for that category of disability. It was argued on behalf of Union of India with reference to the post of driver that since the said post is not suitable to be manned by a person suffering from blindness, the above interpretation of the section would be against the administrative exigencies. Such an argument is wholly misconceived. A given post may not be identified as suitable for one category of disability, the same could be identified as suitable for another category or categories of disability entitled to the benefit of reservation. In fact, the second part of the section has clarified this situation by providing that the number of vacancies equivalent to 1% for each of the aforementioned three categories will be filled up by the respective category by using vacancies in identified posts for each of them for the purposes of appointment.

SECTION 33 DOES NOT REFER TO IDENTIFIED POST – SUBMISSION OF UOI REJECTED

38. It has also been submitted on behalf of the appellants herein that since reservation of persons with disabilities in Group C and D has been in force prior to the enactment and is being made against the total number of vacancies in the cadre strength according to the O.M. dated 29.12.2005 but the actual import of section 33 is that it has to be computed against identified posts only. This argument is also completely misconceived in view of the plain language of the said section, as deliberated above. Even, for the sake of arguments, if we accept that the computation of reservation in respect of Groups C and D posts is against the total vacancies in the cadre strength because of the applicability of the scheme of reservation in Groups C and D posts prior to enactment, section 33 does not distinguish the manner of computation of reservation between Groups A and B posts or Groups C and D posts respectively. As such, one statutory provision cannot be interpreted and applied differently for the same subject-matter.

OFFICE MEMORANDUM 2005 MAKES RESERVATIONS FOR DISABLED PERSONS UNCERTAIN AND ARBITRARY

39. Further, if we accept the interpretation contended by the appellants that computation of reservation has to be against the identified posts only, it would result into uncertainty of the application of the scheme of reservation because experience has shown that identification has never been uniform between the Centre and States and even between the Departments of any Government. For example, while a post of middle school teacher has been notified as identified as suitable for the blind and low vision by the Central Government, it has not been identified as suitable for the blind and low vision in some States such as Gujarat and J&K etc. This has led to a series of litigations which have been pending in various High Courts. In addition, Para 4 of the OM dated 29.12.2005 dealing with the issue of identification of jobs/posts in sub-clause (b) states that list of the jobs/posts notified by the Ministry of Social Justice and Empowerment is not exhaustive which further makes the computation of reservation uncertain and arbitrary in the event of acceptance of the contention raised by the appellants.

RESERVATION FOR DISABLED PERSONS APPLIES TO A, B, C, D GROUPS – IT WILL NOT VIOLATE 50% PRINCIPLE

40. Another contention raised by the appellants is that the computation of reservation against the total vacancies in the cadre strength in Groups A and B will violate the rule of 50% ceiling of reservation in favour of SC, ST and OBC as laid down by this Court in *Indra Sawhney* v. *Union of India*, AIR 1993 SC 477. This contention is also not tenable and is against the abovesaid judgment. It is difficult to understand as to how the computation of reservation against total vacancies in the cadre strength in Groups A and B will violate 50% ceiling when its computation on that basis in Groups C and D will not violate the said ceiling. There is no rationale of distinguishing between the manner of computation of reservation with regard to Groups A and B posts on the one hand and manner of computation of reservation with regard to Groups C and D posts on the other on this ground.

RESERVATION FOR SC, ST AND OBC IS VERTICAL WHILE IT IS HORIZONTAL FOR DISABLED PERSONS. 3% RESERVATION FOR DISABLED PERSONS WILL FALL IN THE CATEGORY TO WHICH THEY BELONG

41. A perusal of *Indra Sawhney* (supra) would reveal that the ceiling of 50% reservation applies only to reservation in favour of other Backward classes under article 16(4) of the Constitution of India whereas the reservation in favour of persons with disabilities is horizontal, which is under article 16(1) of the Constitution. In fact, this Court in the said pronouncement has used the example of 3% reservation in favour of persons with disabilities while dealing with the rule of 50% ceiling. Para 95 of the judgment clearly brings out that after selection and appointment of candidates under reservation for persons with disabilities they will be placed in the respective rosters of reserved category or open category respectively on the basis of the category to which they belong and, thus, the reservation for persons with disabilities *per se* has nothing to do with the ceiling of 50%. Para 95 is reproduced as follows:

> "95. ……all reservations are not of the same nature. There are two types of reservations, which may, for the sake of convenience, be referred to as 'vertical reservations' and 'horizontal reservations'. The reservations in favour of Scheduled Castes, Scheduled Tribes and other backward classes [under article 16(4)] may be called vertical reservations whereas reservations in favour of physically handicapped [under clause (1) of article 16] can be referred to as horizontal reservations. Horizontal reservations cut across the vertical reservations – what is called inter-locking reservations. To be more precise, suppose 3% of the vacancies are reserved in favour of physically handicapped persons; this would be a reservation relatable to clause (1) of article 16. The

persons selected against this quota will be placed in the appropriate category; if he belongs to S.C. category he will be placed in that quota by making necessary adjustments; similarly, if he belongs to open competition (O.C.) category, he will be placed in that category by making necessary adjustments. Even after providing for these horizontal reservations, the percentage of reservations in favour of backward class of citizens remains – and should remain – the same......"

WORDING OF THE SECTION IS CLEAR – NO NEED TO READ THE HEADING – SUBMISSION OF RESPONDENT NO. 1 REJECTED

42. Yet another contention raised by the appellants is that the reservation for persons with disabilities must be vacancy based reservation whereas Respondent No. 1 herein contended that it must be post based reservation as laid down by the High Court in the impugned judgment. Respondent No. 1 herein relied upon the heading of section 33 of the Act, *viz.*, 'Reservation of Posts', to propose the view that the reservation policy contemplated under section 33 is post based reservation.

43. It is settled law that while interpreting any provision of a statute the plain meaning has to be given effect and if language therein is simple and unambiguous, there is no need to traverse beyond the same. Likewise, if the language of the relevant section gives a simple meaning and message, it should be interpreted in such a way and there is no need to give any weightage to headings of those paragraphs. This aspect has been clarified in *Prakash Nath Khanna* v. *Commissioner of Income-tax*, (2004) 9 SCC 686. Paragraph 13 of the said judgment is relevant which reads as under:

> "**13.** It is a well-settled principle in law that the court cannot read anything into a statutory provision which is plain and unambiguous. A statute is an edict of the Legislature. The language employed in a statute is the determinative factor of legislative intent. The first and primary rule of construction is that the intention of the legislation must be found in the words used by the Legislature itself. The question is not what may be supposed and has been intended but what has been said.
>
> "Statutes should be construed, not as theorems of Euclid", Judge Learned Hand said, "but words must be construed with some imagination of the purposes which lie behind them". See *Lenigh Valley Coal Co.* v. *Yensavage*. The view was reiterated in *Union of India* v. *Filip Tiago De Gama of Vedem Vasco De Gama* and *Padma Sundara Rao* v. *State of Tamil Nadu*."

COURTS ARE TO INTERPRET THE LAW NOT TO LEGISLATE

44. It is clear that when the provision is plainly worded and unambiguous, it has to be interpreted in such a way that the Court must avoid the danger of a prior determination of the meaning of a provision based on their own preconceived notions of ideological structure or scheme into which the provision to be interpreted is somewhat fitted. While interpreting the provisions, the Court only interprets the law and cannot legislate it. It is the function of the Legislature to amend, modify or repeal it, if deemed necessary.

DELHI HIGH COURT FOLLOWED SABHARWAL JUDGMENT

45. The heading of a section or marginal note may be relied upon to clear any doubt or ambiguity in the interpretation of the provision and to discern the legislative intent. However, when the section is clear and unambiguous, there is no need to traverse beyond those words, hence, the headings or marginal notes cannot control the meaning of the body of the section. Therefore, the contention of Respondent No. 1 herein that the heading of section 33 of the Act is "Reservation of posts" will not play a crucial role, when the section is clear and unambiguous.

46. Further, the respondents heavily relied on a decision of the Constitution Bench in *R.K Sabharwal* v. *State of Punjab*, (1995) 2 SCC 745 to substantiate their contention. Para 6 reads as under:

> "6. The expressions "posts" and "vacancies", often used in the executive instructions providing for reservations, are rather problematical. The word "post" means an appointment, job, office or employment. A position to which a person is appointed.
>
> "Vacancy" means an unoccupied post or office. The plain meaning of the two expressions make it clear that there must be a 'post' in existence to enable the 'vacancy' to occur. The cadre-strength is always measured by the number of posts comprising the cadre. Right to be considered for appointment can only be claimed in respect of a post in a cadre. As a consequence the percentage of reservation has to be worked out in relation to the number of posts, which form the cadre-strength. The concept of 'vacancy' has no relevance in operating the percentage of reservation."

47. Adhering to the decision laid by the Constitution Bench in *R.K. Sabharwal* (supra), the High Court held as follows:—

> 16. The Disabilities Act was enacted for protection of the rights of the disabled in various spheres like education, training, employment and to remove any discrimination against them in the sharing of development benefits *vis-à-vis* non-disabled persons. In the light of the legislative aim it is necessary to give purposive interpretation to section 33 with a view to achieve the legislative intendment of attaining equalization of opportunities for persons with disabilities. The fact that the vacancy-based roster is to be maintained does not mean that 3% reservation has to be computed only on the basis of vacancy. The difference between the posts and vacancies has been succinctly pointed out in the Supreme Court decision in the case of *R.K Sabharwal* v. *State of Punjab*, AIR 1995 SC 1371 wherein it was held that the word "post" means an appointment, job, office or employment, a position to which a person is appointed. "Vacancy" means an unoccupied post or office. The plain meaning of the two expressions make it clear that there must be a 'post' in existence to enable the vacancy to occur. The cadre-strength is always measured by the number of posts comprising the cadre. Right to be considered for appointment can only be claimed in respect of a post in a cadre.
>
> As a consequence the percentage of reservation has to be worked out in relation to the number of posts which form the cadre-strength. The concept of 'vacancy' has no relevance in operating the percentage of reservation.

Therefore, in our opinion, 3% reservation for disabled has to be computed on the basis of total strength of the cadre *i.e.*, both identified as well as unidentified posts...."

SABHARWAL JUDGMENT WAS PRIOR TO 1995 ACT, GOVERNS ONLY RESERVATION RELATING TO SC, ST, OBC

48. However, the decision in *R.K. Sabharwal* (supra) is not applicable to the reservation for the persons with disabilities because in the abovesaid case, the point for consideration was with regard to the implementation of the scheme of reservation for SC, ST and OBC, which is vertical reservation whereas reservation in favour of persons with disabilities is horizontal. We harmonize with the stand taken by the Union of India, the appellant herein in this regard. Besides, the judgment in *R.K. Sabharwal* (supra) was pronounced before the date on which the Act came into force, as a consequence, the intent of the Act must be given priority over the decision in the abovesaid judgment. Thus, in unequivocal terms, the reservation policy stipulated in the Act is vacancy based reservation.

IT IS SHOCKING THAT PERSONS WITH DISABILITIES ARE OUT OF JOB

Conclusion

49. Employment is a key factor in the empowerment and inclusion of people with disabilities. It is an alarming reality that the disabled people are out of job not because their disability comes in the way of their functioning rather it is social and practical barriers that prevent them from joining the workforce. As a result, many disabled people live in poverty and in deplorable conditions. They are denied the right to make a useful contribution to their own lives and to the lives of their families and community.

CENTRAL AND STATE GOVERNMENTS ARE UNDER CONSTITUTIONAL OBLIGATION TO PROTECT THE RIGHTS OF DISABLED PERSONS

50. The Union of India, the State Governments as well as the Union Territories have a categorical obligation under the Constitution of India and under various International treaties relating to human rights in general and treaties for disabled persons in particular, to protect the rights of disabled persons. Even though the Act was enacted way back in 1995, the disabled people have failed to get required benefit until today.

DISABLED PERSONS ARE ENTITLED TO 3% RESERVATION IN ALL GROUPS A, B, C, D ON TOTAL NUMBER OF VACANCIES IN THE CADRE STRENGTH

51. Thus, after thoughtful consideration, we are of the view that the computation of reservation for persons with disabilities has to be computed in case of Groups A, B, C and D posts in an identical manner *viz.*, "computing 3% reservation on total number of vacancies in the cadre strength" which is the intention of the Legislature. Accordingly, certain clauses in the O.M. dated 29.12.2005, which are contrary to the above reasoning are struck down and we direct the appropriate Government to issue new Office Memorandum(s) in consistent with the decision rendered by this Court.

3% RESERVATION FOR DISABLED PERSONS HAS NOTHING TO DO WITH 50% RESERVATION NOR WILL AFFECT IT

52. Further, the reservation for persons with disabilities has nothing to do with the ceiling of 50% and hence, *Indra Sawhney* (supra) is not applicable with respect to the disabled persons.

53. We also reiterate that the decision in *R.K. Sabharwal* (supra) is not applicable to the reservation for the persons with disabilities because in the above said case, the point for consideration was with regard to the implementation of the scheme of reservation for SC, ST and OBC, which is vertical reservation, whereas reservation in favour of persons with disabilities is horizontal.

DIRECTIONS ISSUED TO THE GOVERNMENTS OF CENTRE, STATE AND INSTRUMENTALITIES COVERED BY ARTICLE 12

Directions:

54. In our opinion, in order to ensure proper implementation of the reservation policy for the disabled and to protect their rights, it is necessary to issue the following directions:

(i) We hereby direct the appellant herein to issue an appropriate order modifying the O.M. dated 29.12.2005 and the subsequent O.Ms. consistent with this Court's Order within three months from the date of passing of this judgment.

(ii) We hereby direct the "appropriate Government" to compute the number of vacancies available in all the "establishments" and further identify the posts for disabled persons within a period of three months from today and implement the same without default.

(iii) The appellant herein shall issue instructions to all the departments/ public sector undertakings/Government companies declaring that the non-observance of the scheme of reservation for persons with disabilities should be considered as an act of non-obedience and Nodal Officer in department/public sector undertakings/Government companies, responsible for the proper strict implementation of reservation for person with disabilities, be departmentally proceeded against for the default.

APPEAL DISPOSED OF – APPRECIATION RECORDED

55. Before parting with the case, we would like to place on record appreciation for Mr. S.K. Rungta, learned senior counsel for rendering commendable assistance to the Court. The appeal is disposed of with the above terms.

....CJI
(P. Sathasivam)

....J.
(Ranjana Prakash Desai)

....J.
(Ranjan Gogoi)

New Delhi;
October 8, 2013.

Author's Note: This is a very important Judgment by the Hon'ble Supreme Court to make the Civil Servants answerable to the Constitution and the Laws and to save them from the political interference by the Political Executive for their personal gains.

RELIEFS SOUGHT FOR PRESERVING INTEGRITY, FEARLESSNESS AND INDEPENDENCE OF CIVIL SERVANTS – PETITIONERS EMINENT RETD. CIVIL SERVANTS

T.S.R. Subramanian[1]

v.

Union of India

SUPREME COURT OF INDIA

Civil Original Jurisdiction

Writ Petition (Civil) No. 82 of 2011

With

Writ Petition (Civil) No. 234 of 2011

K.S. Radhakrishan and Pinaki Chandra Ghose, JJ.

JUDGMENT

K.S. Radhakrishnan, J.

1. Article 32 of the Constitution of India has been invoked by few eminent retired civil servants highlighting the necessity of various reforms for preservation of integrity, fearlessness and independence of civil servants at the Centre and State levels in the country. Prayers made in this writ petition are based on various reports and recommendations made by several Committees appointed for improving the public administration. On the basis of various reports, following reliefs are sought in the writ petition:—

(i) Issue a writ in the nature of *mandamus* or any other appropriate writ, order or direction requiring the Respondents to create an "independent" Civil Service Board or Commission both at the Centre and the State based on recommendations by the Hota Committee, 2004 (para 5.09, para 5.11, Main Recommendations No. 38); the 2nd Administrative Reforms Commission 2008 (10th Report, para 9.8); the statement adopted at the Conference of Chief Ministers on Effective and Responsive Administration, 1997;

(ii) Issue a writ in the nature of *mandamus* or any other appropriate writ, order or direction requiring the respondents to fixed tenure for civil servants ensuring stability based on recommendations by Jha Commission 1986 (para 7.2); Central Staffing Scheme, 1996 (para 17.01, para 17.02, para

1. JT 2013 (14) SC 124.

17.03, para 17.12), the 2nd Administrative Reforms Commission (10th Report, para 8.7, para 9.8, para 17.5), Hota Committee Report, 2004 (Main Recommendations No. 39);

(iii) Issue a writ in the nature of *mandamus* or any other appropriate writ, order or direction requiring the respondents to mandate that every civil servant formally record all such instructions/directions/orders/suggestions which he/she receives, not only from his/her administrative superiors but also from political authorities, legislators, commercial and business interests and other persons/quarters having interest, wielding influence or purporting to represent those in authority based on the principles recognized by rule 3(3)(ii)(iii) of the All India Service Conduct Rules, 1968 and as implicitly recognized by the Santhanam Committee Report, 1962 (Section 6, sub-para 33[iii].

NOTICE ISSUED TO STATES/UNION TERRITORIES ALSO

2. This Court, considering the importance of the matter, issued notice to various State Governments and the Union Territories so as to ascertain their views on the various issues raised in this case. Most of the States have filed detailed counter affidavits explaining their stand with regard to the reliefs prayed for in this writ petition.

CREATION OF CIVIL SERVICE BOARDS—SUBMIT PETITIONERS

3. Shri K.K. Venugopal, learned senior counsel appearing for the writ petitioners, referred elaborately to the above-mentioned reports and highlighted the necessity of the creation of a Civil Service Board (for short 'CSB'), both at the Centre and State level, with a degree of independence so that it can make recommendations on all transfers and postings without sacrificing the executive freedom of the Government. Learned senior counsel pointed out that such CSB shall function in a bare advisory capacity and its recommendations will not impose any constraint on the independence of the political authority to effect postings and transfers, including premature transfers.

FIXED TENURE IS ESSENTIAL FOR BETTER PERFORMANCE—SUBMIT PETITIONERS

Learned senior counsel also highlighted the necessity for providing a fixed tenure for civil servants ensuring stability which is highly necessary for implementing various programmes which will have social and economic impact on the society. Learned senior counsel also highlighted the reasons for recording of instructions, directions and orders by the civil servants so that they can function independently and the possibility of arbitrary and illegal decisions could be avoided.

UNION OF INDIA OPPOSES THE SETTING-UP OF CSBs

4. Mr. Paras Kuhad, learned ASG appearing for the Union of India, opposed in principle prayer for setting up of independent CSB at the Centre and the State levels, which, according to the learned ASG, would be interfering with the governmental functions. Learned ASG also submitted that any mechanism within the governmental structure could be thought of, but involvement of any person, howsoever high he may be, who is not part of the Centre or the State Government, would not be advisable, especially in the absence of any such provision in the Constitution or the laws made by Centre and the State Governments.

DRAFT BILL, 2010 ON THE SUBJECT PENDING CONSIDERATION BEFORE THE CENTRAL CABINET – SUBMISSION OF UOI

Learned ASG also submitted that based on the 2nd Administrative Reforms Committee (ARC), a Draft Bill entitled "Civil Services Performance Standards and Accountability Bill, 2010" was provided incorporating certain recommendations in the above-mentioned reports. Further, it was pointed out that the draft Cabinet Note for the introduction of the said Bill in the Parliament is under consideration of the Central Government.

FIXED TENURE WAS INITIATED IN 2006 – SUBMISSION OF UOI

Further, it was also submitted that for fixing the minimum tenures of cadre post in the Indian Administrative Service was initiated in November, 2006 by the Department of Personnel and Training. Cadre controlling authorities of the Indian Police Service and Indian Foreign Service were also requested to take necessary follow-up action for fixing the minimum tenures in the cadre post for the Indian Police Service and Indian Foreign Service. During the process of consultation, it was pointed out that comments of the State Governments were sought on the proposal of fixing minimum tenure of posting of IAS Officers. 13 State Governments agreed with the proposal, while some States did not agree. The matter was further discussed in the meeting with the Chief Secretary/Principal Secretaries of the States concerned on 31.5.2007 and again on 4.7.2008 in Delhi. Notification providing for two years minimum tenure for IAS posting having been issued for 13 States/Joint Cadres. Reference was also made to study report of "Centre for Good Governance", Hyderabad and it was stated that the same is under consideration with the Central Government. With regard to the prayer for recording of instructions/directions, etc., it was pointed out that the requirements are provided under the All India Service Conduct Rules.

CENTRAL SERVICE BOARDS ALREADY SET-UP IN UTTAR PRADESH – SUBMISSION OF STATES

5. Learned counsels appearing for the State Governments and the Union Territories have also placed their stand on various reliefs sought for in this writ petition. Learned standing counsel appearing for the State of Uttar Pradesh submitted that the State has already established Civil Service Boards in terms of the Government orders dated 24.12.2001 and 19.5.2007, which is meant to operate with respect to IAS and Provisional Civil Services, Indian Police Services and Provisional Police Services and for Indian Forest Services and their feeder services. Over and above, the State has also formulated transfer policy dated 15.5.2008.

MAHARASHTRA GOVERNMENT ALSO PASSED AN ACT, IN 2005 – SUBMISSION OF STATES

Learned counsel appearing for the State of Maharashtra also made reference to the Maharashtra Government Servants Regulations of Transfers and Prevention of Delay in Discharge of Official Duties Act, 2005 and submitted that the Act provided for transfer of Government servants and prevention of delay in discharge of official duties.

RELIEFS SOUGHT BASED ON HOTA COMMITTEE REPORT, 2004 AND OTHER REPORTS

6. Reliefs prayed for in this writ petition are based on the Hota Committee Report, 2004, 2nd Administrative Reforms Commission (10th Report), 2008. 2nd Administrative Service Commission (15th Report), the Report of the Committee on Prevention of Corruption, Santhanam Committee Report, etc. We have gone through those reports in detail.

HOTA COMMITTEE APPOINTED IN 2004 – TERMS OF REFERENCE

A. CIVIL SERVICE BOARD (CSB):

7. The Government of India on 3rd February, 2004, appointed the Hota Committee to examine the whole gamut of Civil Service reforms and the terms of reference of the Committee were as follows:—

"(i) Making the Civil Service responsive and citizen-friendly;

- transparent;
- accountable; and
- ethical

in its (a) actions and (b) interface with the people,

(ii) Making the civil service e-governance friendly.

(iii) Putting a premium on intellectual growth of civil servants and on upgrading their domain knowledge,

(iv) Protecting the civil service against wrongful pressure exerted by

(a) administrative superiors;

(b) political executives;

(c) business interests; and

(d) other vested interests.

(v) Changes, if any necessary, in the various All India Services Rules and Central Civil Rules to provide a statutory cover to the proposed civil service reforms.

(vi) Changes in rules governing the disciplinary proceedings against civil servants to decentralize the process as far as practicable, and to make the disposal of such proceedings time-bound.

(vii) Any other matter that the Committee may consider relevant to the subject of civil service reforms."

HOTA COMMITTEE RECOMMENDED SETTING-UP OF CSBs – FINAL AUTHORITY POLITICAL EXECUTIVES – SETTING UP OF OMBUDSMAN ALSO RECOMMENDED

8. On establishment of Indian Civil Services Board, the Hota Committee made the following recommendations:—

"5.09 We found that some States complied with the recommendations of the Conference of Chief Ministers and set up Civil Services Boards/Establishment Boards with Chief Secretary of the State as the Chairman and other senior officials of the State as Members. But the Boards set up by executive order in different States have failed to inspire confidence as more often than not, they have merely formalized the wishes of their Chief Ministers in matters of transfer of officials. We are firmly of the view that a Civil Services Act has to be enacted to make the Civil Services Board/Establishment Board both in the States and in the Government of India statutory in character. In the proposed set up in the Government of India, the Appointments Committee of the Cabinet will be the final authority for transfer of officers under the Central Staffing Scheme. The same principle of fixed tenure should apply to senior officers, who are not under the Central Staffing Scheme, but are working under the Government of India for which the Departmental Minister in charge is the final authority for transfer. The Chief Minister will be the final authority for transfer of all Group 'A' officers of State Service and AIS officers serving in connection with affairs of the State. If a Chief Minister does not agree with the recommendations of the Civil Services Board/Establishment Board, he will have to record his reasons in writing. An officer transferred before his normal tenure even under orders of the Chief Minister can agitate the matter before a three-member Ombudsman. The Chairperson of the Ombudsman will be a retired official of proven honesty and integrity. The other two members can be on part-time basis from among serving officers. In all such premature transfers the Ombudsman shall send a report to the Governor of the State, who shall cause it to be laid in an Annual Report before the State Legislature. The Ombudsman may also pay damages to the officer so transferred to compensate him for dislocation and mental agony caused due to such transfer. We are conscious that we are recommending a statutory barrier to frequent transfer of senior officials but the matter has come to such a pass that it requires a statutory remedy. We also clarify that the Chief Minister as the highest political executive has the final powers to order transfer of an officer before his tenure is over.

5.10 We are also of the opinion that postings of all Group 'B' officers must be done by the Head of the Department in a State and the same tenure rule shall be given a statutory backing. We were advised by some witnesses that only the Chief Minister's orders for transfer should be taken in case of Group 'A' officers/officers of All India Services and no Minister of a State should have any powers to order a transfer or approve a proposal for transfer of any official either of any State Service or of the All India Service. We agree with the view, as in our opinion owing to reasons of political expediency or even due to unwholesome reasons, Ministers in States often are not able to make proper use of the power vested in them for transfer of their departmental officers. If a Minister has cogent reasons to ask for transfer of an official before he completes his tenure, he will move the Civil Services Board to be set up under the new Civil Services Act and the Civil Services Board, with its views on report of inquiry by a designated officer, shall submit the case to the Chief

Minister for final orders. Thus, in a State Government, a Minister's proposal for transfer of any officer of Group 'A'/Group 'B' will be formally decided by the Chief Minister of the State.

5.11 In our opinion, Civil Services Boards must be set up in all States on similar lines as at the Centre. The Central Act should have a provision to enable the States to adopt the law and make it applicable in the States, without going through the long process of drafting a new law and getting it passed in the Legislature. The Civil Services Board in a State – chaired by the Chief Secretary and comprising senior officers – shall perform the functions relating to transfer, empanelment, promotion, and deputation of officers performed by the Establishment Board of Government of India/Special Committee of Secretaries of Government of India, both of which are chaired by the Cabinet Secretary. Under article 309 of the Constitution, Parliament may also enact a Civil Services Act setting up a Civil Services Board for the Union Government which will perform the functions being performed at present by the Establishment Board presided over by the Cabinet Secretary. The Civil Services Act may also provide for a Special Committee of Secretaries to prepare panel of names for appointment for posts of Additional Secretaries and Secretaries to Government of India. Under the new Civil Services Act, a Cabinet Minister/ Minister of State with independent charge in Government of India may be given a time limit to accept/send back proposals for the Establishment Board regarding posting of officers with his observations. In any particular case, if the Establishment Board after giving the views of the Minister in-charge its utmost consideration does not change its original recommendation, the Cabinet Secretary may send proposals of the Establishment Board with observations of the Minister in charge through the Home Minister, a Member of the ACC to the Prime Minister, who heads the ACC for a final decision.

5.12 *Inter alia*, a Civil Services Board of a State shall also perform functions of recommending officers of All India Service/Group 'A1 service of the State for transfer to different posts under the State Government. It would be expedient before an officer is sought to be transferred in the public interest when he has not completed his tenure, that an administrative inquiry of a summary nature is held to ascertain if the transfer is justified as a matter of public policy. The administrative inquiry will be conducted as expeditiously as possible by a designated officer nominated by the Civil Services Board. In appropriate cases, the Civil Services Board may also direct the officer to proceed on leave on full pay and allowances till the administrative inquiry is over and a decision is taken regarding his transfer. The designated officer to conduct the inquiry will be ordinarily the Reporting Officer of the officer sought to be transferred. The Civil Services Board on receipt of the report of inquiry of the designated officer shall advise the Chief Minister regarding justification for transfer of the officer in the public interest before his normal tenure is over. Ordinarily the Chief Minister is expected to agree with the recommendations of the Civil Services Board as transfer of an official is a routine administrative matter on which a Civil Services Board must have a decisive role. But if the Chief Minister does not agree with the Civil Services Board and orders transfer of an official before his tenure is over, he may have to record in writing reasons for such transfer. If the official is transferred before his tenure without adequate justification, he will have the right to approach a three-member Civil Service Ombudsman set-up for the purpose.

Recommendation 38: In the proposed Civil Service law the highest political executive shall continue to be the final authority to order transfer of any officer before his tenure is over; but he will be expected to give due consideration to Report of the Administrative Inquiry/views of the Civil Service Board/ Establishment Board and record reasons on the need for premature transfer of an officer.

It is reiterated that the political executive shall have the final authority to transfer an officer at any stage in the public interest. An officer aggrieved by order of premature transfer can agitate the matter before a three-Member Ombudsman, who may, where suitable, award monetary compensation to the aggrieved officer. The constitution of the Ombudsman will be the same as the Ombudsman proposed for the Disputes Redressal Council as at para 6.19 of this Report. The President/Governor shall receive reports from the Ombudsman and shall lay an Annual Report on such transfers on the table of the Legislature. There should be a suitable provision in the law to enable States to adopt it and make it applicable in the States without going through the long process of drafting a law and get it passed in the Legislature. (Para 5.03 to 5.10)"

SECOND ADMINISTRATIVE REFORMS COMMISSION IN ITS REPORT 2008 ALSO SUGGESTED INDEPENDENT 'CENTRAL CIVIL SERVICES AUTHORITY' FOR RESPONSIBLE, EFFECTIVE, ACCOUNTABLE AND SUSTAINABLE ADMINISTRATION

9. The 2nd Administrative Reforms Commission was set up by the President reflecting the Resolution dated 31st August, 2005 passed by the Government of India. The Commission was set up to suggest measures to achieve a preemptive responsible, accountable, sustainable and effective administration for the country at all levels of the government. The tenure of the Committee was extended from time to time and the Committee submitted its report in the year 2008. On the question of the setting up of the independent CSB, the Committee has made the following recommendations:

"9.7.1 The Commission suggests that an independent 'Authority' should deal with matters of assignment of domains, preparing panels for posting of officers at the level of SAG and above, fixing tenures for various posts, deciding on posts which could be advertised for lateral entry etc. As this Authority would be performing the above-mentioned crucial tasks, it would be necessary to ensure its independence by giving it a statutory backing and stipulating that it should be headed by an eminent person with experience of public affairs to be appointed by the Prime Minister in consultation with the Leader of the Opposition in the Lok Sabha. The Authority should have a full time Member-Secretary of the rank of Secretary to Government of India, and persons of eminence in public life and professionals with acknowledged contributions to society as Members of the Authority. This Authority, to be named as the Central Civil Services Authority, should be constituted under the proposed Civil Services Act. As the constitution of the Central Civil Services Authority under a new law may take some time, the said Authority may be constituted, initially, under executive orders."

10. Para 9.8.e. also refers to the composition of the Committee which reads as follows:—

"9.8.e. A Central Civil Services Authority should be constituted under the proposed Civil Services Bill. The Central Civil Services Authority shall be a five-member body consisting of the Chairperson and four members (including the member-secretary).

The Authority should have a full time Member-Secretary of the rank of Secretary to Government of India. The Chairperson and members of the Authority should be persons of eminence in public life and professionals with acknowledged contributions to society. The Chairperson and members of the Authority shall be appointed by the President on the recommendations of a Committee consisting of the Prime Minister and the Leader of the Opposition in the Lok Sabha.

(*Explanation.*—Where the Leader of the Opposition in the Lok Sabha has not been recognized as such, the Leader of the single largest group in the Opposition in the Lok Sabha shall be deemed to be the Leader of the Opposition)."

SECOND ADMINISTRATIVE REFORMS COMMISSION IN ITS FIFTEENTH REPORT (APRIL, 2009) ALSO RECOMMENDED CONSTITUTION OF 'CENTRAL CIVIL SERVICES AUTHORITY'

11. The Second Administrative Reforms Commission Fifteenth Report (April 2009) has also made various suggestions in order to provide legislative backing to these measures, the Commission has recommended enactment of a Civil Services Law which will cover all personnel holding civil posts under the Union. The Commission recommended for the constitution of a Central Civil Service Authority, among other things, which reads as follows:

"VIII. **Constitution of the Central Civil Services Authority**:

(i) The Central Government shall, by notification in the Official Gazette, constitute a body to be known as the Central Civil Services Authority to exercise the powers conferred on, and to perform the functions assigned to it, under this Act.

(ii) The Central Civil Services Authority shall be a five-member body consisting of the Chairperson and four members (including the member-secretary). The Authority should have a full time Member-Secretary of the rank of Secretary to Government of India. The Chairperson and Members of the Authority should be persons of eminence in public life and professionals with acknowledged contributions to society. The Chairperson and members of the

Authority shall be appointed by the President on the recommendations of a Committee consisting of the Prime Minister and the Leader of the Opposition in the Lok Sabha.

(*Explanation.*—Where the Leader of the Opposition in the Lok Sabha has not been recognized as such, the Leader of the single largest group in the opposition in the Lok Sabha shall be deemed to be the Leader of the Opposition).

2.4.2.5 Subsequently, in its Report on "Refurbishing of Personnel Administration" (the Tenth Report), the Commission suggested a detailed procedure for placement of officers at the middle and top management levels in the Union Government. It calls for the constitution of a Central Civil Service Authority by law, which will be an independent five-member body consisting of persons of eminence in public life and professionals with acknowledged contributions to Society. This Authority will be empowered to deal with a large number of issues concerning civil services such as assignment of domain to officers, preparing panels for posting at the levels of Joint Secretary and above, fixing tenures for senior assignments and such other matters that may be referred to it by the Union Government. The Commission is of the view that there should be a similar Civil Services law and a State Civil Services Authority for each State. The mandate and functions of the State Body would largely coincide with those prescribed under the proposed Union Civil Services Law. This Authority should deal with issues of appointment and tenure of higher officials of all ranks in the State Governments including the Chief Secretary, Principal Secretaries, Engineer-in-Chiefs and the Principal Chief Conservator of Forests. However, till the time the proposed law is enacted and the State Civil Service Authority is constituted, recommendations made at para 2.14.2.5 above may be immediately adopted by all the State Governments.

2.4.2.6 Recommendations:

(a) After enactment of the State Civil Services Law on the lines of the proposed Union enactment, the proposed State Civil Service Authority should deal with matters concerning appointment and tenure of senior officers of all ranks in the State Governments (including the Chief Secretary, Principal Secretaries, Engineer-in-Chiefs, other Agency Heads and Principal Chief Conservator of Forests).

(b) Till the time that such an Authority is constituted, the following mechanism may be adopted for appointment of the Chief Secretary and Principal Conservator of Forests in the States:—

- There should be a collegium to recommend a panel of names to the Chief Minister/Cabinet for these two posts. For the post of Chief Secretary, this collegium may consist of:

  (a) a Minister nominated by the Chief Minister,

  (b) the Leader of the Opposition in the State Legislative Assembly, and

(c) the incumbent Chief Secretary. For the selection to the post of Principal Chief Conservator of Forests the collegiums may consist of,

(a) The Minister In-charge of Forests,

(b) the leader of Opposition in the State Legislative Assembly, and

(c) the Chief Secretary.

- There should be a fixed tenure of atleast two years for both these posts.
- The selection for the post of Chief Secretary and Principal Chief Conservator of Forests should be widened to include all officers above a specified seniority (*e.g.*, 30 years). All officers with a seniority higher than a prescribed limit should be eligible to be a part of the panel.

(c) As regards the appointment and tenure of the Director-General of Police, the recommendations made by the Commission in its Report on "Public Order" at para 5.2.3.7 should be implemented."

DISCUSSION BY THE SUPREME COURT

12. We have elaborately referred to the Report of the Hota Committee, Report of the 2nd Administrative Commission, 2008-2009, which highlighted the necessity of creation of an independent CSB at the Centre as well as the State level.

THE CENTRAL STAFFING SCHEME,1996 HIGHLIGHTED FIXED TENURE FOR STABILITY IN ADMINISTRATION

B. FIXED TENURE:

13. Various Committees have also recommended and highlighted the necessity of providing fixed tenure for a civil servant so as to ensure stability and efficiency of administration. The Central Staffing Scheme, 1996, highlighted the necessity of a fixed tenure to provide certain degree of stability to the administration. Reference in this regard may be made to paras 17.01, 17.02, 17.03, 17.12 and 17.13 and the same are extracted hereinbelow for easy reference:

"17.01 The fixed tenure of deputation of posting under the Central Government is the heart of the Central Staffing Scheme. Rotation between the Centre and the States, Central Ministries and parent cadres, and headquarters and the field, provide a certain degree of pragmatism to policy formulation and programme implementation from the Central Ministries. Based on the experience gained so far, the periods of tenure at the different levels have been prescribed as under:—

(i) Under Secretary 3 years

(ii) Deputy Secretary 4 years

(iii) Director 5 years

(iv) Joint Secretary 5 years.

17.02 An officer holding the post of Joint-Secretary or equivalent, when appointed to a post under the Government of India at the level of Additional

Secretary, would have a tenure of 3 years from the date of appointment as Additional Secretary subject to a minimum of 5 years and maximum of 7 years of combined tenure as Joint Secretary and Additional Secretary. Where an officer remains on leave (either from the Centre or from his Cadre authority or both) on the expiry of his tenure as Joint Secretary till his appointment as Additional Secretary, the leave period shall be counted as tenure deputation. Additional Secretary 4 years, except for cases covered under the previous heading.

Secretary No fixed tenure.

17.03 Every officer shall revert at the end of his tenure as indicated above on the exact date of his completing his tenure. He will, however, have a choice to revert to his cadre on the 31st May previous to the date of the end of his tenure in case personal grounds such as children's education etc., necessitate such reversion. No extension after completion of the full tenure would be allowed.

17.12 (a) Officers of the Indian Foreign Service appointed to posts under the Central Staffing Scheme would have a tenure of three years.

(b) They shall not normally be relieved, except with the approval of the appointments Committee of the Cabinet from a Central Staffing Scheme post before their tenure.

17.13 No lateral shifts of officers from one Ministry/Department to another will normally be considered. However, in the case of Private Secretary to Ministers the policy followed would be:—

(a) The redeployment of a Private Secretary in the same Ministry/Department as Deputy Secretary or Director is discouraged.

(b) The Private Secretary (to Minister) who has been empanelled for holding post of Joint Secretary at the Centre should also not be considered for relocation in the same Ministry/Department and the officer should be posted to some other Ministry/Department."

UNANIMITY FOR FIXED TENURE FOR CIVIL SERVANTS

14. The 2nd Administrative Reforms Commission (10th Report) also speaks of the same in paras 8.5.11, 8.5.12, 8.5.14, 8.7(e)-(g), 9.8(e)-(g) and 17.5(VIII) and the same are extracted hereinbelow for easy reference :

"8.5.11. There appears to be unanimity on the point that it is necessary to give a fixed tenure to a civil servant in his/her post. In fact, the Draft Public Services Bill, 2007 has stipulated in clause 16(e) that "The Central Government shall fix a minimum tenure for cadre posts, which may be filled on the basis of merit, suitability and experience."

8.5.12 In clause 22, the Bill enjoins the Cadre Controlling Authorities to "notify within a period of six months from the coming into force of this Act, norms and guidelines for transfers and postings to maintain continuity and predictability in career advancement and acquisition of necessary skills and experiences as well as promotion of good governance. Transfers before the specified tenure should be for valid reasons to be recorded in writing. Provided that the normal tenure of all public servants shall not be less than two years."

8.5.14 The Commission is of the view that the Central Civil Services Authority (discussed in detail in Chapter 9) should be charged with the responsibility of fixing the tenure for all civil service posts under the Union Government. At present, the functions of the Authority are envisaged as advisory under the provisions of the Draft Public Services Bill, 2007. This needs to be changed, and so far as the fixation of tenure is concerned, it is suggested that the decision of the Authority should be binding on the Government. The Authority should also be given the responsibility to monitor postings and place before Parliament a periodic evaluation of the actual average tenure for each post and for the Central Government as a whole. Establishment of State Civil Service Authorities for the States with similar responsibilities needs to be urgently taken up by the State Governments where tenures are much less stable. The details of the State Civil Services Authorities would be examined by the Commission in its Report on 'State Administration'.

8.7(e)-(g) **Placement at Middle Management Level**

[.......]

(e) The Central Civil Services Authority should be charged with the responsibility of fixing tenure for all civil service positions and this decision of the Authority should be binding on Government.

(f) Officers from the organised services should not be given 'non-field' assignments in the first 8-10 years of their career.

(g) State Governments should take steps to constitute State Civil Services Authorities on the lines of the Central Civil Services Authority.

9.8(e)-(g) **Placement at Top Management Level**

[......]

(e) A Central Civil Services Authority should be constituted under the proposed Civil Services Bill. The Central Civil Services Authority shall be a five-member body consisting of the Chairperson and four members (including the member-secretary). The Authority should have a full time Member-Secretary of the rank of Secretary to Government of India. The Chairperson and members of the Authority should be persons of eminence in public life and professionals with acknowledged contributions to society. The Chairperson and members of the Authority shall be appointed by the President on the recommendations of a Committee consisting of the Prime Minister and the Leader of the Opposition in the Lok Sabha.

(*Explanation.*—Where the Leader of the Opposition in the Lok Sabha has not been recognized as such, the Leader of the single largest group in the Opposition in the Lok Sabha shall be deemed to be the Leader of the Opposition).

(f) The Central Civil Services Authority should deal with matters of assignment of domains to officers, preparing panels for posting of officers at the level of Joint Secretary and above, fixing tenures for senior posts, deciding on posts which could be advertised for lateral entry and such other matters that may be referred to it by the Government.

(g) A similar procedure should be adopted for filling up vacancies at SAG level and higher in the central police agencies. For example, in the Central Para-Military Forces the senior positions should be opened to competition from officers of the CPMFs, IPS and the Armed Forces (including those completing their Short Service Commissions). Similarly for the intelligence agencies officers from the armed forces as well as the CPOs with experience in the field of intelligence should be considered for postings at higher levels in the intelligence agencies.

17.5 **Recommendations**

"A new Civil Services Bill may be drafted. The following salient features may be included in the proposed Bill.

[.......]

VIII. Fixation of Tenures: All senior posts should have a specified tenure. The task of fixing tenures for various posts may also be assigned to this independent agency – Central Civil Services Authority."

15. The 2nd Administrative Reforms Commission (15th Report), 2009 also speaks of the same in paras 2.4.1.2 and 2.4.2.4 and the same is extracted below for ready reference:—

"2.4.1.2 In order to provide legislative backing to these measures, the Commission has recommended enactment of a Civil Services Law which will cover all personnel holding civil posts under the Union. As recommended at paragraph 17.5 of this Report, the proposed law has the following salient features:

[.....]

V. Fixation of Tenure: All senior posts should have a specified tenure. The task of fixing tenures for various posts may also be assigned to this independent agency – Central Civil Services Authority.

[.....]

IX. Functions of the Central Civil Services Authority.

The Central Authority shall discharge the following functions:

[.....]

vi. Fix the tenure for posts at the 'Senior Management Level' in Government of India.

2.4.2.4 For appointments to the posts of the Chief Secretary and the Principal Conservator of Forest, the Commission communicated the following interim suggestions to the Government in December 2007:—

(i) There should be a collegium to recommend a panel of names to the Chief Minister/Cabinet for these two posts. For the post of Chief Secretary, this collegium may consist of

  (a) a Minister nominated by the Chief Minister,

  (b) the Leader of the Opposition in the State Legislative Assembly, and

  (c) the incumbent Chief Secretary.

For the selection to the post of Principal Chief Conservator of Forests the collegiums may consist of:

(a) The Minister In-charge of Forests,

(b) the leader of Opposition in the State Legislative Assembly, and

(c) the Chief Secretary.

(ii) There should be a fixed tenure of two years for both these posts.

(iii) The selection for the post of Chief Secretary and Principal Chief Conservator of Forests should be widened to include all officers above a specified seniority (*e.g.*, 30 years). All officers with seniority higher than a prescribed limit should be eligible to be a part of the panel."

HOTA COMMITTEE ALSO RECOMMENDED 'CODE OF ETHICS' AND 'FIXED TENURE'

16. The Hota Committee Report, 2004 also highlights the same as its main Recommendation No. 39 which reads as follows:—

"(39). The proposed comprehensive law on the Civil Services shall incorporate, *inter alia*, a Code of Ethics and a statutory minimum tenure in a post to an officer. Under the proposed law, if an officer is sought to be transferred before his tenure, there would be an expeditious administrative inquiry by a designated senior officer to be earmarked for this purpose. This can be dispensed with if the transfer is on promotion/deputation/foreign training. In all other cases, the Report of Inquiry with the views of the Civil Service Board/Establishment Board would be put up to the Chief Minister if officer of the All India Services other civil services work in the States, or the Appointments Committee of the Cabinet if the officers work under the Central Staffing Scheme. For the officers of the other Central Services working in Ministries/Departments but not under the Central Staffing Scheme, the new law will prescribe tenure with a provision for administrative inquiry before an officer is sought to be transferred except on specified grounds."

ORAL DIRECTIONS/ORDERS BY POLITICAL EXECUTIVE TO CIVIL SERVANTS MAJOR REASON FOR FAILURE IN PROPER ADMINISTRATION

C. Recording of Instructions and Directions:

17. Petitioners have highlighted the serious predicament on which the civil servants are placed when they are asked to implement governmental decisions,on oral directions, suggestions, instructions etc. Much of the deterioration of the standards of probity and accountability, according to the Petitioners, can be traced to practice of issuing and acting on verbal instructions or oral orders which are not recorded.

SANTHANAM COMMITTEE PROVIDED SOLUTION TO IT

This issue was addressed by the Santhanam Committee way back in 1962. Paragraphs 6.20 and 6.21 deal with those aspects, which are given below for easy reference:

"6.20. We have already mentioned the existence of 'contactmen' and 'touts'. Obviously these do not include genuine representatives of commercial and industrial firms. In this regard our recommendations are:—

(i) No official should have any dealings with a person claiming to act on behalf of a business or industrial house or an individual, unless he is properly accredited, and is approved by the Department, etc. concerned. Such a procedure will keep out persons with unsavoury antecedents or reputation. There should, of course, be no restriction on the proprietor or manager etc. of the firm or the applicant himself approaching the authorities.

(ii) Even the accredited representatives should not be allowed to see officers below a specified level – the level being specified in each organization after taking into consideration the functions of the organizations, the volume and nature of the work to be attended to, and the structure of the organization. However, care should be taken to limit permissible contacts to levels at which the chances of corruption are considered to be small. This would often mean that no contact would be permitted at the level of subordinate officers.

(iii) There should be some system of keeping some sort of record of all interviews granted to accredited representatives.

(iv) There should be a fairly senior officer designated in each Department to which an applicant etc., may go if his case is being unreasonably delayed.

It is necessary that a proper procedure should be devised in consultation with the Central Vigilance Commission for accrediting and approval by the department. Before granting approval the antecedents of the person proposed to be accredited should, if possible, be verified. In any case no person who is not definitely employed by an established undertaking who will be responsible for his contact and actions should be approved.

6.21. It is also desirable that officers belonging to prescribed categories who have to deal with these representatives should maintain a regular diary of all interviews and discussions with the registered representatives whether it takes place in the office or at home. The general practice should be that such interviews should be in the office and if it takes place at home, reasons should be recorded. Any business or discussion which is not so recorded should be deemed to be irregular conduct, of which serious notice should be taken by the superiors.

ALL INDIA SERVICES (CONDUCT) RULES, 1968 PROVIDES FOR WRITTEN DIRECTIONS/ORDERS ONLY

18. Further, we also notice the All India Services (Conduct) Rules, 1968, which also states that the directions of the officials superior shall ordinarily be in writing. Rule 3(3) of the above-mentioned Rules reads as follows:—

3(3) (i) No member of the Service shall, in the performance of his official duties, or in the exercise of powers conferred on him, act otherwise than in his own best judgment to be true and correct except when he is acting under the direction of his official superior.

(ii) The direction of the official superior shall ordinarily be in writing. Where the issue of oral direction becomes unavoidable, the official superior shall confirm it in writing immediately thereafter.

(iii) A member of the Service who has received oral direction from his official superior shall seek confirmation of the same in writing, as early as possible and in such case, it shall be the duty of the official superior to confirm the direction in writing.

Explanation I.—A member of the Service who habitually fails to perform a task assigned to him within the time set for the purpose and with the quality of performance expected of him shall be deemed to be lacking in devotion to duty within the meaning of the sub-rule (1);

Explanation II.—Nothing in clause (i) of sub-rule (3) shall be construed as empowering a Government servant to evade his responsibilities by seeking instructions from or approval of, a superior officer or authority when such instructions are not necessary under the scheme of distribution of powers and responsibilities."

STATEs/UTs HESITANT ON FIXED TENURES AND CONSTITUTION OF INDEPENDENT CSB

19. We, in this respect, point out that the response of certain States and Union Territories in the matter of creation of an independent CSB, fixed tenure of civil servants and recording of directions, are neither consistent nor positive. But generally, they have welcomed the suggestion for fixation of tenure to the rider that in certain exceptional circumstances, the State Governments should have the power to transfer a person prematurely before completion of the tenure. Few States have welcomed the suggestion that every Civil Servant should record all the instructions and directions received.

INDEPENDENT CSB WILL INTRUDE IN THE FUCTIONING OF POLITICAL EXECUTIVE – PLEAD UOI AND THE STATEs

20. Union and the State Governments apprehend that creation of an independent CSB or institutional arrangement for regulating transfers and postings of officers would be an intrusion into the executive function of the Centre and State Governments headed by the political executives, who are directly responsible to the people. Further, they have also taken up a stand that the said arrangement would lead to a dual line of control, creating complexities in managing administrative functions and affecting efficiency of civil servants.

THREE YEARS TENURE IS ALREADY THE EXISTING POLICY

With regard to frequent transfers of officers, they have taken up the stand that there is already a clear cut policy that except in cases of promotion, in the interest of work and administrative reasons, transfer and posting will be done only after completion of three years of tenure. Few States have issued directions, to get written directions in case of oral directions of Superior Officers in line with rule 3(3)(ii)-(iii) of All India Services (Conduct) Rules, 1968.

ARTICLES 309 TO 312 OF THE CONSTITUTION DEAL WITH CIVIL SERVANTS

21. Chapter XIV of the Constitution of India deals with services under the Union and the States. Article 309 deals with the recruitment and conditions of service of persons serving the Union or the State, which expressly made subject to the other provision of the Constitution of India. In terms of article 309 appropriate Legislature, Parliament or the State Legislature is empowered to legislate, to regulate the recruitment and conditions of service of persons appointed to public services and post them in connection with the affairs of the Union or of any State. In terms of the proviso to article 309, number of rules have been made from time to time by the Union and the State Governments and they govern and regulate the public services in India. Article 310 of the Constitution provides for all members of the civil services of the Union and All India Services to be held in civil post at the pleasure of the President and all members of the civil services of the State at the pleasure of the Governor of the State. Article 311 provides certain safeguards regarding dismissal, removal or reduction in rank of persons employed in civil capacity. Article 312 provides constitution of All India Services.

POWERS OF UPSC AND STATE PSCs ALREADY ENCROACHED BY POLITICAL EXECUTIVE

Articles 318 to 333 deal with the Union Public Service Commission (UPSC) and State Public Service Commissions (PSCs). Article 320 stipulates that it shall be the duty of the Union and the State PSCs to conduct the examinations for appointment to the services of the Union and services of the State, respectively.

22. UPSC or the State PSCs are to be consulted in all matters relating to the method of recruitment to civil services and on the principles to be followed in making appointments to civil services and posts and in making promotions and transfers from one service to another. Of late, the UPSC and PSCs are being denuded of their powers of consultation while making promotions and transfer from one service to another. Article 323 lays down that it shall be the duty of the UPSC to present annually to the President a report of the work done by the Commission and on receipt of such report the President shall cause a copy thereof together with the memorandum, explaining as regard the cases, if any, where advice of the Commission was not accepted, the reasons for such non-acceptance, to be laid before the House of Parliament. Similar provision also exists for the State PSCs. Article 323A authorizes Parliament to set up administrative tribunals regarding disputes with regard to recruitment and conditions of service, appointed to public services. Parliament in exercise of its powers under article 309 enacted the All India Service Act, 1951, which authorizes Union Government in consultation with the State Governments, to make rules for the regulations of conditions of service of persons appointed to All India Services.

CONSTITUTIONAL POWER OF POLITICAL EXECUTIVE IN THE CENTRE AND THE STATES

23. Part V of the Constitution deals with the Union. Article 53 states that the executive power of the Union shall be vested in the President and shall be exercised by him either directly or through officers subordinate to him in accordance with this Constitution. Article 154 of Chapter VI of the Constitution states that the executive power of the State shall be vested with the Governor and shall be exercisable by him either directly or through officers subordinate to him in accordance with the Constitution. Article 73 of the Constitution states that subject to the provisions of the Constitution executive power of the Union shall extend to matters with respect to which Parliament has power to make laws and to the exercise of such rights, authority and jurisdiction, as exercisable by the Government of India by virtue of any treaty or any agreement. Article 163 of the Constitution states that there shall be a Council of Ministers, the Chief Minister as the head to aid and advice the Governor in exercise of his functions, except insofar as he is by or under this Constitution required to exercise his functions or any of them with his discretion.

ROLES OF POLITICAL EXECUTIVE AND CIVIL SERVANTS ARE DEFINED IN THE CONSTITUTION

24. The above are the constitutional provisions which generally deal with the power of the executive. The principles governing the roles and responsibilities of political executive and civil servants, are therefore, constitutionally defined and also based on the basis of various rules framed by the President and Governor for the conduct of business in the Government. Ministers are responsible to the people in a democracy because they are the elected representatives of the Parliament as well as the General State Assembly. Civil servants have to be accountable, of course to their political executive but they have to function under the Constitution, consequently they are also accountable to the people of this country.

CIVIL SERVANTS HAVE TAKEN OATH OF LOYALTY TO THE CONSTITUTION – THEREFORE, ANSWERABLE TO IT

25. Paragraph 15.1.3 of the report of the 2nd Administrative Reforms Committee (2008) reads as follows:

> "A healthy working relationship between Ministers and civil servants is critical for good governance. While the principles governing the roles and responsibilities of Ministers and civil servants are well-defined in political theory, in the actual working of this relationship this division of responsibility becomes blurred with both sides often encroaching upon the other's sphere of responsibility. In any democracy, Ministers are responsible to the people through Parliament and therefore the civil servants have to be accountable to the Ministers. However, an impartial civil service is responsible not only to the government of the day but to the Constitution of the land to which they have taken an oath of loyalty. At the same time, implementing the policies of the duly elected government is a core function of civil servants. That is why the division of responsibility between the civil servants and ministers needs to be more clearly defined. A framework in which responsibility and accountability is well-defined would be useful."

CIVIL SERVANTS MUST WORK TRANSPARENTLY IN PUBLIC INTEREST BEFITTING THEIR CONSTITUTIONAL OATH

26. Civil servants, as already indicated, have to function in accordance with the Constitution and the laws made by the Parliament. In the present political scenario, the role of civil servants has become very complex and onerous. Often they have to take decisions which will have far reaching consequences in the economic and technological fields. Their decisions must be transparent and must be in public interest. They should be fully accountable to the community they serve. Many of the recommendations made by the Hota Committee, various reports of the

2nd Administrative Reforms Commission, 2008 and Santhanam Committee Report have highlighted various lacunae in the present system which calls for serious attention by the political executive as well as the law makers.

CIVIL SERVANTS MUST FUNCTION WITHOUT POLITICAL INTERFERENCE

27. We find it, however, difficult to give a positive direction to constitute an independent CSB at the Centre and State Level, without executive control, which Hota Committee has recommended to be statutory in nature, that too, comprising of persons from outside the Government. Petitioners placed considerable reliance on the judgment of this Court in *Prakash Singh* v. *Union of India*, (2006) 8 SCC 1 and urged that similar directions be given to insulate, to at least some extent, the civil servants from political/executive interference.

CSB WITHOUT GOVERNMENT CONTROL NOT POSSIBLE – MUST CONSIST OF HIGH RANKING SERVING OFFICERS – NOT OF RETIRED

Retired persons, howsoever eminent they may be, shall not guide the transfers and postings, disciplinary action, suspension, reinstatement, etc. of civil servants, unless supported by law enacted by the Parliament or the State Legislature.

28. CSB, consisting of high ranking in service officers, who are experts in their respective fields, with the Cabinet Secretary at the Centre and Chief Secretary at the State level, could be a better alternative (till the Parliament enacts a law), to guide and advise the State Government on all service matters, especially on transfers, postings and disciplinary action, etc., though their views also could be overruled, by the political executive, but by recording reasons, which would ensure good governance, transparency and accountability in governmental functions.

PARLIAMENT MUST ENACT LAW FOR SETTING-UP CSBs

Parliament can also under article 309 of the Constitution enact a Civil Service Act, setting up a CSB, which can guide and advice the political executive transfer and postings, disciplinary action, etc. CSB consisting of experts in various fields like administration, management, science, technology, could bring in more professionalism, expertise and efficiency in governmental functioning.

DIRECTIONS TO THE CENTRE/STATES TO SET-UP CSBs

29. We, therefore, direct the Centre, State Governments and the Union Territories to constitute such Boards with high ranking serving officers, who are specialists in their respective fields, within a period of three months, if not already constituted, till the Parliament brings in a proper legislation in setting up CSB.

AT PRESENT NO STABILITY OF TENURE

30. We notice, at present the civil servants are not having stability of tenure, particularly in the State Governments where transfers and postings are made frequently, at the whims and fancies of the executive head for political and other considerations and not in public interest.

CENTRE AND SOME STATES IMPLEMENTED THE POLICY OF TENURE POSTS

The necessity of minimum tenure has been endorsed and implemented by the Union Government. In fact, we notice, almost 13 States have accepted the necessity of a minimum tenure for civil servants. Fixed minimum tenure would not only enable the civil servants to achieve their professional targets, but also help them to function as effective instruments of public policy.

REPEATED SHUFFLING/TRANSFER DANGEROUS TO GOOD GOVERNANCE

Repeated shuffling/transfer of the officers is deleterious to good governance. Minimum assured service tenure ensures efficient service delivery and also increased efficiency. They can also prioritize various social and economic measures intended to implement for the poor and marginalized sections of the society.

DIRECTIONS ISSUED TO STATES/UTs TO IMPLEMENT MINIMUM TENURE POLICY WITHIN 3 MONTHS

31. We, therefore, direct the Union, State Governments and Union Territories to issue appropriate directions to secure providing of minimum tenure of service to various civil servants, within a period of three months.

32. We have extensively referred to the recommendations of the Hota Committee, 2004 and Santhanam Committee Report and those reports have highlighted the necessity of recording instructions and directions by public servants.

DETERIORATION IN PROBITY AND ACCOUNTABILITY BECAUSE OF INTERFERENCE BY POLITICAL EXECUTIVE

We notice that much of the deterioration of the standards of probity and accountability with the civil servants is due to the political influence or persons purporting to represent those who are in authority. Santhanam Committee on Prevention of Corruption, 1962 has recommended that there should be a system of keeping some sort of records in such situations.

ORDERS FROM SUPERIORS SHOULD BE IN WRITING

Rule 3(3)(iii) of the All India Service Rules specifically requires that all orders from superior officers shall ordinarily be in writing. Where in exceptional circumstances, action has to be taken on the basis of oral directions, it is mandatory for the officer superior to confirm the same in writing. The civil servant, in turn, who has received such information, is required to seek confirmation of the directions in writing as early as possible and it is the duty of the officer superior to confirm the direction in writing.

CIVIL SERVANTS MUST WORK ON WRITTEN ORDERS – THEY NEED PROTECTION ALSO FROM ARBITRARY PRESSURE

33. We are of the view that the civil servants cannot function on the basis of verbal or oral instructions, orders, suggestions, proposals, etc. and they must also be protected against wrongful and arbitrary pressure exerted by the administrative superiors, political executive, business and other vested interests. Further, civil servants shall also not have any vested interests. Resultantly, there must be some records to demonstrate how the civil servant has acted, if the decision is not his, but if he is acting on the oral directions, instructions, he should record such directions in the file. If the civil servant is acting on oral directions or dictation of anybody, he will be taking a risk, because he cannot later take up the stand, the decision was in fact not his own. Recording of instructions, directions is, therefore, necessary for fixing responsibility and ensure accountability in the functioning of civil servants and to uphold institutional integrity.

CITIZENRY MUST HAVE ACCESS TO INFORMATION

RTI Act and Civil Servants

34. Democracy requires an informed citizenry and transparency of information. Right to Information Act, 2005 (RTI Act) recognises the right of the citizen to secure access to information under the control of public authority, in order to promote transparency and accountability in the working of every public authority. Section 3 of the Act confers right to information to all citizens and a corresponding obligation under section 4 on every public authority to maintain the records so that the information sought for can be provided.

ORAL ORDERS, IF NOT RECORDED DEFEAT RIGHTS UNDER RTI ACT – INCREASE CHANCES OF CORRUPTION

Oral and verbal instructions, if not recorded, could not be provided. By acting on oral directions, not recording the same, the rights guaranteed to the citizens under the Right to Information Act, could be defeated. The practice of giving oral directions/instructions by the administrative superiors, political executives etc. would defeat the object and purpose of RTI Act and would give room for favouritism and corruption.

DIRECTIONS ISSUED – TO BE COMPLIED WITHIN 3 MONTHS

35. We, therefore, direct all the State Governments and Union Territories to issue directions like rule 3(3) of the All India Services (Conduct) Rules, 1968, in their respective States and Union Territories which will be carried out within three months from today.

WRIT PETITIONS DISPOSED OF

36. The Writ Petitions are, accordingly, disposed of with the above directions.

....................................J.

(K.S. Radhakrishnan)

....................................J.

(Pinaki Chandra Ghose)

New Delhi,

October 31, 2013.

SUBJECT INDEX

•••